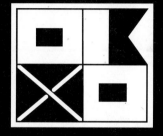

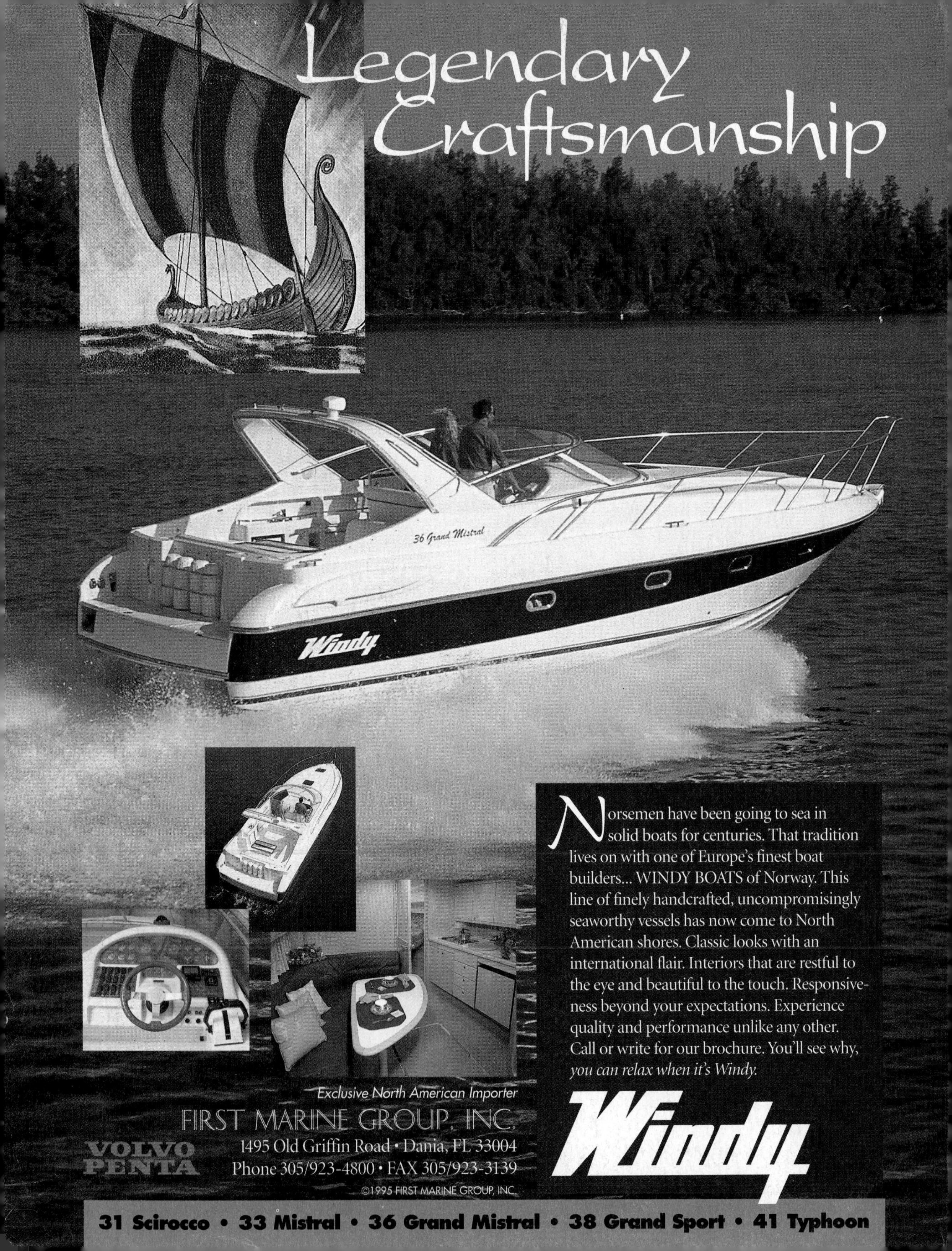
Legendary Craftsmanship
36 Grand Mistral
Windy
Norsemen have been going to sea in solid boats for centuries. That tradition lives on with one of Europe's finest boat builders... WINDY BOATS of Norway. This line of finely handcrafted, uncompromisingly seaworthy vessels has now come to North American shores. Classic looks with an international flair. Interiors that are restful to the eye and beautiful to the touch. Responsiveness beyond your expectations. Experience quality and performance unlike any other. Call or write for our brochure. You'll see why, you can relax when it's Windy.
Exclusive North American Importer
FIRST MARINE GROUP, INC.
1495 Old Griffin Road • Dania, FL 33004
Phone 305/923-4800 • FAX 305/923-3139
©1995 FIRST MARINE GROUP, INC.
VOLVO PENTA
Windy
31 Scirocco • 33 Mistral • 36 Grand Mistral • 38 Grand Sport • 41 Typhoon

Even Viking's high caliber competition can't build a yacht in the class of the Viking 43' Sportfish and 43' Express Yacht. Whether one chooses to cruise in ultimate style and comfort in the 43' Express Yacht or compete in world-class sportfishing tournaments with the 43' Sportfish, the performance and wide open spaces of the new 43' brings new levels of fun and function to the sport.

While people marvel at the 43's striking exterior, her real beauty lies beneath the surface. The 43' Open is built on Viking's renowned modified V-hull and is powered by twin turbo-charged diesels for ultra-fast, efficient, smooth power (30+ knots) with precise handling and unrivaled seakindliness.

Nothing compares to the visibility, control and dry ride a Captain experiences at the centerline command station, surrounded by guests or fishing buddies, while being just steps from her expansive cockpit, stand-up engine room and elegant, opulent interior.

The 43' Sportfish can be delivered tournament ready. Both models are available with one or two staterooms. Most importantly, either 43' gives an experienced yachtsman the pleasure and confidence of making the right choice. A Viking.

THE VIKING 43'
EXPRESS YACHT.
KEEP AN
OPEN MIND.
THE VIKING 43'
SPORTFISH.
viking 43 SF
Viking Yachts Rte 9 New Gretna, NJ 08224
(609) 296-6000 Fax (609) 296-3956
viking
yachts
For those who know better.

1996
EDITION

The McKnew/Parker

Consumer's Guide to

FAMILY & EXPRESS CRUISERS

From the Editors of the POWERBOAT GUIDE

Ed McKnew & Mark Parker

International Marine
Camden, Maine

PUBLISHED BY
International Marine
A Division of The McGraw-Hill Companies
Camden, ME 04843
1-800-822-8158

COMPILED BY
American Marine Publishing, Inc.
P.O. Box 30577
Palm Beach Gardens, FL 33420
1-800-832-0038

ISBN 0-07-045495-7

Printed and bound in the United States of America.

Table of Contents

Contents, cont.

Contents, cont.

Contents, cont.

Contents, cont.

Contents, cont.

Contents, cont.

Contents, cont.

Contents, cont.

Contents, cont.

Introduction

This book is written to help buyers sort through the hundreds of different production family and express cruisers, 25 to 63 feet in length, currently available on the nation's new and used markets. Over three hundred popular models are reviewed in these pages, with prices ranging from the affordable to the truly opulent. For each, we have included complete factory specifications together with floorplan options, real-world performance data, production history, engine choices and production updates. Throughout, the authors' opinions are freely expressed. Advertising hype notwithstanding, some boats are simply better than others and those that stand out at either extreme are occasionally noted. No attempt has been made to maliciously abuse a particular model, however, and the comments represent nothing more or less than the opinions of the authors. Needless to say, the services of experienced marine professionals are strongly recommended in the sale or purchase of any boat.

The prices quoted in this book reflect the market conditions projected by our staff for 1996. Those wishing to establish a consistent pattern for depreciation will be disappointed: we know of no such schedule. Rather, we have evaluated each model on its own merits and assigned values based on our own research and experience. While we are aware of the prices other appraisal guides assign to various models, we are often in disagreement with those values and believe that our estimates are more reflective of actual resale values. **It is very important to review the section, ABOUT THESE PRICES, on page 256 before referencing the assigned values.** And remember, no matter what the various price guides (including ours) might say, the fact remains that the only real value of a boat is what someone is willing to pay for it on a given day.

The CONSUMER'S GUIDE TO FAMILY & EXPRESS CRUISERS, 25' TO 63', is one of several annual marine publications written by Ed McKnew and Mark Parker. The series is a spin-off of the hugely successful POWERBOAT GUIDE, a marine industry reference compiled annually for the exclusive use of yacht brokers, dealers, lenders and marine surveyors.

We sincerely hope you will find the information in this book to be useful, and we welcome any comments you might care to offer regarding the content or the character of this publication. ❑

About the Authors

Ed McKnew has been involved in the marine industry since the mid-1970s, first as a yacht broker and later as the owner of several brokerage operations in Michigan and Texas. He holds a business degree from Oakland University in Rochester, Michigan, and worked for several years in the trucking industry before becoming a yacht broker in 1976. Ed currently lives and works in Palm Beach Gardens, Florida, where he and his partner own and operate American Marine Publishing. When he's not writing about boats, Ed spends his spare time pursuing his long-standing interest in the American Civil War.

Mark Parker has been a boating enthusiast before he can remember. A graduate of Southwest Texas State University with a degree in marketing, Mark held a USCG Masters license and has captained several large sportfishing boats. He is a native of Texas and worked as a broker in both Texas and Florida for twelve years. He and Ed McKnew began researching the original POWERBOAT GUIDE in 1987, and he has co-edited the project since then. He currently works full time with American Marine Publishing. Mark and his wife, Sherri, reside in Palm Beach Gardens, Florida.

Acknowledgments

We wish to thank the following individuals for their generous support. These are the people who were there to lend assistance in the beginning. Without their help this series of books would never have been published.

Floyd Appling, Jr.

Bill Burgstiner

Steve & Delores Brown

Top & Sandy Cornell

George & Helene Gereke

Edward & Betty Groth

Freddy & Patti Hamlin

How to Use This Book

For the most part, the contents of this book are straightforward and easily understood. Before launching into the pages, however, we strongly suggest that you take a few moments and review the following points. Failure to do so is likely to result in some confusion and misunderstanding.

Factory Specifications
The specifications listed for each model are self-explanatory although the following factors are noted:

1) *Clearance* refers to bridge clearance, or the height above the waterline to the highest point on the boat. Note that this is often a highly ambiguous piece of information since the manufacturer may or may not include such things as an arch, hardtop, or mast. Use this figure with caution.
2) *Weight* is a factory-provided specification that may or may not be accurate. Manufacturers differ in the way they compute this figure. For the most part, it refers to a dry boat with no gear.
3) *Designer* refers to the designer of the hull only.
4) *NA* means that the information is not available.

Performance Data
Whenever possible, performance figures have been obtained from the manufacturer or a reliable dealer or broker. When such information was unavailable, the authors have relied upon their own research together with actual hands-on experience. The speeds are estimates and (in most cases) based on boats with average loads of fuel, water, options and gear.

All speeds are reported in knots. Readers in the Great Lakes or inland waterways may convert knots to miles-per-hour by multiplying a given figure by 1.14.

Cruising Speeds, Outboard Engines
On average, we calculate the cruising speed of an outboard engine at about 4,000 rpm, or 1,200–1,500 rpm off a motor's top rpm rating.

Cruising Speeds, Gas Engines
Unless otherwise noted, the cruising speed for gas-powered inboard (or stern drive) boats is calculated at 3,000–3,200 rpm.

Cruising Speeds, Diesel Engines
The cruising speeds for diesel-powered boats are calculated as follows:

1) Detroit (2-stroke) Diesels: about 200–250 rpm off the top rpm rating.
2) Other (4-stroke) Diesels: about 350–400 rpm off the manufacturer's maximum rpm rating.

Floorplans
When there are two or more floorplans, the most recent layout comes last.

Pricing Information

Used boat prices have been compiled from 1975, the base year for our calculations. Boats whose production runs were previous to that year are noted in the Price Schedule with four asterisks (****).

In the Price Schedule, six asterisks (******) indicate that we have insufficient data to render a value for a particular year.

While diesel engines nearly always add significant value to a boat, there are some cases where the differences in the type or horsepower of diesel engines installed in a particular model will seriously affect the average resale value. Those cases in which we believe the diesel options do indeed affect the value of an individual boat have been noted in the Price Schedule.

The Retail High is the average selling price of a clean, well-equipped and well-maintained boat with low-to-moderate engine hours. Boats with an exceptional equipment list or those with unusually low hours will usually sell at a figure higher than the published Retail High.

The Retail Low is the average selling price of a boat with below-average maintenance, poor equipment, high-time engines, or excessive wear. High-time boats in poor condition will generally sell for less than the published Retail Low.

Used boats located in the following markets are generally valued at 10–15% higher than published prices:

1) Great Lakes
2) Pacific Northwest
3) Inland Rivers & Lakes

The prices presented in this book reflect our best estimates of used boat prices for the model year 1996. They are intended for general use only and are not meant to represent exact market values.

Frequently Asked Questions

In an effort to clear away some of the confusion regarding the purchase of a new or used family cruiser, we have listed below some of the most common questions asked by potential buyers. The answers presented to these questions are our own and we welcome responses from others who hold differing views. For the most part, however, we believe the information presented here will address several important issues confronting buyers of boats listed in this publication.

What's the difference between a Family Cruiser and an Express Cruiser?

For the purposes of this book, we define a Family Cruiser as having either a flybridge or a hardtop, and we define an Express Cruiser as an open-style design without a flybridge or hardtop.

Experienced boaters will note that many of the selections we have made in the Guide to Family & Express Cruisers are in fact well-known fishing boats. The Bertram 37 Convertible, for example, is a superb fisherman as are the Tiara 3600 Open and the Viking 38 Convertible. We include these models (and several others like them) because—aside from being excellent fishing boats—they make fine cruising boats as well. Indeed, many such models are purchased every year for their cruising attributes with little consideration given to their offshore fishing capabilities.

I hear a lot of brokers talking about deep-V hulls. Should I be looking for this in my next boat?

The majority of manufacturers of over-30-foot designs build their boats on modified-V hulls because it provides owners with a good combination of performance, stability, and economy. Other builders specialize in more performance oriented designs for better rough-water capabilities. It's true that deep-V designs offer superior rough water performance but at a cost. They tend to roll more at trolling speeds (especially in a beam sea), and they're more sensitive to the added weight of a flybridge. They also require more power to get up on plane, although there's no serious penalty in cruising economy once they're up and running.

Aside from their excellent headsea capabilities, deep-V hulls generally track much better than a modified-V design of similar length and displacement. A Sea Ray 370 Sundancer, for example, will require a lot less steering effort in a quartering or following sea than a Trojan 36 Convertible or a Carver 27 Santego—low-deadrise boats with relatively flat bottoms. Less stable at slow speeds, the deep-V is a more stable design at cruising speeds.

Note that while deep-V hulls involve some compromise in larger boats (over 30 feet) they are generally the standard in smaller designs.

Beam is important to my family since we want as much interior volume as possible in a boat. Some of the wide-beam models we've been aboard recently are huge inside. Just how much is *too much* beam?

Although modern production boats clearly have more beam than their predecessors, many yacht designers still consider one foot of beam for each three feet of length close to the ideal length-to-beam ratio for yachts under fifty-five feet. Having said that, the fact is that most modern production boats have beams that exceed that 3-1 ratio. It's not unusual, for example, to see a 36-footer with a 13-foot beam or, say, a 45-footer with a 16-foot beam.

A boat with an unusually wide beam will be a more stable platform than a similiar-size boat with a normal beam. The additional underwater drag of the wide-beam boat, however, almost always results in a loss of performance and operating efficiency. Finally, boats with exceptionally wide beams are slow to execute turns and sometimes behave poorly in a following sea.

Should I be looking for a boat with diesel engines?

In many cases the answer is yes. Diesels are seldom installed as standard equipment in family or express cruisers under 40 feet although they are usually offered as an option.

Range is often a factor in a cruising yacht and diesels can deliver up to 50% more mileage than the same boat with gasoline engines. It should be noted, however, that it is not at all uncommon to see gas-powered boats over 40 feet in the Great Lakes and inland waterways where range is of less importance. Indeed, for boaters with short seasons and limited cruising grounds the cost of diesels just doesn't make sense.

In a smaller family cruiser or express cruisers the choice between gas and diesel is easy: gas engines are more popular by a wide margin. The added expense of diesels in a 35-foot boat could easily add up up to a quarter of the purchase price. Fortunately, diesels are becoming more affordable as new technology allows manufacturers to reduce both the size and weight of diesel engines while increasing their performance.

In resolving this question, keep in mind that the resale value of a diesel-powered boat will often go a long way toward justifying the added up-front expense.

I know that engine hours are important but what constitutes a lot of hours on a particular set of motors?

This is always a hard question to answer, so we'll just offer up some general guidelines. When it comes to gas engines (inboards and I/Os), most dealers and brokers figure those with over 1,000 hours are probably tired. With turbocharged diesels 3,500 hours is a lot of running time, and with naturally aspirated diesels it's not uncommon to pile up 5,000 hours before an overhaul is required.

The tragedy is that many of today's ultra-high-performance diesels never see 2,000 hours before an overhaul. Sometimes this is a manufacturer problem but premature marine diesel death usually results from improper owner care and maintenance. Lack of use and poor exercise habits may be the number-one killer. Humidity (moisture) on cylinder components can be avoided with regular running and engine heaters. Diesel engines should be run under a load whenever possible. If your mechanical surveyor suggests new oil, fuel, or water hoses, do it. Trying to save money here can be expensive.

Having said that, it's important to note that there are far too many variables to make any buying decisions based upon engine hours alone. It's imperative to have the diesels in a used boat surveyed just as you have the boat itself professionally examined before reaching a final decision. Surveying gas engines is easier and less expensive than surveying diesel engines. While we highly recommend a marine mechanic for the job, an auto mechanic can take cylinder compressions and pass judgement on the internal condition of an inboard gas engine. When it comes to evaluating outdrives and outboard engines, however, a qualified marine mechanic is essential.

Determining the actual hours on an engine (or a set of engines) can be difficult. There are generally hour meters installed in boats over 25 feet but they're not always found in smaller gas-powered boats. Even if you have access to all the service records, we strongly suggest that you rely on an expert to evaluate the engines in any boat you have a serious interest in owning.

I'm in the market for a 30' express cruiser. My broker's telling me to buy a boat with inboard engines rather than stern drives. Yet I see plenty of express cruisers this size with stern drives. Is he giving me good advice?

With a couple of exceptions, we think your broker is providing some excellent advice. While it's certainly true that stern drives (also called inboard/outboards, or I/Os) are getting bigger and more powerful every year, the fact remains that their popularity in boats over 30 feet is generally limited to buyers seeking performance over longevity.

A 30-foot express cruiser with straight inboards will require less overall maintanance simply because there are no outdrives to service every year. That's especially in salt water where outdrives are susceptible to galvanic corrosion— a big reason why stern drive boats are kept out of the water as much as possible when they're not being used.

I'm looking at a boat with prop pockets. What are the advantages and disadvantages?

Prop pockets are used to reduce shaft angles which often results in improved fuel economy and engine efficiency at cruising speeds. Manufacturers like Sea Ray and Phoenix have used them for years. A secondary benefit to owning a hull with prop pockets is evident—the ability to operate with less fear of clipping a prop in shallow waters.
One criticism we've often heard of boats with prop pockets is that they don't back

down as well since they lack the "bite" that a more exposed propeller can get. Most experienced captains agree that backing a boat with prop pockets into a slip takes a little more finesse (or throttle) than with a conventional hull.

Should I reject a boat with bottom blisters?

Generally, no. Blisters can almost always be repaired although the process can require a fair amount of time and expense. With that in mind, it is rare indeed to see a blistering problem so severe that it actually effects the integrity of the hull.

While some boats tend to re-blister again and again, most bottoms properly dried and protected should remain blister-free for five years or longer.

Can I rely on the boat tests that I read in the national magazines?

Yes, they're usually accurate as far as they go. For example, the performance figures—speeds at various rpm rates, fuel burn data, etc.—are quite reliable, although it's always wise to keep in mind that these are new boats with light loads and plenty of factory preparation. Don't look for a lot of hard-hitting criticism in these tests, however, because boating magazines (including ours) depend upon boat manufacturers for a major part of their advertising revenues.

We've read a lot of boat tests over the years. In our opinion, the best and most comprehensive are conducted by Boating magazine. Sea and Sport Fishing also have some excellent reviews.

How important is a lower helm?

That depends upon your location. A lower helm is a great convenience—a luxury, actually—when you're getting an early start on a chilly morning or trying to stay dry on a wet, windy day. For visibility, however (and to avoid seasickness), most skippers prefer the bridge station for heavy weather running in spite of the physical discomforts.

Aside from the added expense (which can be considerable), a lower helm takes up valuable room in the salon which would otherwise be devoted to living space. Not surprisingly, Inside helms are most commonly seen in northern climates, especially in the Great Lakes and the Pacific Northwest. On the other hand, a lower helm in Florida (or along the Gulf Coast) is often a hindrance to a boat's resale value since it may be viewed as a useless and unnecessary feature.

Are freshwater boats really worth more?

Sure, no question about it. Salt water is hard on a boat, especially the gelcoat, electronics, paint, metalwork, and engine room components. And while nearly all diesel-powered boats have closed cooling systems, the same is not always true of gas engines. In a saltwater environment it's wise to look for a boat with a closed cooling system since it usually lengthens engine life. Another reason why freshwater boats often bring a premium price has to do with the fact that they generally have fewer engine hours. The boating season in most freshwater regions is shorter than many of the largest saltwater boating areas. Furthermore, the majority of freshwater vessels spend their winters out of the water—many in a protected environment with reduced exposure to the corrosive effects of sun, wind and rain.

As might be imagined, a well-maintained saltwater vessel is probably a better investment than a poorly maintained freshwater boat. One final factor that equalizes the values between the two is equipment. An East or West Coast saltwater boat is often fitted out with better cruising equipment and more elaborate electronics than a similar Great Lakes or inland waters vessel.

Should I avoid a boat if the manufacturer has gone out of business or is currently undergoing hard times?

No! There are plenty of good used boats on the market from manufacturers who couldn't survive the poor economy of the past several years. The parts you will need from time to time are always available from catalog outlets or suppliers. Engine parts, of course, are easily secured from a number of sources. Generally speaking, there are no components used in a production model that cannot be replaced (or repaired) by a good yard.

Note that many of the most popular models on today's brokerage market were built by companies now out of business.

For resale, should I only consider a brand of boat with big-name market recognition?

There is no question that certain popular brands have consistently higher resale values. There are, however, many designs from small or regional builders that are highly sought after by knowledgeable boaters. Often, the market for these models is tighter and generally less saturated than the high production designs—a factor that often works to a seller's advantage.

Most of the boats I've been considering are equipped with 454-cid Crusader or MerCruiser gas inboards. I'm told these are marinized versions of " big-block" Chevy truck engines. How much fuel can I expect to burn with these motors?

There are several variables to consider when trying to figure the probable fuel consumption of a boat with a given set of engines—weight and beam, gearing, the condition of the bottom, seas, etc. That said, a pair of 454-cid engines running at full cruising speed (3,000–3,200 rpms) can be expected to burn in the neighborhood of 28–32 gallons per hour. Pushing most inboard gas engines beyond 3,200 rpm results in a dramatic fall-off in fuel economy since the other two barrels of the carburetors are then activated.

If I decide to buy a used boat, should I use a broker?

If you have plenty of time on your hands you could locate a good boat at a fair price without a broker. Unless you find a boat for sale by owner, you end up working with a broker anyway—the listing agent.

When choosing a broker consider that you are about to spend a large amount of money. Do your homework and end up with an agent that you feel has your long-term interests at heart. You're not paying for his time and expertise until you purchase a boat through him. Keeping many brokers in competition against one another often results in no one giving you the time and attention that you'll require.

Useful Terms

Abaft—behind

Athwartships—at a right angle to the boat's length

Bulkhead—an upright partition separating compartments in a boat

Bulwark—a raised portion of the deck designed to serve as a barrier

Chine—the point at which the hullsides and the bottom of the boat come together

cid—referring to the cubic inch displacement of an engine, e.g., 454-cid gas engine

Coaming—vertical surface surrounding the cockpit

Cuddy—generally refers to the cabin of a small boat

Deadrise—the angle from the bottom of the hull (not the keel) to the chine

Deep-V Hull—a planing hull form with at least 17° of deadrise at the transom and a fairly constant "V" bottom shape from stem to stern.

Displacement Hull—a hull designed to go through the water and not capable of planing speed

Forefoot—the underwater shape of the hull at the bow

Freeboard—the height of the sides of the hull above the waterline

gph—gallons per hour (of fuel consumption)

Gunwale (also gunnel)— the upper edge of the sheerline

Hull Speed—the maximum practical speed of a displacement hull. To calculate, take the square root of the LWL (waterline hull length) and multiply by 1.34.

Knot—one nautical mile per hour. To convert knots to statute mph, multiply by 1.14.

Modified-V Hull—a planing hull form with less than 17° of transom deadrise

Nautical Mile—measurement used in salt water. A nautical mile is 6,076 feet.

Planing Speed—the point at which an accelerating hull rises onto the top of the water. To calculate a hull's planing speed, multiply the square root of the waterline length by 2.

Semi-Displacement Hull—a hull designed to operate economically at low speeds while still able to attain efficient planing speed performance

Sheerline—the fore-and-aft line along the top edge of the hull

Sole—a nautical term for floor

Statute Mile—measurement used in fresh water. A statute mile equals 5,280 feet.

Tender—refers to (a) a dinghy, or (b) lack of stability

Directory of Yacht Brokers & Dealers

(Sorted Alphabetically by State)

ALABAMA

A&M Yacht Sales
5004 Dauphin Island Pkwy.
Mobile, AL 36605
334-471-6949; Fax 334-479-4625
Hatteras, Viking, Bertram

KV Yacht Brokerage
27844 Canal Rd., Sportsman's Marina
Orange Beach, AL 36561
205-981-9600; Fax 205-981-9602

Marine Brokerage Service
201 Blount Ave.
Guntersville, AL 35976
205-582-8529; Fax 205-582-1656

The Marine Group
Orange Beach Marina, PO Box 650
Orange Beach, AL 36561
205-981-9200; Fax 205-981-9137

ARIZONA

Action Marine
1366 W. Broadway
Mesa, AZ 85210
602-964-6463; Fax 602-969-3026
Luhrs, Mainship

CALIFORNIA

Ballena Bay Yacht Brokers
1150 Ballena Blvd., #121
Alameda, CA 94501
510-865-8601; Fax 510-865-5560
Krogen

Bayside Yacht Sales
164 Marina Drive
Long Beach, CA 90803
310-430-3131; Fax 310-493-4333
DeFever, Krogen

Bill Gorman Yachts
1070 Marina Village Pkwy., #100
Alameda, CA 94501
510-865-6151; Fax 510-865-1220

Cays Boat Sales
509 Grand Caribe Isle
Coronado, CA 92118
619-424-4024; Fax 619-575-7716

Cays Boat Sales
2384 Shelter Island Dr.
San Diego, CA 92106
619-523-3666; Fax 619-523-3670

City Yachts
10 Marina Blvd.
San Francisco CA 94123
415-567-8880; Fax 415-567-6725
West Bay

Darlene Hubbard Yacht Broker
1715 Strand Way
Coronado, CA 92118
800-435-3188; Fax 619-435-3189

Fleming Yachts
510 - 31st Street, #H
Newport Beach, CA 92663
714-723-4225; Fax 714-723-4093
Fleming

Fraser Yachts
2353 Shelter Island Dr.
San Diego, CA 92106
619-225-0588; Fax 619-225-1325

Fraser Yachts
3471 Via Lido
Newport Beach, CA 92663
714-673-5252; Fax 714-673-8795

Fraser Yachts
320 Harbor Dr.
Sausalito, CA 94965
415-332-5311; Fax 415-332-7036

Lager Yacht Brokerage Corp.
400 Harbor Dr. #C
Sausalito, CA 94965
415-332-9500; Fax 415-332-9503

Lemest Yacht Sales
24703 Dana Drive
Dana Point, CA 92629
714-496-4933; Fax 714-240-2398

Newmarks Yacht & Ship Brokers
210 Whalers Walk
San Pedro, CA 90731
310-833-0887; Fax 310-833-0979

Newport Boats
1880 Newport Blvd.
Costa Mesa, CA 92627
714-642-8870; Fax 714-642-9824
Maxum

Newport Yacht Brokers
Box 5741, 400 S. Bayfront
Newport Beach, CA, 92662
714-723-1200; Fax 714-723-1201

Newport Yacht Sales
13555 Fiji Way
Marina del Rey, CA 90292
310-301-0020; Fax 310-821-8755

Newport Yacht Sales
3404 Via Oporto, #203
Newport Beach, CA 92663
714-675-1800; Fax 714-675-9533

Norcal Yachts
1070 Marina Village Pkwy., #103
Alameda, CA 94501
510-814-8560; Fax 510-814-8563

Oceanic Yacht Sales
308 Harbor Dr.
Sausalito, CA 94965
415-331-0533; Fax 415-331-1642
Grand Banks

Offshore Yachts
3412 Via Oporto, Suite 203
Newport Beach, CA, 92663
714-673-5401; Fax 714-673-1220

Passage Yachts
1220 Brickyard Cove Rd.
Point Richmond, CA 94801
510-236-2633; Fax 510-234-0118
Beneteau, Tiara

Yacht Broker & Dealer Directory

Peter Crane Yacht Sales
6 Harbor Way, Suite 106
Santa Barbara, CA 93109
805-963-8000; Fax 805-966-0722

Price & Bell Yacht Brokers
3005 Peninsula Rd.
Channel Islands Harbor, CA 93035
805-984-8550; Fax 805-984-8552

R.D. Snyder Yachts
1231 Shafter St.
San Diego, CA 92106
619-224-2464; Fax 619-224-7396

Richard Boland Yacht Sales
1070 Marina Village Pkwy., #107
Alameda, CA 94501
510-521-6213; Fax 510-521-0118
Viking, Ocean, Riviera

San Diego Yacht Sales
2525 Shelter Island Dr.
San Diego, CA 92106
619-523-1000; Fax 619-221-0308
Hylas

Seaward Yacht Sales
101 Shipyard Way, Suite K
Newport Beach, CA 92663-4447
714-673-5950; Fax 714-673-1058
Vitech, Nordic, Tayana

Southshore Yacht Sales
997 G Street
Chula Vista, CA 91910
619-427-3357; Fax 619-427-6549

Southwestern Yacht Sales
1500 Quivira Way
San Diego, CA 92109
619-224-4102; Fax 619-224-7874
Beneteau, Sabreline

Summit Marine Boat Centers
1700 Verne Roberts Circle
Antioch, CA 94509
510-777-9300
Bayliner

Superior Yacht Sales
Pier 40, South Beach Harbor
San Francisco, CA 94117
415-543-2650; Fax 415-543-2677
Vitesse

Superior Yacht Sales
29 Embarcadero Cove
Oakland, CA 94606
510-534-9492; Fax 510-534-9495
Vitesse

The Crow's Nest
2515 Shelter Island Dr.
San Diego, CA 92106
619-222-1122; Fax 619-222-3851
Bertram, Hatteras, Tiara

The Crow's Nest
2801 W. Coast Hwy., #260
Newport Beach, CA 92663
714-574-7600; Fax 714-574-7610
Bertram, Hatteras, Tiara

Tocci Yachts
3 Marina Plaza
Antioch, CA 94509
510-706-0292; Fax 510-706-0281
Carri Craft, Holiday Mansion

Trident Yacht Sales
43 Embarcadero Cove
Oakland, CA 94606
510-261-2792; Fax 510-261-2794

Warner Boat Sales
4695 Admiralty Way
Marina del Rey, CA 90292
310-822-0688; Fax 310-822-6411
Mediterranean

Wescal Yachts
16400 Pacific Coast Hwy., #106
Huntington Beach, CA 92649
310-592-4547; Fax 310-592-2960

Yachtline International
3810 W. Channel Islands Blvd. #I
Oxnard, CA 93035-4001
805-985-8643; Fax 805-985-3889
Ocean Alexander

Yamaha Marina Del Rey
13555 Fiji Way
Marina del Rey, CA 90292
310-823-8964; Fax 310-821-0569
Tiara, Wellcraft

CONNECTICUT

Boats Incorporated
133 East Main Street
Niantic, CT 06357
203-739-6251; Fax 203-739-3394
Grady White, Albemarle, Boston Whaler, Parker

Boatworks Yacht Sales
Dauntless Shipyard, Box 668
Essex, CT 06426
203-767-3013; Fax 203-767-7178
Sabreline, Grand Banks

Boatworks Yacht Sales
95 Rowayton Ave.
Rowayton, CT 06853
203-866-0882; Fax 203-853-4910
Sabreline, Grand Banks

Chan Moser Yachts
123 Downs Ave.
Stamford, CT 06902
203-324-4479; Fax 203-348-4540

Coastal Marine
143 River Rd., Box 228
Cos Cob, CT 06807
203-661-5765; Fax 203-661-6040
Albin

Eastland Yachts
33 Pratt St.
Essex, CT 06426
203-767-8224; Fax 203-767-9094

Jensen Yacht Sales
142 Ferry Rd.
Old Saybrook, CT 06475
203-395-1200; Fax 203-395-1465
Carver, Holiday Mansion

North East Yachts
54 Riverview St.
Portland, CT 06480
203-342-1988; Fax 203-342-4132
Blackfin, Bertram

Northrop & Johnson of Essex
P.O. Box 190
Essex, CT 06426
203-767-0149 ; Fax 203-767-0878

Norwalk Cove Marina
Beach Road
East Norwalk, CT 06855
203-838-2326; 800-243-2744 ; Fax 203-838-9258
Hatteras, Azimut

Norwest Marine
130 Water St.
South Norwalk, CT 06854
203-853-2822
Luhrs, Regulator, Wahoo!

Portland Boat Works
1 Grove St.
Portland, CT 06480
203-342-1085; Fax 203-342-0544
Post, Tiara

Yacht Broker & Dealer Directory

Rex Marine Center
144 Water St.
South Norwalk, CT 06854
203-866-5555; Fax 203-866-2518
Stamas, Formula, Island Packet

Sail Westbrook
PO Box 1179
Westbrook, CT 06498
203-399-5515; Fax 203-399-8076

FLORIDA

Alliance Marine
2608 N. Ocean Blvd.
Pompano Beach, FL 33062
305-941-5000; Fax 305-782-4911
Legacy

American Trading Industries
500 SE 17th St., #220
Ft. Lauderdale, FL 33316
305-522-4254; Fax 305-522-4435

Ameriship Corporation
3285 SW 11th Ave.
Ft. Lauderdale, FL 33315
305-463-7957; Fax 305-463-3342
Exporter, Contender

Atlantic Pacific Cruising Yachts
2244 SE 17th St.
Ft. Lauderdale, FL 33316
305-463-7651; Fax 305-779-3316
Vagabond, Ultimate

Atlantic Yacht & Ship
850 NE 3rd St., #210
Dania, FL 33004-3402
305-921-1500; Fax 305-921-1518

Bassett Boat Co.
700 NE 79th Street
Miami, FL 33138
305-758-5786
Sea Ray

Boger Yacht Sales
2305 Beach Blvd
Jacksonville Beach, FL 32250
904-247-7966; Fax 904-247-7972

Bradford International Yacht Sales
3151 State Road 84
Ft. Lauderdale, FL 33312
305-791-2600; Fax 305-791-2655

Bruce A. Bales Yacht Sales
1635 S. Miami Rd., #2
Ft. Lauderdale, FL 33316
305-522-3760; Fax 305-522-4364

Cape Yacht Brokerage
800 Scallop Dr.
Port Canaveral, FL 32920
407-799-4724; Fax 407-799-0096
Beachcat

Catamaran Sales
1650 SE 17th St., #207
Ft. Lauderdale, FL 33316
305-462-6506; Fax 305-462-6104
Euphoric, Privilege

Charles Morgan Associates
200 Second Ave. S.
St. Petersburg, FL 33701
813-894-7027; Fax 813-894-8983

Coast Marine
230 Eglin Parkway SE
Ft. Walton Beach, FL 32548
904-244-3333; Fax 904-243-2433
Wellcraft, Excell, Cruisers

Coastal Yacht Sales
300 S. Duncan Ave., Ste. 189
Clearwater, FL 34615
813-593-7900; Fax 813-449-9743
Ocean

Complete Yacht Services
3599 E. Indian River Dr.
Vero Beach, FL 32963
407-231-2111; Fax 407-231-4465
Grand Banks, Sabreline

Custom Brokerage Yacht Sales
11422 SW 87th Terrace
Miami, FL 33173
305-598-9875; Fax 305-598-2239

Dave Pyles Yacht Sales
2596 SW 23rd Terrace
Ft. Lauderdale, FL 33312
305-583-8104; Fax 305-797-7669

Daytona Marina & Boatworks
645 S. Beach St.
Daytona Beach, FL 32114
904-253-6266; Fax 904-253-8174

East-West Yachts
10 Avenue A, Ft. Pierce Yacht Center
Ft. Pierce, FL 34950
407-466-1240; Fax 407-466-1242
Brokerage

East-West Yachts
800 N. Flagler Dr.
West Palm Beach, FL 33401
407-655-2323; Fax 407-655-2310
Brokerage

Eastern Yacht Sales
1177 Avenue C
Riviera Beach, FL 33404-6943
407-844-1100; Fax 407-844-8946
Freedom, Beneteau, Tollycraft, Whaler, J Boats, Catalina

Edgewater Yacht Sales
PO Box 34227
Pensacola, FL 32507
904-492-2588; Fax 904-492-3334

Fairline Marine
201 SE 15th Terrace, #210
Deerfield Beach, FL 33441
305-481-3569; Fax 305-481-2433
Fairline (Squadron and Phantom)

First Marine Group
1495 Old Griffin Rd.
Dania, FL 33004
305-923-4800; Fax 305-923-3139
Apache, Baha

Fish Tale Marina
7225 Estero Blvd.
Ft. Myers Beach, FL 33931
813-463-4448; Fax 813-765-1419
Blackfin, Grady White, Fountain

Florida Yacht Charters & Sale
1290 Fifth Street at Miami Beach Marina
Miami Beach, FL 33139
305-532-8600; Fax 305-672-2039
Albin, Hunter

Fraser Yachts
2230 SE 17th St.
Ft. Lauderdale, FL 33316
305-463-0600; Fax 305-763-1053
Benetti, Christensen, Vitech, Custom

Gilman Yacht Sales
1212-A U.S. Hwy 1
North Palm Beach, FL 33408
407-626-1790; Fax 407-626-5870

Grand Lagoon Yacht Brokers
3706 Thomas Dr.
Panama City Beach, FL 32408
904-233-4747; Fax 904-233-4741

Yacht Broker & Dealer Directory

Great American Marine
11620 Cleveland Ave.
Ft. Myers, FL 33901
813-277-9919
Donzi, Excel

H&H Yacht Sales
450 Basin St.
Daytona Beach, FL 32114
904-255-0744; Fax 904-253-8842
Brokerage Services

Hal Jones & Co.
1900 SE 15th St.
Ft. Lauderdale, FL 33316
305-527-1778; Fax 305-523-5153
Grand Banks

Hatteras of Lauderdale
401 SW 1st Ave.
Ft. Lauderdale, FL 33301
305-462-5557; Fax 305-462-0029
Hatteras, Tiara

Helms • Kelly • MacMahon Int'l Yachting
1650 SE 17th St., Suite 101
Ft. Lauderdale, FL 33316
305-525-1441; Fax 305-525-1110
Brokerage Services

Herb Phillips Yacht Sales
1535 SE 17th St., #117B
Ft. Lauderdale, FL 33316
305-523-8600; Fax 305-523-8609
Striker

HMY Yacht Sales
850 NE 3rd. St.
Dania, FL 33004
305-926-0400; Fax 305-921-2543
Post, Hines-Farley, Viking, Cabo

HMY Yacht Sales
2401 PGA Blvd., Suite 190
Palm Beach Gardens, FL 33410
407-775-6000; Fax 407-775-6006
Post, Cabo

Kenyon Power Boats
19400 U.S. 19 North
Clearwater, FL 34624
813-539-7444; Fax 813-531-7098
Bayliner, Maxum, SeaCat, Starcraft

Lazzara Int'l Yacht Brokerage
5300 W. Tyson Ave.
Tampa, FL 33611
813-835-5300; Fax 813-835-0964
Brokerage

Luxury Yacht Corp.
1900 SE 15th Street
Ft. Lauderdale, FL 33316
305-764-3388; Fax 305-763-8852
Mainship, Vantare, Mikelson

Merrill-Stevens Yacht Sales
1270 NW 11th St.
Miami, FL 33125
305-858-5911; Fax 305-858-5919

Merritt Yacht Brokers
2040 SE 17th St
Ft. Lauderdale, FL 33316
305-761-1300; 800-446-6695; Fax 305-463-8617

Naples Boat Mart
829 Airport Road North
Naples, FL 33963
813-643-2292; Fax 813-643-6197
Luhrs, Regal

Naples Yacht Brokerage
774 12th Ave. South
Naples, FL 33940
941-434-8338; Fax 941-434-6848

New Wave Marine Center
13255 Biscayne Blvd. NE
North Miami, FL 33181
305-892-2628; Fax 305-892-0444
Regal, Century

Offshore Yacht & Ship Brokers
404 Riberia St.
St. Augustine, FL 32084
904-829-9224; Fax 904-825-4292

OKB Marine
3427 S. Orange Ave.
Orlando, FL 32806
407-859-2628; Fax 407-856-0512
Hydrasports, Glastron

Ortega Yacht Sales
3420 Lake Shore Blvd.
Jacksonville, FL 32210
904-388-5547; Fax 904-384-8400
Sabreline

Oviatt Marine
850 NE 3rd St., Suite 201
Dania, FL 33004
305-925-0065; Fax 305-925-8822
DeFever

Palm Beach Yacht Brokerage
226 Royal Palm Beach
Palm Beach, FL 33480
407-835-8393; Fax 407-835-4214

Palm Beach Yacht Club
800 N. Flagler Dr.
West Palm Beach, FL 33401
407-655-2323; Fax 407-655-2310

Power Yacht Sales International
PO Box 654101
Miami, FL 33265-4101
305-661-2095; Fax 305-661-3518

Prestige Yachts
600 Barracks St., Suite 102
Pensacola, FL 32501
904-432-6838; Fax 904-432-8999
Tiara, Silverton

Reel Deal Yachts
2550 S. Bayshore Dr.
Coconut Grove, FL 33133
305-859-8200; Fax 305-854-8044
Donzi, Mako, Blackfin, Luhrs, Egg Harbor, Mainship

Rhodes Yacht Brokers
2901 NE 28th Court
Lighthouse Point, FL 33064
305-941-2404; Fax 305-941-2507

Richard Bertram, Inc.
3660 NW 21st Street
Miami, FL 33142
305-633-9761; Fax 305-634-9071
Bertram, Ocean Alexander

Richard Bertram, Inc.
801 Seabreeze Blvd.
Ft. Lauderdale, FL 33316
305-467-8405; Fax 305-763-2675
Bertram, Ocean Alexander

Richard Bertram, Inc.
2 Fishing Village Dr.
Key Largo, FL 33037
305-367-3267; Fax 305-367-2128
Bertram, Ocean Alexander

Richard Bertram, Inc.
2385 PGA Blvd.
Palm Beach Gardens, FL 33410
407-625-1045
Bertram, Ocean Alexander

Royal Yacht & Ship Brokers
3859 Central Ave.
St. Petersburg, FL 33713
813-327-0900; Fax 813-327-7797

Rybovich-Spencer Group
4200 N. Dixie
West Palm Beach, FL 33407
407-844-4331; Fax 407-844-8393

Yacht Broker & Dealer Directory

Shear Yacht Sales
2401 PGA Blvd., Suite 182
Palm Beach Gardens, FL 33410
407-624-2112; Fax 407-624-1877
Island Gypsy, Novatec, Tollycraft

Singer Island Yacht Sales
11440 U.S. Highway 1
Palm Beach Gardens, FL 33408
407-622-0355; Fax 407-622-0339

South Florida Marine Yacht Brokerage
4800 N. Federal Hwy., Suite 113B
Boca Raton, FL 33431
407-750-5155; Fax 407-750-8533

Stella Marine
2385 PGA Blvd.
Palm Beach Gardens, FL 33410
407-624-9950; Fax 407-624-9949
Carver, Pursuit, Albemarle, Pro-Line

Stella Marine
250 SW Monterey
Stuart, FL 34994
407-287-1101; Fax 407-287-8445
Carver, Pursuit, Albemarle, Pro-Line

Striker Yacht Corporation
1535 SE 17th St., #117B
Ft. Lauderdale, FL 33316
305-523-8600; Fax 305-523-8609
Striker

Stuart Yacht
450 SW Salerno Rd.
Stuart, FL 34997
407-283-1947; Fax 407-286-9800

Sunny Isles Boat Sales
3450 N. Federal Hwy.
Lighthouse Point, FL 33064
305-784-1501; Fax 305-784-1960
Chaparral, Silverton

Sunshine Yacht Sales
20533 Biscayne Blvd., Suite 4-156
North Miami Beach, FL 33180
305-949-2248; Fax 305-944-7173

Taber Yacht Sales
Pirates Cove Marine,
PO Box 1687
Port Salerno, FL 34992
407-288-7466; Fax 407-288-7476

The Allied Marine Group
401 SW 1st Ave.
Ft. Lauderdale, FL 33301
305-462-5527; Fax 305-462-0029
Hatteras, Tiara

The Boatworks
6921 - 14th Street West (U.S. 41)
Bradenton, FL 34207
813-756-1896; Fax 813-753-9426
Bayliner, Wellcraft, Mako, Blackfin, Century

The Marine Group of Palm Beach
2401 PGA Blvd., Suite 164
Palm Beach Gardens, FL 33410
407-627-9500; Fax 407-627-9503

United Derecktor Gunnell
901 SE 17th St., #205
Ft. Lauderdale, FL 33316
305-524-4616; Fax 305-524-4621

Universal Yacht
1645 SE 3rd Ct., Suite 214
Deerfield Beach, FL 33441-4465
305-420-0229; Fax 305-420-0117

Walker's Yacht Sales
1006 N. Barfield Dr.
Marco Island, FL 33937
813-642-6764; Fax 813-642-0476
Luhrs, Formula, Pursuit, Tiaar

Walker's Yacht Sales
895 - 10th St. South
Naples, FL 33940
813-262-6500; Fax 813-262-6693
Luhrs, Formula, Pursuit, Tiara

Walsh Yachts
1900 S.E. 15th Street
Ft. Lauderdale, FL 33316
305-525-7447; Fax 305-525-7451
Ferretti

Wayne Roman Yachts
155 E. Blue Heron Blvd.
Riviera Beach, FL 33404
407-844-5000; Fax 407-844-0124

West Florida Yachts
4880 - 37th St. South
St. Petersburg, FL 33711
813-864-0310; Fax 813-867-6860

Woods & Oviatt
Pier 66 Marina, 2301 SE 17th St.
Ft. Lauderdale, FL 33316
305-463-5606; Fax 305-522-5156
Brokerage Services

Yacht Brokerage USA
125 Basin St. at Halifax Harbor Marina
Daytona Beach, FL 32114
904-253-9353; Fax 904-253-0401

Yacht Perfection
1133 Bal Harbor Blvd., #1141
Punta Gorda, FL 33950
813-637-8111; Fax 813-637-9918

Yacht Sales International
300 Alton Rd.
Miami Beach, FL 33139
305-534-3226; Fax 305-534-2924
Ocean

Yachtmasters
290 Coconut Ave.
Sarasota, FL 34236
813-366-3722; Fax 813-365-8411
Brokerage

ZK Yacht
850 NE 3rd Street, Ste. 209
Dania, FL 33004
305-923-7441; Fax 305-923-7477
Brokerage Services

GEORGIA

Robert P. Minis, Inc.
102 McIntosh Dr.
Savannah, GA 31406
912-354-6589; Fax 912-354-6589
Brokerage Services

ILLINOIS

Class Sea Yachts
207 N. Hager
Barrington, IL 60010
708-382-2100; Fax 708-381-1265
Post

Harborside Marina
27425 South Will Rd.
Wilmington, IL 60481
815-476-2254
Bluewater, Nordic Tugs, Cruisers

Larsen Marine Service
1663 N. Elston Ave.
Chicago, IL 60614
312-993-7711; Fax 312-772-0891
Tiara

INDIANA

H&M Yacht Brokerage
1 Newport Dr.
Michigan City, IN 46360
219-879-7152
Brokerage Services

Yacht Broker & Dealer Directory

Kentuckiana Yacht Sales
700 East Market St.
Jeffersonville, IN 47131
812-282-7579; Fax 812-282-8020
Jefferson, Gibson, Mainship

IOWA

Anderson Marine at Dubuque Marina
Eagle Point Ext.
Dubuque, IA 52001
319-582-3653; Fax 319-582-0941
Bayliner, Wellcraft

River Bend Yacht Sales
2363 W. Dale Ct.
Bettendorf, IA 52722-2147
319-355-2726; Fax 319-355-0938
Brokerage Services

LOUISIANA

Competition Marine
2233 Lafayette Ave.
Harvey, LA 70059
504-366-8021
Stamas

Mayer Yacht Services
PO Box 840060
New Orleans, LA 70184
504-945-2268; Fax 504-942-2708
Brokerage Services

MAINE

Casco Bay Yacht Exchange
239 US Rt. 1
Freeport, ME 04032
207-865-4016; Fax 207-865-0759
Brokerage Services

Hinckley Yacht Brokerage
Box 699, Shore Rd.
Southwest Harbor, ME 04679
207-244-5531; Fax 207-244-9833
Hinckley

North Star Yacht Sales
DiMillo's Marina, Long Wharf
Portland, ME 04101
207-879-7678; Fax 207-879-1471

The Yacht Connection
14 Ocean Street
South Portland, ME 04106
207-799-3600; Fax 207-767-5937
Brokerage Services

MARYLAND

Anchor Yacht Basin
1048 Turkey Point Rd.
Edgewater, MD 21037
410-269-6674; Fax 410-798-6782
Phoenix, Dawson

Arnold C. Gay Yacht Sales
"C" Street, PO Box 538
Solomons, MD 20688
410-326-2011; Fax 410-326-2012
Brokerage

Burr Yacht Sales
1106 Turkey Point Rd
Edgewater, MD 21037
410-798-5900; Fax 410-798-5911
Fleming, Bertram

Cherry Yachts
2830 Solomons Island Rd.
Edgewater, MD 21037
410-266-3801; Fax 410-266-3805

Gemini Marine Group
326 1st Street, #32
Annapolis, MD 21403
800-525-5105; Fax 410-267-6127

Jackson Marine Sales
PO Box 483, Hances Point
North East, MD 21901
410-287-9400; Fax 410-287-9034
Onset, Mercury & OMC

Martin Bird & Associates
326 First Street
Annapolis, MD 21403
410-268-1086; Fax 410-268-0942

Nautilus Yacht Sales
Skipjack Cove Yachting Resort
PO Box 56
Georgetown, MD 21930
410-275-1100, 800-654-BOAT;
Fax 410-275-1133
Brokerage Services

Oxford Yacht Agency
317 S. Morris St.
Oxford, MD 21654
410-226-5454; Fax 410-226-5244
Grand Banks

Reynolds Yacht Sales
PO Box 147
Georgetown, MD 21930
410-648-5347; Fax 410-648-5263
Brokerage Services

Riverside Marine
11051 Pulaski Hwy
White Marsh, MD 21162-1813
410-686-1500
Bayliner

Solomons Yacht Brokerage
PO Box 380, 255 "A" Street, Town Center Marina
Solomons, MD 20688
410-326-6748; Fax 410-326-2149
Brokerage Services

Tidewater Yacht Sales
64A Old South River Rd.
Edgewater, MD 21037
410-224-3100; Fax 410-224-6919
Bayliner, Fountain

Warehouse Creek Yacht Sales
301 Pier One Rd.
Stevensville, MD 21666
410-643-7878; Fax 410-643-7877
Cruisers

William Magness Yachts
301 Pier One Rd., #103
Stevensville, MD 21666
410-643-8434; Fax 410-643-8437
Brokerage Services

Yacht-Net Ltd.
1000 West St.
Annapolis, MD 21401
410-263-0993; 800-822-9303;
Fax 410-267-7967
Brokerage Services

MASSACHUSETTS

Alden Yachts, Power & Sail
Allen Harbor Marine
335 Lower County Rd.
Harwich Port, MA 02646
508-432-0353; Fax 508-432-0487
Pursuit, Tiara

Boston Yacht Sales
275 River St.
North Weymouth, MA 02191
617-331-2400; Fax 617-331-8215
Hatteras, Viking, Sabreline, Brokerage

Brewer Yacht Sales
14 Union Street
Plymouth, MA 02360
508-746-4500
Grand Banks

Yacht Broker & Dealer Directory

Burr Bros. Boats
309 Front St.
Marion, MA 02738
508-748-0911; Fax 508-748-1557
Boston Whaler, Sun Fish/Laser, Avon, Dyer

Buzzards Bay Yacht Sales
PO Box 369
Westport Point, MA 02791
508-636-4010; Fax 508-636-5929
Brokerage Services

Cataumet Boats
Route 28A
Bourne, MA 02532
508-563-7102; Fax 508-563-5157
Grady White, Albemarle, Brendan

Dudley Yacht Sales
42 Fiddler's Cove Marina
North Falmouth, MA 02556
508-564-4100; Fax 508-564-4129
Brokerage Services

Gary Voller's Yacht Sales
Barnstable Marine Freezer Rd.
Barnstable, MA 02630
508-362-3626; Fax 508-362-8011
Brokerage

Gifford Marine Co.
676 Dartmouth St.
South Dartmouth, MA 02748
508-996-8288; Fax 508-997-9705
Grady White, Tiara

Green Harbor Marina
PO Box 338, Dyke Rd., Rt. 139
Green Harbor, MA 02041
617-837-1181
Rampage

Hyannis Marina
21 Arlington St.
Hyannis, MA 02601
508-775-5662; Fax 508-775-0851
Sea Ray, Formula

Hyannis Yacht Sales
157 Pleasant St.
Hyannis, MA 02601
508-790-2628; Fax 508-790-0996
Cabo, Ocean, Luhrs, Regulator

Nauset Marine
Box 357, Route 6A
Orleans, MA 02653
508-255-0777; Fax 508-255-0373
Nauset

Northrop & Johnson
43 Water St.
Beverly, MA 01915
508-921-6600; Fax 508-921-6691
Brokerage Services

Thomas Marine
R-24 Ericsson St.
Dorchester, MA 02122
617-288-1000; Fax 617-282-5728
Sea Ray

Wells Yachts
91 Front St.
Marblehead, MA 01945
617-631-3003; Fax 617-639-2503
Tiara, Pursuit, Catalina, J-Boats

MICHIGAN

Barrett Boat Works
821 W. Savidge St.
Spring Lake, MI 49456
616-842-1202; Fax 616-842-5735
Brokerage Services

Bay Harbor Marina
5309 E. Wilder Rd.
Bay City, MI 48707
517-684-5010
Silverton, Pro-Line, Cruisers

Colony Marine
6509 M-29 Hwy., Box 388
Algonac, MI 48001
810-794-4932; Fax 810-794-2147
Sea Ray

Eldean Boat Sales, Ltd.
2223 South Shore Dr.
Macatawa, MI 49434
616-335-5843; Fax 616-335-5848
Grand Banks, Bertram, Ocean

Harbor Boat Shop, The
13240 West Bayshore Dr.
Traverse City, MI
49684
616-922-3020; Fax 616-922-3003

Irish Boat Shop
PO Box 259
Harbor Springs, MI, 49740
616-526-6226; Fax 616-526-5565
Boston Whaler, Sea Ray

Irish Boat Shop
1300 Stover Rd.
Charlevoix, MI 49720
616-547-9967; Fax 616-547-4129

Jefferson Beach Marina
24400 E. Jefferson
St. Clair Shores, MI 48080
810-778-7600; Fax 810-778-4766
Viking Yachts, Sunseeker, Fountain, Formula, Maxum, Bayliner Yachts
Brokerage Services

John B. Slaven, Inc.
Box 864, 31300 N. River Rd.
Mt. Clemens, MI
810-463-0000; Fax 810-463-4317
Brokerage

McMachen Marine
30099 South River Rd.
Mt. Clemens, MI 48045
810-469-0223; Fax 810-469-1646
Tiara, Sea Ray, Tollycraft
Brokerage Services

Onekama Marine
Portage Lake
Onekama, MI 49675
616-889-4218; Fax 616-889-3398
Silverton, Larson, Cruisers

Pier 33
3000 - 28th St. SW
Grand Rapids, MI 49418
616-538-3314
Pro-Line, Brokerage Services

Superbrokers of Traverse City
12719 SW Bayshore Dr., #9
Traverse City, MI 49684
616-922-3002; Fax 616-922-3013
Brokerage Services

Toledo Beach Marina
11840 Toledo Beach Rd.
LaSalle, MI 48145
313-847-3823; Fax 313-243-3815
Hatteras, Silverton, Pro-Line

MINNESOTA

Harris Yacht Sales
6351 St. Croix Trail N., #141
Stillwater, MN 55082-6973
612-439-2000; Fax 612-439-3859
Brokerage Services

Owens Yacht Sales
371 Canal Park Dr.
Duluth, MN 55802
800-879-2684; Fax 218-722-4730
Worldwide Charters, Brokerage

Yacht Broker & Dealer Directory

NEW HAMPSHIRE

Marine USA
5 Route 101A, #8
Amherst, NH 03031
603-673-0024
Bayliner

Northeast Yachts
2456 Lafayette Rd.
Portsmouth, NH 03801
603-433-3222; Fax 603-431-2817
Brokerage Services

NEW JERSEY

Bob Massey Yacht Sales
1668 Beaver Dam Rd.
Pt. Pleasant, NJ 08742
908-295-3700; Fax 908-892-0649
Jefferson, Onset

Clarks Landing Marina
PO Box 2182
Ocean City, NJ 08226-8182
609-898-9889; Fax 609-390-1260
Luhrs, Pursuit, Blackfin, Bertram
Brokerage Services

Clarks Landing Marina
847 Arnold Ave.
Pt. Pleasant, NJ 08742
908-899-5559; Fax 908-899-5572
Luhrs, Pursuit, Pro-Line, Bertram

Comstock Yacht Sales
704 Princeton Ave
Brick Town, NJ 08724
908-899-2500; Fax 908-892-3763
Post, Silverton, Regulator, Tiara

Integrity Marine
9401 Amherst Ave.
Margate City, NJ 08402
800-435-2337; Fax 609-487-1716
Post

Seaport Yacht Sales
94 East Water St.
Toms River, NJ 08753
908-286-2100
Tollycraft

South Jersey Marine Brokers
602 Green Ave.
Brielle, NJ 08730
908-223-2200; Fax 908-223-0211
Viking, Cabo, Ocean

Sportside Marine
1627 "F" Street
South Belmar, NJ 07719
908-280-2111; Fax 908-280-1011
Brokerage

Total Marine
411 Great Bay Blvd.
Tuckerton, NJ 08087
609-294-0480
Phoenix, Powerplay

NEW YORK

Bruce Tait & Assoc. Yacht Sales
Waterfront Marina, Bay Street
Sag Harbor, NY 11963
516-725-4222; Fax 516-725-9886

City Island Yacht Sales
673 City Island Ave.
City Island, NY 10464
718-885-2300; Fax 718-885-2385

Fred Chall Marine
1160 Merrick Rd.
Copaigue, NY 11726
516-842-7777; Fax 516-842-7998
Hatteras, Wellcraft

Fred Chall Marine
124 Woodcleft Ave.
Freeport, NY 11520
516-546-8960; Fax 516-546-8888
Hatteras

McMichael Yacht Brokers
447 E. Boston Post Rd.
Mamaroneck, NY 10543
914-381-5900; Fax 914-381-5060
Nauticat, J-Boats

Orange Boat Sales
51-57 Route 9W
New Windsor, NY 12553
914-565-8530; Fax 914-565-2706
Baja, Thompson, Regal, Rinker, Bayliner, Pro-Line, Maxum

Owasco Marine
377 Owasco Rd.
Auburn, NY 13021
315-253-0693; Fax 315-253-2104
Celebrity, Glastron, Crestliner

Rowe Boats International
1 Coastland Dr.
Plattsburgh, NY 12901
518-563-1400; Fax 518-563-1400
Marine Trader Intl., Catalina/Capri, Dyer

Rowland Boats & Motors
1598 North Highway
Southampton, NY 11968
516-283-3444; Fax 516-283-3489
Carolina Classic, Regulator, Wahoo, Carolina Skiff, Sailfish

Security Marine Yacht & Boat Sales
1 World's Fair Marina
Flushing Meadows, NY 11368
718-478-7600; Fax 718-533-8530
Brokerage

Star Island Yacht Club
PO Box 2180
Montauk, NY 11954
516-668-5052; Fax 516-668-5503
Tiara, Shamrock, Phoenix

Star Island Yacht Club
116 Woodcleft Ave.
Freeport, NY 11520
516-623-6256; Fax 516-868-7332
Tiara, Shamrock, Phoenix

Surfside 3 Marina
846 S. Wellwood Ave.
Lindenhurst, LI NY 11757
516-957-5900; Fax 516-957-8099
Carver, Sea Ray

Van Schaick Island Marina
South Delaware Ave.
Cohoes, NY 12047
518-237-2681; Fax 518-233-8355
Carver, Trojan, Mainship

WhiteWater Marine
5500 Sunrise Highway
Sayville, NY 11782
516-589-2502; Fax 516-567-4855
Parker, Maxum, Stingray

Woodcleft Marine
195 Woodcleft Ave.
Freeport, NY 11520
516-868-1730
CrownLine

NORTH CAROLINA

70 West Marina
Highway 70
Morehead City, NC 28557
919-726-5171; Fax 919-726-9993
Tiara, Jersey, Albemarle

Yacht Broker & Dealer Directory

Baker Marine
6 Marina St.
Wrightsville Beach, NC 28480
910-256-8300; Fax 910-256-9542
Grand Banks, Hatteras, Tiara

Beaufort Yacht Sales
328 Front St.
Beaufort, NC 28516
919-728-3155; Fax 919-728-6715
Viking, Freedom, Valient

Causeway Marina
300 Morehead Ave., Box 2366
Atlantic Beach, NC 28512
919-726-6977; Fax 919-726-7089
Stamas

Harbourside Yachts
PO Drawer 896
Wrightsville Beach, NC 28480
910-350-0660; Fax 910-350-0506
Carver, Blackfin, Luhrs, Trojan

McCotters Marina
Route 7, Box 221
Washington, NC 27889
919-975-2174

Pages Creek Marina
7000 Market St.
Wilmington, NC 28405
910-799-7179; Fax 910-799-1096
Mako

Quay & Associates
PO Box 397
Atlantic Beach, NC 28512
919-247-2280; Fax 919-247-1194

The Boat Rack
7865 Spinnaker Bay Dr.
Sherrills Ford, NC 28673
704-478-2118; Fax 704-478-2628
Silverton

OHIO

Allcraft Marine
4505 Kellogg Avenue
Cincinnati, OH 45226
513-533-8800
Silverton

Coastal Marine & Yacht Sales
1805 W. Lakeshore Dr.
Port Clinton, OH 43452
419-732-2150; Fax 419-732-8820
Tollycraft, Wellcraft, Ocean

Island Yacht Sales
4236 E. Moore's Dock Rd.
Port Clinton, OH 43452
419-797-9003; Fax 419-797-6846

Lake & Bay Yacht Sales
PO Box 237
Marblehead, OH 43440
419-798-8511; Fax 419-798-8511
Egg Harbor, Phoenix

Lakeside Marine
1000 N. Erie Beach Rd.
Lakeside, OH 43440
419-798-4406; Fax 419-798-4089
Tiara, Pursuit

North Shore Boat Brokerage
1787 Merwin
Cleveland, OH 44113
216-241-2237

Progressive Marine Consultants
7130-C Harbor Rd.
Lakeside, OH 43440
419-732-8191; Fax 419-734-9679
Blackfin

Progressive Marine Consultants
111 East Shoreline Dr.
Sandusky, OH 44870
419-627-1177; Fax 419-627-0406
Brokerage Services

The Flerlage Marine Company
2233 Eastern Ave.
Cincinnati, OH 45202
513-221-2233; Fax 513-872-5287
Sea Ray, Harbor Master

Treasure Cove Marina
2555 NE Catawba
Port Clinton, OH 43452
419-797-4492; Fax 419-797-6450
Sea Ray

Treasure Cove Marina
5782 Heisley Rd.
Mentor, OH 44060
216-942-2544
Sea Ray

OKLAHOMA

Cedar Port Marina
Hwy. 28, Box 546
Disney, OK 74340
800-435-8250; Fax 918-435-8390
Silverton, Maxum, Powerquest

Yacht Links
Applegate Cove Marina
HC61, Box 308
Sallisaw, OK 74955
918-775-4522; Fax 918-775-4538
Brokerage Services

OREGON

Compass Point Yachts
1521 N. Jantzen Ave.
Portland, OR 97217
503-286-7070; Fax 503-286-7077
Silverton, Ocean Alexander

Northwest Boat Center
719 N. Marine Dr.
Portland, OR 97217
503-289-9338

Oregon Yacht Sales
2305 NW 133rd Place
Portland, OR 97229
503-285-5586; 503-799-5028
Fax 503-690-0824
Tollycraft, Tiara, Queenship, Symbol, Ocean
New Jersey, Fountain

RHODE ISLAND

Alden Yacht Brokerage
1909 Alden Landing
Portsmouth, RI 02871
401-683-4285; Fax 401-683-3668
Alden Yachts, Power & Sail

Black Watch Brokerage
One Little Harbor Landing
Portsmouth, RI 02871
401-683-5777; Fax 401-683-5620
Brokerage Services

Brewer's Yacht Sales
222 Narragansett Blvd.
Portsmouth, RI 02871
401-683-3977; Fax 401-683-0696

Eastern Yacht Sales
One Lagoon Rd.
Portsmouth, RI 02871
401-683-2200; Fax 401-683-0961
Brokerage Services

Eastern Yacht Sales of RI
One Masthead Dr.
Warwick, RI 02886
401-885-2400; Fax 401-885-2457
Tollycraft, Catalina, Beneteau

Yacht Broker & Dealer Directory

Island Gypsy Yacht Sales, Ltd.
138 Wharf Rd.
Warwick, RI 02889
401-737-2233; Fax 401-737-2207
Island Gypsy

Newport Yacht Services
PO Box 149
Newport, RI 02840
401-846-7720; Fax 401-846-6850

Northrop & Johnson
19 Brown & Howard Wharf
Newport, RI 02840-3471
401-848-5500; Fax 401-848-0120

Standish Boat Yard
1697 Main Road
Tiverton, RI 02878
401-624-4075; Fax 401-624-3438
Cape Dory, Albin

The Point Boat Co.
360 Gooseberry Rd.
Wakefield, RI 02880
401-789-7189; Fax 401-783-5350
Albin

Twin City Marine
600 High St.
Central Falls, RI 02863
401-723-6100
Four Winns, Cruisers, Quest

SOUTH CAROLINA

American Yacht Sales
1880 Andell Buffs Blvd.
Johns Island, SC 29455
803-768-9660; Fax 803-768-7300
Luhrs, Mainship, Albemarle, Shamrock, Cobia

Berry-Boger Yacht Sales
Box 36, Harbour Place, #101
N. Myrtle Beach, SC 29597
803-249-6167; Fax 803-249-0105
Wellcraft, Gibson

DYB Charters & Yacht Sales
14 New Orleans Rd., Suite 14
Hilton Head, SC 29928
803-785-4740; Fax 803-785-4827
Catalina, Gamefisherman

Hilton Head Yachts, Ltd.
PO Box 22488
Hilton Head Island, SC 29925
803-686-6860; Fax 803-681-5093

Sea Ray of Charleston
4415 Sea Ray Dr.
North Charleston, SC 29405
803-747-1889
Sea Ray

Wilkins Boat & Yacht Co.
1 Harbour Place
N. Myrtle Beach, SC 29582
803-249-6032; Fax 803-249-6523
Sonic

TENNESSEE

Erwin Marine Sales
1940 Hixson Marina Rd.
Hixson, TN 37343
615-843-0232; Fax 615-843-0233
Sea Ray, Harbor Master, Marinette, Formula

Fox Road Marina, LLC
1100 Fox Rd.
Knoxville, TN 37922
615-966-9422; Fax 615-966-9475
Holiday Mansion

Hatteras of Nashville
341 Hill Ave.
Nashville, TN 37210
615-254-9107
Hatteras

Jim Bennett Yacht Sales
Route 4, Box 532
Iuka, TN 38852
601-423-9999; Fax 601-423-3339
Bluewater, Carver

Leader Marine
722 E. College St.
Dickson, TN 37055
615-446-3422; Fax 615-446-9819
Cruisers

Loret Marine
PO Box 556
Harrison, TN 37341
615-344-8331; Fax 615-344-6275
Carver, Monterey, Four Winns

Peer Gynt Enterprises
6421 Fairest Dr.
Harrison, TN 37341
615-344-5628; Fax 615-344-0960
Brokerage

Phil's Marine Sales
4935 Highway 58, Suite C
Chattanooga, TN 37416
615-892-0058; Fax 615-894-3281

VIP Yachts
11211 Crown Point Dr.
Knoxville, TN 37922
615-693-3039; Fax 615-675-2144
Bluewater

TEXAS

Boats Unlimited
1900 Shipyard Dr.
Seabrook, TX 77586
713-334-2559
Brokerage Services

Coastal Yacht Brokers
715 Holiday Dr. North
Galveston, TX 77550
409-763-3474; Fax 713-488-8782

Fox Yacht Sales
Box 772, Island Moorings Marina
Port Aransas, TX 78373
512-749-4870; Fax 512-749-4859
Bertram, Blackfin
Brokerage Services

Houston Yacht Sales
585 Bradford Ave., Suite B
Kemah, TX 77565
713-334-7094; Fax 713-334-4936
Hatteras, Marlin, Ocean

Jay Bettis & Company
2509 NASA Road 1
Seabrook, TX 77586
713-474-4101; Fax 713-532-1305
DeFever, Shamrock, Mainship

Ron's Yacht Brokerage
1101 Shipyard Dr., Box 621
Seabrook, TX 77586
713-474-5444; Fax 713-474-7024

Sea Lake Yachts
1500 FM 2094, Box 1611
Kemah, TX 77565
713-334-1993; Fax 713-334-4795
Brokerage Services

Vega Yacht Sales
4106 NASA Road 1
Seabrook, TX 77586
713-326-5588; Fax 713-532-1275
Brokerage Services

Weaver & Cameron
2511B NASA Rd. 1, Suite 200
Seabrook, TX 77586
713-326-1111; Fax 713-532-3075
Brokerage Services

Yacht Broker & Dealer Directory

VIRGINIA

Atlantic Yacht Brokers
932 Laskin St., Suite 200
Virginia Beach, VA 23451
804-428-9000; Fax 804-491-8632
Ocean Yachts, Cabo

Bluewater Yacht Sales
25 Marina Rd.
Hampton, VA 23669
804-723-0793; Fax 804-723-3320
Hatteras, Viking

Casey Marine
1021 W. Mercury Blvd.
Hampton, VA 23666
804-591-1500; Fax 804-826-5557
Pro-Line, Baja, Robolo, Maxum, Luhrs

Coastal Yacht Sales
Rt. 1210
Gloucester Point, VA 23062
804-642-3732; Fax 804-642-4966
Brokerage Services

Commonwealth Yachts
PO Box 1070
Gloucester Point, VA 23062
804-642-2156; Fax 804-642-4766
Brokerage Services

Dominion Yacht Brokers
2100 Marina Shores Rd.
Virginia Beach, VA 23455
804-481-0533; Fax 804-481-0056
Brokerage Services

Dozier's Dockyard
PO Box 388
Deltaville, VA 23043
804-776-6711; Fax 804-776-6998

Norton's Yacht Sales
PO Box 220, Route 636
Deltaville, VA 23043
804-776-9211; Fax 804-776-9044
Luhrs, Hunter, Silverton

Tidewater Yacht Sales
10A Crawford Parkway
Norfolk, VA 23704
804-393-6200; Fax 804-397-1193
Bayliner, Fountain

Virginia Yacht Brokers
424 E. Queen St.
Hampton, VA 23669
804-722-3500; Fax 804-722-7909
Brokerage Services

WASHINGTON

AAA Yacht Finders
2415 "T" Ave., Suite 3
Anacortes, WA 98221
360-299-2628; 800-704-2628
Fax 360-293-3246
Brokerage Services

Alliance Yacht Sales
2130 Westlake Ave. North
Seattle, WA 98109
206-283-8111; Fax 206-283-4200
Offshore

Bayside Yacht & Ship Sales
1724 #2 W. Marine View Dr.
Everett, WA 98201
206-258-2790

Bellingham Yacht Sales
1801 Roeder Ave.
Bellingham, WA 98225
800-671-4244; Fax 360-671-0992
Sabreline (Motoryachts 34'-49')

Breakwater Marina
5603 Waterfront Dr.
Tacoma, WA 98407
206-752-6663; Fax 206-752-8291
Hershine

Elliott Bay Yachting Center
2601 West Marina Pl., #D
Seattle, WA 98199
206-285-9563; Fax 206-281-7636
Brokerage Services

Fraser Yachts
1500 Westlake Ave. N.
Seattle, WA 98109
206-282-4943; Fax 206-285-4956
Brokerage Services

Gig Harbor Yacht Sales
Box 528, 3119 Harborview Dr.
Gig Harbor, WA 98335
206-851-2674; Fax 206-858-2674

Intrepid Yacht Sales
2144 Westlake Ave. North
Seattle, WA 98109
206-282-0211; Fax 206-281-8250
Grand Banks, Eastbay

Intrepid Yacht Sales
1015 Thomas Glenn Dr., #1
Bellingham, WA 98225
360-676-1248; Fax 360-676-9059
Grand Banks, Eastbay

Lake Union Yacht Sales
3245 Fairview Ave E. #103
Seattle, WA 98102
206-323-3505; Fax 206-323-4751
Island Gypsy, Catalina
Brokerage Services

Marina Yacht Sales
1500 Westlake Ave. N., Suite 8
Seattle, WA 98109
206-298-9900; Fax 206-270-9045
Brokerage Services

Murray Wasson Marine Sales
4224 Marine View Dr.
Tacoma, WA 98422
206-927-9036; Fax 206-927-9034
Albin

Nordic Northwest Yacht Brokerage
2046 Westlake
Seattle, WA 98109
206-282-8847; Fax 206-282-5951
Nordic Tugs

Olympic Boat Centers
16340 Aurora Ave. North
Seattle, WA 98113
206-363-5562
Bayliner

Olympic Boat Centers
13200 Bel-Red Rd.
Bellevue, WA 98005
206-454-9929
Bayliner

Olympic Boat Centers
10 East Allison St.
Seattle, WA 98102
206-322-3880
Bayliner

Olympic Boat Centers
6610 - 16th St. East
Fife, WA 98424
206-922-0303
Bayliner

Olympic Boat Centers
6790 Martin Way
Olympia, WA 98506
206-491-1679
Bayliner

Pacific Boatland
11704 Hwy. 99
Vancouver, WA 98686
206-573-0621
Cruisers

Yacht Broker & Dealer Directory

Picks Cove Marine Center
1940 East D Street
Tacoma, WA 98421
206-572-3625
Symbol

San Juan Yacht Sales
PO Box 69
Anacortes, WA 98221
360-293-4117; Fax 360-293-6683
Symbol

Skipper Cress Yacht Sales
1019 Q Ave., Suite B
Anacortes, WA 98221
800-996-9991; Fax 360-293-7874
Nordic Tugs

Sundance Yacht Sales
1001 NE Boat St.
Seattle, WA 98103
206-633-2850
Carver

Yarrow Bay Yacht Sales
5207 Lake Washington Blvd. NE
Kirkland, WA 98033
206-822-6066
Cruisers

WISCONSIN

Bay Marine of Sturgeon Bay
PO Box 229
Sturgeon Bay, WI 54235
414-743-6526
Cruisers

Cal Marine
1024 Bay Shore Dr.
Sister Bay, WI 54234
414-854-4521; Fax 414-854-5137
Tiara, Silverton, Powerquest, Pursuit

Emerald Yacht Ship Mid America
1933 S. First St.
Milwaukee, WI 53204
414-671-1110; Fax 414-671-1211
Brokerage Services, New Construction

Fox River Marina
P.O. Box 1006
Oshkosh, WI 54902
414-235-2340
Wellcraft, Cruisers

Lakeside Marina
902 Taft Ave.
Oshkosh, WI 54901
414-231-4321; Fax 414-231-0004
Bayliner, Carver, Chaparral, Larson

Professional Yacht Sales
451 S. Second St.
Prescott, WI 54021
715-262-5762; Fax 715-262-5658
Mainship, Holiday Mansion

Shipyard Marine
164 South Shore Dr.
Washington Island, WI 54246
414-847-2533
Albemarle, Navigator

Skipper Buds
N 10 W 24850 Silvernail Rd
Pewaukee, WI 53072
414-544-1200
Hatteras, Sea Ray, Chris Craft

Sturgeon Bay Yacht Harbor
306 Nautical Drive
Sturgeon Bay, WI 54235
414-743-3311; Fax 414-743-4298
Ocean/Alexander, Thunderbird/Formula

Tinus Marine
307 Forest St.
Oconomowoc, WI 53069
414-567-7533; Fax 414-567-8677
Fountain

Marine Surveyor Directory

Professional Surveyor Associations

ABYC ....American Boat & Yacht Council
ASA ....American Society of Appraisors
AIMS ....American Institute of Marine Surveyors
NAMI ....National Association of Marine Investigators
NAMS ....National Association of Marine Surveyors
NFPA ....National Fire Protection Association
SAMS ....Society of Accredited Marine Surveyors
SNAME ....Society of Naval Architects & Marine Engineers

ALABAMA

Michael Schiehl
M.J. Schiehl
PO Box 1990
Orange Beach, AL 36561-1990
334-981-6611; Fax 334-981-2611
NAMS

Donald Smith
Port City Marine Services
3263 Demetroplis Rd., Ste. 8C
Mobile, AL 36693
334-661-5426; Fax 334-460-9898
SAMS (AMS), ABYC

CALIFORNIA

Hans Andersen
Anderson Int'l. Marine Surveyors
433 North H St., Ste. G
Lompoc, CA 93436
805-737-3770; Fax 805-737-3773
SAMS (AMS)

Clark Barthol, CMS
Clark Barthol Marine Surveyors
27 Buccaneer St.
Marina del Rey, CA 90292
310-823-3350; Fax 310-827-7883
NAMS, ABYC

Thomas Bell
Thomas Bell & Associates
1323 Berkeley Street, #A
Santa Monica, CA 90404-2503
310-306-1895
SAMS (AMS), ABYC, NAMI, ASA

Roby Bessent
Pacific Marine Surveyors
PO Box 3111
Long Beach, CA 90803
310-434-5711; Fax 310-434-5711
NAMS, ABYC

Christopher Bishop
James E. Dillon & Assoc.
175 Filbert St., Ste. #201
Oakland, CA 94607
510-452-2866; Fax 510-452-2875
NAMS

John Bonner
John Bonner & Assoc.
131 Steuart St., Ste. #650
San Francisco, CA 94105
415-495-0778; Fax 415-495-6120
NAMS

Robert Bornholdt
Marine Surveyor
1310 Rosecrans
San Diego, CA 92106
619-224-2944

Archibald Campbell
Campbell's Marine Survey
340 Countryside Drive
Santa Rosa, CA 95401
707-542-8812; Fax 707-542-8812
SAMS (AMS), ABYC, ASME, SNAME

Carl Colditz
Giannotti Marine Services
1631 Spinnaker Dr., #204
Ventura, CA 93001
805-658-8836; Fax 805-658-8953
NAMS

William Engstrom
Marine Surveyor
1251 W. Sepulveda Blvd., #160
Torrance, CA 90502
310-534-4345; Fax 310-534-4345
NAMS

James Enzensperger
Pacific Cargo Inspection Bureau
1490 - 66th Street
Oakland, CA 94608-1014
510-420-1386; Fax 510-420-0660
NAMS

John Flachsenhar, Jr.
Marine Surveyor
1067 Shafter St.
San Diego, CA 92106
619-223-8167
NAMS

William Hansen
Fireman's Fund Insurance Co.
PO Box 3136
San Francisco, CA 94119
415-541-4434; Fax 415-541-4441
NAMS

Marvin Henderson
Marvin Henderson Marine Surveyors
2727 Shelter Island Dr., #C
San Diego, CA 92106
619-224-3164; Fax 619-588-7607
NAMS, ABYC, NFPA, SNAME

Richard Jacobson
J.A. Jacobson & Assoc.
1324 N. Avalon Blvd.
Wilmington, CA 90744
310-834-4553

Marine Surveyor Directory

Bill Jewell
American Marine Consultants
5055 N. Harbor Dr., Ste. D
San Diego, CA 92106
619-223-7380
ASNE, ABYC

Douglas Johnstone
Admiralty Marine Surveyors
920 N. Avalon Blvd.
Wilmington, CA 90744
310-835-7139; Fax 310-835-9161
NAMS

Chris Kieffer
Marine Surveyor
1310 Rosecrans St., #K
San Diego, CA 92106
619-224-2944

Jack Mackinnon
Marine Surveyor
PO Box 335
San Lorenzo, CA 94580-0335
510-276-4351; Fax 510-276-9237
SAMS (AMS), ABYC

Douglas Malin
Malin Marine Surveyors
5942 Edinger Ave., #113
Huntington Beach, CA 92649
714-897-6769; Fax 714-897-6769
SAMS (AMS), ABYC, NFPA

Albert Milani, CMS
Ocean Marine Consultants, Inc.
664 Santana Rd.
Novato, CA 94945
415-892-4385; Fax 415-892-4385
NAMS, SNAME

Don Parish
Marine Surveyor
4140 Oceanside Blvd., #159-320
Oceanside, CA 92056
619-721-9410
ABYC

Kent Parker
Marine Surveyor
PO Box 2604
San Rafael, CA 94912
415-457-5312

Gerald Poliskey
G.A. Poliskey & Associates
5014 Esmond Ave.
Richmond, CA 94805
510-236-1793; Fax 510-236-1797
SAMS (AMS), NAMS, SNAME, ABYC, NFPA

Capt. Joseph W. Rogers
Rogers & Assoc., Certified Marine Surveyors
400 Dolores St., #A - Yacht Harbor
Santa Cruz, CA 95062
408-475-4468; Fax 408-475-4468
NAMS, ASA

Todd Schwede
Todd Schwede & Associates
2390 Shelter Island Dr., #220
San Diego, CA 92106
619-226-1895; Fax 619-223-8942
SAMS (AMS), NAMI, ABYC

Rod Whitfield
R.J. Whitfield & Associates, Inc.
7011 Bridgeport Circle
Stockton, CA 95207-2357
209-956-8488; Fax 209-956-8490
SAMS (AMS), NAMI, ABYC

Stanley Wild
Stan Wild & Associates
1912 Stanford St.
Alameda, CA 94501
510-521-8527; Fax 510-521-8196
NAMS

Donald Young
Donru Marine Surveyors & Adjusters
32 Cannery Row
Monterey, CA 93940
408-372-8604; Fax 408-373-2294
SAMS (AMS), ABYC

CONNECTICUT

Robert Hughes
Marine Surveyor
88 Eastwood Rd.
Groton, CT 06340
203-446-9473

Art Kelsey
Marine Surveyors Bureau
23 Riverside Dr., #B1
Clinton, CT 06413
203-399-9309; Fax 203-399-4996
NAMS, ABYC, NFPA

James Taylor
Taylor Yacht Surveys
#5 The Laurels
Enfield, CT 06082
203-749-7400

FLORIDA

Mel Allen
Allen's Boat Surveying & Consulting
638 North U.S. Hwy 1, Suite 207
Tequesta, FL 33469-2397
407-747-2433; Fax 407-745-3245
SAMS (AMS), ABYC, NFPA

William Ballard
Ballard & Assoc., Inc.
18845 SW 93rd Ave.
Miami, FL 33157
305-252-8008; Fax 305-255-4681
SAMS (AMS)

Dennis Brown
Marine Surveyor
414 Sandpiper Dr.
Satellite Beach, FL 32937
407-779-9750
ABYC, NFPA

Pete Brown
Marine Surveyor
11340 - 7th St., East
St. Petersburg, FL 33706-3038
813-367-2489
NAMS

C.H. Brown, Jr.
Marine Surveyor
2925 Lake Pineloch Blvd.
Orlando, FL 32806
407-843-8138

Brett Carlson
Carlson Marine Surveyors & Adjusters
1002 NE 105th St.
Miami Shores, FL 33138
305-891-0445; Fax 305-891-8446
SAMS (AMS)

Clyde Carter
Darling & Co., Marine Surveyors
PO Box 8703
Longboat Key, FL 34228
813-922-5341
SAMS (SA), ABYC, NFPA

Charles Corder
Chapman School of Seamanship
4343 SE St. Lucie Blvd.
Stuart, FL 34997
407-283-8130; Fax 407-283-2019
SAMS (AMS)

Marine Surveyor Directory

Ric Corley
Capt. Tom Corley & Son Marine Surveyors
1701 Grant Avenue
Panama City, FL 32401
904-784-9939; Fax 904-233-4982
SAMS (AMS), ABYC, NFPA, NAMS, NAMI

Jerome Cramer
Slakoff, Cramer & Associates
1524 S. Andrews Ave., Suite 215
Ft. Lauderdale, FL 33316
305-525-7930; Fax 305-525-7947
SAMS (AMS)

Tom Drennan
Continental Marine Consultants, Inc.
618 North US Hwy #1, Suite 301
North Palm Beach, FL 33408
407-844-6111; Fax 407-844-7152
NAMS

Capt. Larry C. Dukehart
Marine Surveyor & Consultant
PO Box 1172
Islamorada, FL 33036-1172
305-664-9452; Fax 305-664-9453
SAMS (AMS), ABYC, NFPA, NAMI

Tom Fexas
Tom Fexas Yacht Design, Inc.
333 Tressler Dr., Suite B
Stuart, FL 33497
407-287-6558; Fax 407-287-6810
NAMS

Dean Greger
Coastal Marine Surveyors
23 Winston Dr.
Belleair, FL 34616
813-581-0914
ABYC

William King
Atlantic Marine Survey
6201 SE Monticello Terrace
Hobe Sound, FL 33455-7383
407-545-0011; Fax 407-545-1025
SAMS (AMS), ABYC

Drew Kwederas
Global Adventure Marine Associates
4120 NE 26th Ave.
Ft. Lauderdale, FL 33308
305-566-4800; Fax 305-566-4802
ABYC, NFPA, SNAME, ASNE, NACE

Veronica Lawson
Veronica M. Lawson & Associates
PO Box 1201
Naples, FL 33939
813-434-6960; Fax 813-649-1374
NAMS, SNAME, ABYC, NFPA

Capt. F. Michael McGhee
Black Pearl Marine Specialities, Inc.
6695 NW 25th Terrace
Ft. Lauderdale, FL 33309
305-970-8305; Fax 305-970-8303
ABYC, NFPA, ASA, AIMS

Marty Merolla
Marty Merolla Certified Marine Surveyor, Inc.
4300 SE St. Lucie Blvd., #128
Stuart, FL 34997
407-286-4880; Fax 407-221-9408
NAMS

Downing Nightingale, Jr.
North Florida Marine Services, Inc.
3360 Lakeshore Blvd.
Jacksonville, FL 32210
904-384-4356; Fax 904-384-4356
SAMS (AMS), AMS

Allen Perry
Ocean Adventures, Inc.
453 Spinnaker Dr.
Naples, FL 33940
813-261-5466
SAMS (SA), ABYC, NAMS

Henry Pickersgill
Henry W. Pickersgill & Co., Inc.
26231 MTN Lake Rd.
Brooksville, FL 34602
800-348-8105; Fax 904-754-1789
NAMS

Thomas Price
Price Marine Services, Inc.
9418 S.E. Sharon St.
Hobe Sound, FL 33455-6833
407-546-0928; Fax 407-546-1503
SAMS (AMS), ABYC, NFPA

John Reeve
Reeve Marine Associates, Inc.
P.O.Box 4202
Tequesta, FL 33469
407-747-5493
SAMS (SA), ABYC

Mark Rhodes
Rhodes Marine Surveyors
4701 N. Federal Hwy., Ste 340, Box C-8
Lighthouse Point, FL 33064-6563
305-946-6779; Fax 305-783-0057
SAMS (AMS), ABYC, NFPA

Mike Rhodes
Rhodes Marine Surveyors
4701 N. Federal Hwy., Ste 340, Box C-8
Lighthouse Point, FL 33064-6563
305-946-6779; Fax 305-783-0057
SAMS (AMS), ABYC, NFPA

Edward Rowe
Ed Rowe & Associates
1821 SW 22nd Ave.
Ft. Lauderdale, FL 33312
305-792-6062; Fax 305-792-8404
SAMS (AMS), ABYC

Robert Russo
Jacksonville Towing and Salvage Corp.
2268 Mayport Rd., #118
Atlantic Beach, FL 32250
904-249-0309; Fax 904-247-3366
SAMS (SA)

James Sanislo
C&J Marine Surveyors
4163 Frances Dr.
Delray Beach, FL 33445
407-495-4920; Fax 407-495-8701
SAMS (AMS)

Norman Schreiber II
PO Box 350247
Ft. Lauderdale, FL 33335
305-537-1423; Fax 305-761-9087
NAMS, SNAME, ABYC, NFPA

James Shafer
Harbor Marine Services
979 Sultan Dr.
Port St. Lucie, FL 34953
407-340-5570; Fax 407-340-5570
SAMS (SA), ABYC, NAMI

Ronald Silvera
R.E. Silvera & Associates
1904 SW 86th Ave.
North Lauderdale, FL 33068
305-720-8660
SAMS (AMS), SNAME, ABYC, ASA

Eugene Sipe, Jr.
Nautical Services Technologies
424 Production Blvd., #70
Naples, FL 33942-4723
813-434-7445; Fax 813-947-5175
SAMS (AMS)

Ed Stanton
Rhodes Marine Surveyors
4701 N. Federal Hwy., Ste 340, Box C-8
Lighthouse Point, FL 33064-6563
305-946-6779; Fax 305-783-0057
SAMS (AMS), ABYC, NFPA

Mickey Strocchi
Strocchi & Company
PO Box 16541
Jacksonville, FL 32245-6541
904-398-1862; Fax 904-398-1868
SAMS (AMS)

Marine Surveyor Directory

Donald Walwer
D&G Marine, Inc.
58 Ocean Blvd.
Naples, FL 33942
813-643-0028; Fax 813-643-0028
SAMS (AMS)

Ted Willandt
Marine Network
4211 Harbour Island Dr.
Jacksonville FL 32225
904-641-3334
SAMS (AMS), ABYC, NAMI

Dick Williamson
Professional Marine Surveys, Inc.
7491-C5 N. Federal Hwy, #232
Boca Raton, FL 33487
407-272-1053
SAMS (AMS), ABYC, NFPA

GEORGIA

Ronald Collins
Marine Surveyor
26 North End Dr.
Brunswick, GA 31525
912-262-0448

HAWAII

Dennis D. Smith
Marine Surveyors & Consultants, Inc.
677 Ala Moana Blvd., Ste. 812
Honolulu, HI 96813
808-545-1333
SAMS (AMS)

Alfred Gallant, Jr.
Marine Surveyor
47-457 Aiai Place
Kaneohe, HI 96744

IOWA

Michael Baxter
U.S. Inland Marine Surveying
1599 Vail Ave.
Muscatine, IA 52761
319-263-6235
NAMS

ILLINOIS

Lee . H Asbridge
Marine Surveyor
440 N. McClurg Ct., #313
Chicago, IL 60611
312-527-1774; Fax 312-464-9640
SAMS (AMS), ABYC, NFPA

Chris Kelly
Professional Yacht Services
733 Sheridan Rd.
Winthrop Harbor, IL 60096
800-535-0072; Fax 708-872-0073
SAMS (SA), ABYC, NFPA, NAMI

James Singer
Marine Surveyor
1854 York Lane
Highland Park, IL 60035
708-831-9157; Fax 708-831-9155
SAMS (AMS), ABYC, NAMI

INDIANA

Chris McNamara
McNamara Marine Surveys, Inc
702 Domke Dr.
Valparaiso, IN 46383-7816

KENTUCKY

Jim Hill, CMS
Marine Surveyor
187 Dogwood Hills Club Rd.
Gilbertsville, KY 42044
800-967-6646

Gregory Weeter
Riverlands Marine Surveyors
935 Riverside Dr.
Louisville, KY 40207
502-897-9900; Fax 502-897-9910
NAMS, ABYC

LOUISIANA

Stanhope Hopkins
Stanhope Hopkins Surveyors
PO Box 15141
New Orleans, LA 70175-5141
504-895-2667

Larry Strouse
Bachrach Wood, Peters & Assoc., Inc.
PO Box 7415
Metairie, LA 70010-7415
504-454-0001; Fax 504-454-3257
NAMS

Albert Westerman
Albert B. Westerman & Co.
2800 Sells St.
Metairie, LA 70003-3543
504-888-8865; Fax 504-455-7960
NAMS, SNAME, ABYC

MAINE

Carl Beal
Casco Marine Consultants, Inc.
5 Ledgeview Ln., RFD Five
Brunswick, ME 04011
207-729-6711; Fax 207-729-6547
SAMS (AMS)

Malcolm Harriman
Marine Surveyor
8 Country Club Rd.
Manchester, ME 04351
207-622-2049
SAMS (AMS)

Malcolm Harriman
Marine Surveyor
PO Box 5151
Elsworth, ME 04605
207-667-1157
SAMS (AMS)

MARYLAND

Thomas Brittain
Marine Surveyor
8809 Thomas Lea Terr.
Gaithersburg, MD 20879
301-948-0015
NAMS, ABYC, SSCD

Peter Hartoft
Hartoft Marine Survey, Ltd.
PO Box 3188, 310 Giddings Ave.
Annapolis, MD 21403
410-263-3609
ABYC, NAMS, MTAM

Frederick Hecklinger
Frederick E. Hecklinger, Inc.
17 Hull Ave.
Annapolis, MD 21403
410-268-3018
NAMS

Michael Kaufman
Kaufman Design, Inc.
PO Box 4219
Annapolis, MD 21403
410-263-8900; Fax 410-263-3459
NAMS

Woodrow Loller
Woodrow W. Loller, Inc.
204 Washington Ave.
Chestertown, MD 21620
410-778-5357; Fax 410-778-5357
NAMS, ABYC

Marine Surveyor Directory

Catherine C. McLaughlin
Marine Surveyor
29142 Belchester Rd.
Kennedyville, MD 21645
410-348-5188; Fax 410-348-5657
SAMS (AMS), ABYC, NFPA, NAMI, ASA

Capt. Michael Phil Heuman, Jr.
Heuman & Assoc.
3707 Paca Avenue
Abingdon, MD 21009
800-794-8258; 800-458-8258; Fax 410-538-6498
NFPA, ABYC, ASA

Michael L. Previti
Previti Marine Surveyor & Consultant Inc.
PO Box 1210
Solomons, MD 20688
410-326-0826; 800-823-0866; Fax 410-326-0826
ABYC

Richard Stimson
R.M. Stimson & Associates
7074 Bembe Beach Rd., #102
Annapolis, MD 21403
410-268-0080; 800-278-4676; Fax 410-268-0080
NAMS, ABYC

Capt. Wright
KIS Marine
5830 Hudson Wharf Rd.
Cambridge, MD 21613
410-228-1448
SAMS (SA)

MASSACHUSETTS

Donald B. Pray
Donald B. Pray Associates
PO Box 66
South Weymouth, MA 02190
617-335-3033; 800-454-7729
Fax 617-331-0607
SAMS (AMS), ABYC, NFPA

Edwin Boice
Robert N. Kershaw, Inc.
25 Garden Park
Braintree, MA 02184
617-843-4550; 800-537-742
Fax 617-849-6653
NAMS, SAMS (AMS)

J. Raymond Gaffey
Robert N. Kershaw, Inc.
25 Garden Park
Braintree, MA 02184
617-843-4550; 800-537-7429
Fax 617-849-6653

Robert Kershaw
Robert N. Kershaw, Inc.
25 Garden Park
Braintree, MA 02184
617-843-4550; 800-537-7429
Fax 617-849-6653
NAMS, SAMS (AMS)

Christopher Leahy
Leahy Associates
PO Box 6313
North Plymouth, MA 02362
508-746-5971; Fax 508-279-0130
SAMS (SA), ABYC, NFPA, NAMI

Joseph Lombardi
Manchester Yacht Survey
PO Box 1576
Manchester, MA 01944
800-253-7458; Fax 508-526-8390
SAMS (AMS), ABYC, SNAME

Capt. Norman LeBlanc
Yacht Surveyor
23 Congress St.
Salem, MA 01970
508-744-8289; Fax 508-741-4365
SAMS (AMS)

Allen Perry
Ocean Adventures, Inc.
419 Sippewissett Rd.
Falmouth, MA 02540
508-540-5395; Fax 508-540-0560
SAMS (SA), ABYC, NAMS

Norman Schreiber II
Transtech - Marine Division
140 Wendward Way
Hyannis, MA 02601
508-775-0183
SNAME, ABYC, NFPA

Ronald Tarr
Harris Associates
9 Rocky Neck Ave.
Gloucester, MA 01930
508-281-6600; Fax 508-281-2460
SAMS (AMS), ABYC

Donald Walwer
D&G Marine, Inc.
PO Box 635
North Eastham, MA 02651
508-255-2406; Fax 508-255-2406
SAMS (AMS)

MICHIGAN

Jim Cukrowicz
Personal Marine Services
52671 CR 388
Grand Junction, MI 49056
616-434-6396; Fax 616-637-4040
SAMS (AMS)

Capt. A. John Lobbezoo
Great Lakes Marine Surveyors, Inc.
PO Box 466, 16100 Highland Dr.
Spring Lake, MI 49456-0466
616-842-9400; Fax 616-842-9401
SAMS (AMS), ABYC, NFPA

Robert McCarthy, Jr.
Robert McCarthy, Marine Surveyor
30060 South River Rd.
Mt. Clemens, MI 48045
313-468-8390

Terry Purdie
Marine Surveyors Company
25025 Jefferson Ave.
St. Clair Shores, MI 48080
313-773-8859

MINNESOTA

A. William Fredell
Marine Surveyor
408 Quarry Lane
Stillwater, MN 55082
612-439-5795
SAMS (AMS)

Paul Liedl
Croix Marine Consultants
531 Mariner Dr.
Bayport, MN 55003
612-439-7748
SAMS (SA), ABYC

John Rantala, Jr.
Rantala Marine Surveys & Services
1671 - 10th Ave, #2
Newport, MN 55055
612-458-5842
SAMS (AMS), ABYC

MISSISSIPPI

Edna Rae Andre
Rush Andre Marine Surveyor & Consultant
414 McGuire Circle
Gulfport, MS 39507
601-863-5962; Fax 601-865-9776
SAMS (SA), ABYC, NFPA, NAMI

Marine Surveyor Directory

Robert Payne
Marine Management, Inc.
PO Box 1803
Ocean Springs, MS 39564
601-872-2846; Fax 601-872-2846
NAMS, ABYC

MISSOURI

Jim Hill, CMS
Marine Surveyor
3653 Boston Farm Rd.
St. Louis, MO 63044
800-967-6646

Peter Merrill
Merrill Marine Services
12231 Manchester Rd.
St. Louis, MO 63131
314-822-8002; Fax 314-822-1232
NAMS

William Wolter
Cairo Marine Service
209 S. Broadway, #161
Cape Girardeau, MO 63701
618-734-4370

NEW HAMPSHIRE

Capt. David A. Page
Marine Surveyor/Adjuster
2456 LaFayette Rd.
Portsmouth, NH 03801
603-433-1568; Fax 603-427-0876
SAMS (AMS), ABYC, NAMI, NFPA

Donald B. Pray
Donald B. Pray Associates
PO Box 340
Madison, NH 03849
603-367-8208; 800-454-7729
SAMS (AMS), ABYC, NFPA

NEW JERSEY

Charles Batten
Argo Marine Surveys
895 Briarcliff Drive
Toms River, NJ 08753

William Campbell
W.J. Campbell, Marine Surveyor
9 Gate Rd.
Tabernacle, NJ 08088
609-268-7476; Fax 609-268-2421
NAMS, SNAME

Frank Christiansen
Frank Christiansen Associates
280 Highway 35
Red Bank, NJ 07701-5900
908-530-7700; Fax 908-530-4716
NAMS

Capt. Rob Cozen
Certified Marine Surveyor
108 Ridge Rd.
Cherry Hill, NJ 08002
609-429-5508
USSA, ABYC, NAMI, SNAME

John Klose
Bayview Associates
PO Box 368
Barnegat Light, NJ 08006
609-494-7450
SAMS (AMS)

David Talbot
Talbot Marine Survey, Inc.
404 Maxon Ave.
Pt. Pleasant, NJ 08742

NEW YORK

Capt. Shawn Bartnett
Bartnett Marine Services, Inc.
52 Ontario St.
Honeoye Falls (Rochester), NY 14472
716-624-1380; Fax 716-624-4168
NAMS, ABYC, NFPA, SNAME, NAMI

Richard Belt
Marine Surveyors Bureau
2055 Merrick Rd., #386
Merrick, NY 11566
516-683-1199; Fax 914-684-9870
NAMS, ABYC, NFPA

Ward Bury
Marine Surveyor
PO Box 2247
Liverpool, NY 13089
315-461-8627; Fax 315-461-8627
SAMS (AMS), ABYC, NFPA

Rocco Citeno
Long Island Marine Surveyor, Inc.
PO Box 542
Sayville, NY 11782
516-589-6154; Fax 516-589-6154
ABYC, NFPA

Donald Cunningham
McGroder Marine Surveyors
Box 405, 228 Central Ave.
Silver Creek (Buffalo), NY 14136
716-934-7848; Fax 716-934-7849
NAMS, ABYC, NFPA

Capt. Jim Dias
Marine Surveyors Bureau
215 Central Ave.
White Plains, NY 10606
800-426-2825; Fax 914-684-9870
NAMS, SAMS (AMS), ABYC, NFPA

John Fitzgibbon
McGroder Marine Surveyors
Box 405, 228 Central Ave.
Silver Creek (Buffalo), NY 14136
716-934-7848; Fax 716-934-7849
NAMS, ABYC, NFPA

William Foster
Marine Surveyor
185 Harrison Place
Staten Island, NY 10310
718-816-0588; Fax 718-816-0588
SAMS (SA), ABYC, NFPA, NAMI

Joseph Gaigal
Suffolk Marine Surveying
RFD 1, Box 174G
St. James, NY 11780
516-584-6297; Fax 516-584-2265
SAMS (AMS), ABYC, NFPA, NAMI,SNAME

James Gambino
Marine Surveyor
66 Browns Blvd.
Ronkonkoma, NY 11779
516-588-5308; 800-381-1779
SAMS (SA), ABYC, NFPA, NAMI

Chris Garvey
Garvey & Scott Marine
15 Trail Rd.
Hampton Bays, NY 11946
516-723-3510; Fax 516-723-3510
SAMS (AMS), ABYC

Walter Lawrence
Lawrence Marine Services
PO Box 219
Alton, NY 14413
315-483-6680; Fax 315-483-6734
SAMS (SA)

William Matthews
Admiralty Marine Surveyors & Adjusters
PO Box 183
Westhampton, NY 11977-0183
516-288-3263; Fax 516-288-0253
NAMS, SNAME, ABYC

Marine Surveyor Directory

Daniel Merin
Daniel Merin, Marine Surveyor
PO Box 128
Chatham, NY 12037
518-392-2518; Fax 518-392-6287
SAMS (SA), ABYC

Capt. H.L. Olsen
Olsen Marine Surveyors Co.
PO Box 283
Port Jefferson, NY 11777
516-928-0711; Fax 516-928-0193
SNAME

William Reilly
Marine Surveyor
249 City Island Ave.
City Island, NY 10464
718-829-2365; 718-885-1617; Fax 718-829-2365
SAMS (AMS), SNAME

Paul Robinson
Marifax Marine Services
21 Swanview Dr.
Patchogue, NY 11772
516-654-3300; Fax 516-654-3300
SAMS (AMS), ABYC

Roy Scott Garvey & Scott Marine Surveyors
32 Colony Rd.
Port Jefferson Station, NY 11776
516-476-1010; Fax 516-331-8552
SAMS (AMS), ABYC

Kenneth Weinbrecht
Ocean Bay Marine Services
PO Box 668
Yaphank, NY 11980
516-924-4362; Fax 516-924-4381
SAMS (AMS), ABYC, NFPA, NAMI

NORTH CAROLINA

Rob Eberle
Eberle Marine Surveys
PO Box 124
New Bern, NC 28560
919-633-4280; Fax 919-635-1912
SAMS (AMS), ABYC

Carl Foxworth
Industrial Marine Claims, Inc.
9805 White Cascade Dr.
Charlotte, NC 28269
704-536-7511; Fax 803-651-7425
SAMS (AMS), ABYC, NAMI, NFPA

James C. Harper
James C. Harper & Associates
PO Box 494
Wrightsville Beach, NC 28480
919-452-0768
NAMS, SNAME

OHIO

Glen Kreis
Marine Surveyor
10558 Ridgevale Dr.
Cincinnati, OH 45240
513-851-5878

OKLAHOMA

Thomas Benton
Accredited Marine Surveyor
RR 3, Box 178-5
Cleveland, OK 74020
918-243-7689; Fax 918-243-7235
SAMS (AMS), NAMI, ABYC, NFPA

OREGON

Steven Cox
Marine Surveyors Northwest
7776 SW Barnard Dr.
Beaverton, OR 97007
503-641-4604

PENNSYLVANIA

Einar Groething
Technical Maritime Services
204 N. Benjamin Dr.
West Chester, PA 19382-1946
610-436-5110; Fax 610-436-5119
NAMS, M.E.

William Major
Bristol Yacht Services, Inc.
110 Mill St.
Bristol, PA 19007
215-788-0870; Fax 215-788-0790
SAMS (AMS), ABYC

RHODE ISLAND

Robert Daigle, SA
Marine Surveyor
141 Plain Road
North Kingstown, RI 02852
401-295-8061
SAMS (SA)

Richard Learned
Learned & Associates
84 Gateway Rd.
North Kingstown, RI 02852
401-294-9232; Fax 401-294-9710
ASA, ABYC, NAMI

Donald B. Pray
Donald B. Pray Associates
PO Box 1224
Newport, RI 02840
401-423-2774; 800-454-7729
Fax 401-423-0934
SAMS (AMS), ABYC, NFPA

Jon Stolte
Marine Surveyors Bureau
580 Thames St., #255
Newport, RI 02840
401-596-0101; Fax 203-399-4996
NAMS, ABYC, NFPA

SOUTH CAROLINA

Carl Foxworth
Industrial Marine Claims, Inc.
515 Creekside Dr.
Murrells Inlet, SC 29576
803-651-2800; Fax 803-651-7425
SAMS (AMS), ABYC, NAMI, NFPA

TENNESSEE

James Robbins
Marine Surveyor
1793 The Lane Road
Cookeville, TN, 38506-8756
615-537-6743, 615-537-6719
SAMS (AMS)

Rudolf H. Roemer
World Class Marine Services
3515 St. Elmo Ave.
Chattanooga, TN 37409
615-267-8557; Fax 615-267-8452
NAMS, SNAME

TEXAS

Bobby Brown
Blue Water Surveyors, Inc.
5009 Marcus Dr.
Flower Mound, TX 75028
214-355-1389; Fax 214-355-1758
SAMS (SA), ABYC

Marine Surveyor Directory

Peter Davidson
Able Seaman Marine Surveyors
320 S. Chaparral St.
Corpus Christi, TX 78401
512-884-7245; Fax 512-882-6631
SAMS (AMS), ABYC, NFPA, NAMI

James Merritt
Tangent Development Co.
1715 Harlequin Run
Austin, TX 78758
512-266-9248; Fax 512-835-8938
SAMS (AMS), ABYC, NAMI, SNAME, USSA

John B. Oliveros
Marine Surveyor
127 Marlin St.
Galveston, TX 77550
409-763-3123
NAMS, ABYC

Dale Vandermolen
C & V Marine Surveyors
PO Box 31174
Corpus Christi, TX 78463
512-855-3801
NAMS

VERMONT

William Talbott
Marine Surveyor
RD Box 2450
N. Ferrisburg, VT 05473
802-425-2973
NAMS

VIRGINIA

Bill Coker
Entre Nous Marine Services
PO Box 1865
Hampton, VA 23669
804-723-2883; Fax 804-867-7206
ABYC, NFPA, SAMS (SA)

L. Wayne Hudgins
Wolftrap Marine Surveying
Route 666
Hallieford, VA 23068
804-725-3410
SAMS (SA), ABYC

Stephen Knox
Knox Marine Consultants
355 Crawford St., #601
Portsmouth, VA 23704-2823
804-393-9788; Fax 804-393-9789
NAMS

Danny Reynolds
Aetna Casualty and Surety
5040 Corporate Woods Dr.
Virginia Beach, VA 23462
804-671-2757; Fax 804-671-2791
NAMS

George Zahn, Jr.
Ware River Associates
5604 Roanes Wharf Rd.
Gloucester, VA 23061
804-693-4329; Fax 804-693-4329
SAMS (AMS), SNAME, ABYC, NFPA

WASHINGTON

Matthew Harris
Reisner, McEwen & Harris
1333 Lincoln St., #323
Bellingham, WA 98226
360-647-6966; Fax 360-733-9022
NAMS, SAMS (AMS), ABYC

Capt. David L. Jackson
Marine Surveyors & Consultants
909 3rd St.
Anacortes, WA 98221
360-293-4528; Fax 360-293-0366
NAMS

John Marples
Marples Marine Services
4530 Se Firmont Dr.
Port Orchard, WA 98366
206-871-5634
NAMS

Jay McEwen
Reisner, McEwen & Assoc., Inc.
2500 Westlake Ave. North, #D
Seattle, WA 98109
206-285-8194; Fax 206-285-8196
NAMS, ABYC, ASA

Steve Nelson
Marine Surveyor
PO Box 1356
Friday Harbor, WA 98250-1356
206-392-1670

Ronald Reisner
Reisner, McEwen & Assoc., Inc.
2500 Westlake Ave. North, #D
Seattle, WA 98109
206-285-8194; Fax 206-285-8196
NAMS, SAMS (AMS)

WISCONSIN

Chris Kelly
Professional Yacht Services
2132 - 89th Street, #1
Kenosha, WI 53143
800-535-0072; Fax 708-872-0073
SAMS (SA), ABYC, NFPA, NAMI

Edward Montgomery
Northern Marine Survey Co.
1014 John Avenue
Superior, WI 54880
715-394-6848
ABYC

CANADA

Timothy McGivney
Aegis Marine Surveyors, Ltd.
745 Clark Dr.
Vancouver, B.C., Canada V5L 3J3
604-251-2210; Fax 604-254-0515
NAMS, ABYC, SNAME

Barry Smith
Barry D. Smith & Company
#9-323 Governors Ct.
New Westminster, B.C., Canada V3L 5S6
604-522-2877
NAMS

1996 EDITION

The McKnew/Parker

Consumer's Guide to

FAMILY & EXPRESS CRUISERS

ALBIN 27 DIESEL CRUISER

SPECIFICATIONS

Length	26'9"	Cockpit	NA
Length WL	24'4"	Water	30 gals.
Beam	9'8"	Fuel	72/100 gals.
Draft	2'6"	Hull Type	Semi-Disp.
Weight	6,800#	Designer	Joe Puccia
Clearance	NA	Production	1983–Current

The Albin 27 Cruiser is a descendant of the Swedish-built Albin 25, one of the best-selling small craft ever designed. Because of her salty appearance and sturdy construction, the Albin 27 has been popular for a number of years with family cruisers seeking a small, easily handled, and economical boat with the privacy of an aft-cabin layout. Hull construction is solid fiberglass, and a full-length keel provides protection for the running gear in shallow waters. While the Albin's twin-cabin accommodations are necessarily basic (she is, after all, only 27 feet), they are nonetheless adequate for two undemanding couples. Perhaps her best feature is the center-cockpit layout with inboard seating and protected helm. Built in the U.S., the Albin 27 Cruiser is inexpensive to operate and requires relatively little maintenance. Several 4- and 6-cylinder diesel engines have been available over the years, and all will provide an economical 2–3 gph at moderate cruising speeds of 10–12 knots. Note that bow thrusters and additional fuel are standard in newer models. ❑

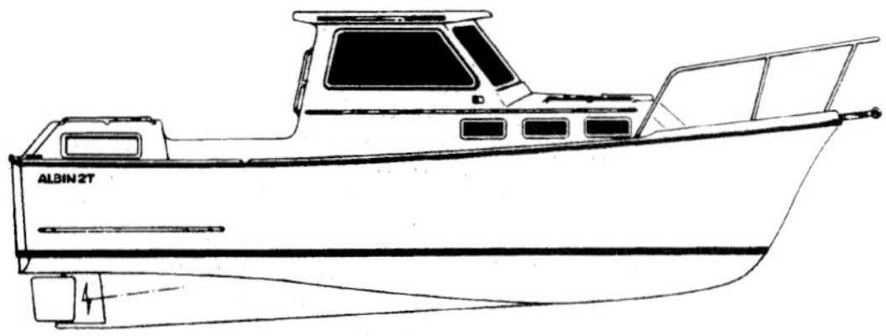

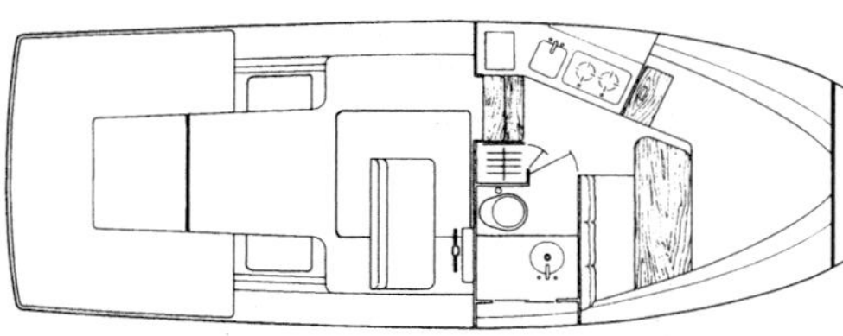

See Page 257 for Pricing Informationn

ALLMAND 34 CLASSIC

SPECIFICATIONS

Length	34'0"	Water	120 gals.
Beam	11'0"	Fuel	170 gals.
Draft	2'8"	Hull Type	Deep-V
Weight	12,000#	Deadrise Aft	NA
Clearance	12'2"	Designer	Allmand
Cockpit	NA	Production	1971–81

The Allmand 34 is an all-fiberglass family cruiser with a roomy interior, decent performance (for her era), and a better-than-average ride in a chop. In order to maximize interior volume, the Allmand 34's deckhouse is set well forward giving her a slightly awkward look. These were affordable family cruisers during the '70s, and quite a number were sold. There were several interior layouts offered, but most were arranged with a single stateroom forward, galley and dinette down, and a standard lower helm. The teak and mica laminates used in the 34 make for a rather dated interior by today's standards. While she's not designed as a fisherman, her cockpit is suitable for a couple of light-tackle anglers. The bridge is small, and the sidedecks are narrow. The Allmand 34 was offered as a flybridge sedan (the "Classic" pictured above), or as a Sportfish model with a much larger cockpit. Diesels were available, but most were sold with 225-hp gas inboards, which cruise around 17 knots and reach a top speed of 25 knots. ❑

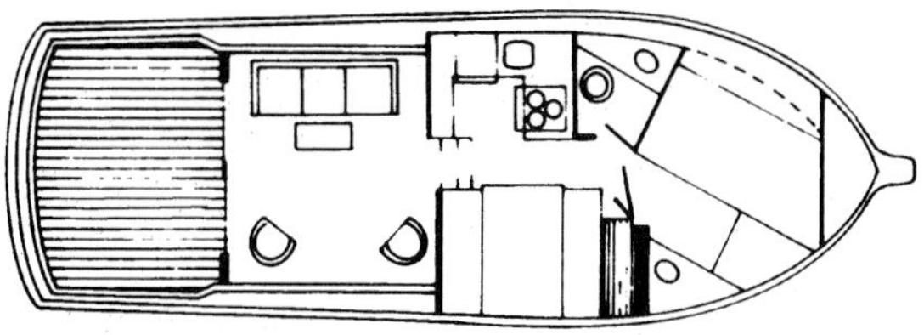

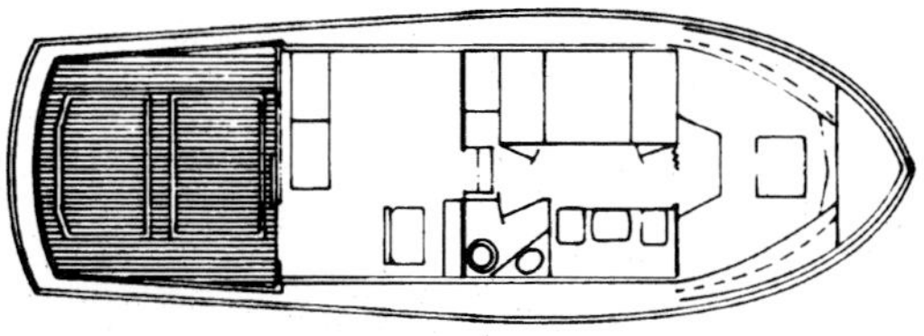

See Page 257 for Pricing Information

ATLANTIC 34 SPORTSMAN

SPECIFICATIONS

Length	34'0"	Fuel	300 gals.
Beam	12'0"	Cockpit	NA
Draft	3'0"	Hull Type	Modified-V
Weight	13,500#	Deadrise Aft	16°
Clearance	8'0"	Designer	J. Scopinich
Water	40 gals.	Production	1988–92

Until the 34 Sportsman came along, Atlantic Yachts had been known primarily for their line of trawler-style cruisers and motor yachts. It came as a surprise, then, to see their first new design in years fall into the sportfisherman category. A popular model with good handling qualities, she was built on a solid fiberglass hull with a modified-V bottom and generous flare at the bow. Her large bi-level cockpit was offered in several deck configurations for use as an express cruiser or sportfisherman. A centerline hatch on the bridgedeck provides decent access to the motors. Below, the cabin accommodations are laid out in the conventional manner with V-berths forward, an enclosed head with shower, small galley, and a dinette seating area. Standard gas 454-cid engines cruise the Sportsman at 25 knots and reach a top speed of 31–32 knots. Optional 300-hp GM 8.2 diesels cruise around 27 knots and reach 31 knots top. A total of 77 Atlantic 34s were built before production ended in 1992. ❑

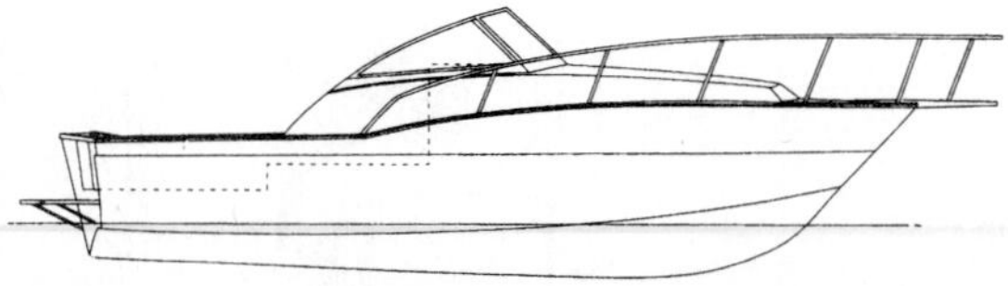

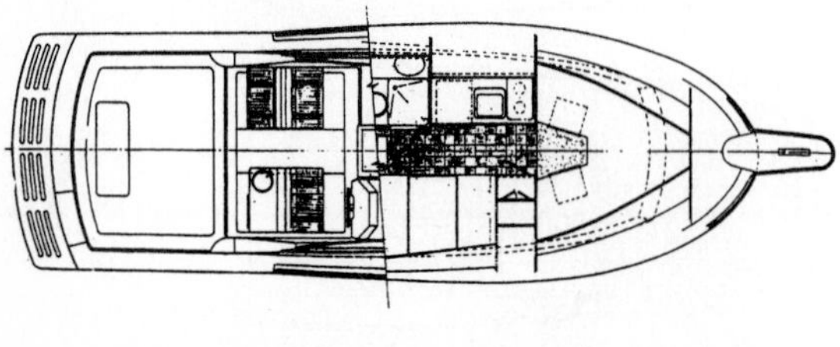

See Page 257 for Pricing Information

BAYLINER 2556 COMMAND BRIDGE

SPECIFICATIONS

Length	25'0"	Water	30 gals.
Beam	9'6"	Fuel	102 gals.
Draft, Up	1'11"	Hull Type	Deep-V
Draft, Down	3'3"	Deadrise Aft	18.5°
Weight	5,685#	Designer	Bayliner
Clearance	8'0"	Production	1986–94

Introduced in 1986 as the 2560 Trophy (which implied she was a fishing boat), Bayliner marketing execs changed the name of this model to 2556 Ciera Command Bridge in 1988. She's a well-proportioned small sedan with a spacious two-stateroom interior and a cockpit large enough to accommodate a couple of light-tackle anglers. Like all Bayliner models, she's built on a solid fiberglass hull and her relatively wide beam results in a surprisingly roomy boat for her size. Inside, the portside dinette is raised above the cabin sole in order to provide space below for a private midship cabin with a double bed. A lower helm and complete galley were standard along with a small stand-up head and shower. Standard features include an inside helm, transom platform, folding swim ladder, 30-gal. in-deck fish box, rod holders, rod storage port and starboard, and tackle drawers. Note that this is a small boat to carry a flybridge, and she's designed for inland and coastal use only. A single 300-hp stern drive engine will cruise at 17 knots and deliver about 28 knots top. ❑

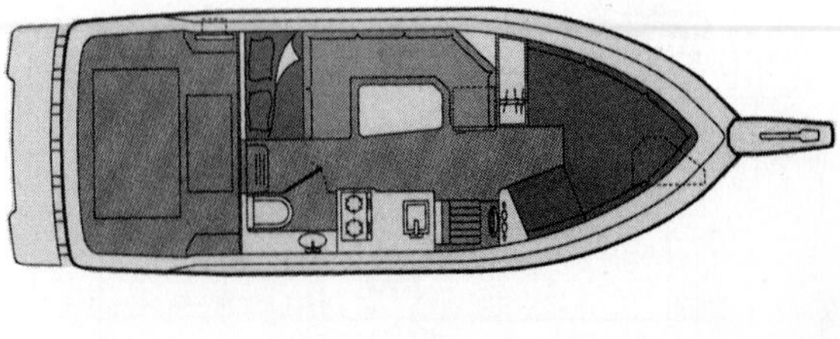

See Page 257 for Pricing Information

BAYLINER 2650/2655 CIERA SUNBRIDGE

SPECIFICATIONS

Length ....26'1"	Water ....35 gals.
Beam..............................9'6"	Fuel ....105 gals.
Draft, Up ....1'8"	Hull Type ....Deep-V
Draft, Down ....3'3"	Deadrise Aft....................19°
Weight.......................5,100#	Designer ....Bayliner
Clearance ....9'2"	Production 1988–90

The Bayliner 2655 Ciera Sunbridge (originally called the *2650* Ciera Sunbridge) is a straightforward mid-cabin weekender with modern styling and a maxi-interior layout. There were no options offered for this model (except air conditioning), and they all have the same hull graphics, sport arch, and interior colors. The cabin walls and overhead are carpeted—an inexpensive approach to finishing out the interior. With nine-feet-six-inches of beam, the 2655 Ciera is a roomy boat. The mid-cabin is tucked below the bridgedeck and comes with sitting headroom, a privacy curtain and opening ports. When the dinette is converted there are sleeping accommodations for four adults and two kids. At 5,100 lbs., the 2655 is a light boat for her size (especially considering that she's not a trailerable model), and the performance with a single stern drive engine is impressive. The standard 5.7-litre stern drive engine cruises at 17 knots (about 26 knots top), and the optional 7.4-litre engine cruises at 20+ and delivers 35–36 knots wide open. Note that since 1991 Bayliner has had two additional 2655 Ciera Sunbridge models—both trailerable. ❑

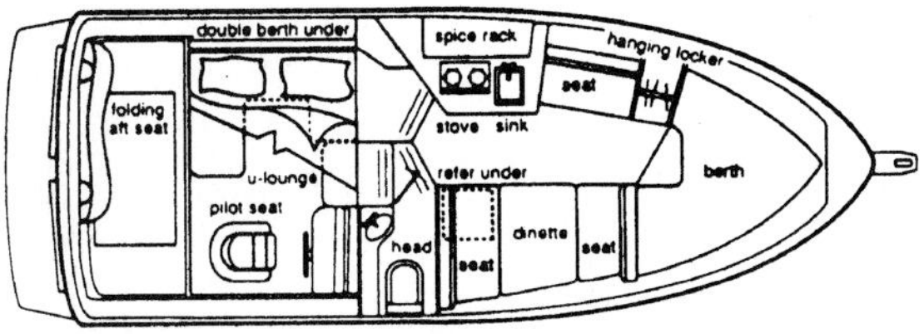

See Page 257 for Pricing Information

BAYLINER 2450/2455/2651/2655 SUNBRIDGE

2450/2455 Ciera Sunbridge (1984–89)

2651/2655 Ciera Sunbridge (1991–93)

SPECIFICATIONS

Length, 2450 ....24'5"	Fuel ....55 gals.
Length, 2566 ....25'7"	Water ....13 gals.
Beam................................8'0"	Clearance ....6'6"
Draft, Up.........................1'8"	Hull Type ....Deep-V
Draft, Down ....3'3"	Deadrise Aft....................20°
Weight........................4,300#	Production 1984–93

Bayliner's most popular trailerable cruiser for many years, this model began production in 1984 when she was introduced as the 2450 Ciera Sunbridge. She became the 2651 Ciera Sunbridge in 1990 when a new integral swim platform and a revised floorplan were added, and—finally—Bayliner changed the model name to 2655 in 1991. Lightly built and inexpensive to own, she came with a long list of standard equipment and ranked among the best buys in her class. Inside, the mid-cabin floorplan will sleep four and includes a small galley, a removable dinette table, and a stand-up head. Not surprisingly, stowage space is limited. An L-shaped lounge seats four opposite the helm, and a bench seat at the transom folds away for access to the engine. Additional features include a fully cored hull, bow pulpit, and swim ladder. Among several engine options offered over the years, a single 205-hp MerCruiser will cruise the Bayliner 2566 Ciera Sunbridge at an economical 20 knots (about 8 gph) and reach a top speed of 30–31 knots. ❏

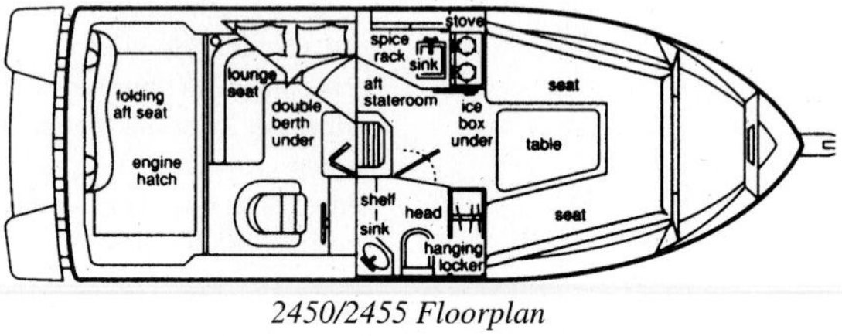

2450/2455 Floorplan

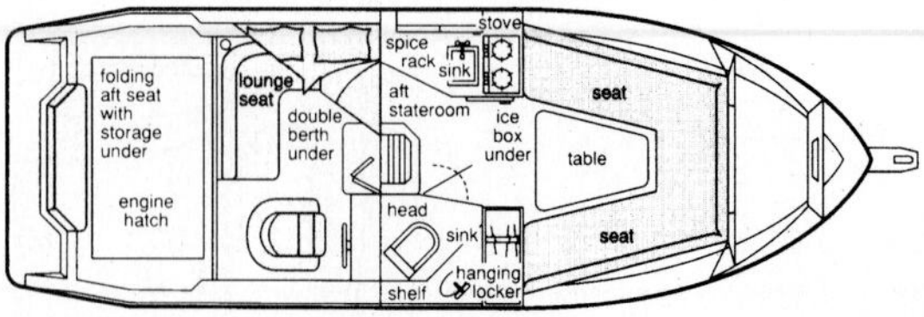

2651/2655 Floorplan

See Page 257 for Pricing Information

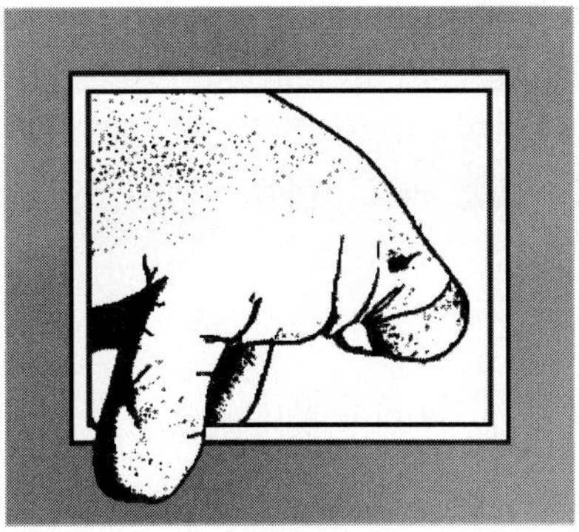

Get Your M.A. (Manatee Awareness) Degree In Recreational Watersports:

Tips To Protect Manatees

There are many things YOU can do to protect manatees from a watercraft collision or other human-related injuries:

✤ Wearing polarized sunglasses can help eliminate the glare of the sun and helps boaters to see below the water's surface.

✤ Stay in deep water channels when boating. Avoid boating over seagrass beds and shallow areas where manatees might be feeding (but be aware that manatees also use deep water channels when traveling).

✤ Look for a snout, back, tail, or flipper breaking the surface of the water, or a swirl or a flat spot on the water that is created by the motion of the manatee's paddle-shaped tail when it dives or swims.

✤ If you see a manatee when operating a powerboat, remain a safe distance away — 50 feet is suggested. If you want to observe the manatee, cut the motor, but do not drift over the animal.

✤ If you like to jet-ski, water-ski, or participate in high-speed water sports, choose areas that manatees do not, or cannot frequent, such as a landlocked lake.

✤ Obey posted speed zone signs and keep away from posted manatee sanctuaries.

✤ Keep your litter on board your vessel. Recycle it or throw it in a trash container when you get back on shore.

✤ Discard monofilament line or hooks properly. Discarding monofilament line into or onto the waters of the state of Florida is against the law.

✤ Look, but don't touch manatees. If manatees become accustomed to being around people, it can alter their behavior in the wild, perhaps causing them to lose their natural fear of boats and humans, and this may make them susceptible to harm. Passive observation is the best way to interact with manatees and all wildlife.

✤ Resist the urge to feed manatees or give them water. Remember, passive observation!

✤ When swimming or diving, the key words are _________ ___________ (right! passive observation). You may not know it, but your presence might accidentally separate a mother manatee and calf or keep a manatee away from its warm water source — both of which are potentially life-threatening situations.

✤ Call the Manatee Hotline at 1-800-DIAL-FMP if you happen to spot an injured, dead, tagged, or orphaned manatee, or if you see a manatee that is being harassed.

Save the Manatee® Club
500 N. Maitland Avenue • Maitland, FL 32751
1 - 800 - 432 - JOIN

BAYLINER 2655 CIERA SUNBRIDGE

SPECIFICATIONS

Length w/Pulpit	27'9"	Water	25 gals.
Beam	8'5"	Waste	13 gals.
Draft, Up	1'4"	Clearance	7'4"
Draft, Down	3'1"	Hull Type	Modified-V
Weight	4,970#	Deadrise Aft	16°
Fuel	70 gals.	Production	1994–Current

The most recent version of Bayliner's super-popular 2655 Ciera Sunbridge series (see previous pages for earlier models) is 5" wider than her immediate predecessor with improved styling (note the stylish wraparound windshield) and increased cabin headroom. Built on a solid fiberglass hull, the compact-but-complete mid-cabin floorplan is arranged with a small galley, a forward dinette/V-berth, an enclosed stand-up head and shower, and a big aft berth with a hanging locker and storage. While the interior accommodations are certainly adequate, Bayliner designers have clearly placed the emphasis of the 2655 Ciera in the spacious cockpit where there's comfortable seating for four adults on an L-shaped lounge opposite the helm. There are molded steps on both sides of the cockpit for access to the narrow but usable sidedecks. For additional seating, a pull-out aft cockpit bench seat is optional. The engine is under the cockpit sole which raises manually on twin gas-lift assisters. The optional 235/5.7-litre MerCruiser stern drive will cruise at 19 knots and reach a top speed of around 31-32 knots. ❑

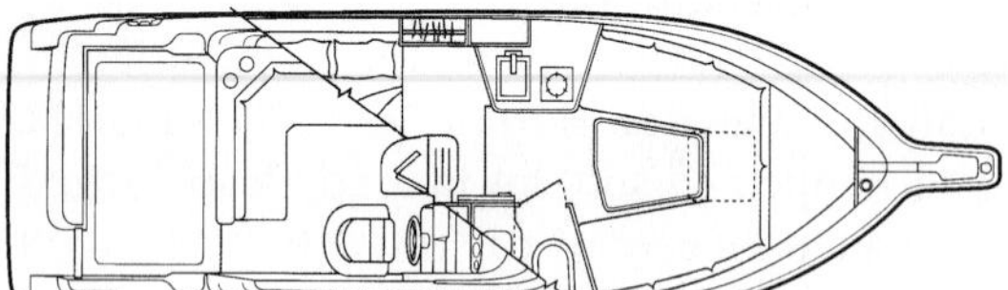

See Page 258 for Pricing Information

BAYLINER 2850 COMMAND BRIDGE

SPECIFICATIONS

Length	27'7"	Water	30 gals.
Beam	10'0"	Fuel	120 gals.
Draft, Up	1'11"	Hull Type	Deep-V
Draft, Down	3'3"	Deadrise Aft	NA
Weight	5,775#	Designer	Bayliner
Clearance	6'8"	Production	1983–89

A popular boat for several years, the Bayliner 2850 Command Bridge (called the *Ciera* Command Bridge in 1988–89) was marketed as a stylish and affordable family sedan primarily designed for coastal and inland cruising. She's built on a cored hull with a realtively wide beam and moderate freeboard—a good-looking design with a stylish profile. Inside, the original floorplan had a single stateroom with a convertible dinette to port, a convertible settee opposite, and a privacy door forward. In 1986, a new mid-cabin interior layout was introduced with a second stateroom positioned ahead of the aft bulkhead and below the dinette settee. A wide ten-foot beam makes the 2850 Command Bridge a roomy boat inside. Standard featured included a lower helm, sport arch (on later models), swim platform, and swim ladder. Not surprisingly, storage space is at a premium. There's seating for four aft of the helm on the console. Built on a lightweight hull, most were sold with a single 260-hp Volvo stern drive engine which provides very adaquate performance. She'll cruise easily at 17–18 knots and reach a top speed of about 27 knots. ❑

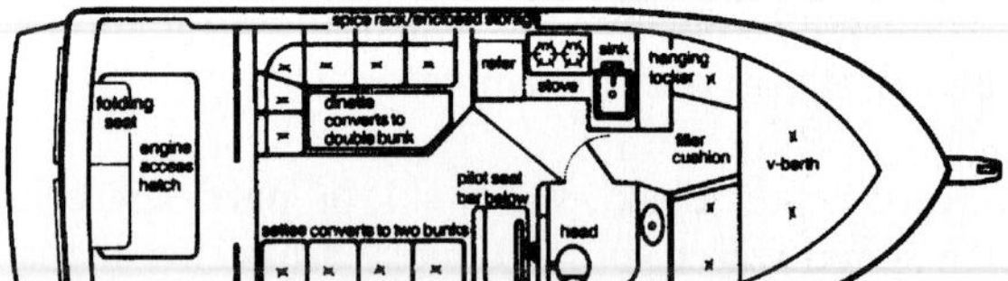

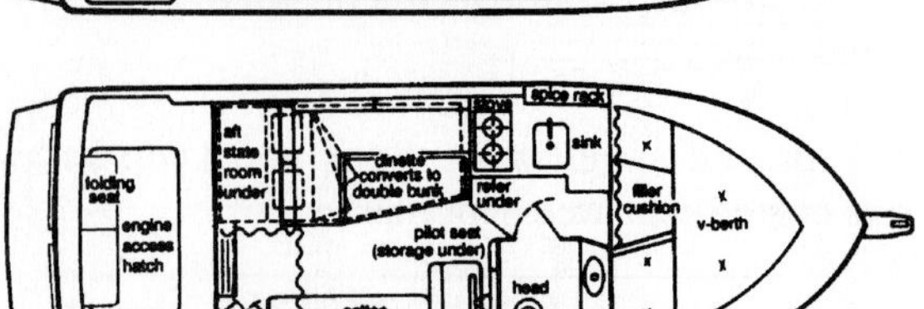

See Page 258 for Pricing Information

BAYLINER 2850 CONTESSA SUNBRIDGE

SPECIFICATIONS

Length	27'5"	Water	30 gals.
Beam	10'0"	Fuel	120 gals.
Draft, Up	1'11"	Hull Type	Deep-V
Draft, Down	3'3"	Deadrise Aft	NA
Weight	5,775#	Designer	Bayliner
Clearance	6'8"	Production	1983–89

Bayliner has had their share of popular boats over the years, and the 2850 Contessa Sunbridge was certainly one of them. Introduced in 1983, she was marketed as a budget-priced family cruiser with sleek styling, a wide beam, and a spacious mid-cabin layout. The Contessa is a roomy boat below with good headroom thanks to her raised foredeck and elevated helm. Berths for six are provided together with a stand-up head compartment, decent counter space, and a full-size galley. The cockpit has plenty of lounge seating for guests, and visibility from the helm position is excellent. In 1986, the deckhouse was redesigned and raised slightly, and the interior was completely rearranged with a U-shaped dinette to port replacing the previous dinette forward. Built on a lightweight hull, most were sold with a single 260-hp Volvo stern drive engine. She'll cruise easily at 18 knots and reach a top speed of 26–27 knots. (Note that she was called the 2850 Ciera Sunbridge in 1988 and the 2855 Ciera Sunbridge in 1989.) ❑

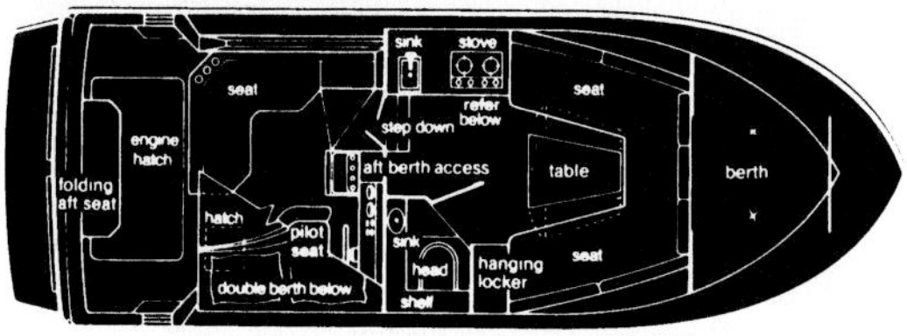

Contessa Floorplan (1983–87)

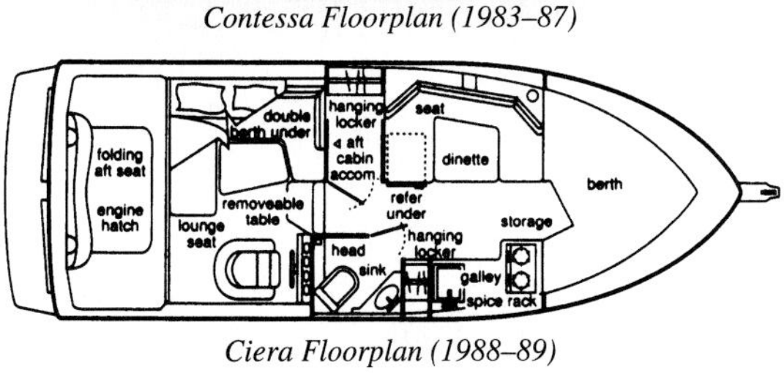

Ciera Floorplan (1988–89)

See Page 258 for Pricing Information

BAYLINER 2855 SUNBRIDGE (EARLY)

SPECIFICATIONS

Length	28'1"	Water	35 gals.
Beam	9'6"	Fuel	102 gals.
Draft, Up	1'8"	Hull Type	Deep-V
Draft, Down	3'3"	Deadrise Aft	18°
Weight	6,510#	Designer	Bayliner
Clearance	9'2"	Production	1991–93

The 2855 Ciera Sunbridge is a practical family cruiser with a mid-cabin floorplan and a rather innovative salon layout. Bayliner engineers designed a wraparound dinette lounge for this model with a removable jump seat for access to the V-berth—a great entertaining arrangement with pit-style seating for a crowd. The dinette converts in the normal fashion to a double berth, and both the forward and mid-cabin sleeping areas are fitted with privacy curtains. Topside, a big L-shaped lounge seat (with removable table) provides guest seating opposite the helm. A shower is built into the transom, and a fold-down ladder is available for swimmers. The standard 230-hp MerCruiser I/O will cruise at 17 knots (around 25 knots top), and the optional 300-hp motor will deliver 19 knots at cruise and about 30 knots wide open. Note that there was an earlier 2855 Ciera Sunbridge model offered in 1989 (see the 2850 Contessa Sunbridge for details), and an all-new design with the same name was introduced in 1994. ❑

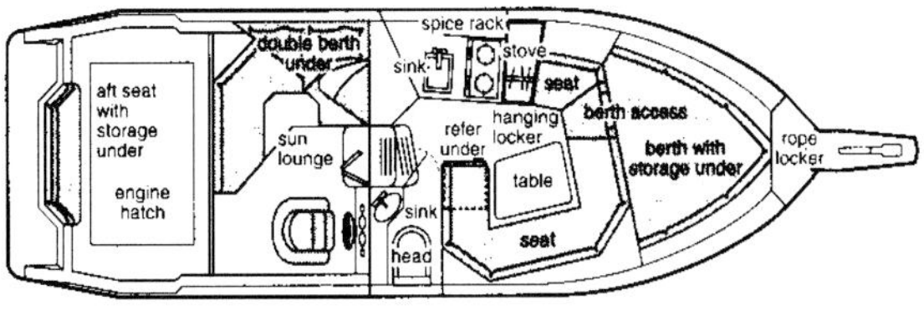

See Page 258 for Pricing Information

BAYLINER 2855 SUNBRIDGE

SPECIFICATIONS

Length	30'31"	Water	35 gals.
Beam	9'7"	Fuel	102 gals.
Draft, Up	1'8"	Hull Type	Deep-V
Draft, Down	3'4"	Deadrise Aft	22°
Weight	6,510#	Designer	Bayliner
Clearance	8'6"	Production	1994–Current

One of Bayliner's more popular cruisers, the 2855 Sunbridge was completely redesigned for 1994 with a sleek new profile, a smoother ride, and a revised interior with a bigger galley area and more storage space. The hull is basically the same as the earlier 2855 with an extra inch in the beam for more interior volume and additional transom deadrise for a better ride in a chop. The mid-cabin floorplan of the 2855 Sunbridge is arranged with double berths fore and aft and a convertible dinette which can sleep two kids. Privacy curtains separate both sleeping areas, and headroom is adaquate throughout most of the cabin. Outside, big U-shaped lounge (with a removable table) is opposite the helm. Lacking sidedecks, a windshield walk-through provides access to the foredeck. Additional features include a slide-out jumpseat behind the companion lounge, transom door, sport arch and colorful hull graphics. A good performer with a single 7.4-litre MerCruiser I/O (optional), the 2855 Sunbridge will cruise at 20 knots and reach 30 knots wide open. ❑

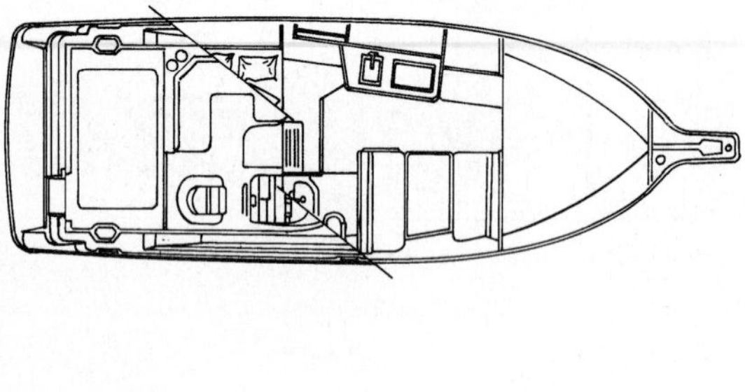

See Page 258 for Pricing Information

BAYLINER 2955 SUNBRIDGE

SPECIFICATIONS

Length	28'8"	Water	30 gals.
Beam	10'6"	Fuel	120 gals.
Draft, Up	2'0"	Hull Type	Deep-V
Draft, Down	3'6"	Deadrise Aft	20°
Weight	7,400#	Designer	Bayliner
Clearance	9'6"	Production	1988–90

Introduced as the Bayliner 2950 Avanti in 1988, this is yet another example of why Bayliner so dominates the entry level end of the boating market. Fully equipped (there were no options except air conditioning), a new 2955 Avanti Sunbridge delivered for about $50,000 in 1989/90—less by far than any of the more upscale competition. Not surprisingly, a lot of 2955s were sold during her production run, and they are quite common on today's aftermarket. With her 10-foot, 6-inch beam, the 2955 Avanti is a wide boat for her size with roomy cabin accommodations and an abundance of cockpit space. The mid-cabin floorplan will sleep four adults and two kids and includes a stand-up head with shower and a small galley. Note the absence of a privacy door in the forward stateroom. Too, the swim platform is a bolt-on affair rather than a modern integral design. A single 340-hp I/O was standard (16 knots cruise and 28 top), and twin 260-hp MerCriuisers were optional (21–22 knots cruise/33 top). Engine access with the twins is tight. ❑

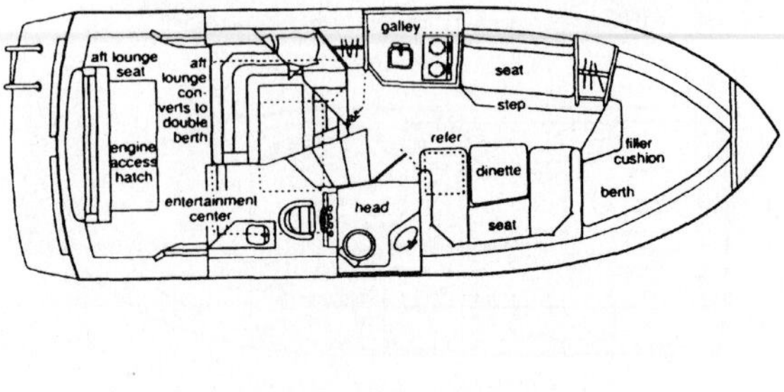

See Page 258 for Pricing Information

BAYLINER 2958 COMMAND BRIDGE

SPECIFICATIONS

Length	28'8"	Water	29 gals.
Beam	10'6"	Fuel	121 gals.
Draft, Up	2'0"	Hull Type	Deep-V
Draft, Down	3'6"	Deadrise Aft	20°
Weight	8,750#	Designer	Bayliner
Clearance	11'8"	Production	1988–90

A stylish family cruiser with an affordable price tag to go with her rakish lines, the Bayliner 2958 Command Bridge is a roomy boat inside thanks to her wide 10-foot, 6-inch beam. Construction is solid fiberglass and, at just under 9,000 lbs., she's a light boat for her size. The salon dimensions are made even larger by placing the bulkhead well aft into what would otherwise have been cockpit space. A private mid-cabin is located below the dinette. Only a curtain provides privacy in the forward stateroom. The lower helm was standard. While the cockpit is small, the bridge accommodations are generous with plenty of guest seating. The radar arch, swim platform, and bow pulpit were all standard along with a low, entry-level price tag. A large opening hatch in the cockpit provides access to the motors where working space is at a premium. Twin 230-hp stern drive engines (standard) give the 2985 Command Bridge a cruising speed of 19 knots and a top speed of around 29 knots. (Note that she was called the 2950 Avanti Command Bridge in 1986.) ❑

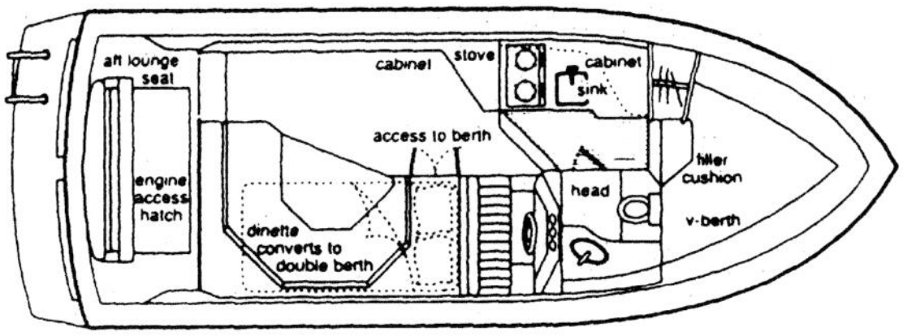

See Page 258 for Pricing Information

BAYLINER 3055 SUNBRIDGE

SPECIFICATIONS

Length	30'7"	Water	36 gals.
Beam	10'0"	Fuel	125 gals.
Draft, Up	1'6"	Hull Type	Modified-V
Draft, Down	3'0"	Deadrise Aft	14°
Weight	8,000#	Designer	Bayliner
Clearance	8'9"	Production	1991–94

A bargain-priced express cruiser with a stylish profile, the 3055 Ciera Sunbridge (originally called the 3055 Avanti Sunbridge) has been a popular model for Bayliner since her introduction in 1991. A ten-foot beam is about average for a thirty-footer, and the 3055 Sunbridge is not a notably roomy boat below for her length. She has a fairly straightforward mid-cabin floorplan with a convertible dinette, a small galley (the refrigerator is placed under the dinette seat), and head with shower. Both staterooms have curtains for privacy. The cockpit is well-arranged with lounge seating opposite the helm and a wet bar behind the helm seat. The engine access hatch in the cockpit has gas assist springs, and the transom platform has a folding swim ladder and a built-in shower. Like all Bayliner products, most everything was standard in the 3055 Sunbridge (except air conditioning), and there were practically no options. A good-looking boat, a standard 300-hp MerCruiser I/O will cruise at 17 knots and reach a top speed of 26–27 knots. ❑

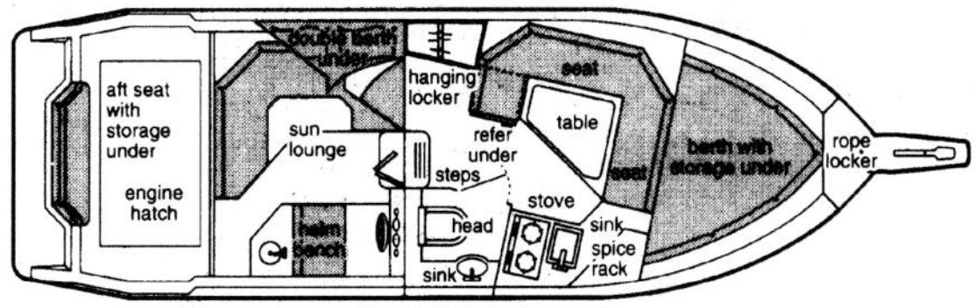

See Page 258 for Pricing Information

BAYLINER 3058 COMMAND BRIDGE (EARLY)

SPECIFICATIONS

Length	30'7"	Water	36 gals.
Beam	10'0"	Fuel	125 gals.
Draft, Up	1'6"	Hull Type	Modified-V
Draft, Down	3'0"	Deadrise Aft	14°
Weight	8,200#	Designer	Bayliner
Clearance	11'8"	Production	1991–92

There are two different 3058 Command Bridge models. The first (pictured above) lasted just two years in production before being replaced by an all-new model with a revised floorplan and beamier hull. Marketed as an inexpensive sport cruiser, the original 3058 is a better-looking boat than her sucessor but suffers from a rather unorthodox interior layout. In typical Bayliner fashion, the mid-cabin entryway is located aft of the salon settee—a suitable use of salon space perhaps in a larger boat, but, in this thirty-footer, the salon dimensions become too confining, especially with the standard lower helm. There are berths for six when the dinette is converted, and a privacy curtain is provided for the forward stateroom. Storage space is at a premium. Outside, the integral swim platform with molded port and starboard steps is a nice feature. The flybridge has seating for two or three guests. A standard 300-hp MerCruiser I/O will cruise at 17 knots and reach a top speed of 26–27 knots. Twin engines were optional. ❑

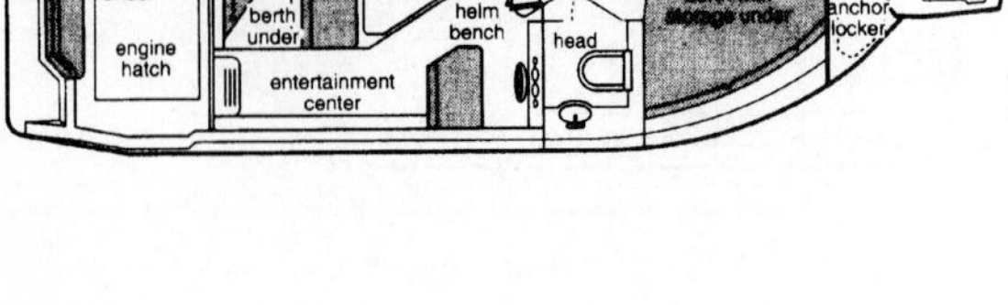

See Page 258 for Pricing Information

BAYLINER 3058 COMMAND BRIDGE

SPECIFICATIONS

Length	30'4"	Water	36 gals.
Beam	10'10"	Fuel	180 gals.
Draft, Up	1'11"	Hull Type	Modified-V
Draft, Down	3'2"	Deadrise Aft	15°
Weight	9,200#	Designer	Bayliner
Clearance	10'0"	Production	1992–93

The second Bayliner 3058 Command Bridge pictured above is a completely different boat from the earlier 3058 Command Bridge (1991–92). The styling is dramatically different, and this newer model has nearly a foot more beam than her predecessor. Most notable, however, is the fact that she's basically a three-piece boat with the hull and liner joining into a single fiberglass mold forming the swim platform, cockpit, house, bridge, and foredeck. (Pacemaker did this some years ago on their 30-foot Sportfisherman.) The benefits are reduced cost, a more rigid structure, and the end of leaks, but the boat's lines are pretty plain. Nonetheless, she's a roomy boat below, and her mid-cabin floorplan features berths for six with a stand-up head, lower helm, fully equipped galley, and a privacy door for the mid-cabin. Engine access is excellent, and the hatches are assisted by gas struts. The bridge can seat two or three guests no problem. Standard 180-hp twin stern drives will cruise around 18 knots, and optional 235-hp Mercs will cruise at 21–22 and reach 33 knots top. ❑

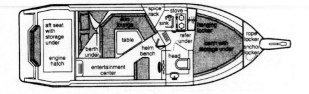

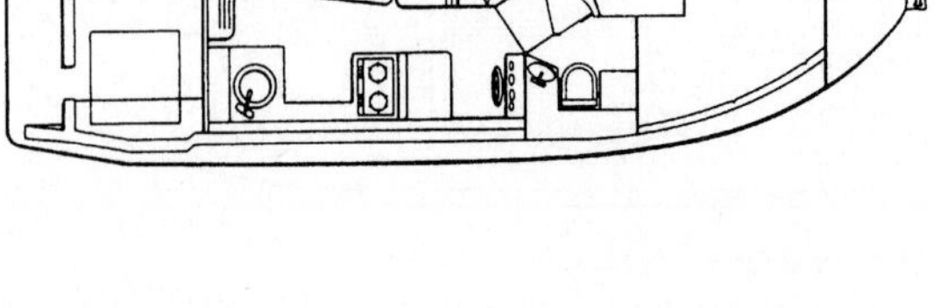

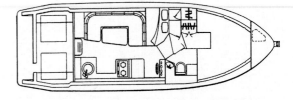

See Page 258 for Pricing Information

BAYLINER 3255 AVANTI SUNBRIDGE

SPECIFICATIONS

Length w/Platform........35'2"	Fuel........................180 gals.
Hull Length...............32'11"	Water.......................35 gals.
Beam............................11'0"	Clearance....................11'0"
Draft, Up.......................1'9"	Hull Type.........Modified-V
Draft, Down..................3'0"	Deadrise Aft...................16°
Weight.....................11,000#	Production.......1995–Current

A couple of unusual styling features incorporated into the new Bayliner 3255 Avanti Sunbridge combine to give this boat a somewhat distinctive appearance. First of course is the reverse radar arch (considered a radical design in the U.S. before Sea Ray began using the concept a few years ago in a few of their express cruisers), and the second attention-getter is the somewhat surprising absence of an integrated swim platform—the current rage in express cruiser designs. In most respects, the 3255 is a fairly conservative family express with an affordable price tag to go with her generous interior accomodations. The mid-cabin floorplan is arranged with double berths fore and aft (both cabins can be closed off for privacy), and there's a full galley, convertible dinette and a good-size hanging locker in the salon. Outside, a U-shaped settee is opposite the helm in the bi-level cockpit along with a small wet bar and a transom door. The sidedecks are reasonably wide, and foredeck access is easy. Twin 300-hp MerCruiser stern drives (optional) cruise at 19–20 knots and deliver top speeds of around 32 knots. ❑

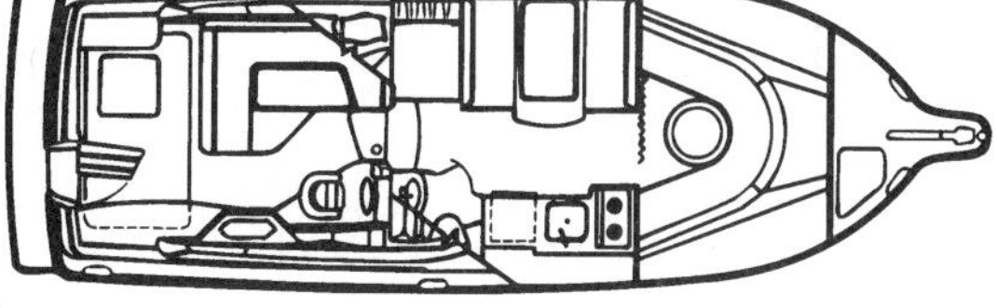

See Page 258 for Pricing Information

BAYLINER 3258 COMMAND BRIDGE

SPECIFICATIONS

Length w/Platform........35'2"	Fuel........................180 gals.
Hull Length...............32'11"	Water.......................52 gals.
Beam............................11'0"	Clearance....................11'7"
Draft, Up.......................1'9"	Hull Type.........Modified-V
Draft, Down..................3'0"	Deadrise Aft...................16°
Weight.....................11,900#	Production.......1995–Current

Dramatic styling has become a hallmark of Bayliner convertible designs since the late 1980s and the 3258 Avanti Command Bridge is no exception. With her rakish lines and aggressive profile, she'll be an attractive choice for budget-minded buyers looking for a spacious flybridge sedan at an affordable price. The cabin window treatment is very Euro-style—easily her most distinctive feature—and the small cockpit virtually guarantees an exceptionally roomy interior layout. The 3258 Avanti utilizes a somewhat unusual mid-stateroom floorplan with an elevated lower helm and settee forward, and both the galley and dinette aft in the salon.This provides for a notably large galley, but the layout comes up a bit short when it comes to salon space. Visability from the lower helm is excellent, and storage space is impressive for a boat this size. The flybridge, with the helm forward, will seat three. Additional features include a transom door and swim platform, easy engine access, radar arch,and an integral pulpit. Twin 300-hp MerCruiser stern drive engines (optional) will cruise the Bayliner 3258 Avanti Command Bridge at a steady 19 knots cruise with a top speed of about 30 knots. ❑

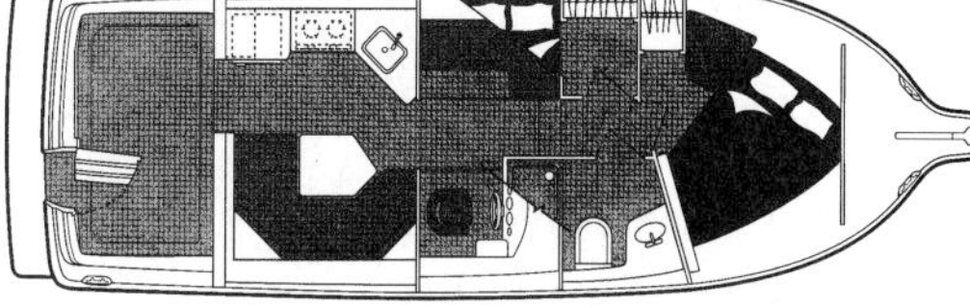

See Page 258 for Pricing Information

BAYLINER 3288 MOTOR YACHT

SPECIFICATIONS

Length	32'1"	Water	65 gals.
Length WL	28'10"	Fuel	200 gals.
Beam	11'6"	Hull Type	Modified-V
Draft	2'11"	Deadrise Aft	6°
Weight	13,800#	Designer	D. Livingston
Clearance	13'10"	Production	1981–Current

A popular model for many years, Bayliner calls their 3288 a Motor Yacht—quite a stretch in describing a straightforward 32-foot flybridge sedan. (For the record, she was introduced as the Bayliner 3270 Explorer in 1981; became the Bayliner 3270 MY in 1987; and evolved into the 3288 MY in 1989.) Marketed as an affordable family cruiser, she features an innovative interior layout with a small midships stateroom below the salon dinette. Note the standard lower helm. The 3288's fully cored hull results in a lightweight and extremely fuel-efficient package. The engines are set well aft with short shafts turning small wheels in prop pockets. Engine access is via two cockpit hatches—a tight fit. Twin 4-cylinder diesel engines were originally offered in the 3270, however in recent years the 140-hp Hino diesels were standard. Built on a lightweight and nearly flat-bottom hull, speeds are not fast (about 15 knots at cruise and 17–18 knots top), but the cruising economy is better than a mile per gallon—very impressive indeed. ❑

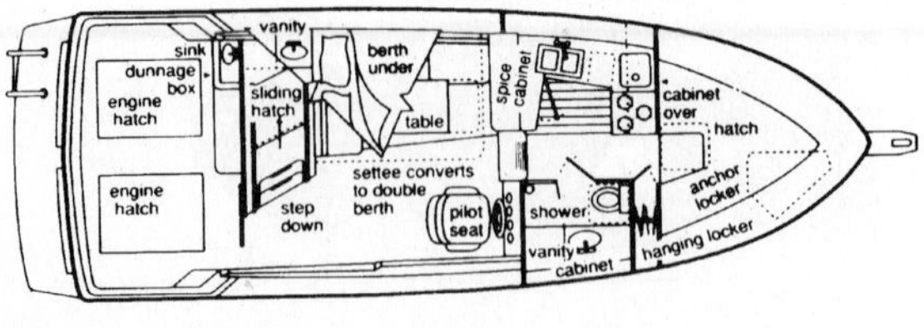

See Page 258 for Pricing Information

BAYLINER 3350 MONTEGO

SPECIFICATIONS

Length	32'3"	Fuel	220 gals.
Beam	11'5"	Cockpit	53 sq. ft.
Draft	3'0"	Hull Type	Modified-V
Weight	12,500#	Deadrise Aft	17°
Clearance	13'2"	Designer	Bayliner
Water	70 gals.	Production	1974–78

During most of her production years, the 3350 Montego was the largest boat in the Bayliner fleet. Her spacious interior is the result of using V-drives to move the engines aft in the hull. While the Montego's mid-galley floorplan allows space for two private staterooms forward, the salon, with its lower helm station, serving bar, and built-in dinette, is a tight fit. Note the stall shower in the head. The interior of each cabin is finished with plastic laminates, vinyl wall coverings, and teak trim. Two large in-deck hatches in the cockpit sole provide access to the engines and V-drive units. Additional features include wide sidedecks, a large bridge, and a swim platform. Twin 250-hp Chrysler gas engines provide a cruising speed of 17–18 knots and a top speed of about 27 knots. (The Montego was also available with I/Os.) Fuel economy is close to a mile per gallon, but the small fuel tanks limit range to less than 200 miles. With a deep 17° of transom deadrise, the 3350 Montego delivers a surprisingly comfortable ride in a chop. ❑

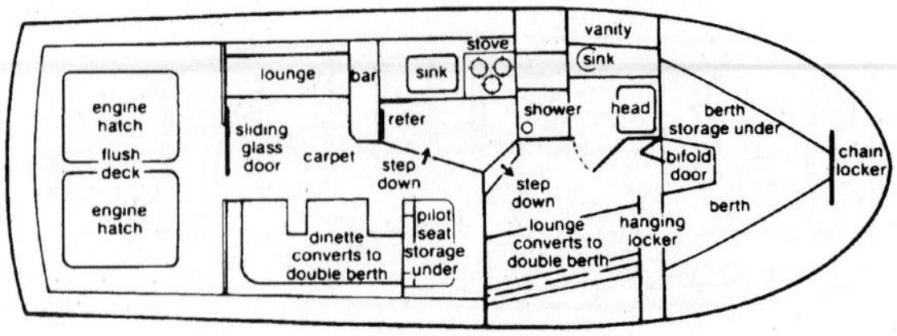

See Page 258 for Pricing Information

BAYLINER 3450/3485/3785 SUNBRIDGE

3450/3485 Avanti

3785 Avanti

SPECIFICATIONS

Length	33'9"	Water	50 gals.
Beam	12'10"	Fuel	205 gals.
Draft	3'0"	Hull Type	Modified-V
Weight	12,000#	Deadrise Aft	NA
Clearance	9'6"	Designer	Bayliner
Cockpit	NA	Production	1987–90

With all of her model designations, this is a tough boat to follow. From 1987 to 1988, she was called the Bayliner 3450 Avanti Sunbridge. In 1989 she became the 3485 Avanti (same basic boat), and in 1990—the last year of production—she was called the 3785 Avanti. (Notably, the 3785 featured a new integral swim platform and a longer hull length.) Like most other sportboats, she has plenty of sex appeal with her colorful hull graphics, Med-style bow rail, oval ports, and sweptback radar arch. The hull is fully cored to save weight, and side exhausts serve to keep the noise down and gas fumes out of the cabin. With nearly 13 feet of beam, the Avanti is a roomy boat below with spacious accommodations including a mid-cabin stateroom. The interior is finished with colorful fabrics and oak trim. Access to the engines and V-drive units is via removable hatches in the cockpit sole. Standard 330-hp gas engines will cruise the Avanti around 20 knots with a top speed of 27–28 knots. ❑

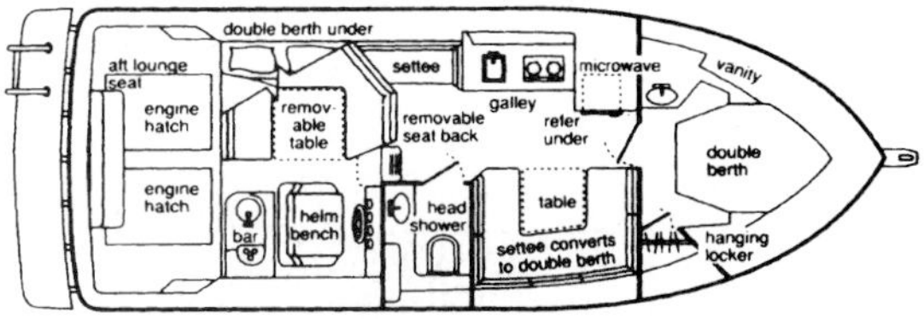

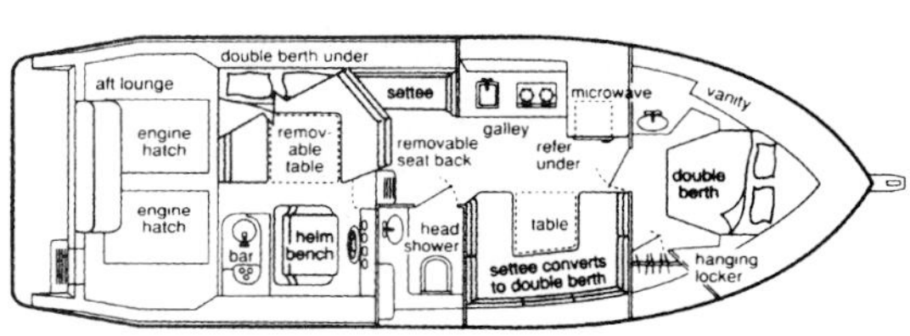

See Page 258 for Pricing Information

BAYLINER 3486 CONVERTIBLE

SPECIFICATIONS

Length	33'9"	Fuel	315 gals.
Beam	12'10"	Cockpit	NA
Draft	3'0"	Hull Type	Modified-V
Weight	13,900#	Deadrise Aft	NA
Clearance	15'0"	Designer	Bayliner
Water	65 gals.	Production	1987–89

Introduced in 1987 as the Bayliner 3460 Trophy, the Bayliner 3486 Convertible is an inexpensive and versatile family cruiser with a distinctive Med-style profile. She was conceived as a fishing boat, but her bold hull graphics and lightweight construction had limited appeal in the hard-core fishing community. She does have a fair-size cockpit, however, with a standard bait station with livewell and sink, two in-deck fishboxes, and a transom door. Inside, the two-stateroom floorplan is arranged with a small mid-cabin below the dinette and an offset double berth in the forward stateroom. The lower helm was standard. The interior is a blend of white fiberglass surfaces, colorful fabrics, and teak paneling and trimwork. Outside, the motors and V-drives are located beneath the cockpit sole. Note that the flybridge was redesigned in 1989. Engine access (two small in-deck hatches) is tight and so is the working space. Twin 330-hp inboard gas engines will cruise the Bayliner 3486 at around 20 knots. Top speed is 27–28 knots. Note the short production run. ❑

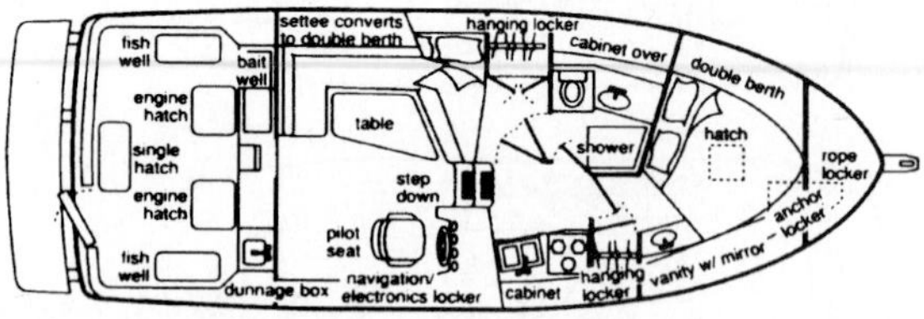

See Page 258 for Pricing Information

BAYLINER 3550 BRISTOL

SPECIFICATIONS

Length	35'0"	Fuel	400 gals.
Beam	13'1"	Cockpit	70 sq. ft.
Draft	3'2"	Hull Type	Modified-V
Weight	16,000#	Deadrise Aft	16°
Clearance	11'6"	Designer	Bayliner
Water	150 gals.	Production	1978–81

The Bayliner 3550 Bristol was an affordably priced family cruiser with a sporty profile and several innovative design features. Beginning with an unusually large flybridge, the Bristol has a unique fold-down walkway (complete with handrail) with steps leading directly from the bridge to the foredeck. Inside, the spacious floorplan is arranged with the galley on the salon level and two staterooms below, each with a double berth. With the salon settee converted into a double berth at night, the Bayliner 3550 can sleep up to three couples. A separate stall shower is fitted in the double-entry head, and wraparound cabin windows provide excellent outside visibility. While the interior accommodations are expansive, the cockpit is small. Additional features include wide sidedecks, standard lower helm, transom gate, and very good storage. An average performer, standard twin 330-hp gas engines (with V-drives) will cruise the Bayliner 3550 Bristol at 18–19 knots and reach a top speed of around 27 knots. With her generous 400-gallon fuel capacity, the cruising range is an impressive 250 miles. ❑

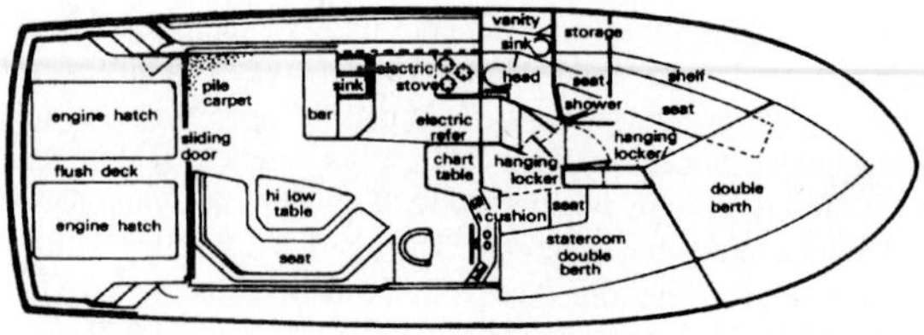

See Page 258 for Pricing Information

BAYLINER 3250/3255/3555 SUNBRIDGE

3250/3255 Avanti Sunbridge

3555 Avanti Sunbridge

SPECIFICATIONS

Length	34'7"	Water	50 gals.
Beam	11'5"	Fuel	205 gals.
Draft, Up	2'4"	Hull Type	Deep-V
Draft, Down	3'8"	Deadrise Aft	19°
Weight	10,200#	Designer	Bayliner
Clearance	9'0"	Production	1988–94

Because they change their model designations so often, it's always confusing to follow any Bayliner product that stays in production for more than a few years. Here's the story of this boat: introduced in 1988 as the 3250 Avanti Sunbridge (with a 31-foot, 6-inch LOA), the name was changed to 3255 Avanti in 1989. She became the 3555 Avanti Sunbridge in 1990 when a new integral swim platform added length and pizzaz to her lines. This has been a popular sport cruiser for Bayliner, and aside from some minor decor updates, the mid-cabin interior layout has remained unchanged from the original. Notably, the forward stateroom is fitted with a vanity and a privacy door (the mid-cabin has only a curtain). Outside, there's guest seating opposite the helm and engine access hatches in the cockpit. Twin 230-hp MerCruiser I/Os (that's right, I/Os in a 35-footer!) cruise efficiently at 21 knots and reach 29 top. The Avanti's fit and finish is pretty average, but the price is low, and she is a good-looking boat. ❑

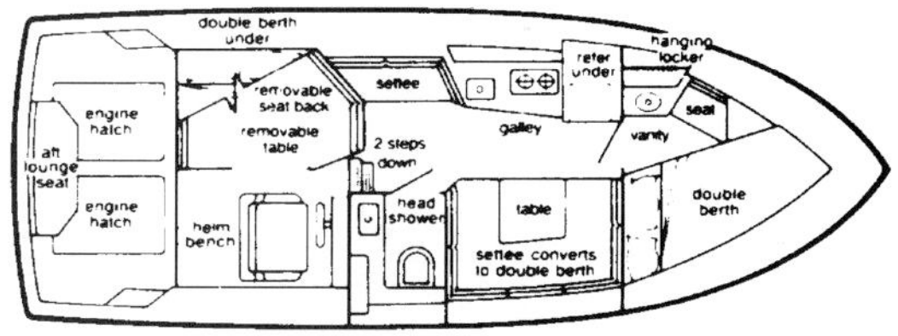

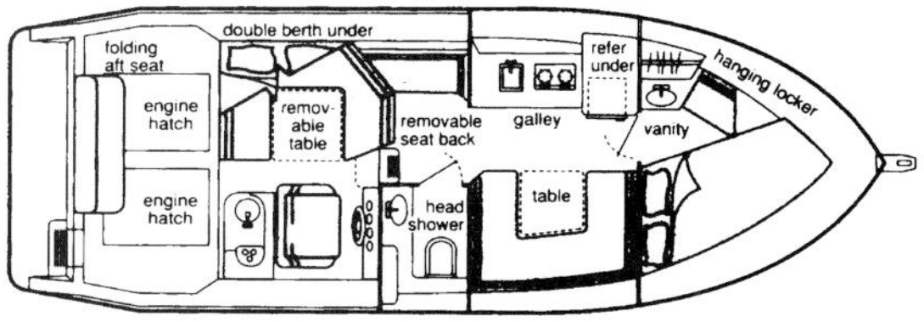

See Page 258 for Pricing Information

BAYLINER 3688 MOTOR YACHT

SPECIFICATIONS

Length	36'1"	Fuel	250 gals.
Beam	12'2"	Cockpit	NA
Draft	2'11"	Hull Type	Modified-V
Weight	13,700#	Deadrise Aft	14°
Clearance	13'10"	Designer	Bayliner
Water	96 gals.	Production	1992–94

Built on a conventional modified-V hull with prop pockets, the Bayliner 3688 Motor Yacht (actually a flybridge sedan) is an inexpensive family cruiser with a rakish profile and a very innovative mid-cabin floorplan. In an unusual design configuration, portside steps located just inside the salon door lead down to the mid-cabin, where there's partial standing headroom and a built-in vanity. Both staterooms are fitted with double berths. Privacy for the forward stateroom is limited to a sliding curtain, and the absence of a stall shower in the head is regrettable. The salon—with its built-in settee and standard lower helm—is well-arranged, but the wide walkarounds and relatively narrow beam of the 3688 limit the interior dimensions. Additional features include a stylish integral swim platform with shower and transom door, port and starboard cockpit steps, and a comfortable flybridge with seating for six. Twin 200-hp US Marine diesels (with V-drives) were standard. No racehorse, the Bayliner 3688 MY will cruise economically at 15 knots (1 mpg) and reach a top speed of 17–18 knots. ❑

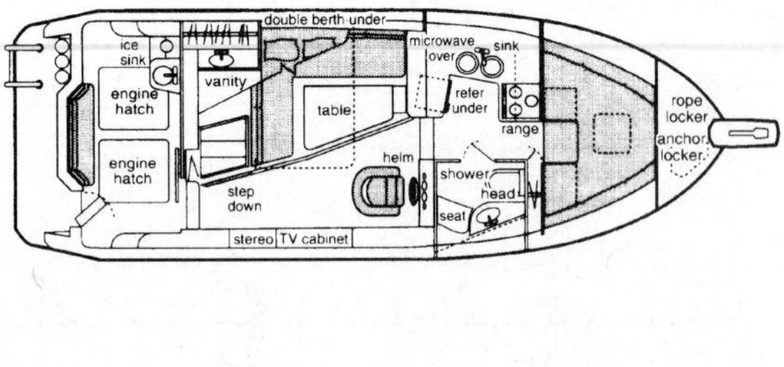

See Page 259 for Pricing Information

BAYLINER 3888 MOTOR YACHT

SPECIFICATIONS

Length	38'2"	Fuel	304 gals.
Beam	13'5"	Cockpit	NA
Draft	3'2"	Hull Type	Modified-V
Weight	17,500#	Deadrise Aft	6°
Clearance	14'10"	Designer	Bayliner
Water	80 gals.	Production	1983–94

Long a popular and good-selling boat for Bayliner, the 3888 Motor Yacht is generally recognized as a good value for those seeking a comfortable family cruiser at an affordable price. (Note the 3870 model designation was changed to the current 3888 in 1989.) Although not a motor yacht in the accepted sense of the word, she is a roomy flybridge sedan with plenty of interior volume and cruising comforts that families will love. The hull is fully cored, and the transom deadrise is a fairly flat 6 degrees. She features an innovative mid-cabin layout, and there are separate heads for each stateroom. Early models were powered with twin 135-hp Mitsubishi 6-cylinder diesels, but these engines were dropped in 1986 in favor of U.S. Marine 175-hp diesels—an update that boosted the cruising speed from 14 to 17 knots. The current 200-hp diesels cruise around 18+ knots. Fuel consumption at cruising speeds is a startling 14–15 gph, which makes the 3888 MY an extremely fuel-efficient boat. A successful model, about a thousand have been built. ❑

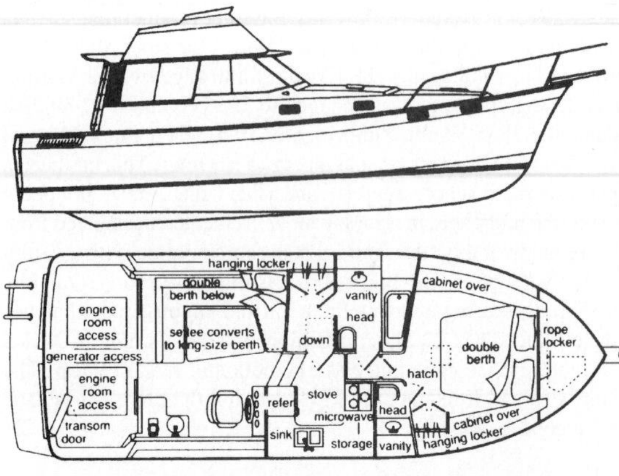

See Page 259 for Pricing Information

BAYLINER 3988 MOTORYACHT

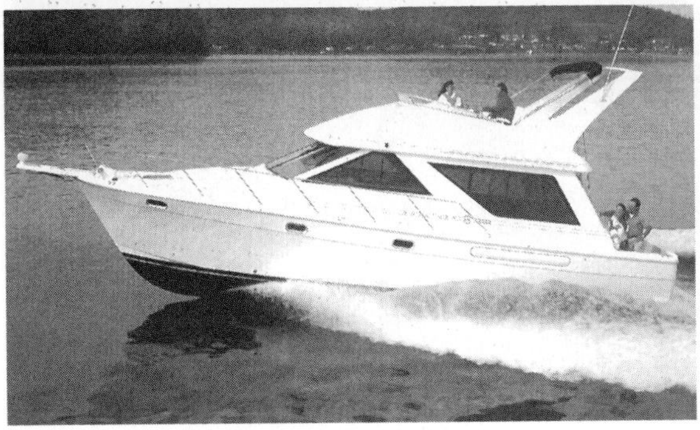

SPECIFICATIONS

Length	39'0"	Clearance	14'10"
Beam	13'11"	Cockpit	NA
Draft	3'2"	Hull Type	Modified-V
Weight	21,000#	Deadrise Aft	7°
Fuel	296 gals.	Designer	Bayliner
Water	100 gals.	Production	1995–Current

Pilothouse designs have become increasingly popular in recent years thanks to their clean lines, practical layouts, and versatile all-weather cruising capabilities. The 3988 Motoryacht combines the many virtues of a true pilothouse design with the scaled down price tag common to all Bayliner products. Aside from her appealing profile (the aggressive window treatment is especially stylish), the wide open interior of the 3988 seems large for a 40-footer. The floorplan is typical of a raised pilothouse boat with the galley aft of the lower helm and a mid stateroom located beneath the elevated portside settee. The salon, which is on the cockpit level, is designed around an L-shaped settee with plenty of built-in teak cabinetry. Forward, the owner's stateroom contains a private head (with a tub), and the mid stateroom has direct access to a second smaller head. Note that the generous interior dimensions of the 3988 result in a very small cockpit. Optional 240-hp Hino diesels will cruise the Bayliner 3988 at 18–19 knots with a top speed of about 24 knots.❑

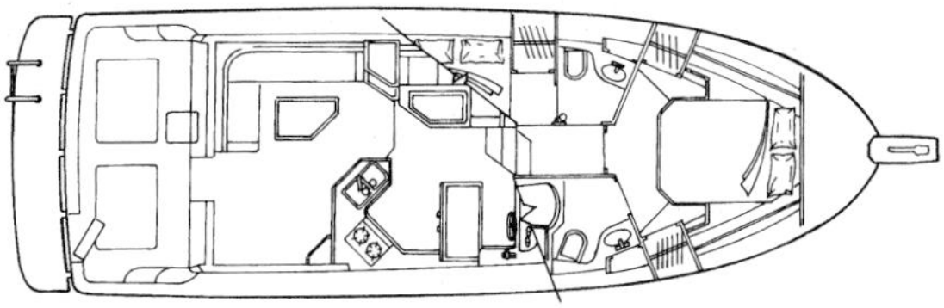

See Page 259 for Pricing Information

BAYLINER 4050 BODEGA

SPECIFICATIONS

Length	40'0"	Fuel	400 gals.
Beam	14'0"	Cockpit	NA
Draft	3'8"	Hull Type	Modified-V
Weight	23,000#	Deadrise Aft	14°
Clearance	NA	Designer	D. Watson
Water	114 gals.	Production	1978–83

While the boxy, high-freeboard profile of the Bayliner 4050 Bodega has often been remarked upon, few will dispute her generous accommodations. A total of three staterooms are provided (including a unique aft cabin with its own head) together with a large step-down salon. Although the emphasis is clearly on interior comforts, the outdoor entertainment areas are equally generous and include a huge 150-sq.-ft. flybridge. A unique fold-down ladder leading from the bridge to the foredeck is a popular feature found in later models. A relatively light boat for her size, her solid fiberglass hull is designed with a shallow keel, average beam and moderate deadrise at the transom. Additional features include a portside lower helm with deck access door, a surprisingly roomy salon, and double berths in two of the staterooms. Storage space is limited and the absence of a separate stall shower in either head is lamentable. No racehorse, standard 350-hp gas engines cruise the Bayliner Bodega at 15–16 knots with a top speed of about 25 knots. ❑

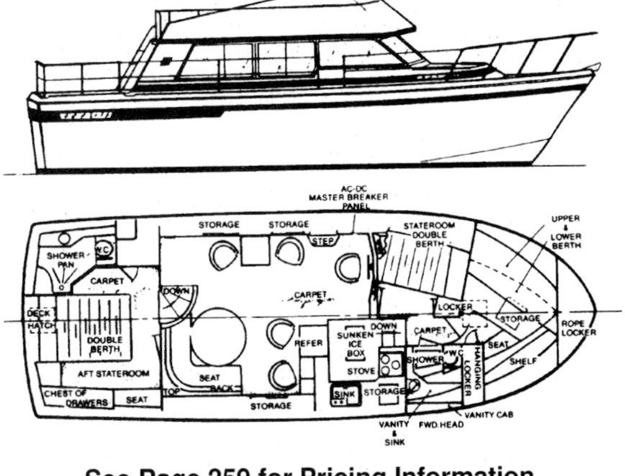

See Page 259 for Pricing Information

BAYLINER 4388 MID CABIN MY

SPECIFICATIONS

Length	43'1"	Water	100 gals.
Length WL	NA	Fuel	300 gals.
Beam	14'3"	Hull Type	Modified-V
Draft	3'0"	Deadrise Aft	14°
Weight	19,000#	Designer	Bayliner
Clearance	13'6"	Production	1991–94

With her sleek Euro-style profile and rakish appearance, the Bayliner 4388 Motor Yacht combined the big-boat accommodations most cruising families expect in a boat this size with a surprisingly affordable price. She's built on a solid fiberglass hull with a relatively wide beam and an integrated swim platform. Her two-stateroom interior is arranged with the U-shaped galley forward of the salon and on the same level which results in a wide open and very comfortable layout. The owner's stateroom is forward, and a small mid-stateroom (with partial standing headroom) is tucked below the galley. Note the common shower stall between the two heads. While the interior accommodations are generous, the cockpit is quite small. Additional features include a spacious flybridge, good access to the engines, and a standard lower helm station. Standard 240-hp V-drive diesels cruise the 4388 MY at 19–20 knots and deliver a top speed of 25 knots. A light boat for her size, the small 300-gallon fuel capacity limits her cruising trange. ❑

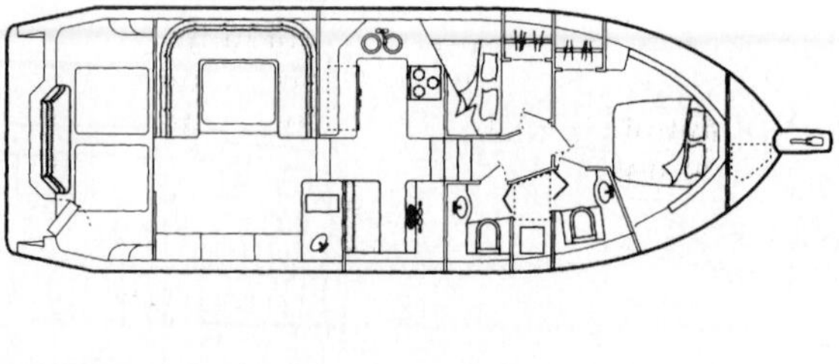

See Page 259 for Pricing Information

BERTRAM 28 BAHIA MAR

SPECIFICATIONS

Length .... 28'6"	Fuel .... 185/240 gals.
Beam .... 11'0"	Cockpit .... 85 sq. ft.
Draft .... 2'8"	Hull Type .... Deep-V
Weight .... 11,700#	Deadrise Aft .... 23°
Clearance .... 7'10"	Designer .... D. Napier
Water .... 48 gals.	Production 1985–92

The Bertram 28 Bahia Mar shares the same hull as the Bertram 28 FBC and SF models. Easily recognized in a crowd, her low-profile deckhouse and wraparound windshield reflect a distinctive European styling influence. The Bahia Mar is a superb sea boat, and her deep-V hull and low center of gravity result in superior offshore performance and handling characteristics. Equally at home as an offshore fisherman or pocket cruiser, she features a large, unobstructed cockpit with low freeboard and a basic (but well-finished) cabin layout offering overnight accommodations for two. Visibility from the helm position is good, and sightlines are excellent in all directions. The original raised engine boxes were eliminated in the 1986 models in favor of a flush deck; either way, service access to the motors is good. An impressive performer, standard 260-hp MerCruiser gas engines will cruise the 28 Bahia Mar around 23 knots and reach a top speed of 32–33 knots. Twin 230-hp Volvo diesels (28 knots cruise) became optional in 1992. The fuel capacity was increased in 1986 to 240 gallons. ❑

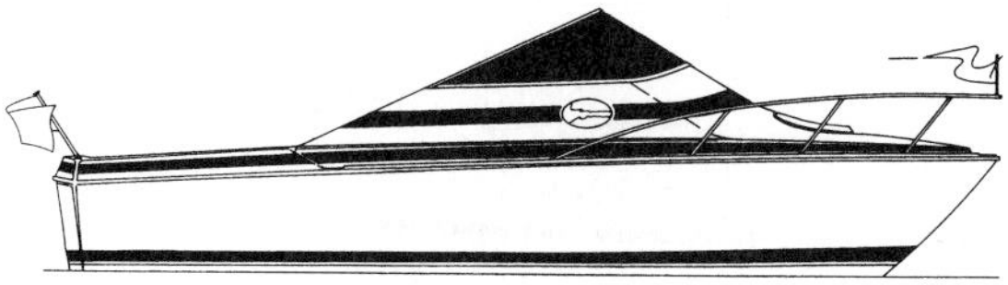

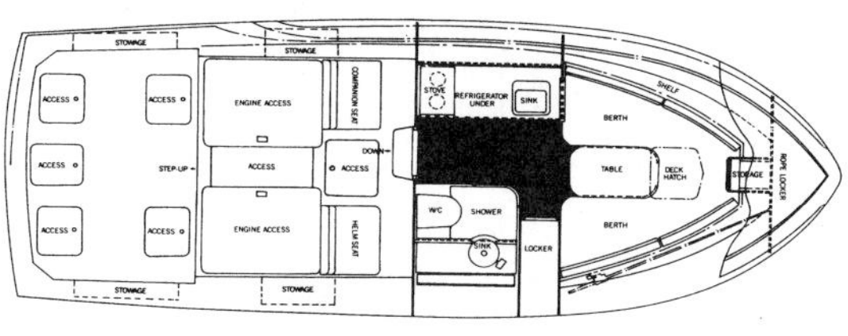

See Page 259 for Pricing Information

BERTRAM 28 MOPPIE

SPECIFICATIONS

Length	28'6"	Fuel	234 gals.
Beam	11'0"	Cockpit	85 sq. ft.
Draft	2'7"	Hull Type	Deep-V
Weight	10,400#	Deadrise Aft	23°
Clearance	7'1"	Designer	D. Napier
Water	27 gals.	Production	1987–94

The latest in a long string of Bertram 28-footers, the Moppie is a very stylish inboard runabout with the quality engineering expected of a Bertram product. Her sleek profile is attractively accented with painted windshield frame and bowrails, and the Moppie has the modern sportboat "look" popular with many of today's performance-boat buyers. She's built on the standard Bertram 28 deep-V hull with solid fiberglass construction and a steep 23° of transom deadrise. Aside from her superb handling characteristics, the Moppie's primary attraction is her expansive and versatile bi-level cockpit layout. The lower level has a generous 85 sq. ft. of fishing space with plenty of room for a fighting chair. In a practical design application, the galley is concealed in molded lockers abaft the helm and companion seats in the cockpit. The cabin accommodations are basic with a head and V-berths. A good performer with standard 260-hp MerCruiser gas engines, the 28 Moppie will cruise around 24 knots and reach 31–32 knots top. Optional 230-hp Volvo diesels cruise at 28 knots. ❑

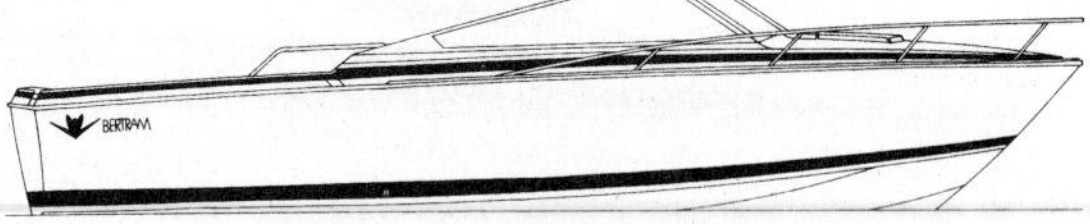

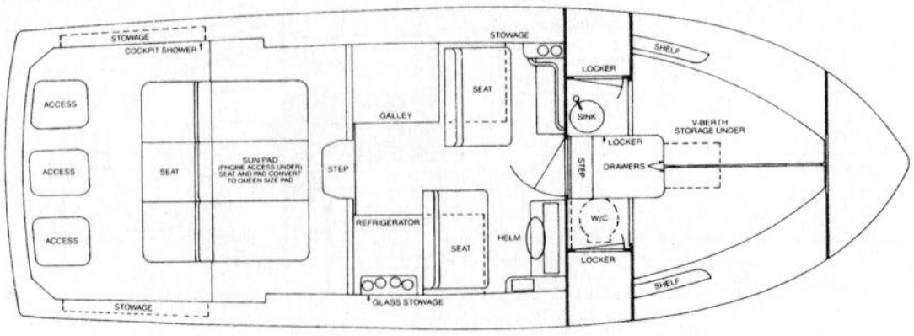

See Page 259 for Pricing Information

BERTRAM 30 MOPPIE

Sport Cruiser

Sportfish

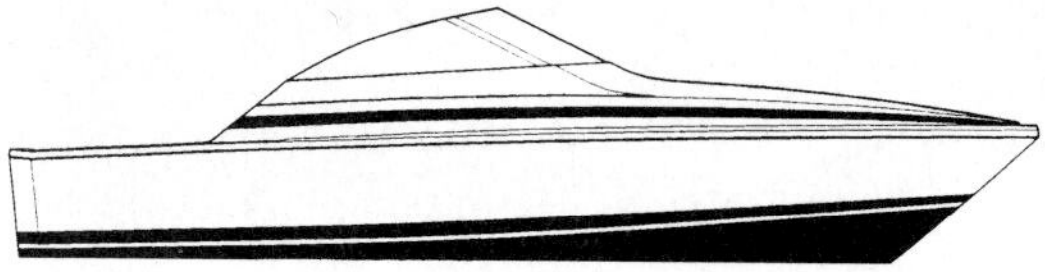

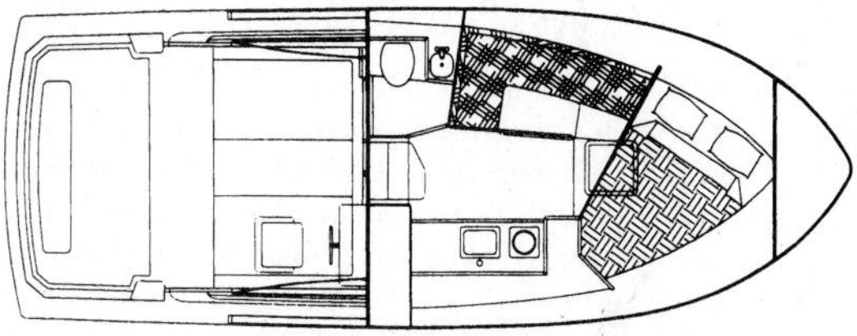

Standard Deck Layout

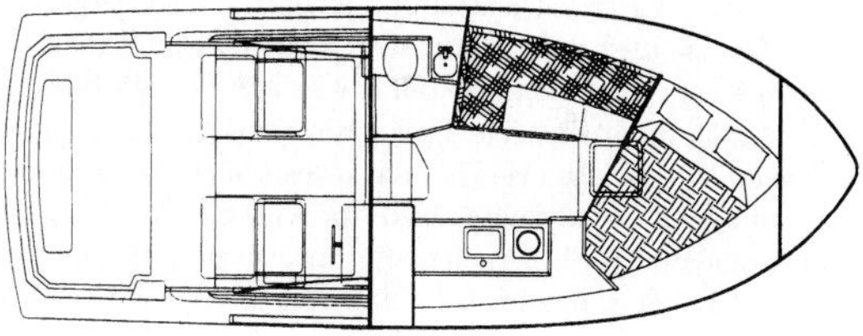

Optional Sportfish Layout

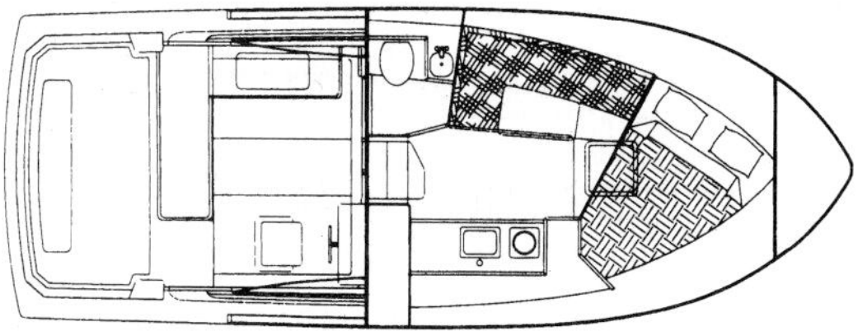

Optional Sport Cruiser Layout

SPECIFICATIONS

Length	30'6"	Fuel	275 gals.
Beam	11'3"	Cockpit	50 sq. ft.
Draft	2'11"	Hull Type	Deep-V
Weight	12,500#	Deadrise Aft	18.5
Clearance	NA	Designer	Bertram
Water	40 gals.	Production	1994–Current

Designed to appeal to cruisers as well as anglers, the Bertram 30 Moppie is a good-looking inboard express with a sleek profile to go with her rugged construction. Employing the hull from the Bertram 30 FBC (1984–85), the Moppie's clean lines offer plenty of sex appeal without the integral swim platform and molded pulpit common in other modern express boats. Three deck plans make her adaptable to fishing, cruising, or daytime activities. The standard layout has a helm seat and a wide-open bridge; the Sport Cruiser features a large L-shaped settee opposite the helm; and the Sportfish version comes with a companion seat, bait prep center, washdowns and rod holders. The interior is the same for all three versions with a double berth forward, a small galley, dinette, and a stand-up head with shower. Access to the motors (which are below the bridgedeck) is very good. Standard 454-cid gas engines will cruise the Moppie at 23 knots and reach 31 top. Optional 291 Cummins (or 300-hp Cats) will cruise at 27 knots (31 top), and 340-hp Cats will cruise about 30 knots and reach 33 wide open. ❑

See Page 259 for Pricing Information

BERTRAM 31 BAHIA MAR

SPECIFICATIONS

Length	30'7"
Beam	11'2"
Draft	2'9"
Weight	9,400#
Clearance	8'3"
Water	18 gals.
Fuel	222 gals.
Cockpit	147 sq. ft.
Hull Type	Deep-V
Deadrise Aft	23°
Designer	Ray Hunt
Production	1966–81

Built on the legendary Bertram 31 deep-V hull with a steep 23° of deadrise at the transom, the 31 Bahia Mar is an open sport-cruiser design with a large fishing cockpit and basic interior accommodations for two. Bahia Mars have attracted a remarkable following among serious anglers who have come to appreciate her numerous fishing attributes. The 31 Bahia Mar is a stable fishing platform and ranks with the best modern designs when it comes to overall fishability. Her completely open cockpit arrangement puts the helm close to the action, and the cockpit itself is much larger than in most other sportfishermen of her size. Visibility from the helm is another feature fisherman have come to admire—sightlines are excellent in all directions. The Bahia Mar is considered a superb all-round utility boat, and many have seen years of operation in charter and dive-boat fleets. Engine boxes provide easy access to the motors. Standard 330-hp gas engines cruise around 23 knots and reach about 33 knots top. Several diesel options were offered over the years. ❑

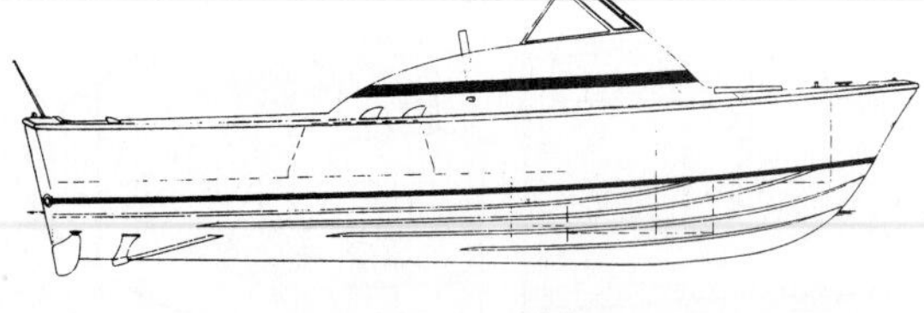

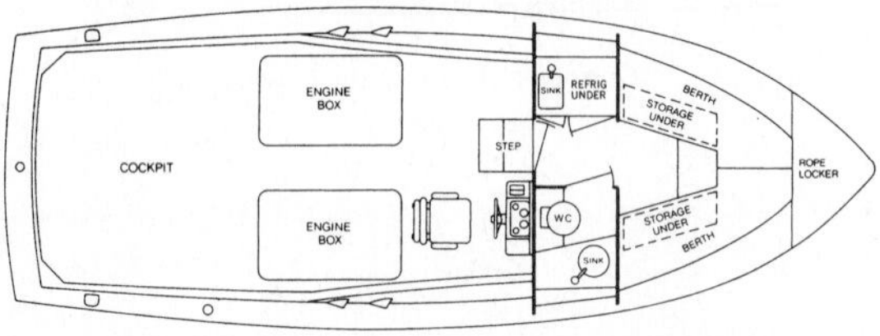

See Page 259 for Pricing Information

BERTRAM 33 FLYBRIDGE CRUISER

SPECIFICATIONS

Length	33'0"
Beam	12'6"
Draft	3'0"
Weight	22,800#
Clearance	12'6"
Fresh Water	70 gals.
Fuel, Gas	250/315 gals.
Fuel, Dsl.	255 gals.
Cockpit	72 sq. ft.
Hull Type	Deep-V
Deadrise Aft	17°
Production	1977–92

The Bertram 33 FB Cruiser is a particularly flexible boat that can provide adequate service as a weekend fisherman while still offering excellent cruising accommodations. Combined with her deep-V hull, the 33 FBC's high deckhouse makes for a tender boat offshore. She was originally offered with a single-stateroom layout until a more popular two-stateroom interior became standard in 1980. In 1981 a new tournament flybridge was added, and in 1984 a teak interior decor replaced the woodgrain mica cabinetry. The Bertram 33 II version (introduced in 1988) has a restyled flybridge and an oak interior. Changes in 1990 included a revised layout with a stall shower in the head. In 1992, a varnished maple interior became standard (teak was optional). Twin 454-cid gas engines will cruise the Bertram 33 around 19 knots. Optional 260-hp Cats cruise at 22 knots, and the newer 320-hp Cats cruise at 25–26 knots (30 knots top). Note that the fuel capacity was increased for the gas models in 1980, although late diesel-powered 33s were still fitted with a 255-gallon tank. ❑

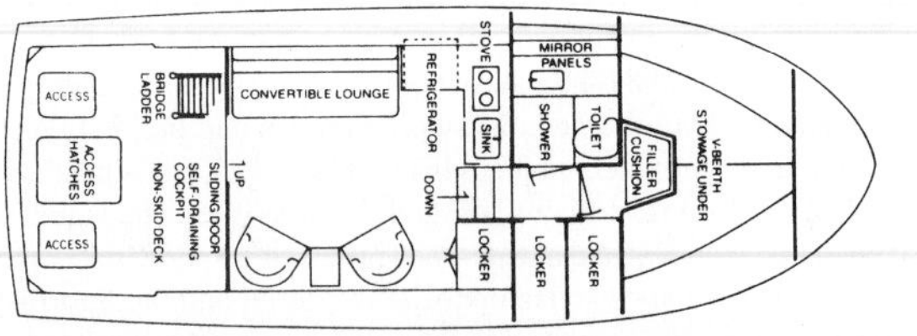

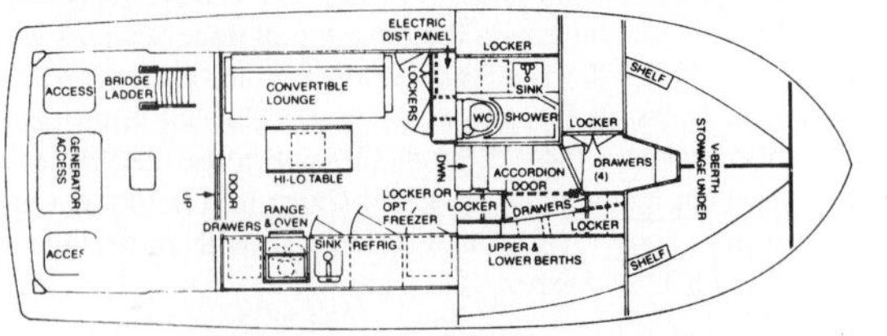

See Page 259 for Pricing Information

BERTRAM 43 MOPPIE

SPECIFICATIONS

Length ... 43'4"	Cockpit ... 106 sq. ft.
Beam ... 15'0"	Clearance ... 9'1"
Draft ... 4'8"	Hull Type ... Deep-V
Weight ... 38,290#	Deadrise Aft ... 17°
Fuel ... 546 gals.	Designer ... Bertram
Water ... 160 gals.	Production ... 1995–Current

Production express fishermen over forty feet have become popular in recent years and the new Bertram 43 Moppie is tough competition. This is certainly one of the best-looking boats Bertram has ever built. Like all Bertrams, she's heavily constructed on a rugged deep-V hull. Two different deck layouts are available: the cruising version has a radar arch and wraparound seating in the cockpit, and the sportfishing version has a completely unobstructed cockpit with a transom fish box, direct cockpit access to the engine room, rod storage, and a transom door and gate. Below decks, the Moppie's maplewood interior is arranged with a huge galley (with excellent storage), berths for four adults, and a spacious head with separate stall shower. Additional features include a molded bow pulpit, a double-wide helm seat with lounge seating opposite, and wide sidedecks. A good sea-boat, the 43 Moppie will cruise at a fast 27 knots with standard 550-hp 6V92 diesels and reach 30+ knots top. First available in 1996, the new 625-hp DDEC 6V92s will cruise at an honest 28 knots with a full tower and load. ❑

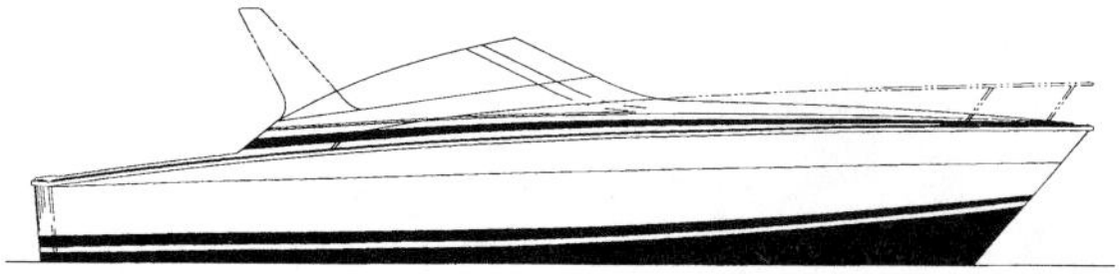

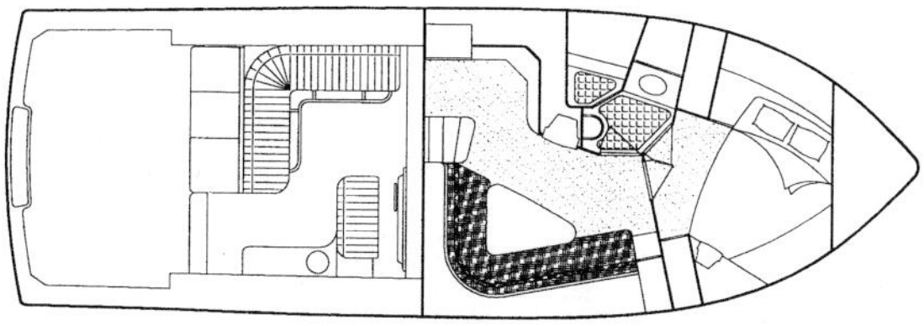

Sportfishing Version

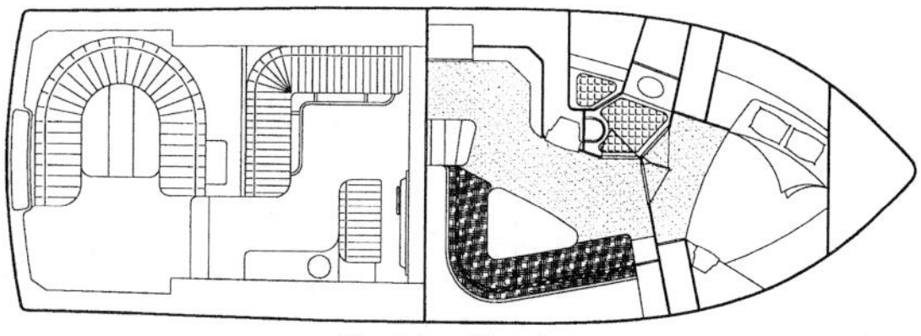

Cruising Version

See Page 259 for Pricing Information

BERTRAM 46 MOPPIE

SPECIFICATIONS

Length ....46'0"	Fuel ....650 gals.
Beam ....14'11"	Cockpit.................106 sq. ft.
Draft ....4'8"	Hull Type ....Deep-V
Weight.....................42,000#	Deadrise Aft...................17°
Clearance ....9'1"	Designer ....Dave Napier
Water ....135 gals.	Production 1993–Current

Introduced in 1993, the Bertram 46 Moppie is built on a stretched 43 Convertible hull with cored hullsides, a wide beam, and a fairly steep 17° of transom deadrise. This is one of the bigger express cruisers to be found, and she's designed to meet the needs of fishermen and upscale sportcruisers alike. Offered with a choice of two floorplans, the single-stateroom layout (with two heads — very unusual) is aimed at the sportfish market while the two-stateroom layout is more suited for cruising activities. Either way, there's seating on the bridgedeck for a small crowd, and the sportfish version includes molded tackle centers in the cockpit. Until 1995, the Moppie had reversed engines with V-drive-like shaft couplers. The current engines, however, are straight inboards. Also in 1995, the genset was moved from under the cockpit into the more protected environment of the engine room. A good-running boat and a comfortable ride in a chop, a pair of 735-hp 8V-92s will cruise the Bertram 46 Moppie at a fast 28–29 knots and reach top speeds in the neighborhood of 32 knots. ❑

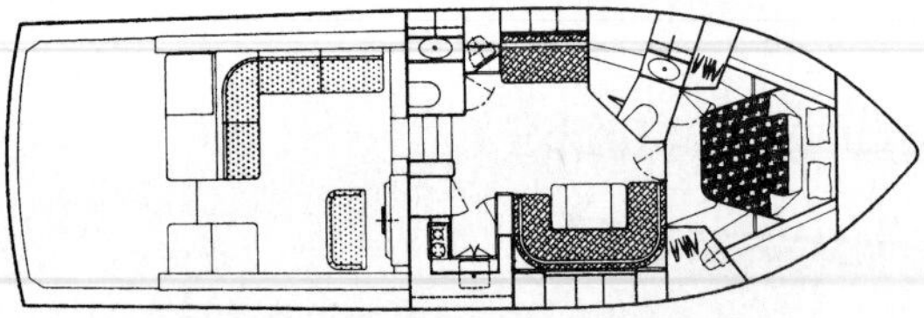

Single Stateroom w/Sport Option (1993–94)

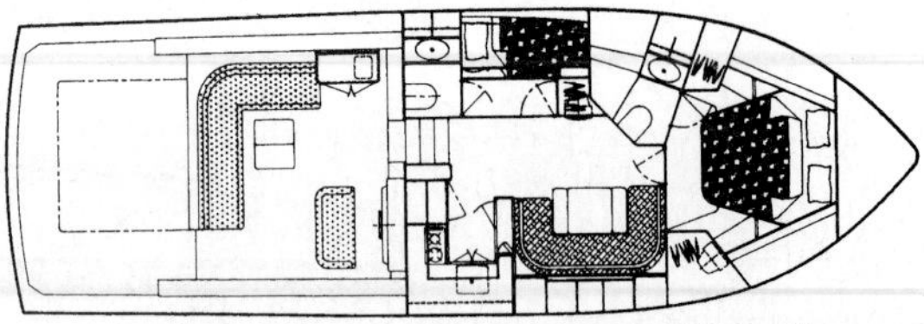

Double Stateroom Cruising Layout (1993–94)

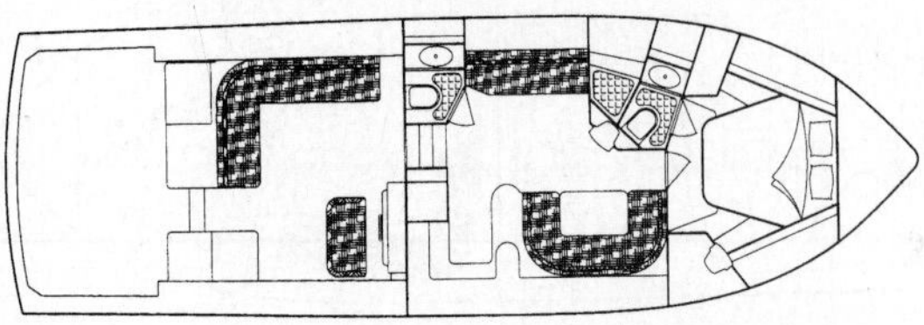

Single Stateroom w/Sport Option (1995)

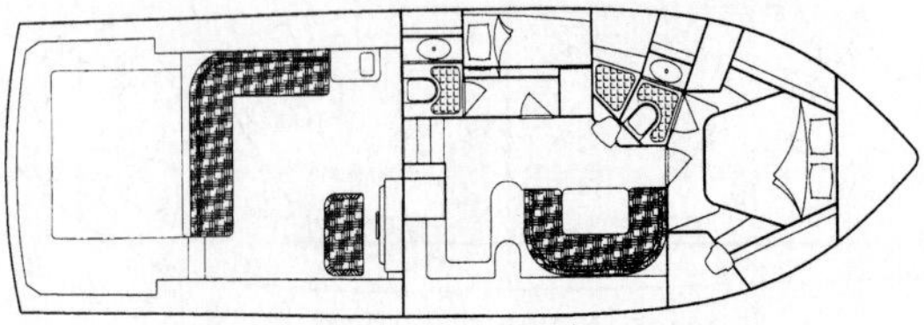

Double Stateroom Cruising Layout (1995)

See Page 259 for Pricing Information

BLUE SEAS 31

SPECIFICATIONS

Length	30'8"	Water	80 gals.
Length WL	29'2"	Fuel	200 gals.
Beam	11'6"	Cockpit	NA
Draft	3'0"	Hull Type	Semi-Disp.
Weight	11,000#	Designer	R. Lowell
Clearance	9'2"	Production	1988–91

The Blue Seas 31 was one of the last introductions for the Hinterhoeller Yachts, the Canadian builder best known for their high-quality series of Nonsuch sailboats. She was introduced at the 1988 Toronto boat show by the original builder, the Blue Seas Boat Co. of Clinton, Ontario. Production under the Hinterhoeller nameplate commenced in late 1989. A lobster-boat design with a Downeast heritage, the Blue Seas was built on a single-piece hull with three watertight compartments, a nearly plumb bow, rounded bilges, and a full-length keel. Inside, a privacy door separates the salon from the lower level galley and stateroom—very unusual. Originally offered with a shortened deckhouse and larger cockpit, the "long house" version became standard in later models. Her roomy cockpit provides plenty of space for deck chairs or light-tackle fishing. The single 210-hp Cummins diesel engine will cruise economically at 14 knots and reach a top speed of around 17–18 knots. Offered with or without a flybridge, the Blue Seas 31 is well-constructed and very easy on the eye. ❑

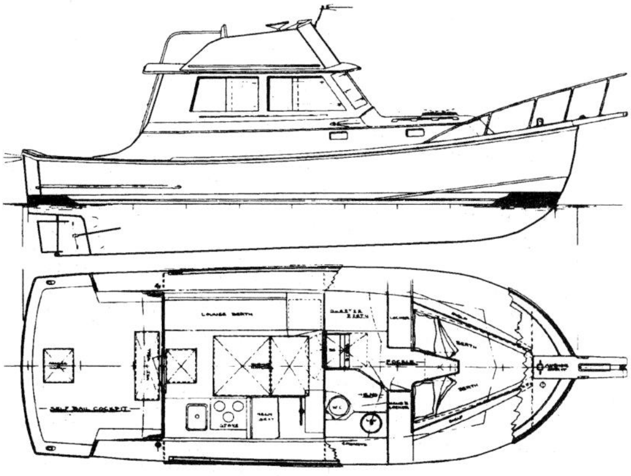

See Page 259 for Pricing Information

BRENDAN 32 SEDAN

SPECIFICATIONS

Length	32'10"	Fuel	260 gals.
Beam	12'0"	Cockpit	NA
Draft	2'9"	Hull Type	Modified-V
Weight	13,500#	Deadrise Aft	NA
Clearance	11'3"	Designer	W. Schultz
Water	80 gals.	Production	1986–Current

Built by the Shannon Boat Co. (the well-ragarded sailboat builder) until 1990, the Brendan 32 is available as a Sport Sedan (pictured above with a flybridge) or as an open express without a flybridge. Constructed on a modified-V hull with cored hullsides, the Brendan 32 is designed primarily as a small family cruiser although her cockpit is large enough for some light-tackle fishing. A transom door is standard, and there are two in-deck fish boxes in the cockpit sole. The belowdecks layout is arranged with the galley and dinette down and a lower helm in the small salon. The well-crafted teak woodwork (including a teak parquet sole) and a full 360° view creates an open and very traditional interior. The flybridge is very small for a boat this size and, while well-arranged at the helm, it's definitely not designed for a crowd. Twin 205-hp GM 6.2 diesels have been most popular engines over the years. With these engines the Brendan 32 will cruise around 18 knots and reach 23 knots wide open. More recent models with 210-hp Cummins will run 1–2 knots faster. About forty have been built to date. ❑

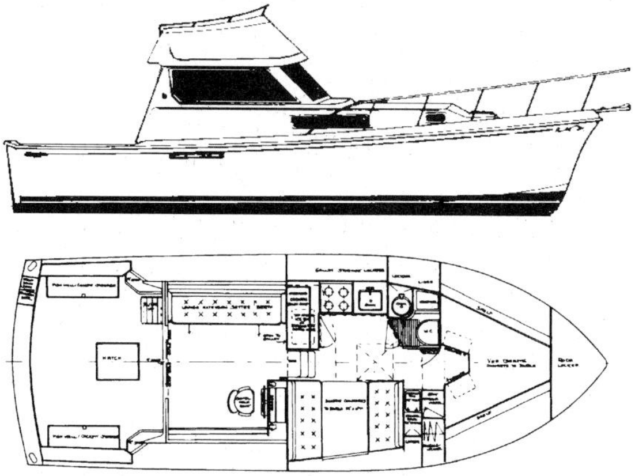

See Page 259 for Pricing Information

Cabo 35 Express

"...the best production inboard 35-foot fishing boat the world has to offer."

Dean Travis Clarke ***Sportfishing magazine***

"You'll find everything aboard the Cabo that you'd ever expect to find in the cockpit of a top flight 50-foot sportfishing convertible..." ***Dean Clarke***

A boat you can love

Dean Travis Clarke has seen and run a lot of sportfishing boats. As executive editor of *Sport Fishing* magazine, Dean has evaluated the performance, handling and fishability of nearly the entire gamut of sportfishing boats on the market today. In Dean's words, "There are plenty of great boats to like out there, but when you start talking love, over the period of a lifetime there are very few...those who've spent their lives on boats will fall for this boat just as sure as ebb follows flood."

It's perfect for light tackle

Pam Basco is an internationally known angler who has captured seven world records on light tackle and was named by the IGFA as one of the outstanding anglers of the year in 1993. When searching for the ideal boat to try for a new world record for blue marlin on 8# test, Pam selected the Cabo 35. In her words, "The boat does great. We raised an awful lot of fish in two days, including 2 striped marlin, 11 blues and one sail. And the way it maneuvers and backs down, it's perfect for light tackle."

A war chest of fishing features

"You'll find everything aboard the Cabo that you'd ever expect to find in the cockpit of a top flight 50-foot sportfishing convertible: Bait prep station, bait freezer, live well, tackle storage center and rod storage for 19 rods are all standard fare. When you go aboard the Cabo, lift one of the big lids to a fishbox in the cockpit, then do something you know you shouldn't--let it fall shut. The hatches fit into their gasketed and drained lips so well that rather than slamming shut, the lid quietly goes 'boomph'."

Superior construction

"No boat, no matter how beautiful, is worth the effort if it isn't durable. Only the finest ingredients go into a Cabo: Vinylester resin for greater osmotic blistering protection, biaxial nonwoven fiberglass roving and balsa core from the waterline up offer strength with light weight in the hull, while the bottom is solid fiberglass. All hidden areas, like bilges and inside cabinets, are ground and then gelcoated for a smooth, flawless finish. Put your face right against the hull of a Cabo: Look for indentations, bumps and finish flaws. You won't find any."

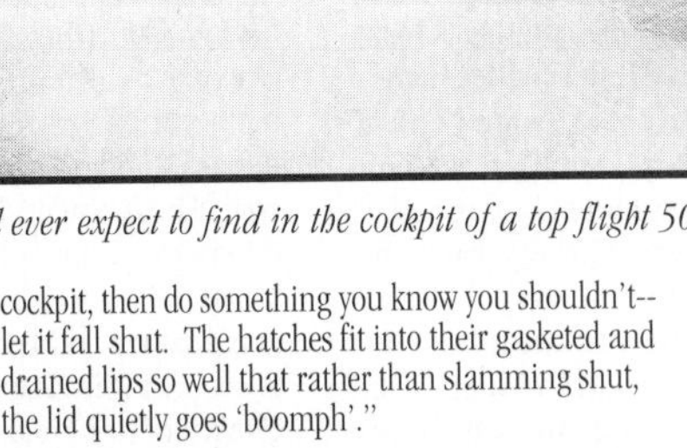

Engine access without equal

"Touch a button at the threshold to the helm deck and the entire deck rises on electrically activated hydraulic rams, revealing the impressive power center--impressive mainly for its organization. Every single hose, wire, pipe and fitting in the engine room is run and labeled individually. All functions are segregated with the plumbing on one side, everything electrical on the other side..."

The best the world has to offer

"At the moment, Cabo arguably provides the best production inboard 35-foot fishing boat the world has to offer." Dean is not alone in his assessment of the Cabo 35. Other experts in the industry and professional anglers agree that the Cabo may be the finest 35-foot sportfishing boat ever.

To receive unedited full color reprints of test reports run by the experts at *Boating, Saltwater Sportsman, Sportfishing, Marlin* and *Powerboat Reports,* call, write or FAX:

CABO™ Sportfishers
by **Cat Harbor Boats, Inc.**
9780 Rancho Road
Adelanto CA. 92301
Fax. (619)246-8970
Phone 800 647-8236

CAT® Diesel Power

CABO 31 EXPRESS

SPECIFICATIONS

Length w/Pulpit..........33'2"	Water.......................80 gals.
Hull Length..................31'0"	Clearance........................NA
Beam.............................12'5"	Hull Type................Deep-V
Draft...............................3'2"	Deadrise Aft................18.5°
Weight......................19,500#	Headroom.......................6'6"
Fuel.........................320 gals.	Production....1995–Current

Introduced in mid 1995, the new Cabo 31 Express is a top-quality offshore fisherman with tremendous eye appeal to go with her-superb performance. She's built on an easy-riding deep-V hull with a wide beam, a sharp entry, and balsa coring in the hullsides. While the Cabo is obviously designed for serious anglers, the upscale cabin accommodations are surprisingly spacious for a boat of this type with berths for four adults, a complete galley area, decent storage, and an enclosed, stand-up head and shower. The interior is finished with varnished teak woodwork, and headroom is more than adequate throughout. Outside, the entire helm deck can be raised hydraulically for access to the motors. An L-shaped settee is opposite the helm, and the windshield has a center vent. Cockpit features include a bait prep center, transom fishbox, rod storage, fresh and salt water washdowns, and a transom door with gate. Among several engine options (gas engines are standard), twin 300-hp Cats will cruise the Cabo 31 Express at 25 knots and reach a top speed of about 30 knots. Note the generous 320-gallon fuel capacity. ❑

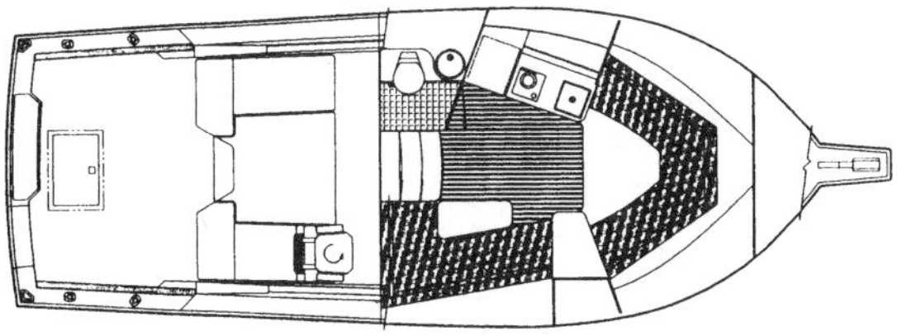

See Page 259 for Pricing Information

CABO 35 FLYBRIDGE SF

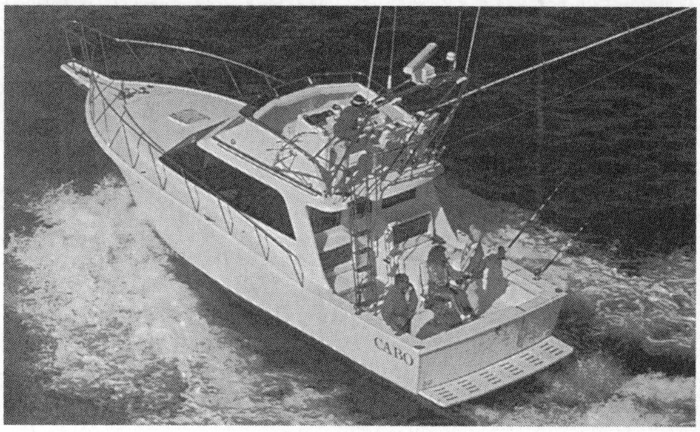

SPECIFICATIONS

Length w/Pulpit..........37'6"	Water......................100 gals.
Hull Length.................34'6"	Fuel.........................400 gals.
Beam.............................13'0"	Cockpit....................80 sq. ft.
Draft...............................2'6"	Hull Type................Deep-V
Weight.....................21,000#	Deadrise Aft................17.5°
Clearance......................11'3"	Production....1992–Current

A good-looking boat with a low-slung appearance and a huge cockpit, the Cabo 35 is a very popular design with a lot of built-in quality and sex appeal. She's built on a deep-V hull with a relatively wide beam and cored hullsides. Her low profile is the result of placing the motors in cockpit engine boxes, thus allowing the salon sole to be set low in the hull. Considering her oversized cockpit, the Cabo's interior is surprisingly spacious. The galley-up layout includes an 8-foot settee with hidden rod storage in the salon and an island berth in the stateroom, while the galley-down floorplan has a stall shower in the head. (There's a large storage area beneath the salon sole.) Additional features include two in-deck fish boxes, transom door and gate, good cabin headroom, single-lever helm controls, and wide side decks with sturdy rails. A popular boat since the day she hit the market (over 60 have been sold to date), optional 375-hp Cats will cruise the Cabo 35 at 27 knots and reach around 32 knots top. Note the generous 400-gallon fuel capacity. ❑

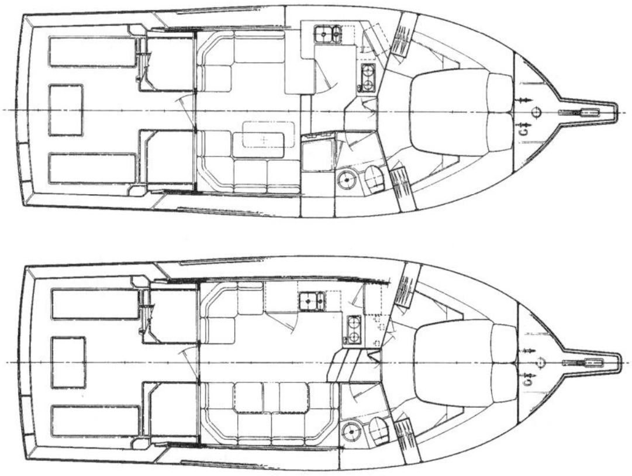

See Page 260 for Pricing Information

CABO 35 EXPRESS SF

SPECIFICATIONS

Length w/Pulpit..........37'6"	Water......................188 gals.
Hull Length ....34'6"	Fuel..........................400 gals.
Beam..............................13'0"	Cockpit....................80 sq. ft.
Draft ....2'6"	Hull Type ....Deep-V
Weight ....18,000#	Deadrise Aft................17.5°
Clearance......................11'3"	Production 1993–Current

Using the hull of the Cabo 35 Flybridge model, the Cabo 35 Express is a rugged express fisherman with the kind of family-style interior accommodations that most dedicated fishboats lack. She's constructed on a deep-V hull with a relatively wide beam and Airex-cored hullsides. The Cabo's floorplan is arranged with a full-size double berth forward along with a roomy galley and dinette. Throughout, the Corian countertops, teak joinerwork, and upscale appliances combine to present an attractive and extremely well-crafted interior decor. Outside, the cockpit is big for a 35-footer and comes standard with a bait prep center, transom door, two in-deck storage boxes, cockpit coaming, and washdowns. An L-shaped settee is opposite the helm, and the entire bridgedeck lifts hydraulically for excellent access to the motors. A good performer with plenty of eye appeal (as well as an upscale price), optional 422-hp Cats will cruise at 29 knots and reach around 33 knots top. A good-selling boat, over 40 have been built to date. ❑

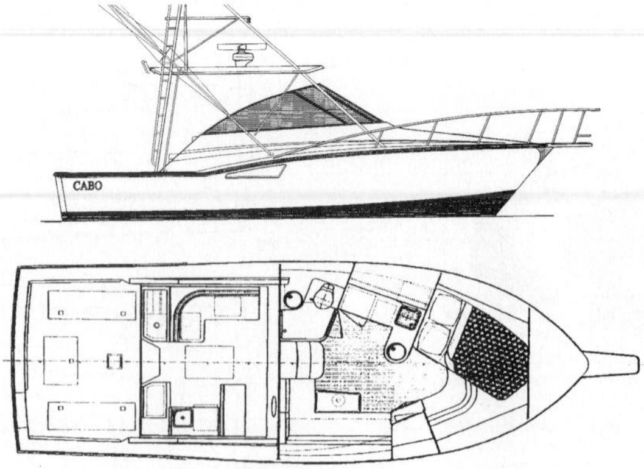

See Page 260 for Pricing Information

CALIFORNIAN 35 CONVERTIBLE

SPECIFICATIONS

Length ....34'11"	Fuel ....300 gals.
Beam ....12'4"	Cockpit ....NA
Draft ....3'2"	Hull Type ....Modified-V
Weight ....18,000#	Deadrise Aft ....15°
Clearance ....10'8"	Designer ....J. Marshall
Water ....75 gals.	Production 1985–87

A stylish and good-looking boat, the 35 Convertible was introduced during the time of Wellcraft's ownership of Californian Yachts. A sporty profile and a unique window treatment give the 35 a distinctive look and make her an easy boat to spot in a crowd. She was built on the same hull used for the Californian 35 Motor Yacht—a conservative modified-V design with moderate beam and a short skeg below. Equally at home as a family cruiser or weekend fisherman, the interior of the Californian 35 is quite spacious, and the grain-matched teak cabinetry is impressive. Berths for four are provided, and a stall shower is fitted in the head. The relatively small cockpit can support some light-tackle fishing, although a step along the cabin bulkhead prevents the installation of a tackle center. Molded cockpit steps lead to wide sidedecks making foredeck access easy and secure. Gas engines were standard, but 210-hp Cat diesels proved a popular option. At a 17-knot cruising speed, the Cats burn just 15 gph—better than 1 mpg. ❑

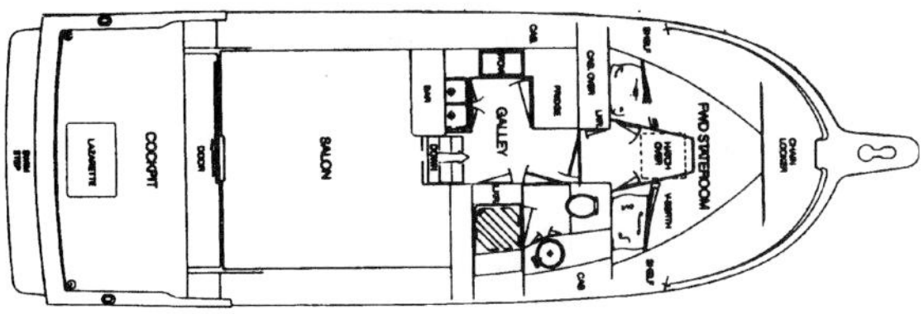

See Page 260 for Pricing Information

CALIFORNIAN 38 CONVERTIBLE

SPECIFICATIONS

Length ....37'8"	Fuel ....400 gals.
Beam ....13'3"	Cockpit ....NA
Draft ....3'6"	Hull Type ....Modified-V
Weight ....25,000#	Deadrise Aft ....15°
Clearance ....14'6"	Designer ....J. Marshall
Water ....100 gals.	Production 1984–87

The Californian 38 Convertible is a modern and good-looking family cruiser with attractive styling and above-average finish work. (Interestingly, a lot of bow flare was used to create what appears to be a broad, trawler-style foredeck.) She's built of solid fiberglass on a low-deadrise hull with moderate beam and a shallow skeg below. Like all Californian models, the sidedecks of the 38 Convertible are notably wide with molded steps in the cockpit for easy access. The standard two-stateroom interior is arranged with an in-line galley to port opposite a built-in settee. Both staterooms are fitted with double berths, and there's a stall shower in the head. The woodwork is very good. Outside, the cockpit is large enough for the occasional fishing venture, however there are no in-deck storage bins, and the step along the salon bulkhead prevents the installation of a molded tackle center. Twin 210-hp Caterpillar diesels will cruise around 15 knots (18–19 knots top), and the larger 300-hp Cats will cruise at 21 knots and deliver 25 top. ❑

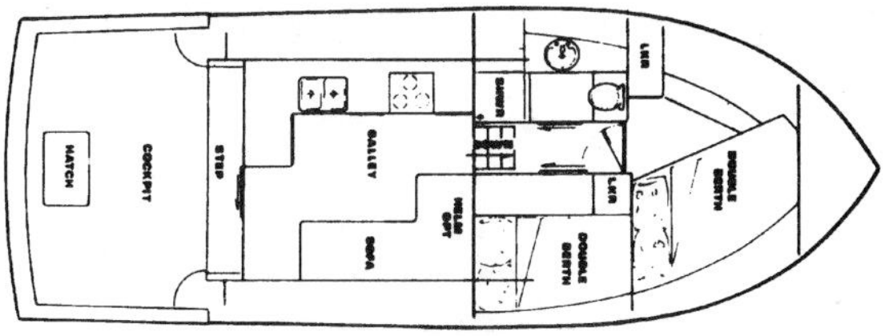

See Page 260 for Pricing Information

CALIFORNIAN 44 VENETI

SPECIFICATIONS

Length w/Pulpit........47'10"	Water......................190 gals.
Hull Length.................44'0"	Fuel.........................400 gals.
Beam.............................15'2"	Hull Type.........Modified-V
Draft................................4'0"	Deadrise Aft....................15°
Weight......................25,000#	Designer............J. Marshall
Clearance.....................10'0"	Production.............1988–89

Although she's dated by many of today's high-style production sportboats, the 44 Veneti remains a fairly popular boat on the used markets thanks of her big-boat appearance and roomy interior accommodations. Notably, she was one of the early applications of the integral reverse transom in an express boat design. The hull, also used in many other Californian models, is solid fiberglass. Inside, the floorplan is arranged with two private staterooms and two full heads—an unusual layout (most big express boats have a single stateroom and head) resulting in salon dimensions that are smaller than average for a boat this size. While visibility from the elevated helm is good, the console—with its various levels of gauges and switches—is best described as confusing. Additional features include a big engine room, cockpit wet bar, wide sidedecks, and good storage. No racehorse in spite of her sleek profile, twin 375-hp Caterpillar diesels will cruise the Californian 44 Veneti at 20–21 knots and reach a top speed of about 24 knots. ❑

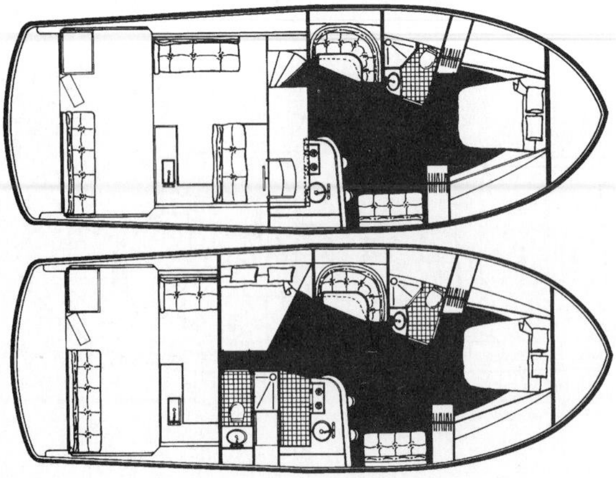

See Page 260 for Pricing Information

CAMANO 28

SPECIFICATIONS

Length w/Pulpit..........31'0"	Water........................75 gals.
Hull Length.................28'0"	Fuel...........................75 gals.
Beam.............................10'6"	Hull Type...........Semi-Disp.
Draft...............................3'3"	Deadrise Aft......................8°
Weight........................8,000#	Designer............B. Warman
Aft Deck.................40 sq. ft.	Production....1990–Current

For those who enjoy a little character in their boat, we present the Camano 28, a slick little sedan cruiser from British Columbia with a distinctive profile and a very practical layout. She's heavily built on an efficient semi-displacement hull with a wide beam, cored hullsides, and an unusually wide prop-protecting keel. (Indeed, the keel cavity is big enough to contain the engine, which keeps the weight down low for added stability.) The Camano's no-nonsence interior is well-finished and her trolly-style foredeck windows are unique. With the galley located down, the salon is unusually large for a 28' sedan cruiser. A lower helm is standard. With her wide beam, the Camano is able to carry a relatively large flybridge without difficulty. Overall, her upright bow and curved transom give her a salty, easy-on-the-eyes workboat profile. A single 150-hp Volvo diesel will cruise the Camano 28 easily at 12 knots (4 gph) and reach 16–17 knots wide open. Note that a bow thruster is standard. ❑

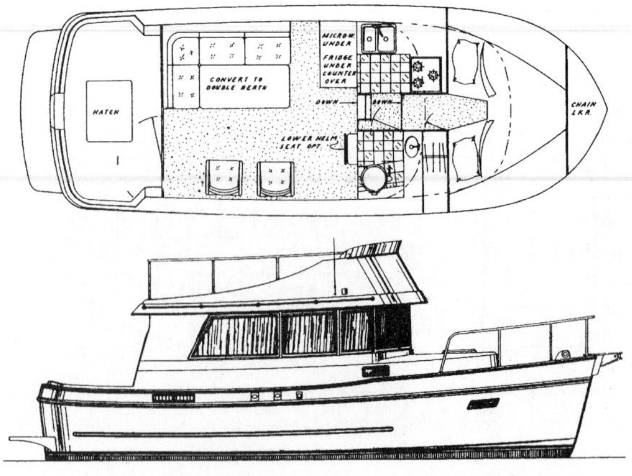

See Page 260 for Pricing Information

CAPE DORY 28

Cape Dory 28 Flybridge

Cape Dory 28 Open Fisherman

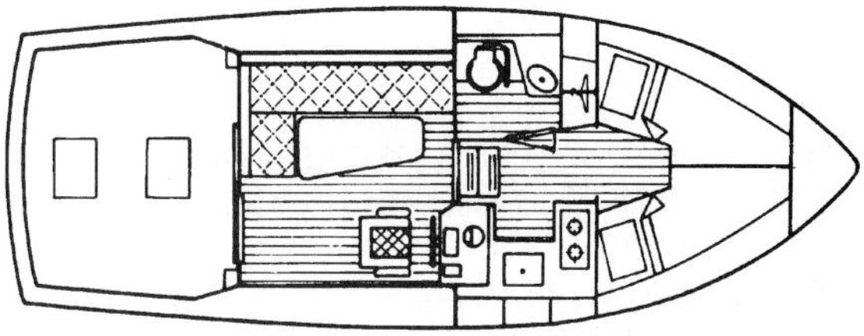

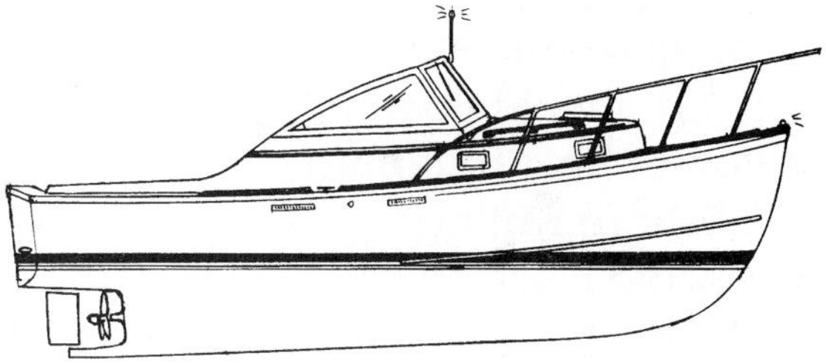

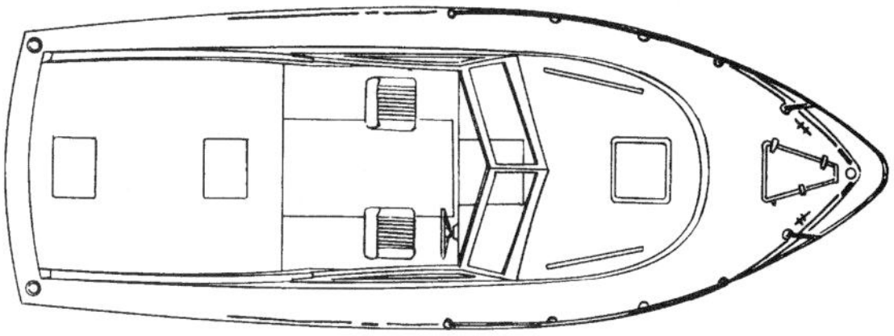

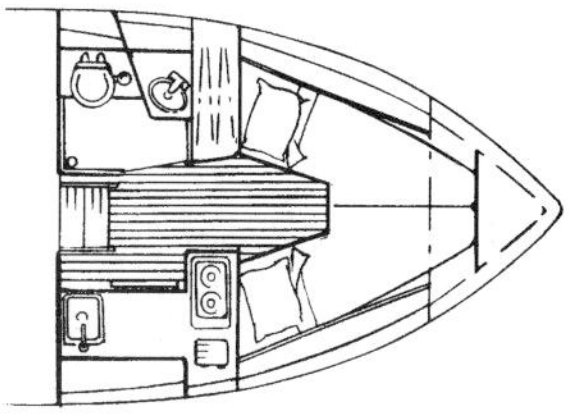

SPECIFICATIONS

Length	27'11"	Water	45 gals.
Length WL	25'11"	Fuel	76 gals.
Beam	9'11"	Cockpit	56 sq. ft.
Draft	2'11"	Hull Type	Semi-Disp.
Weight	8,000#	Designer	Cape Dory
Clearance	11'2"	Production	1985–Current

A popular boat since her introduction in 1985, the Cape Dory 28 is a classy Downeast-style cruiser with a traditional lobster-boat character to go with her modern construction. This boat has been available in several configurations over the years (the 28 Flybridge has been the most popular), and a number have been built for commercial applications. She's built on an easy-riding semi-displacement hull with moderate beam, rounded bilges, and a fully protected prop. Both the Flybridge and Open Fisherman share a similar single-stateroom layout with V-berths forward and a good-sized galley and head compartment. The traditional teak interior woodwork is attractive and well-crafted throughout. Notable features include wide sidedecks, good service access to the engine, and sliding cabin windows in the Flybridge model. Most Cape Dory 28s have been fitted with the optional 200-hp Volvo diesel (about 14 knots cruise/17 knots top) rather than the once-standard single gas engine. Over 220 Cape Dory 28s (mostly flybridge models) have been built to date. Newport Shipyards purchased the molds late in 1994 and modified the underbody to improve performance. ❑

See Page 260 for Pricing Information

LEARN AT THE HELM

Chapman
SCHOOL OF SEAMANSHIP

Whether you seek a career as a professional mariner, or want more confidence in operating your own power or sail boat . . . no one is better equipped to teach you than Chapman boating professionals.

From small boat handling to professional mariner training, Chapman School offers boating and maritime education programs throughout the year at our waterfront campus in Stuart, Florida.

- Professional Mariner Training
- Yacht & Small Craft Surveying
- Recreational Boating
- Power Boat Handling
- Offshore Sailing
- Marine Electronics
- Marine Engine Maintenance
- Custom Courses
- Private Lessons

For more information, please call:

407-283-8130
or
800-225-2841

The Chapman School is also your source for professional crew placement. Call today to hire a Chapman graduate.

The Chapman School is a not-for-profit educational institution and admits students of any sex, race, color, and national or ethnic origin.

THIS SINGLE PARENT NEEDS YOUR HELP.

Alone on a moonlit night, she will entrust her children to a sandy hole on a lonely beach. And without your help, most of them will die. You can help by adopting her — a Sea Turtle of your very own. The adoption fee, a $100 donation to fund scientists' work at Mote Marine Laboratory, will help us hatch and release as many as 1,000 more baby turtles. It's important work — work that could rescue an entire species — and you can help. Join our "Adopt-A-Turtle" program today.

THAT DOLPHIN OFF YOUR BOW COULD BE ONE YOU HELPED SAVE.

Rescuing stranded dolphins — and learning how to save them from disease and pollution — is a major effort at Mote Marine Laboratory. It's important work, but it doesn't come cheap. We need your support to do more. Please donate to help us continue this important research. Because the dolphin dancing off your bow could be one you personally helped save.

MOTE MARINE LABORATORY
1600 Thompson Parkway, Sarasota, Florida 34236
1-800-691-MOTE

CAPE DORY 30 POWER YACHT

SPECIFICATIONS

Length	30'3"	Fuel	230 gals.
Beam	12'0"	Hull Type	Modified-V
Draft	3'0"	Deadrise Aft	13°
Weight	12,500#	Designer	Clive Dent
Clearance	12'3"	Production	1990–91
Water	62 gals.		1995–Current

A good-looking boat with her upright profile and traditional styling, the Cape Dory 30 combines planing-speed performance with a classic Downeast design in a very attractive package. She's built on a hard-chine, modified-V hull (not the semi-displacement design usually associated with New England-style boats) with a wide beam, a full-length keel, and balsa-cored hullsides. The single-stateroom floorplan (with a walkaround island berth forward) features a full teak-and-holly sole with an ash ceiling and plenty of teak trim. A lower helm was optional. The engine room is big for a 30-footer, and three hatches in the salon sole make access easy. Additional features include big wraparound (opening) cabin windows, teak covering boards in the cockpit, a double-entry head compartment, teak bow pulpit, and wide sidedecks. Chrysler 275-hp gas engines were standard, however nearly all Cape Dory 30s were sold with the twin 200-hp Volvo diesels (19–20 knots cruise/around 22 knots top). Note that the molds were aquired by Nauset Marine in 1994, and new models are available on a semi-custom basis. ❑

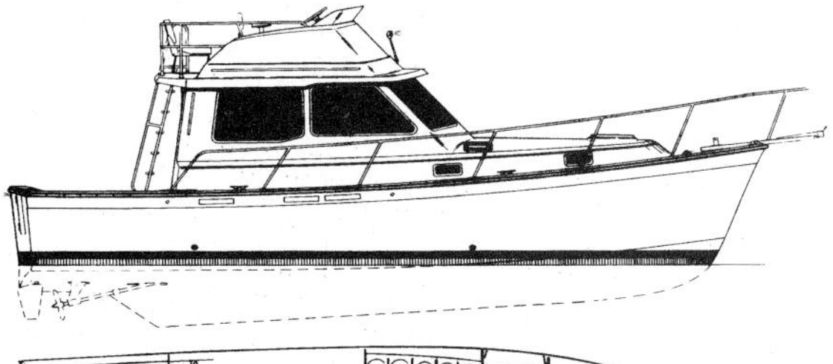

See Page 260 for Pricing Information

CAPE DORY 33 POWER YACHT

SPECIFICATIONS

Length	32'10"	Fuel	260 gals.
Beam	12'2"	Cockpit	65 sq. ft.
Draft	2'11"	Hull Type	Modified-V
Weight	13,500#	Deadrise Aft	15°
Clearance	12'8"	Production	1988–92
Water	100 gals.		1995–Current

The Cape Dory 33 is an attractive Downeast-style flybridge cruiser with a traditional profile and surprisingly brisk performance. She's constructed on a modified-V hull with a full-length (prop-protecting) keel and balsa coring in the hullsides. Inside, the 33's salon is completely surrounded by large cabin windows and paneled with teak. Visibility from the lower helm is excellent, and a full 6 feet, 4 inches of headroom makes the salon seem larger than it really is. While the Cape Dory 33's floorplan is fairly conventional for a boat of this size, the finish work and detailing are noteworthy. The forward stateroom was offered with V-berths or an optional island berth. The cockpit is large enough to satisfy the needs of most weekend anglers, and the flybridge has bench seating aft of the helm for a couple of guests. The Cape Dory 33 has been offered with several single or twin engine options, gas or diesel. Among them, a pair of 200-hp Volvos will cruise at 17 knots and reach 21 knots top. Note that the molds were aquired by Nauset Marine in 1994, and new models are currently available on a semi-custom basis. ❑

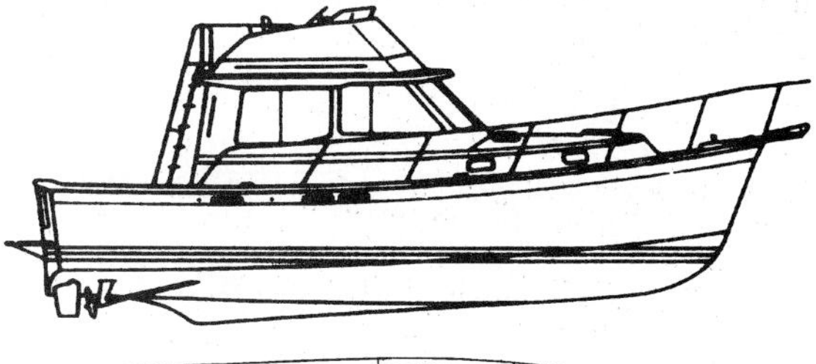

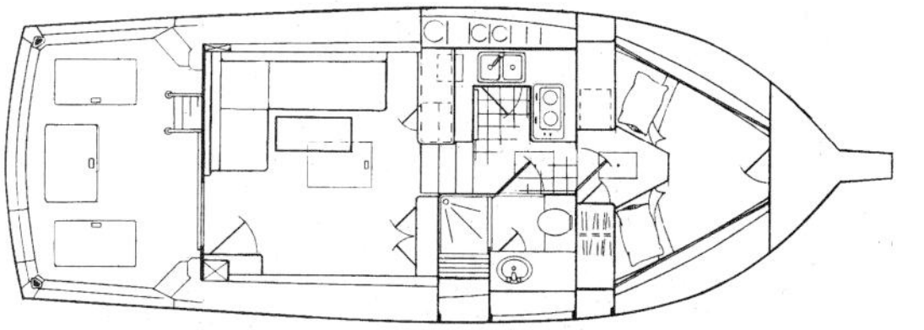

See Page 260 for Pricing Information

CAPE DORY 36 POWER YACHT

SPECIFICATIONS

Length ....35'9"	Fuel ....350 gals.
Beam ....13'6"	Cockpit ....77 sq. ft.
Draft ....3'6"	Hull Type ....Modified-V
Weight ....18,000#	Deadrise Aft ....16°
Clearance ....13'0"	Designer ....Clive Dent
Water ....100 gals.	Production 1988–90

The Cape Dory 36 is one of those better-quality semi-production boats whose high-end price restricted her appeal to a relatively small market of upscale buyers. She's a good-looking design with her stylish profile and distinctive Downeast character, and her lines seem particularly well-proportioned for a 36-footer. Her modified-V hull features a deep, full-length (prop-protecting) keel, a fairly wide beam and balsa-coring in the hullsides. The interior of the Cape Dory 36 shows the traditional teak woodwork and attention to detail long identified with this builder. A practical two-stateroom layout with mid-level galley and V-berths forward was standard, and a dinette option (replacing the guest stateroom) was optional. The large cabin windows make the interior seem larger than it actually is. Designed as a cruising boat, the 77 sq. ft. cockpit is big enough for a couple of light-tackle anglers and comes with a transom door and teak covering boards. Twin 340-hp gas engines were standard, and they'll cruise the Cape Dory 36 at about 19 knots. Optional 250-hp GM 8.2 diesels cruise at 19–20 knots.❑

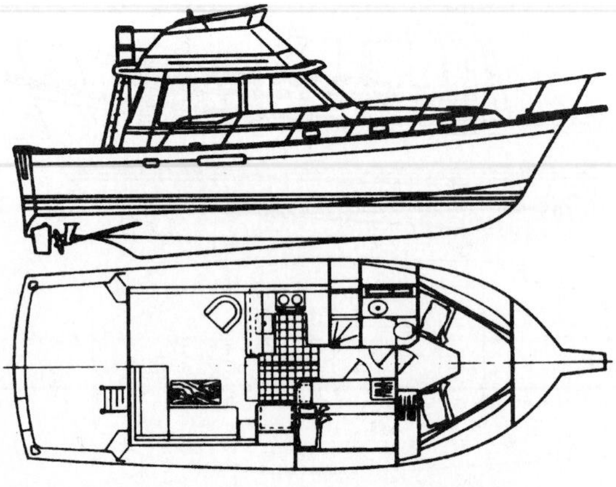

See Page 260 for Pricing Information

CAPE DORY 40 EXPLORER

SPECIFICATIONS

Length ....40'0"	Fuel ....400 gals.
Beam ....13'10"	Cockpit ....NA
Draft ....3'9"	Hull Type ....Modified-V
Weight ....25,000#	Deadrise Aft ....14°
Clearance ....13'3"	Designer ....Dave Gerr
Water ....170 gals.	Production 1992–Current

With her distinctive trawler profile and upright deckhouse, the 40 Explorer is the latest in the Cape Dory series of Downeast-style cruisers. She's constructed on a modified-V hull with cored hullsides and a long keel that protects the running gear. Belowdecks, the big, wide-open salon seems spacious for a 40-footer until the small cockpit dimensions are noted. A full lower helm (with deck access door) is standard, and the woodwork—including the teak-and-holly flooring—is impressive throughout. There are two staterooms and two heads (both sharing a common shower stall—very unusual) on the lower level, and the master stateroom is particularly comfortable and roomy. Topside, the flybridge is arranged with the helm forward and guest seating aft. Additional features include underwater exhausts, a teak cockpit sole, extra-wide sidedecks, a roomy engine room and a transom door. Note the offset bridge ladder. A classy boat with a good deal of eye appeal, standard 300-hp Cats 3116 diesels will cruise the Cape Dory 40 efficiently at 18 knots and reach a top speed of 23–24 knots. ❑

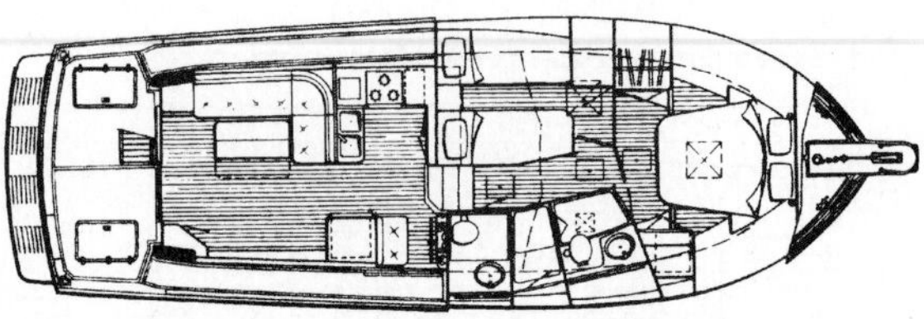

See Page 260 for Pricing Information

CARVER 25 ALLEGRA

SPECIFICATIONS

Length Overall............28'0"	Water.......................20 gals.
Hull Length.................25'0"	Fuel........................103 gals.
Beam...............................9'6"	Hull Type...............Deep-V
Draft...............................3'3"	Deadrise Aft...................19°
Weight.......................5,100#	Designer...................Carver
Clearance.......................8'9"	Production.............1989–90

Smallest of two Allegra models from Carver during 1989–90, the 25 Allegra is a wide-body sport cruiser with racy lines, a roomy cockpit and a compact interior. Construction is solid fiberglass, and the curved windshield, bold hull graphics and stylish integral swim platform add much to her modern Eurostyle appearance. The cockpit provides enough lounge space for sunbathing with bench seating aft and a walk-thru to the molded swim platform. Below, the Allegra's small cabin (most of her LOA is devoted to cockpit space) contains a U-shaped dinette forward that converts into a big double berth, a tiny head and an equally tight galley. The galley is hidden under folding panels to create extra counter space. Headroom is about 5 feet, 5 inches. The engine compartment is at the transom under the stern seat. At the touch of a button the entire seat assembly hinges upward for engine service. A good performer, twin 231-hp Volvo stern drives will cruise the Allegra at a brisk 26–27 knots and deliver a top speed of about 35 knots. ❑

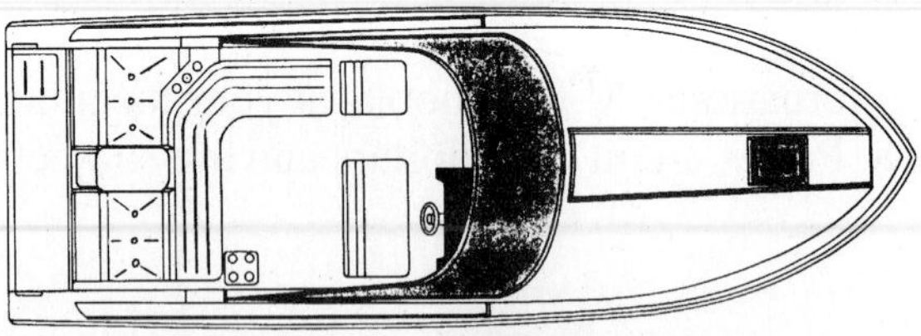

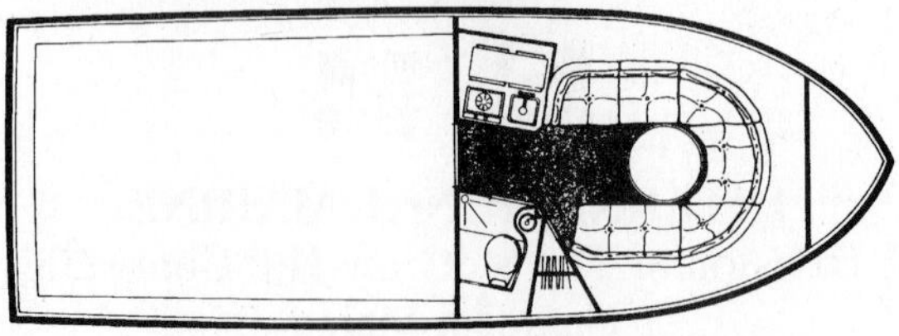

See Page 260 for Pricing Information

CARVER 250 MID CABIN EXPRESS

SPECIFICATIONS

Length w/Pulpit .... 27'4"	Water .... 25 gals.
Hull Length .... 24'2"	Clearance .... 7'1"
Beam .... 8'6"	Hull Type .... Deep-V
Draft, Drive Down .... 3'0"	Deadrise Aft .... 18°
Weight .... 6,100#	Designer .... Carver
Fuel .... 74 gals.	Production 1995–Current

The smallest boat in the current Carver fleet, the 250 Mid Cabin is also the only trailerable boat offered by this well-known Wisconsin builder. Like all Carver models, hull construction is solid fiberglass and, at 6,100 lbs., the 250 is heavy indeed for a trailerable 25-footer. (Including a trailer, fuel, and gear, the tow weight is close to 7,000 lbs.) A very unique feature of the mid-cabin floorplan is the location of the circular head compartment on the boat's centerline where the headroom is best. An extended settee wraps around the starboard side of the interior which adds more seating capacity than other small cruisers. Outside, the helm is particularly stylish and well designed. A molded-in step provides foredeck access through a windshield opening, and the rear cockpit seat folds away for extra space. Additional features include a double-wide helm seat, a molded pulpit, and cockpit storage. A good performer in spite of her heavy displacement, a single MerCruiser 7.4 liter I/O (optional) will cruise the Carver 250 Mid-Cabin at 25 knots and reach about 40 knots wide open. ❑

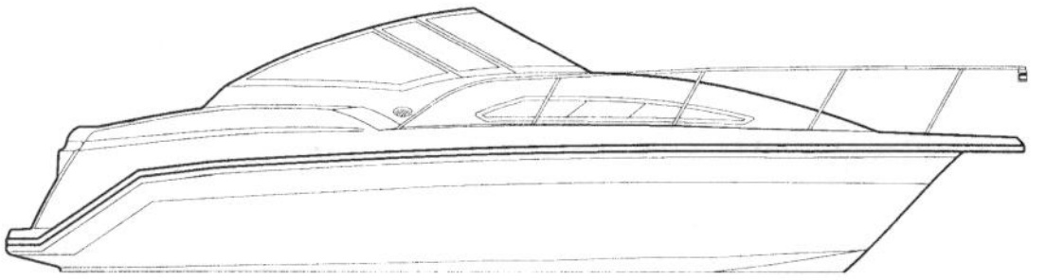

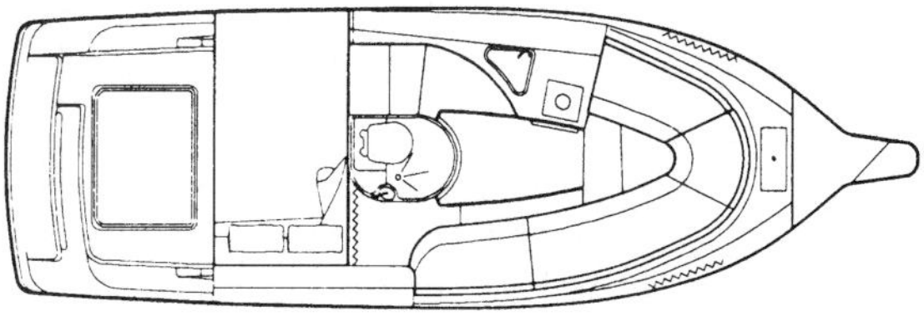

See Page 260 for Pricing Information

CARVER 26 SANTA CRUZ

SPECIFICATIONS

Length	25'8"	Cockpit	NA
Beam	8'0"	Clearance	8'9"
Draft	2'10"	Hull Type	Modified-V
Weight	5,400#	Deadrise Aft	16°
Fuel	100 gals.	Designer	Carver
Water	46 gals.	Production	1980–87

You can count the number of *trailerable* flybridge sedans on one hand and for good reason. They're generally heavy and difficult to trailer, launching is a pain in the ass, and a 26-footer with a narrow 8-foot beam becomes unstable in a hurry with a couple of people on the bridge. Nonetheless, Carver built this model for a long time, and she's actually a rather stylish boat considering her built-in limitations. Hull construction is solid fiberglass and, although the interior accommodations are cramped, Carver designers managed to include all the amenities necessary for weekend family cruising including a lower helm, an enclosed, stand-up head compartment and berths for four adults. A privacy curtain separates the V-berths from the rest of the cabin and headroom is about 6 feet throughout. Outside, the roomy cockpit is a pleasant surprise, and the bench seat at the transom can be converted into a sun lounge. Side decks are practically nonexistent. All power options were single engine, and an inboard was available. A single 260-hp MerCruiser stern drive will cruise at 18–19 knots and top out at about 28 knots. ❑

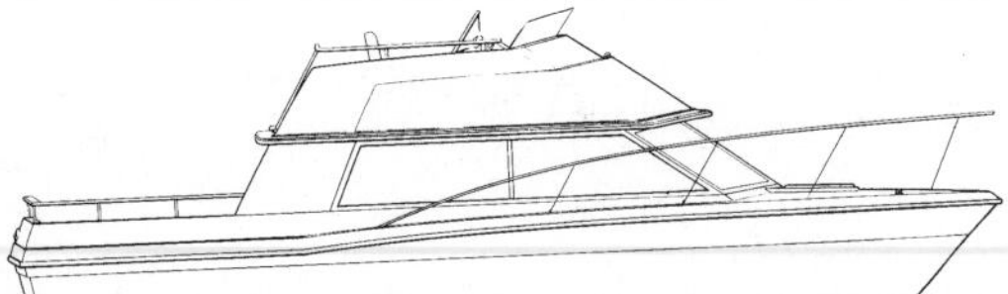

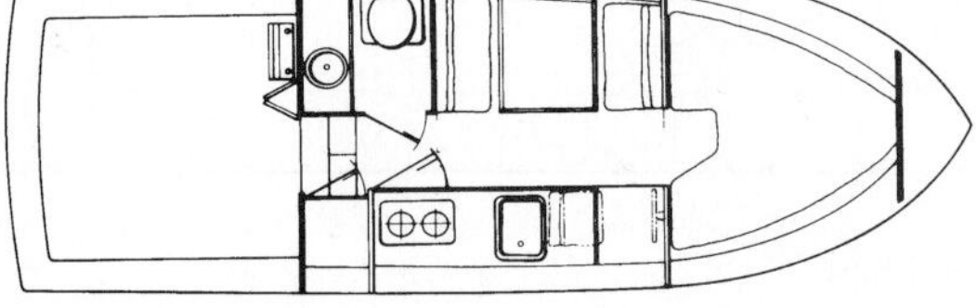

See Page 260 for Pricing Information

CARVER 26 MONTEREY

SPECIFICATIONS

Length	25'8"	Cockpit	NA
Beam	8'0"	Clearance	8'9"
Draft	2'10"	Hull Type	Modified-V
Weight	5,300#	Deadrise Aft	16°
Fuel	100 gals.	Designer	Carver
Water	46 gals.	Production	1981–84

Obviously dated by today's express cruiser standards, the Carver 26 Monterey (or the 2687 Monterey to be exact) was actually a rather stylish design in her day with attractive hull graphics and an inexpensive price tag to go with her wide open interior. Construction was solid fiberglass, and an eight-foot beam made the Monterey trailerable in every state. (At 5,300 lbs., however, she's a heavy load.) The interior was designed to accommodate the needs of a cruising family with berths for four, a stand-up head compartment, a well-arranged galley and a convertible dinette. Storage space is at a premium, but the large cabin windows provide an abundance of natural lighting below making the interior seem more spacious than many other small cruisers in her class. Visabilty from the helm is very good and, while cockpit space is limited, a companion seat and bench seating at the transom were standard. Among several single engine inboard and I/O installations, the popular 260-hp MerCruiser stern drive will cruise the Carver 26 Santa Cruz at a respectable 18–19 knots with a top speed of about 29 knots. ❑

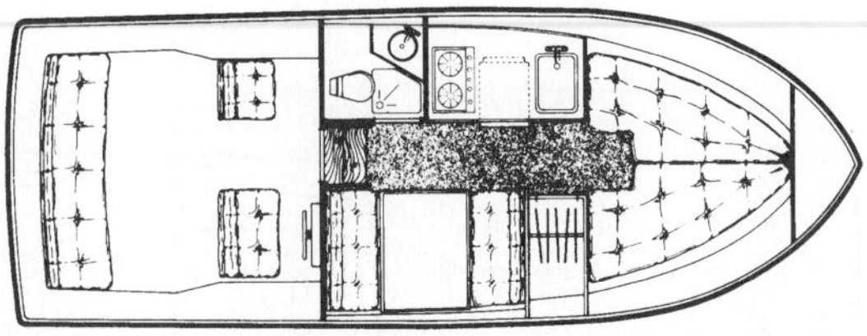

See Page 260 for Pricing Information

CARVER 26 MONTEGO

SPECIFICATIONS

Length ....25'8"	Cockpit ....NA
Beam ....8'0"	Clearance ....8'10"
Draft ....2'10"	Hull Type ....Modified-V
Weight ....5,300#	Deadrise Aft ....16°
Fuel ....98 gals.	Designer ....Carver
Water ....41 gals.	Production 1985–87

Based on the earlier 26 Monterey (previous page) and sharing nearly identical specifications and a very similar profile, the Carver 26 Montego is a very different boat below with a mid-cabin layout and a lot more room. Carver's designers extended the cabin full width, eliminating the side decks but adding more headroom foward and an aft cabin floorplan in place of the Monterey's conventional layout. The mid-cabin is accessed via a privacy door in the angled bulkhead and features a stand-up dressing area in addition to a small settee. The V-berth forward is fitted with a dinette, and while the galley is very compact and storage is limited, the head compartment is quite spacious and comes with a shower. Outside, the cockpit features a lounge and removable table with seating for four. Standard features include twin sun pads on the foredeck, bow pulpit and swim platform. Because there are no side decks, foredeck access is best achieved through the forward-most deck hatch—an awkward procedure at best. A single 260-hp MerCruiser I/O will cruise at 18–19 knots and deliver a top speed of 29 knots.

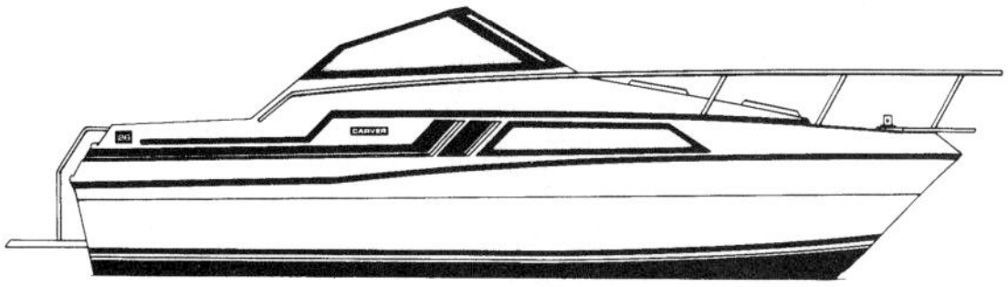

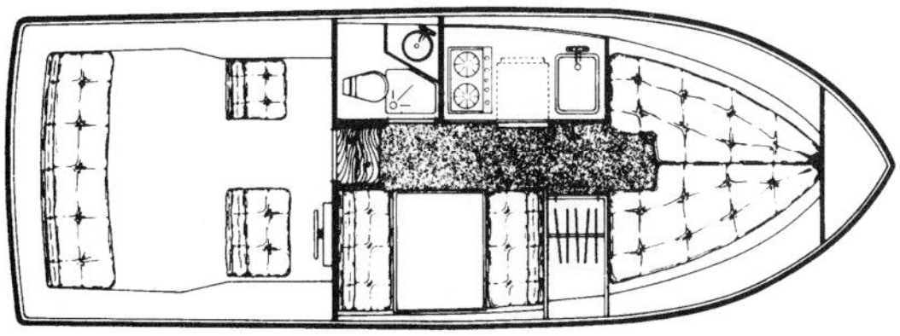

See Page 260 for Pricing Information

CARVER 26 COMMAND BRIDGE/280 SEDAN

SPECIFICATIONS

Length w/Pulpit ....29'11"	Water ....40 gals.
Hull Length ....27'9"	Fuel ....120 gals.
Beam ....9'6"	Hull Type ....Modified-V
Draft ....2'4"	Deadrise Aft ....15°
Weight ....8,500#	Designer ....Carver
Clearance ....8'0"	Production 1991–Current

Although she's best known as the 280 Sedan, this model was originally introduced in 1991 as the Carver 26 Command Bridge—a good-looking small inland cruiser with clean-cut lines and a sporty profile. (She became the 280 Sedan in 1993 when Carver began including swim platforms in their length measurments.) Notably, this is one of the smallest production flybridge cruisers available in today's market. She's a beamy boat for her length, and the house is carried well forward in order to maximize interior space. The cabin is bright and well-arranged with wraparound windows, good headroom throughout, and plenty of seating. A lower helm is a popular option. Fortunately, Carver designers left some room in the floorplan for a fair-size cockpit. Topside, the compact flybridge will seat two passangers aft of the helm. A heavy boat, single or twin stern drives are offered, and most will probably be fitted with the latter for the performance advantage. Twin MerCruiser or Volvo V-6 stern drives will cruise the Carver 280 Sedan at 18–20 knots and reach 30+ wide open. ❑

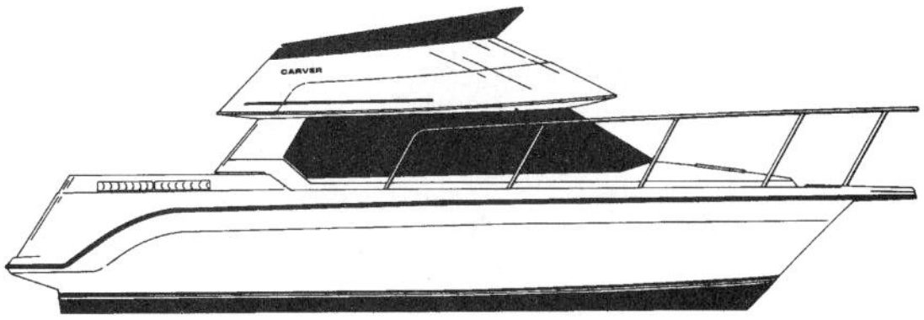

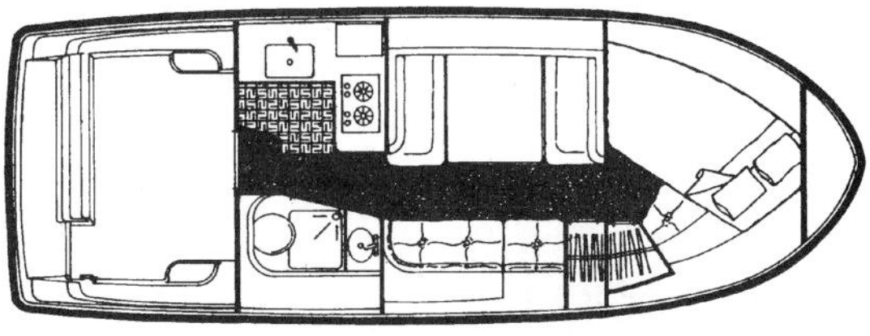

See Page 260 for Pricing Information

CARVER 27/530/300 MONTEGO

SPECIFICATIONS

Length w/Platform.......29'2"	Water........................41 gals.
Hull Length..................27'3"	Fuel.........................120 gals.
Beam..............................10'0"	Hull Type.........Modified-V
Draft...............................2'10"	Deadrise Aft......................8°
Weight........................6,900#	Designer....................Carver
Clearance........................9'0"	Production..............1986–93

A long-running model in the Carver fleet and a popular boat with owners, the 27 Montego was also known as the 530 Montego during 1991–92 and as the 300 Montego in 1993. Carver packed some impressive living space into this 27-foot hull, but her raised foredeck and high freeboard give her a decidedly overfed appearance. While the cabin accommodations are less extravagant than those of her sistership, the 27 Santego, they are nonetheless completely suitable for weekend cruisers. Headroom is adequate throughout; privacy curtains are provided for both sleeping areas; and the galley actually has some decent counter space—a rarity in a small cruiser. Outside, the cockpit is spacious for a 27-footer with bench seating at the transom and a walk-thru to the swim platform. Note that the Montego's original swim platform (pictured above) was replaced in 1990 with a more elaborate bolt-on unit. Twin 205-hp V-6 stern drives (among several engine packages) will cruise the 27 Montego at 22–23 knots and deliver 33+ knots wide open.❑

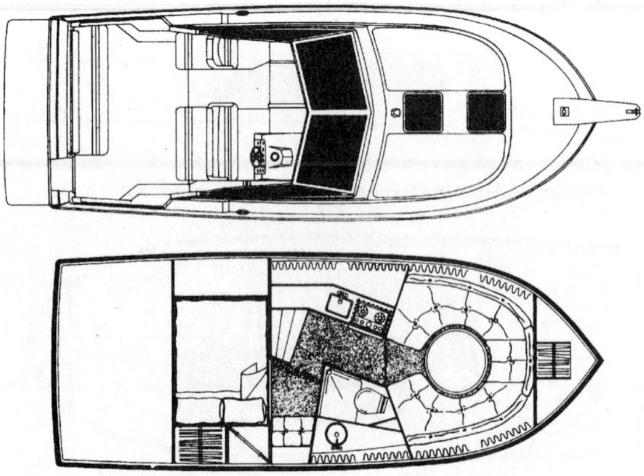

See Page 260 for Pricing Information

CARVER 27/630/300 SANTEGO

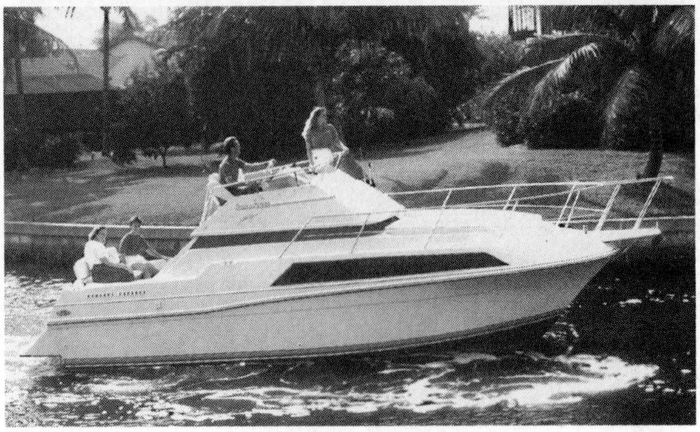

SPECIFICATIONS

Length w/Platform.......29'2"	Water........................41 gals.
Hull Length..................27'3"	Fuel.........................100 gals.
Beam..............................10'0"	Hull Type.........Modified-V
Draft...............................2'8"	Deadrise Aft......................8°
Weight........................8,400#	Designer....................Carver
Clearance........................9'2"	Production..............1988–93

A popular model, the Carver 27 Santego (called the 630 Santego during 1991–92 and the 300 Santego in 1993) is a modern mid-cabin family cruiser with an unusually spacious interior and a slightly topheavy profile. In order to gain interior volume, Carver engineers extended the Santego's cabinsides to the hull's full width. The result is a cavernous single-level cabin with an athwartship wraparound dinette forward and hidden Vee berths. With the dinette converted, there are berths for six together with a compact galley and stand-up head with shower. The excellent 6-foot, 3-inch headroom is the result of her raised foredeck (which in turn accounts for her bulky profile). There's bench seating in the cockpit and lounge seating on the flybridge opposite the helm. Sunpads can be fitted to the foredeck and a cockpit hatch provides access to the motors. Note the bolt-on swim platform. A heavy boat for her size, twin V-6 stern drives (205-hp) cruise the 27 Santego at 19–20 knots and reach a top speed of just over 30 knots. ❑

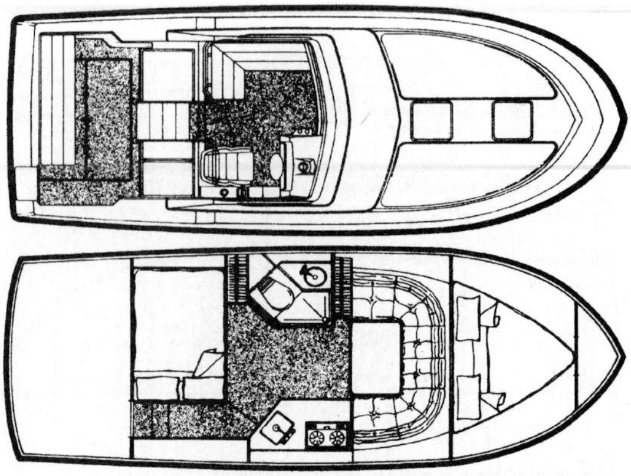

See Page 260 for Pricing Information

CARVER 2866 SANTA CRUZ

SPECIFICATIONS

Length	28'4"	Water	30 gals.
Beam	10'4"	Fuel	160 gals.
Draft	3'5"	Hull Type	Modified-V
Weight	7,630#	Deadrise Aft	11°
Clearance	9'6"	Designer	Carver
Cockpit	70 sq. ft.	Production	1976–82

The 2866 Santa Cruz is a low-profile coastal and inland fisherman with compact interior accommodations and a relatively spacious cockpit. Popular with light-tackle anglers, she was constructed on a solid fiberglass hull with moderate beam and a relatively flat 11 degrees of transom deadrise. The Santa Cruz enjoyed a long production run for Carver, and she remained pretty much the same boat throughout with only minor cosmetic updates and alterations. Her single-level floorplan is arranged three steps down from the cockpit level and includes berths for four, a complete mini-galley and a stand-up head with shower. Most were sold with a lower helm. The engines are accessed below the cockpit, and the flybridge has guest seating for two. Not an expensive boat, her outside teak trim and interior decor are clearly dated by today's standards. Several inboard and stern drive engine options were offered over the years. Among them, twin 230-hp gas engines will cruise the 2866 Santa Cruz at 16–17 knots and attain a top speed of around 22 knots. ❑

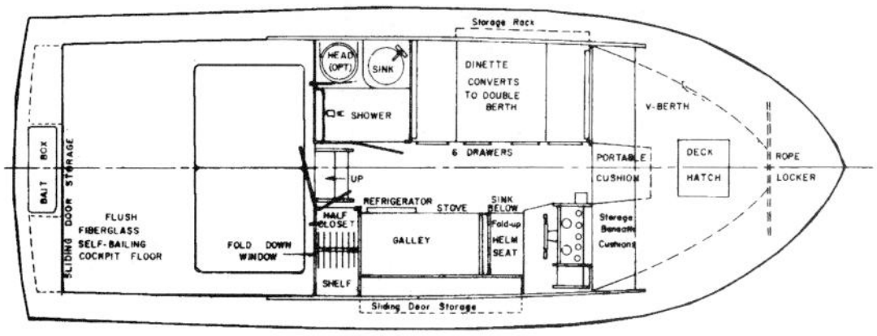

See Page 260 for Pricing Information

CARVER 28 MARINER & VOYAGER

SPECIFICATIONS

Length	28'0"	Fuel	150 gals.
Beam	11'1"	Cockpit	NA
Draft	2'10"	Hull Type	Modified-V
Weight	10,300#	Deadrise Aft	10°
Clearance	9'11"	Designer	R. MacNeill
Water	51 gals.	Production	1983–90

Enjoying a long production run, the Carver 28 remains one of the more popular family sedans ever built. She was offered in either a Voyager or Mariner model, the difference being the choice of interior floorplans. The Mariner layout has the galley and head forward, whereas in the Voyager they're located aft (just inside the salon door), and the Voyager also has a lower helm. Carvers are well-known for their spacious floorplans, and the 28 Convertible is no exception: there's seating in the salon for a small crowd; the head is surprisingly large; and the cockpit is roomy enough to handle a couple of deck chairs or anglers. The flybridge on this boat is huge with seating for six and a table that converts into a full-width sun pad. (Underway, the weight of six—or even four—persons on the bridge will make her very tender—guaranteed!) A hard ride in a chop, standard 220-hp gas engines (with V-drives) will cruise the Carver 28 Convertible at 18 knots and reach 26–27 knots wide open. ❑

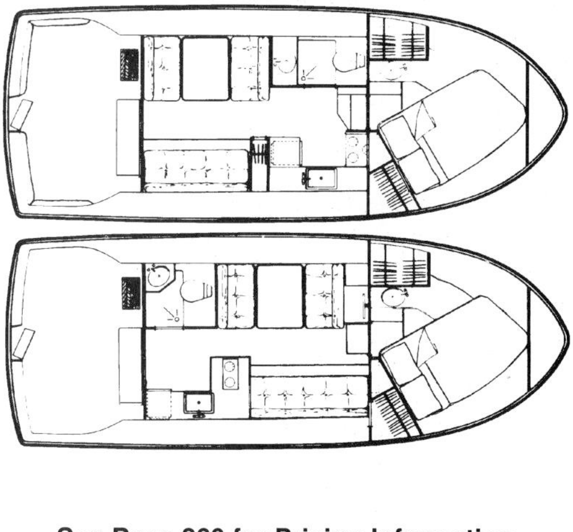

See Page 260 for Pricing Information

CARVER 28 RIVIERA

SPECIFICATIONS

Length	28'0"	Water	52 gals.
Beam	11'1"	Fuel	160 gals.
Draft	2'10"	Hull Type	Modified-V
Weight	8,900#	Deadrise Aft	10°
Clearance	9'3"	Designer	R. MacNeill
Cockpit	NA	Production	1983–89

There have only been a few 28-foot boats built with two stateroom interiors. The Carver 28 Riviera is one of these—a beamy little cruiser with an overfed profile and cramped accommodations. Nonetheless, she was a popular model for Carver. In the eyes of most owners, the best part about the boat is her open-air center cockpit with its wraparound windshield. The driver has good helm visibility in all directions, the side windshields provide some weather protection, and there's seating for six around a dinette table and jump seat. When the weather turns sour, snap on the camper-style canvas enclosure panels and keep on going. With the cockpit table converted, there are a total of six berths in three separate sleeping areas. Twin 220-hp gas engines are located below the cockpit sole, and routine access is difficult thanks to an unwieldy hatch cover. A wet boat and a hard ride in a chop, the cruising speed of the Carver 28 Riviera is 20 knots, and the top speed is around 28 knots. ❑

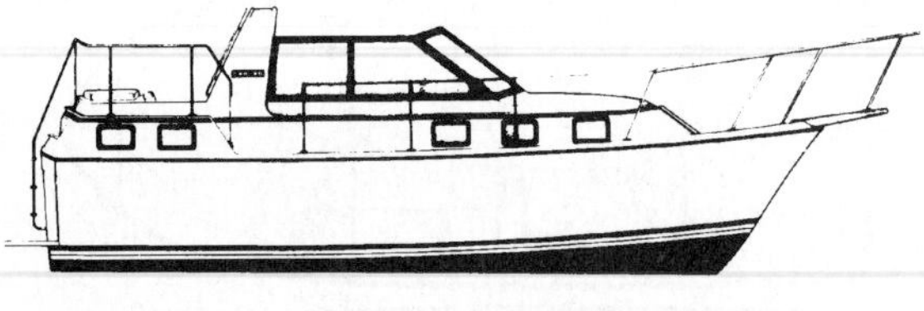

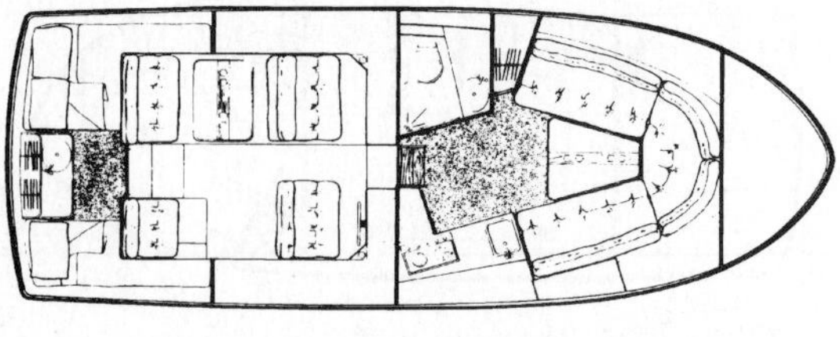

See Page 261 for Pricing Information

CARVER 28/300 SEDAN

SPECIFICATIONS

Length Overall	30'6"	Water	51 gals.
Length w/Platform	30'6"	Fuel	150 gals.
Beam	11'10"	Hull Type	Modified-V
Draft	2'11"	Deadrise Aft	16°
Weight	12,500#	Designer	Carver
Clearance	9'1"	Production	1991–93

The Carver 28 Sedan (called the 300 Sedan in 1993) is one of the largest 28-foot boats in the business. Indeed, her nearly 12-foot beam is more common to a 33-footer. (Note that she's built on the same hull as Carver's 28-foot Aft Cabin model.) A well-styled cruiser designed for coastal and inland waters, the interior is surprisingly spacious for a boat of this size. Two floorplans are available—one with a lower helm and the other without. Notably, there's a privacy door for the stateroom rather than just a curtain. Berths are provided for up to six in either layout. The generous interior accommodations of the Carver 28 come at the expense of a very small cockpit. Topside, the flybridge is huge with guest seating that converts into a sun lounge. Hatches in the cockpit sole provide access to the engines, and the V-drives are reached through the salon sole. Optional 260-hp gas engines will cruise the Carver 28 Sedan at 17 knots and reach 26–27 knots top. ❑

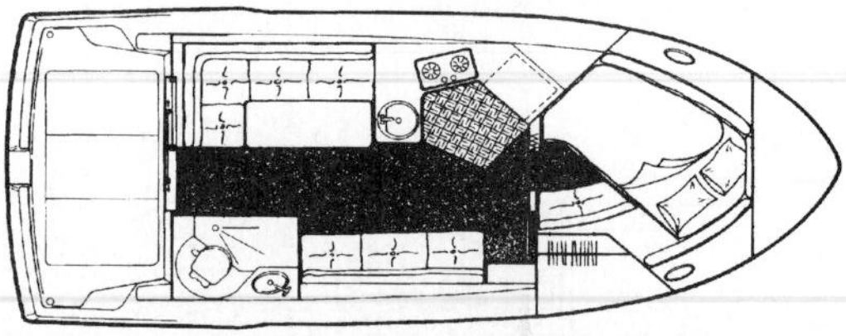

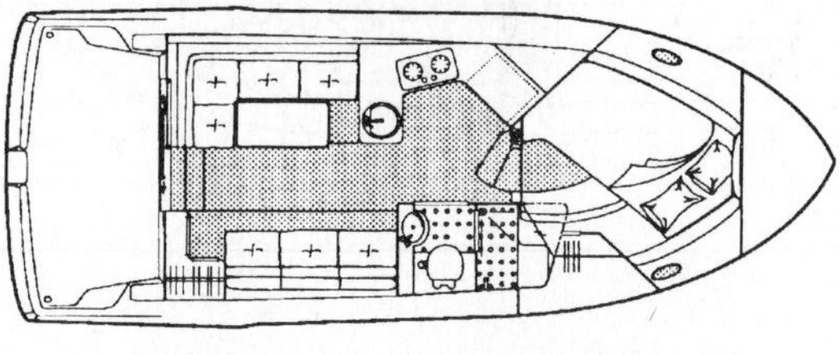

See Page 261 for Pricing Information

CARVER 25 MONTEGO/280 EXPRESS

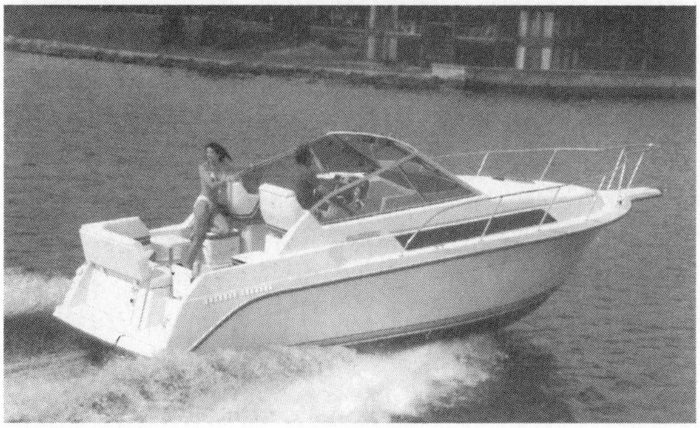

SPECIFICATIONS

Length Overall ....29'10"	Water ....25 gals.
Length w/Platform.......28'0"	Fuel ....100 gals.
Beam................................9'6"	Hull Type ....Deep-V
Draft ....3'3"	Deadrise Aft....................19°
Weight ....5,900#	Designer....................Carver
Clearance ....8'9"	Production.......1988–Current

The 280 mid-Cabin Express actually began life in 1988 when she was introduced as the Carver 25 Montego, an affordable mid-cabin cruiser with modern lines and room enough for two couples. Built on a solid fiberglass hull and sporting an integral swim platform, Carver redesigned this boat for 1993 dropping the Montego designation and re-introduced her as the new 280 Express. The hull remained the same but the 280 has a redesigned deckhouse, curved windshield, and a new (and much improved) interior floorplan with the head aft (rather than in the middle of the cabin as before) and a starboard-side dinette. Where the original 25 Montego slept four, the 280 Express can sleep six. The cockpit hasn't changed: a cut-out in the transom leads to the swim platform, and a bench seat and table are standard. Available with single or twin stern drives, a 280 Express fitted with a single 300-hp MerCruiser will cruise at 18–19 knots and reach about 32 knots top. Note that she was called the 528 Montego in 1991 and 1992. ❑

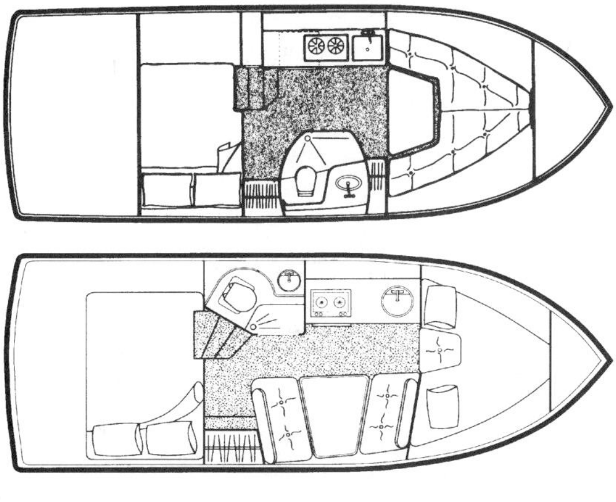

See Page 261 for Pricing Information

CARVER 30 ALLEGRA

SPECIFICATIONS

Length Overall.............34'0"	Water ....51 gals.
Hull Length ....30'8"	Fuel ....150 gals.
Beam..............................11'0"	Hull Type ....Deep-V
Draft ....3'1"	Deadrise Aft....................18°
Weight ....10,950#	Designer....................Carver
Clearance ....8'5"	Production 1989–90

Like the 25 Allegra, the Carver 30 Allegra features a sportier look and a greater emphasis on cockpit accommodations than previous Carver models. Her topheavy profile (the result of an elevated foredeck) is mostly offset by the long sweptback windshield and steeply raked reverse arch. She's built on a solid fiberglass hull with moderate beam and a steep 18 degrees of deadrise aft. There's a lot of cockpit space in the Allegra—more than most other express boats her size—and this is a really fun boat for daytime family cruising. A wet bar was standard, and a U-shaped lounge aft of the companion seat is big enough for several guests. Because the Allegra was designed for open-air activities, her interior is smaller than other 30-footers, although still well-arranged and efficient. Berths are provided for four, and the stateroom has a privacy door (rather than a curtain). Twin 231-hp Volvo stern drives were standard in the Allegra. She'll cruise at 20 knots and reach a top speed of around 33 knots. ❑

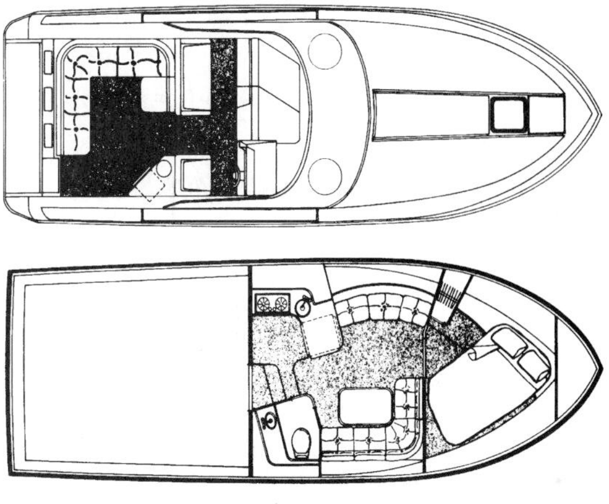

See Page 261 for Pricing Information

CARVER 310 SANTEGO

SPECIFICATIONS

Length Overall	33'5"	Water	66 gals.
Hull Length	31'3"	Clearance	9'10"
Beam	10'10"	Hull Type	Modified-V
Draft	2'8"	Deadrise Aft	NA
Weight	8,400#	Designer	Carver
Fuel	130 gals.	Production	1994–Current

Those seeking a maxi-volume family cruiser with the amenities of a small apartment will find much to like in the 310 Santego. She's built on a beamy, modified-V hull with an integral swim platform and bow pulpit and relatively high freeboard. Note the absence of side decks; the Santego's full-width cabin is extended to the hullsides resulting in a notably spacious and wide-open interior. Stepping below from the small cockpit, the floorplan is arranged on a single level with the owner's stateroom forward and lounge seating on both sides of the salon. The starboard dinette converts to a double berth, and the portside lounge converts to an upper and lower bunk and includes a privacy curtain. Additional features include a double-wide helm seat with guest seating forward, good engine access, cockpit shower, transom door and swim platform with storage lockers. Available with V-drive or stern drive power, twin 4.3-litre Volvo I/Os will cruise at 18 knots (about 30 knots top), and 5.7-litre inboards cruise at 22 knots and reach 33 knots top. ❑

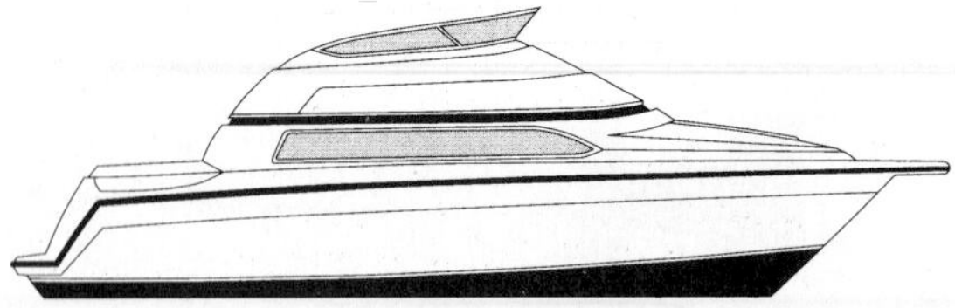

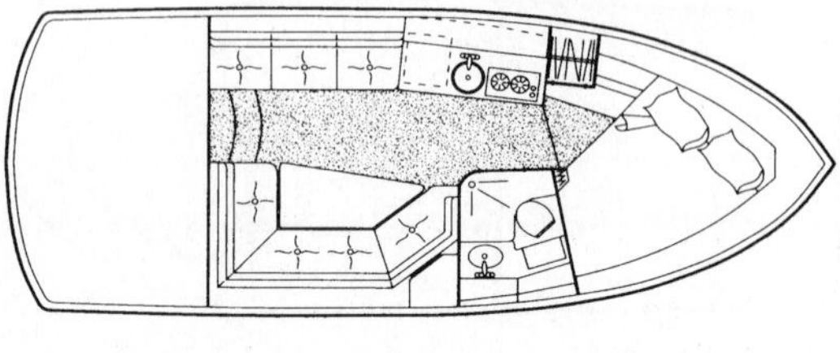

See Page 261 for Pricing Information

CARVER 310 MID-CABIN EXPRESS

SPECIFICATIONS

Length Overall	33'5"	Water	50 gals.
Length w/Platform	31'3"	Clearance	9'7"
Beam	10'10"	Hull Type	Modified-V
Draft	2'8"	Deadrise Aft	NA
Weight	8,100#	Designer	Carver
Fuel	180 gals.	Production	1995–Current

Carver designers have applied some unusual styling features to the new 310 Mid-Cabin, and the result is a hull and deck profile with more dips and curves than just about anything else on the market. Construction is solid fiberglass and a wide beam and relatively high freeboard combine to provide a very roomy interior. Two floorplans are available. The standard layout has a spacious salon with an extra-large L-shaped lounge that converts to a double berth with privacy curtain. The alternate floorplan offers a mid-cabin stateroom at the expense of a smaller salon. The owner's stateroom features a large double berth and private access to the head. Outside, the cockpit has a double-wide helm seat with a wet bar opposite. The wrap-around seating aft of the helm converts to a sun lounge. Additional features include a foredeck sun pad, walk-thru windshield, side exhausts, and radar arch. Available with V-drive or stern drive power, optional 5.8-litre Volvo I/Os will cruise at 25 knots (about 42 knots top), and 5.7-litre Crusader inboards cruise at 22 knots (32 knots top). ❑

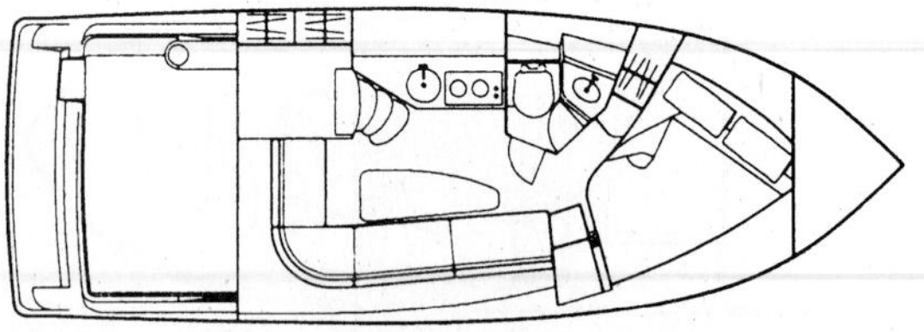

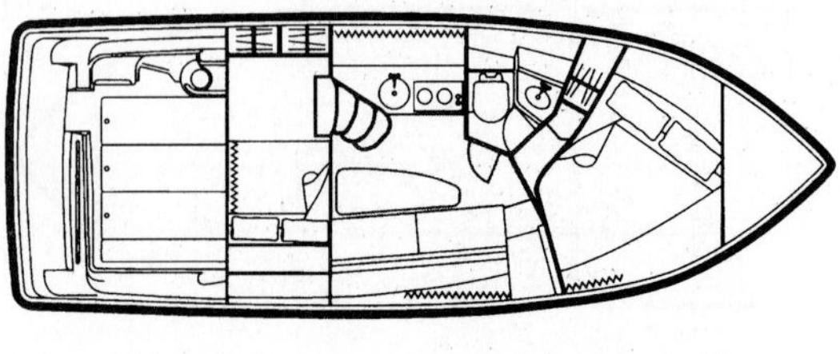

See Page 261 for Pricing Information

CARVER 32 CONVERTIBLE

SPECIFICATIONS

Length	32'0"	Fuel	220 gals.
Beam	11'7"	Cockpit	57 sq. ft.
Draft	2'10"	Hull Type	Modified-V
Weight	12,600#	Deadrise Aft	10°
Clearance	11'6"	Designer	R. MacNeill
Water	84 gals.	Production	1984–93

Enough Carver 32 Convertibles have been sold since 1984 to make this a popular and well-known model in most boating markets. While the 32's styling is admittedly conservative, the belowdecks layout is innovative. Interior volume is increased by using V-drives to locate the engines beneath the cockpit rather than below the salon sole. Hidden beneath the raised dinette, the Carver 32 features a mini-stateroom with limited standing headroom and a private access door from the galley. With that, she's an honest two-stateroom boat—rare in any 32-footer. The compact galley is down from the salon level and includes a nearly full-size refrigerator. Note the sepatate stall shower in the head. A sliding glass door leads into the cockpit, where a transom door and swim platform were standard. Two lift-out hatches in the cockpit sole provide good service access to the engines, and the entire deck can be removed when necessary. Twin 270-hp gas engines will cruise the Carver 32 Convertible around 17 knots, and she'll reach 26–27 knots wide open. ❑

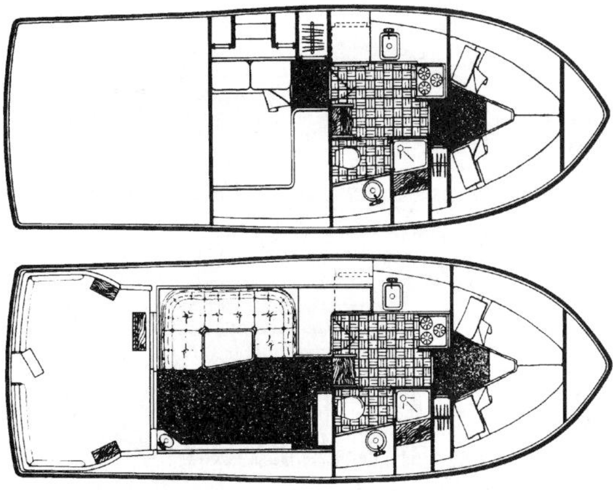

See Page 261 for Pricing Information

CARVER 32/330 MARINER

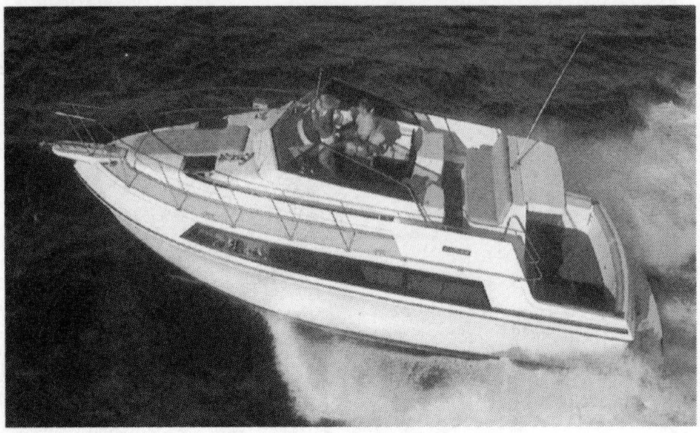

SPECIFICATION

Length Overall	35'5"	Water	92 gals.
Hull Length	32'3"	Fuel	192 gals.
Beam	12'4"	Hull Type	Modified-V
Draft	2'9"	Deadrise Aft	6°
Weight	12,000#	Designer	R. MacNeill
Clearance	10'10"	Production	1985–Current

The Carver 32 Mariner was introduced in 1985 as a downsized version of her sistership, the popular 36 Mariner. (Since 1993 she's been called the Carver 330 Mariner.) Her unorthodox appearance has drawn a lot of abuse over the years, but over 650 of these boats have been sold, which says something about Carver's ability to please the public. Her great appeal as a family cruiser is the enormous single-level step-down interior that successfully uses every possible square inch of space available in the hull. The result is a truly social boat with an apartment-size salon featuring facing settees. (Natural lighting is poor, however, because the cabin windows are so tiny.) A ladder in the salon provides convenient inside access to the flybridge which is another huge entertainment center in itself. Standard 270-hp gas engines (with V-drives) are located beneath the cockpit. A thirsty and fairly hard-riding boat in a chop, the Mariner burns around 20 gph at a modest cruising speed of 16 knots. The top speed is around 25–26 knots. ❑

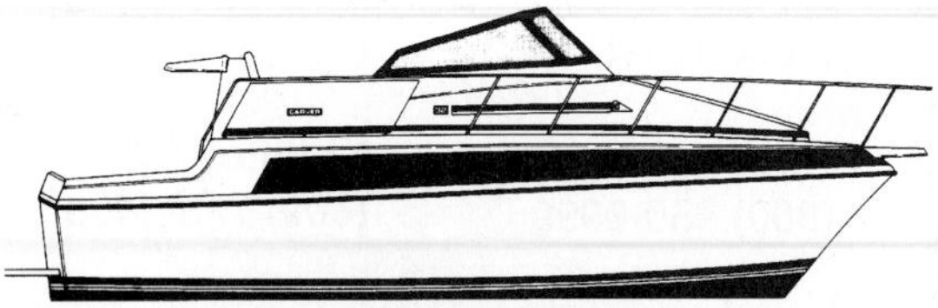

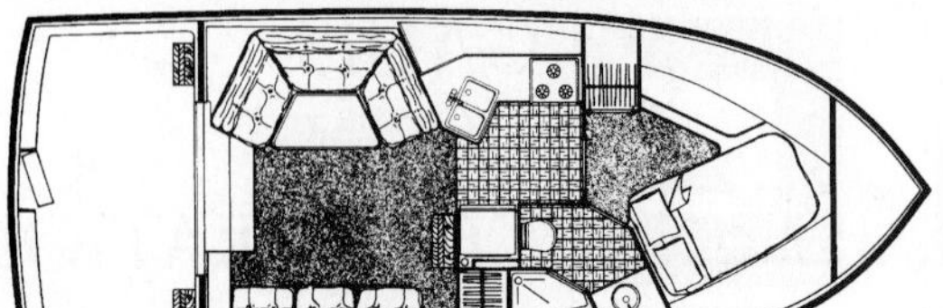

See Page 261 for Pricing Information

CARVER 32 MONTEGO

SPECIFICATIONS

Length	32'3"	Water	92 gals.
Beam	12'4"	Fuel	192 gals.
Draft	2'9"	Hull Type	Modified-V
Weight	13,000#	Deadrise Aft	6°
Clearance	9'0"	Designer	R. MacNeill
Cockpit	NA	Production	1987–91

Carver's 32 Montego sport cruiser was built using the hull originally designed for the 32 Mariner—a wide, flat-bottom affair with a fairly sharp entry, shallow keel, and solid fiberglass construction. While not known as an especially efficient design, it does have the advantage of offering considerable beam with which to work. The Montego combines a sportboat profile with a comfortable interior layout, and the result is a practical weekend family cruiser. Her full-width floorplan is spacious for a boat of this type and features a mid-stateroom beneath the bridgedeck. The galley is forward in the salon, and a double-entry head with stall shower provides private access from the forward stateroom. The cabin is attractively decorated with textured wall coverings, Formica counters, and stylish fabrics. Standard 270-hp gas engines (with V-drives) will cruise the Carver 32 Montego around 15–16 knots, and the optional 350-hp Crusaders will cruise 20 knots and reach 29–30 knots wide open. Note that in her final production year she was called the 534 Montego. ❑

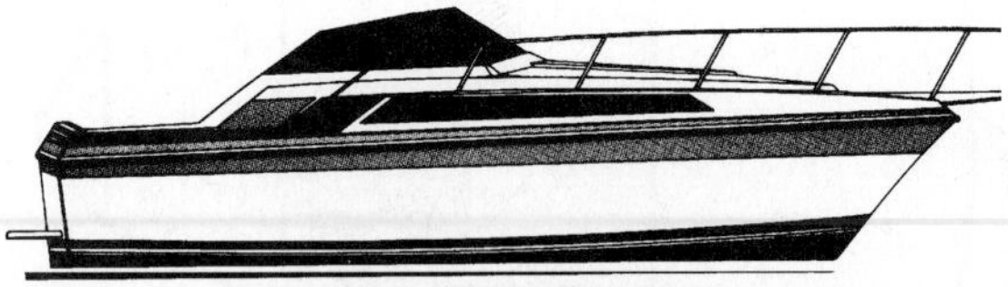

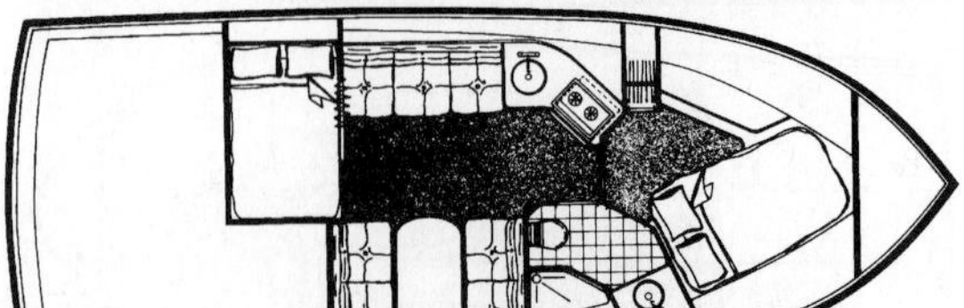

See Page 261 for Pricing Information

CARVER 320 VOYAGER

SPECIFICATIONS

Length Overall	35'0"	Water	56 gals.
Length w/Platform	32'2"	Fuel	188 gals.
Beam	11'10"	Hull Type	Modified-V
Draft	2'11"	Deadrise Aft	16°
Weight	13,000#	Designer	Carver
Clearance	9'11"	Production	1994–Current

The Carver 320 Voyager is a traditional family cruiser with a stylish profile to go with her generous accommodations. She's built on a solid fiberglass hull with a wide beam and a steep 16 degrees of deadrise at the transom. The Voyager is a roomy boat inside and Carver offers her in a choice of layouts: with a lower helm or without. (Without the helm, there's room for a stall shower in the head and additional hanging locker space.) Either way, the stateroom has an offset double berth (and a privacy door), and the dinette and salon sofa convert into double berths. Outside, the integral swim platform features a built-in fender rack and a hideaway boarding ladder. Access to the engines and V-drives is via hatches in the cockpit sole. The oversize flybridge of the 320 Voyager has the helm forward and guest seating for five. The sidedecks are narrow and foredeck access is heel-to-toe. Twin 350-cid Crusader gas engines will cruise at 17 knots and deliver a top speed of 27–28 knots. ❑

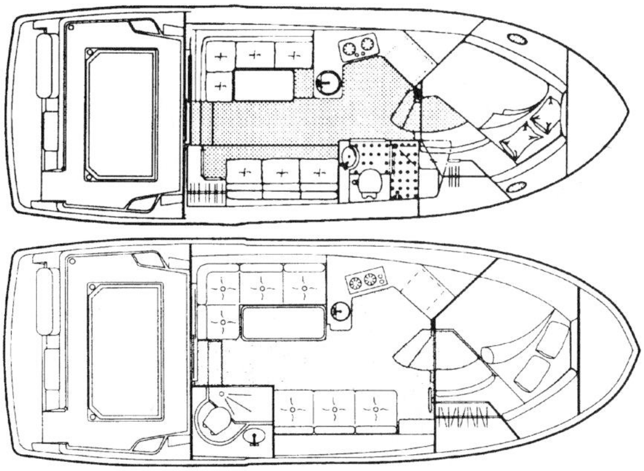

See Page 261 for Pricing Information

CARVER 33 MARINER

SPECIFICATIONS

Length	32'6"	Fuel	145 gals.
Beam	12'0"	Cockpit	NA
Draft	2'6"	Hull Type	Modified-V
Weight	11,620#	Deadrise Aft	NA
Clearance	NA	Designer	Carver
Water	75 gals.	Production	1975–84

Long a popular boat, the Carver 33 Mariner sold well for a decade, and today they're commonly found in many of the nation's coastal and inland waters. Known primarily for her huge interior layout and boxy appearance, the original 33 Mariner was built with a plywood superstructure (1975–76), while later models are all fiberglass in construction. Stepping down into the single-level floorplan, one is immediately impressed with the spacious dimensions of the combined salon and galley area. Obviously designed as a family cruiser, the Carver 33 Mariner features a stall shower in the head and a unique bulkhead ladder in the salon for direct access to the bridge. (A cockpit ladder is available as well, but the interior passage is a more convenient and quicker route.) The Mariner's flybridge is massive and features an L-shaped lounge, which can be converted into an outdoor double berth when the weather is right. Sidedecks are practically non-existent. Several engine options (with V-drives) were offered, and most provide cruising speeds from 17–20 knots and top speeds to around 27 knots. ❑

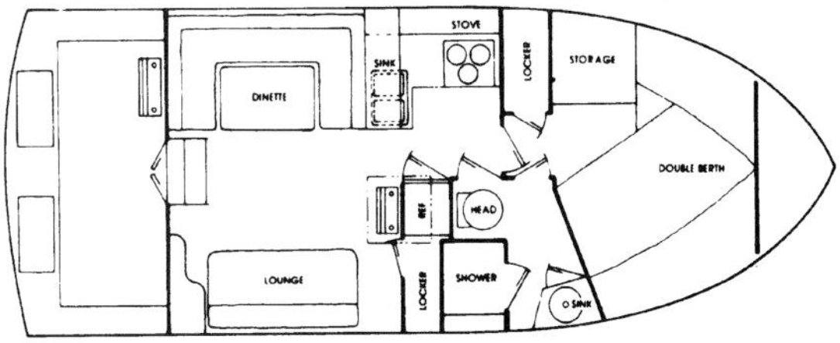

See Page 261 for Pricing Information

CARVER 33 VOYAGER

SPECIFICATIONS

Length	32'9"	Fuel	200 gals.
Beam	12'0"	Cockpit	45 sq. ft.
Draft	2'3"	Hull Type	Modified-V
Weight	13,000#	Deadrise Aft	NA
Clearance	11'9"	Designer	Carver
Water	70 gals.	Production	1977–81

Not a pretty sight with her awkward lines and three-story profile, the Carver 33 Voyager clearly has little to recommend from the standpoint of exterior styling. Her best features are inside, where a large and expansive interior seem all but impossible in just a 33-foot hull. Admittedly, the Voyager's floorplan dimensions aren't notably generous by today's maxi-beam standards. She was, however, one of the earlier boats to use an angled bulkhead in the forward stateroom to permit a double berth rather than conventional V-berths—a now-common design trick. The lower helm was standard; there are berths for six when the dinette is converted; and a separate shower stall is fitted in the head compartment. With so much of the boat's LOA devoted to interior living space, the cockpit is necessarily small. Several engine choices were offered in the Carver 33 Voyager over the years, all with V-drives. The cruising speed with the popular 270-hp Crusader gas engines is 16–17 knots, and the top speed is around 24 knots. ❑

See Page 261 for Pricing Information

CARVER 30/634/340 SANTEGO

SPECIFICATIONS

Length Overall	33'7"	Water	48 gals.
Length w/Platform	30'0"	Fuel	150 gals.
Beam	11'0"	Hull Type	Deep-V
Draft	3'1"	Deadrise Aft	19°
Weight	11,150#	Designer	Carver
Clearance	14'10"	Production	1988–94

Introduced in 1988 as the Carver 30 Santego and called the 634 Santego during 1991–92, this popular family cruiser is easily one of the roomiest boats to be found in this size range. Her heavy-set profile may be inelegant, but the accommodations of the 340 Santego are impressive. Using the full width of the boat's hull (sidedecks are extremely narrow), the salon is completely open with facing settees and excellent headroom. The entire floorplan is on a single level which adds to the impression of size and space. The flybridge is equally large for a 30-footer. Note that a walk-thru bridge (for improved foredeck access) was introduced in 1991 in the 634 model. There's room in the cockpit for a couple of deck chairs, and hatches in the sole provide good access to the motors. Originally designed in 1988, the Santego's bolt-on swim platform is a disappointment in today's market. Available with inboard (V-drive) or stern drive (except for '94) engines, 454-cid V-drives cruise at 22-23 knots, 32 knots top. ❑

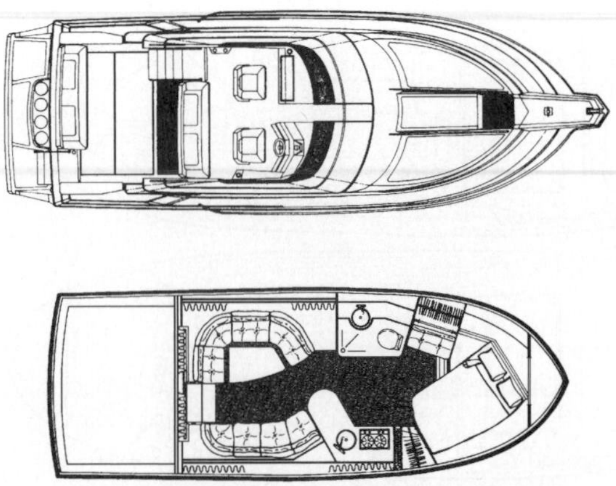

See Page 261 for Pricing Information

CARVER 34/350/370 VOYAGER

34/350 Voyager with Bolt-On Swim Platform

370 Voyager with Integral Swim Platform

SPECIFICATIONS

LOA (34 & 350) ....39'0"	Water ....100 gals.
LOA (370) ....40'1"	Fuel, Std. ....280 gals.
Beam..............................13'3"	Fuel, Opt. ....340 gals.
Draft ....2'7"	Hull Type ....Modified-V
Weight ....17,000#	Deadrise Aft....................11°
Cockpit....................40 sq. ft.	Production 1992–Current

Introduced in 1992 as the 34 Voyager, the 350 Voyager (and the current 370 Voyager introduced in 1993) will appeal to those who appreciate the versatility of a raised pilothouse layout—even a small one. With both galley and dinette on the bridgedeck level, the Voyager still manages to include two private staterooms forward and a comfortable salon in a rather expansive and well-arranged floorplan. The cockpit, on the other hand, is quite small with room for just a couple of deck chairs. Notable features include a huge flybridge with seating for six (including a sun lounge), transom door, stall shower in the head, and a handy pass-thru port from the galley to the bridge. With the optional 340 gal. fuel capacity the Voyager has good range, especially when equipped with diesel engines. Standard 454-cid gas engines will cruise at a comfortable 18–19 knots (about 28 knots top), and optional 210-hp Cummins diesels cruise economically at 18 knots (24 knots top). Note that the 350 Voyager ceased production in 1993. ❑

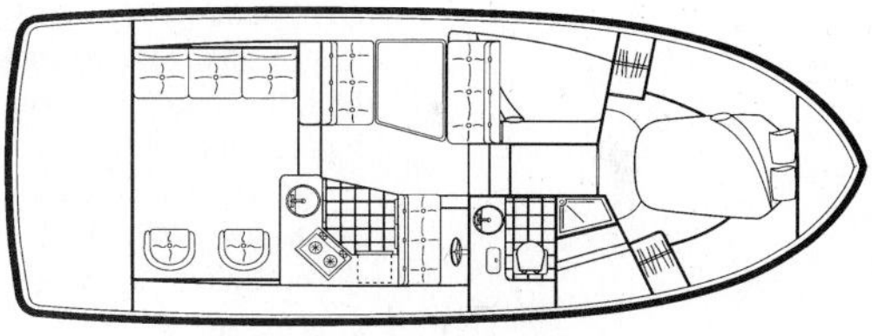

Original 34/350 Floorplan

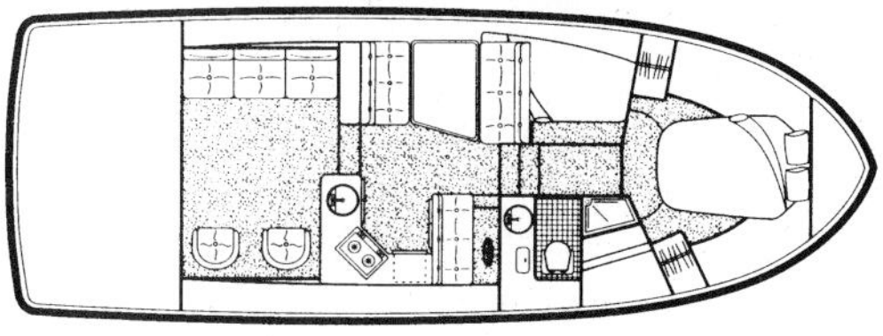

370 Floorplan (1993–94)

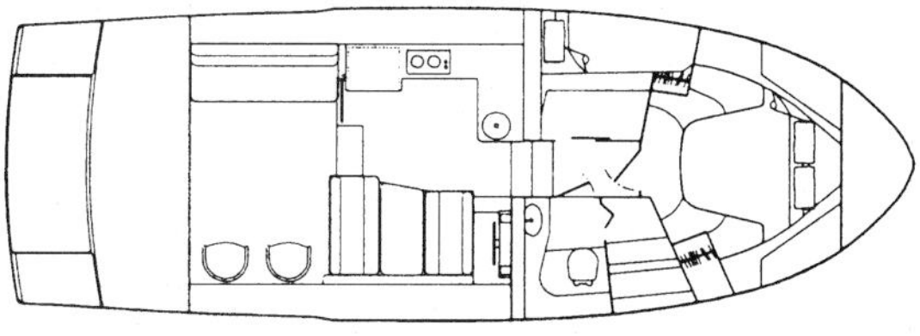

370 Floorplan (1995–Current)

See Page 261 for Pricing Information

CARVER 36 MARINER

SPECIFICATIONS

Length	35'7"	Water	103 gals.
Length WL	31'4"	Fuel	274 gals.
Beam	12'6"	Hull Type	Modified-V
Draft	3'2"	Deadrise Aft	8°
Weight	19,500#	Designer	R. MacNeill
Clearance	13'6"	Production	1984–88

The huge interior of the Carver 36 Mariner comes as a surprise to most first-time observers. Her dockside profile may be a little hard on the eye, but the belowdecks accommodations and huge flybridge are seldom matched in other boats her size. An outstanding design from the standpoint of space engineering, the 36 Mariner was a very successful model for Carver and led to the introduction in 1985 of the smaller and similarly styled 32 Mariner. She was built on the flat-bottom dual mode hull originally used for the Carver 36 Aft Cabin. Inside, her wide open interior is arranged on a single level, down from the cockpit level. Using the full width of the boat's hull, the Mariner's vast interior can handle the demands of a very large family indeed. The performance is not terribly impressive: 15–16 knots at cruise and 25 knots at the top with standard 350-hp gas engines. With both the motors and the fuel tanks located under the cockpit, trim tabs are useful to keep the Mariner's bow down at cruising speeds. ❑

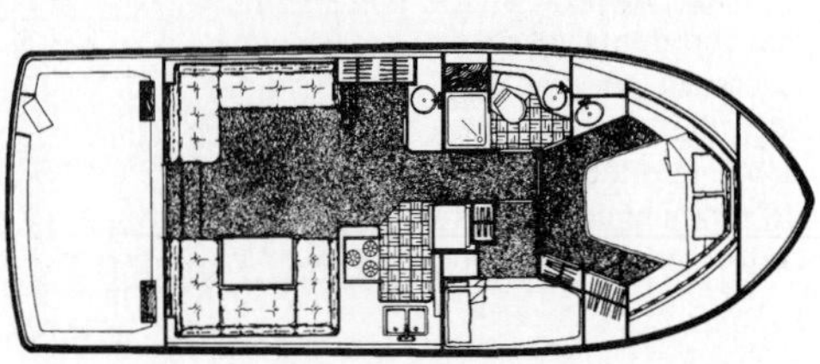

See Page 261 for Pricing Information

CARVER 38 SANTEGO

SPECIFICATIONS

Length	37'6"	Water	92 gals.
Length WL	32'7"	Fuel	265 gals.
Beam	14'0"	Hull Type	Modified-V
Draft	3'5"	Deadrise Aft	12°
Weight	19,000#	Designer	R. MacNeill
Clearance	14'3"	Production	1988–90

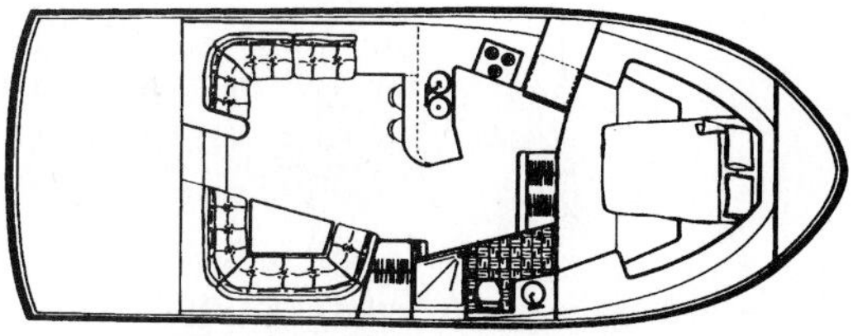

Original Single Stateroom Floorplan

Big brother to the 380 Santego and featuring an almost-identical floorplan, the Carver 38 Santego was one of the early sedan bridge designs that have since become popular with buyers. She was constructed on a moderate-deadrise hull with balsa coring in the hullsides and a solid glass bottom. The Santego is a great boat for entertaining, and she has one of the slickest bridge layouts imaginable. Guest seating surrounds the elevated helm console, and a cutout forward reveals a set of molded steps leading to the foredeck—a real necessity since there are no sidedecks. Below, the Santego's single-level interior uses the full width of the hull to create a cavernous main salon. A two-stateroom floorplan was introduced in 1990 as an alternative to the original single-stateroom layout. The cockpit is roomy enough, but the bolt-on swim platform is a disapointment. For power, the Santego uses 454-cid gas engines (with V-drives) located beneath the cockpit sole. Cruising speed is a lackluster 14-15 knots, and the top speed is around 24 knots. ❑

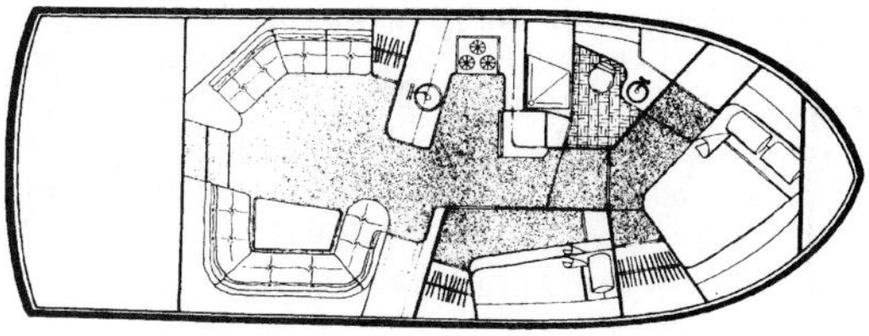

Two-Stateroom Floorplan (1990–94)

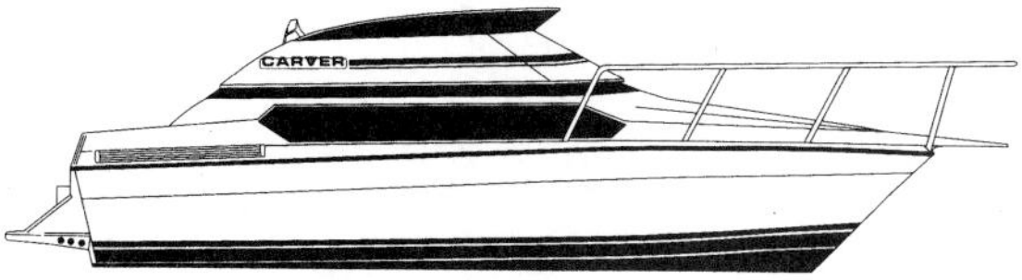

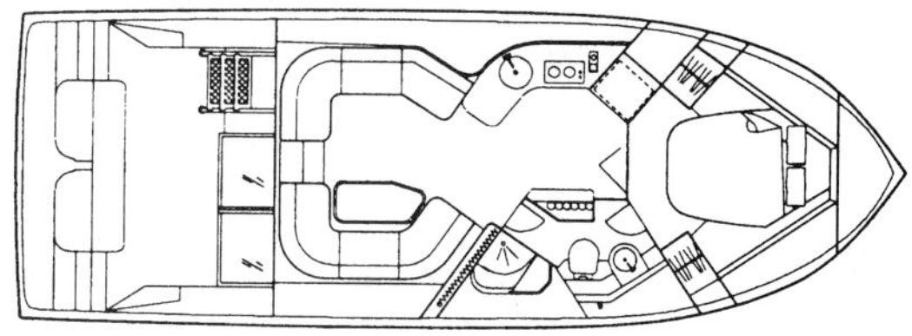

Current Standard Floorplan

See Page 261 for Pricing Information

CARVER 34/638/380 SANTEGO

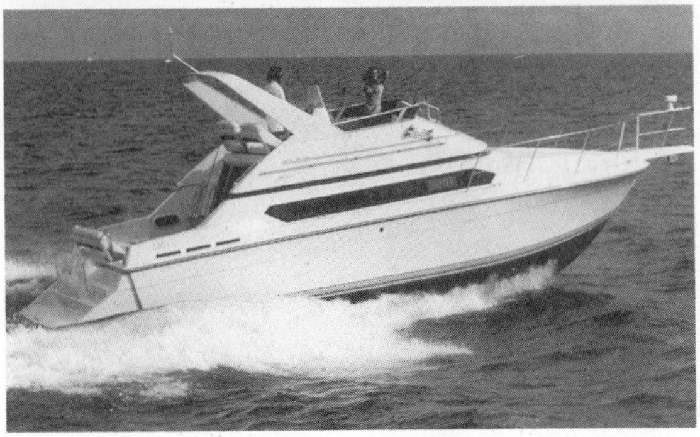

SPECIFICATIONS

Length Overall	41'10"	Water	101 gals.
Hull Length	34'9"	Fuel	200 gals.
Beam	13'2"	Hull Type	Deep-V
Draft	3'4"	Deadrise Aft	19°
Weight	16,000#	Designer	Carver
Clearance	15'0"	Production	1989–Current

Introduced as the 34 Santego in 1989, Carver called this boat the 638 Santego in 1992 and finally settled on the 380 Santego designation in 1993. She's built on the same solid fiberglass deep-V hull used for her sistership, the 35 Montego. While the layouts of these two boats appear similar, the Santego eliminates the Montego's mid-cabin floorplan in favor of a more expansive salon with facing wraparound settees and twin dinettes. Inside and out, the Santego's party-time accommodations are more than just a little impressive in a boat of this size. There's seating for a crowd on the huge flybridge where a walk-thru folds down to reveal a centerline stairway to the foredeck. It's unfortunate that Carver never retooled this design to include an integral (rather than bolt-on) swim platform. Twin hatches in the cockpit sole provide good access to the motors and V-drives. A good-riding boat in a chop, standard 454-cid gas engines will cruise the Santego at 18 knots and reach 26–27 knots wide open.

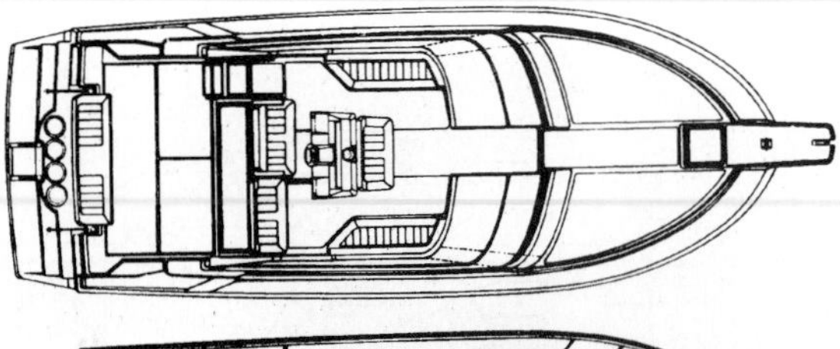

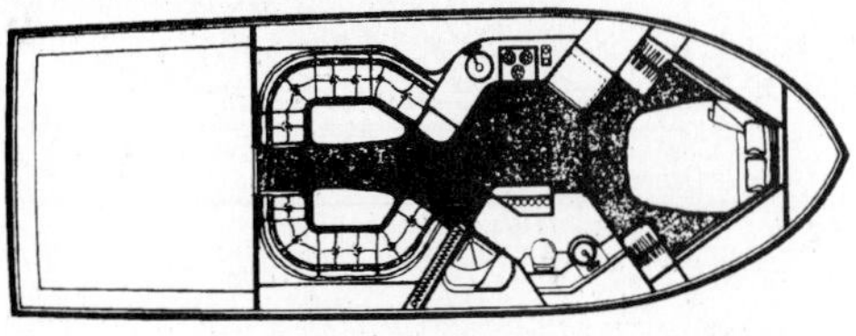

See Page 261 for Pricing Information

CARVER 380 EXPRESS

SPECIFICATIONS

Length	38'5"	Fuel	250 gals.
Beam	13'2"	Cockpit	NA
Draft	3'4"	Hull Type	Deep-V
Weight	16,000#	Deadrise Aft	19°
Clearance	15'11"	Designer	Carver
Water	91 gals.	Production	1990–94

A boat of many names (she was introduced as the Carver 35 Montego in 1990, and during 1991–92 she was the Carver 538 Montego), the 380 Express is a traditional mid-cabin cruiser with a sportboat profile and a roomy interior. Because she's built on a deep-V hull (Carvers are generally built on low-deadrise bottoms), her ride is quite good in a chop. A wide beam combined with a single-level floorplan makes the Montego a roomy boat below. Headroom is good throughout thanks to the raised foredeck, however the small cabin windows result in a somewhat dark interior, and the absence of natural lighting is immediately apparant. Outside, the cockpit is arranged with L-shaped guest seating opposite the helm and includes a wet bar and bench seating at the transom. The Montego's downside is her bolt-on swim platform—an effort at modernizing her plain-Jane looks. A good-running boat, 454-cid gas inboards with V-drives will cruise at 16–17 knots and reach a top speed of around 25 knots. ❑

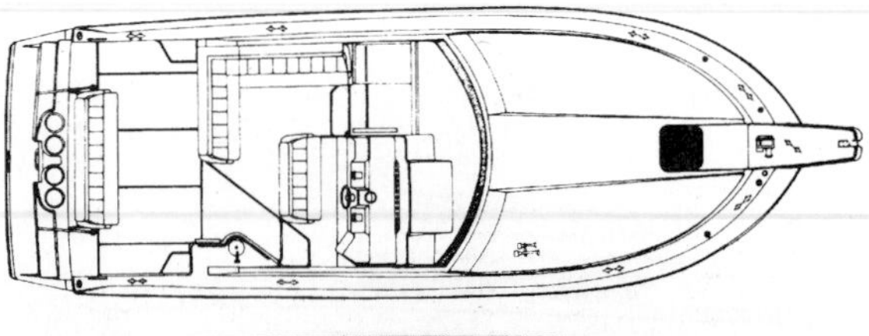

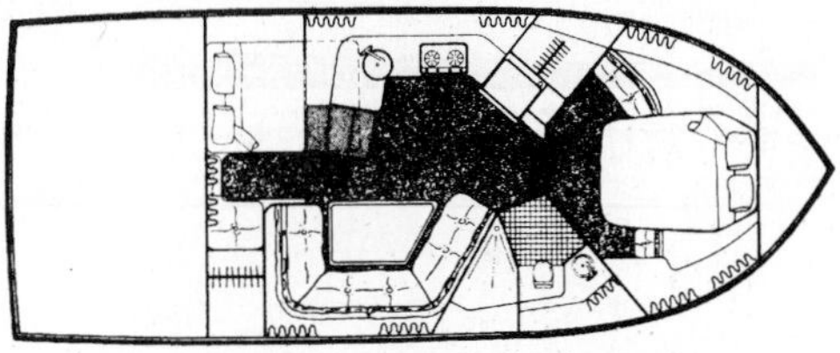

See Page 261 for Pricing Information

CELEBRITY 245/265 SPORT CRUISER

SPECIFICATIONS

Length w/Pulpit .... 26'5"	Fuel .... 80 gals.
Hull Length .... 24'2"	Water .... 35 gals.
Beam .... 8'6"	Clearance .... 6'3"
Draft, Up .... 1'7"	Hull Type .... Modified-V
Draft, Down .... 3'0"	Deadrise Aft .... 18°
Weight .... 5,700#	Production 1992–Current

The Celebrity 265 Sport Cruiser is a maxi-cube trailerable cruiser with an affordable price and practical accommodations. (Note that she was called the 245 Sport Cruiser in 1993.) Built on a solid fiberglass hull, the Sport Cruiser weighs in at a hefty 5,700 lbs. and, with a trailer, her towing weight approaches 7,000 lbs. With her chunky appearance, she's not the most graceful boat on the water, but she does have a couple of features that will appeal to perspective buyers. The companionway, for example, is on the centerline which makes entering the cabin a lot easier than negotiating the circular steps of a port-side entry. Too, most of the Sport Cruiser's hull length is devoted to a big cockpit which is great for enjoying the outdoors. On the downside, the cabin is quite small. Additional features include a windshield walk-thru for bow access, three opening ports in the aft cabin, a molded pulpit and near-standing headroom below. A competent performer, a single 245-hp 5.7-litre Volvo I/O will cruise the Celebrity 265 at about 20 knots with a top speed of around 30 knots. ❑

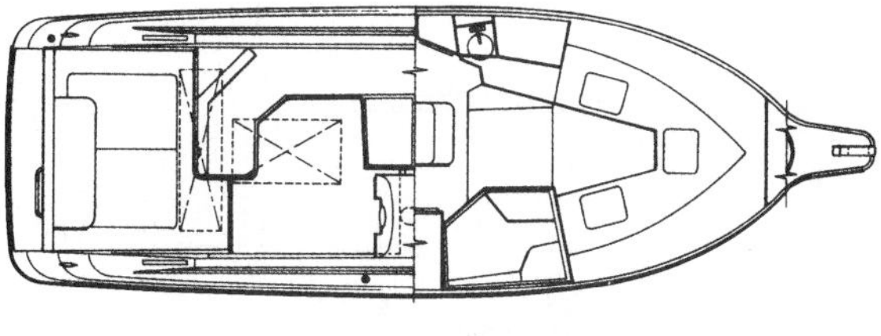

See Page 262 for Pricing Information

CELEBRITY 26 CROWNLINE 268/270 SPORT CRUISER

SPECIFICATIONS

Length w/Pulpit .... 29'7"	Fuel .... 118 gals.
Hull Length .... 26'8"	Water .... 17 gals.
Beam .... 9'9"	Clearance .... 7'6"
Draft, Up .... 2'2"	Hull Type .... Modified-V
Draft, Down .... 3'0"	Deadrise Aft .... 18°
Weight .... 8,500#	Production 1987–91

Introduced in 1987 as the 26 Crownline, Celebrity called this model the 268 Sport Cruiser in 1989 and the 270 Sport Cruiser in 1990–91. While her styling is dated by current standards, she was a popular boat for Celebrity and enjoyed a long production run before being replaced in 1992. She rides on a solid fiberglass hull with high freeboard and a relatively sharp 18 degrees of transom deadrise. Note the droop-nose profile and dramatic hull graphics. The mid-cabin interior is arranged with double berths fore and aft and a pull-out settee which can sleep two adults. Privacy curtains separate the sleeping areas from the salon, and headroom in the galley and head compartment is about 6 feet. Storage is provided by an assortment of drawers, bins, and cabinets located throughout the main cabin. There's plenty of seating outside including a double-wide helm seat and two folding bench seats in the aft part of the cockpit. A transom door and teak swim platform were standard. A good-running boat, optional twin 260-hp MerCruiser stern drives will cruise at 25 knots and reach a top speed of around 40 knots. ❑

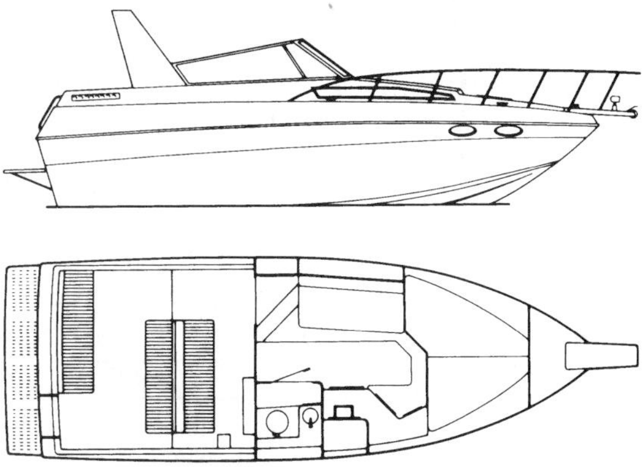

See Page 262 for Pricing Information

CELEBRITY 285/290/310 SPORT CRUISER

SPECIFICATIONS

Length w/Pulpit	31'0"	Clearance	9'0"
Hull Length	28'5"	Water	22 gals.
Beam	10'4"	Fuel	137 gals.
Draft, Up	2'5"	Hull Type	Modified-V
Draft, Down	3'3"	Deadrise Aft	18°
Weight	8,800#	Production	1989–Current

Introduced in 1989 as the 285 Sport Cruiser, Celebrity engineers completely reworked the boat in 1990 with a new deckhouse and interior as well as a new redesigned bottom — the 285 obviously had some shortcomings that needed fixing. Now called the 290 Sport Cruiser and sporting a much-improved profile, she lasted for four years (1990–93) until she was again updated in 1994 with a new integral swim platform replacing the bolt-on platform of the 290. Today she's called the 310 Sport Cruiser — a fairly conventional express cruiser with a mid-cabin floorplan and a stylish profile. Hull construction is solid fiberglass and her 10-foot, 4-inch beam is about average for a 30-footer. The 290/310 floorplan has remained essentially unchanged over the years aside from decor and hardware upgrades. Both staterooms can be separated from the main cabin with privacy curtains and headroom is better than 6 feet. Outside, there's seating for six in the bi-level cockpit. Note that the side decks are narrow on this boat and foredeck access is not easy. Twin 350-cid MerCruiser stern drives will cruise the Celebrity 290/310 at 22–23 knots and reach a top speed of 37+ knots. ❑

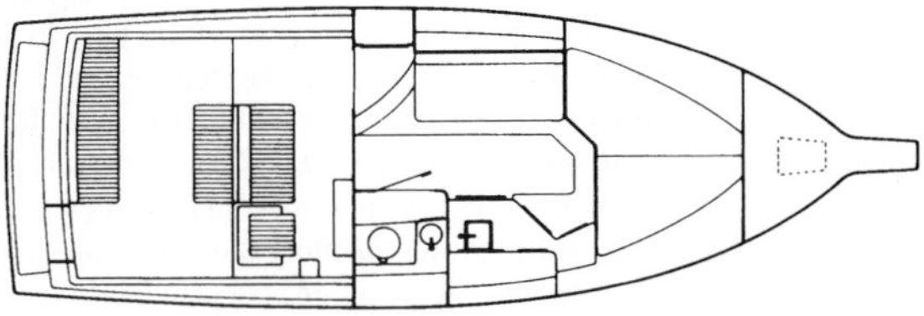

285 Floorplan

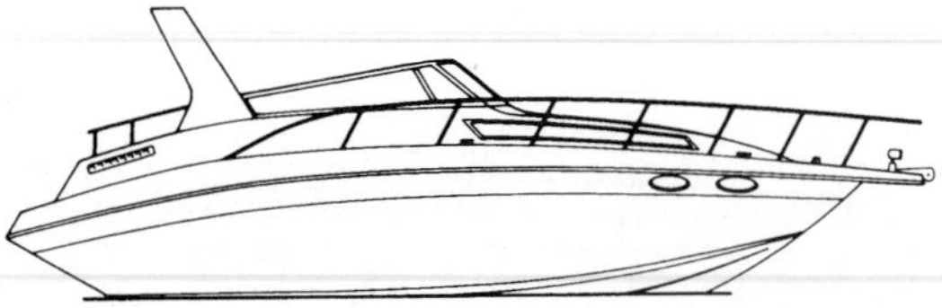

285 Profile

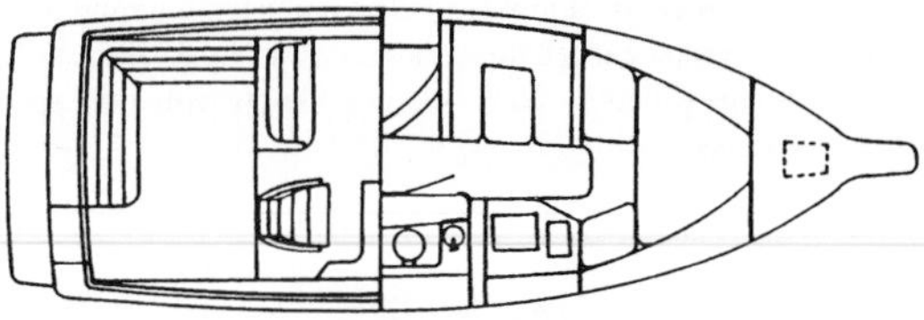

290 Floorplan

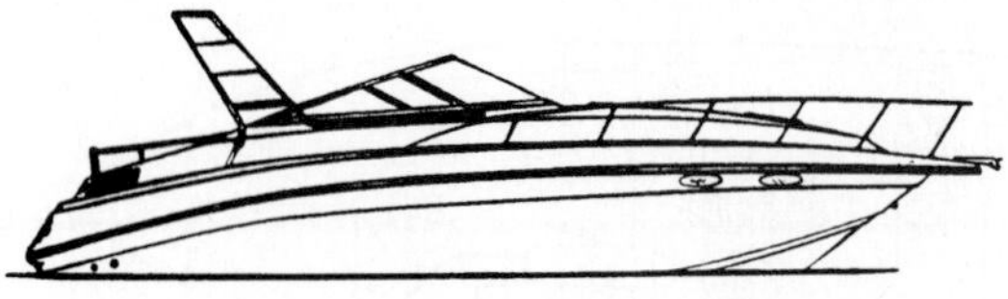

290/310 Profile

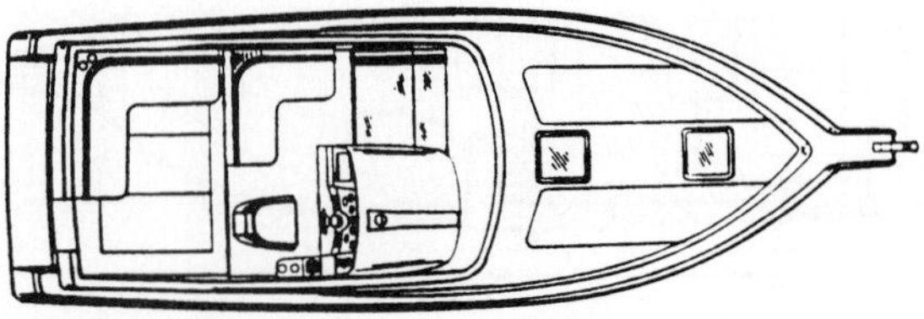

310 Floorplan

See Page 262 for Pricing Information

CHAPARRAL SIGNATURE 26/27

SPECIFICATIONS

Length w/Pulpit..........28'5"	Clearance.......................9'8"
Hull Length..................26'2"	Water........................25 gals.
Beam................................9'0"	Fuel.........................105 gals.
Draft, Up.........................2'1"	Hull Type...............Deep-V
Draft, Down...................2'9"	Deadrise Aft...................20°
Weight......................6,120#	Production.......1992–Current

Called the Chaparral Signature 26 when she was introduced in 1992, the Signature 27 pictured above is the second Chaparral product to carry this model designation. (The original 1988–1991 Signature 27 was trailerable and came with a narrower beam.) Featuring good-quality materials and traditional construction, the Signature 27 is priced slightly above the average for sport cruisers her size. An elevated foredeck provides marginal headroom below but at the expense of a somewhat topheavy exterior appearance. Set up to sleep four, the straightforward layout is arranged with a circular dinette/V berth forward, a compact galley and head, and a snug mid-cabin stateroom aft. The fabrics, hardware, appliances, and furnishings are first-rate throughout. Outside, an L-shaped lounge is opposite the helm, and a hideaway bench seat is fitted at the transom. With no windshield opening and narrow sidedecks, foredeck access is difficult. Among several single and twin stern drive engine options, a single 300-hp 7.4-litre MerCruiser will cruise the Signature 27 at 22 knots and reach about 32 knots top. ❑

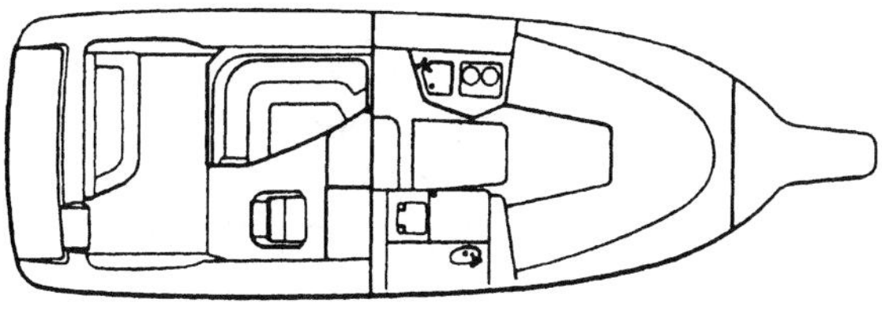

See Page 262 for Pricing Information

CHAPARRAL SIGNATURE 28/29

SPECIFICATIONS

Length w/Pulpit........31'11"	Clearance.........................9'4"
Hull Length...................29'3"	Water.........................30 gals.
Beam...............................9'9"	Fuel..........................121 gals.
Draft, Up.......................1'11"	Hull Type.................Deep-V
Draft, Down....................2'9"	Deadrise Aft....................20°
Weight.......................7,200#	Production........1991–Current

The Signature 29 (originally called the Chaparral Signature 28) is a classy sport cruiser with a practical layout to go with her affordable price tag. She's built in Georgia on a rugged deep-V hull with cored hullsides and moderate beam. Her modern styling is accented with a molded bow pulpit and an integrated swim platform, but like most mid-cabin cruisers under 30 feet with standing cabin headroom, her raised foredeck results in a slightly topheavy profile. Inside, the floorplan is a departure from the usual mid-cabin configuration. Chaparral designers have included a circular dinette/settee on the centerline, just aft of the V berths. The mid-cabin includes a stand-up entryway and a privacy door rather than just a curtain. The bi-level cockpit is arranged with an L-shaped lounge opposite the helm and (fold-away) bench seating at the transom. A single 7.4-litre stern drive will cruise the Chaparral 29 around 19–20 knots (32 top), and twin 5.0-litre small blocks will cruise at 23–24 knots and reach a top speed of around 38 knots. ❑

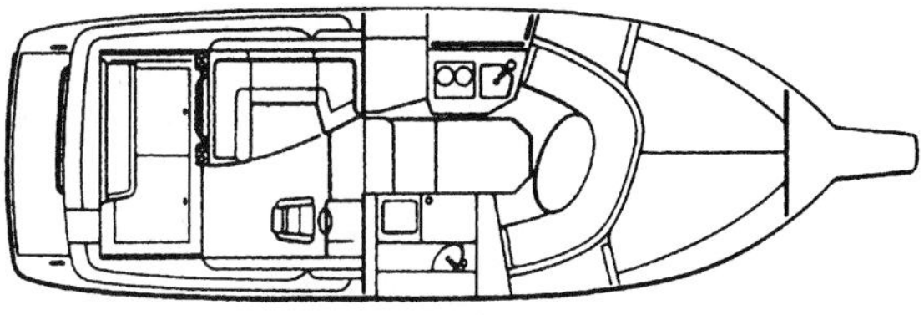

See Page 262 for Pricing Information

CHAPARRAL SIGNATURE 30/31

SPECIFICATIONS

Length w/Pulpit..........33'2"	Clearance........................9'4"
Hull Length..................30'6"	Water........................40 gals.
Beam..............................10'9"	Fuel.........................150 gals.
Draft, Up........................1'11"	Hull Type.........Modified-V
Draft, Down...................2'9"	Deadrise Aft....................17°
Weight........................9,750#	Production....1990–Current

Chaparral has a reputation for quality products and the Signature 31 (originally called the Chaparral Signature 30) is one of the more sophisticated express cruisers in her size range. This is a well-styled sportboat with a molded bow pulpit, flowing lines, modest hull graphics, and a fashionable integrated swim platform. Her mid-cabin interior is finished with upscale fabrics and furnishings throughout, and the detailing is above average. Both sleeping areas are fitted with privacy curtains, and the large dinette converts to sleep two adults. Outside, the cockpit is flush from the transom forward—rare in a mid-cabin cruiser. The L-shaped lounge opposite the helm converts (with the aid of an insert) into a sunpad, and the bench seat at the transom folds away into the transom bulkhead when not in use. The helm console was redesigned in 1993 (among a few other upgrades). A good performer, twin 230-hp MerCruiser (or 250-hp Volvo) stern drives will cruise the Signature 31 at 19–20 knots and reach about 33 knots wide open. ❑

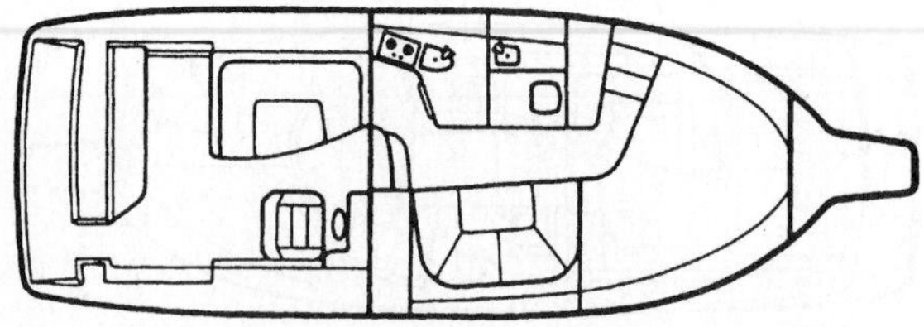

See Page 262 for Pricing Information

CHAPARRAL LASER 32

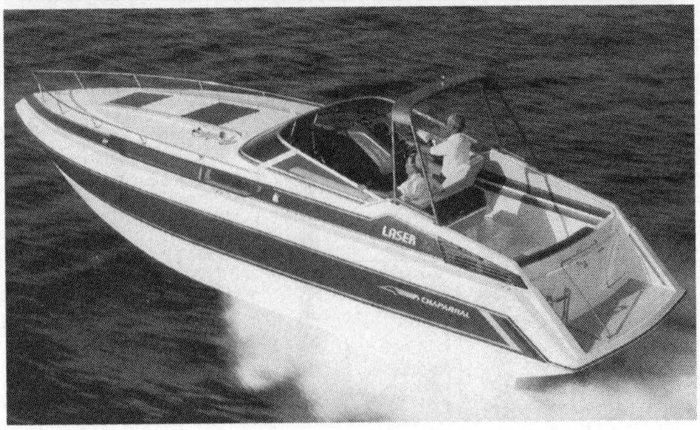

SPECIFICATIONS

Length...........................32'2"	Water........................34 gals.
Beam..............................10'8"	Fuel.........................218 gals.
Draft...............................3'6"	Hull Type.........Modified-V
Weight......................10,500#	Deadrise Aft....................12°
Clearance........................8'9"	Designer...........J. Opperude
Cockpit............................NA	Production.............1988–91

The first wide-beam cruiser for Chapparal (all of their previous models had been trailerable), the Laser 32 is a high-performance mid-cabin express with a curved windshield and stylish integrated swim platform to complement her colorful sportboat profile. (Note the absence of a bow pulpit—a design touch growing in popularity in recent years.) Heavily constructed on a fully cored hull with a modest 12 degrees of transom deadrise, the Laser is quick to accelerate but a hard ride in a chop. The interior is arranged with double berths fore and aft (each sleeping area has a privacy curtain) and a well-appointed salon with a convertible dinette and facing settee. The galley is compact and so is the mid-cabin, but the head is big enough for a shower. Outside, an L-shaped lounge is across from the helm and additional guest seating is provided at the transom. A good-running boat, twin 260-hp stern drives will cruise the Laser 32 at a fast 28 knots and reach a top speed of 40+ knots. ❑

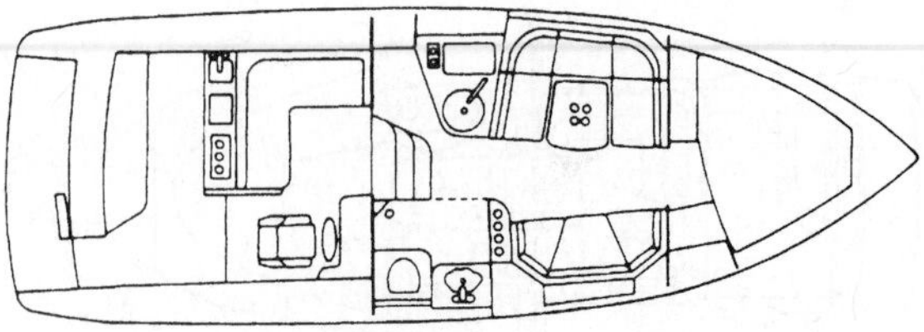

See Page 262 for Pricing Information

CHRIS CRAFT 25 CATALINA

SPECIFICATIONS

Length	25'4"
Beam	9'9"
Draft	2'3"
Weight	4,600#
Clearance	7'6"
Water	10 gals.
Fuel	50/75 gals.
Cockpit	NA
Hull Type	Modified-V
Deadrise Aft	15°
Designer	Chris Craft
Production	1974–86

The Chris 25 Catalina Express is surely one of the most popular and durable small family cruisers ever produced. She was built on a solid fiberglass hull, and her nearly 10-foot beam gives the 25 a good deal of interior volume for such a small boat. The cabin accommodations include V-berths forward, a compact galley, stand-up head with sink, convertible dinette and ample storage lockers and bins—an efficient layout for a boat of this size and a big reason for the Catalina's success over the years. Outside, the cockpit is large enough for light-tackle fishing or a few deck chairs, and removable hatches in the cockpit sole provide good engine access. Visibility from the helm is excellent, and the sidedecks are wide enough to get safely forward. Nearly all of the 25 Catalinas were fitted with a single 225/230-hp gas engine. A rugged little boat, the cruising speed is 17–18 knots, and the top speed is 25 knots. Note that models previous to 1980 carried only 50 gallons of fuel. ❑

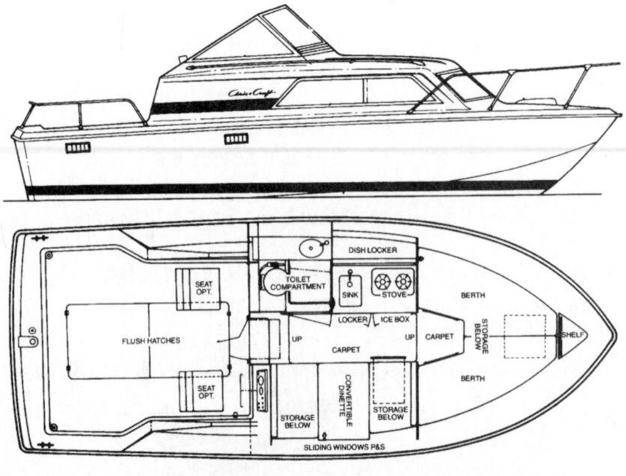

See Page 262 for Pricing Information

CHRIS CRAFT 262 AMEROSPORT

SPECIFICATIONS

Length w/Platform	30'4"
Hull Length	26'0"
Beam	9'6"
Draft, Up	2'3"
Draft, Down	3'7"
Weight	6,400#
Water	25 gals.
Fuel	100 gals.
Hull Type	Deep-V
Deadrise Aft	NA
Designer	Chris Craft
Production	1988–90

The good news about the 262 Amerosport is that she's a good-looking boat with a modern profile. (She was in fact the first Amerosport to have an integral swim platform when she came out in 1988—a small distinction perhaps, but we'll note it for the record anyway.) Here's the bad news: Amerosports were pretty cheap boats with below-average quality. Indeed, Chris Craft had to recall a number of early 262s when owners began reporting problems with hull cracking. The interior is roomy enough, and the mid-cabin layout is well-arranged and efficient, etc., but the fabrics, hardware and fixtures did not compare well with the more upscale competition. There are berths for six (with the dinette converted), a small galley with under-counter refrigeration, and a stand-up head with shower. Outside, the cockpit is arranged with a double-wide seat at the helm and bench seating aft. Note the tubular radar arch. A single 275-hp Volvo stern drive will cruise the 262 Amerosport at 18–19 knots and reach around 28 knots top. ❑

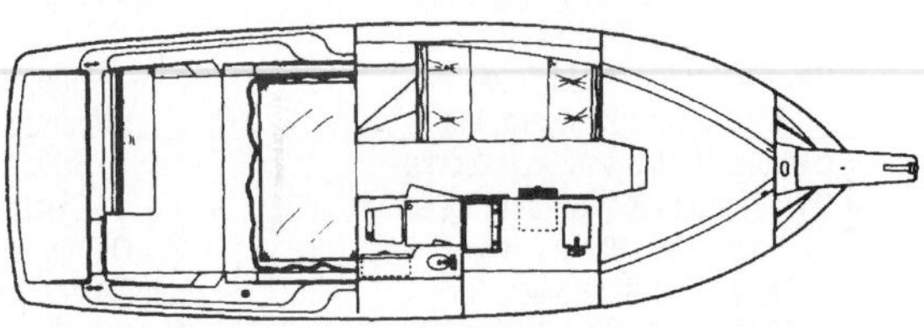

See Page 262 for Pricing Information

CHRIS CRAFT 262/26 CROWNE

SPECIFICATIONS

Length ....25'7"	Water ....20 gals.
Beam ....8'6"	Clearance ....NA
Draft, Up ....1'10"	Hull Type ....Modified-V
Draft, Down ....3'2"	Deadrise Aft ....15°
Weight ....5,100#	Designer ....Chris Craft
Fuel ....54 gals.	Production 1993–Current

With her rounded corners and sculptured profile, the Chris Craft 26 Crowne (note that she was called the 262 Crowne in 1993–94) is a bold entry into the small trailerable cruiser market. Indeed, those looking for something different from the traditional mid-cabin cruiser will find the Crowne's futuristic look to be a departure from the norm. She's built on a solid fiberglass hull with moderate transom deadrise (most other cruisers her size have deep-V hulls) and high freeboard. The interior is arranged with a dinette/V-berth forward and a small aft cabin with sitting headroom and a large opening port. A compact galley is opposite the enclosed head which has standing headroom and a shower. Outside, cockpit seating consists of a side-facing lounge opposite the elevated helm and a semi-circular lounge with a removable cocktail table in the starboard corner. Additional features include a handsome instrument panel, good access to the engine beneath the cockpit sole, and a very wide swim platform. The standard 5.8-litre OMC stern drive will cruise the 26 Crowne at 18 knots (about 30 knots top). ❑

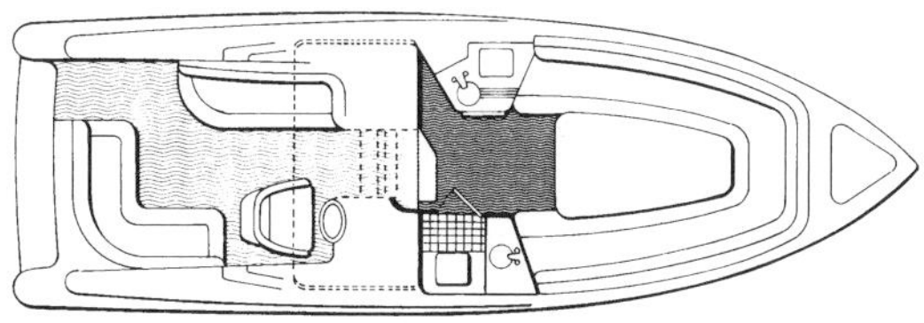

See Page 262 for Pricing Information

CHRIS CRAFT 258/268/27 CONCEPT

SPECIFICATIONS

Length ....27'0"	Fuel ....80/97 gals.
Beam ....9'0"	Hull Type ....Deep-V
Draft ....3'0"	Deadrise Aft ....20°
Weight ....5,000#	Designer ....Chris Craft
Water ....20 gals.	Production 1992–Current

The Chris 258/268/27 Concept Cruiser is best described as part cruiser and part performance boat. (She was called the 258 Concept when she was introduced in 1992 and became the 27 Concept in 1995.) A good-looking little cruiser with sleek sport-boat lines, the Concept is built on a deep-V hull with modest beam and a relatively steep 20 degrees of deadrise at the transom. She's a stand-out performer capable of going fast through some rough water. Since the aim of the Concept is outdoor entertainment, most of her length is devoted to an expansive cockpit layout with wraparound lounge seating for a crowd (the seat bottom pulls out to form a sun-pad). A hideaway ladder folds down over the companionway door and allows access through the windshield to the foredeck—very resourceful. Below, her compact cabin features a stand-up head and a convertible dinette. A single 310-hp stern drive will cruise the Concept at 22 knots (36 top) and optional twin 5.0-litre stern drives will cruise at a fast 29 knots (40+ knots top). Note that the fuel was increased to 97 gallons in 1995. ❑

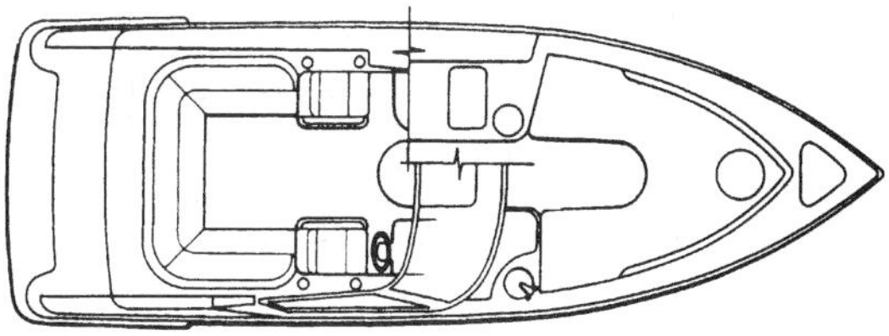

See Page 262 for Pricing Information

CHRIS CRAFT 28 CATALINA

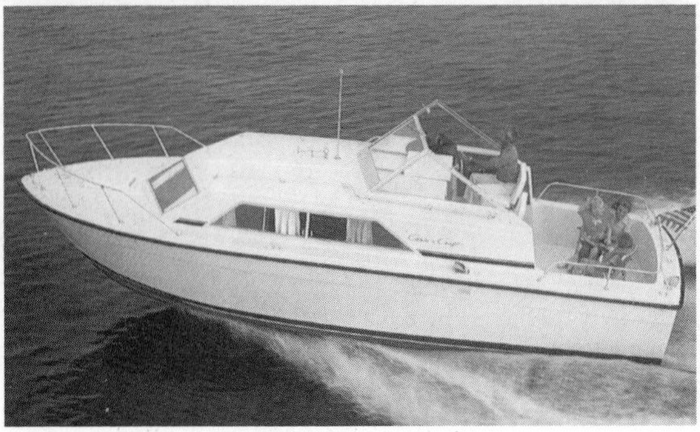

SPECIFICATIONS

Length	28'11"	Water	25 gals.
LWL	24'5"	Fuel	100/125 gals.
Beam	10'9"	Cockpit	65 sq. ft.
Draft	2'5"	Hull Type	Modified-V
Weight	7,000#	Deadrise Aft	15°
Clearance	8'6"	Production	1978–85

The 28 Catalina (along with her sistership, the 25 Catalina) formed the backbone of Chris Craft's presence in the small family cruiser market for many years. Sharing a similar profile and hull design with the smaller 25-foot Catalina, the Chris 28 Catalina has a larger interior with overnight accommodations for six. Primarily designed as a weekend cruiser, the cockpit area can easily be used for casual fishing as well as swimming or diving activities. The hull of the 28 Catalina—a modified-V form with moderate beam and a substantial 15 degrees of deadrise aft—is notable for its dry and comfortable ride. (The 280 model has a single engine, and the 281 has twins.) Performance with a single 230-hp gas motor is 17–18 knots at cruise and 25 knots wide open. With twin engines, speeds increase to around 21 knots at cruise and 30 knots top. Twin engine models carry 125 gallons of fuel; single engine models carry 100 gallons. Note that the Chris Craft 291 Catalina is basically the same boat with a flybridge. ❑

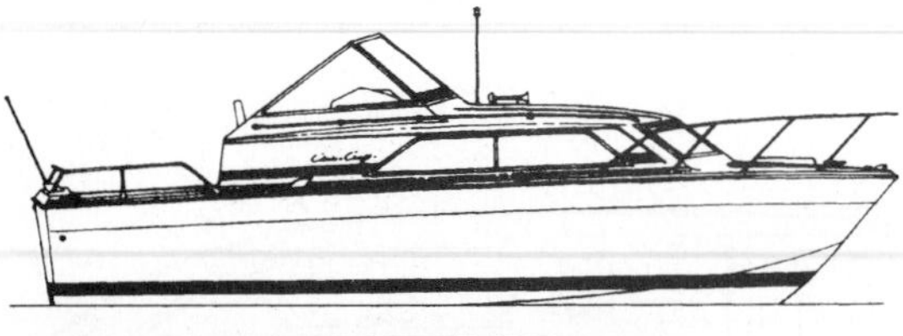

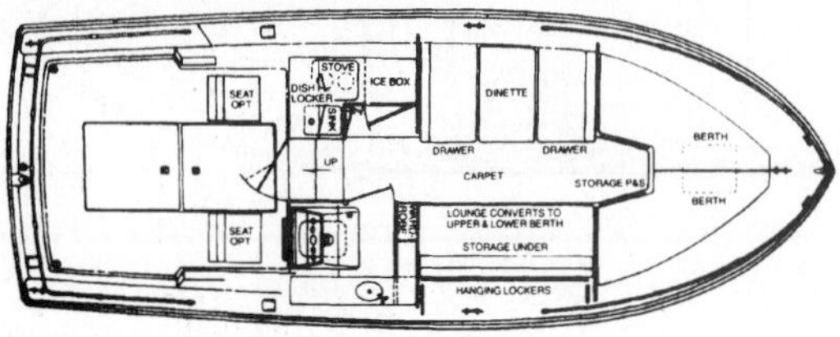

See Page 262 for Pricing Information

CHRIS CRAFT 284 AMEROSPORT

SPECIFICATIONS

Length w/Pulpit	31'3"	Water	25 gals.
Hull Length	27'9"	Fuel	150 gals.
Beam	10'2"	Hull Type	Deep-V
Draft	2'9"	Deadrise Aft	NA
Weight	8,214#	Designer	Chris Craft
Clearance	9'0"	Production	1987–90

Introduced in 1987 when Eurostyle express cruiser sales were really beginning to heat up, the Chris 284 Amerosports's bolt-on swim platform and unattractive hull graphics did little to distinguish her from the more upscale sportboat competition. Hull construction is solid fiberglass, and a fairly wide beam gives the 284 a spacious interior for her size. The mid-cabin floorplan is arranged in the conventional manner with berths for six. Like other Amerosport models of her era, the interior fixtures, hardware and decor items are below average in quality. With the companionway offset to port, guest seating in the forward part of the cockpit is limited to the double-wide helm seat—a not-uncommon arrangement in express boats this size. A tubular radar arch became optional in 1989, and in 1990 (her last year of production) the "SE" model had a traditional swim platform rather than the bolt-on appendage of earlier models. A good-running boat, twin Volvo 271-hp Duoprop I/Os will cruise the 284 Amerosport at a fast 27 knots and deliver 40 knots wide open. ❑

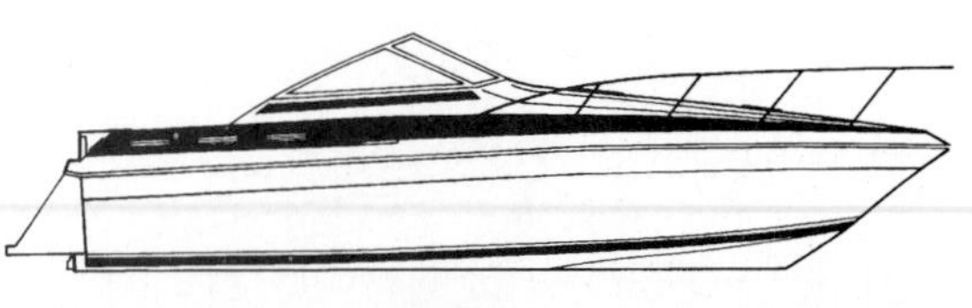

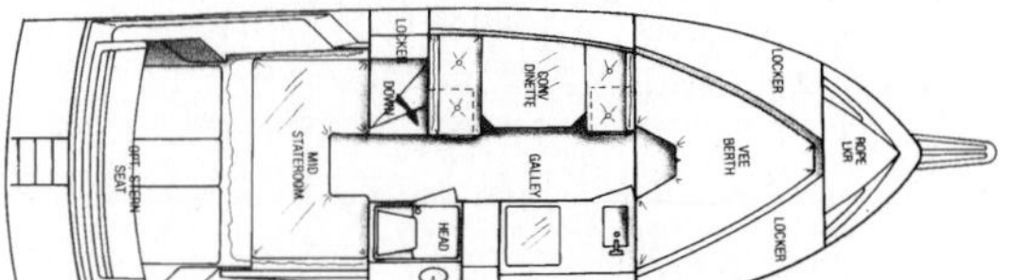

See Page 262 for Pricing Information

CHRIS CRAFT 292 SUNBRIDGE

SPECIFICATIONS

Length	28'11"	Water	25 gals.
Beam	10'9"	Fuel	125 gals.
Draft	2'3"	Hull Type	Modified-V
Weight	7,800#	Designer	Chris Craft
Clearance	9'4"	Production	1986–89

Introduced as a replacement for the aging 28 Catalina—and built on the 28 Catalina's hull—the 292 Sunbridge is a versatile family boat with an attractive profile and an unusual amount of room for a 29-foot cruiser. The hull is solid fiberglass, and her wide beam results in a very roomy interior. Note that the deckhouse is set well forward to allow space aft for a large cockpit. The single-level floorplan is almost the same as the older 28 Catalina with berths for six and good headroom throughout. The (very) small galley will handle most basic food-prep necessities, and the stand-up head is equipped with a shower. Topside, the flybridge has seating for the helmsman and up to four guests. Lift-out hatches in the cockpit sole provide good access to the twin 220-hp Crusader gas engines. An efficient performer, the Chris 292 Sunbridge will cruise easily at 19 knots at just 17 gph—excellent economy indeed. The top speed is about 28–29 knots depending upon the load. ❑

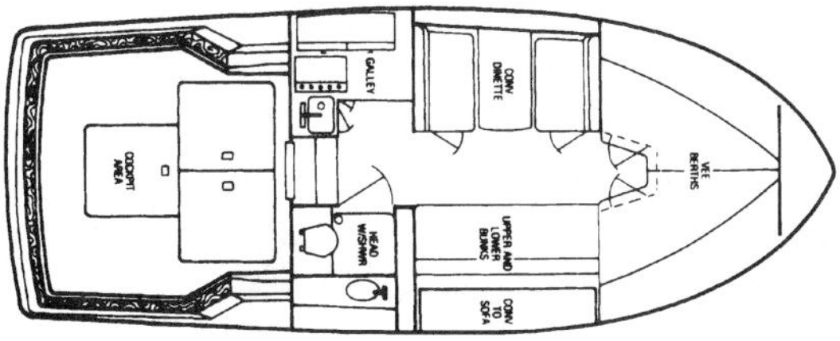

See Page 262 for Pricing Information

CHRIS CRAFT 302/30 CROWNE

SPECIFICATIONS

Length w/Pulpit	31'6"	Clearance	9'6"
Hull Length	29'5"	Water	25 gals.
Beam	10'0"	Fuel	100 gals.
Draft, Up	1'10"	Hull Type	Modified-V
Draft, Down	3'2"	Deadrise Aft	16°
Weight	8,400#	Production	1991–Current

The introduction of the Crowne series in 1991 was an effort by Chris Craft to resurrect the company's declining family cruiser sales. A distinctive boat, the 302 Crowne (she became the 30 Crowne in 1995) owes her good looks to a molded bow pulpit, a curved wraparound windshield, circular foredeck hatches, and an integral swim platform. The original mid-cabin floorplan (with an offset double berth forward) was completely revised in 1992. The companionway stairs are a series of welded steps that create a more open and very futuristic look. The galley and head are small, and the dinette table can be interchanged with two small cockpit tables. Outside, the sports car-style helm console is unique. The U-shaped cockpit lounge can seat six. A wet bar is standard, and fender racks are built into the swim platform. Additional features include decent sidedecks, radar arch, and a molded bow pulpit. Twin 351-cid stern drives will cruise the Crowne at 17 knots (33–34 knots top) and optional 454-cid I/Os will cruise at 20 knots and top out around 40 knots. ❑

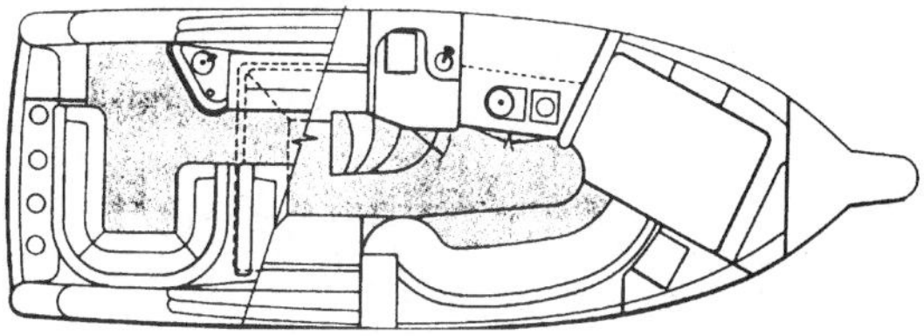

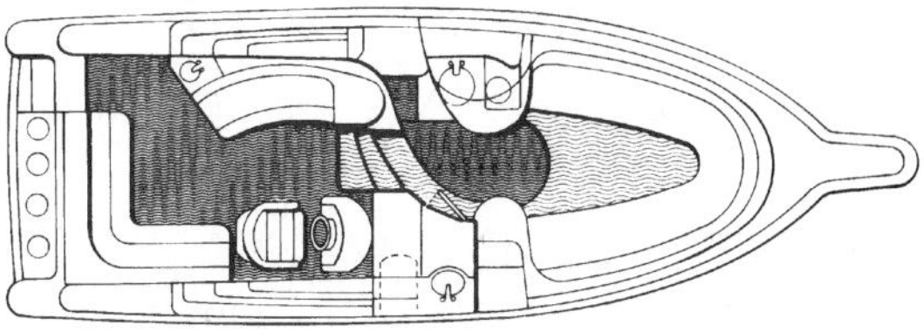

See Page 262 for Pricing Information

CHRIS CRAFT 310 CATALINA

SPECIFICATIONS

Length	30'10"	Fuel	150 gals.
Beam	11'9"	Cockpit	90 sq. ft.
Draft	2'3"	Hull Type	Modified-V
Weight	11,704#	Deadrise Aft	5°
Clearance	NA	Designer	Chris Craft
Water	35 gals.	Production	1979–81

For a boat that remained in production for only three years, there seem to be a lot of 310 Catalinas spread around the nation's marinas. Key to her popularity among owners is space—not only is the cockpit large enough for fishing, but the interior is surprisingly open for a 31-footer. The spacious accommodations of the Catalina are the result of moving the deckhouse well forward and trading the convenience of a foredeck for the benefits of more interior space. The lines suffer a little, but the versatile layout of the Catalina can't be denied. Inside, the lack of a bulkhead separating the V-berth from the main cabin adds to the impression of volume. Visibility from the semi-enclosed lower helm is good, and both seats fold away for access to the engines. The flybridge is small with limited guest seating. A hard ride in a chop, twin 250-hp gas engines deliver a cruising speed of around 20 knots and a top speed of 26–27 knots. With just 150 gallons of fuel, range is limited. ❑

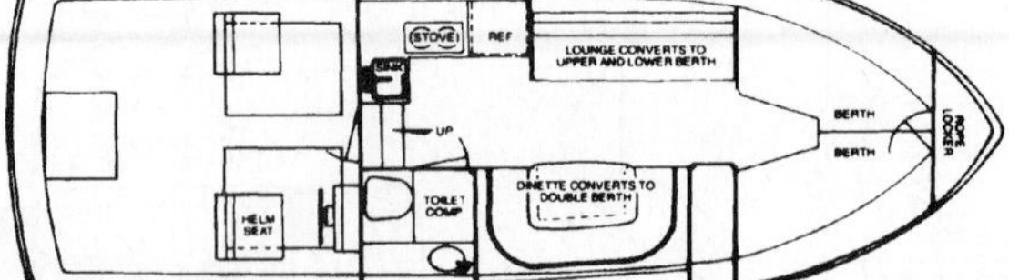

See Page 262 for Pricing Information

CHRIS 320/322 AMEROSPORT EXPRESS

SPECIFICATIONS

Length w/Pulpit..........34'7"	Water........................50 gals.
Hull Length................31'11"	Fuel.........................200 gals.
Beam............................11'11"	Hull Type ....Deep-V
Draft ....2'7"	Deadrise Aft..................NA
Weight.....................12,000#	Designer ....S. Leonard
Clearance ....10'9"	Production 1987–90

The Chris Craft 320 Amerosport Express (called the 322 Amerosport in 1989 and the 320 EC in 1990) is a straightforward family cruiser with a traditional sportboat profile and a spacious interior. Hull construction is solid fiberglass, and her beam is wide for a 32-footer. Surprisingly, the 320/322 Amerosport lacks the mid-cabin floorplan seen in most other express cruisers her size. The galley and head are aft (where they're easily accessed from the cockpit), and a curtain provides privacy in the stateroom. Outside, the single-level cockpit is arranged with elevated helm and companion seats with bench seating at the transom. A centerline hatch in the cockpit sole provides good access to the motors, and molded cockpit steps port and starboard make boarding easy. Note the unattractive bolt-on reverse swim platform. A radar arch and bow pulpit were standard. Standard 270-hp Crusader inboard gas engines (without the V-drives required in mid-cabin designs) will cruise the 320/322 Express at 19 knots (29–30 knots top). Optional 350-hp Crusaders will cruise at 22 knots and reach 33–34 knots wide open. ❑

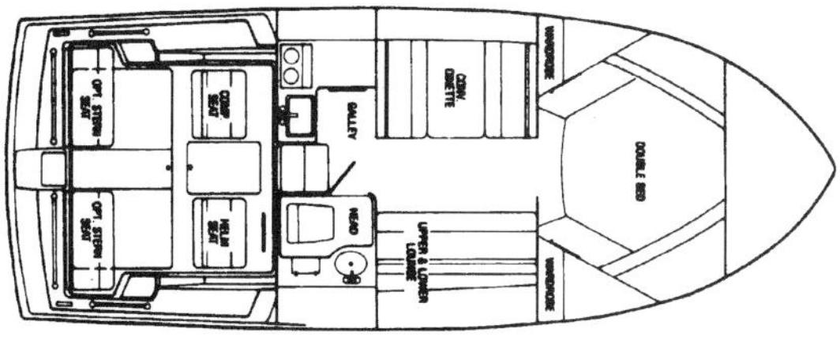

See Page 262 for Pricing Information

CHRIS 320 AMEROSPORT SEDAN

SPECIFICATIONS

Length ....31'11"	Water........................50 gals.
Beam............................11'11"	Fuel.........................200 gals.
Draft ....2'8"	Hull Type ....Modified-V
Weight.....................12,000#	Deadrise Aft..................NA
Clearance ....10'9"	Designer ....S. Leonard
Cockpit............................NA	Production 1987–90

A distinctive boat with a rakish profile and aggressive styling, the 320 Amerosport (note that she was called the 322 Catalina in 1990) had a moderately successful four-year production run before Chris Craft dropped her from the line-up in 1991. She was built on a conventional modified-V hull with solid fiberglass construction and a relatively wide beam. Inside, the Amerosport's mid-cabin floorplan is arranged with a second "stateroom" tucked below the elevated salon dinette. A lower helm was optional, and the wide beam and 360-degree cabin windows make for a spacious and wide-open interior. The original teak woodwork was updated in 1990 to light oak. Outside, the cockpit comes with built-in bench seating at the transom, and the flybridge has the helm forward with guest seating aft. Note the bolt-on reverse swim platform. Additional features include fairly wide sidedecks and a separate stall shower in the head. With a pair of 270-hp gas engines the Amerosport Sedan will cruise about 19 knots and reach 26 knots top. ❑

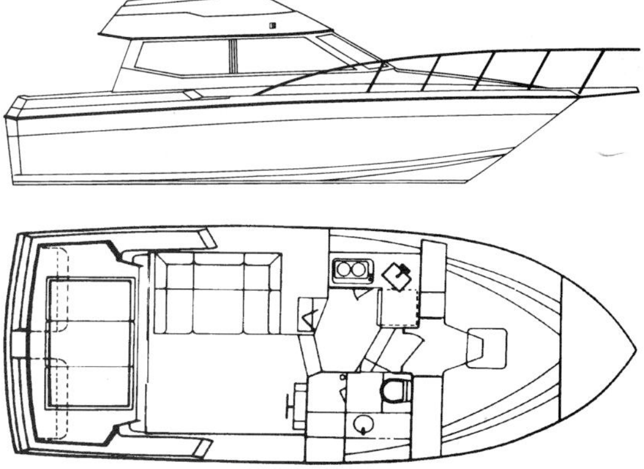

See Page 262 for Pricing Information

CHRIS CRAFT 322/340 CROWNE
30/34 CROWNE

SPECIFICATIONS

Length w/Pulpit........34'10"	Weight, 332................9,500#
Hull Length..................32'8"	Fuel.........................180 gals.
Beam..............................11'0"	Water........................35 gals.
Draft, 340......................2'11"	Hull Type ....Deep-V
Draft, 332.........................3'2"	Deadrise Aft....................18°
Weight, 340.............10,000#	Production...........1993–Current

Power options are all that separate the 30 and 34 Crowne: the 30 has stern drives, and the 34 has V-drive inboards. (Note that the 30 Crowne was called the 322 until 1995, and the 34 Crowne was called the 340.). Both are built on solid fiberglass hulls with moderate beam and a fully integrated swim platform and pulpit. A centerline companionway leads down into the Crowne's spacious interior where the mid-cabin floorplan will sleep six adults. A curved settee—elevated from the salon sole—dominates the main cabin, and the fore and aft sleeping areas both have privacy curtains. Headroom and ventilation are excellent. Cockpit seating is comprised of a big U-shaped lounge aft and a single settee opposite the double-wide helm seat. Additional features include a cockpit wet bar, a wide swim platform with fender racks, oval ports and (in the 340 model) side-dumping exhausts. The 30 (322) Crowne, with twin 235-hp OMC stern drives, will cruise at 19–20 knots, and the 34 (340) Crowne, with a pair of 300-hp Volvo inboards, will cruise at about 24 knots. ❑

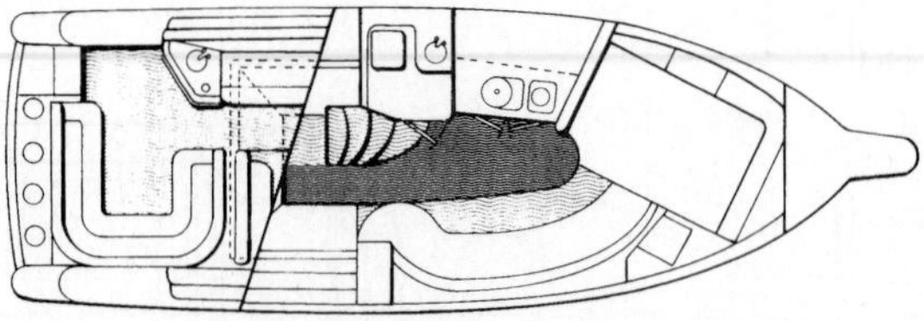

See Page 263 for Pricing Information

CHRIS CRAFT 33 CORINTHIAN

SPECIFICATIONS

Length ....33'1"	Fuel ....230 gals.
Beam ....12'4"	Cockpit ....81 sq. ft.
Draft ....2'4"	Hull Type ....Modified-V
Weight ....11,976#	Deadrise Aft ....NA
Clearance ....10'6"	Designer ....Chris Craft
Water ....40 gals.	Production 1971–80

The Chris 33 Corinthian began life in 1971 as the Chris Craft 33 Coho, a gigantic six-sleeper (in those days) topped with an oversized bridge. A popular boat, the Coho (which had a low-deadrise fiberglass hull and flybridge, vinyl-covered wooden decks, and a wooden superstructure) lasted until 1976 when the interior was revised, and she became the all-fiberglass Chris 33 Offshore. Finally, in 1978 the name was again changed to Corinthian—this time with no apparent interior or styling changes. All told, the boat remained in production for a decade which says a lot about her popularity. Thanks to her extended single-level cabin layout the Corinthian is surprisingly roomy below. The raised cockpit is also quite large (for a 33-foot boat), and hatches in the sole provide good access to the engines. A lower helm was standard, and the flybridge is very spacious with seating for five. A hard riding boat in a chop, twin 250-hp gas engines will cruise the 33 Corinthian at a respectable 19 knots with a top speed of 26–27 knots. ❑

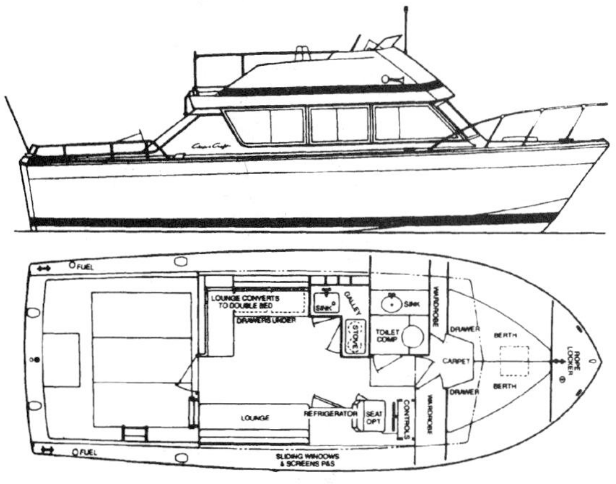

See Page 263 for Pricing Information

CHRIS CRAFT 33 CATALINA

SPECIFICATIONS

Length ....33'1"	Fuel ....270 gals.
Beam ....12'5"	Cockpit ....NA
Draft ....2'4"	Hull Type ....Modified-V
Weight ....14,800#	Deadrise Aft ....NA
Clearance ....12'5"	Designer ....Chris Craft
Water ....40 gals.	Production 1974–80

Introduced in 1974 as the 33 Sport Sedan, the Chris 33 Catalina earned a good reputation over the years as a durable mid-size family cruiser in spite of her stiff ride. Dated by today's standards, enough were sold to keep used models in circulation for a long time to come. Her conservative interior layout includes a small salon with lower helm and sofa, dinette and galley down, and overnight accommodations for six. Note the double-entry head compartment. (Early 33 Sport Sedan models had a two-stateroom floorplan with the galley up in the salon.) Wraparound cabin windows provide good ventilation and allow for excellent natural lighting inside. A sliding glass door opens to the cockpit where a ladder leads up to a very small flybridge. The hull is built of solid fiberglass with balsa coring in the decks and cabintop. Long out of production, used Chris Craft 33 Catalinas can still offer a lot of boat for a budget-minded family seeking a roomy cruiser. Twin 250-hp gas engines will cruise around 18 knots. ❑

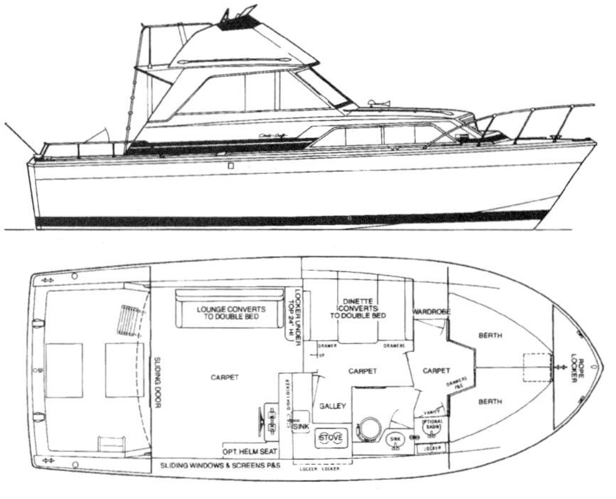

See Page 263 for Pricing Information

CHRIS CRAFT 332 EXPRESS

SPECIFICATIONS

Length	33'0"	Fuel	250 gals.
Beam	12'1"	Cockpit	NA
Draft	2'9"	Hull Type	Deep-V
Weight	11,560#	Deadrise Aft	18°
Clearance	7'11"	Designer	Chris Craft
Water	50 gals.	Production	1981–86

A popular boat for Chris Craft in the early 1980s, the 330 Commander Express is unusual in that she was built on a true deep-V hull—a rare platform for a family cruiser. Deep-Vs tend to be somewhat unstable in a beam sea (at slow speed), and they aren't usually noted for their fuel efficiency, but they do have superb handling qualities in heavy seas—a characteristic that quickly sets the 332 apart from the competition. She underwent several updates over the years, including the addition of an arch in 1983 and, in 1986 (the last year of production), a revised floorplan was introduced with a settee opposite the dinette, and a new swim platform was added at the transom. While her interior isn't particularly roomy for her size, the 332 has one of the largest cockpits found in any 33-footer. Indeed, the oversize cockpit more than compensates for the compact cabin accommodations. With big-block 454-cid gas engines, she'll cruise comfortably around 21–22 knots and reach a top speed of 30+ knots. ❑

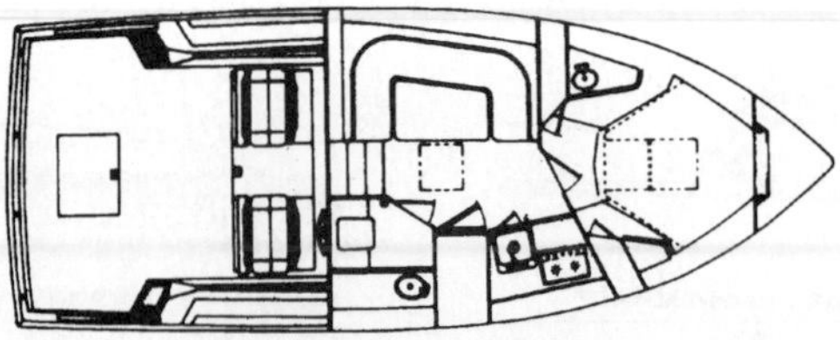

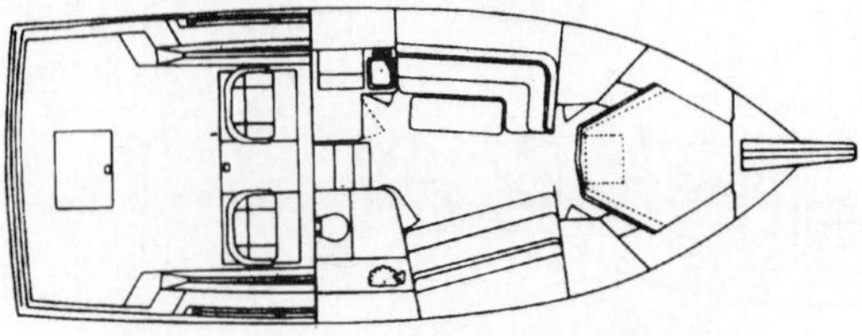

See Page 263 for Pricing Information

CHRIS CRAFT 333 SEDAN

1981–83

1984–87

SPECIFICATIONS

Length	33'0"	Clearance	NA
Beam	12'1"	Cockpit	NA
Draft	2'9"	Hull Type	Deep-V
Weight	13,000#	Deadrise Aft	18°
Water	50 gals.	Designer	Chris Craft
Fuel	250 gals.	Production	1981–87

Sharing the same sea-eating deep-V hull used in the production of the 332 Express, the Chris Craft 333 Sedan is a capable family cruiser with a distinctive profile and an unusually open cabin layout. Construction is solid fiberglass, and her relatively wide beam creates a roomy interior with berths for six and good headroom throughout. While the salon itself isn't particularly large (a lower helm was standard, and later models had a built-in lounge), the wide-open galley/dinette area three steps down delivers genuine apartment-size accommodations seldom seen in a boat this size. In 1984, the deckhouse was redesigned for a more modern appearance, and the cabin windows were dramatically restyled. In 1986—the last year of production—a revised flybridge relocated the helm further aft and added bench seating forward of the console. A good-running boat in a variety of sea conditions, standard 454-cid gas engines will cruise the Chris 333 Sedan comfortably at 20 knots and deliver a top speed in the neighborhood of 30 knots. ❑

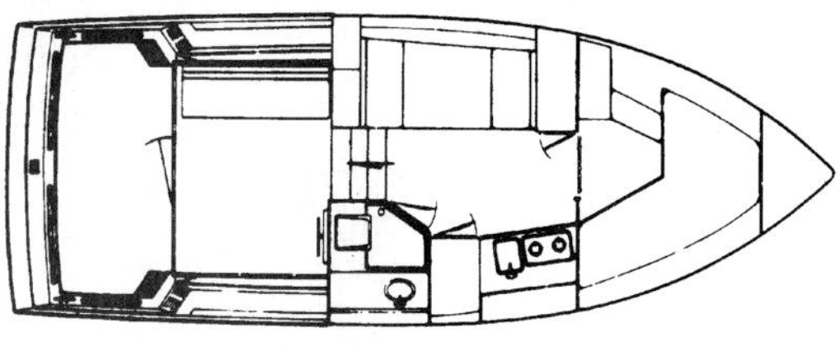

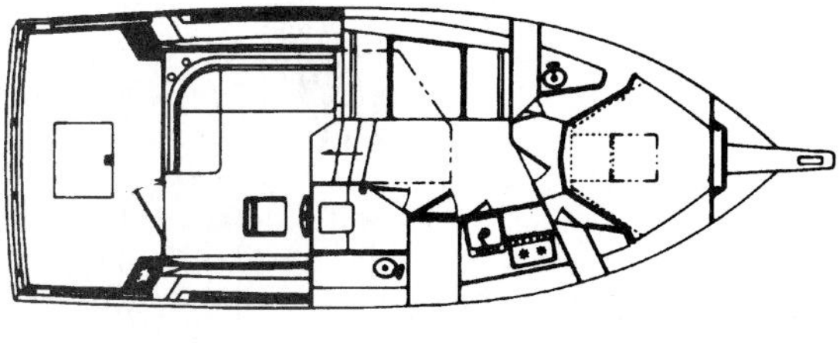

See Page 263 for Pricing Information

CHRIS CRAFT 336 MID-CABIN

SPECIFICATIONS

Length	33'0"	Water	50 gals.
Beam	12'1"	Fuel	250 gals.
Draft	2'9"	Hull Type	Deep-V
Weight	12,360#	Deadrise Aft	18°
Clearance	7'11"	Designer	Chris Craft
Cockpit	NA	Production	1983–86

The growing popularity of mid-cabin family cruisers in the early 1980s prompted Chris Craft to rework the interior of their 332 Express in order to create the look-alike 336 Mid-cabin. Indeed, it's difficult to tell the difference between the two boats until you step aboard and confront the raised bridgedeck of the 336. The interior dimensions are about average for a 33-footer, and there were no changes to the basic layout over the years other than cosmetic updates. Both sleeping areas are fitted with privacy doors (rather than curtains), and a vanity is fitted in the forward stateroom. Since the motors have beem moved aft in the 336 (to accommodate the mid-cabin floorplan), V-drives must be used to deliver the power. Three removable hatches in the cockpit sole provide excellent engine access (although the bench seat must first be removed). A good offshore performer thanks to her deep-V hull, optional 340-hp gas engines will cruise the Chris 336 at 21 knots and reach a top speed of around 30 knots. ❑

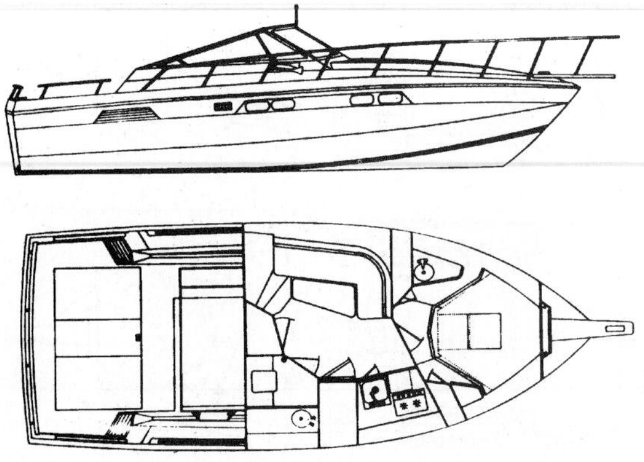

See Page 263 for Pricing Information

CHRIS CRAFT 360 EXPRESS

SPECIFICATIONS

Length	38'7"	Fuel	300 gals.
Beam	13'0"	Cockpit	NA
Draft	3'0"	Hull Type	Deep-V
Weight	15,000#	Deadrise Aft	18°
Clearance	NA	Designer	D. Fletcher
Water	50 gals.	Production	1988–92

Introduced in 1987 as the 370 Amerosport, the 360 Express is a well-styled family weekender with an attractive profile and an unusual mid-cabin layout. She was built on a deep-V, solid fiberglass hull with moderate beam and an integrated swim platform. The original Amerosport floorplan with a circular dinette lasted just a year before being replaced with a more open arrangement featuring semi-circular mid-cabin seating that reaches well into the salon—very different indeed, and it makes the cabin seem huge. On the downside, the 360's all-modular interior suffers from inconsistent detailing (the fabrics, hardware, and furnishings are obviously inexpensive), and there's only a curtain for privacy in the forward stateroom rather than a solid door. The bi-level cockpit is very spacious with plenty of guest seating, a transom door, and a built-in wet bar. A radar arch and bow pulpit were standard. A good-running boat in a chop, standard 454-cid gas engines will cruise the 360 Express around 18 knots with a top speed of 26-27 knots. ❑

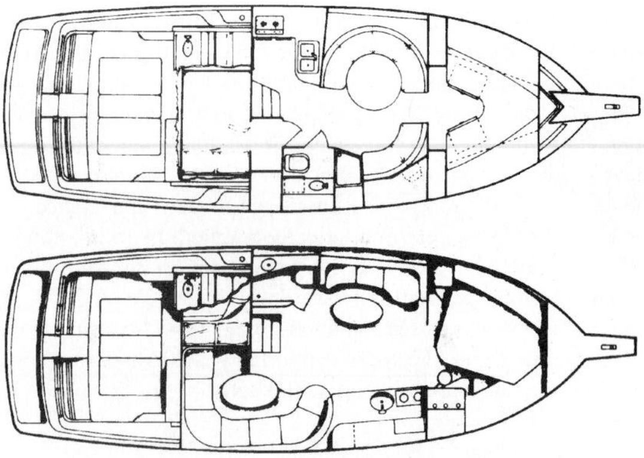

See Page 263 for Pricing Information

CHRIS CRAFT 360 SPORT SEDAN

1973–84

1985–86

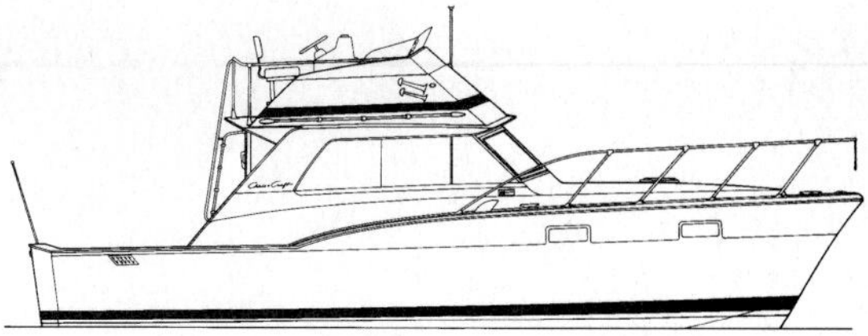

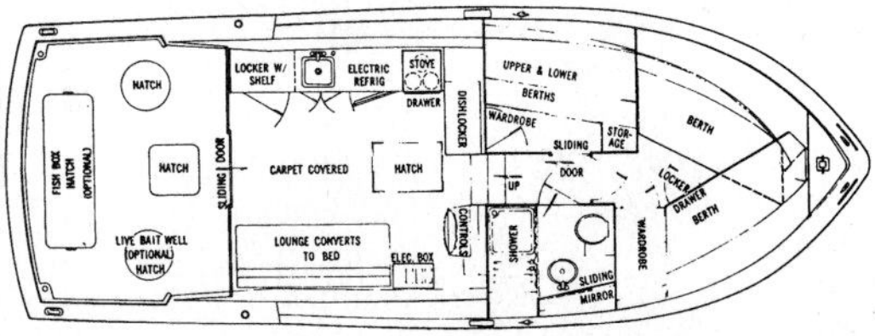

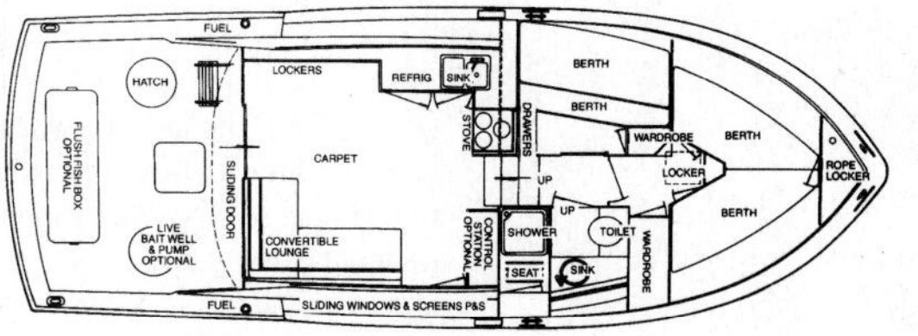

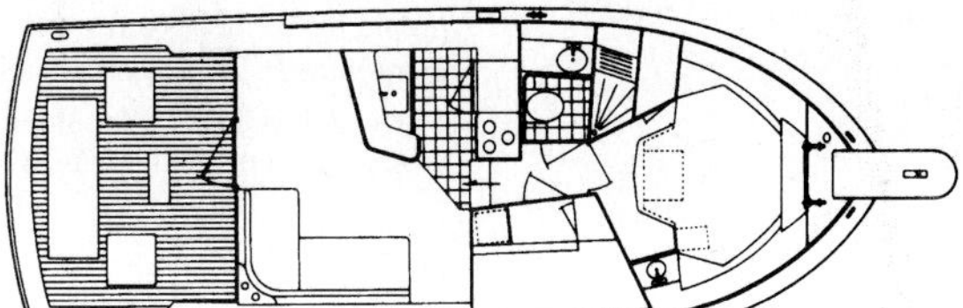

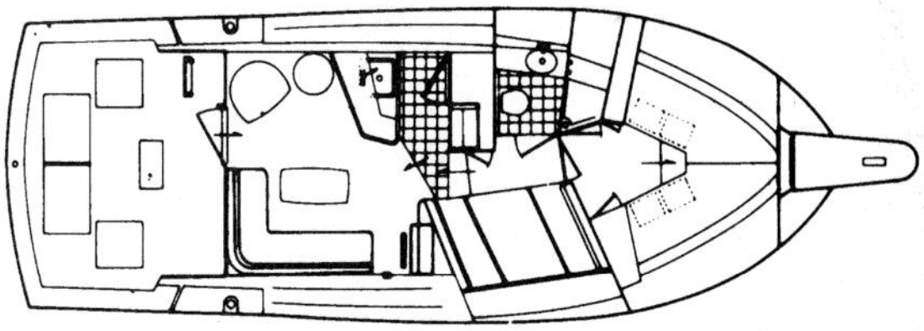

SPECIFICATIONS

Length ....36'0"	Fuel ....300/400 gals.
Beam ....13'0"	Cockpit ....NA
Draft ....3'2"	Hull Type ....Modified-V
Weight ....22,600#	Deadrise Aft ....NA
Clearance ....11'11"	Designer ....Chris Craft
Water ....75/100 gals.	Production 1973–86

A long-time favorite with fishermen and family cruisers alike, the Chris 360 Sport Sedan enjoyed an unusually long production run (for a Chris Craft), and they remain reasonably popular today on the used markets. Introduced in 1973 as the 36 Tournament SF (she became the 360 Commander in 1981), she had a practical two-stateroom, galley-up interior until 1984 when a single-stateroom floorplan with a dinette became standard. Construction is solid fiberglass, and her low deadrise hull generates good lift but produces a stiff ride in a chop. The profile of the original 36 (pictured above, top) remained the same until 1985 when the deckhouse and flybridge were dramatically restyled. An increase in fuel capacity (to 400 gallons) in 1983 improved the range considerably. Standard 454-cid gas engines will cruise at about 18 knots with a top speed of 27–28 knots. Among numerous diesel options, the 300-hp Cat (or 320-hp Cummins) diesels bring the cruising speed up to approximately 23 knots and the top speed to 26–27 knots. ❑

See Page 263 for Pricing Information

CHRIS CRAFT 380 CONTINENTAL

SPECIFICATIONS

Length	39'7"	Water	77 gals.
Hull Length	35'5"	Fuel	300 gals.
Beam	12'6"	Hull Type	Modified-V
Draft	3'1"	Deadrise Aft	15°
Weight	14,500#	Designer	J. Douglas
Clearance	10'3"	Production	1993–Current

Innovation is great, and there's never enough of it, but innovation is not what the 380 Continental is about. This is glitz over practicality—the triumph of modern art over nautical common sense. The styling from the arch forward is as modern (and handsome) as it gets, but the semi-circular stern makes an otherwise well-proportioned boat seem a little chopped off. Not surprisingly, the transom treatment also eats into the 380's usable cockpit space. Below, there are no bulkheads in the wide-open interior, so floor-to-ceiling track curtains are used to divide up the cabin into separate sleeping quarters. Note that the helm is on the centerline. (The old-fashioned instrument cluster is pretty slick). The foredeck is reached through a door in the windshield. Anchor handling is interesting: lacking a pulpit, the anchor is retrieved through a bow port. The Continental's extra-wide swim platform has storage lockers and a hot/cold shower. A heavy boat, standard 460-cid gas engines with V-drives will cruise around 16 knots and reach 28 knots wide open. ❑

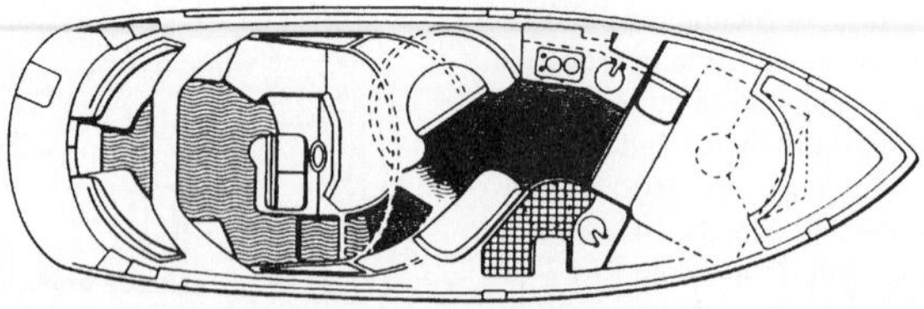

See Page 263 for Pricing Information

CHRIS 412 AMEROSPORT EXPRESS

SPECIFICATIONS

Length ....38'9"	Fuel ....380 gals.
Beam ....14'0"	Cockpit ....80 sq. ft.
Draft ....3'2"	Hull Type ....Modified-V
Weight ....15,000#	Deadrise Aft ....NA
Clearance ....9'5"	Designer ....R. Avery
Water ....100 gals.	Production 1987–90

When the Chris Craft 412 Amerosport was introduced in 1987, she was one of the bigger production express cruisers available on the market. Actually a 39-footer, she was built on a solid fiberglass hull with moderate beam and, while her lines are still modern by today's sportboat standards, her bolt-on swim platform and overdone hull graphics are less than appealing. Inside, the downscale furnishings and inexpensive decor of the 412 compare poorly with most of the competition. Privacy curtains (rather than doors) are used to separate the fore and aft sleeping areas from the salon, and the roomy head compartment stands in contrast to a rather compact galley. Outside, the driver's helm position is a bit low, and forward visibility—especially on hard acceleration—is not the best. The cockpit is arranged with facing U-shaped settees with a removable table and seating for eight to ten passengers. Standard 454-cid gas engines will cruise the Chris 412 Amerosport at a steady 17–18 knots and deliver a top speed of about 27 knots. ❑

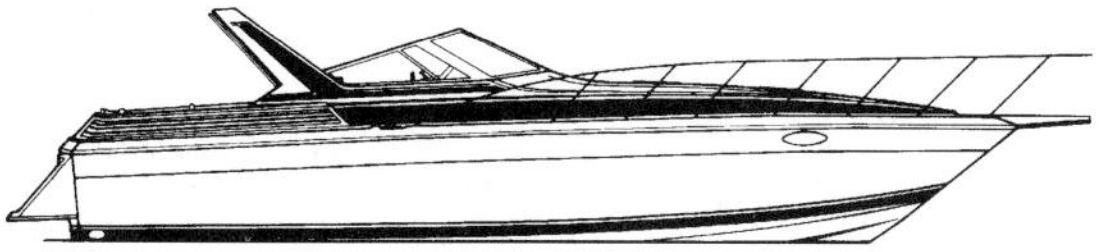

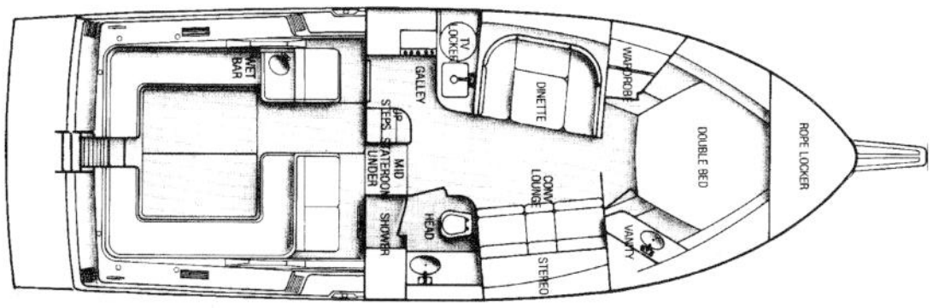

See Page 263 for Pricing Information

CHRIS CRAFT 421 CONTINENTAL

SPECIFICATIONS

Length ....43'3"	Water ....108 gals.
Beam ....13'6"	Fuel ....350 gals.
Draft ....3'2"	Hull Type ....Modified-V
Weight ....18,700#	Deadrise Aft ....17°
Clearance ....13'11"	Designer ....Chris Craft
Cockpit ....NA	Production 1993–Current

A very unusual design with her sloped-foredeck profile and semicircular cockpit, the Chris 421 Continental is a budget-priced family cruiser for those who appreciate unorthodox styling. She's built on a solid fiberglass, modified-V hull with moderate beam, prop pockets, and a fairly steep 17 degrees of transom deadrise. The two-stateroom floorplan is arranged on a single level with excellent headroom and plenty of overhead lighting to compensate for the absence of cabin windows. The oversize galley may occasionally be useful, but it eats up cabin space that might otherwise be used for additional seating. If the interior is a little small for a 42-footer, the cockpit dimensions are relatively spacious, although the oval transom design still consumes a lot of square footage. The engine compartment (beneath the cockpit sole) is a tight fit. Additional features include a spacious flybridge, molded foredeck seating, and a big swim platform. No racehorse, standard 300-hp gas inboards (with V-drives) will cruise the Chris 421 around 14–15 knots, and optional 320-hp Volvo diesels cruise around 21 knots. ❑

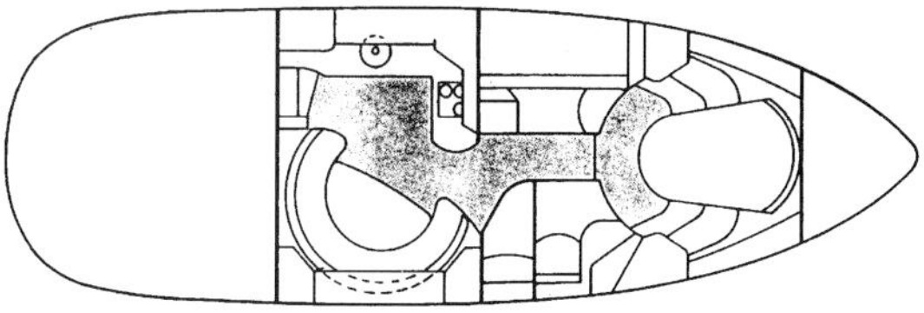

See Page 263 for Pricing Information

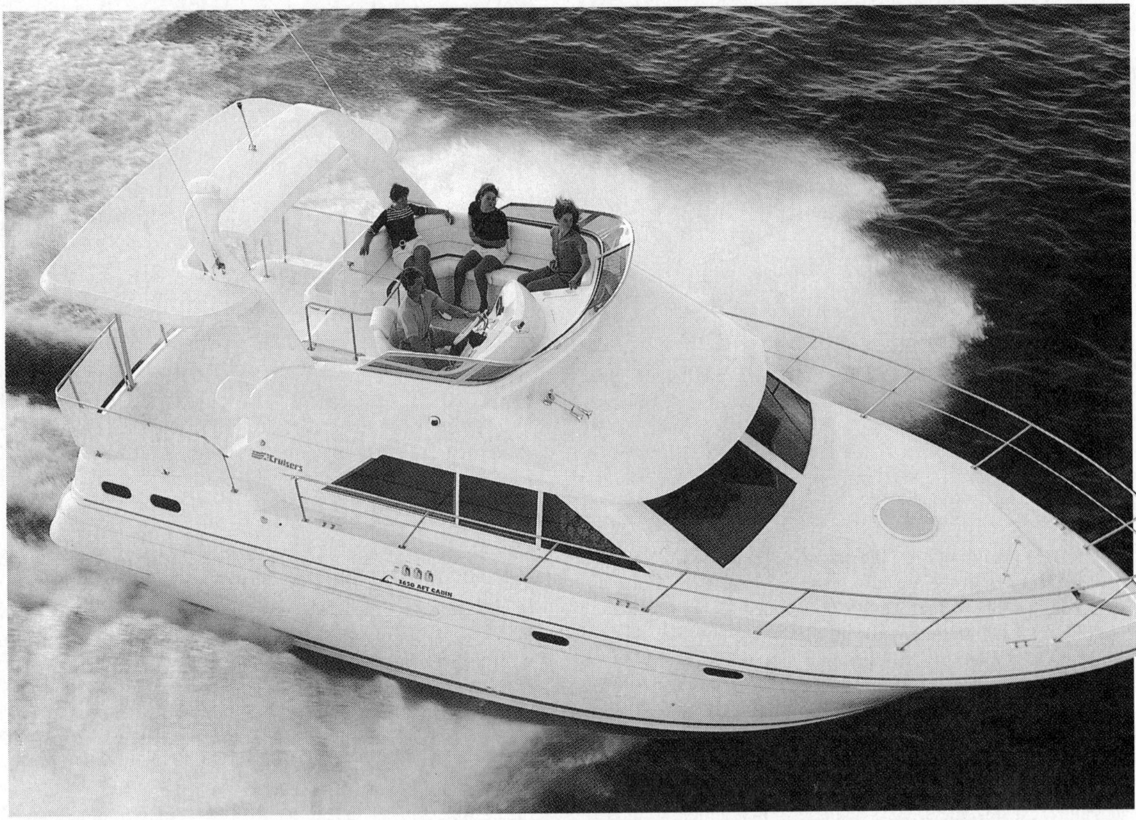

CRUISERS 2420 ARIA

SPECIFICATIONS

Length w/Pulpit..........25'8"	Fuel..........................80 gals.
Hull Length.................24'0"	Water........................20 gals.
Beam...............................8'6"	Clearance........................6'6"
Draft, Up.........................1'7"	Hull Type................Deep-V
Draft, Down...................2'9"	Deadrise Aft..................NA
Weight.......................5,500#	Production.......1994–Current

A good-looking small cruiser with a sporty profile (in spite of her high freeboard), the most striking feature about the Cruisers 2420 Aria is her unusually large cockpit. Indeed, her cockpit dimensions are those of the average 30-footer, and she's clearly aimed at buyers who place a premium on open-air activities rather than interior accommodations. The Aria is built on a solid fiberglass, modified deep-V hull with moderate (trailerable) beam and an integrated swim platform. There are berths for two below along with an enclosed (very small) head and a compact galley with sink and storage. The headroom is a full 6 feet in the cabin. Lacking sidedecks, a walk-thru in the windshield allows access to the bow platform. The huge, single-level cockpit is designed with seating for eight adults and features a built-in wet bar and ice box, in-deck storage and a removable cocktail table. Note that the low-profile windshield doesn't provide much wind protection at the helm. With a single 245-hp/5.7-litre Volvo stern drive the Aria will cruise at 21 knots and reach around 33 knots wide open. ❑

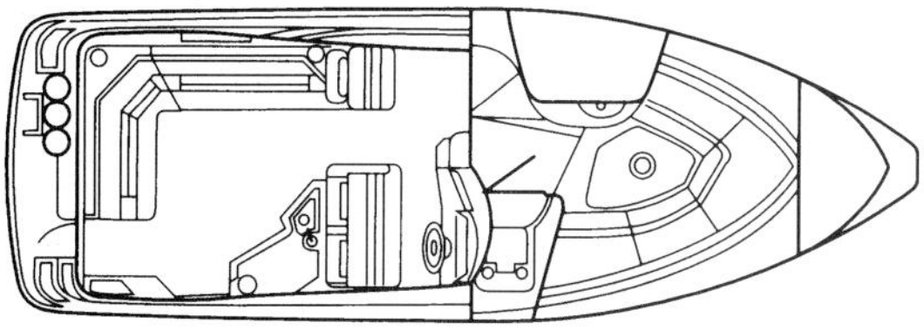

See Page 263 for Pricing Information

CRUISERS 2470 ROGUE

SPECIFICATIONS

Length w/Pulpit..........25'8"	Fuel..........................80 gals.
Hull Length.................24'0"	Water........................20 gals.
Beam...............................8'6"	Clearance......................6'11"
Draft, Up.........................1'7"	Hull Type................Deep-V
Draft, Down...................2'9"	Deadrise Aft..................NA
Weight.......................5,700#	Production.......1994–Current

The Cruisers 2470 Rouge is an affordable and well-crafted mid-cabin express whose rakish sportboat styling helps to overcome her topheavy profile. She's built on a solid fiberglass, modified deep-V hull with moderate (trailerable) beam and an integrated swim platform. The reason for her high freeboard can be found inside the cabin where the headroom is better than 6 feet—an unusual feature in a 24-footer. The Rogue's mid-cabin floorplan is arranged in the usual way with a dinette/V-berth forward, a double berth in the aft cabin, a small galley and an enclosed head and shower. Four opening ports and a large deck hatch provide cabin ventilation. Outside, the cockpit has a double-wide helm seat along with lounge seating and a removable cockpit table at the transom. A walk-through windshield (with two molded steps and a handrail) provides easy access to the foredeck sun pads, and fender racks are built into the swim platform. With a single 245-hp Volvo Duoprop stern drive, the 2470 Rouge will cruise at 20 knots and reach a top speed of about 32 knots. ❑

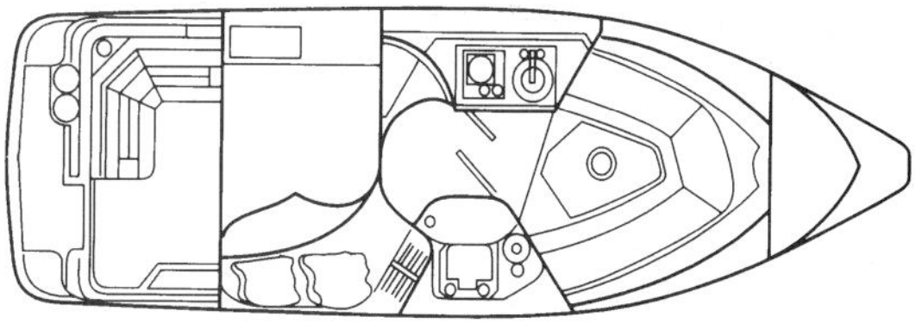

See Page 263 for Pricing Information

CRUISERS 2660 VEE SPORT

SPECIFICATIONS

Length	26'1"	Water	31 gals.
Beam	10'0"	Fuel	120 gals.
Draft	3'0"	Hull Type	Deep-V
Weight	6,600#	Designer	Jim Wynn
Clearance	9'10"	Deadrise Aft	22°
Cockpit	NA	Production	1979–91

Obviously dated by today's sportboat standards, the 2660 Vee Sport (called the Cruisers 266 Vee Sport from 1979–87) enjoyed a good deal of popularity during her long 12-year production run. She was built in a solid fiberglass hull with a wide beam, and her raised foredeck gave her a somewhat chubby profile. The original floorplan had the dinette to port; since 1984, the galley has been to port. Note that instead of a mid-cabin layout, the Vee Sport has a quarter berth—very unusual. While the interior is quite spacious for a 26-footer (and notably well-appointed with good quality hardware and furnishings), the cockpit dimensions are on the stingy side. Aside from cosmetic updates (interior decor, helm console, hull graphics, etc.), the 2660 Vee Sport remained relatively unchanged over the years. The swim platform and teak bow pulpit were standard. Among several possible engine choices, twin 350-cid stern drives will cruise the 2660 Vee Sport comfortably at 27–28 knots and reach a top speed of around 40 knots. ❑

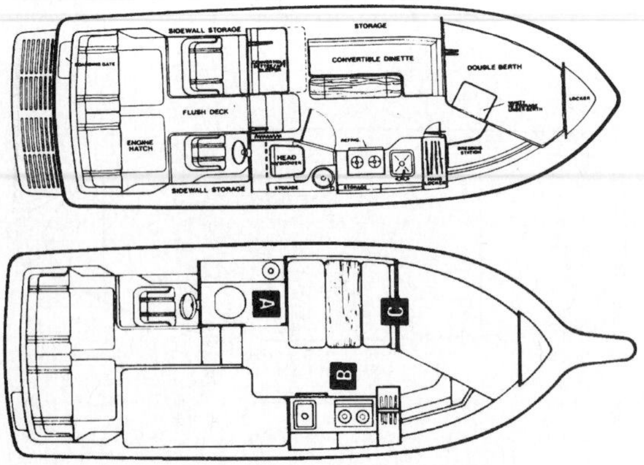

See Page 263 for Pricing Information

CRUISERS 2670 ROGUE

SPECIFICATIONS

Length w/Pulpit	26'0"	Clearance	7'6"
Hull Length	24'6"	Water	20 gals.
Beam	9'6"	Fuel	95 gals.
Draft, Up	2'0"	Hull Type	Deep-V
Draft, Down	3'5"	Deadrise Aft	24°
Weight	6,100#	Production	1991–Current

The 2670 Rogue succeeds in packing as much living space into as small package as any 26-footer in the business today. She's built on the same solid fiberglass deep-V hull as the larger 2870 Rouge and, with a full 9 feet, 6 inches of beam, the cockpit and interior accommodations are very generous. Her stylish mid-cabin interior includes berths for four with a stand-up head (located amidships where headroom is best) and a compact galley area. Guest seating for six is provided in the cockpit including a double-wide seat at the helm. There are no sidedecks so access to the foredeck is via a molded step and a walk-through in the windshield. A boxy boat because of her relatively high freeboard, Cruisers designers eliminated the cabin windows in 1994 and replaced them with a pair of oval ports on both sides of the hull. Consequently, the loss of outside natural lighting results in a rather closed-in feeling below. Among several engine choices, a single 454-cid MerCruiser stern drive will cruise the 2670 Rouge at 20 knots and reach around 32 knots top. ❑

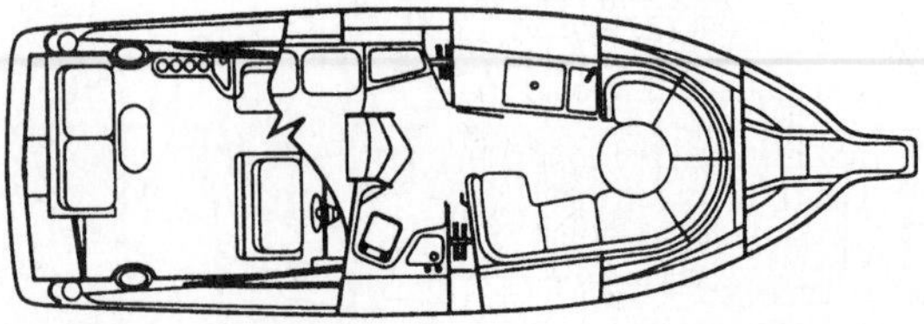

See Page 263 for Pricing Information

CRUISERS 2870 HOLIDAY
CRUISERS 2870/2970 ROGUE

SPECIFICATIONS

Length w/Pulpit	28'8"	Water	30 gals.
Hull Length	26'0"	Fuel	120 gals.
Beam	9'6"	Hull Type	Deep-V
Draft	3'2"	Deadrise Aft	24°
Weight	7,800#	Designer	Cruisers
Clearance	8'8"	Production	1990–95

While there are few truly good-looking express cruisers under 30 feet (standing cabin headroom usually results in excessive freeboard in a small boat), the 2970 Rouge is certainly one of the more stylish of the lot. Introduced in 1990 as the Cruisers 2870 Holiday, she's a well-built family cruiser with solid fiberglass hull construction, a good cockpit layout and a fairly roomy interior. The Rogue's mid-cabin floorplan includes a compact galley as well as wraparound salon seating and adequate stowage. The interior fabrics, hardware and furnishings are impressive for their overall quality and appearance. Outside, the cockpit can seat eight and includes a wet bar and a fold-down jump seat hidden in the back of the helm seat. There's a sunpad for the foredeck, but getting there is difficult since there are practically no sidedecks. Note that she became the 2970 Rouge in 1995 when the transom door was moved to port. Among several engine options, twin 350-cid Volvo stern drives will provide a cruising speed of 24 knots and a top speed of 36 knots.❑

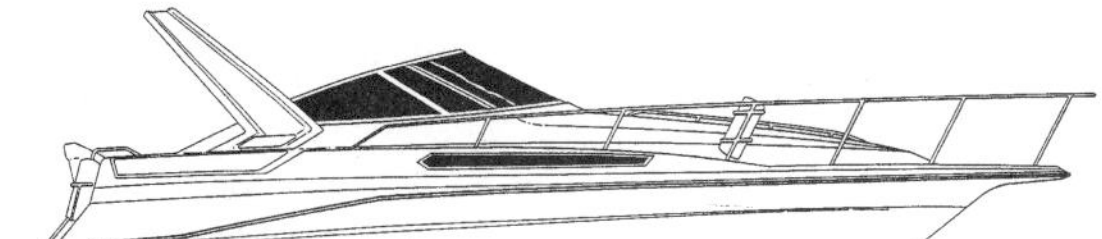

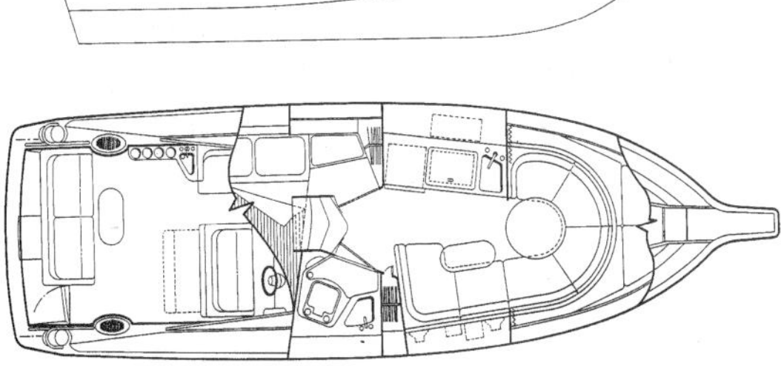

See Page 264 for Pricing Information

CRUISERS 296 AVANTI VEE

SPECIFICATIONS

Length	28'8"	Water	45 gals.
Length WL	24'11"	Fuel	200/250 gals.
Beam	10'8"	Hull Type	Deep-V
Draft	2'9"	Deadrise Aft	17°
Weight	9,000#	Designer	Jim Wynne
Clearance	7'5"	Production	1984–87

Introduced in 1984, the 296 Avanti Vee was a stylish and fairly popular express cruiser for Cruisers for several years. Built on a solid fiberglass hull with prop pockets and a relatively (by today's standards) beam, her interior is somewhat unusual in that the dinette is placed aft in the salon beneath the raised helm—almost a mid-cabin layout but not quite. An offset double berth is fitted into the stateroom forward with a draw curtain for privacy. The choice of fabrics and hardware was made with care, and the boat has a good quality appearance throughout. A distinguishing feature of the 296 Avanti Vee is her positive foam flotation—a rarity in a boat this size. Helm visibility is excellent, and the cockpit is large enough for several guests. There's a walk-thru in the transom, and the radar arch was standard. Twin 260-hp gas engines provide a cruising speed of 19–20 knots and a top speed of around 30 knots. Note that the Cruisers 291 Sea Devil (1984–85) is the same boat in sportfishing trim. ❑

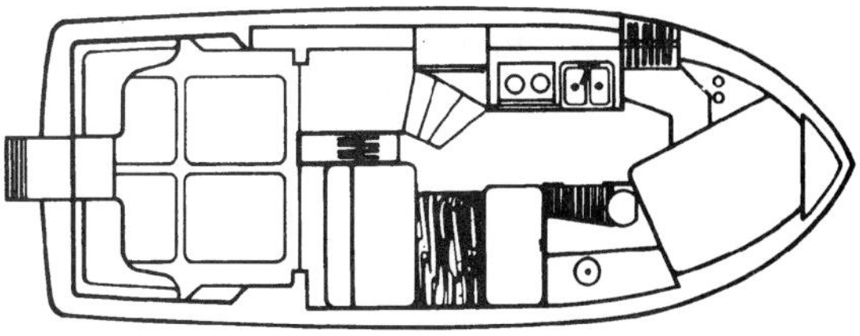

See Page 264 for Pricing Information

CRUISERS 2970 ESPRIT

SPECIFICATIONS

Length ....28'8"	Water ....45 gals.
Length WL ....24'11"	Fuel ....200/250 gals.
Beam ....10'8"	Hull Type ....Deep-V
Draft ....2'9"	Deadrise Aft ....17°
Weight ....9,000#	Designer ....Jim Wynne
Clearance ....7'5"	Production 1986–91

Introduced as the Cruisers 297 Elegante in 1986, the 2970 Esprit was a popular boat for Cruisers during her 5-year production run. She has the same exterior profile as the 296 Avanti Vee but differs below with her mid-cabin floorplan and berths for six. To achieve the 2970's increased interior volume, Cruisers engineers used V-drives to locate the engines aft in the hull, which freed up the additional space necessary for the mid-cabin layout. The 2970 is built on a solid fiberglass hull with moderate beam, prop pockets, and the hull is filled with foam flotation. Below, the contemporary decor features teak paneling and good-quality hardware and appliances. Both fore and aft staterooms have draw curtains for sleeping privacy rather than doors. The view from the elevated helm is good, although trim tabs are occasionally required to keep the running angles down. The radar arch and swim platform were standard. Twin 260/270-hp gas engines will cruise the 2970 Esprit around 20 knots with a top speed of 29–30 knots. ❑

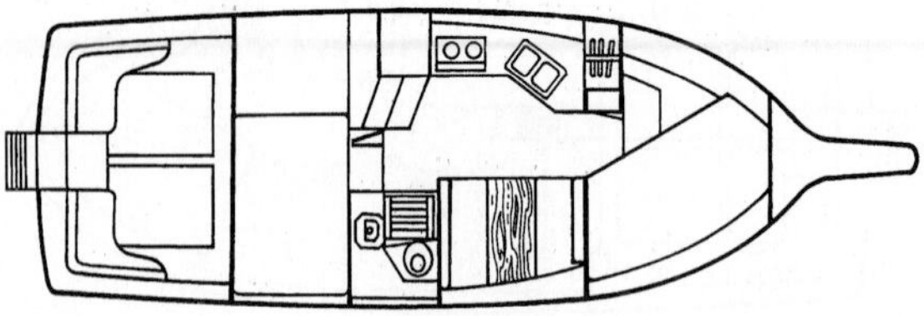

See Page 264 for Pricing Information

CRUISERS 288/298 VILLA VEE 2980 ESPRIT

SPECIFICATIONS

Length ....28'8"	Water ....45 gals.
Length WL ....24'11"	Fuel ....150/180 gals.
Beam ....10'8"	Hull Type ....Deep-V
Draft ....2'9"	Deadrise Aft ....17°
Weight ....9,500#	Designer ....Jim Wynne
Clearance ....9'5"	Production 1978–90

Equally well-known as the 288 Villa Vee (1978–83) and the 298 Villa Vee (1984–87), the Cruisers 2980 Esprit is a distinctive family sedan with attractive lines and a surprisingly roomy interior layout featuring a real salon—a rarity in such a small boat—together with a big cockpit and overnight accommodations for four. Her basic portside galley layout remained pretty much the same until 1989, when Cruisers engineers rearranged the floorplan and in the process moved the galley to starboard. Because many of these boats were sold in northern climates, a lower helm was a common option. A popular boat for Cruisers, she enjoyed an unusually long 12-year production run. She was built on a deep-V hull with moderate beam and prop pockets for reduced shaft angles. A good performer, she'll cruise around 18 knots with the small 230-hp gas engines (26 knots top). With the 260-hp motors, the cruising speed is about 20 knots, and the top speed is 29–30 knots. ❑

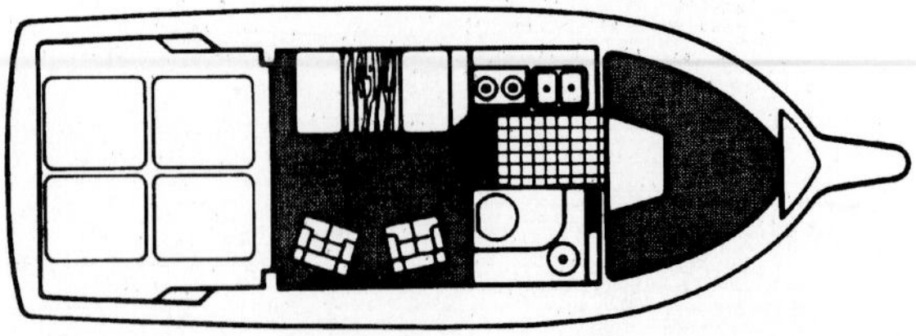

See Page 264 for Pricing Information

CRUISERS 3020/3120 ARIA

SPECIFICATIONS

Length w/Pulpit..........30'8"	Clearance. ....9'4"
Hull Length ....28'8"	Water. ....32 gals.
Beam.............................10'6"	Fuel. ....200 gals.
Draft, Down ....3'0"	Hull Type. ....Deep-V
Draft, Up.........................2'1"	Deadrise Aft...................20°
Weight.......................8,800#	Production 1992–Current

Sharing the same fully cored hull as the 3070 Rouge, the Aria stands out from other 30-foot express cruisers for her enormous cockpit. Indeed, about two-thirds of her LOA is devoted to cockpit space, and the result is a superb dayboat with room for a party-size gathering. The entire aft cockpit perimeter is lined with seating that folds away and disappears in the inwales. With all of the seat sections fully deployed, the cockpit becomes a giant sunlounge. Most of the galley is located in the cockpit, and molded steps next to the helm provide foredeck access via a walkthrough in the windshield. A huge storage bin is located beneath the cockpit. The compact interior is well-finished and includes a mini-galley and enclosed head. A mid-cabin berth is optional beneath the helm; otherwise that space is used for storage. A great-looking boat, twin 5.7-litre stern drives will cruise at 21 knots (35 top), and optional 454-cid engines will cruise at 25 knots (about 40 knots wide open). ❑

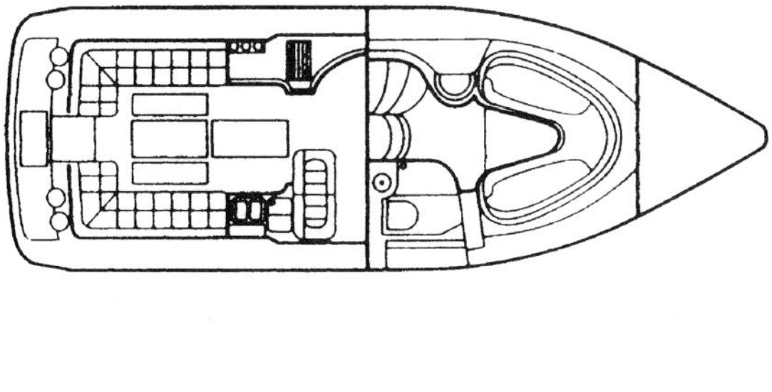

See Page 264 for Pricing Information

CRUISERS 3070 ROGUE

SPECIFICATIONS

Length w/Pulpit..........30'8"	Clearance. ....8'9"
Hull Length ....28'8"	Water. ....35 gals.
Beam.............................10'6"	Fuel. ....170 gals.
Draft, Down ....3'0"	Hull Type. ....Deep-V
Draft, Up.........................2'1"	Deadrise Aft...................20°
Weight.......................9,800#	Production 1990–94

The 3070 Rouge comes in at (or near) the top of the class when it comes to popular and well-designed 30-foot express cruisers with stern drive power. Her lines are remarkably sleek in spite of the raised foredeck. Inside, the mid-cabin interior is very roomy with top-quality fabrics, hardware, and furnishings throughout; and although the cockpit isn't huge compared to other boats her size, it's fitted with a good-looking helm console, plenty of guest seating, a wet bar, and shower. Perhaps the most distinguishing features of the 3070 Rouge are her rounded deck hatches, the circular foredeck sunpad, and the molded fender racks at each corner of the boat—a thoughtful and innovative touch. Cabin ventilation is excellent thanks to nine opening ports and hatches, all with screens. Clearly a well-built boat, standard 230-hp stern drives will cruise easily at 20 knots (32–33 knots top), and optional 300-hp motors will cruise the 3070 Rogue at about 24 knots and deliver a top speed of 40+ knots. ❑

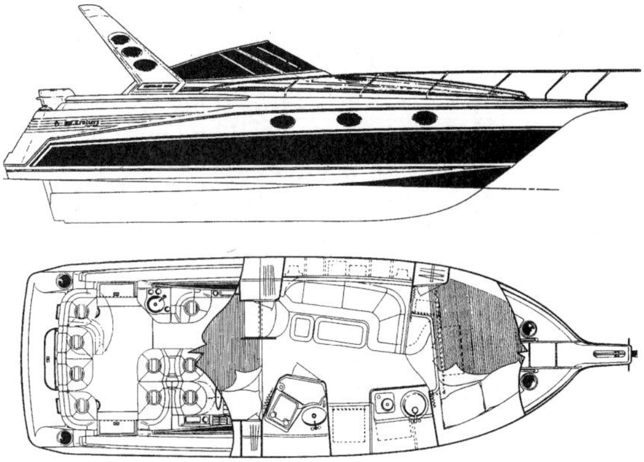

See Page 264 for Pricing Information

CRUISERS 3175 ROGUE

SPECIFICATIONS

Length.....32'8"	Fuel.....163 gals.
Hull Length.....30'8"	Water.....32 gals.
Beam.....10'6"	Clearance w/Arch.....9'10"
Draft, Up.....2'1"	Hull Type.....Deep-V
Draft, Down.....3'0"	Deadrise Aft.....20°
Weight.....9,300#	Production.....1995–Current

The 3175 Rouge is an affordably priced 30-footer with a couple of design features not seen in other express cruisers her size. Although her 10-foot, 6-inch beam is narrow for a modern 30-footer, the absence of any sidedecks provides for a more open interior than one might otherwise expect. Too, note that the unique shape of the bow pulpit makes it more a part of the hull than simply a molded extension of the deck. Finally, more than half of the 3175's overall length is devoted to the interior. The result is a good-looking exterior profile with a long foredeck and a somewhat small cockpit. The mid-cabin floorplan includes double berths fore and aft, a compact galley area, and a stand-up head with (surprise!) a separate stall shower. Additional features include a walk-through windshield, foredeck sun pad, and a wet bar and wraparound lounge seating in the cockpit. Note that the hull is fully cored, even the bottom. Twin 245-hp/5.7-litre Volvo stern drives will cruise the 3175 at 22 knots and reach a top speed of about 35 knots. ❑

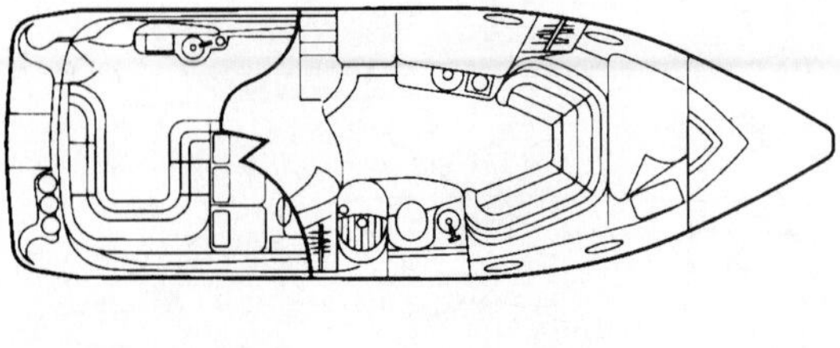

See Page 264 for Pricing Information

CRUISERS 3260/3270 ESPRIT

SPECIFICATIONS

Length.....30'10"	Water.....45 gals.
Beam.....10'10"	Fuel.....200/250 gals.
Draft.....2'10"	Hull Type.....Modified-V
Weight.....10,500#	Deadrise Aft.....18°
Clearance.....7'0"	Designer.....Jim Wynne
Cockpit.....NA	Production.....1988–94

The Cruisers 3260 and 3270 Esprit models are styled alike outside with the difference being the mid-cabin layout in the 3270 compared to the dinette arrangement in the 3260. The popularity of the mid-cabin floorplan kept the 3270 in production, while the 3260 was dropped in 1990. Most people find the exterior lines of these family express cruisers to be quite attractive with better-than-average glasswork and detailing. Both models feature the upscale interior decors and quality furnishings one expects in a Cruisers boat. There are berths for six in the mid-cabin 3270, while the 3260 model sleeps four. Note the curved wraparound windshield, oval hull ports, radar arch, and stylish integral swim platform. With the standard 350-cid Crusader gas engines, the Cruisers 3260/3270 Esprit models will cruise at 19–20 knots and reach a top speed of 30 knots. Note that the 3270 uses V-drives, while straight drives are used in the 3270. Also, with 250 gallons of fuel capacity, the 3260 has an additional 50 gallons over her sistership. ❑

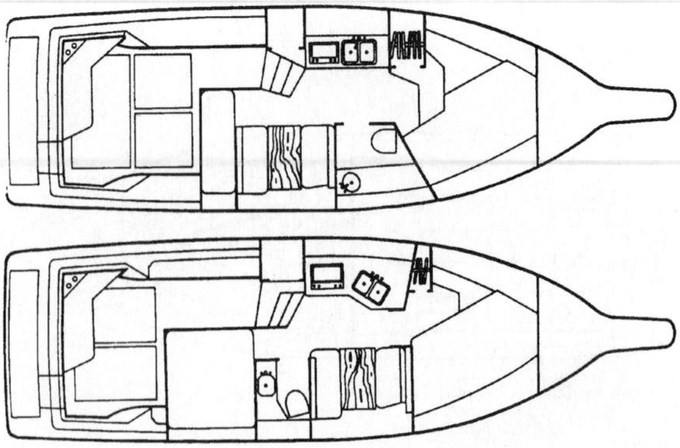

See Page 264 for Pricing Information

CRUISERS 336 ULTRA VEE

SPECIFICATIONS

Length ....32'10"	Water ....70 gals.
Beam ....11'10"	Fuel ....250/300 gals.
Draft ....2'9"	Hull Type ....Deep-V
Weight....................11,500#	Deadrise Aft....................18°
Clearance ....8'6"	Designer ....Jim Wynne
Cockpit....................NA	Production 1983–88

With her overfed profile and unappealing hull graphics, the 336 Ultra Vee is no award-winner when it comes to styling. That said, the appeal of the Cruisers 336 lies in her unique interior and superior construction. Inside, the Ultra Vee's mid-cabin is actually the master stateroom with partial standing headroom, a privacy door, and direct access to the head—a completely innovative floorplan made possible by the radically elevated cockpit sole. Major updates in 1985 included an additional 50 gallons of fuel capacity and the introduction of a more upscale and modern (de-teaked, in other words) interior decor. A good-running boat in a headsea with unsurpassed helm visability, the Ultra Vee's combination of deep-V hull, moderate beam, and considerable freeboard causes her to roll a bit at low speeds, especially with a few people in the cockpit. A good-running boat, speeds are around 22 knots at cruise and 30–31 knots top with the standard 350-hp inboard gas engines. Note that positive foam flotation placed throughout the hull makes the 336 Ultra Vee unsinkable. ❑

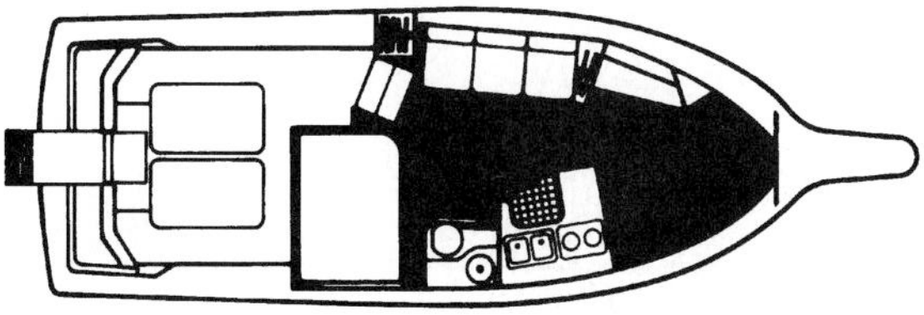

See Page 264 for Pricing Information

CRUISERS 3370 ESPRIT

SPECIFICATIONS

Length ....32'10"	Water ....70 gals.
Beam ....11'10"	Fuel ....300 gals.
Draft ....2'9"	Hull Type ....Deep-V
Weight....................11,500#	Deadrise Aft....................18°
Clearance ....8'6"	Designer ....Jim Wynne
Cockpit....................NA	Production 1986–94

Built on the same deep-V, prop-pocket hull as the 336 Ultra Vee, the Cruisers 3370 Esprit trades the private mid-cabin (with standing headroom) floorplan found in the 3360 for additional salon seating and a much more open and spacious interior layout. Two matching L-shaped settees dominate the interior of the 3370 with seating for as many as eight guests—a grand arrangement for those who enjoy entertaining. The price for the excellent cabin headroom (an honest 6 feet, 4 inches) is the elevated foredeck profile of the 3370. The decor is well-appointed with quality fabrics and furnishings, and it's evident that this is not an inexpensive boat compared to much of the competition. Notably, the hull is packed with sufficient flotation to keep her from sinking—a very unusual safety feature in a boat this size. A good-running boat in a chop, the cruising speed of the 3370 Esprit with twin 454-cid Crusader gas engines is about 21 knots, and the top speed is around 30 knots. ❑

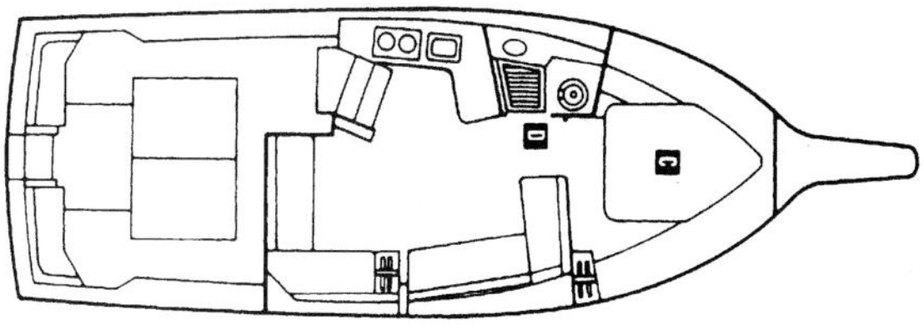

See Page 264 for Pricing Information

CRUISERS 3380 ESPRIT

SPECIFICATIONS

Length	32'10"	Water	70 gals.
Beam	11'10"	Fuel	300 gals.
Draft	2'10"	Hull Type	Deep-V
Weight	13,000#	Deadrise Aft	18°
Clearance	11'6"	Designer	Jim Wynne
Cockpit	NA	Production	1985–94

It's doubtful that many 3380 Esprits have been sold on the strength of sex appeal. The elimination in 1991 of most of the hull graphics did much to improve her otherwise ungainly profile. Indeed, the 3380 Esprit's claim to owner popularity has to do with her quality construction (nothing feels cheap or flimsy in this boat) and a practical family layout. The mid-cabin interior is arranged with double berths in both staterooms and a stall shower in the head. There are berths for a total of six, and most were sold with the optional lower helm. Outside, the cockpit comes with built-in bench seating at the corners. The oversized flybridge has the helm forward with a wraparound settee aft. An average performer with 454-cid gas engines, she'll cruise around 20 knots and reach 29–30 knots wide open. (Note that she was called the Cruisers 338 Chateau Vee from 1985–87.) Like other Cruisers models, the hull is built with positive foam flotation for safety in the event of an accident. ❑

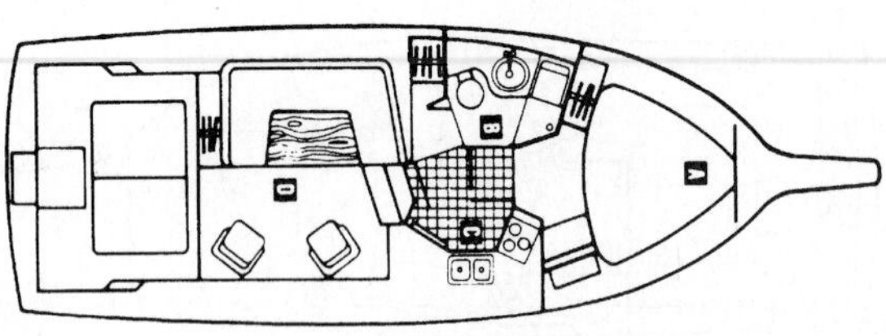

See Page 264 for Pricing Information

CRUISERS 3570 EXPRESS

SPECIFICATIONS

Length w/Pulpit	37'4"	Water	70 gals.
Hull Length	35'0"	Clearance	8'2"
Beam	13'0"	Hull Type	Deep-V
Draft	3'5"	Deadrise Aft	17°
Weight	16,000#	Designer	Cruisers
Fuel	300 gals.	Production	1995–Current

Innovation is an abused term in the marine industry where even minor features are touted as design breakthroughs. In the case of the 3570 Esprit, however, it's fair to say that this really is a boat that's different and, yes, innovative. Beginning with the unusual helm seating in the cockpit, and featuring a wide-open mid-cabin interior with no forward bulkhead (unusual on a 35-footer), the Esprit offers something different in a sea of me-too express cruiser designs. In this floorplan, the owner's stateroom is aft with a walkaround queen berth and a full 6 feet of headroom—almost unheard of in a mid-cabin boat. The extra headroom comes from raising the bridgedeck two steps above the cockpit level, a design scheme which also results in a better view from the helm. The exterior styling is crisp and handsome in spite of the raised deck profile, and the gracefully integrated bow platform is unique. Built on a fully cored hull with prop pockets, the Esprit will cruise at 18 knots with V-drive 320-hp MerCruisers and top out at around 30 knots. ❑

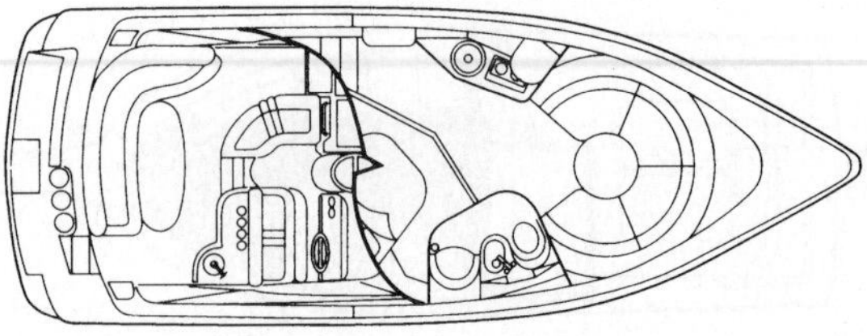

See Page 264 for Pricing Information

CRUISERS 3670/3675/3775 ESPRIT

SPECIFICATIONS

Length	35'3"	Water	110 gals.
Beam	13'0"	Fuel	300 gals.
Draft	2'10"	Hull Type	Mod. Deep-V
Weight	17,500#	Deadrise Aft	17°
Clearance	9'7"	Designer	Jim Ginter
Cockpit	NA	Production	1989–Current

The Cruisers 3670 Esprit—and the more recent 3675 model introduced in 1991, and the current 3775 (since 1995)—are all basically the same boat on the outside with different mid-cabin interior layouts. A popular model with a modern sportcruiser profile and better-than-average detailing, she's built on a beamy hull with prop pockets and a relatively steep 17 degrees of deadrise at the transom. Several floorplans have been used over the years. The original 3670 model had a U-shaped dinette to port and a walkaround double berth forward. The 3675, on the other hand, has had two floorplans: the first was a very open arrangement with no dinette and an offset berth in the forward stateroom, while the current layout brings back a small dinette as well as a centerline double berth but in a more fashionable decor package. (In 1993 Cruisers dropped the 3670 model completely.) Outside, the cockpit is extremely well-arranged with seating for a crowd. Standard 454-cid gas engines (with V-drives) will cruise the Cruisers 3675 Esprit at 19 knots and reach a top speed of 29–30 knots. ❑

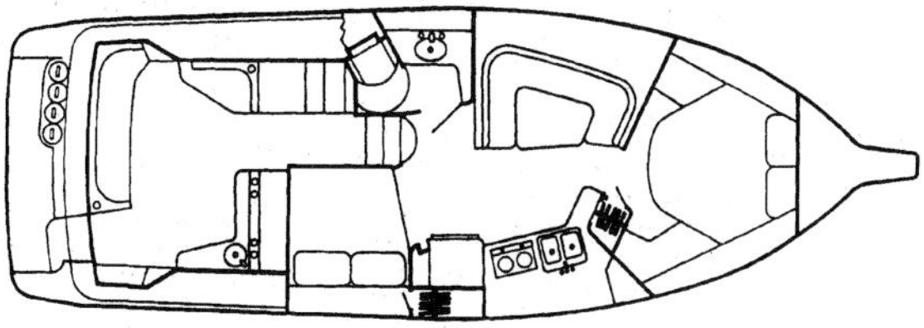

3660 Floorplan

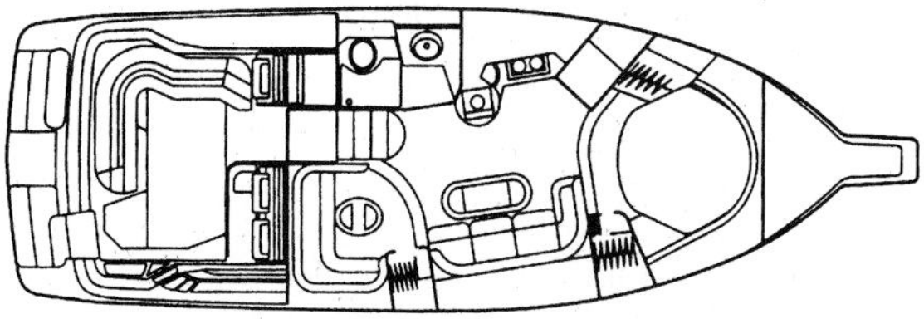

3675/3775 Mid-Cabin Floorplan

See Page 264 for Pricing Information

CRUISERS 4280/4285 EXPRESS BRIDGE

1988–91

1992–95

SPECIFICATIONS

Length	42'0"	Fuel	400 gals.
Beam	14'6"	Cockpit	91 sq. ft.
Draft	3'6"	Hull Type	Modified-V
Weight	27,000#	Deadrise Aft	16°
Clearance	13'3"	Designer	Jim Wynne
Water	160 gals.	Production	1988–95

For those who enjoy their socializing on a grand scale, the 4280/4285 Express Bridge is loaded with features not usually expected in a mid-size cruiser. Restyled for 1992, she's still no award winner when it comes to looks. (Indeed, we've been calling this boat a party barge since she came out in 1988.). Inside, however, the expansive full-width interior is laid out on a single-level, providing unusually comfortable living accommodations. The 4280 and 4285 designations refer to the floorplans: the original 4280 is a two-stateroom arrangement with two heads and a small galley, and the 4285 floorplan, introduced in 1990, has only a single-stateroom but a much larger galley and salon. (Just to make it more confusing, the 4280 layout was updated in 1992.) Topside, there's seating for a crowd on the massive bridge which is easily the social focus of the boat. Molded steps on both sides of the cockpit lead up to the bridge—very convenient. Her modified-V hull is fully cored and includes prop pockets for reduced shaft angles. Standard gas engines provide a sluggish 13 knots at cruise (about 20 knots top). With optional 375-hp Cats or 400-hp 6V53s the Express Bridge will cruise at 20 knots and reach a top speed of around 24 knots. ❑

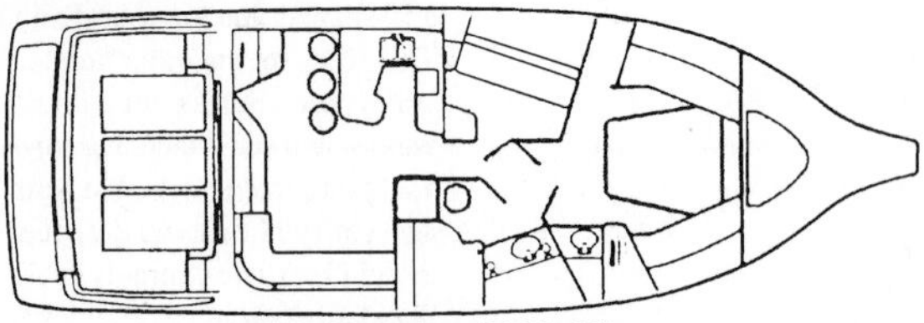

4280 Floorplan (1988–91)

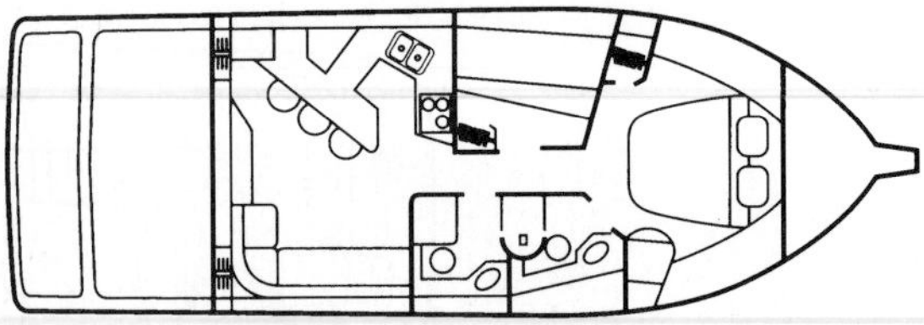

4280 Floorplan (1992–94)

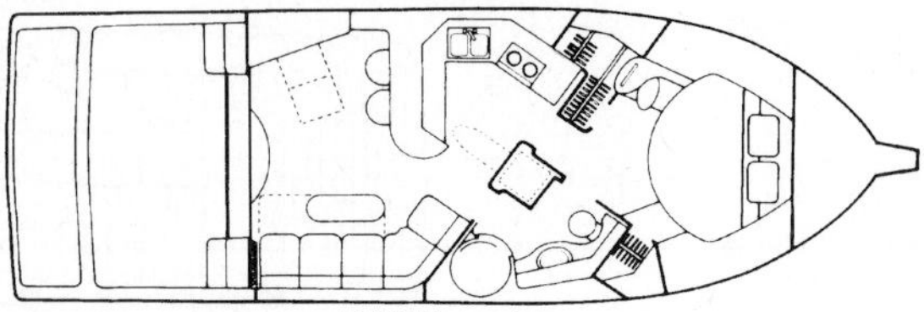

4285 Floorplan

See Page 264 for Pricing Information

DORAL 270 PRESTANCIA

SPECIFICATIONS

Length w/Pulpit..........27'1"	Clearance........................8'8"
Hull Length..................25'4"	Water........................28 gals.
Beam................................9'6"	Fuel.........................106 gals.
Draft, Up.........................1'7"	Hull Type.........Modified-V
Draft, Down...................2'9"	Deadrise Aft....................17°
Weight.......................7,175#	Production.............1989–95

Those seeking an upscale weekend cruiser with conservative lines and better-than-average quality would do well to consider the Canadian-built Doral 270. (Introduced as the 270 Monticello, the name was changed to Prestancia in 1991.) She's actually a 25-footer (not counting the pulpit), and her wide beam and elevated foredeck deliver a good deal of living space below for such a small boat. Berths for six are provided in a traditional mid-cabin layout with a stand-up head compartment and a small galley with plenty of storage. Considering how roomy the cabin is, it's surprising how much living space Doral engineers were able to design into the 270's cockpit. Outside, an L-shaped lounge across from the helm comes with a built-in wet bar, and a hidden cockpit shower is located near the transom gate. Additional features include a foredeck sunpad, molded pulpit, radar arch, and a wide swim platform. A good-running boat, twin 205-hp V-6 MerCruiser stern drives will cruise the Doral 270 at a brisk 24 knots and reach 35+ top. ❑

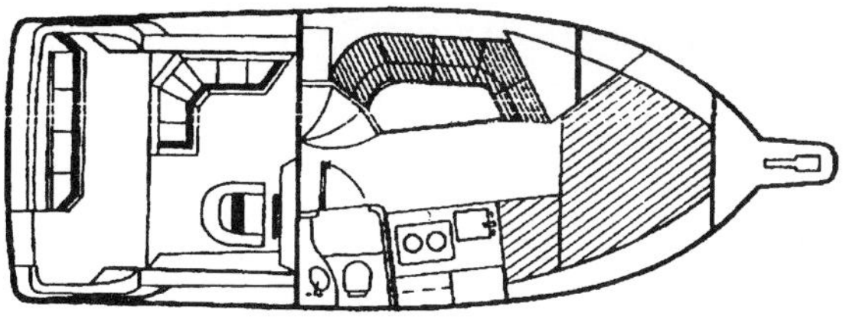

See Page 264 for Pricing Information

DORAL 300 PRESTANCIA

SPECIFICATIONS

Length w/Pulpit..........30'3"	Water........................34 gals.
Hull Length..................28'0"	Fuel.........................136 gals.
Beam..............................10'0"	Hull Type................Deep-V
Draft..............................2'11"	Deadrise Aft....................18°
Weight.......................8,275#	Designer...............D. Collier
Clearance........................9'2"	Production.............1989–95

A popular boat before Doral folded in 1992, the 300 Prestancia was subsequently manufactured by Cadorette until production ended in 1995. Built in Quebec on a fully-cored, deep-V hull, her 10-foot beam is quite wide considering that this is really a 28-foot boat. While she lacks the modern integrated swim platform of her more stylish competitors, the Prestancia's lines benefit from her curved windshield, subdued hull graphics, radar arch and molded bow pulpit. The interior is wide open with privacy curtains for both staterooms and a big dinette lounge with seating for a crowd. The mid-cabin horseshoe lounge coverts into a huge 6-foot, 8-inch double berth at night with plenty of room for two adults. Seating for six is provided in the cockpit (a bench seat is hidden in the transom), and a convenient hot-and-cold shower is recessed into the transom as well. A well finished boat, standard 4.3-litre MerCruiser I/Os will cruise the 300 Prestancia at a modest 16–17 knots (about 28 top), and optional 5.7-litre I/Os will cruise at 24 knots and reach 40 knots top. ❑

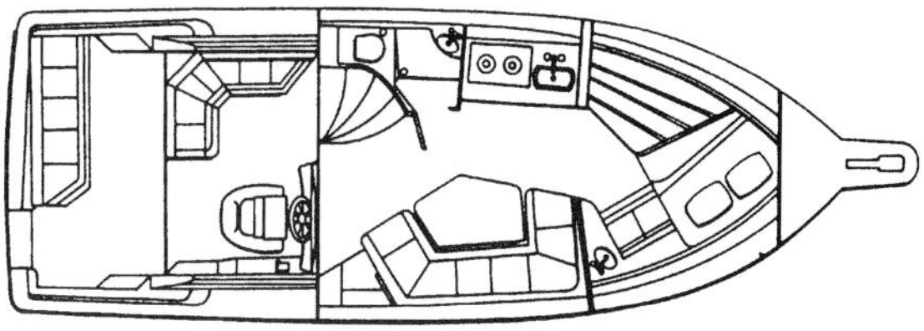

See Page 264 for Pricing Information

DORAL 350 BOCA GRANDE

SPECIFICATIONS

Length w/Pulpit..........35'8"	Fuel........................260 gals.
Beam.............................12'6"	Cockpit............................NA
Draft................................3'0"	Hull Type.........Modified-V
Weight......................13,900#	Deadrise Aft...................17°
Clearance.....................10'0"	Designer.....................Doral
Water........................80 gals.	Production..............1990-92

For those who have an appreciation for quality and don't mind paying for it, the Doral 350 is an impressive mid-sized express cruiser. She's built in Canada and currently represents the largest offering in Doral's fleet. Features include a stylish curved windshield, molded pulpit, foredeck sunpad, a huge hydraulically activated cockpit hatch for engine access, and an innovative power helm seat that can serve as a stand-up bolster when the seas pick up. The conventional mid-cabin floorplan of the Boca Grande is open and spacious, with a curtain providing limited privacy in the forward stateroom. The mid-cabin has pit-style lounge seating and an adjustable dinette table, and the head has a separate shower stall. A good-looking cruiser with meticulous detailing and finish, Doral's decision to employ a conventional transom design rather than a Hollywood-glitz Euro-transom is slightly refreshing. Built on a fully cored hull and driven through V-drives, she'll cruise around 17–18 knots with standard 454-cid MerCruisers gas engines and reach 28 knots wide open. ❑

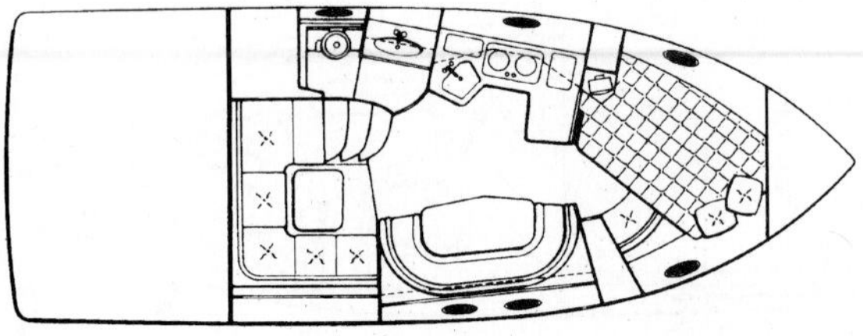

See Page 265 for Pricing Information

DUFFY 35 SPORT CRUISER

SPECIFICATIONS

Length..........................35'1"	Fuel, Std. ....100 gals.
Length WL...................33'4"	Fuel, Opt. ....200 gals.
Beam...........................11'11"	Cockpit............................NA
Draft...............................3'3"	Hull Type.........Modified-V
Weight.....................12,000#	Designer...............S. Lincoln
Water........................50 gals.	Production....1983–Current

Designed with a greater emphasis on speed than most other Downeast-style boats of her type, the Duffy 35 is a well-built, semi-custom cruiser with distinctive lines and tremendous eye appeal. She's constructed on a solid fiberglass, modified-V hull with a fine entry, hard chines aft, and a full-length keel which provides protection for the underwater gear. Like most of the true Downeast designs, a fully equipped Duffy 35 is priced at the higher end of the market for boats in her size range. Aside from good looks and traditional charm, her great attraction is a superb blend of New England craftsmanship and lasting value. The Duffy is a versatile boat with a cockpit large enough for serious fishing and an efficient interior layout well-suited for extended cruising. Features include a deckhouse galley, complete lower helm station, a large stall shower, and excellent access to the engine. A seaworthy and economical boat, a single Cat 375-hp diesel will produce a surprisingly fast cruising speed of 24 knots and a top speed of around 28 knots. ❑

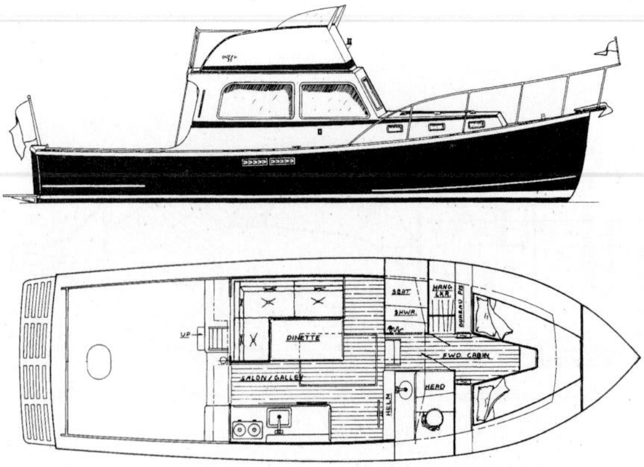

See Page 265 for Pricing Information

DUFFY 42 SPORT CRUISER

SPECIFICATIONS

Length	42'0"	Fuel	500 gals.
Beam	14'6"	Cockpit	NA
Draft	4'6"	Hull Type	Semi-Disp.
Weight	24,000#	Designer	S. Lincoln
Water	100 gals.	Production	1985–Current

A classic lobster boat profile and a high level of craftsmanship have made the Duffy 42 Sport Cruiser one of the more popular Downeast cruisers currently on the market. These are rugged semi-custom boats with cored hulls and a full length keel below—sea-worthy designs with beautiful sheers, protected running gear, and generous cockpits. There are several versions of the Duffy 42, and each can be built to a buyer's specifications. The two-stateroom, galley-up floorplan of the FB Cruiser (pictured above) features an island berth forward and bunk berths in the guest cabin. A lower helm is standard, and the conservative interior decor is functional and well-finished. Engine room access is very good, and a transom door and swim platform are standard. Most of the Duffy 42s built for private use (many are used commercially) have been powered with a single 375-hp Cat which delivers a 14-15-knot cruising speed and around 18 knots wide open. Cruising range is an impressive 500+ miles. A class act, used Duffy 42s (which are rare) are considered premium boats on the used markets. ❑

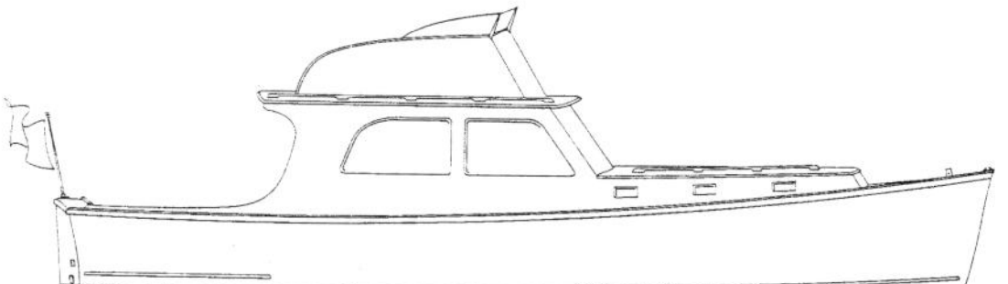

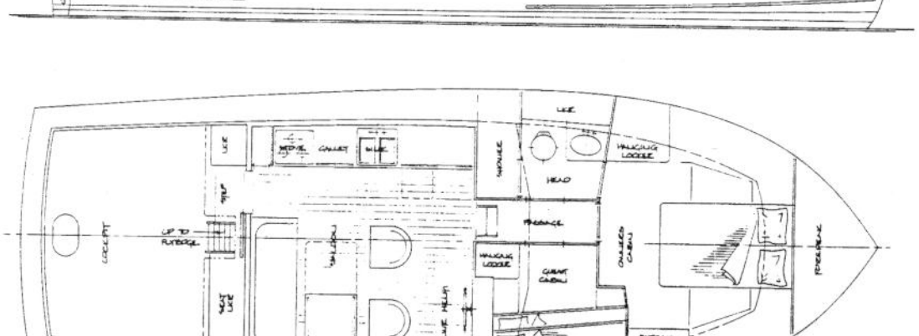

See Page 265 for Pricing Information

DYER 29

Trunk Cabin

Bass Boat

SPECIFICATIONS

Length	28'6"	Fuel	110 gals.
Beam	9'5"	Cockpit	NA
Draft	2'6"	Hull Type	Semi-Disp.
Weight	6,700#	Deadrise Aft	NA
Clearance	6'0"	Designer	Nick Potter
Water	24 gals.	Production	1955–Current

Designed for cruising, fishing, or as a general utility boat, the durable Dyer 29 is a industry classic. Indeed, there are those who think she's one of the most alluring small boats ever designed. Production began over 35 years ago making her the longest-running fiberglass model in the business. Each of the over 300 sold has been customized to some extent and no two are exactly alike. At only 6,700 lbs., the Dyer would be considered a light boat were it not for her narrow beam. She's built on a soft-chined hull with a fine entry, protected prop, and an uncommonly graceful sheer. The ability of the hull to tackle heavy sea conditions is legendary. Those who own Dyers tolerate her tight cabin quarters and inconvenient engine box and delight in the fingertip control and positive response of this easily driven hull. Among numerous engine options, a single 200-hp Volvo diesel will cruise the Dyer 29 efficiently at 16 knots (7 gph) and reach a top speed of 20–21 knots. In addition to the popular Trunk Cabin and Bass Boat models (pictured above), the 29 is available in hardtop and express versions. ❑

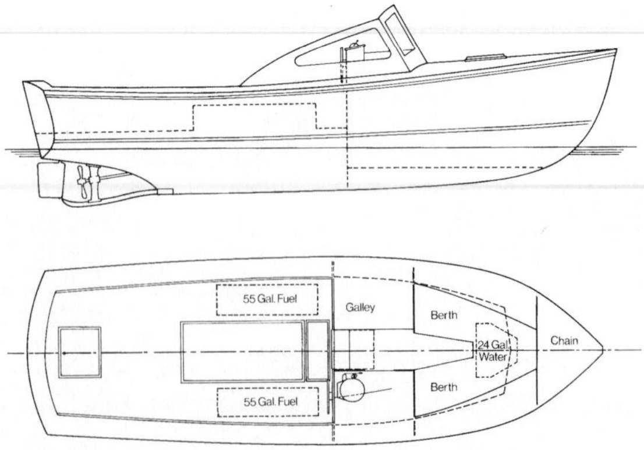

See Page 265 for Pricing Information

EGG HARBOR 33 SEDAN

1971–77

1978–81

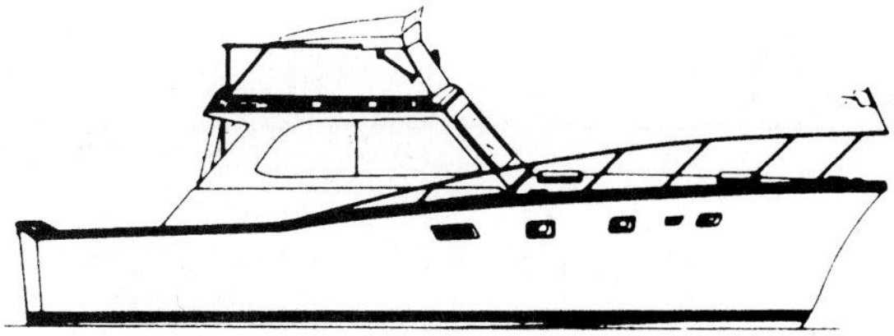

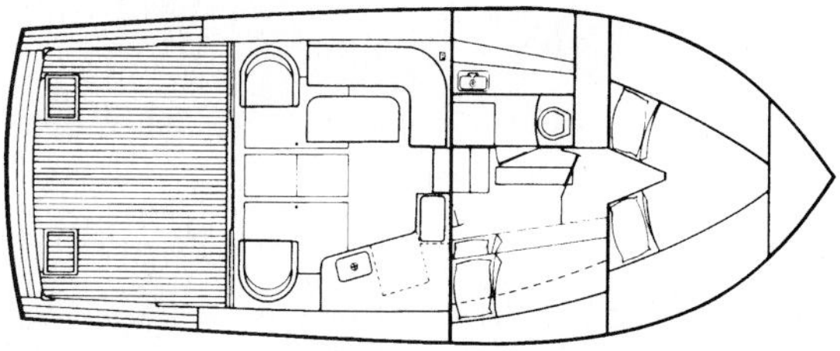

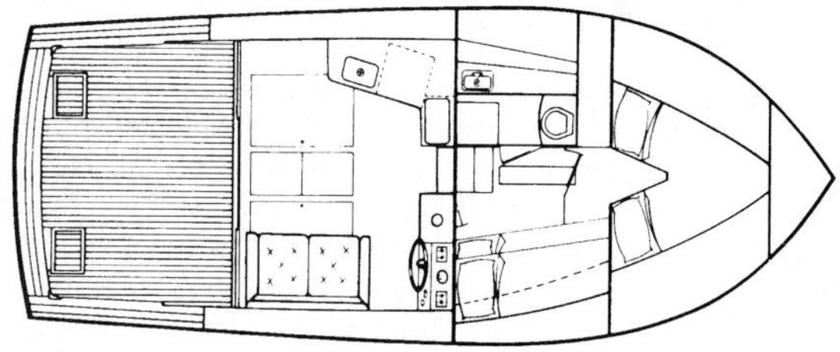

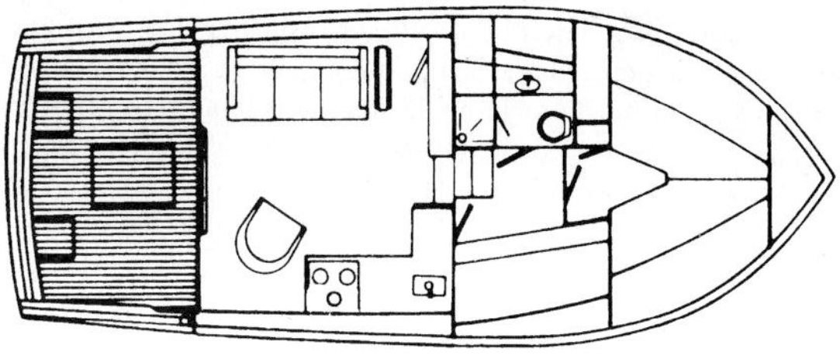

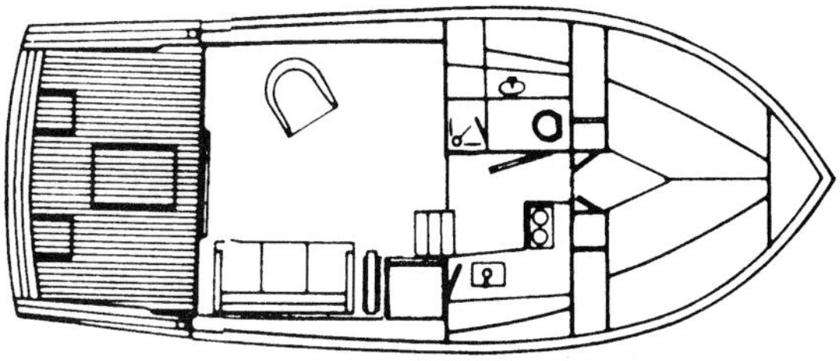

SPECIFICATIONS

Length ....33'0"	Fuel ....216 gals.
Beam ....13'2"	Cockpit ....NA
Draft ....2'9"	Hull Type ....Modified-V
Weight.....................13,000#	Deadrise Aft ....8°
Clearance ....NA	Designer ....Egg Harbor
Water ....50 gals.	Production 1971–81

The 33 Sedan was the first fiberglass hull ever built by the Egg Harbor Yacht Company. Designed primarily as a family cruiser, she was constructed with a mahogany deck and superstructure until 1978 when the switch was made to all-fiberglass construction. The standard floorplan arrangement has a two-stateroom layout with the galley in the salon. A galley-down version was offered in later models, and the head was also redesigned to accommodate a separate stall shower. Although the cockpit is small, and the range is limited, the great appeal of the Egg Harbor 33 Sedan lies in her graceful profile, rich mahogany interior, and the extensive use of exterior teak including teak covering boards and a solid teak cockpit sole. Her appearance improved dramatically when the fiberglass deck and house were introduced, and she remained in production until replaced in 1982 with the all-new Egg Harbor 33 Convertible. Twin 270-hp Crusader engines will cruise the Egg 33 at a modest 15–16 knots, and she'll reach a top speed of about 23 knots. ❑

See Page 265 for Pricing Information

ELLIS 32 CRUISER

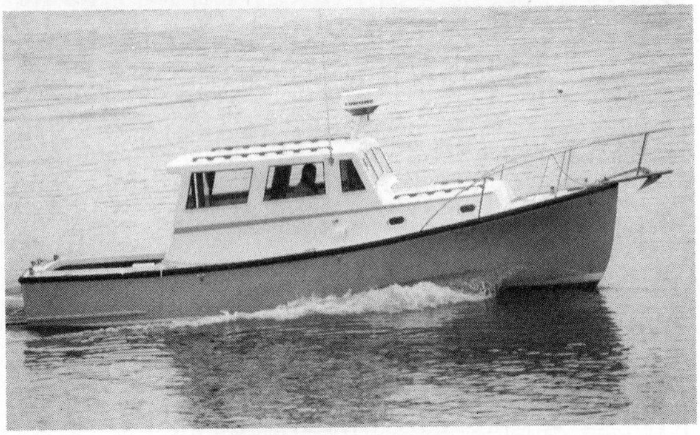

SPECIFICATIONS

Length	32'1"	Fuel	160 gals.
Beam	11'9"	Cockpit	NA
Draft	3'9"	Hull Type	Semi-Disp.
Weight	13,000#	Deadrise Aft	NA
Water	25 gals.	Designer	R. Ellis
Clearance	NA	Production	1991–Current

The Ellis Boat Company is an old-time builder of hand-crafted cruisers and lobster boats operating from a small yard in Manset, Maine. The 32 is the newest and largest of their designs. Offered in flybridge and bass boat models in addition to the hardtop pictured above, the solid fiberglass hull is a semi-displacement design with a deep, prop-protecting keel and generous beam. The Ellis 32 is a straightforward, basic boat with a pretty trunk cabin profile, superb detailing, and plenty of traditional teak trim. She's a roomy boat inside with accommodations for up to six depending on the floorplan. Note that the galley is located just inside the salon door, where it's easily accessed from the cockpit. The forecabin has two large V-berths, and the seat back of the settee opposite the large head folds up to create an upper berth. The ceilings are light ash, and the teak and holly cabin sole throughout the interior is impressive. Built on a semi-custom basis, a single 300-hp Volvo diesel will cruise at 18 knots (23–24 knots top). ❑

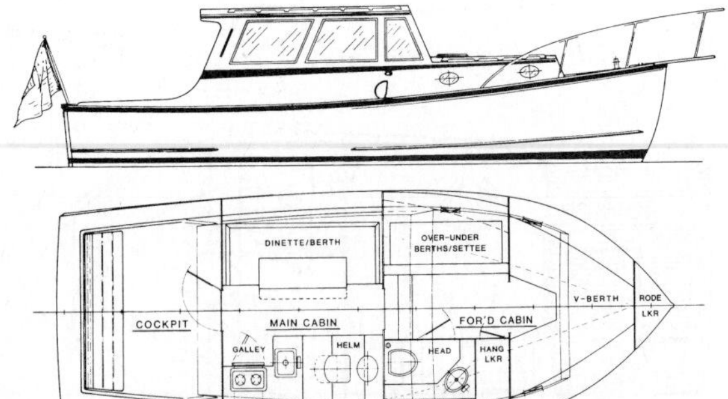

See page 265 for Pricing Information

EXCEL 26 SE

SPECIFICATIONS

Length	27"5"	Fuel	77 gals.
Hull Length	26'0"	Water	22 gals.
Beam	8'6"	Clearance	6'6"
Draft, Up	1'7"	Hull Type	Deep-V
Draft, Down	3'4"	Deadrise Aft	20°
Weight	5,000#	Production	1994–Current

When it comes to price, the Excel 26 SE is tough competition for most other boats her size on the market. There are no options — the equipment list and even the color scheme is the same on every boat — and the result is a super inexpensive trailerable package that budget-minded buyers will certainly find attractive. Hull construction is solid fiberglass, and at only 4,000 lbs. the 26 SE is a very light boat for her size. The basic mid-cabin floorplan is arranged with double berths fore and aft, a compact galley, and an enclosed, stand-up head with vanity and shower. Considering her relatively narrow beam, the cabin seems surprisingly open and comfortable. Outside, the cockpit will seat up to eight, and the bench seat opposite the helm converts into a sun lounge. Lacking sidedecks, a walk-through windshield provides access to the bow. Note that there's very little space at the helm for electronics. A single 225-hp Volvo stern drive cruises the Excel 26 at 25 knots with a top speed of 32 knots—not bad for a single-engine 26-footer. ❑

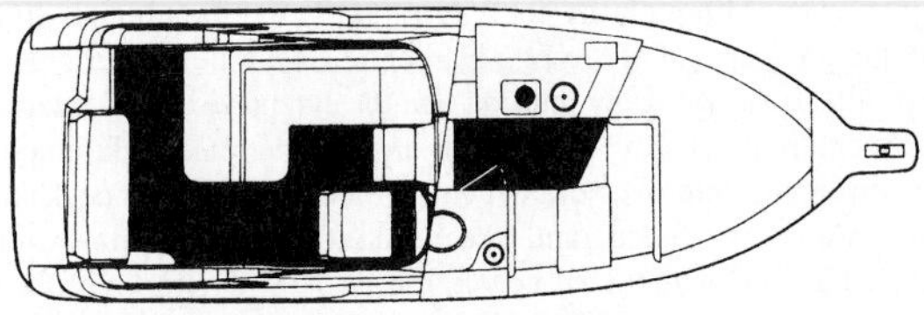

See page 265 for Pricing Information

FEXAS 42 SPORT SEDAN

SPECIFICATIONS

Length	41'9"	Cockpit	NA
Length WL	37'9"	Water	200 gals.
Beam	13'0"	Fuel	400 gals.
Draft	3'0"	Hull Type	Semi-Disp.
Weight	24,000#	Designer	Tom Fexas
Clearance	10'4"	Production	1982–91

The Fexas 42 was built in Taiwan on a soft-chined hull with a somewhat narrow beam, with a fine entry, and shallow keel. The hull is fully cored, and she weighs in at a frugal 24,000 lbs. What sets the Fexas 42 apart from most other mid-size sedan models is her superb styling. Note the rakish fore and aft bridge overhangs and distinctive stepped salon windows. While several floorplans have been offered over the years, most 42s were delivered with a two-stateroom teak interior with a lower helm and single head. The salon dimensions—while adequate—are limited by the relatively narrow beam and wide sidedecks. The flybridge is arranged with the helm forward and facing settees fore and aft. A good performer with standard 300-hp Cat 3116 diesels, the Fexas 42 will cruise efficiently at 21 knots and deliver a top speed of around 24–25 knots. Early models powered with 260-hp GM 8.2s are a knot or two slower. Note that she's also been imported as the Mikelson and Ultimate 42. ❑

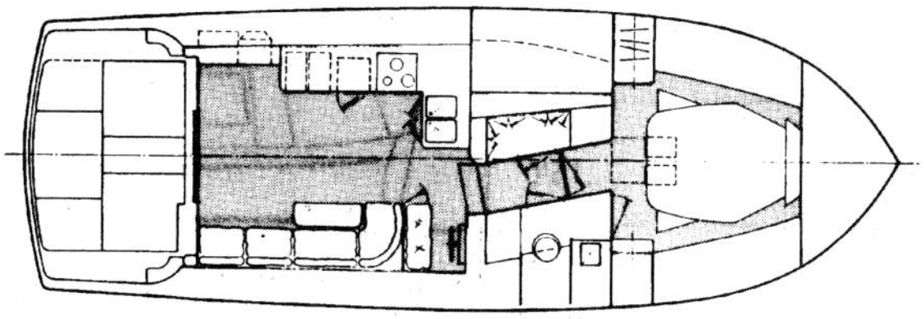

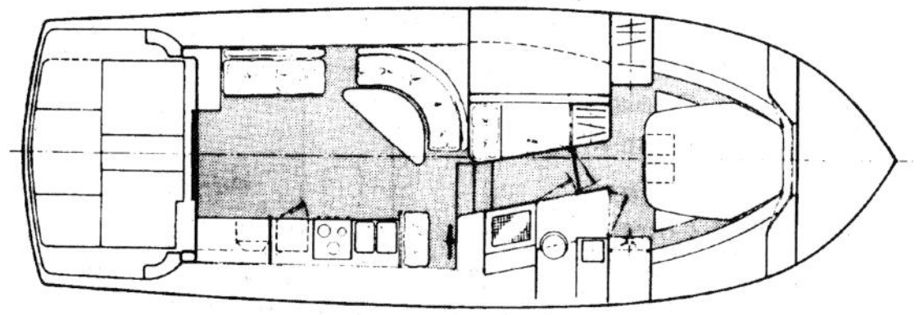

See Page 265 for Pricing Information

FORMULA 26 PC

SPECIFICATIONS

Length w/Pulpit..........30'5"	Water........................32 gals.
Hull Length..................26'0"	Clearance........................8'6"
Beam................................8'6"	Hull Type................Deep-V
Draft, Down.................2'11"	Deadrise Aft....................20°
Weight........................8,200#	Designer................J. Adams
Fuel...........................90 gals.	Production.............1988–93

A popular boat with a long production run, the Formula 26 PC is a well-built express cruiser with an rakish profile and distinctive hull graphics. She's obviously dated by today's sportboat designs (note the bolt-on swim platform and bow pulpit), but with her 8-foot, 6-inch beam and comfortable mid-cabin interior, the 26 PC is still one of the more livable mid-size family cruisers around. She's also trailerable—the largest ever built by Formula—but at close to 9,000 lbs. (including trailer) she's definately no lightweight. Hull construction is solid fiberglass, and the deep-V bottom of the 26 PC insures a stable and comfortable ride in a chop. There are berths for six below along with a stand-up head and a small galley. Privacy curtains separate the fore and aft sleeping areas, and the fabrics, hardware and interior appliances are first rate. Additional features include fold-away cockpit seating, a wide swim platform, and a motorized hatch in the cockpit sole for engine access. A single 330-hp stern drive will cruise the Formula 26 PC at 18 knots (about 28 knots top), and twin 205-hp I/Os run about 3–4 knots faster. ❑

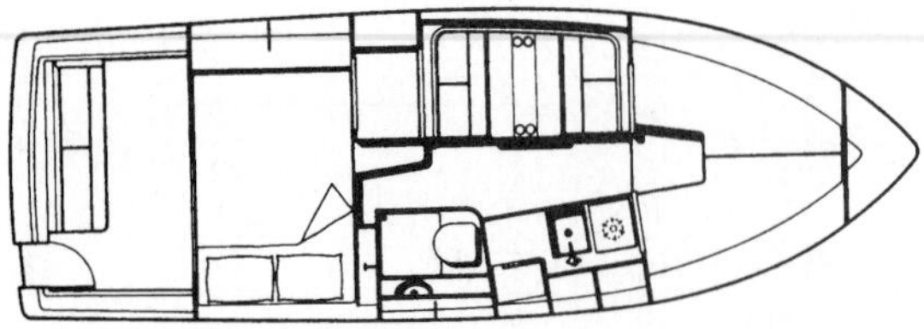

See page 265 for Pricing Information

FORMULA 27 PC

SPECIFICATIONS

LOA...............................28'2"	Water........................26 gals.
Hull Length.................27'0"	Fuel.........................107 gals.
Beam..............................9'7"	Hull Type................Deep-V
Draft...............................3'1"	Deadrise Aft....................18°
Weight.......................9,000#	Designer................J. Adams
Clearance.......................8'8"	Production....1994–Current

The Formula 27 PC is a good-looking express cruiser with an upscale price tag to go with her sporty appearance. Built on a solid fiberglass, deep-V hull, her 9,000 lb. displacement is heavy for a 27-footer. Her mid-cabin floorplan is arranged with a built-in entertainment center facing the dinette in addition to a large head, a stylish pod-type galley, and berths for four. This is an impressive and beautifully designed interior with quality hardware, furnishings, and fabrics throughout. Lacking sidedecks (foredeck access is via a cut-out in the windshield), the full-width cockpit is roomy indeed and comes with a double-wide helm seat, tilt wheel, wet bar, and a stow-away aft bench. An electrically activated in-deck hatch provides access to the engine compartment. The anchor is hidden in the anchor locker—no unsightly bow pulpit required. Additional features include a radar arch, an adjustable cocktail table for the cockpit with filler cushion, and a tilt steering wheel. Twin 180-hp/4.3-litre stern drives will cruise the 27 PC at 18 knots (about 33 knots top), and optional 235-hp/5.7-litre I/Os will cruise at 26 knots (43–44 knots wide open). ❑

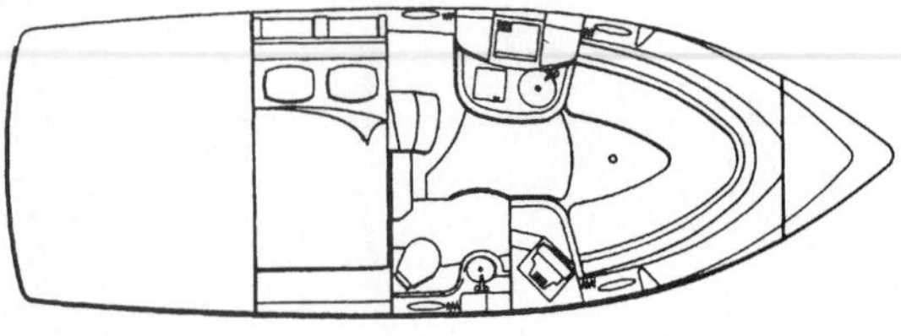

See Page 265 for Pricing Information

FORMULA 28 PC

SPECIFICATIONS

Length w/Pulpit..........30'6"	Water........................39 gals.
Hull Length.................28'0"	Fuel.........................160 gals.
Beam.............................10'0"	Hull Type...............Deep-V
Draft..............................2'10"	Deadrise Aft...................24°
Weight.......................7,850#	Designer...............J. Adams
Clearance.......................8'4"	Production.............1985–87

Mid-cabin layouts were rapidly gaining in buyer acceptance in the mid-1980s, and Formula was one of many manufacturers to incorporate this floorplan in their evolving line of express cruisers. Obviously dated by today's Eurostyle sportboats, the 28 PC was considered an upscale boat during her production years, and her above-average construction and stylish hull graphics have allowed her to age gracefully. She's a roomy boat below thanks to her wide beam, and the layout is well-arranged. The forward stateroom is separated from the salon by a folding privacy door, and a section of the upholstered wall separating the two cabins is actually a sliding panel: leave it down for a more open salon. The aft cabin includes facing settees and game table which convert to a double bed at night. Outside, L-shaped lounge seating is opposite the helm, and the engine compartment (the hatch raises hydraulically) is huge. A good performer, twin 260-hp stern drives will cruise the Formula 28 PC at 23 knots and reach 35 knots top. ❑

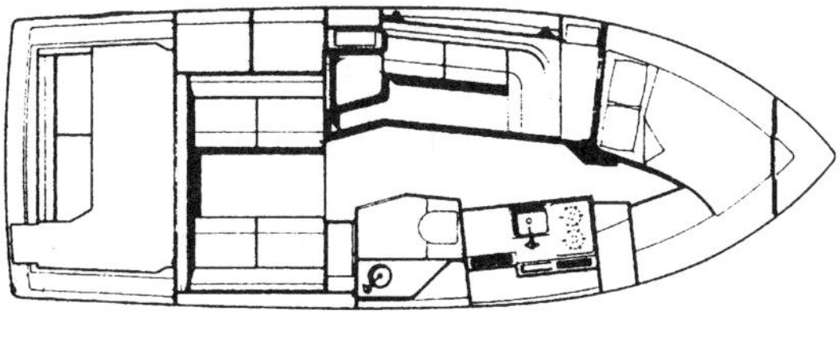

See Page 265 for Pricing Information

FORMULA 29 PC

SPECIFICATIONS

Length w/Pulpit..........33'9"	Water........................50 gals.
Hull Length.................29'0"	Fuel.........................165 gals.
Beam.............................10'7"	Hull Type...............Deep-V
Draft..............................2'6"	Deadrise Aft...................20°
Weight.......................9,700#	Designer...............J. Adams
Clearance.......................8'9"	Production.............1988–92

Introduced in 1988 as a replacement for the 28 PC, the Formula 29 PC is basically an enlarged version of her predecessor with additional beam and weight, a little less transom deadrise, and improved styling (note the curved windshield and swept-back radar arch). Inside, the mid-cabin layout is essentially unchanged, although the fabrics and wall coverings are brighter. Indeed, the interior of the 29 PC is very inviting, with good-quality cabinetry and hardware throughout. The galley has plenty of counter space, and there's enough room in the head to take a comfortable shower. Headroom in the main cabin is excellent. To create a more open cabin, curtains are used (rather than doors) for privacy in both staterooms. In the cockpit, the helm seat swivels to face aft, and the back seat slides into a transom recess for access to the motors. (The deck raises automatically to expose a big engine compartment.) Twin MerCruiser or Volvo 350-cid stern drives will cruise at 21 knots and reach 33–34 knots top. This is an especially good-handling boat. ❑

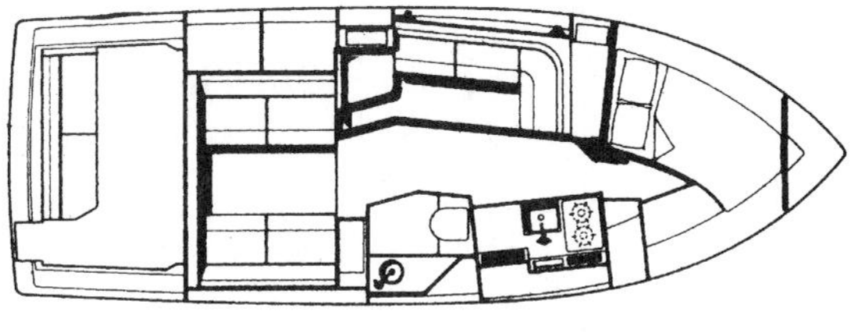

See Page 265 for Pricing Information

FORMULA 31 SC EXPRESS

SPECIFICATIONS

Length	31'4"	Water	45 gals.
Beam	12'0"	Fuel	200 gals.
Draft	2'6"	Hull Type	Deep-V
Weight	10,500#	Deadrise Aft	18°
Clearance	8'4"	Designer	J. Adams
Cockpit	NA	Production	1981–85

Aside from her reversed arch, the most striking feature of the Formula 31 SC is her wide beam—wider in fact than any other family cruiser her size in the early 1980s. Built of solid fiberglass on a constant deadrise deep-V hull, the 31 SC's trunk cabin appearance is clearly dated (modern express designs incorporate a raised foredeck profile), although the generous cabin headroom is a big plus. The floorplan is arranged with a double berth in the forward stateroom (with a folding privacy door), a big U-shaped dinette, and facing settee. While the galley is compact, the head compartment is quite large. Outside, the single-level cockpit is very spacious for a boat this size, with double-wide helm and companion seats and removable bench seating aft. Additional features include wide sidedecks, teak swim platform, and teak covering boards. A good-handling boat thanks to her deep-V hull, optional 350-hp inboards will cruise the Formula 31 SC at 18-19 knots cruise and about 27 knots top. ❑

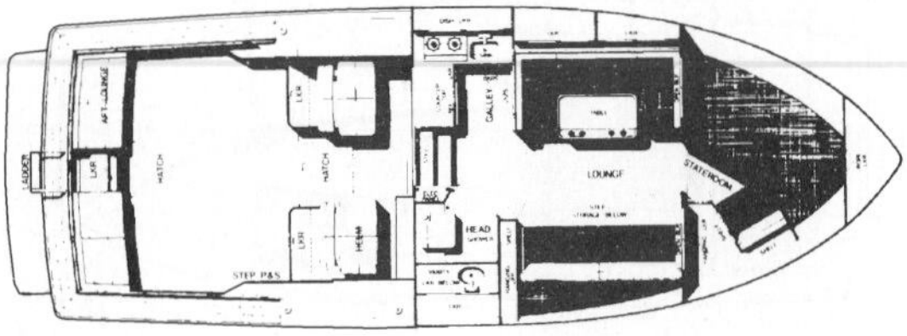

See Page 265 for Pricing Information

FORMULA 31 PC

SPECIFICATIONS

Length w/Pulpit	*34'0"*	Water	50 gals.
Hull Length	31'0"	Fuel	180 gals.
Beam	11'0"	Hull Type	Deep-V
Draft	3'2"	Deadrise Aft	19°
Weight	11,730#	Designer	J. Adams
Clearance	9'3"	Production	1993–95

Although a 31-foot express cruiser with stern drives isn't unusual in today's market, there are many who prefer inboard power in a boat this size. That said, the Formula 31 PC ranks near the top of the list when it comes to construction and performance, and her styling is impressive in spite of her relatively high freeboard. Like all of Formula's PC series, the 31 is built on a modern deep-V bottom, and both the swim platform and pulpit are an integral part of the hull. Inside, the mid-cabin floorplan is organized in the conventional manner, with berths for six, a large head, and privacy curtains for both staterooms. Not surprisingly, the hardware, fabrics, furnishings, and appliances are first-rate. Outside, the cockpit is arranged with a fore-and-aft lounge opposite the double-wide helm seat. The bench seating aft folds away, and a motorized hatch provides access to the (tight) engine compartment. A fast boat with twin 7.4-litre stern drive MerCruisers, the cruising speed is 24 knots and the top speed is 36 knots. ❑

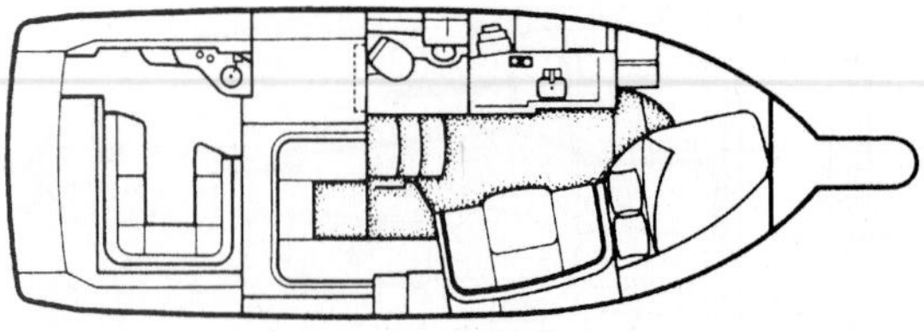

See Page 265 for Pricing Information

FORMULA 34 PC

SPECIFICATIONS

LOA ....37'0"	Water ....60 gals.
Hull Length ....34'0"	Fuel ....230 gals.
Beam.............................12'0"	Hull Type ....Deep-V
Draft ....2'6"	Deadrise Aft...................18°
Weight......................13,000#	Designer ....J. Adams
Clearance ....9'3"	Production 1991–Current

A well-built boat with plenty of sex appeal to go with her sport-boat image, the Formula 34 PC has been a popular boat for Thunderbird since her introduction in 1991. Like all of Formula's PC (Performance Cruiser) designs, she's built on a constant dead-rise, deep-V hull with average beam and solid fiberglass construction. The mid-cabin interior will sleep six and comes with an island berth in the forward stateroom and convertible facing settees in the aft cabin. Both staterooms have privacy curtains, and a bi-fold door in the head isolates the shower from the vanity. A triple-wide companion seat is opposite the helm, and the entire aft part of the huge cockpit can be turned into a giant sunken sunpad. Note that the 34 PC was available only with stern drives until 1994 when inboards (with V-drives) became standard. A good performer, twin 454-cid Volvo or MerCruiser I/Os will cruise at 21–22 knots (about 34 knots top). Cruising speeds for the 454-cid MerCruiser inboards are about a knot or two slower. ❑

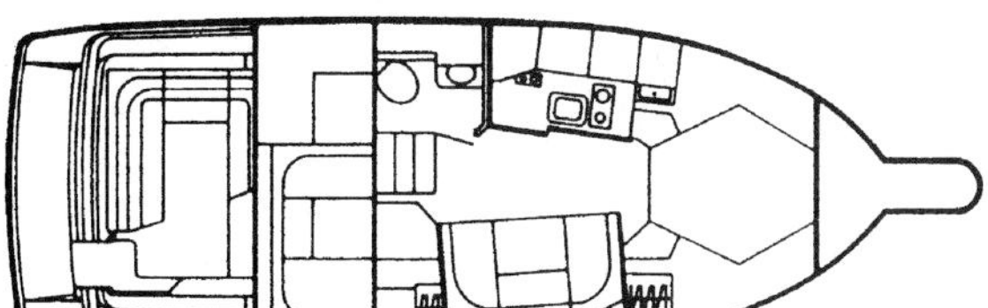

See Page 265 for Pricing Information

FORMULA 35 PC

SPECIFICATIONS

LOA ....40'0"	Water ....50 gals.
Hull Length ....35'0"	Fuel ....275 gals.
Beam.............................12'0"	Hull Type ....Deep-V
Draft ....2'8"	Deadrise Aft...................20°
Weight......................13,750#	Designer ....J. Adams
Clearance ....10'2"	Production 1986–89

Largest of the Formula Performance Cruiser (PC) fleet in the late 1980s, the 35 PC is a roomy family express cruiser with a still-attractive profile and a comfortable mid-cabin interior layout. Construction is solid fiberglass, and her deep-V hull is designed with side-dumping exhausts and prop pockets at the transom. Below, the wide-open floorplan includes a superb U-shaped galley area—one of the best we've seen in any express boat this size—and a step-down mid-cabin with facing settees which convert into a big double bed at night. There's a centerline island berth in the forward stateroom (with only a draw curtain for nighttime privacy), and all of the fabrics, hardware, furnishings, and appliances are first rate. The cockpit is arranged with a big L-shaped lounge opposite the helm and fold-away bench seating at the transom. Accessed via a motorized hatch lift, twin 454-cid MerCruiser gas engines (with V-drives) will cruise the Formula 35 PC at 21–22 knots and reach a top speed of around 31 knots. ❑

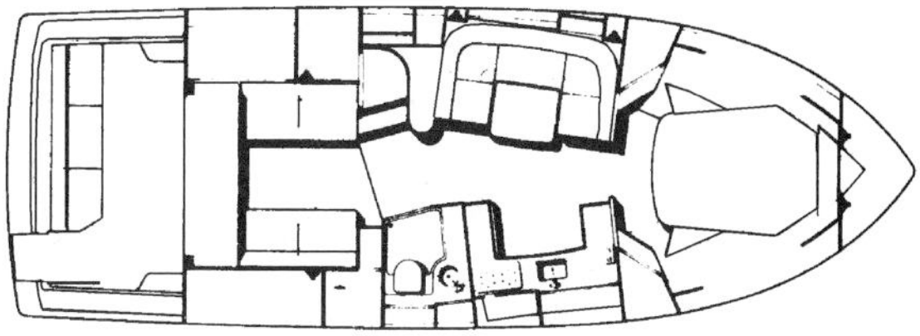

See Page 265 for Pricing Information

FORMULA 36 PC

SPECIFICATIONS

Length Overall	38'3"	Water	60 gals.
Hull Length	36'0"	Fuel	300 gals.
Beam	13'3"	Hull Type	Deep-V
Draft	2'8"	Deadrise Aft	18°
Weight	17,600#	Designer	J. Adams
Clearance	10'9"	Production	1990–95

A good-selling model during her six-year production run, the Formula 36 PC is an upscale cruiser with plenty of eye appeal to go with her roomy interior. She's built of solid fiberglass on a beamy deep-V hull with fairly high freeboard and prop pockets at the transom. Inside, the mid-cabin floorplan is arranged in the conventional manner with an island bed in the forward stateroom (with a door for privacy) and facing settees in the step-down aft cabin. There's a built-in entertainment center on the aft bulkhead above the mid-cabin facing the salon—very innovative. In the cockpit, a big L-shaped lounge is opposite the helm, and a hydraulically operated hatch provides outstanding access to the engine compartment. Unlike most modern mid-cabin designs, the Formula 36 PC does not have V-drives—a big plus in our book. Standard 454-cid gas engines will cruise at a moderate 17 knots and reach 26–27 knots top. Note that in 1990 (only) Formula offered an Express version of the 36 PC without the mid-cabin but with a huge engine room and extra storage. ❑

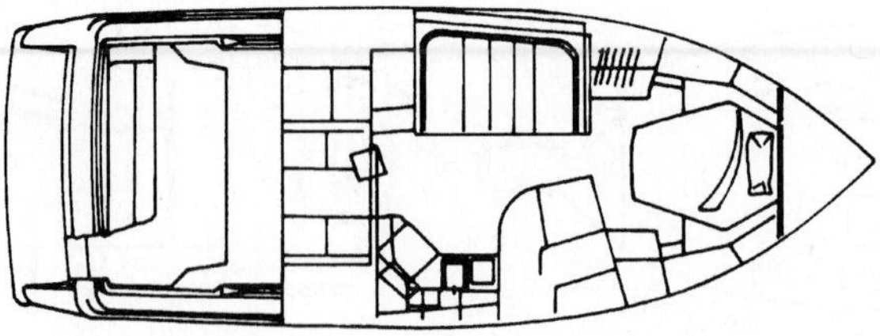

See Page 266 for Pricing Information

FOUR WINNS 258 VISTA

SPECIFICATIONS

Length	25'4"	Water	20 gals.
Beam	8'6"	Clearance	6'9"
Draft	3'3"	Hull Type	Modified-V
Weight	5,730#	Deadrise Aft	17°
Cockpit	NA	Designer	T. Weinstadt
Fuel	75 gals.	Production	1994–Current

The Four Winns 258 Vista is a well-arranged trailerable cruiser with a modern profile (note the absence of a bow pulpit) and an affordable price. She's built on a solid fiberglass, modified-V hull that incorporates the bottom of the swim platform as part of the running surface. Below deck, the mid-cabin floorplan features a full galley with sink, stove, refrigerator and counter space. Wraparound seating forward doubles as a V-berth and, with a removable table, converts into a four-place dinette. The enclosed head has standing headroom and includes a vanity and shower. The mid-cabin serves as a second stateroom with a double berth and privacy curtain. The cockpit of the 258 has a double-wide (reversible) helm seat and wraparound lounge seating aft. Engine access is through a floor hatch and, since there are no walkarounds, a walk-through windshield provides access to the bow. Additional features include a wide swim platform with swim ladder and a walk-through transom. A single 255-hp 5.8-litre OMC stern drive engine will provide a cruising speed of 18 knots (about 30 knots top). ❑

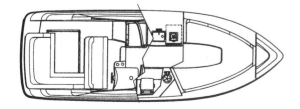

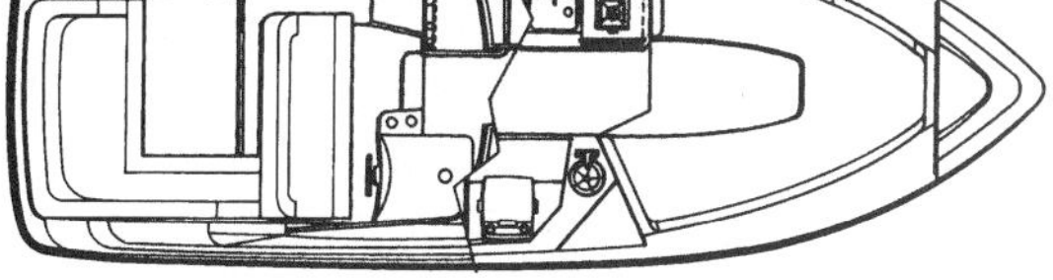

See Page 266 for Pricing Information

FOUR WINNS 265 VISTA

SPECIFICATIONS

Length w/Pulpit	26'2"	Water	20 gals.
Hull Length	24'7"	Clearance w/Arch	8'0"
Beam	8'6"	Hull Type	Deep-V
Draft	3'3"	Deadrise Aft	NA
Weight	6,000#	Designer	Four Winns
Fuel	85 gals.	Production	1990–93

No longer in production, the 265 Vista remains as the largest trailerable cruiser ever built by Four Winns. She's constructed on a solid fiberglass, deep-V hull with a sharp entry and an integral swim platform. The mid-cabin floorplan of the 265 Vista is arranged with an open V-berth/dinette forward followed by a small galley to port and an enclosed head to starboard. Aft, under the bridgedeck, is a queen-sized berth with a privacy curtain and storage shelves. Sliding cabin windows and four opening ports at the bow provide good cabin ventilation, and the headroom in the galley is about 6 feet. In the cockpit, a curved settee opposite the helm rotates to face the afterdeck. The bench seat at the transom has a kick-up extension for sunbathing, and a transom door leads to a wide swim platform with a boarding ladder. Note that the walkarounds are very narrow. A single 260-hp 5.7-litre OMC stern drive will cruise the 265 Vista at 18 knots (32 top), and twin 175-hp 5.0-litre OMCs will deliver a 23-knot cruising speed and top speed of about 36 knots. ❑

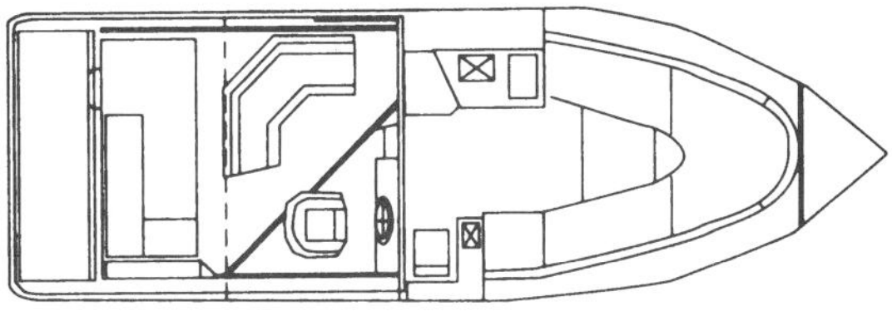

See Page 266 for Pricing Information

FOUR WINNS 275/278 VISTA

SPECIFICATIONS

Length	27'2"	Cockpit	NA
Beam	9'4"	Clearance w/Arch	8'6"
Draft	3'3"	Hull Type	Modified-V
Weight	7,400#	Deadrise Aft	17°
Fuel	110 gals.	Designer	Four Winns
Water	38 gals.	Production	1994–Current

The Four Winns 278 Vista (called the 275 Vista in 1994) is a maxi-cube pocket cruiser with a modern profile (note the absence of a bow pulpit) and an affordable price. Like most family boats her size, her modified-V hull provides a stable and comfortable ride in a variety of weather conditions. The Vista's accommodations are evenly divided between a roomy and well-arranged cockpit and the full-width cabin with its conventional mid-cabin floorplan. There are double berths fore and aft, and both sleeping areas have a curtain for privacy. The galley (often an afterthough on many small cruisers) is very complete with plenty of storage and counter space. There's a shower in the stand-up head, and the dinette table converts into a kid-sized berth. Outside, visability from the double-wide helm seat is excellent. Additional features include a walk-through windshield for bow access, space in the helm for flush-mounted electronics, and fold-away bench seating at the transom. Twin 200-hp/5.0-lite OMC stern drives (optional) will cruise the Vista 278 at 24–25 knots (about 38 knots top). ❑

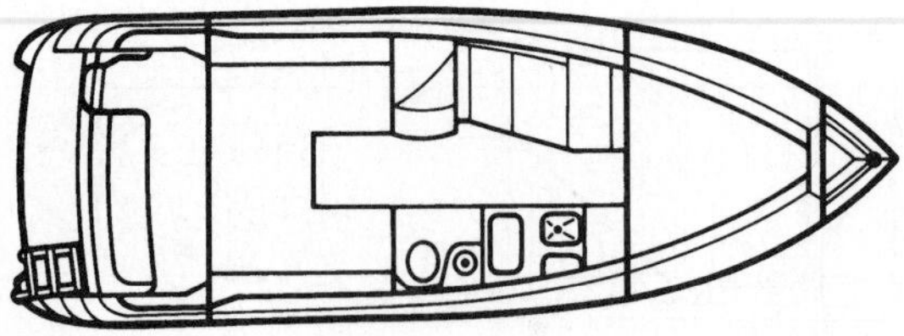

See Page 266 for Pricing Information

FOUR WINNS 285 EXPRESS

SPECIFICATIONS

Length	28'11"	Water	35 gals.
Beam	10'2"	Fuel	140 gals.
Draft	3'3"	Hull Type	Deep-V
Weight	9,060#	Deadrise Aft	19°
Clearance	8'6"	Designer	Four Winns
Cockpit	NA	Production	1991–93

No longer in production, the Four Winns 285 Express remains a good-looking express cruiser with a rakish profile (note the circular deck hatches and dramatic hull graphics) and roomy accommodations. She's built on an easy-riding, deep-V hull with cored hullsides, a relatively wide beam, and a solid fiberglass bottom. While most family cruisers this size are built with mid-cabin interiors, the 285 Express is unique in that she offered a choice of two layouts. The standard floorplan (and the most popular) has a wraparound lounge/dinette/V-berth forward with seating for six adults. An alternate layout has a separate dinette in the salon and a double berth forward. Outside, the passanger seat opposite the helm rotates to face the cockpit (a useful feature), and wide walkarounds make getting to the bow easy and safe. Additional features include fold-away bench seating at the transom, good access to the engines, and a swim ladder with an assist rail. Among several engine options, twin 245-hp/351-cid OMC stern drives will cruise the 285 Express at 24–25 knots and reach 40 knots top. ❑

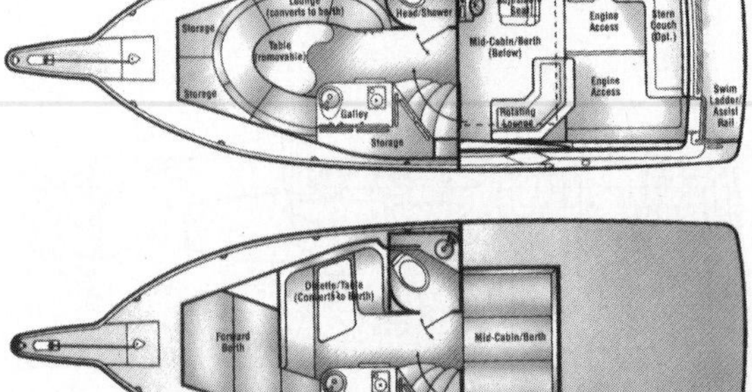

See Page 266 for Pricing Information

FOUR WINNS 315/325 EXPRESS

SPECIFICATIONS

Length w/Pulpit..........30'6"	Water.......................35 gals.
Hull Length..................28'6"	Fuel.........................150 gals.
Beam..............................11'0"	Hull Type.........Modified-V
Draft.....................2'10"/3'4"	Deadrise Aft....................19°
Weight......................11,700#	Production, 315......1988–93
Clearance.......................9'0"	Production, 325......1991–93

The 1988 introduction of the Four Winns 315 Vista (she became the 325 Express in 1993) was a big step up for a company whose reputation had previously been made in the trailerable-boat business. The 325 model (pictured above) is an inboard version of the original 315 with V-drives and a slightly lengthened hull with prop pockets. Both are heavily built on a maxi-beam hull with cored hullsides and a solid fiberglass bottom. The sidedecks are quite wide, and the molded pulpit, curved windshield, and integral swim platform contribute to her sportboat profile. With her wide beam, the cabin dimensions are quite spacious for a 29-footer. Both the 315 and 325 share an identical mid-cabin interior with berths for six, a small head, and compact galley. (The 315 received some cosmetic updates and a new helm in 1990.) For performance, a pair of 5.7-litre stern drives will cruise the 315 Express at 20 knots (30 knots top), and optional 7.4-litre I/Os will cruise at 24 knots. The 325 Express with 270-hp inboards will cruise at 18 knots and reach 27–28 knots wide open. ❑

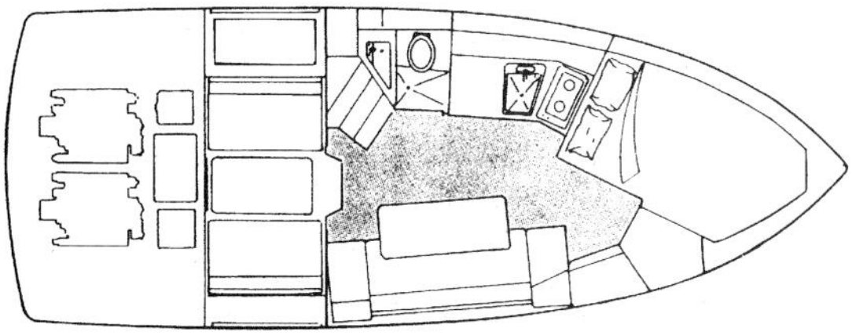

See Page 266 for Pricing Information

FOUR WINNS 365 EXPRESS

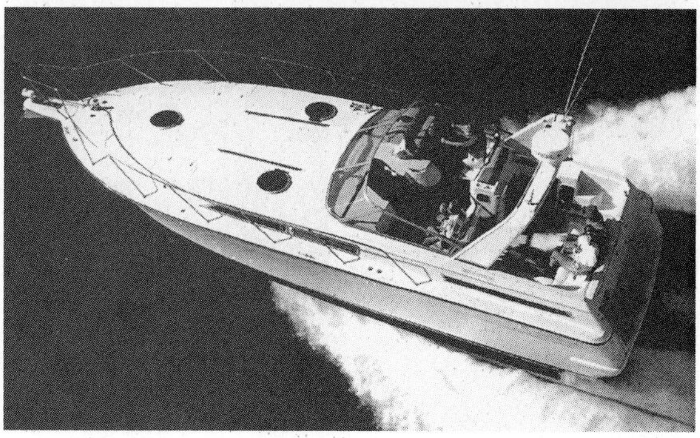

SPECIFICATIONS

Length w/Pulpit..........36'0"	Fuel.........................315 gals.
Beam.............................13'2"	Cockpit...........................NA
Draft...............................3'2"	Hull Type.........Modified-V
Weight......................18,600#	Deadrise Aft....................16°
Clearance.....................10'4"	Designer...............Blackwell
Water.......................98 gals.	Production.............1991–94

The Four Winns 365 is another of the good-looking mid-cabin express cruisers increasingly popular in today's sportboat market. Indeed, it's becoming difficult to distinguish one from another, but the 365 does have something none of the others can claim—an optional Jacuzzi spa hidden below the island berth in the forward stateroom! She's built on a conventional modified-V hull with a relatively wide beam and prop pockets aft. Note the long, sweeping foredeck of the 365—the helm is well aft in this boat, thus reducing cockpit space in favor of an unusually spacious and wide-open interior. Notable features include hidden foredeck lockers, a unique fold-away dinette table, excellent access to the engines and generator, tilt steering wheel, side exhausts, good sidedecks, and a unique air induction system designed to lower the risk of cockpit fumes. Crusader 350-hp gas inboards (with V-drives) will cruise the Four Winns 365 at a respectable 18–19 knots (about 32 knots top), and optional 300-hp Cummins diesels cruise at 20 knots and deliver around 30 knots wide open. ❑

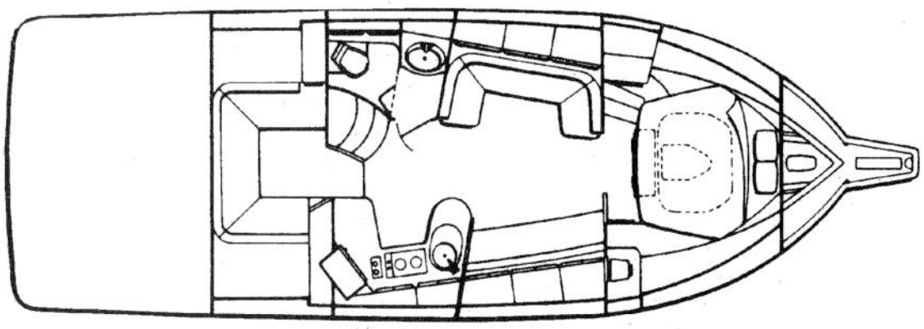

See Page 266 for Pricing Information

HATTERAS 36 SEDAN CRUISER

SPECIFICATIONS

Length	36'6"	Fuel	355 gals.
Beam	13'7"	Cockpit	NA
Draft	3'9"	Hull Type	Modified-V
Weight	25,500#	Deadrise Aft	18°
Clearance	12'6"	Designer	Jim Wynne
Water	115 gals.	Production	1986–87

Not remembered as a particularly successful model (production lasted only two years), the Hatteras 36 Sedan is basically the same boat as the Hatteras 36 Convertible (1983–87) with a larger interior and smaller cockpit dimensions. Hull construction is solid fiberglass, and the hull is designed with moderate beam, a shallow keel, and prop pockets. Two mid-galley interior layouts were available in the 36 Sedan: a dinette floorplan with a single stateroom and a two-stateroom arrangement without the dinette. Either way, the head compartment is very large and includes a separate stall shower. The interior is finished with traditional teak woodwork throughout, and it's notable that a lower helm option was never offered. While the salon is quite roomy for a 36-footer, the cockpit is too small for any serious fishing activities. Additional features include a big flybridge, good engine access, and fairly wide sidedecks. An unexciting performer with standard 350-hp Crusader gas engines, the Hatteras 36 Sedan will cruise at 15 knots and reach a top speed in the neighborhood of 24 knots. Diesels were optional and faster. ❑

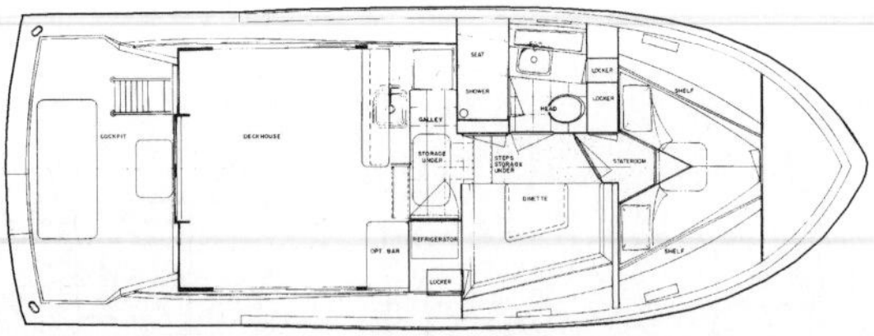

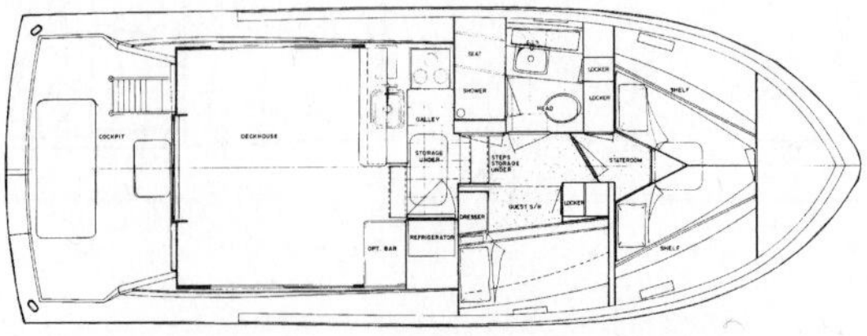

See Page 266 for Pricing Information

HATTERAS 39 SPORT EXPRESS

SPECIFICATIONS

Length ....39'0"	Clearance ....NA
Beam..............................13'5"	Cockpit.................103 sq. ft.
Draft ....4'8"	Hull Type ....Modified-V
Weight.....................29,500#	Deadrise Aft......................9°
Fuel ....458 gals.	Designer ....Hatteras
Water ....117 gals.	Production 1995–Current

Tiara started the trend toward big, dual-purpose (fish or cruise) express boats with the introduction in 1991 of their 4300 Open. Viking and Bertram have since come out with 43-footers, and Hatteras introduced the 39 Sport Express in 1995. She is unquestionably a beautiful boat—perhaps the best in her class when it comes to styling. (The cruising version, with curved bridgedeck seating and a sport arch, is pictured above.) She's built on the same deep-draft hull used for the Hatteras 39 Convertible with moderate beam, a flared bow and cored hullsides. The Sport Express is a big boat on the outside with a party-size bridgedeck and a cockpit large enough to handle a full-size chair. (Note that the standard version has L-shaped settees on the bridgedeck—rather than the circular lounge—and no arch.) Cockpit features include an in-deck fishbox, molded tackle center, transom door and direct access to the engine room. Inside, the single-stateroom floorplan will sleep six and comes complete with a stall shower in the head. Optional 465-hp 6-71s provide a respectable 24 knots at cruise and 28–29 knots wide open. ❑

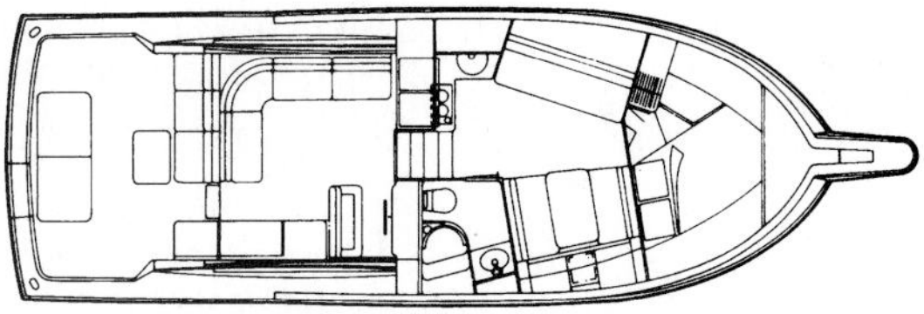

Standard Layout with L-shaped Seating

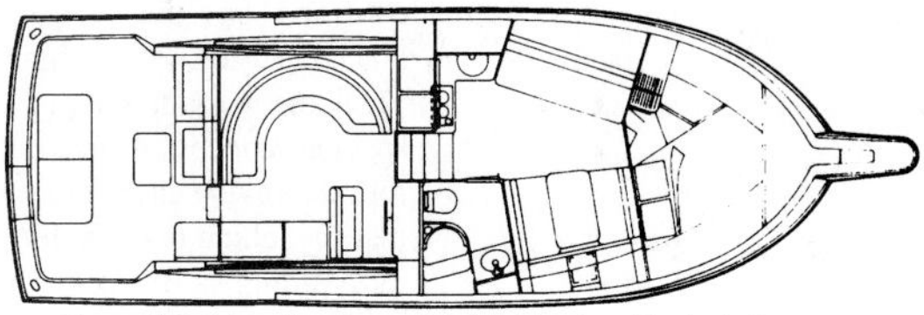

Curved Bridge Seating with Aft-Facing Cockpit Lounge

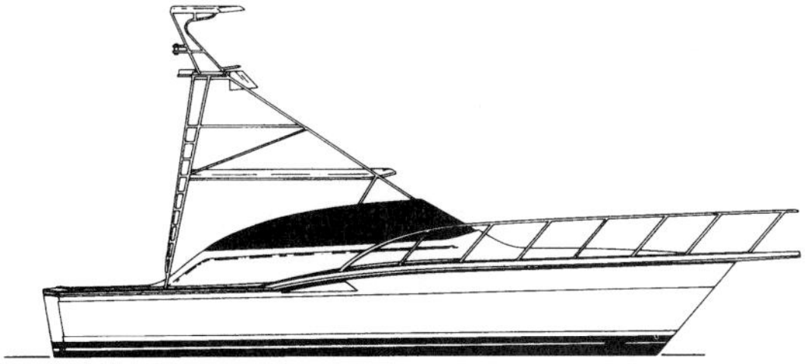

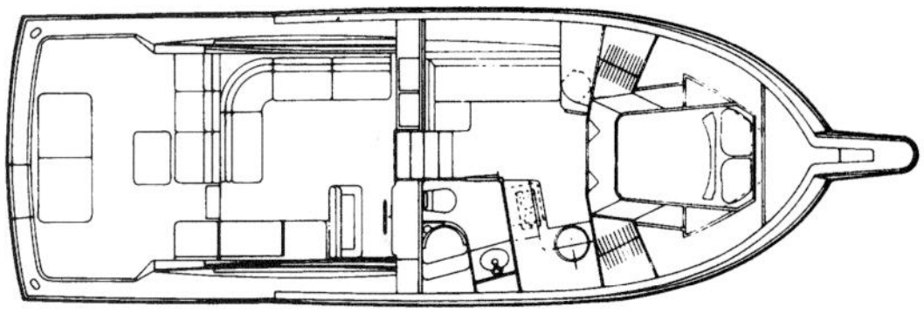

Centerline Queen Berth and Expanded Lounge Area

See Page 266 for Pricing Information

HINCKLEY TALARIA 39/42

SPECIFICATIONS

Length ....41'9"	Water ....110 gals.
Length WL....................38'7"	Clearance ....12'6"
Beam..............................13'8"	Hull Type...........Semi-Disp.
Draft ....4'4"	Deadrise Aft.......................5°
Weight......................22,000#	Designer...............S. Lincoln
Fuel ....400 gals.	Production.......1990–Current

The Hinckley Talaria 42 is an elegant and finely crafted Downeast cruiser for those who can afford such a luxury from one of America's pre-eminent boatbuilders. (Note that the Talaria was introduced in 1990 as a 39-footer—same boat, but with a smaller cockpit.) She's built on a fully cored semi-displacement hull with a flared bow and a long, prop-protecting keel. Designed for comfortable cruising, the traditional teak interior of the Talaria is available in a single-stateroom, galley-down configuration, or with the galley up and two staterooms (not shown). A lower helm station is standard, and large wraparound cabin windows and excellent headroom make the salon seem larger than her measurements might suggest. The joinerwork, fixtures, and hardware are, of course, flawless. The spacious cockpit is large enough for fishing, and very wide walkarounds provide easy access to the bow. Additional features (among many) include underwater exhausts, a teak cockpit sole, and twin teak sliding salon doors. A single 425-hp Cat diesel provides an economical cruising speed of 16–17 knots (about 22 knots top). ❑

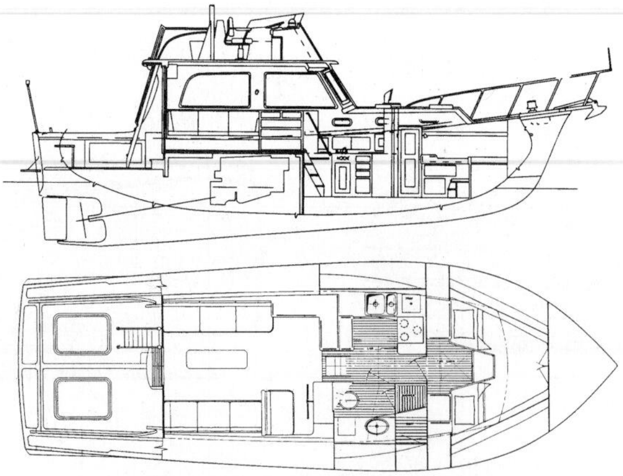

See Page 266 for Pricing Information

LARSON 250 CABRIO

SPECIFICATIONS

Length w/Pulpit	27'0"	Waste	4 gals.
Beam	8'6"	Clearance	7'1"
Draft	2'10"	Hull Type	Modified-V
Weight	4,900#	Deadrise Aft	18°
Fuel	80 gals.	Designer	Larson
Water	20 gals.	Production	1994–95

With her clean profile and overnight accommodations for four, the Larson 250 Cabrio combines an affordable price with easy trailerability in an attractive sportboat package. Built on a solid fiberglass hull with moderate deadrise and a relatively wide beam, her mid-cabin interior includes a V-berth/dinette forward, a small gelley with sink and refrigerator, and an enclosed head compartment and shower. Four opening ports and an overhead deck hatch provide ventilation. The aft cabin has a double berth and an opening port. Outside, the Cabrio's roomy single-level cockpit is one of the best in her class with comfortable seating for six adults. (Note that the centerline companionway is much more convenient than the awkward portside entryway found in many competitive models.) A bow pulpit, transom door and swim ladder are standard. A single 235-hp/5.7-litre MerCruiser stern drive cruises at 20 knots (about 30 knots top), and an optional 300-hp/7.4-litre MerCruiser will cruise the 250 Carbrio at a brisk 24–25 knots and deliver a top speed in the neighborhood of 35 knots. ❑

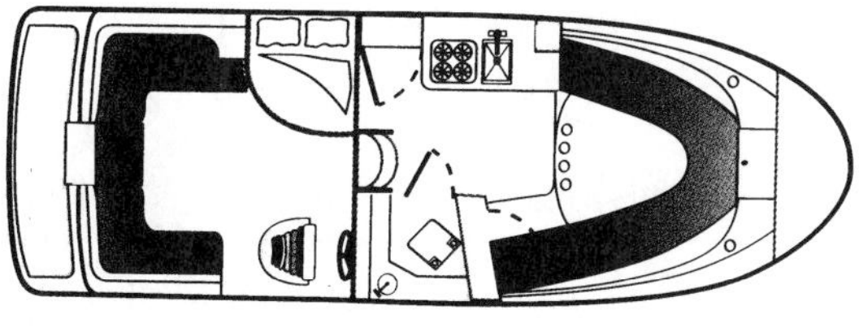

See Page 266 for Pricing Information

LARSON 260 CABRIO

SPECIFICATIONS

Length	27'2"	Water	20 gals.
Beam	9'6"	Fuel	80 gals.
Draft	2'9"	Hull Type	Modified-V
Weight	4,900#	Deadrise Aft	18°
Clearance	7'1"	Designer	H. Schoell
Cockpit	NA	Production	1992–93

An innovative design with her circular transom seating and centerline helm position, the 260 Cabrio is a classy little family cruiser with a stylish profile to go with her affordable price. Hull construction is solid fiberglass and—like other Larson models—the Cabrio rides on one of Harry Schoell's patented Delta-Conic hulls. She's a beamy boat for her length, and the wide-open interior is attractively arranged with staterooms fore and aft, a compact galley, and a stand-up head with shower. Outside, the focus is on the cockpit layout: Larson engineers rejected the conventional in their decision to place the helm amidships (improved visibility) and to employ wraparound semi-circular seating at the transom. This innovative arrangement results in a deeper swim platform and generous seating, but the rounded transom design eats up a lot of useful cockpit space. Among several engine options, a single 454-cid MerCruiser or Volvo stern drive will cruise the 260 Cabrio at 17–18 knots and reach a top speed of around 30 knots. Note the (very) limited fuel capacity. ❑

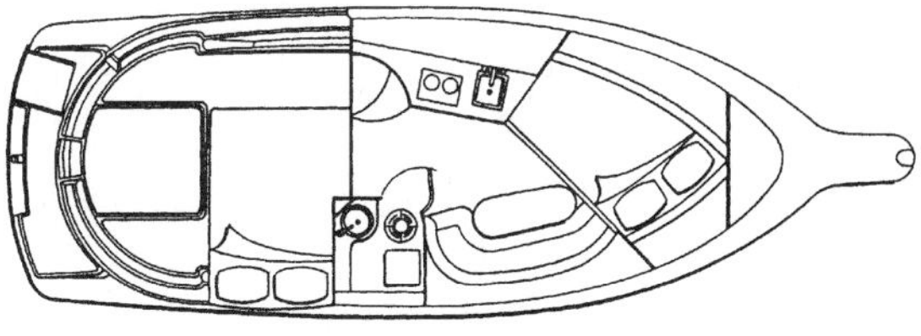

See Page 266 for Pricing Information

LARSON 270 CABRIO

SPECIFICATIONS

Length .....27'3"	Water .....20 gals.
Beam .....9'0"	Fuel .....100 gals.
Draft .....2'10"	Hull Type .....Modified-V
Weight .....7,800#	Deadrise Aft .....18°
Clearance .....9'0"	Designer .....H. Schoell
Cockpit .....NA	Production 1989-93

This boat has had several names over the years. Introduced in 1989 as the Milano 27, during 1990–91 she was called the Mirado 270, and for 1992–93 she was known as the 270 Cabrio. A popular model for Larson, she's a straightforward express cruiser with modern sportboat lines and a well-arranged interior. Note the fully integrated swim platform, oval ports and the sleek Euro-style curved windshield. A sun pad is recessed into the foredeck and the cockpit—with its curved lounge seating and standard wet bar—offers excellent visibility from the raised helm. Inside, the mid-cabin layout includes a small galley, a stand-up head compartment, and privacy curtains for both staterooms. Additional features include a double-wide helm seat, good cabin storage, and backrests for the transom seats (a welcome touch). Among several engine options offered over the years, a single 454-cid MerCruiser or Volvo stern drive will cruise the 270 Cabrio at 19 knots, and twin 350-cid I/Os will cruise in the 25-knot range. The fuel capacity is limited. ❑

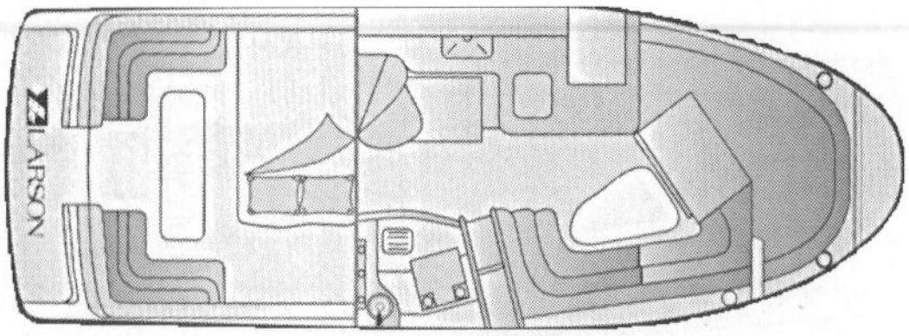

See Page 266 for Pricing Information

LARSON 280 CABRIO

SPECIFICATIONS

Length w/Pulpit .....28'11"	Water .....33 gals.
Beam .....10'0"	Fuel .....125 gals.
Draft .....2'10"	Hull Type .....Modified-V
Weight .....7,200#	Deadrise Aft .....18°
Clearance .....9'4"	Designer .....H. Schoell
Cockpit .....NA	Production 1994–Current

A good-looking sport cruiser, the Larson 280 Cabrio is a modern and well-appointed express with a moderate price tag to go with her roomy accommodations. She's built on a unique modified-V hull bottom with an amidships "step" that divides the hull into fore and aft sections—what Larson calls a Duo-Delta Conic hull. (The effect of this hull on performance is dramatic as shown in the speeds below.) The mid-cabin layout of the 280 includes double berths in both sleeping areas (with draw curtains for privacy), a good-size galley, and a curved dinette. With a wide ten-foot beam, there's a surprising amount of room below and the Formica cabinetry and oak trim present an upscale impression. Above deck, the cockpit is arranged with a removable L-shaped lounge and a double-wide, back-to-back seat at the helm. Additional features include a tilt wheel, decent sidedecks, a power-assist engine hatch, and a walk-thru transom. While several twin-engine stern-drive options are available, performance with a single 300-hp 7.4-litre MerCruiser I/O is excellent: 21 knots at cruise and 36–37 knots top. ❑

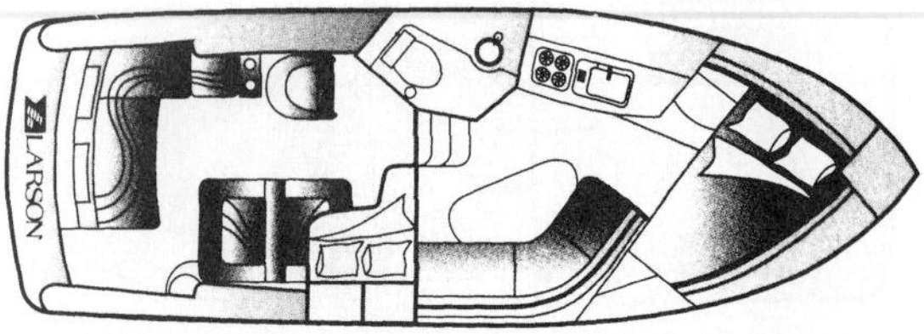

See Page 266 for Pricing Information

LARSON 300/310 CABRIO

SPECIFICATIONS

Length w/Pulpit	32'6"	Water	30 gals.
Hull Length	29'11"	Fuel	170 gals.
Beam	10'6"	Hull Type	Modified-V
Draft	2'10"	Deadrise Aft	14°
Weight	9,500#	Designer	H. Schoell
Clearance	7'4"	Production	1991–Current

The 310 Cabrio is the flagship of the current Larson fleet, and she's basically a redesign of an earlier model, the Larson Contempra 300 (1989–90). Originally called the 300 Cabrio, she was renamed for 1995 as the 310. While her exterior appearance hasn't changed a lot over the years, the Cabrio's brighter and more open interior is a big improvement from the Contempra's somewhat confining layout. Actually, there have been two floorplans for the Cabrio since her 1991 introduction. The original layout had an island berth in the forward stateroom and a very long galley (with lots of counter space) to starboard. In 1994, an offset berth forward opened the salon even further and allowed the introduction of a big U-shaped settee. Outside, the cockpit is arranged with a double-wide (reversible) helm seat, a covered wet bar (very slick), and a gas-assist engine hatch in the sole. Among several engine options, twin 205-hp/5.0-litre MerCruiser stern drives will cruise the Larson 310 Cabrio at an efficient 23 knots (about 35 knots top), and a pair of 235-hp/5.7-litre engines will deliver a top speed of 37–38 knots. ❑

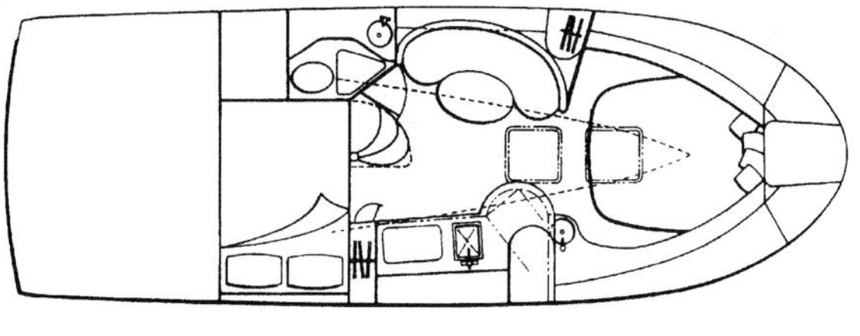

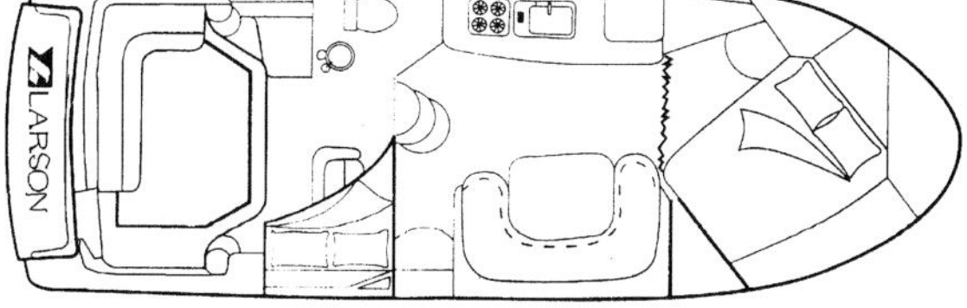

See Page 266 for Pricing Information

LIMESTONE 24

24 Cuddy Cabin

24 Express Cruiser

SPECIFICATIONS

Length .... 23'6"	Fuel, EC .... 97 gals.
Beam .... 9'2"	Water .... 16 gals.
Hull Draft .... 1'5"	Hull Type .... Deep-V
Weight, Open .... 4,700#	Deadrise Aft .... 22°
Weight, EC .... 5,000#	Production 1987–90
Fuel, Open .... 75 gals.	.... 1993–Current

The Limestone 24 is an extremely well-built small cruiser with outstanding performance and the kind of timeless good looks that will ensure her resale value for years to come. She was originally built by Hinterhoeller Yachts, an Ontario firm best-known for their series of Nonsuch sailboats. Medieros (also Ontario-based) picked up the molds following Hinterhoeller's demise and reintroduced her in 1993. A Mark Ellis, deep-V design with a wide beam and fully-cored construction, the Limestone has always been offered in Cuddy Cabin and Express Cruiser models. With her small cabin (basically a V-berth and Porta-Potti), the Cuddy version has the larger cockpit although—with her jackshaft drive system—much of the space is consumed by an engine box. The Express Cruiser, on the other hand, is a conventional stern drive design with a varnished teak interior with a stand-up head and galley. Notable features (and there are many) include opening vent panels in the windshield and superb glasswork and joinerwork. A single 5.7-litre engine will cruise either model at 25 knots (35 knots top), and a 7.4-litre motor will run 4–5 knots faster. ❑

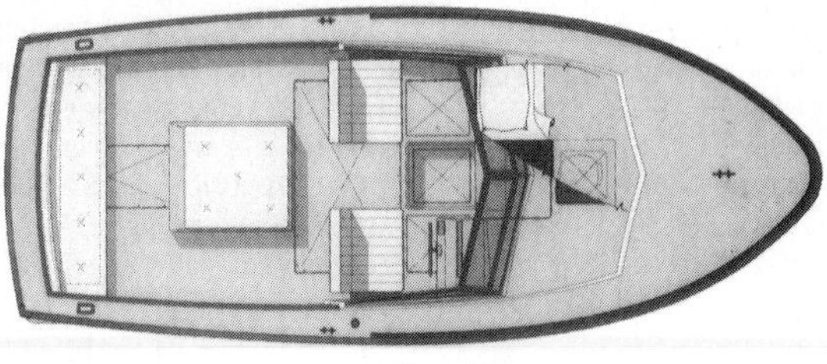

Cuddy Cabin

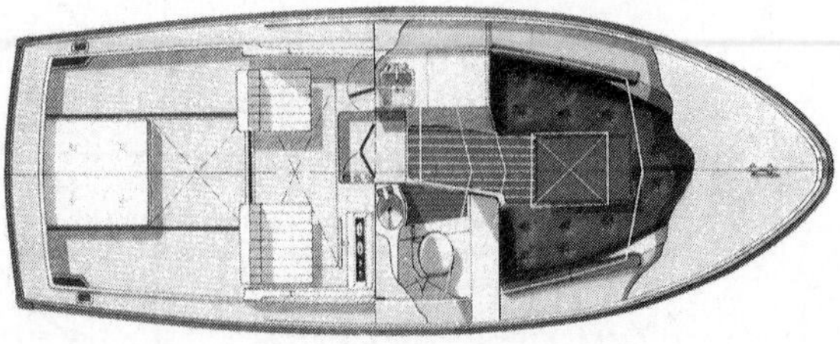

Express Cruiser

See Page 266 for Pricing Information

LITTLE HARBOR 36/40

SPECIFICATIONS

Length	36'2"	Water	120 gals.
Length WL	29'7"	Fuel	300 gals.
Beam	11'0"	Hull Type	Deep-V
Draft	3'1"	Deadrise Aft	16°
Weight	16,000#	Designer	Hunt
Clearance	8'0"	Production	1990–Current

For those who can afford the cost of a custom-built yacht, the Little Harbor 40 is a high-tech masterpiece of classic American styling and modern construction. Built thru '92 as a 36-footer, she features a traditional trunk cabin foredeck and a relatively narrow beam. The vacuum-bagged, balsa-cored hull uses Kevlar and S-glass laminates. (The hull is a true deep-V, although deadrise at the transom is just 16 degrees.) Because these are semi-custom yachts, there are a variety of layouts an owner might choose from to personalize his boat. In any case, expect to see plenty of varnished teak cabinetry belowdeck, Corian countertops in the head, and top-quality hardware and furnishings throughout. The bi-level cockpit is arranged with a dinette to port, and lift-up helm and companion sections provide excellent access to the engine room. A handsome boat by any standard (note the stylish teak-framed windshield), the cockpit can be adapted to serious sportfishing pursuits. Several diesel options are offered. Typically, 300-hp Cummins diesels will cruise the Little Harbor 36 at a comfortable 24–25 knots. ❑

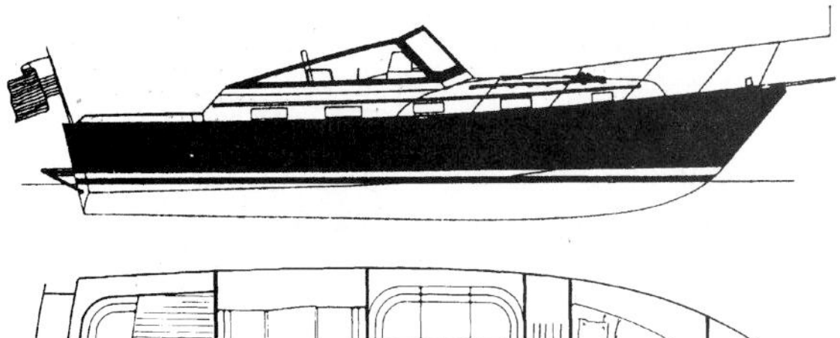

See Page 266 for Pricing Information

LUHRS ALURA 30

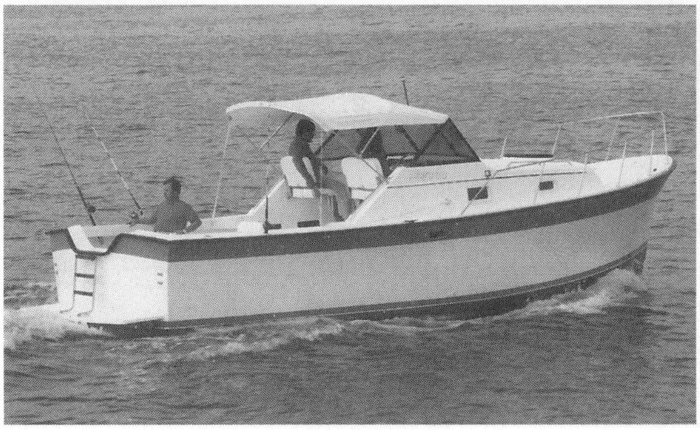

SPECIFICATIONS

Length	30'0"	Water	38 gals.
Length WL	28'0"	Fuel	196 gals.
Beam	10'3"	Cockpit	110 sq. ft.
Draft	2'11"	Hull Type	Semi-Disp.
Weight	7,800#	Designer	Luhrs
Clearance	NA	Production	1987–90

Featuring a distinctive Downeast profile, the Alura 30 is a versatile weekender with a large cockpit and comfortable cabin accommodations. She's built of solid fiberglass on a semi-displacement hull with a sweeping sheer and moderate beam. A long keel provides a measure of prop protection while ensuring good handling characteristics at low speeds. Although not considered a beamy boat, the cockpit is exceptionally large and includes built-in baitwells and fish boxes. Helm visibility is good, and the windshield can be opened for ventilation. The wide sidedecks are notable. Inside, the cabin layout is clean and simple, and the teak and holly sole is especially attractive. Two people can cruise aboard this boat for a few days without problem. A good all-purpose design, the Alura 30 will do well as a dive boat or as an inexpensive fisherman and weekend cruiser. Note that the keel was redesigned in 1988 to reduce vibration problems. Her single 270-hp gas engine provides an efficient cruising speed of 14–15 knots and a top speed of around 22 knots. ❑

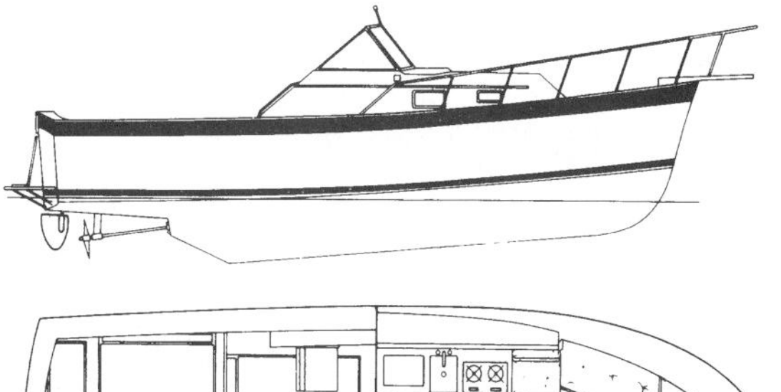

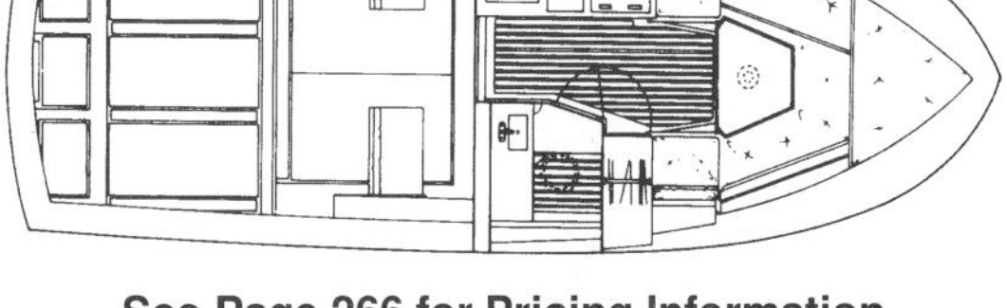

See Page 266 for Pricing Information

LUHRS 3400 MOTOR YACHT

SPECIFICATIONS

Length	34'0"	Fuel	300 gals.
Beam	12'6"	Cockpit	NA
Draft	3'2"	Hull Type	Modified-V
Weight	13,500#	Deadrise Aft	15°
Clearance	22'0"	Designer	J. Fielding
Water	60 gals.	Production	1990–92

It's interesting to note that the Luhrs 3400 MY was built on the same hull used for Tournament 340 and 342 models—an easy-riding modified-V affair with moderate beam and solid fiberglass construction. Luhrs engineers gave the 3400 a lot more interior volume by moving the salon bulkhead well aft into the cockpit and designing the new layout with a modern Eurostyle decor. The result is a spacious family cruiser with the galley and dinette down, wraparound windows in the salon, a complete entertainment center, and a walkaround island berth in the stateroom. Calling this boat a Motor Yacht is wishful thinking at its best; the 3400 is actually a flybridge sedan with larger-than-average interior dimensions. The cockpit is too small for any serious fishing activities, but the flybridge is huge and includes a convenient walkthrough to the foredeck (which compensates for the boat's somewhat narrow sidedecks). Standard 454-cid Crusader gas engines will cruise the Luhrs 3400 MY at 19–20 knots and reach about 28 knots wide open. Twin 300-hp Cummins diesels are optional. ❑

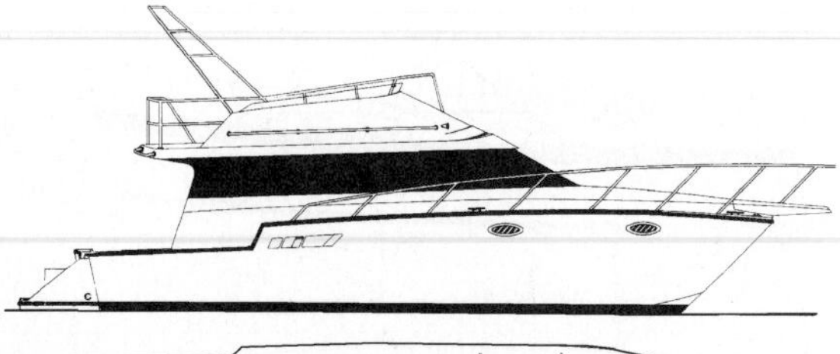

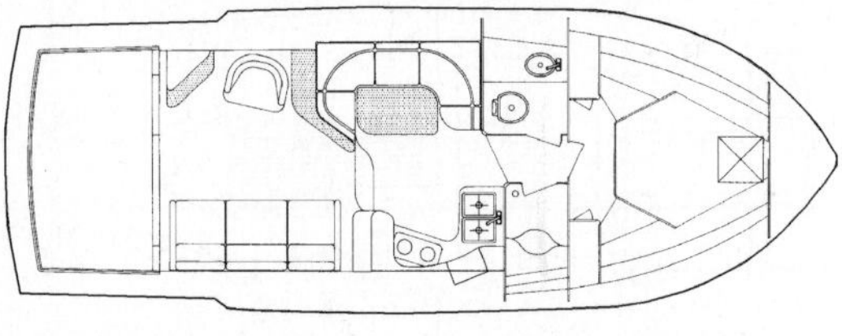

See Page 266 for Pricing Information

LUHRS 3420 MOTOR YACHT

SPECIFICATIONS

Length	34'0"	Fuel	300 gals.
Beam	12'6"	Cockpit	50 sq. ft.
Draft	3'2"	Hull Type	Modified-V
Weight	13,500#	Deadrise Aft	15°
Clearance	22'0"	Designer	Luhrs
Water	60 gals.	Production	1991–93

Closely resembling the 3400 MY, the Luhrs 3420 has a larger cockpit, a smaller salon, and a revised flybridge layout without the foredeck walk-thru. Hull construction is solid fiberglass—the same tried-and-true design first used for the Luhrs 340. Inside, the single-stateroom floorplan is arranged with the mid-level galley open to the salon. Note that the head is divided with the shower stall to starboard. The interior is attractively finished with colorful fabrics and accented with a modest amount of teak trim. Outside, the cockpit is small—useful for entertaining and cruising but not suitable for any serious fishing pursuits. Guest seating is provided forward of the helm console on the flybridge, and the aluminum arch was standard. Additional features include a built-in entertainment center, oak parquet galley sole, fish box, washdown, cockpit bridge overhang, and a swim platform with molded bait well. Twin 454-cid gas engines will cruise the Luhrs 3420 MY at 19–20 knots and reach a top speed of around 28 knots. ❑

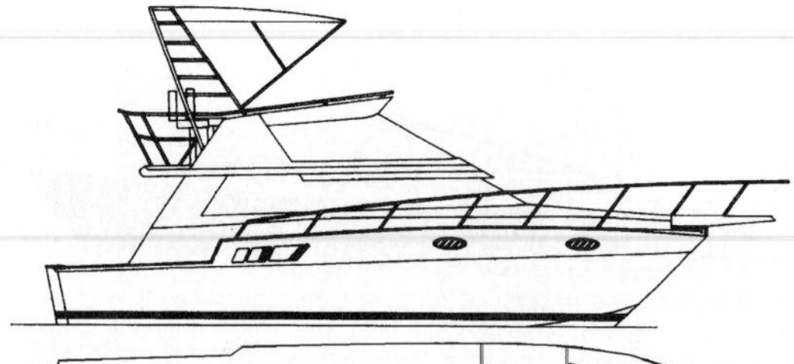

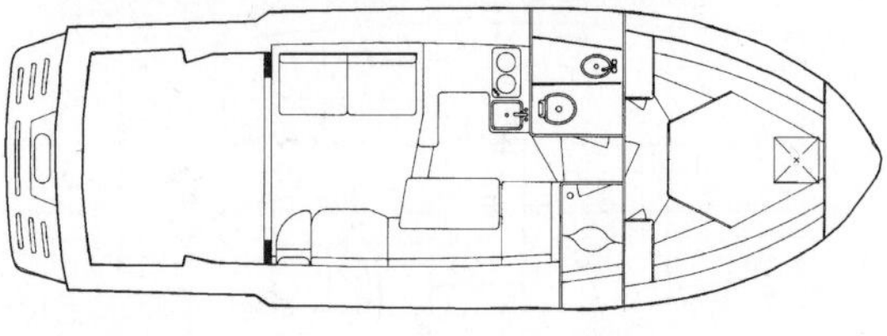

See Page 266 for Pricing Information

LUHRS ALURA 35

SPECIFICATIONS

Length ....35'5"	Fuel ....260 gals.
Beam ....12'2"	Cockpit ....NA
Draft ....2'11"	Hull Type ....Modified-V
Weight ....12,800#	Deadrise Aft ....NA
Clearance ....NA	Designer ....Luhrs
Water ....55 gals.	Production 1988–89

The appealing Downeast character of the Alura 30 is missing from the more recent Alura 35. Here, the styling is more contemporary, and the accent is on the sportboat image. As such, the Alura 35 was designed to appeal to the price-conscious buyer. She's a straightforward express design without the curved windshield, radar arch, or the integral swim platform found in many of today's modern sportboats. What the Alura 35 does provide is a lot of boat for the money. If not plush, the mid-cabin interior accommodations are nonetheless roomy and very comfortable. The decor is light and airy, and the teak-and-holly cabin sole is especially attractive. Outside, the 35's large bi-level cockpit is well-suited to the demands of family cruisers as well as weekend anglers. A small tackle center is behind the helm seat; a swim platform was standard; and foredeck access is easy thanks to the wide sidedecks. Twin 270-hp Crusader gas engines will cruise the Alura 35 at around 17 knots with a top speed of 25–26 knots. ❑

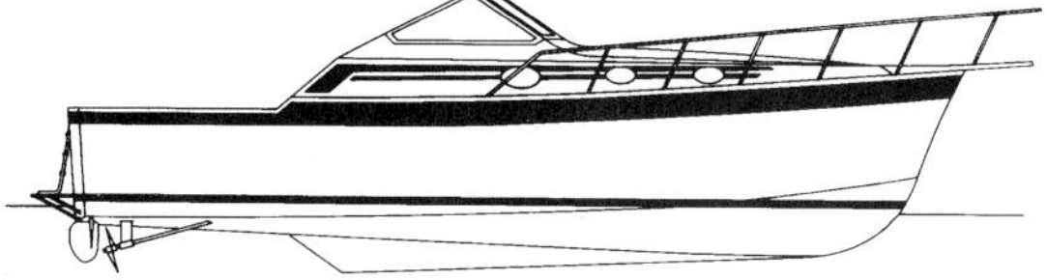

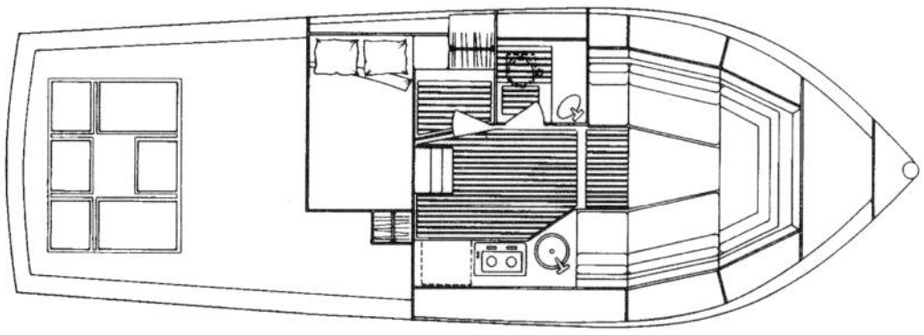

See Page 266 for Pricing Information

MAINSHIP 47

MAINSHIP 40

MAINSHIP 31

MAINSHIP 31 SEDAN BRIDGE

SPECIFICATIONS

L.O.A.	33'3"	Water	50 gals.
Hull Length	31'3"	Fuel	200 gals.
Beam	11'10"	Hull Type	Modified-V
Draft	2'10"	Deadrise Aft	NA
Weight	16,000#	Designer	Mike Peters
Clearance	14'4"	Production	1994–Current

While the chief attraction of the 31 Sedan Bridge may well be her attractive styling and big flybridge, those who step below will be immediately impressed with the spacious interior packed into this 31-foot hull. Like all sedan bridge designs, the sunken floorplan is the result of moving the engines aft where V-drives permit their installation beneath the cockpit sole. The result is a wide open interior arranged more or less on a single level from the salon forward. There are two staterooms in this layout, so the galley ends up in the salon opposite a big L-shaped settee. Note the double-entry head compartment. Outside, molded steps lead up to the bridge with its wraparound guest seating and unusual portside helm position. With very narrow sidedecks, a convenient walk-thru in the bridge coaming leads to the foredeck. The cockpit comes with molded bench seating, and the entire sole lifts for engine access. Twin 454-cid (340-hp) gas engines will cruise the Mainship 31 at 20 knots and reach a top speed of about 30 knots. ❑

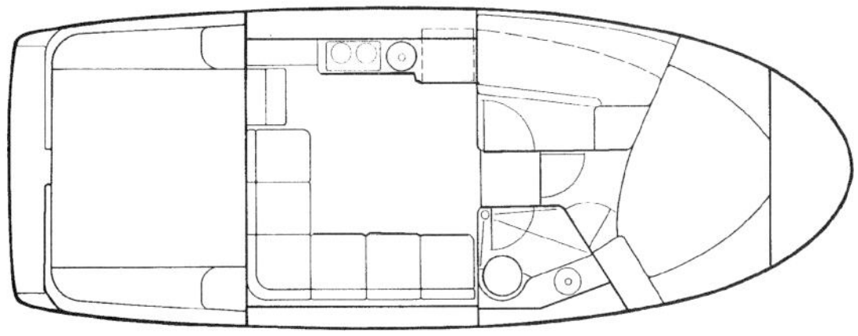

See Page 266 for Pricing Information

MAINSHIP 34 SEDAN

SPECIFICATIONS

Length	34'0"	Water	50 gals.
LWL	NA	Fuel	220 gals.
Beam	11'11"	Cockpit	80 sq. ft.
Draft	2'10"	Hull Type	Semi-Disp.
Weight	14,000#	Designer	Cherubini
Clearance	13'6"	Production	1978–82

The Mainship 34 Sedan is one of the most popular small cruisers ever built. She was constructed on a solid fiberglass semi-displacement hull design with a fine bow entry and a full-length keel below. First of the Mainship series, the appeal of the 34 Sedan had much to do with her trawler-style profile and affordable price tag, and her greatest attraction remains her superb economy at better than trawler speeds. With a single 160-hp Perkins 6-cylinder diesel, the Mainship's easily driven hull will cruise at 10–11 knots burning only 6 gph. At a more relaxed 7-knot speed, the fuel consumption drops to a remarkable 2 gph. The practical single-stateroom floorplan is well-suited to the needs of a cruising couple. A lower helm was standard in the salon; the galley is large enough for serious food preparation; and a stall shower is included in the head. Outside, the flybridge extends aft to provide weather protection for the cockpit. Considered a low-maintenance boat, the Mainship 34 Sedan continues to enjoy great popularity in most markets. ❑

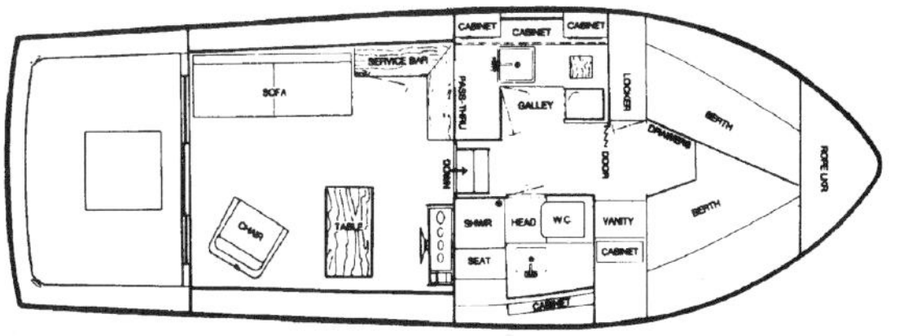

See Page 266 for Pricing Information

MAINSHIP 34 II

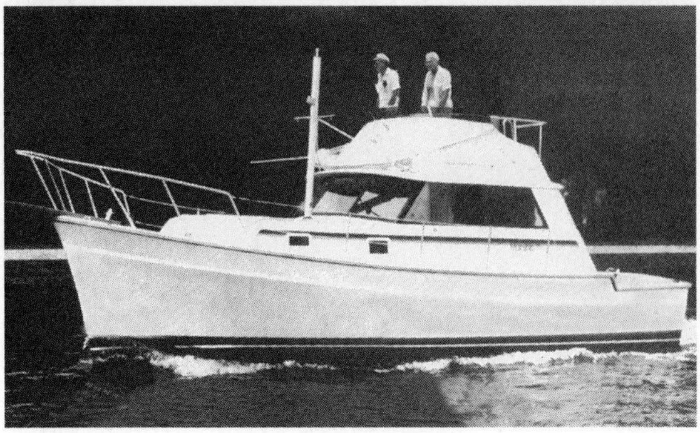

SPECIFICATIONS

Length	34'0"	Water	50 gals.
Length WL	NA	Fuel	220 gals.
Beam	11'11"	Cockpit	78 sq. ft.
Draft	2'10"	Hull Type	Semi-Disp.
Weight	14,000#	Designer	Cherubini
Clearance	13'6"	Production	1980–82

With her trawler-style profile, seakindly hull and attractive interior, the Mainship 34 II is a good all-around family cruiser with a practical layout to go with her superb economy. She's built on the same easily-driven semi-displacement hull used in the production of the original Mainship 34. Inside, the single-stateroom floorplan is arranged with the galley down. The large head comes with a separate stall shower, and V-berths are forward. A lower helm was standard, and there's a pass-through serving counter from the galley below. This is basically the same layout used in the Mainship 34, but the salon is smaller in order to provide for the larger cockpit. Additional features include a roomy engine compartment, wide walkarounds, full wraparound cabin windows, foredeck mast, and teak interior trim. The flybridge is quite small with bench seating for two. Never a big seller, a single turbocharged 160-hp Perkins diesel was standard in the Mainship 34 II. She'll cruise easily around 11 knots (burning just 6 gph) and reach a top speed of 14 knots. ❑

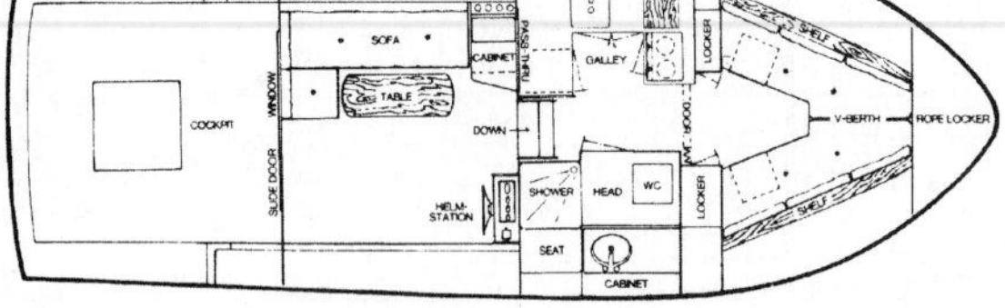

See Page 266 for Pricing Information

MAINSHIP 34 III

SPECIFICATIONS

Length	34'0"	Water	40 gals.
Length WL	NA	Fuel	190 gals.
Beam	11'11"	Cockpit	NA
Draft	3'6"	Hull Type	Semi-Disp.
Weight	14,000#	Designer	Cherubini
Clearance	13'6"	Production	1983–88

The Mainship 34 III is a refined and more stylish version of the original Mainship 34 Sedan. In the 34 III, the salon has been lengthened by some 9 inches to add interior space, and the extended hardtop of the original 34 Sedan was eliminated in favor of a more open cockpit. The same basic interior (updated from teak to light oak trimwork in 1985) was retained with a slightly larger galley and bigger salon windows. The cockpit of the 34 III is somewhat smaller than the earlier Mainship 34, although the transom door and swim platform were made standard. Every Mainship 34 is powered with a single diesel engine (usually a 165-hp or 200-hp Perkins) capable of cruising at 7 knots at 2 gph or 13–14 knots at only 6–7 gph. The fuel efficiency of this coastal cruiser is truly impressive, and used Mainship 34 IIIs are always in demand. In all, over 900 Mainship 34s were built including the original Sedan and 34 II models, and these inexpensive boats remain a benchmark in owner popularity. ❑

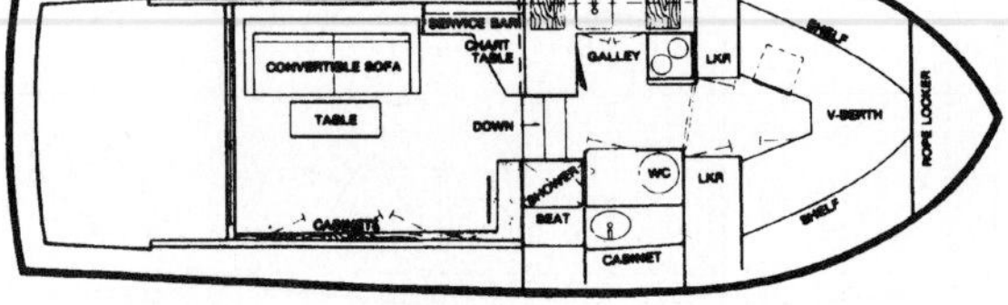

See Page 266 for Pricing Information

MAINSHIP 35 CONVERTIBLE

SPECIFICATIONS

Length	34'11"	Fuel	250 gals.
Beam	12'8"	Cockpit	80 sq. ft.
Draft	2'10"	Hull Type	Modified-V
Weight	16,000#	Deadrise Aft	12°
Clearance	15'0"	Designer	Mike Peters
Water	80 gals.	Production	1988–94

The Mainship 35 Convertible (called the Mediterranean 35 Cockpit until 1992) is a modern family cruising sedan with one of the largest interior layouts in her class. The clean profile of the Mainship 35 speaks for itself—European, streamlined, and very distinctive. Built on a solid glass hull with a shallow deadrise aft, the sleek styling gives the appearance of a bigger boat. The original single-stateroom floorplan was replaced with a two-stateroom dinette layout in 1992, when the boat was restyled. Further updates for 1992 included white windshield frames (replacing the earlier black frames), a bigger flybridge with additional seating, and new interior colors. There are few 35-foot boats with two staterooms and a dinette, and the Mainship even manages a roomy salon—very impressive. The cockpit is small with a transom door, engine compartment hatches, and molded-in bridge steps. Note the single-piece Eurostyle bow rails and step-down window styling. Standard 454-cid Crusader gas engines will cruise the Mainship 35 at 17–18 knots with a top speed of around 28 knots. ❑

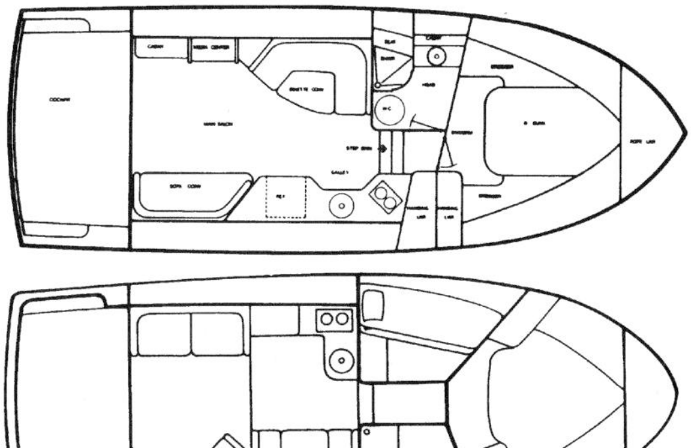

See Page 267 for Pricing Information

MAINSHIP 36 SEDAN

SPECIFICATIONS

Length	36'2"	Fuel	240 gals.
Beam	13'0"	Cockpit	NA
Draft	3'0"	Hull Type	Modified-V
Weight	20,000#	Deadrise Aft	NA
Clearance	11'3"	Designer	Mainship
Water	100 gals.	Production	1986–88

Sharing the same hull as the 36 Double Cabin, the Mainship 36 Sedan (also called the 36 Nantucket) has the interior space and comfort of a much larger boat. Indeed, the salon dimensions are unusually generous due to the fact that the cabin bulkhead is located well aft, increasing the interior dimensions at the expense of cockpit space. A comfortable cruising boat, the profile of the 36 Sedan is on the boxy side. Inside, there are two staterooms on the lower level as well as a stall shower in the head. Both the galley and dinette are located in the salon. The decor features attractive light oak woodwork, and, with the dinette converted, there are berths for six. A second benefit of the extended salon is seen in the spacious flybridge, where L-shaped lounge seating is provided aft of the helm. A good performer with standard Crusader 270-hp gas engines, she'll cruise at 17 knots and reach 25–26 knots wide open. Approximately fifty 36 Mainship Sedans were built during her brief three-year production run. ❑

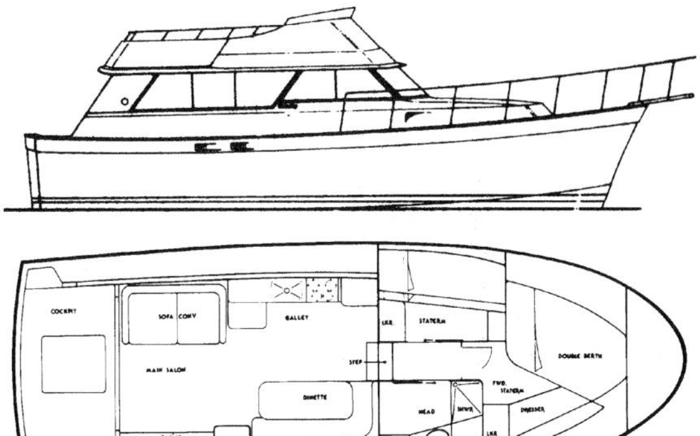

See Page 267 for Pricing Information

MAINSHIP 35 OPEN/36 EXPRESS

SPECIFICATIONS

Length ....36'5"	Water ....75 gals.
Length WL..........NA	Fuel ....250 gals.
Beam..........12'5"	Hull Type ....Modified-V
Draft ....2'8"	Deadrise Aft..........NA
Weight..........13,500#	Designer ....Mike Peters
Clearance ....10'6"	Production 1990–94

The 36 Express (called the Mainship 35 Open when she was introduced in 1990) is a Eurostyle express cruiser with a large cockpit and a practical mid-cabin interior layout. High freeboard and the absence of a curved windshield keep the 36 Express from being a truly attractive design in the eyes of many, and her portside helm location is unusual (most builders place the helm to starboard). Inside, the mid-cabin floorplan (upgraded in 1992) is arranged with double berths in both staterooms, a compact galley, and stall shower in the head compartment. The lack of interior bulkheads adds to the impression of space inside the 36, although there are no privacy doors for the staterooms, just curtains. The real appeal of this boat is the big cockpit with its sexy helm console, contoured sun lounge, walk-through transom, and seating for a crowd. A hatch in the sole provides good access to the engines and V-drives. Crusader 454-cid gas engines will cruise at 19 knots and reach a top speed of 27–28 knots. ❑

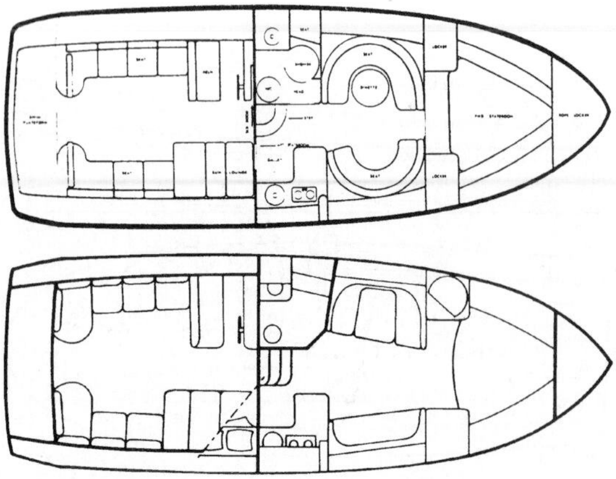

See Page 267 for Pricing Information

MAINSHIP 35 OPEN BRIDGE 36 SEDAN BRIDGE

SPECIFICATIONS

Length ....36'0"	Water ....85 gals.
Length WL..........NA	Fuel ....250 gals.
Beam..........12'5"	Hull Type ....Modified-V
Draft ....2'8"	Deadrise Aft..........12°
Weight..........13,500#	Designer ....Mike Peters
Clearance ....10'0"	Production 1990–92

While maximum interior volume is obviously the theme of this model, the egg-shaped exterior styling of the Mainship 36 Sedan Bridge is very unorthodox. Appearances aside, the full-width interior of this boat is cavernous and ideally suited to entertaining on a grand scale. (Note that she was originally called the Mainship 35 Open Bridge when introduced in 1990.) She's built on a solid fiberglass modified-V hull with average beam and shallow deadrise at the transom. The step-down interior is set well below the cockpit level, and the headroom throughout is extraordinary. Indeed, these are comfortable accommodations for a 36-foot boat, and the single-level floorplan seems completely open. Unfortunately, the cabin windows are very small, and the absence of outside natural lighting is notable. Additional features include a walk-through from the bridge to the foredeck, attractive cherry interior trim, and wraparound bridge seating. Standard 454-cid gas engines will cruise the 36 Sedan Bridge at a respectable 17–18 knots and deliver a top speed of around 28 knots. ❑

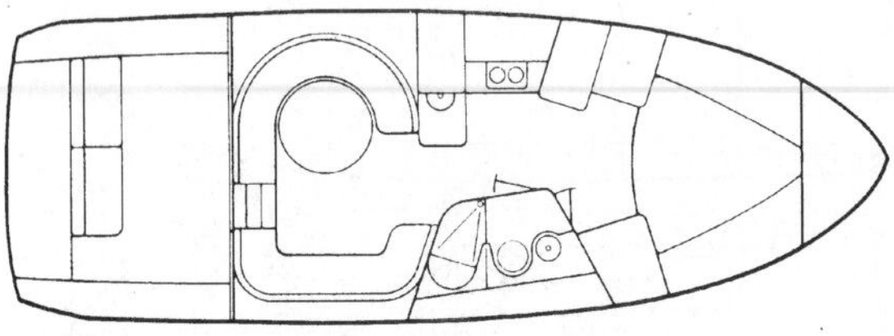

See Page 267 for Pricing Information

MAINSHIP 39 EXPRESS

SPECIFICATIONS

Length .... 39'2"	Water .... 80 gals.
Beam .... 14'1"	Fuel .... 320 gals.
Draft .... 3'4"	Hull Type .... Modified-V
Weight .... 15,000#	Deadrise Aft .... 12°
Clearance .... 8'0"	Designer .... Mike Peters
Cockpit .... NA	Production 1989–94

The 39 Express (originally called the Mainship 39 Open) has the bold and seductive profile of a modern American sportboat, although the absence of a curved windshield is a little disappointing. She was built on a solid fiberglass hull with a wide beam and modest transom deadrise. Inside, the Mainship 39's two-stateroom interior is lavish and quite spacious. The convertible dinette and settee provide seating for a crowd, and outside natural lighting is excellent thanks to a series of translucent overhead deck hatches. The single-level cockpit of the Mainship 39 is huge, with a contoured sun lounge next to the helm, a full wet bar, and wraparound lounge seating for guests. Additional features include a unique bi-level transom design, twin foredeck sun pads, side exhausts, and a radar arch. Note that the sidedecks are extremely narrow on this boat and going forward is a dicey proposition underway. With V-drives and 502-cid Crusader gas engines, the Mainship 39 Express will cruise at 21 knots and reach a top speed of 28–29 knots. ❑

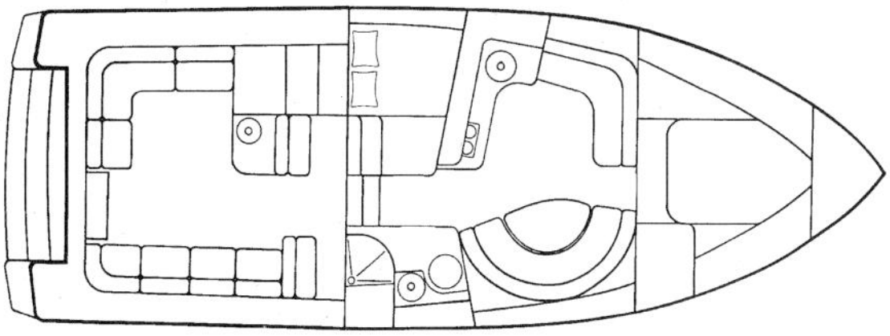

See Page 267 for Pricing Information

MAINSHIP 40 SEDAN BRIDGE

SPECIFICATIONS

Length .... 40'7"	Water .... 93 gals.
Beam .... 13'6"	Fuel .... 310 gals.
Draft .... 2'8"	Hull Type .... Deep-V
Weight .... 20,000#	Deadrise Aft .... 17°
Clearance .... 17'0"	Designer .... Mainship
Cockpit .... NA	Production 1993–Current

Many manufacturers are building sedan bridge boats these days. The principal is simple enough: use V-drives to move the engines aft from under the salon to beneath the cockpit, thus lowering the salon sole and improving the boat's profile while enlarging the accommodations. Of the many sedan bridge models on the market, the Mainship 40 certainly has one of the more attractive profiles. Hull construction is solid fiberglass, and the deck, deckhouse, and bridge are a single-piece mold. The step-down floorplan is arranged with two staterooms forward and a huge head with a stall shower. The wide salon is big for a 40-footer, and the cherry woodwork, pastel fabrics, and Corian countertops combine to create a stylish decor. The cockpit is fairly small and comes with molded seating and two big hatches in the sole for engine access. Topside, the flybridge has a centerline helm with wraparound seating. A cut-out in the bridge coaming provides access to the foredeck. Standard 454-cid gas engines will cruise at a sedate 16 knots and deliver about 26 knots top. ❑

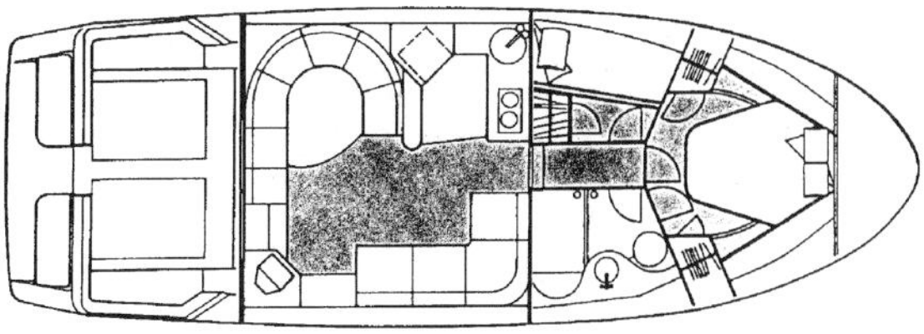

See Page 267 for Pricing Information

MAINSHIP 41 GRAND SALON

SPECIFICATIONS

Length	40'11"	Water	130 gals.
Beam	14'5"	Fuel	375 gals.
Draft	3'6"	Hull Type	Modified-V
Weight	23,000#	Deadrise Aft	12°
Clearance	15'0"	Designer	Mike Peters
Cockpit	NA	Production	1989–90

The Mainship 41 Grand Salon is an unorthodox Euro-style cruiser that might better be described as a floating condo. The design emphasis was obviously on the mega-volume interior. Built on a solid glass hull with a wide beam, there were two versions of the Mainship 41: the Double Cabin with a master stateroom aft, and the Grand Salon with an enormous full-length salon stretching for almost two-thirds of the boat's length. Either layout is impressive with one of the more stylish decor packages ever attempted in a popular-priced production boat. Indeed, the interior of the Mainship 41 was more than just innovative—it was a giant step toward Mainship's vision of the future in mid-size U.S. yacht designs. Unfortunately, the boxy profile and townhouse accommodations failed to impress the market and production lasted only two years. Standard 454-cid gas engines will cruise the Mainship 41 at 16–17 knots (around 25 knots top), and the optional Cat 375-hp diesels cruise around 23 knots and reach 27 knots wide open. ❑

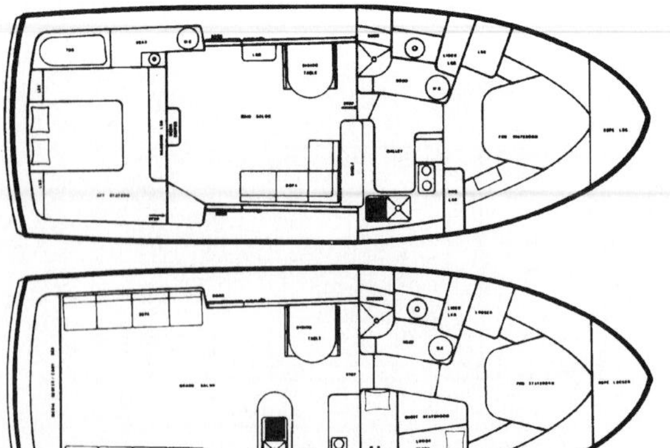

See Page 267 for Pricing Information

MAINSHIP 41 CONVERTIBLE

SPECIFICATIONS

Length	40'11"	Fuel	375 gals.
Beam	14'5"	Cockpit	75 sq. ft.
Draft	3'6"	Hull Type	Modified-V
Weight	22,000#	Deadrise Aft	12°
Clearance	11'4"	Designer	Mike Peters
Water	130 gals.	Production	1989–92

Featuring one of the largest interior layouts found in a boat of this size, the Mainship 41 is a distinctive Eurostyle family cruiser with an affordable price tag to go with her family-size accommodations. Construction is solid fiberglass, and, at just 22,000 pounds, she's a light boat for her size. Her chief attraction is the cavernous interior—an appealing array of stylish appliances, designer fabrics and rounded corners. Originally designed with the dinette open to the salon, an alternate layout (introduced in 1991) has the galley and dinette down from the salon. While the guest stateroom is a tight fit, the master stateroom is quite spacious and fitted with a big pedestal berth. A fold-down transom door with molded boarding steps offers easy access to the swim platform. The flybridge on this boat is huge (note the cockpit overhang). Standard 454-cid gas engines cruise at 15–16 knots and deliver a top speed of around 24 knots. Optional 375-hp Cat diesels will cruise at 22–23 knots and reach 26 knots top. ❑

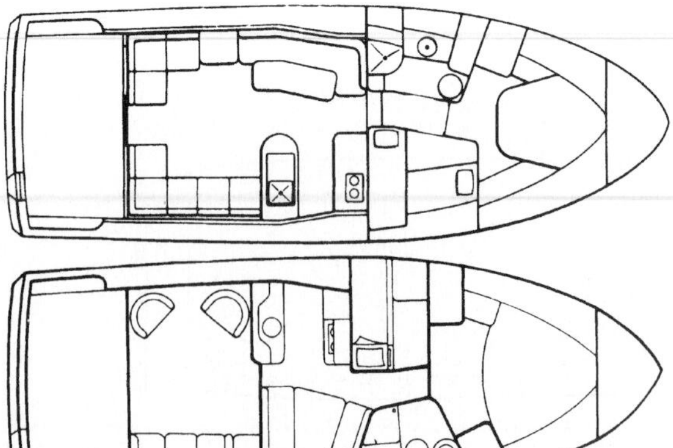

See Page 267 for Pricing Information

MARES 38 CAT

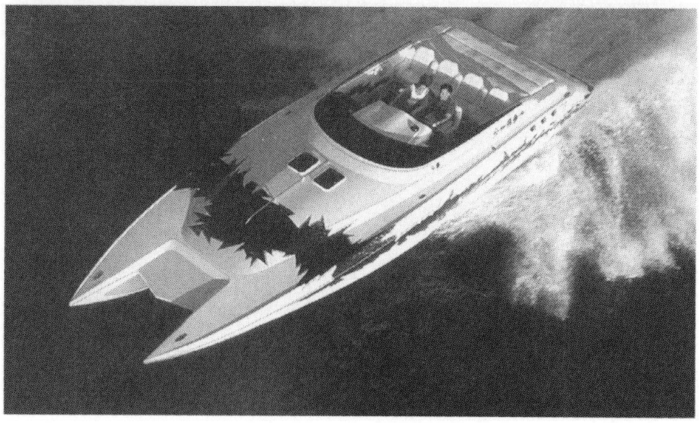

SPECIFICATIONS

Length	38'0"	Water	20 gals.
Beam	11'4"	Fuel	240 gals.
Draft	1'9"	Hull Type	Catamaran
Weight	9,300#	Designer	S. Robson
Clearance	4'8"	Production	1994–Current

The Mares 38 is a high-tech, high-performance catamaran designed for those who like their cruising on the fast side. Built in Florida (the company's main yard is in Brazil), the Mares 38 is clearly aimed at those seeking a fast sport cruiser with an emphasis on performance. The twin hulls create a tapered tunnel of air beneath the center of the boat that acts as a cushion as speed increases. A great ride in a chop, once on plane the ride becomes exceedingly soft and—unlike conventional racing catamarans—the bow sections of each hull are fuller to keep them from digging in when coming off a wave. Below, the cabin accommodations are basic and include a double bed, a stereo, and a small head. The cockpit is arranged with a centerline helm, guest seating for four, and a hydraulically raised sunpad for access to a roomy engine compartment. Among several engine options, a pair of 502-cid MerCruiser stern drives will cruise the Mares 38 efficiently at around 30 knots and reach a blistering 55+ knots wide open. ❑

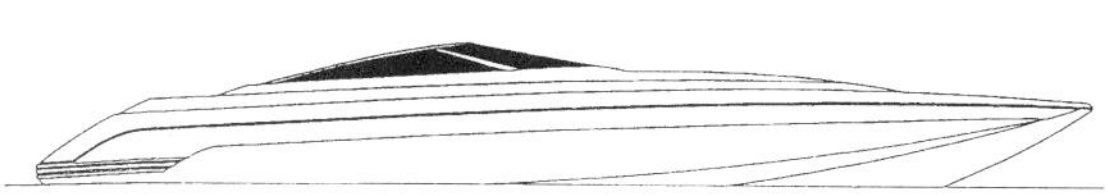

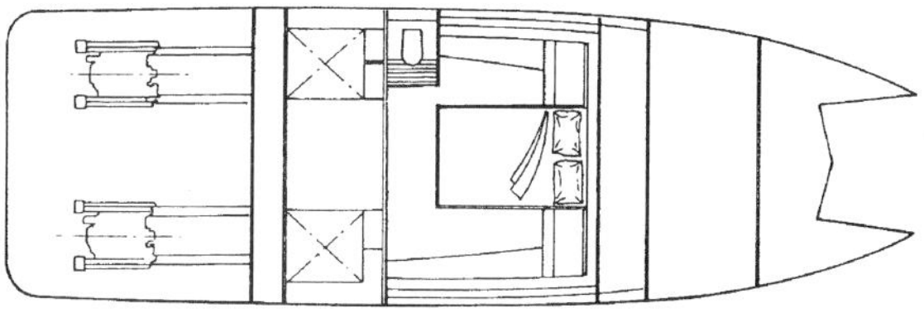

See Page 267 for Pricing Information

MARES 54 CAT

SPECIFICATIONS

Length	54'0"	Water	150 gals.
Beam	17'4"	Fuel	500 gals.
Draft	3'0"	Hull Type	Catamaran
Weight	38,000#	Designer	S. Robson
Clearance	14'6"	Production	1994–Current

At dockside or even at a distance, the Mares 54 has the swept-back profile of a conventional, albeit good-looking, flybridge convertible. It isn't until one gets a closer look (or views her bow-on) that it becomes evident that she's actually a catamaran. Built in New Zeland on a fully cored structure, the Mares 54 combines the efficiencies of asymmetrical hulls with the stability of an extra-wide beam to deliver something quite new to the American power-boat market. The twin hulls create a tapered tunnel of air beneath the center of the boat that acts as a cushion as speed increases. The result is an unusually soft and comfortable ride. Inside, the three-stateroom layout is cavernous, with room in a huge salon for a complete lower helm. Access to the engines is via hatches in the cock-pit sole, and the flybridge can accommodate a small crowd. A good-running and notably efficient boat, 620-hp MAN inboard diesels will cruise the Mares 54 at a fast 28 knots and reach 34–35 knots wide open. ❑

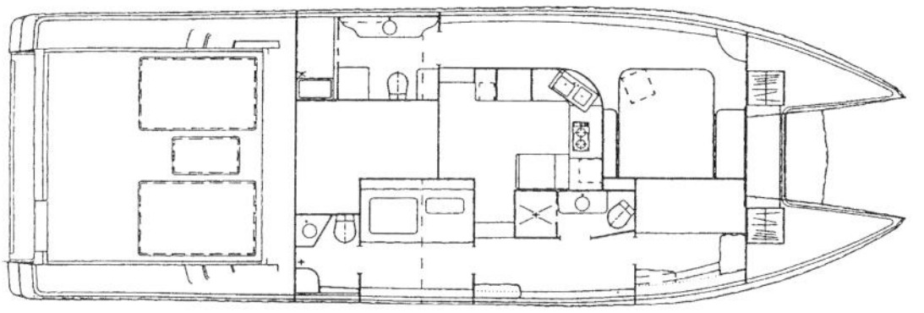

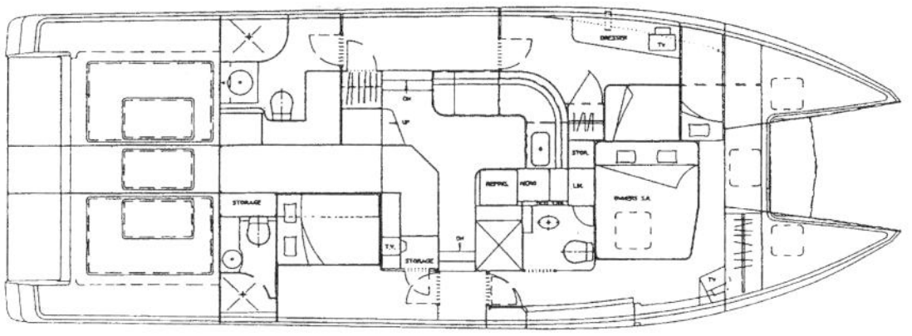

See Page 267 for Pricing Information

MARINETTE 32 SEDAN

SPECIFICATIONS

Length ....32'6"	Fuel ....150 gals.
Beam ....12'0"	Cockpit ....NA
Draft ....2'0"	Hull Type ....Modified-V
Weight ....10,500#	Construction ....Aluminum
Clearance ....9'2"	Designer ....Marinette
Water ....35 gals.	Production 1976–90

A durable and exceedingly popular model, over 1,800 Marinette 32s were built during her long production run. She's constructed of welded marine-grade aluminum, and her conservative 1970s-era styling stands in contrast to her lively performance and practical accommodations. A wide 12-foot beam results in a good deal of living space below. With the dinette and salon settee converted, the Marinette will sleep six in comfort. The salon is quite large for a 32-footer, and the wraparound cabin windows add to the spacious effect. A portside lower helm came standard, and the interior is finished off with teak paneling and woodwork. Additional features include wide sidedecks, foredeck seating, and a roomy engine room. Note than a Flybridge Express version eliminated the salon bulkhead in favor of a semi-open lower helm with an enlarged cockpit. A hardtop model was also available. At only 10,500 lbs., it's no surprise that her performance is brisk. With 260-hp Chrysler gas engines, the Marinette 32 will cruise efficiently at 22 knots and turn 30+ knots at full throttle. ❑

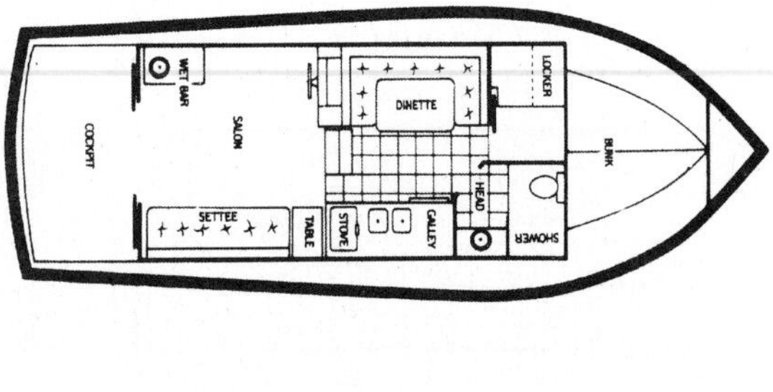

See Page 267 for Pricing Information

MAXUM 2700 SCR

SPECIFICATIONS

Length w/Pulpit ....28'9"	Water ....30 gals.
Beam ....9'8"	Clearance w/Arch ....9'1"
Draft, Up ....1'11"	Hull Type ....Deep-V
Draft, Down ....3'3"	Deadrise Aft ....18.5°
Weight ....6,450#	Designer ....Maxum
Fuel ....102 gals.	Production 1993–Current

The Maxum 2700 is one of the most affordable express cruisers available in a market jam-packed with mid-cabin family boats of this type. Hull construction is solid fiberglass, and her generous transom deadrise results in a stable and comfortable ride in spite of her high freeboard. The 2700 is a big boat on the inside because the full-width cabin eliminates the sidedecks in order to take maximum advantage of the wide beam. The floorplan is arranged in the usual way with double berths fore and aft, a convertible dinette, compact galley and an enclosed head with standing headroom. Privacy curtains separate the sleeping areas from the main cabin. There's seating for six in the cockpit with facing settees aft and a double-wide seat at the helm. Note that the windshield is too low to provide complete wind protection. Twin hatches in the cockpit sole provides good access to the engine(s). The standard 260-hp/5.7-litre MerCruiser stern drive will cruise the Maxum 2700 at 15–16 knots and reach 27 knots top. Optional twin 205-hp/4.3-litre MerCruisers will deliver a 23-knot cruising speed and around 35 knots wide open. ❑

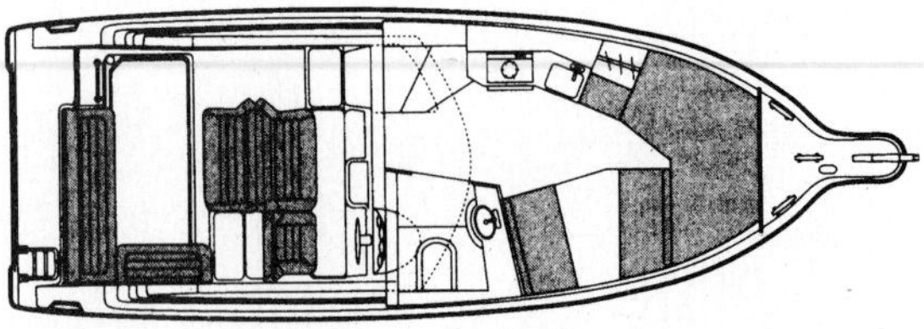

See Page 267 for Pricing Information

MAXUM 3200 SCR

SPECIFICATIONS

Length w/Pulpit	34'9"	Water	36 gals.
Beam	11'0"	Clearance w/Arch	9'6"
Draft, Up	1'6"	Hull Type	Modified-V
Draft, Down	3'0"	Deadrise Aft	16°
Weight	10,800#	Designer	Maxum
Fuel	186 gals.	Production	1994–Current

It might be said that the Maxum 3200 is best described as a lot of boat for the money. Indeed, she's among the least expensive express cruisers to be found in this size range and, with her full-figured shape, the accommodations are quite generous inside and out. Hull construction is solid fiberglass, and the Maxum's 11-foot beam, together with the lack of any sidedecks, results in a big interior for a 32-footer. The mid-cabin layout is arranged in the usual manner with a double berth fore and aft, a convertible dinette, complete galley, and a stand-up head with sink and shower. A curtain forward and a folding door aft separate the sleeping areas from the salon, and the cabin headroom is excellent, even in the aft cabin. Outside, the cockpit is set up with facing settees and a double-wide seat at the helm. A windshield walk-through provides access to the sun pad and bow platform. Note that there's very little space on the console for electronics. Optional 250-hp/5.7-litre MerCruiser stern drives will cruise the Maxum 3200 SCR around 21 knots with a top speed of 30+ knots. ❑

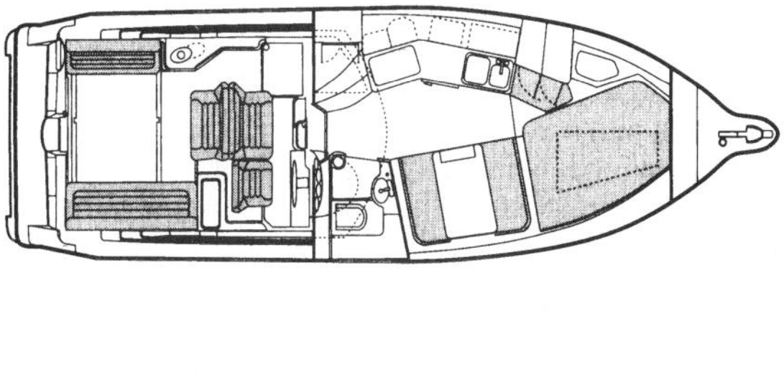

See Page 267 for Pricing Information

MEDITERRANEAN 38 CONVERTIBLE

SPECIFICATIONS

Length w/Pulpit	42'10"	Water	100 gals.
Hull Length	38'4"	Fuel	300/450 gals.
Beam	12'6"	Cockpit	NA
Draft	3'2"	Hull Type	Deep-V
Weight	25,000#	Deadrise Aft	18°
Clearance	11'6"	Production	1985–Current

The Mediterranean 38 is a sturdy-looking flybridge sedan with a good deal of value packed into her low factory-direct price. She's built on a balsa-cored deep-V hull, and the construction involves some 65 individual molds resulting in a finished, gelcoated surface everywhere you look. Two interior layouts are offered with the single-stateroom floorplan being more popular. An overhead compartment in the salon can store six rods and reels. The interior is comprised of laminated teak cabinets and decorator fabrics. Outside, the sidedecks are very wide, and a cockpit tackle center, transom door, and fish box are standard. The step in the sheer was eliminated in 1987, and in 1988 the cockpit was rearranged and the fuel increased to 450 gallons. The flybridge can be ordered with the helm console forward or aft: either way, the bridge dimensions are comparatively moderate. Cummins 300-hp diesels will cruise at an economical 22 knots (27 knots top), and the larger 388-hp Cummins will cruise at 24–25 knots and reach 30 knots wide open. ❑

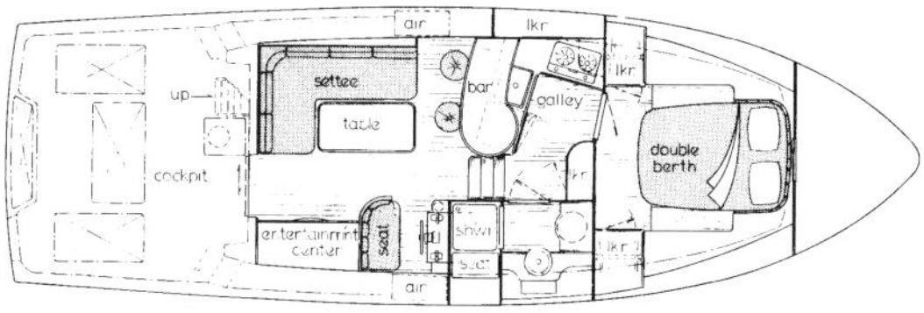

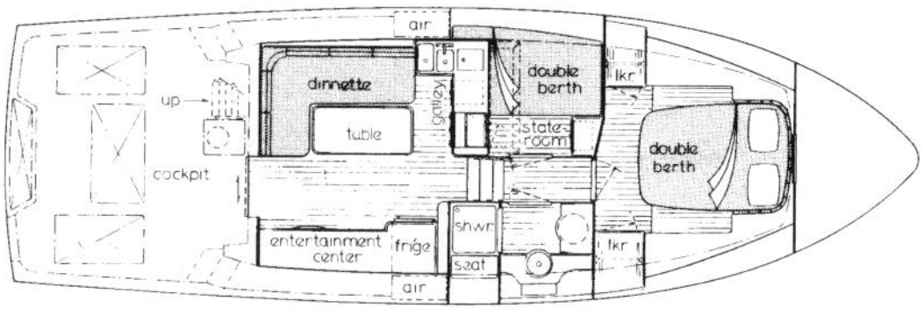

See Page 267 for Pricing Information

MIDNIGHT LACE 40 EXPRESS

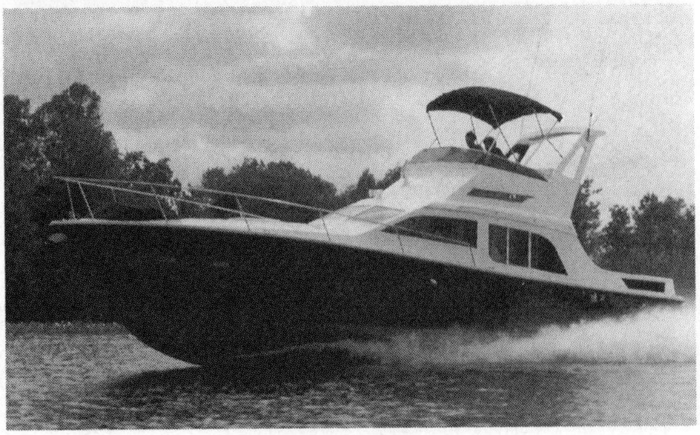

SPECIFICATIONS

Length	40'3"	Water	100 gals.
Length WL	35'4"	Fuel	430 gals.
Beam	13'6"	Hull Type	Modified-V
Draft	3'8"	Deadrise Aft	14°
Weight	19,690#	Designer	Tom Fexas
Clearance	16'0"	Production	1991–94

A very distinctive design with her black hull and sleek, low-profile deckhouse, the Midnight Lace 40 Express is aimed squarely at the market for upscale family cruisers. She was built on a lightweight, fully Divinycell-cored hull with a relatively fine entry and moderate beam. The original two-stateroom floorplan of the Midnight Lace 40 has the galley to starboard in the salon and facing L-shaped settees. A new arrangement introduced in 1992 offered a much-enlarged galley to port and a full-length L-shaped settee opposite. Outside, the cockpit is raised two steps from the salon level, and, while not intended for any serious fishing, it is large enough to satisfy weekend anglers and comes with a standard transom door. Additional features include excellent engine room access under the cockpit, side exhausts, a unique foredeck cockpit, a varnished teak transom, and a stylish helm console with room to flush mount most electronics. A good performer with 300-hp Cummins diesels, she'll cruise efficiently at 23 knots burning only 1 gpm. Top speed is about 27–28 knots. ❑

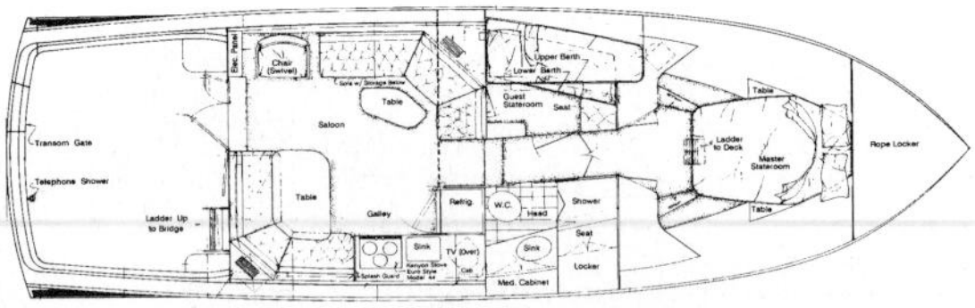

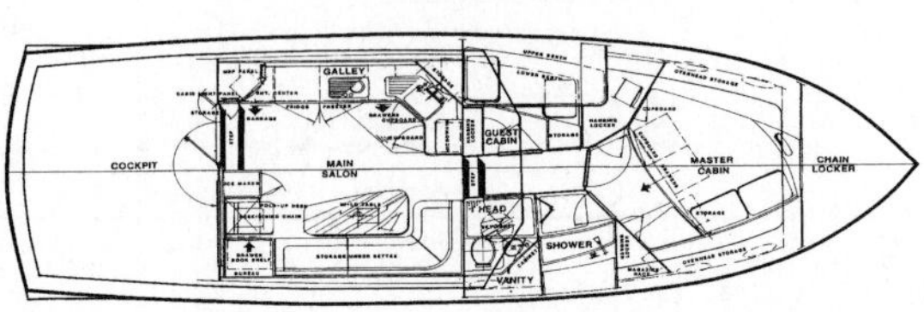

See Page 267 for Pricing Information

MIDNIGHT LACE 44 EXPRESS CRUISER

SPECIFICATIONS

Length	44'0"	Water	130 gals.
Beam	11'0"	Fuel	250 gals.
Draft	2'10"	Hull Type	Modified-V
Weight	15,900#	Deadrise Aft	8°
Clearance	16'0"	Designer	Tom Fexas
Cockpit	NA	Production	1978–89

The Midnight Lace 44 is the boat that put Tom Fexas on the map. The prototype was introduced at the Ft. Lauderdale Boat Show in 1978 and nearly stole the show. Based on the elegant commuter-style boats of the 1920s, the Midnight Lace 44 is a completely modern blend of lightweight cored construction and a highly efficient "penetrating" hull form. She features a very narrow beam with a fine entry, a well-flared bow, and tightly rounded bilges. The Midnight Lace 44s were built in Hong Kong and came with a choice of single- or twin-stateroom floorplans. Originally offered as an express, a flybridge became available in 1979 (although most 44s were sold without it). Note the unique forward cockpit (accessed from the forward stateroom) and the beautiful brightwork of the house. A remarkably classy and efficient boat, standard 220-hp GM 8.2 diesels (driven through V-drives) will cruise the Midnight Lace 44 at 21 knots burning only 14 gph! Top speed is around 25 knots. Larger 260-hp GM 8.2s were optional. ❑

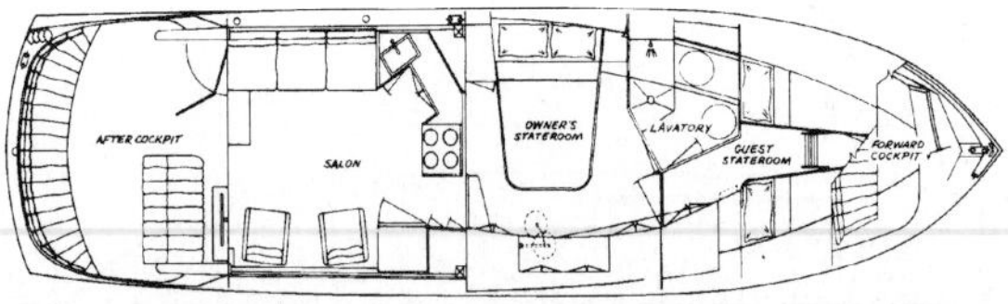

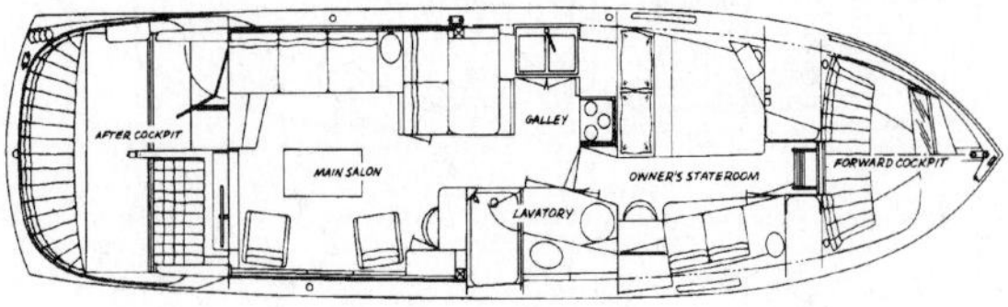

See Page 267 for Pricing Information

MIDNIGHT LACE 52 EXPRESS CRUISER

SPECIFICATIONS

Length	52'6"	Water	230 gals.
Length WL	47'6"	Fuel	480 gals.
Beam	13'0"	Hull Type	Modified-V
Draft	3'0"	Deadrise Aft	8°
Weight	19,850#	Designer	Tom Fexas
Clearance	20'0"	Production	1982–89

Based upon the popular Midnight Lace 44, the Midnight Lace 52 has the same low-profile, commuter-style lines but with a slightly wider beam and a more contemporary interior. The hull and superstructure are fully cored and—at just under 20,000 lbs.—she's a notably lightweight boat for her size. The easily driven hull features a heavily flared bow, a reverse transom, and rounded bilges. Although the interior dimensions are not large, the accommodations are comfortable and finished with traditional teak woodwork. The floorplan has the owner's stateroom forward at the end of the S-shaped passageway, with a small guest cabin to starboard. The engines (with V-drives) are located well aft, below the cockpit. The helm position is elevated, and the classy foredeck cockpit of the original Lace 44 remains in the 52. The flybridge was a popular option, and all but two (of the 16 built) were so equipped. Twin 260-hp 8.2 diesels cruise the Lace 52 efficiently at 20 knots (22 gph) and reach a top speed of 24 knots. ❑

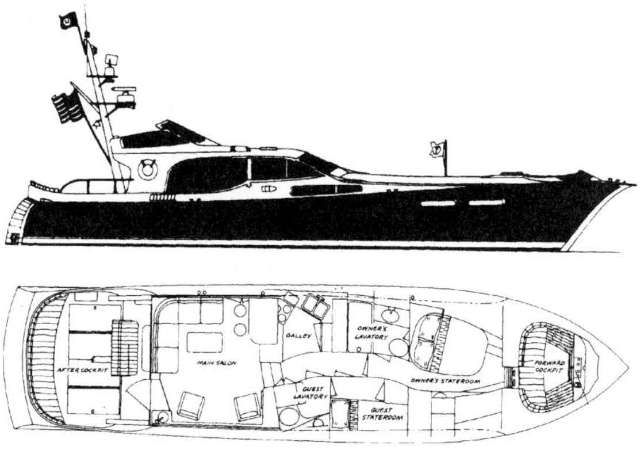

See Page 267 for Pricing Information

MONTEREY 236/246/256 CRUISER

SPECIFICATIONS

Length	24'10"	Water	21 gals.
Beam	8'6"	Clearance w/Arch	8'6"
Draft, Up	1'6"	Hull Type	Deep-V
Draft, Down	2'10"	Deadrise Aft	20°
Weight	4,500#	Designer	Monterey
Fuel	57 gals.	Production	1992–Current

Introduced in 1992 as the 236 Cruiser, Monterey called this boat the 246 Cruiser for 1993–94 and updated her again in 1995 when she was reborn as the Monterey 256 Cruiser. Despite the name changes, this is a small trailerable weekender with an attractive, high-freeboard profile and a surprisingly big interior. Hull construction is solid fiberglass and her deep-V bottom provides a stable and comfortable ride. Designed for coastal and inland use, the Monterey's elevated foredeck results in better that 6 feet of headroom in the cabin—not bad for a 25 foot weekender. The mid-cabin floorplan has a dinette/V-berth forward followed by a compact galley, an enclosed head and shower, and an athwartship double berth in the aft cabin. (Note that there is no opening port in the head.) The cockpit, complete with a slide-out jump seat behind the double-wide helm seat, accommodates six adults. While there are minimum walkarounds, a walk-through in the windshield provides easy access to the bow. A single Volvo 5.7-litre stern drive engine will cruise at 24–25 knots (about 30 knots top). ❑

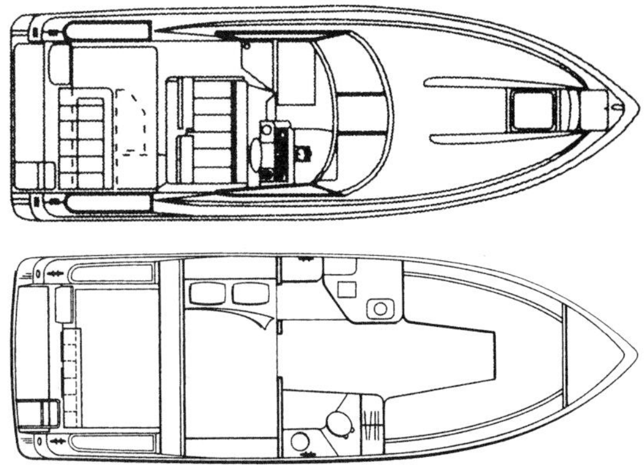

See Page 267 for Pricing Information

MONTEREY 265/276 CRUISER

SPECIFICATIONS

Length w/Pulpit..........29'0"	Fuel..........................100 gals.
Hull Length................26'10"	Water........................32 gals.
Beam.................................9'6"	Clearance w/Arch.........9'2"
Draft, Up.........................1'8"	Hull Type ....Deep-V
Draft, Down ....3'0"	Deadrise Aft...................20°
Weight........................6,500#	Production 1993–Current

The Monterey 276 Cruiser (called the 265 Cruiser for 1993–94) is an affordably priced and well-built weekend cruiser with roomy accommodations and an attractive profile. She's built on a solid fiberglass, deep-V hull with an integral swim platform and bow pulpit and a relatively wide beam. The mid-cabin interior is arranged in the usual way with a U-shaped settee forward that doubles as a V-berth when the table is lowered. The compact galley includes a sink, refrigerator, and stove. Opposite the galley is an enclosed head with shower, and the aft cabin is fitted with a pair of settees and a table that converts into a big double berth. Cabin headroom is almost 6 feet; any more, and the exterior of the 276 Cruiser would have the bloated appearance common to other mid-size cruisers this size. Additional features include a walk-thru windshield (the sidedecks are quite narrow), foredeck sun pad, cockpit wet bar and sport arch. The standard 7.4-litre MerCruiser stern drive will cruise at a brisk 23–24 knots and delivers about 40 knots wide open. ❑

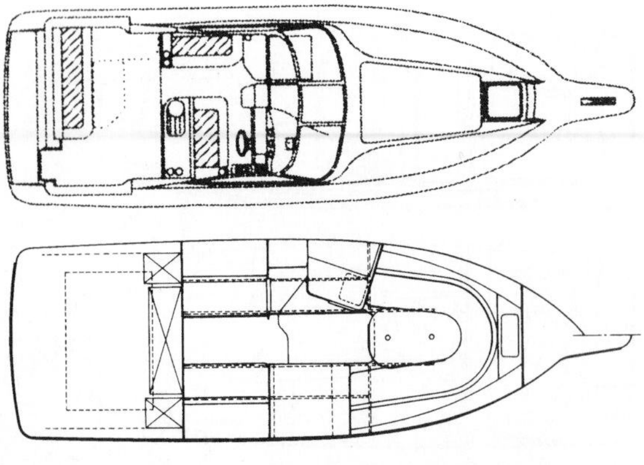

See Page 267 for Pricing Information

MONTEREY 286/296 CRUISER

SPECIFICATIONS

Length w/Pulpit..........31'6"	Fuel..........................140 gals.
Hull Length................28'10"	Water........................44 gals.
Beam...............................10'0"	Clearance w/Arch.........9'4"
Draft, Up.........................1'9"	Hull Type ....Deep-V
Draft, Down ....3'1"	Deadrise Aft...................19°
Weight........................8,000#	Production 1993–Current

A great-looking boat with a well-balanced profile, the 296 Cruiser is Monterey's entry into the highly competitive market for 30-foot stern-drive family weekenders. (Called the 286 Cruiser in 1993–94, the cockpit was revised in 1995 when she became the 296 Cruiser.) Hull construction is solid fiberglass, and her deep-V bottom provides a stable, comfortable ride in most weather conditions. The interior of the 296 is arranged in the usual fashion with double berths for and aft, a convertible dinette, enclosed head and shower and adequate storage. There are facing settees in the mid-cabin with a removable table and a pull-out panel that converts the seats into a huge double berth. Originally designed with a single helm chair, a double-wide helm seat (with an aft-facing bench seat) became standard in 1995. Additional features include a walk-thru windshield, a wide swim platform with fender racks, good main cabin headroom, a sport arch and a molded bow platform. Among several engine options, twin 185-hp/4.3-litre V-6 Volvos will cruise at 23 knots and reach a top speed of around 38 knots. ❑

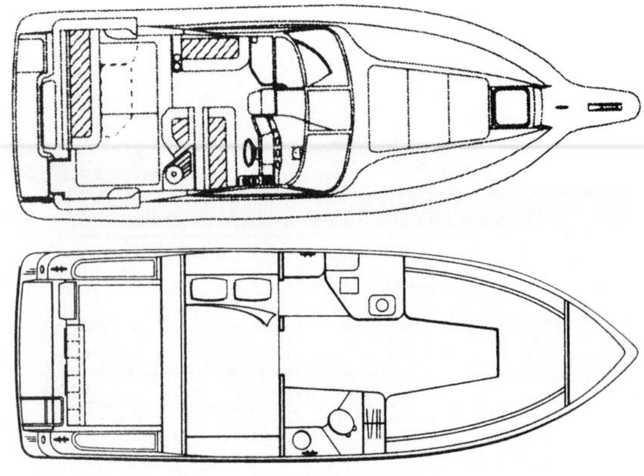

See Page 268 for Pricing Information

NAUSET 35 SPORT CRUISER

SPECIFICATIONS

Length	35'0"	Water	40 gals.
Beam	12'0"	Fuel	150 gals.
Draft	3'0"	Hull Type	Semi-Disp.
Weight	17,000#	Deadrise Aft	NA
Clearance	NA	Designer	R. Lowell
Cockpit	NA	Production	1984–94

Nauset Marine is a well-known New England builder of commercial workboats and custom cruisers, and among their more notable products is the 35 Sport Cruiser, a popular boat the company built for over a decade. She's constructed on the old Bruno-Stillman 35 hull—an extremely popular design used in the production of some 350 boats from 1973 until 1984 when the company closed down. Nauset bought the molds and have since built about forty 35 Sport Cruisers for private use. Construction is solid fiberglass with a single-piece inner liner and a deep, prop-protecting keel. The interior changed little from the original Bruno-Stillman layout but the deckhouse profile was completely new. Features include a standard lower helm, wide sidedecks (well-protected with raised bulwarks and high railings), a prominent bowsprit, and a large cockpit with room for a mounted chair. Among several single- and twin-engine options, a single 375-hp Cat (17–18 knots cruise/24 top) has proven most popular. With her classic profile and seakindly hull, the Nauset 35 is a very appealing design. ❑

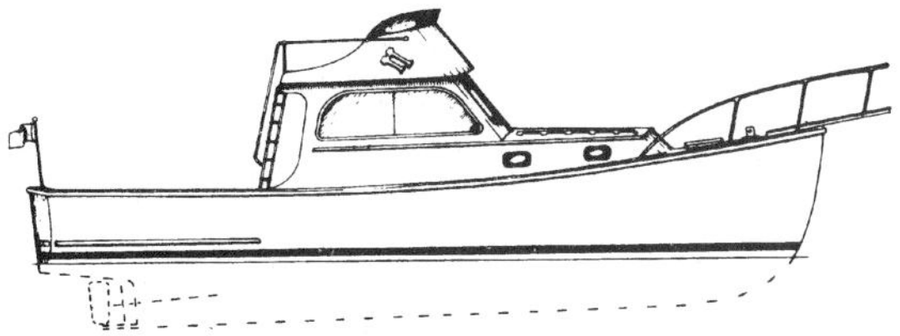

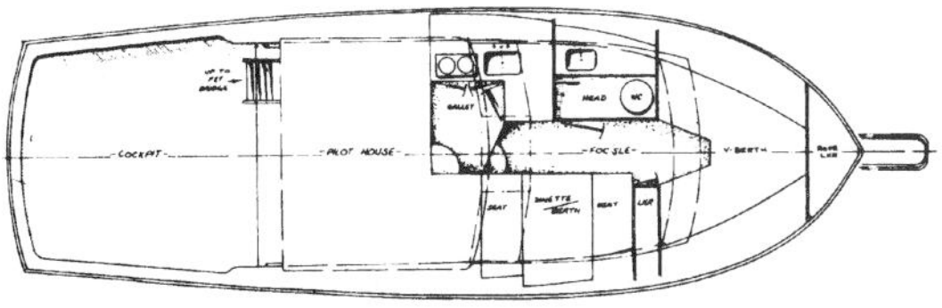

See Page 268 for Pricing Information

OCEAN 35 SPORT FISH & SPORT CRUISER

Sport Fish

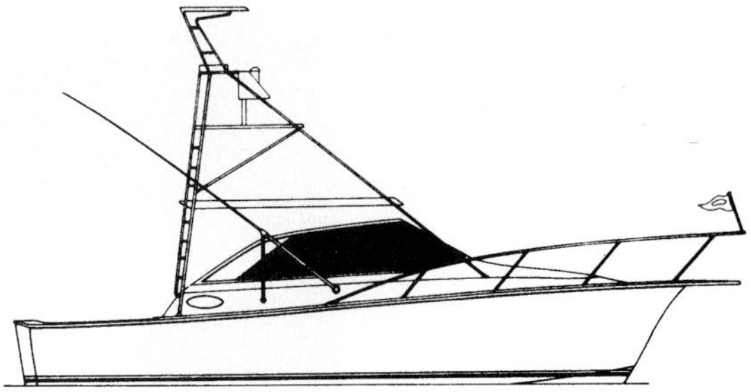

Sport Cruiser

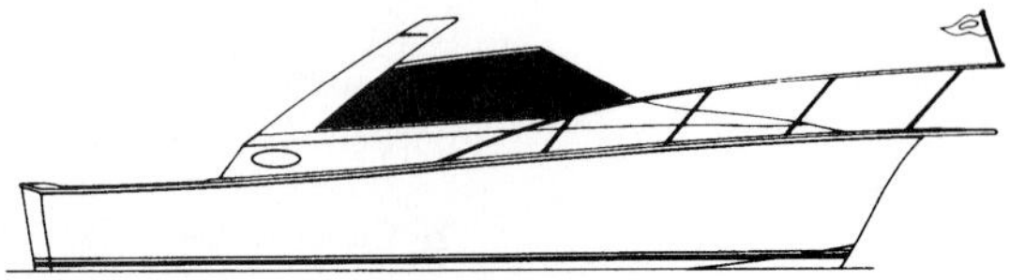

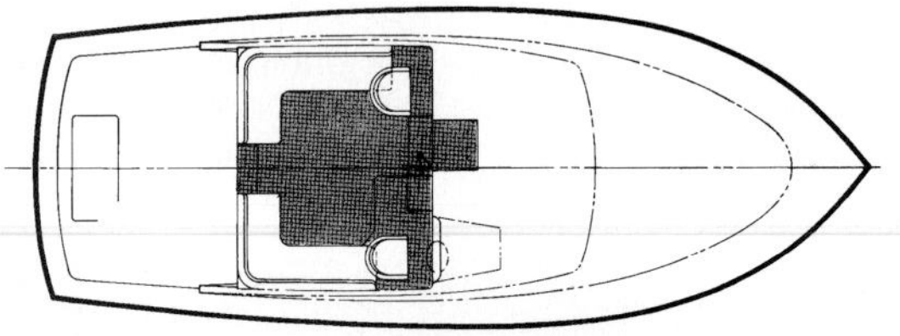

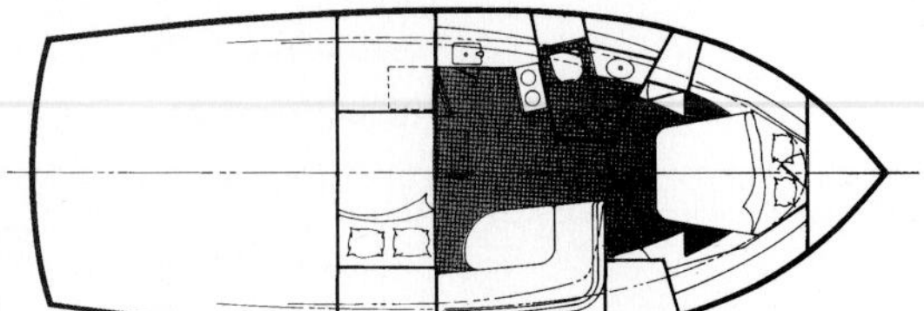

SPECIFICATIONS

Length	35'0"	Fuel	280 gals.
Beam	13'0"	Cockpit	74 sq. ft.
Draft	2'11"	Hull Type	Modified-V
Weight	18,000#	Deadrise Aft	13°
Clearance	8'9"	Designer	D. Martin
Water	55 gals.	Production	1990–92

In general, express-style designs from manufacturers of sportfishing boats tend to be at the high end of the price spectrum. The Ocean 35 Sport Cruiser is unusual in that respect—she's an affordable and competent express cruiser equally at home as a family cruiser or weekend fisherman. Available in a Sportfish version as well as the Sport Cruiser model pictured above, the difference between the two is the extra cockpit seating and radar arch found in the Sport Cruiser and the teak covering boards, tackle lockers, and hinged transom gate of the Sportfish. The interiors are identical in both boats with a centerline double berth in the forward stateroom, a nifty mid-cabin fitted beneath the bridgedeck, a head with shower stall, and a portside galley with dinette opposite. Standard equipment includes air conditioning, generator, washdowns, rod storage, and a bimini with enclosure. Twin 320-hp gas engines will cruise at 22–23 knots and exceed 30 knots wide open. The optional 300-hp Cummins diesels cruise around 26 knots with a top speed of 29–30 knots. ❑

See Page 268 for Pricing Information

OCEAN ALEXANDER 42/46 SEDAN

Ocean Alexander 42 Sedan

Ocean Alexander 46 Sedan

SPECIFICATIONS

Length	42'/46'	Fuel	500 gals.
Beam	14'4"	Cockpit	NA
Draft	3'2"	Hull Type	Modified-V
Weight	23,000/26,000#	Deadrise Aft	NA
Clearance	11'6"	Designer	Ed Monk
Water	150 gals.	Production	1987–94

Beginning as the 390 Sedan in 1985, Alexander Marine stretched the hull a couple of years later to create the 42 Sedan (1987–93) as well as the 46 Sedan model. A popular boat—especially the 42—with plenty of eye appeal, she's built om an easy-riding modified-V hell with a fine entry and cored hullsides. The format of the two models is very similar with the 46 having a slightly larger salon and cockpit than the 42. While neither the Alexander 42 or 46 is particularly beamy, the salon and living areas are well-proportioned and beautifully finished throughout. The layouts of both offer a large salon with the galley and lower helm on the main deck. Two staterooms and one head are forward along with a unique storage room where the engine room access door is found. Updates in 1990 included a restyled superstructure and arch, wider sidedecks, and a revised interior decor. Note that production of the Alexander 46 ended in 1993. Standard 250-hp Cummins will cruise either boat at 14 knots (17–18 knots top), and the optional 425-hp Cats will cruise at 22–23 knots (about 26 top). ❑

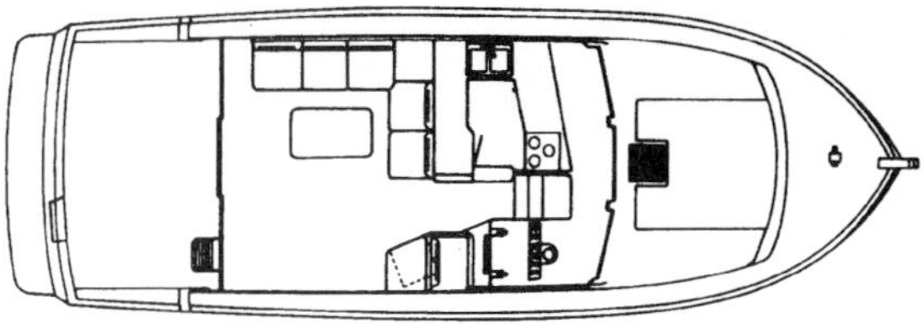

Main Deck Layout

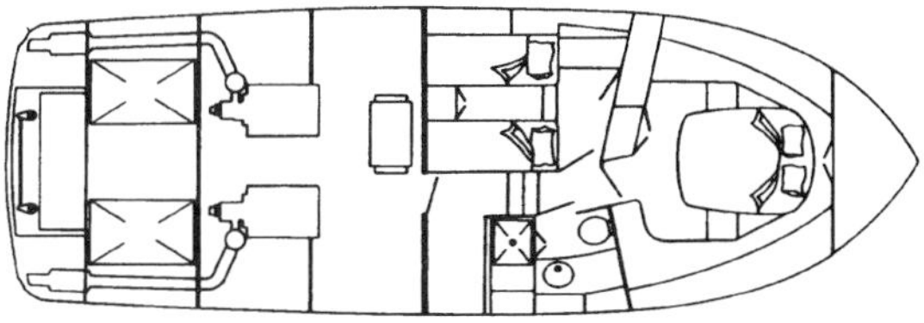

Lower Level Layout

See Page 268 for Pricing Information

PHOENIX 27 WEEKENDER

SPECIFICATIONS

Length	27'3"	Water	24 gals.
Length WL	23'6"	Fuel, Std.	200 gals.
Beam	9'10"	Fuel, Opt.	250 gals.
Draft	1'10"	Hull Type	Deep-V
Weight	7,200#	Deadrise Aft	21°
Clearance	6'9"	Production	1979–94

Long a popular boat, the Phoenix 27 Weekender is a straightforward offshore express without a lot of frills. Construction is solid fiberglass with a full-length inner liner bonded to the hull for added strength. As with other Jim Wynne designs, the Phoenix 27 has propeller pockets recessed into her deep-V hull. Since over half of the boat's length is devoted to the single-level cockpit, the interior is necessarily compact with V-berths, a small galley, and stand-up head with shower. The engines are located under raised engine boxes that double as bait-watching seats. In addition to the Weekender model, the 27 was offered in a "Fishbuster" version (1979–89) with the galley/tackle center located forward and to port in the cockpit (see top layout below). Standard 350-cid gas engines provide a cruising speed of about 23 knots (31+ knots top). Optional 200-hp Volvo diesels will cruise around 25 knots (29-30 top). With a pair of 250-hp Yahama outboards, the 27 Tournament will hit a top speed of 40 knots. ❑

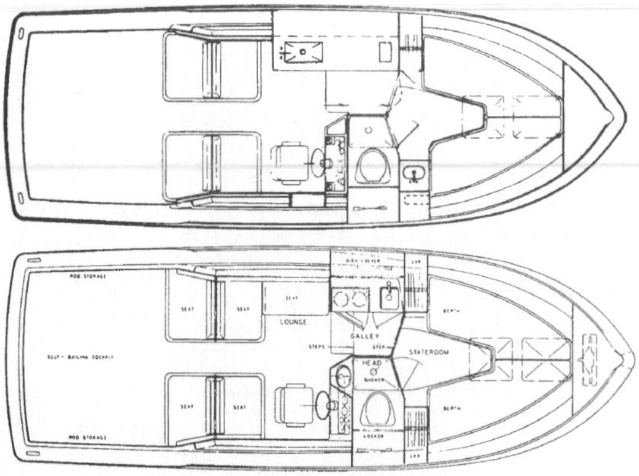

See Page 268 for Pricing Information

PHOENIX 27 TOURNAMENT

SPECIFICATIONS

Length	27'3"	Water	24 gals.
Length WL	23'6"	Fuel, Std.	220 gals.
Beam	9'10"	Fuel, Opt.	290 gals.
Draft	2'0"	Hull Type	Deep-V
Weight	8,200#	Deadrise Aft	21°
Clearance	7'6"	Production	1990–Current

Built on the same hull as the Phoenix 27 Weekender, the 27 Tournament is a good-looking raised-deck open express with a clean and uncluttered fishing layout. She's built on a rugged deep-V hull with prop pockets and a steep 21 degrees of transom deadrise. Her bi-level cockpit eliminates the engine boxes found in the Weekender while providing much-improved helm visibility. Below, the cabin accommodations are centered around a convertible lounge/dinette forward and a small galley to port. There's standing headroom in the head, and the interior is tastefully finished with teak trim and off-white mica laminates. Additional features include a molded bow pulpit, transom door and gate, in-deck fish box, seawater washdown, lockable rod storage under the cockpit coaming, and good access to the engines. Twin 350-cid gas engines are standard (23 knots cruise/30 knots top), and Volvo 200-hp diesels are optional (25 knots cruise/29 knots wide open). A pair of 250-hp Yahama outboards will cruise at 25 knots and reach a top speed of 40 knots. ❑

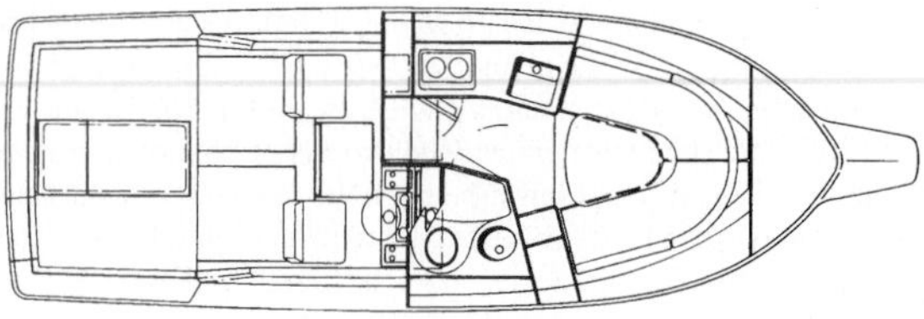

See Page 268 for Pricing Information

PHOENIX BLACKHAWK 909

SPECIFICATIONS

Length w/Pulpit	32'5"	Water	40 gals.
Hull Length	30'1"	Fuel	140 gals.
Beam	10'0"	Hull Type	Modified-V
Draft	1'10"	Deadrise Aft	21°
Weight	9,150#	Designer	Jim Wynne
Clearance	8'0"	Production	1985–94

Phoenix has a reputation for building good fishing boats, so it was a surprise when they introduced the Eurostyle Blackhawk 909 express cruiser in 1985. Built on a solid fiberglass hull with prop pockets, the 909 was a stern-drive boat (a first for any Phoenix model) until 1986 when inboards became available. A molded full-length inner liner—used to create the interior—also adds a good deal of rigidity and strength to the hull. Below deck, a U-shaped lounge/dinette at the bow will seat five and converts into a large double berth at night. Another couple can sleep in the small mid-cabin tucked beneath the bridgedeck. While the absence of interior bulkheads makes the interior seem very open, the lack of natural cabin lighting and ventilation is apparent. Features include a unique sliding transom door, curved windshield, good headroom below, and an integral swim platform and bow pulpit. Twin 350-cid gas inboards cruise at 22 knots (31 knots top). Twin 200-hp Volvo diesels were optional. Note the limited fuel capacity. ❑

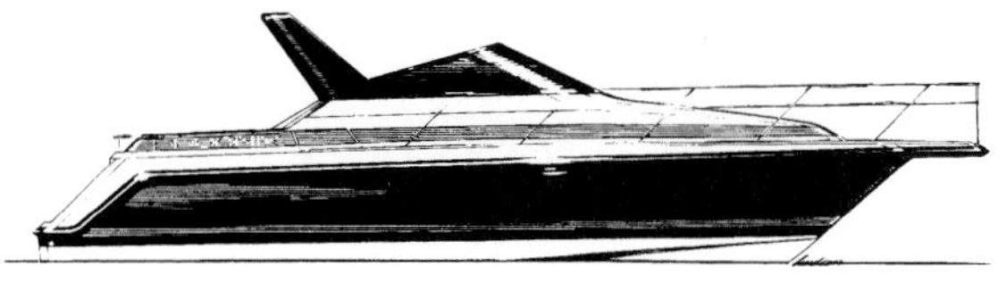

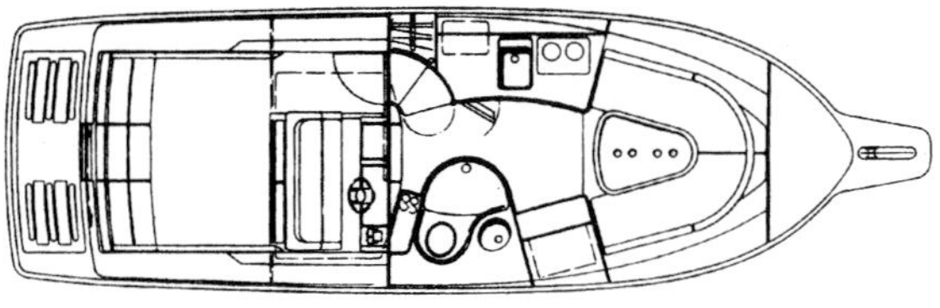

See Page 268 for Pricing Information

PORTSMOUTH 30 CRUISER

SPECIFICATIONS

Length	29'9"	Water	64 gals.
Length WL	28'2"	Fuel	180 gals.
Beam	10'6"	Cockpit	NA
Draft	2'11"	Hull Type	Semi-Disp.
Weight	10,000#	Designer	R. Lowell
Clearance	NA	Production	1989–92

The origins of the Portsmouth 30 go back to 1978 when the late Royal Lowell (perhaps the best-known designer of Downeast boats) drew the lines for the Sisu 30, an inboard fisherman with a reputation for seaworthy and dependable operation. Sisu went out of business in 1987, and the molds were acquired by Portsmouth. Built on a semi-displacement hull with a deep, prop-protecting keel, the Portsmouth hulls are balsa cored, and the boats are turned out on a semi-production basis in New Hampshire. There are several versions of the Portsmouth 30 including sportfisherman, hardtop, and commercial workboat models, however the Cruiser (pictured above) has been the most popular to date. A galley-up and galley-down floorplan are available (both with a single stateroom), and the traditional teak interior woodwork is very appealing. Outside, the cockpit is large enough for some serious fishing, and the sidedecks are protected by high railings. A good-looking boat, a single 250-hp Cummins diesel will cruise the Portsmouth 30 at 16 knots (about 19 knots top). ❑

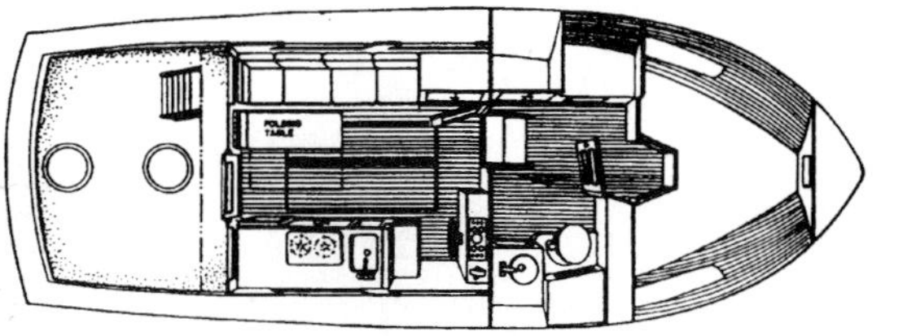

See Page 268 for Pricing Information

PRESIDENT 35 SEDAN

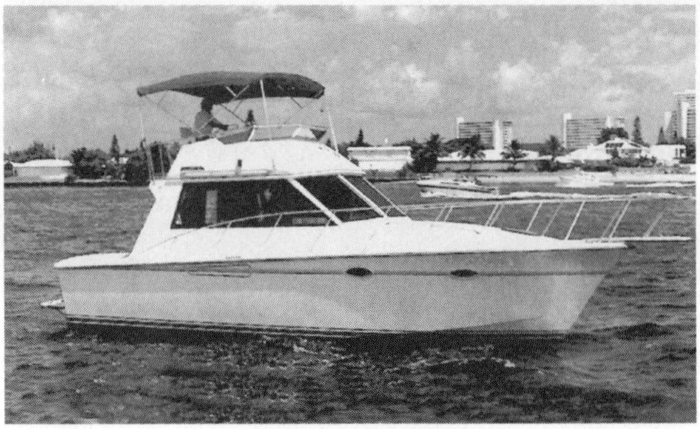

SPECIFICATIONS

Length	34'5"	Water	100 gals.
Beam	12'10"	Fuel, Std.	250 gals.
Draft	3'1"	Hull Type	Modified-V
Weight	18,700#	Deadrise Aft	NA
Clearance	11'7"	Designer	President
Cockpit	NA	Production	1987–92

This conservative flybridge sedan was introduced in 1987 by President as a Sedan Fisherman—a bad idea since few anglers have taken to Taiwan products as serious fishing boats. She's actually a beamy family cruiser (a near-13-foot beam is wide for a 34-footer) with an adequate cockpit and a very spacious all-teak interior. There were two floorplans available for the President 35: a two-stateroom layout with the galley in the salon, and a more open single-stateroom arrangement with the galley down. A lower helm station was optional, and a separate (circular) stall shower is fitted in the head compartment. Both floorplans have V-berths forward. Note that the generator is installed beneath the cockpit sole—not the ideal location in our estimation. The small flybridge is set up with guest seating in front of the helm in the conventional manner. Among several engine options offered over the years, a pair of 225-hp Lehman diesels will cruise the President 35 Sedan at 15–16 knots and reach about 19 knots top. ❑

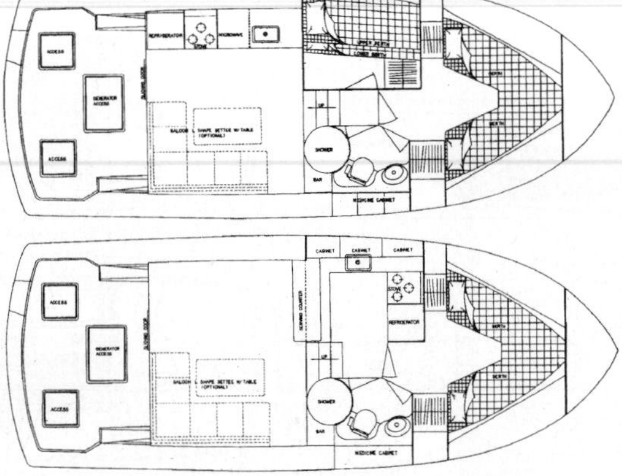

See Page 268 for Pricing Information

REGAL VALANTI 252/256 COMMODORE 256

SPECIFICATIONS

Length w/Pulpit	26'0"	Water	27 gals.
Hull Length	24'6"	Waste	17 gals.
Beam	8'6"	Clearance	8'2"
Draft, Down	2'10"	Hull Type	Deep-V
Weight	5,000#	Deadrise Aft	21°
Fuel	65 gals.	Production	1993–Current

One of the bigger trailerable cruisers on the market and a popular model for Regal, the 256 Commodore was introduced in 1993 as the 252 Valenti, a name that was updated the following year to 256 Valenti. Regardless of what they call her, she's a well-built mid-cabin cruiser with asolid fiberglass, deep-V hull, a maxi-volume interior (there are no sidedecks), and a well-arranged cockpit with room for six adults. There are berths for four below along with a small galley and an enclosed stand-up head. These are surprisingly spacious accommodations for a 25-footer, and the fabrics and appliances are first-rate. The cockpit has a wraparound lounge with a removable table to port (opposite the helm) and fold-away bench seating aft. Additional features include a walk-through windshield with user-friendly access steps, transom door, fender storage in the swim platform and an integral bow pulpit. A good performer in spite of her full-figured profile, she'll cruise at 23 knots with a single 235-hp 5.7-litre Volvo stern drive and reach a top speed of about 32 knots. ❑

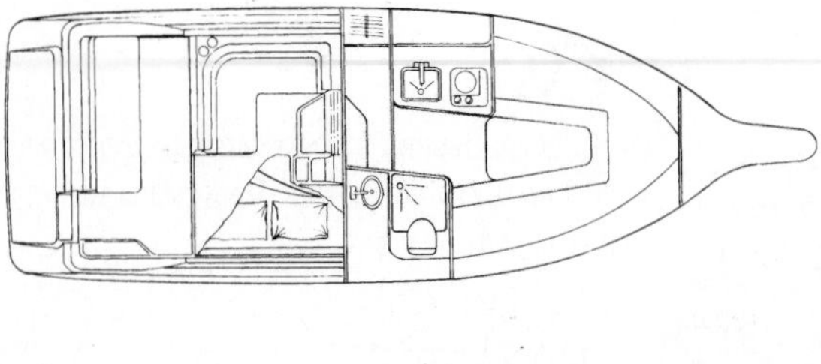

See Page 268 for Pricing Information

REGAL COMMODORE 265/270/276

SPECIFICATIONS

Length w/Pulpit	29'6"	Water	35 gals.
Hull Length	26'10"	Fuel	110 gals.
Beam	9'6"	Hull Type	Deep-V
Draft	2'8"	Deadrise Aft	19°
Weight	6,500#	Designer	Regal
Clearance	9'8"	Production	1990–93

Regal introduced this widebody model in 1990 as the Commodore 265—an upscale family cruiser with a maxi-volume interior to go with her sportboat profile. (Note that she became the Commodore 270 in 1991, and the 276 designation came in 1993.) It isn't just a wide beam that makes her a big boat inside; the cabin headroom is a generous 6 feet, 2 inches thanks to the raised foredeck. Like all Commodore express models, the 265/270/276 is a mid-cabin design with an athwartships queen berth tucked below the helm. A circular dinette dominates the cabin, while the small berth in the forepeak is better suited for kids. Note that a door (not curtains) provides privacy for the aft cabin and its stand-up dressing area. Outside, a companion seat is opposite the helm, and engine access is via hatches in the cockpit sole. Additional features include a molded pulpit, foredeck sunpad, and bench seating at the transom. A standard 454-cid MerCruiser stern drive will cruise at 19–20 knots with a top speed of around 33 knots. ❑

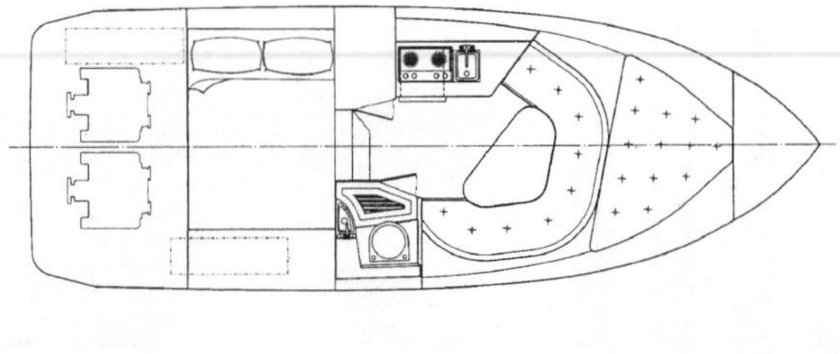

See Page 269 for Pricing Information

REGAL COMMODORE 272

SPECIFICATIONS

Length w/Pulpit	28'6"	Water	27 gals.
Hull Length	26'7"	Fuel	105 gals.
Beam	9'2"	Hull Type	Deep-V
Draft	3'6"	Deadrise Aft	21°
Weight	6,200#	Designer	Regal
Clearance	6'9"	Production	1991–Current

Called the Regal Valanti 260 when she was introduced in 1991, the Commodore 272 is a popular wide-body family cruiser with a modern sportboat profile and a roomy mid-cabin interior. Indeed, the excellent cabin headroom is unusual in a 27-footer—the result of a greatly raised foredeck that gives the boat a somewhat topheavy appearance. Featuring a molded pulpit and integrated swim platform in addition to her curved windshield and colorful graphics, the Commodore 272 is constructed on a deep-V hull with cored hull-sides and bottom. Her interior includes a queen-size aft cabin with privacy curtain, convertible dinette, stand-up head, and compact galley. Outside, the cockpit arranged with a triple-wide helm seat and a windshield walk-thru provides access to the foredeck. The engine hatch—basically the cockpit sole—has an electric lift. Among several stern drive engine options, twin V-6 Volvos will cruise the Commodore 272 around 22 knots (39 knots top), while a single 454-cid MerCruiser will cruise at 20 knots and reach 35 knots. ❑

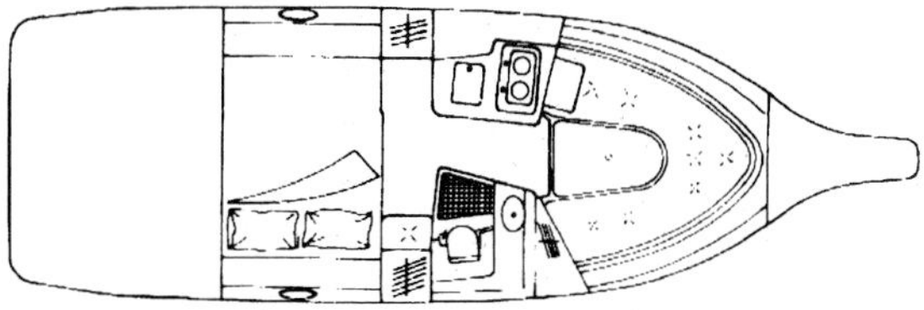

See Page 269 for Pricing Information

REGAL VENTURA 8.3

SPECIFICATIONS

Length	27'6"	Water	24 gals.
Beam	9'1"	Fuel	105 gals.
Draft	2'10"	Hull Type	Deep-V
Weight	5,800#	Deadrise Aft	21°
Clearance	5'6"	Designer	Regal
Cockpit	NA	Production	1993–Current

Aside from her sleek appearance, the most arresting feature of the Regal 8.3 SC is her huge cockpit—about the largest of any sportboat in her class. This is a boat with outdoor entertaining in mind, and the compact interior—with its convertible dinette and small head—seems an afterthought. Built on a deep-V hull with cored hullsides, the 8.3 SC is designed with wraparound guest seating in the cockpit in addition to a wet bar and excellent cockpit storage. The center cushion in the double-wide helm seat locks up to allow the driver to use the seat as a leaning post. Additional features include a walk-thru windshield (with molded access steps), a huge engine compartment with an electrically-raised aft seat/hatch assembly, tilt wheel, and better-than-average construction. A good-running boat, a single 7.4-litre stern drive will cruise at 22 knots and reach a top speed of 38-39 knots. Note that an open bow version with a small enclosed head—the 8.3 SE—is also available. ❑

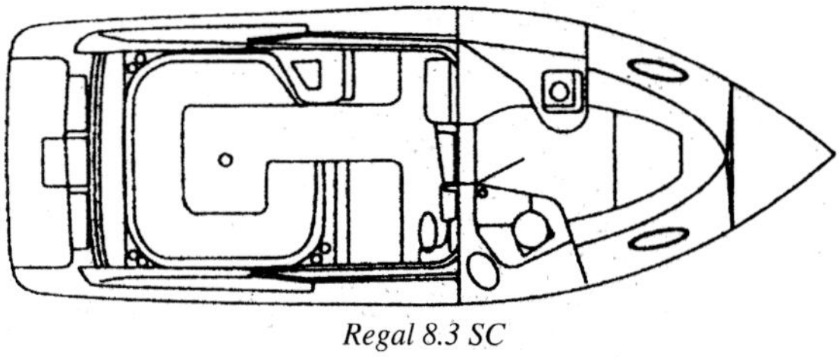

Regal 8.3 SC

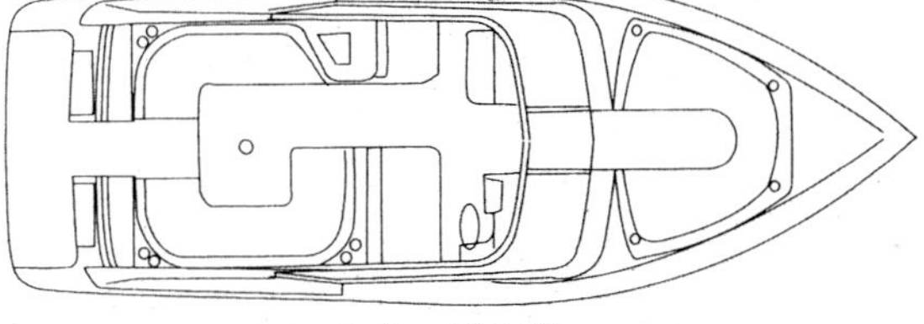

Regal 8.3 SE

See Page 269 for Pricing Information

REGAL COMMODORE 277XL/280XL/290/300

277XL Commodore (1982–87)

280 Commodore (1988–89)

290/300 Commodore (1990-94)

SPECIFICATIONS

LOA, 277XL/280	27'1"	Water	35 gals.
LOA, 290/300	32'5"	Fuel	140 gals.
Beam	10'0"	Hull Type	Modified-V
Draft	3'2"	Deadrise Aft	16°
Weight	8,200#	Designer	Regal
Clearance	9'3"	Production	1982–94

Introduced in 1982 as the Regal 277XL, this model went through more model upgrades and name changes than just about any other boat in the business. After five years of production as the 277XL, Regal redesigned the deckhouse and added a curved windshield in 1988 and re-introduced her as the Commodore 280. In 1990, a new integral swim platform was added—a major styling improvement—and she became the Commodore 290. During 1993 she was sold as the Commodore 300—basically the same boat as the 290 but with a new name to more accurately reflect her longer length with the swim platform. Aside from cosmetic and decor updates, the mid-cabin interior layout remained unchanged until 1994 (the last year of production) when a new mid-cabin floorplan was introduced for the Commodore 300. Built on a solid fiberglass hull with moderate beam, several single and twin stern-drive power options were offered over the years. Among them, a pair of 5.0-litre (4-cylinder) MerCruisers will cruise at 18 knots (about 30 knots top), and the more popular 5.7-litre engines (Volvo or MerCruiser) will cruise around 23 knots (37–38 knots top). ❑

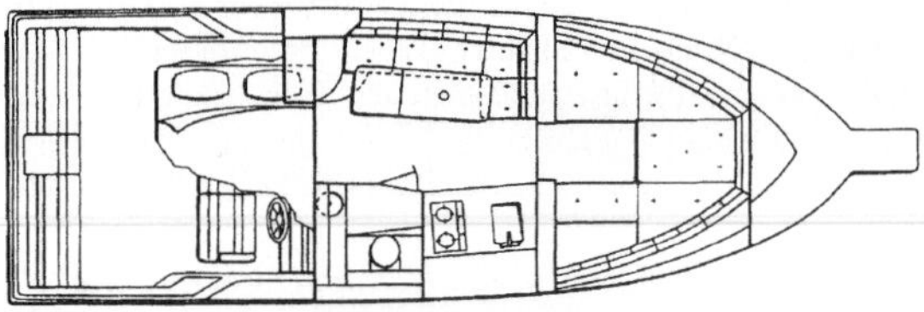

1982–93 Layout

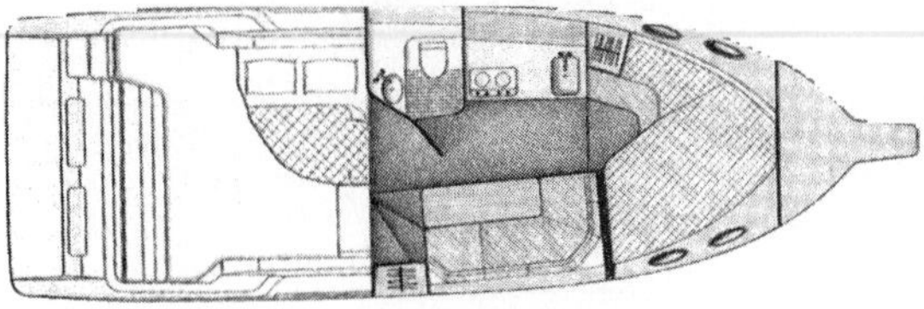

1994 Layout

See Page 269 for Pricing Information

REGAL COMMODORE 292

SPECIFICATIONS

Length ....28'9"	Waste ....30 gals.
Beam ....10'4"	Clearance ....NA
Draft, Down ....3'2"	Headroom ....6'3"
Weight ....8,500#	Hull Type ....Deep-V
Fuel ....150 gals.	Deadrise Aft ....18°
Water ....35 gals.	Production 1995–Current

A well-built boat for those willing to pay a little more, the Commodore 292 is a good-looking stern-drive cruiser with very upscale accommodations. She's built on a solid fiberglass hull with a relatively wide beam and innovative trim tab pods beneath the swim platform. In the European fashion, the 292 is one of a growing number of American-made express cruisers with no bow pulpit. Her plush, maxi-beam interior (there are no sidedecks) includes double berths fore and aft and a convertible dinette in the salon—berths for four adults and two kids. There are privacy curtains for both staterooms, and the rich furnishings and Corian countertops lend a touch of luxury not often seen in a boat this size. The cockpit has a U-shaped lounge aft that converts into a sun pad and fold-away bench seating at the transom. Additional features include a walk-through windshield, a very stylish curved arch, and a recessed anchor windlass (optional). Twin 250-hp 5.7-litre MerCruiser I/Os will cruise the 292 Commodore at 23 knots and reach 37–38 knots wide open. ❑

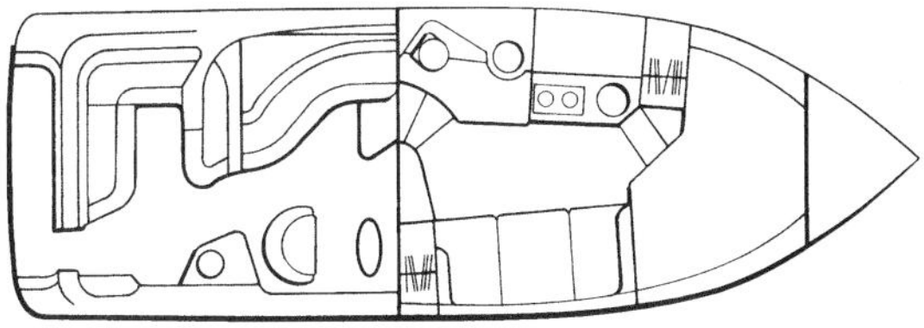

See Page 269 for Pricing Information

REGAL COMMODORE 320

SPECIFICATIONS

Length ....31'10"	Water ....50 gals.
Beam ....11'2"	Fuel ....178 gals.
Draft, Up ....1'8"	Hull Type ....Deep-V
Draft, Down ....2'11"	Deadrise Aft ....19°
Weight ....11,000#	Designer ....Regal
Clearance ....9'4"	Production 1988–92

A good-looking cruiser with stylish graphics and a graceful profile, the Regal Commodore 320 is one of the more elegant mid-cabin sportboats in her class. She's built on a solid fiberglass deep-V hull with average beam and a steep 19 degrees of transom deadrise. Below, the mid-cabin floorplan is arranged in the conventional manner with a convertible dinette and an offset double berth forward. Privacy curtains separate the forward and mid-cabin staterooms from the salon and a deep storage bin is located beneath the mid-cabin berth. The fabrics, furnishings, hardware, and detailing found throughout the Regal 320 are above average. Exterior features include a foredeck sunpad, a deep integrated swim platform with built-in fender storage, tilt wheel, and fairly wide sidedecks. Note that the entire aft part of the deck tilts up electrically for access to the motors. Standard 260-hp stern drives will cruise around 22 knots (35 knots top), and optional 340-hp engines will cruise at 26 knots and reach a top speed of about 42 knots. ❑

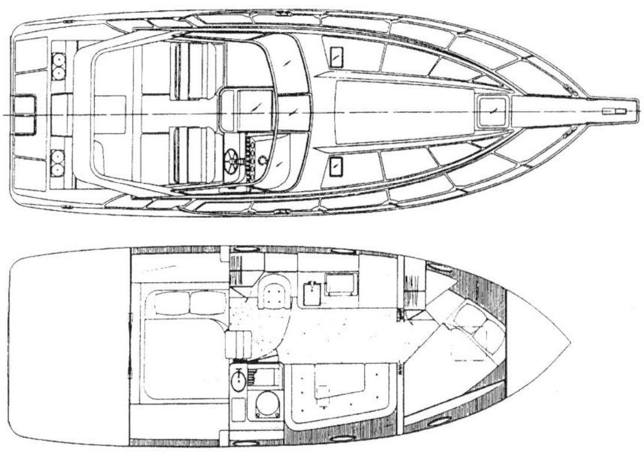

See Page 269 for Pricing Information

REGAL VENTURA 9.8/COMMODORE 322

SPECIFICATIONS

Length ....32'0"	Water ....50 gals.
Beam ....11'2"	Fuel ....178 gals.
Draft ....3'2"	Hull Type ....Deep-V
Weight ....11,000#	Deadrise Aft ....19°
Clearance ....8'6"	Designer ....Regal
Cockpit ....NA	Production 1993–Current

The Commodore 322 (called the Ventura 9.8 until 1995) is a highly Eurostyled express cruiser with a classy profile to go with her mid-cabin accommodations. The absence of a bow pulpit and the aft-raking curve in the arch are innovative touches. The Ventura is built on a deep-V hull with cored hullsides and a solid fiberglass bottom. She's available with stern drives or V-drives; with the latter, there are small prop pockets recessed into the bottom and side-dumping exhausts. Below, the upscale interior of the 9.8 is arranged in the conventional manner with berths for six, a large galley and plenty of storage. A folding door provides privacy for the aft stateroom, while just a curtain separates the forward cabin. The cockpit is set up with a double-wide helm seat, wraparound guest seating aft, and a walk-thru windshield for access to the foredeck. A fast boat with stern drives, twin 300-hp MerCruisers will cruise at 23–24 knots (38 knots top). With V-drive inboards, the same engines will cruise at 20 knots and reach about 35 knots top. ❑

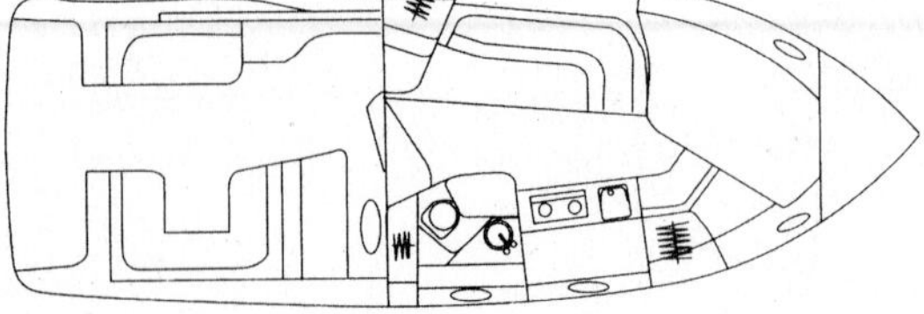

See Page 269 for Pricing Information

REGAL COMMODORE 360/380/400/402

Commodore 360

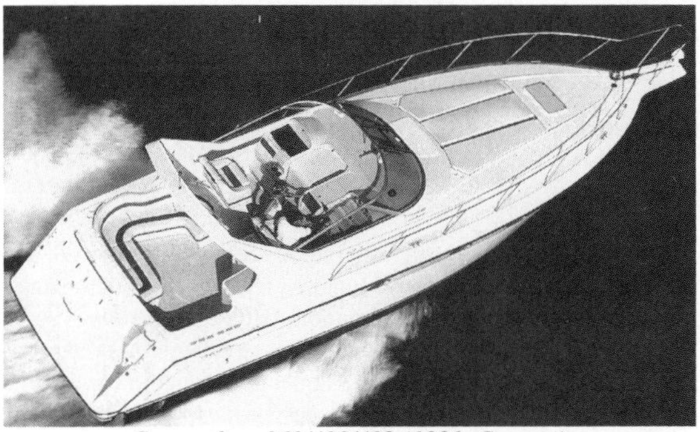

Commodore 360/400/402 (1991–Current)

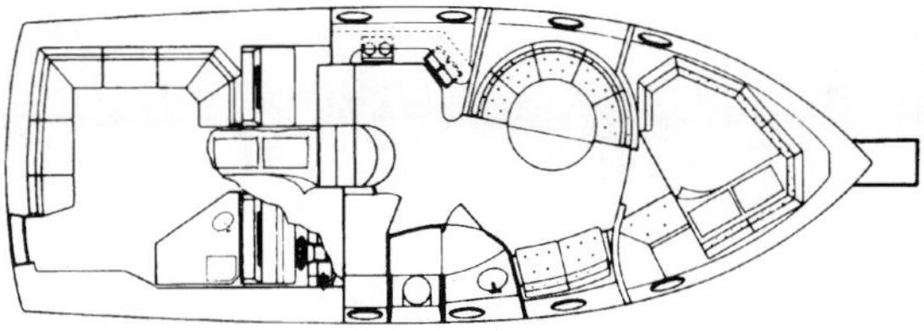

360 Floorplan

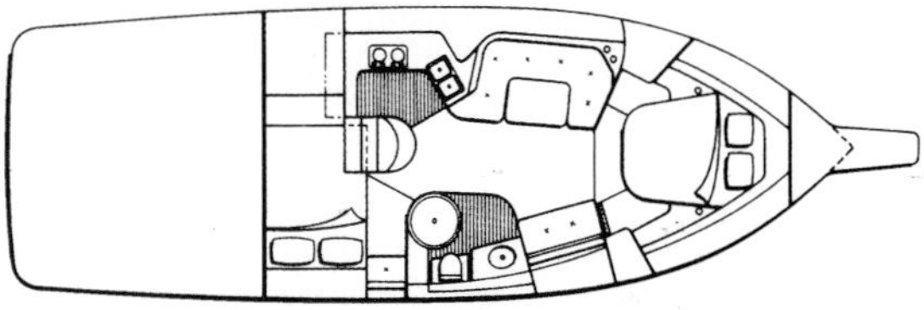

380 Floorplan

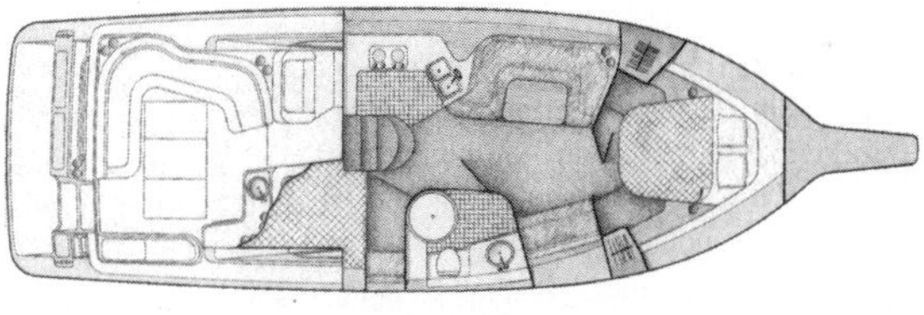

400 Floorplan (1993)

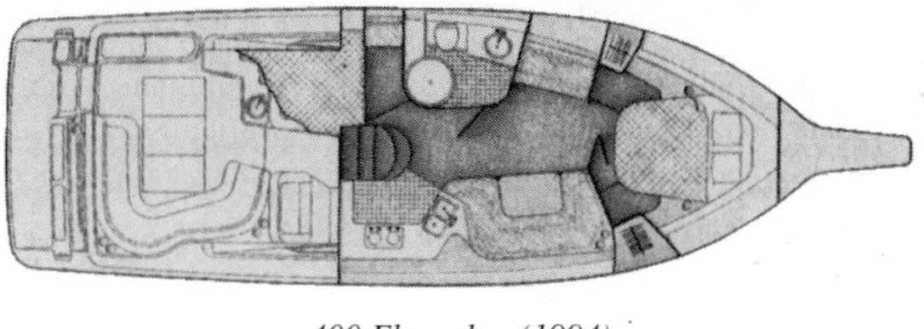

400 Floorplan (1994)

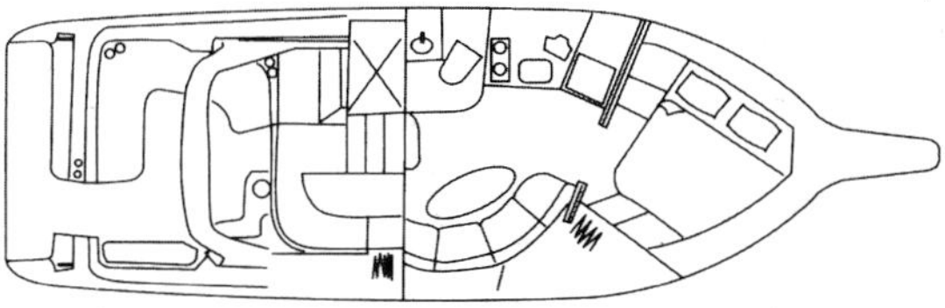

402 Floorplan

SPECIFICATIONS

Length w/Pulpit ....42'0"	Water ....125 gals.
Hull Length ....39'5"	Fuel ....280 gals.
Beam ....13'1"	Waste ....65 gals.
Draft ....3'0"	Hull Type......Mod. Deep-V
Weight......................16,000#	Deadrise Aft....................17°
Clearance ....9'5"	Production 1985–Current

Today's Commodore 402 began life in 1985 as the Commodore 360, a smartly styled mid-cabin express with a decidedly upscale interior to go with her good looks. She's built on a modified deep-V hull with a solid fiberglass bottom, cored hullsides, moderate beam and a well-flared bow. Note that prop pockets are used in conjunction with V-drives to reduce shaft angles and allow for shallow-water operation. A molded pulpit was added to the package in 1990, and in 1991 Regal reintroduced her as the Commodore 380, now with an integral swim platform, redesigned helm console, side exhausts, and a much-improved profile. It's hard to believe, but there have been *five* different floorplans in this model since she was introduced — all with top-quality furnishing and fixtures and excellent detailing. Notable features include standing headroom in the aft stateroom, a super-attractive low profile radar arch, a large hydraulically assisted engine room hatch, side exhausts and a well-arranged cockpit. Standard 300-hp/454-cid gas engines will cruise at 18–19 knots and provide a top speed of about 28 knots. Optional 315-hp Cummins diesels cruise at 26 knots (about 30 knots top).❑

See Page 269 for Pricing Information

RINKER 260/265 FIESTA VEE

SPECIFICATIONS

Length w/Pulpit	28'11"	Water	33 gals.
Beam	8'6"	Waste	27 gals.
Draft, Up	1'9"	Clearance	6'3"
Draft, Down	2'11"	Hull Type	Deep-V
Weight	5,725#	Deadrise Aft	20°
Fuel	75 gals.	Production	1991–Current

The Rinker 260/265 Fiesta Vee is an economy-priced mid-cabin family cruiser with an attractive profile to go with her relatively narrow 8-foot, 6-inch beam. Indeed, she's one of the larger trailerable boats available although you'll need a good-size truck to take advantage of her mobility. Introduced as the 260 in 1991, Rinker engineers updated the sytling, enlarged the galley, and raised the deck four inches in 1994 when the model name was changed to the current 265 Fiesta Vee. Hull construction is solid fiberglass, and her deep-V bottom provides a stable and comfortable ride in a chop. The Fiesta Vee's compact accomodations are efficiently arranged with a V-berth and removable table forward and a stand-up head compartment amidships. The mid-cabin offers good headroom at the entrance, an athwartships double berth, and a small port for ventilation. Outside, a sizeable L-shaped settee is opposite the helm and a molded-in bench seat is set against the transom. A single 5.7-litre MerCruiser I/O will cruise the Rinker 265 at 21 knots (about 33 knots top, and an optional 7.4-litre MerCruiser cruises at 32 knots with a top speed of 42–43 knots. ❑

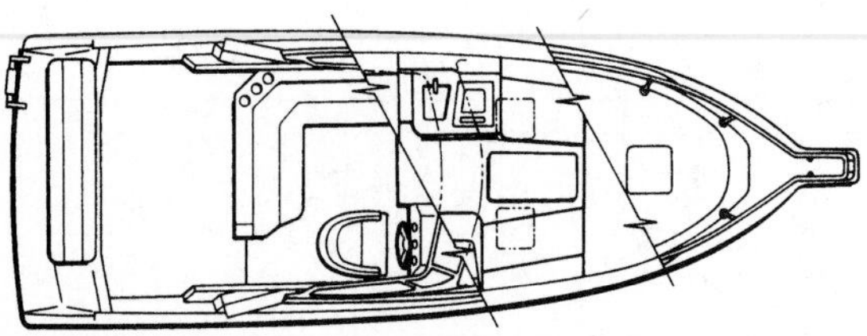

See Page 269 for Pricing Information

RINKER 280 FIESTA VEE

SPECIFICATIONS

Length w/Pulpit	30'2"	Water	33 gals.
Beam	10'0"	Waste	27 gals.
Draft, Up	1'10"	Clearance w/Arch	8'11"
Draft, Down	3'0"	Hull Type	Deep-V
Weight	8,680#	Deadrise Aft	20°
Fuel	120 gals.	Production	1993–Current

Like all Rinker models, the 280 Fiesta Vee is a budget-priced, no-glitz package with a lot of standard features that other manufacturers consider as extra-cost options. Hull construction is solid fiberglass, and her 10-foot beam is about average for an express cruiser her size. She's a good-looking boat with her integral swim platform and curved windshield and, despite the low price, the overall fit and finish is quite good. The 280's mid-cabin floorplan is typical of family cruisers her size with double berths fore and aft, convertible dinette, and a compact galley. Privacy curtains separate the sleeping areas from the salon. Headroom is excellent throughout, and there are plenty of storage bins and lockers. Outside, the cockpit is arranged with a big L-shaped settee opposite the helm and bench seating at the transom. Note that the sidedecks are narrow and foredeck access is no easy matter, especially underway. Twin 180-hp 4.3-liter stern drives will cruise the Rinker 280 around 21 knots (29–30 knots top) and optional 235-hp 5.7-litre Mercs will cruise at 24 knots and reach 37–38 knots wide open. ❑

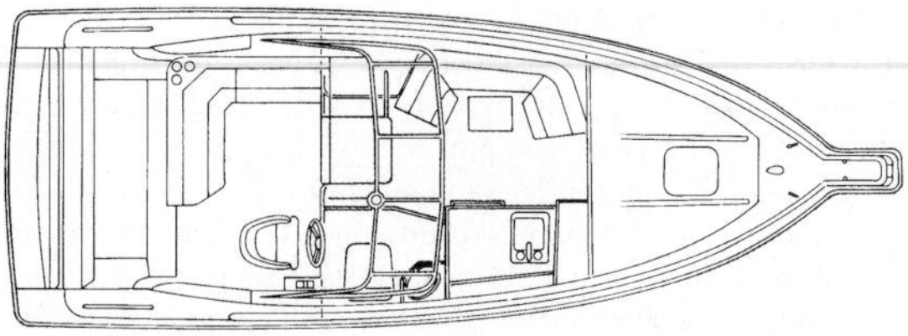

See Page 269 for Pricing Information

RINKER 300 FIESTA VEE

SPECIFICATIONS

Length w/Pulpit........33'11"	Water........................34 gals.
Beam..............................10'6"	Waste........................25 gals.
Draft, Up..........................1'8"	Clearance w/Arch.........9'8"
Draft, Down ....2'10"	Hull Type ....Deep-V
Weight......................10,000#	Deadrise Aft....................18°
Fuel.........................140 gals.	Production 1990–Current

The Rinker 300 Fiesta Vee is a sporty and affordably priced express cruiser with attractive lines and a well-arranged interior. Hull construction is solid fiberglass, and while there are many who would prefer straight inboard engines in a boat this size, stern drives offer better performance and are not at all uncommon in a 30-footer. Inside, the mid-cabin floorplan is laid out in the conventional manner with double berths fore and aft, convertible dinette, a fully equipped galley and a *very* spacious head compartment. Headroom is about 6 feet, 2 inches in the galley area, and storage—including the aircraft-style overhead lockers—is excellent. The aft cabin, with its removable table, is a separate seating area during the day and a privacy curtain separates it from the main salon at night. There's plenty of cockpit seating (the L-shaped lounge opposite the helm will seat four adults), and engine access is very good. Twin 235-hp 5.7-litre MerCruiser stern drives (optional) will cruise the Rinker 300 at an easy 21 knots while delivering a top speed of about 38–39 knots. ❑

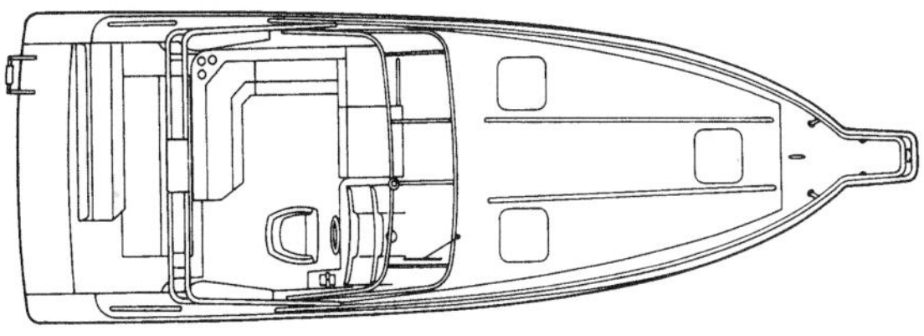

See Page 269 for Pricing Information

SABRELINE 34

SPECIFICATIONS

Length ....34'0"	Fuel.........................250 gals.
Beam.............................12'6"	Cockpit....................70 sq. ft.
Draft ....3'3"	Hull Type ....Modified-V
Weight......................17,800#	Deadrise Aft....................14°
Clearance ....12'8"	Designer ....Sabre
Water......................160 gals.	Production 1991–Current

An upright, slightly Downeast profile and an attractive interior characterize the Sabreline 34 Sedan, a modern trawler-style design from Sabre Yachts. She's built on the same modified-V hull used in the production of the original Sabreline 36 with moderate beam and a shallow keel. Like all Sabre boats (sail or power), there's no shortage of craftsmanship and attention to detail in the way she's put together. Her traditional teak interior is arranged with the galley forward in the salon opposite the lower helm and a walkaround island berth in the stateroom. Everything is carefully arranged with an eye toward practicality and comfort. The large salon windows all open (so does the center windshield forward), and ventilation in this boat is exceptional. The 34 isn't a wide-beam boat, so the interior dimensions are somewhat compact. Features include excellent engine access, stall shower with wet locker (nice touch) and a quiet underwater exhaust system. Economical to operate and a good performer, the Sabreline 34 will cruise at 18 knots with twin 210-hp Cummins diesels. ❑

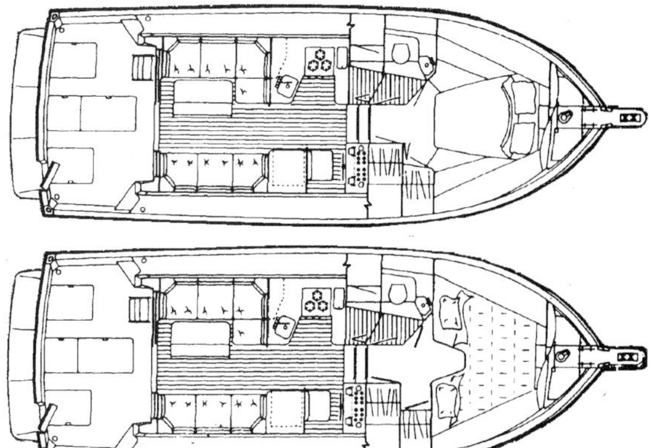

See Page 269 for Pricing Information

SEA RAY 250 SUNDANCER (EARLY)

SPECIFICATIONS

Length w/Pulpit	28'6"	Fuel	99 gals.
Hull Length	25'4"	Water	24 gals.
Beam	8'6"	Headroom	6'2"
Draft, Up	1'8"	Hull Type	Deep-V
Draft, Down	3'0"	Deadrise Aft	19°
Weight	5,100#	Production	1989–91

A popular boat during her three-year production run, the Sea Ray 250 Sundancer is a trailerable family cruiser with a sporty profile and a mid-cabin interior layout. Like most Sea Ray boats, she's built on an easy-riding deep-V hull, and she's one of the early boats in her class to have an integrated swim platform with a walk-thru transom. There are accommodations for four in the cabin along with a complete galley and a stand-up head with shower. Pull-out aft-facing seats and a refreshment center on the back of the helm seat were standard in the cockpit, and visibility from the elevated helm is excellent. The sidedecks are very narrow, and bow access is not easy (more recent express cruiser designs with narrow walkarounds have the advantage of a walk-thru windshield). Additional features include a fold-away aft seat, folding swim ladder, dinette table, adaquate storage and easy access to the engine compartment. A single 260-hp 5.7-litre MerCruiser stern drive will cruise the 250 Sundancer at 19–20 knots (30 knots top), and the 7.4-litre engine is about four knots faster. ❑

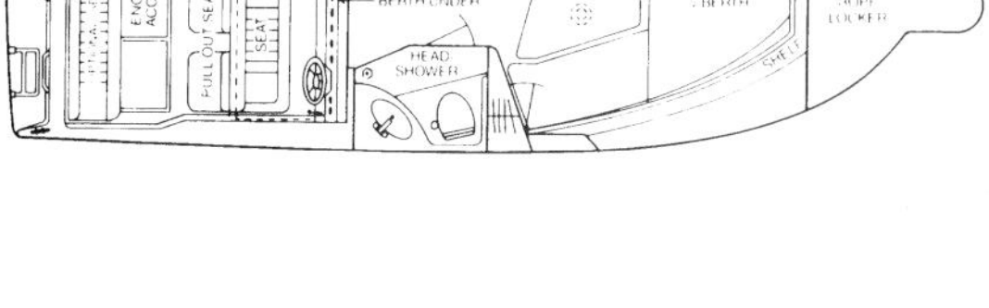

See Page 269 for Pricing Information

SEA RAY 250 SUNDANCER

SPECIFICATIONS

Length w/Pulpit	26'5"	Fuel	70 gals.
Hull Length	24'7"	Water	20 gals.
Beam	8'6"	Waste	28 gals.
Draft, Up	1'6"	Hull Type	Deep-V
Draft, Down	3'0"	Deadrise Aft	19°
Weight	5,000#	Production	1995–Current

A hot-selling boat and the market leader in her class, the Sea Ray 250 Sundancer is a high-style sport cruiser with an innovative cockpit layout and a mid-cabin interior. She's certainly one of the better-looking trailerable boats available in this size range in spite of her relatively high freeboard. There are berths for four below including double beds fore and aft, a complete galley, and an enclosed stand-up head and shower. The cockpit seems large for a 25-footer and includes a unique portside sun lounge in addition to facing bench seats, a built-in cooler, and a walk-through transom. Lacking sidedecks, access to the foredeck is via a windshield walk-through with a molded step built into the sliding companionway door. Additional features include a well-arranged helm console, oval ports, and good storage. Depending on the load, a single 235-hp 5.7-litre MerCruiser stern drive will cruise the 250 Sundancer at an easy 19 knots and reach a top speed of about 29–30 knots. The optional 7.4-litre engine cruises around 22 knots (35 knots top). ❑

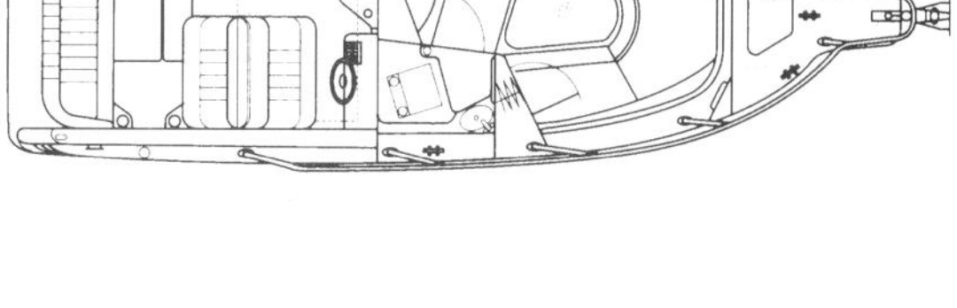

See Page 269 for Pricing Information

SEA RAY 250 EXPRESS CRUISER

SPECIFICATIONS

Length w/Pulpit..........26'2"	Fuel..........70 gals.
Hull Length..........24'7"	Water..........20 gals.
Beam..........8'6"	Waste (Optional)........11 gals.
Draft, Up..........1'6"	Hull Type..........Deep-V
Draft, Down..........3'0"	Deadrise Aft..........20°
Weight..........5,000#	Production..........1993–94

A particularly good-looking boat, the Sea Ray 250 Express Cruiser will appeal to families willing to give up some of the interior amenities usually found in a trailerable cruiser this size in exchange for the open-air advantages of a larger cockpit. Sea Ray altered the traditional express boat layout by moving the dinette table into the cockpit; the smaller cabin allows the placement of the cabin bulkhead further forward which adds up to increased cockpit space. The result is a very roomy, *single-level* cockpit with seating for a small crowd. Note that about half of the cabin bulkhead is removable which transforms the cabin and cockpit into one big open area—a pretty useful design trick. A walk-through windshield (but no step) provides access to the foredeck and bow platform. The extended trunk cabin profile of the 250 EC allows for adequate cabin headroom below without creating the chunky exterior appearance common to many small family boats. A single 5.7-litre stern drive will cruise at 20 knots (33 top), and the optional 7.4-litre engine cruises at around 25 knots (38 knots top.) ❑

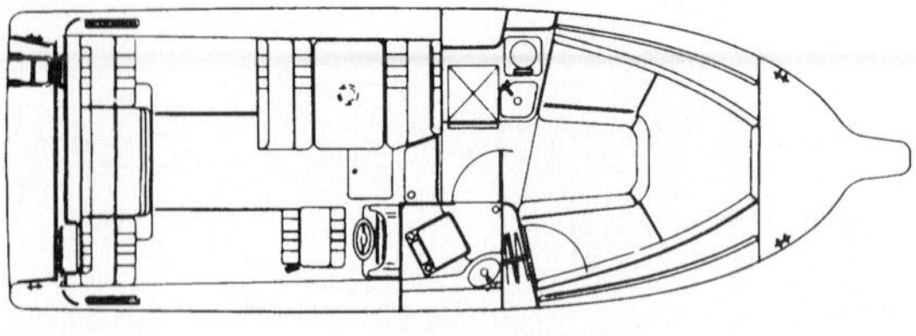

See Page 269 for Pricing Information

SEA RAY 260 CUDDY

SPECIFICATIONS

Length w/Platform.....27'6"	Fuel..........99 gals.
Hull Length..........26'0"	Water..........None
Beam..........8'6"	Hull Type..........Deep-V
Draft, Up..........1'8"	Deadrise Aft..........NA
Draft, Down..........3'0"	Designer..........Sea Ray
Weight..........4,500#	Production..........1989–91

Aside from her sexy sportboat profile, the big attraction of the Sea Ray 260 Cuddy is her oversized cockpit with seating for as many as eight people. This is a good example of the sleek styling that can be achieved in a boat this size when it's not necessary to raise the foredeck in order to have full standing headroom in the cabin. The 260 Cuddy is clearly aimed at those who plan to use their boat for daytime activities. Because the cockpit is so large, the belowdecks accommodations are basic. The full-length V-berth will sleep two adults and a Porta-Potti fits between the bunks. A small galley was optional. Additional features include easy access to the engine (beneath the full-width bech seat), an integral swim platform with ladder, and recessed cockpit storage under the gunnels. Bow access is best achieved through the foredeck hatch. A full cockpit liner makes clean-up easy, and the lack of a bow pulpit enhances her overall profile. A single 5.7-litre stern drive will cruise at 22 knots (35 top), and the 7.4-litre engine cruises at 28–29 knots (40+ knots top.) ❑

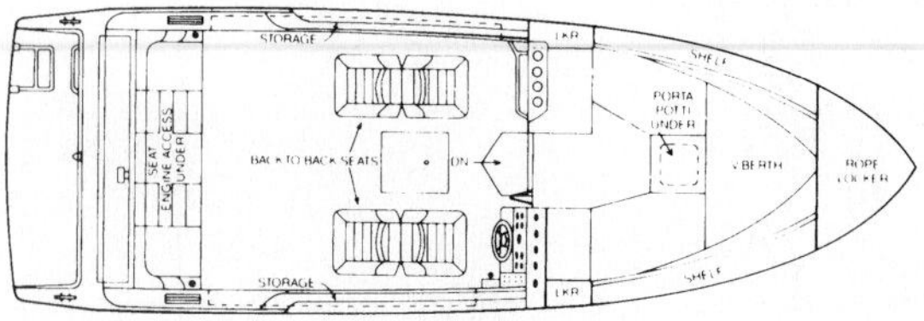

See Page 269 for Pricing Information

37′ SEA RAY SUNDANCER 1991

New '02 T/7.4 FWC MPI 140hrs. 7.5 kw gen 177hrs, vacuflush, ac, heat, cust stereo, new color radar/gps, vinyl seats. Clean, mint. Must see, negotiable $50,000 (CHP23793)

Tony
(917) 804-4060

SEA RAY 260 OVERNIGHTER

SPECIFICATIONS

Length w/Platform	27'6"	Fuel	99 gals.
Hull Length	26'0"	Water	13 gals.
Beam	8'6"	Hull Type	Deep-V
Draft, Up	1'8"	Deadrise Aft	NA
Draft, Down	3'0"	Designer	Sea Ray
Weight	4,500#	Production	1989–91

Like her sistership (the 260 Cuddy Cabin), the Sea Ray 260 Overnighter is a high-style sportboat with a distinctive profile and a versatile pedigree. This is a boat for those who prefer the open-air advantages of a large cockpit and who don't require the accommodations of a full cruising-style cabin. Because the interior is small, the bulkhead is set well forward which results in an extra-large cockpit (compared to most other 26-foot sportboats). There's wraparound seating for four just behind the helm and companion seat, and the entire aft section of the cockpit is consumed by an elevated sundeck — a 5-1/2-foot-deep full-width platform with a kick-up headrest and room for three sunbathers. The cuddy cabin features an alcohol stove, Porta-Potti, a V-berth that sleeps two and a hanging locker. Additional features include fold-down helm and companion seats, a cockpit ice chest and bar, and a big storage bin under the forward section of the sunpad. A single 5.7-litre stern drive will cruise the 260 Overnighter at 22 knots (35 top), and the 7.4-litre engine cruises at around 27–28 knots (40+ knots top.) ❑

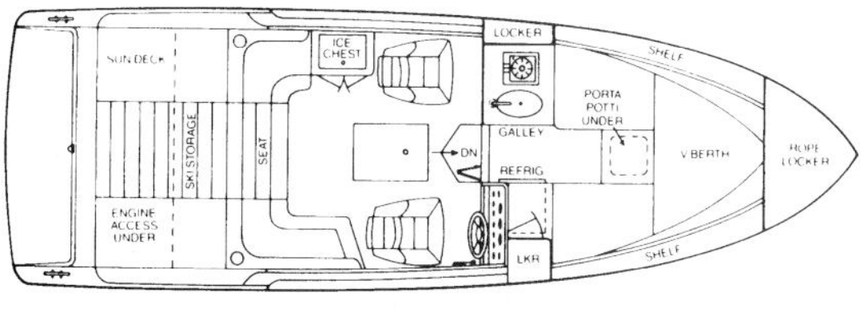

See Page 269 for Pricing Information

SEA RAY 268 SUNDANCER

SPECIFICATIONS

Length w/Platform	27'6"	Fuel	100 gals.
Hull Length	26'0"	Water	24 gals.
Beam	8'6"	Hull Type	Deep-V
Draft, Up	1'8"	Deadrise Aft	NA
Draft, Down	3'0"	Designer	Sea Ray
Weight	4,500#	Production	1986–89

A popular and affordable model, the Sea Ray 268 Sundancer is a trailerable family cruiser with big-boat accommodations and a versatile layout. Her styling is clearly dated by today's express cruiser standards, and the 268 was one of the last Sea Rays to incorporate a bolt-on swim platform rather than a fully integrated platform. Like all Sundancer models, she comes with a versatile mid-cabin floorplan which allows five people to sleep in three separate areas; a V-berth forward, convertible dinette (for a kid), and an aft cabin with a double berth and opening port. Privacy curtains separate the fore and aft sleeping areas, and there's near-standing headroom in the enclosed head. Outside, the cockpit is arranged with a double-wide helm seat, fold-down aft-facing jump seats, and bench seating at the transom. Additional features include radar arch, teak bow pulpit, teak interior trim, and opening cabin windows (that leak a lot). A single 7.4-litre MerCruiser stern drive will cruise the 268 Sundancer at 22–23 knots and reach a top speed of 35 knots. ❑

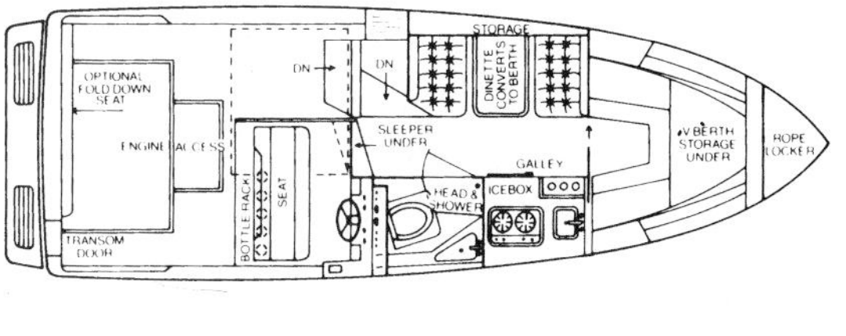

See Page 269 for Pricing Information

SEA RAY 270 AMBERJACK

SPECIFICATIONS

Length w/Pulpit	29'3"	Water	28 gals.
Hull Length	27'7"	Fuel	200 gals.
Beam	10'0"	Cockpit	NA
Draft, Up	1'3"	Hull Type	Deep-V
Drave, Down	2'8"	Deadrise Aft	22°
Weight	7,000#	Production	1986–90

A good-selling boat for Sea Ray, the 270 Amberjack is a roomy express cruiser with an unusually large cockpit to go with her basic cabin accommodations. Construction is solid fiberglass, and her 10-foot beam is wide for a 27-footer. (Note that the maximum beam is carried well aft resulting in plenty of cockpit space but a relatively narrow cabin.) The single-level cockpit is arranged with a fore-and-aft companion seat opposite the helm and fold-away bench seating at the transom. There's a storage bin between the two seats, and additional storage is located under the gunwales. Inside, the cabin is fitted with V-berths, an enclosed stand-up head compartment with shower, and a compact galley area. A single hatch at the transom provides good access to the engines. Additional features include a small transom door, swim platform with ladder, teak bow pulpit, and teak covering boards. Popular 260-hp stern drives will cruise the 270 Amberjack at an easy 23 knots and reach a top speed of 32–33 knots. ❑

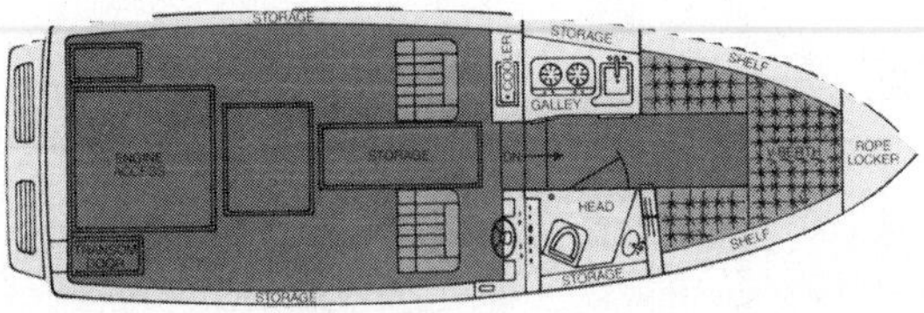

See Page 269 for Pricing Information

SEA RAY 270 SUNDANCER (1982–88)

SPECIFICATIONS

Length w/Pulpit	29'2"	Fuel	120 gals.
Hull Length	27'7"	Clearance	NA
Beam	10'0"	Hull Type	Deep-V
Draft	2'8"	Deadrise Aft	22°
Weight	6,700#	Designer	Sea Ray
Water	28 gals.	Production	1982–88

An extremely popular boat with family-size accommodations and a comfortable ride, the 270 Sundancer enjoyed a long and successful production run for Sea Ray during the 1980s. She's built on a solid fiberglass deep-V hull with a relatively wide beam, and the raised foredeck (for headroom below) doesn't create the bloated exterior profile so common in express cruisers this size. Aside from the normal fabric and decor updates, the mid-cabin interior layout remained unchanged over the years. There are berths for six along with a compact galley and a roomy stand-up head with shower. In 1987, the original mica interior woodwork gave way to teak, and a radar arch became standard. The cockpit is arranged with an elevated double-wide helm seat, in-deck storage, transom door, and bench seating at the transom. A teak bow pulpit and swim platform with ladder were standard. Several stern drive engine options were offered during her production years. The popular 260-hp MerCruisers will cruise the 270 Sundancer at an easy 23 knots and reach a top speed of 35 knots. ❑

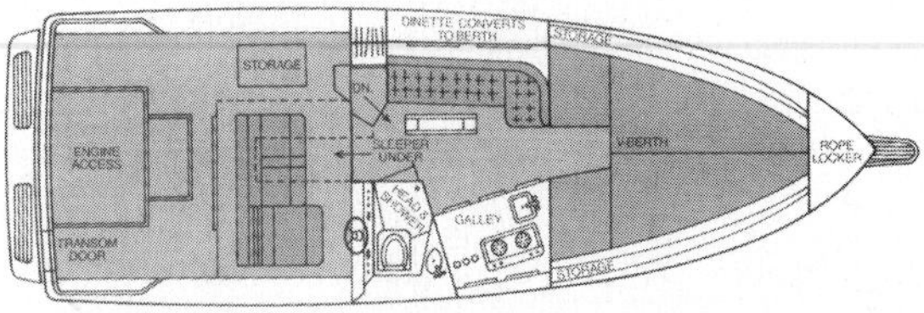

See Page 269 for Pricing Information

SEA RAY 270 SUNDANCER (1992–93)

SPECIFICATIONS

Length w/Pulpit	28'6"	Water	24 gals.
Hull Length	26'9"	Fuel	99 gals.
Beam	8'6"	Hull Type	Deep-V
Draft	3'0"	Deadrise Aft	20°
Weight	5,600#	Designer	Sea Ray
Clearance	7'0"	Production	1992–93

Another in a series of 270 Sundancers from Sea Ray, this particular model evolved from the 250 Sundancer introduced back in 1988. Her 8-foot, 6-inch beam is narrow for a 27-footer, and she can be legally trailed in any state without obtaining a permit. Like all current Sea Ray products, the hull is fully cored, and her deep-V bottom delivers a stable ride in a variety of conditions. A good-looking and affordably priced family cruiser, her integral pulpit and swim platform, attractive hull graphics, and wraparound windshield are in keeping with today's modern sportboat styling. Inside, the mid-cabin floorplan is arranged with V-berths forward with a small galley and head opposite the dinette. The double berth in the aft cabin is big enough for two adults and may be curtained-off for privacy. Cockpit accommodations include a three-person transom settee facing another two-seater behind the helm. The standard 454-cid MerCruiser stern drive engine will cruise at 21 knots (32–33 top), and optional twin V-6 stern drives cruise 23–24 knots (36 top). ❑

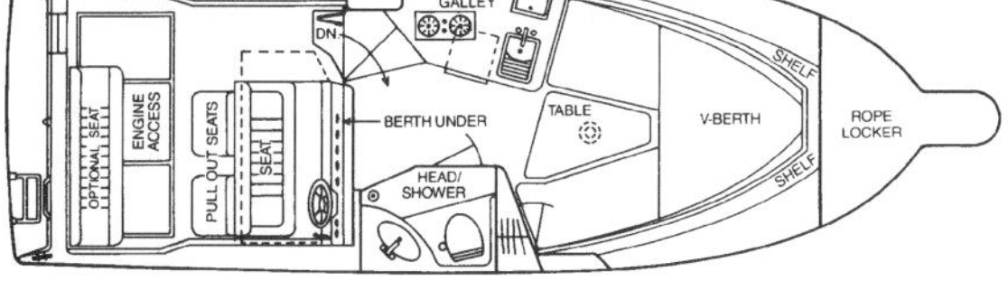

See Page 270 for Pricing Information

SEA RAY 270 SUNDANCER

SPECIFICATIONS

Length w/Pulpit	29'11"	Clearance	7'0"
Hull Length	27'4"	Water	24 gals.
Beam	8'6"	Fuel	100 gals.
Draft, Up	1'11"	Hull Type	Deep-V
Draft, Down	3'0"	Deadrise Aft	20°
Weight	6,100#	Production	1994–Current

A good-looking boat and one of Sea Ray's most popular models, the current 270 Sundancer is built on the same trailerable fully cored hull used in the production of the previous 270 Sundancer, but with a revised deckhouse and cockpit layout. The sliding cabin windows seen in earlier Sundancer models have been replaced with new opening portlights—a dramatic styling improvement. The companionway is on the centerline in this new model, and the old bi-fold companionway door has been replaced with a sliding acrylic door which is easier to operate. Inside, the mid-cabin floorplan is essentially unchanged, although the decor is much improved from the previous 270. There are berths for four along with a small galley and a stand-up head with shower. Storage is marginal, and the mid-cabin berth is large enough to accommodate two adults. On deck, a double helm seat with a full aft-facing seat, refreshment center, and fold-away rear seat are standard. A single 7.4-litre MerCruiser stern drive will cruise at 21-22 knots and reach a top speed of 35 knots. ❑

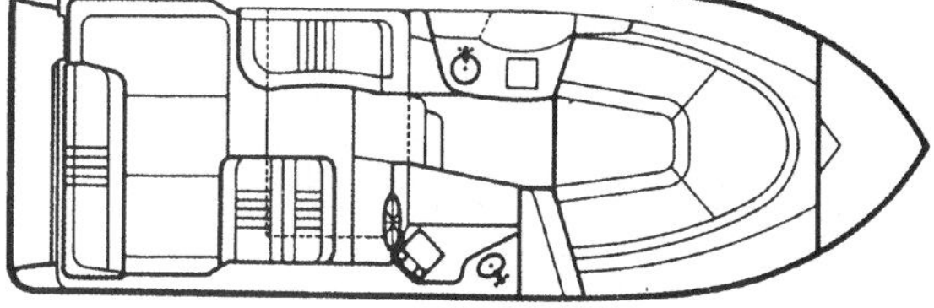

See Page 270 for Pricing Information

SEA RAY 280 SUNDANCER

SPECIFICATIONS

Length w/Pulpit	31'11"
Hull Length	28'0"
Beam	10'6"
Draft	2'8"
Weight	8,000#
Clearance	9'0"
Water	35 gals.
Fuel	120 gals.
Hull Type	Deep-V
Deadrise Aft	20°
Designer	J. Michelak
Production	1989–91

The Sea Ray 280 Sundancer was introduced in 1989 as a replacement for the original and very popular 270 Sundancer (1982–88). A good-looking cruiser with her molded pulpit, curved windshield, and integrated swim platform, the 280 rides on a solid fiberglass deep-V hull with a flared bow and relatively wide 10-foot, 6-inch beam. Not surprisingly, there's a lot of room below, and the Sundancer's wide-open cabin layout delivers comfortable overnight accommodations for as many as six adults. The mid-cabin floorplan is arranged in the conventional manner with V-berths forward and a wide double berth in the aft stateroom. Curtains are used for privacy in both staterooms, and headroom in the salon is a good 6 feet, 2 inches. Topside, visibility from the elevated double helm seat is very good. Note that the companionway is to port. An aft-facing seat and transom settee provide plenty of guest seating in the cockpit. Twin 350-cid stern drives will cruise the 280 Sundancer at a respectable 23 knots and reach a top speed of 35 knots. ❑

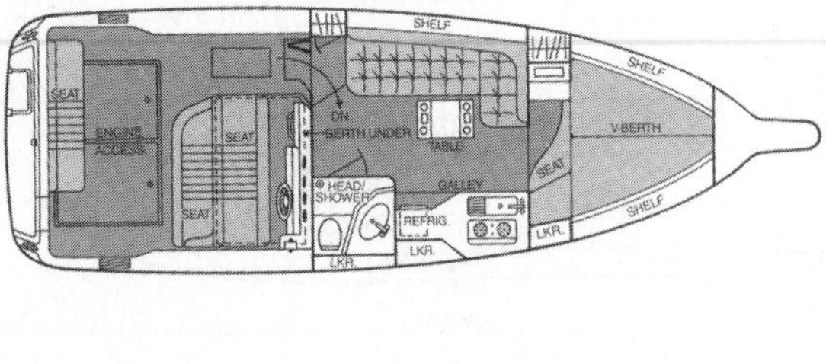

See Page 270 for Pricing Information

SEA RAY 270/290 SUNDANCER

SPECIFICATIONS

Length w/Pulpit	30'6"
Hull Length	28'7"
Beam	9'0"
Draft	3'1"
Weight	5,800#
Water	24 gals.
Fuel	100 gals.
Clearance	NA
Hull Type	Deep-V
Deadrise Aft	20°
Designer	Sea Ray
Production	1990–93

Introduced as the 270 Sundancer in 1990, Sea Ray marketed this model as the 290 Sundancer from 1992–93. She's built on a fully cored deep-V hull, and her integral swim platform, curved windshield and molded pulpit combine to give her the sleek profile common to all recent Sea Ray sportboats. The original mid-cabin floorplan is arranged in the conventional manner, with double berths fore and aft, a full galley, and a stand-up head with shower. Draw curtains are used for privacy in the staterooms, and storage space is at a premium (as it is in just about all family boats this size). In 1993, Sea Ray introduced an alternate floorplan configuration with a big U-shaped dinette to starboard. The cockpit features a standard arch, fold-away stern seating, and a walk-thru transom door. Visibility from the raised double-wide helm seat is very good. A single 454-cid MerCruiser stern drive will cruise the Sea Ray 270 Sundancer at 20 knots and reach a top speed of about 35. ❑

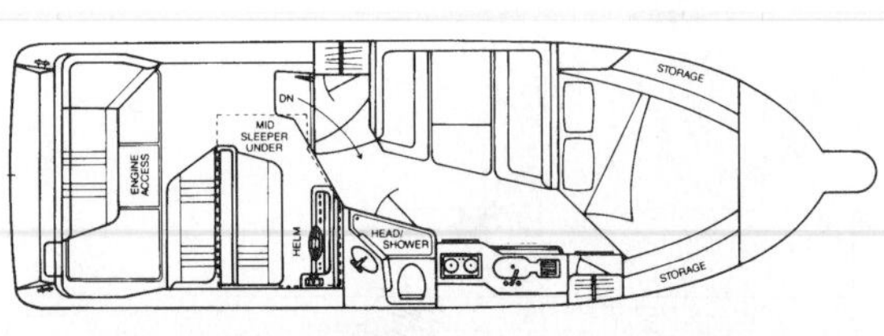

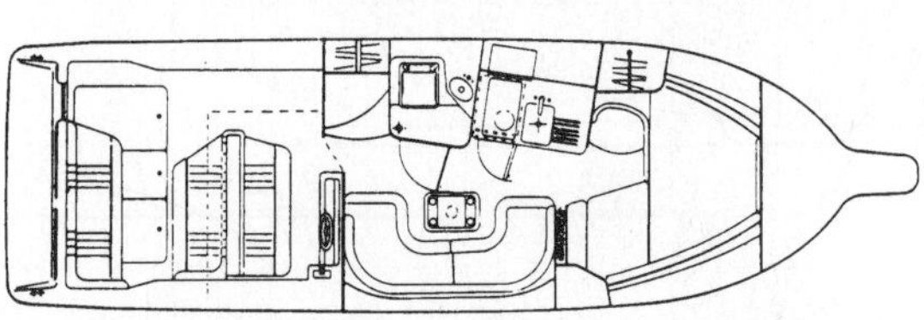

See Page 270 for Pricing Information

SEA RAY 290 SUNDANCER

SPECIFICATIONS

Length w/Pulpit	32'1"	Clearance	8'0"
Hull Length	29'4"	Water	24 gals.
Beam	9'8"	Fuel	130 gals.
Draft, Up	2'0"	Hull Type	Deep-V
Draft, Down	3'9"	Deadrise Aft	21°
Weight	7,700#	Production	1994–Current

The new 290 Sundancer (the original model ran from 1992–93) is a good example of why Sea Ray continually dominates the market for moderately priced express cruisers. A good-looking sportboat (stylish oval portlights have replaced the narrow glass windows used in earlier Sundancer models), she's built on a fully cored deep-V hull with crisp lines and a relatively low foredeck profile. The interior is big for a 29-footer, and a choice of two floorplans is offered: one with a U-shaped dinette/settee and the other with a conventional dinette with facing seats. Both staterooms are fitted with double beds and privacy curtains and storage space—with two hanging lockers—is notable. Outside, the 290's cockpit is arranged with an elevated double-wide helm seat and wraparound guest seating aft, which can be converted into a sun pad. There's a protected chart flat at the helm (very nice) and a walk-thru transom door. A single 454-cid MerCruiser stern drive will cruise the 290 Sundancer at 20 knots and deliver a top speed of about 34. ❑

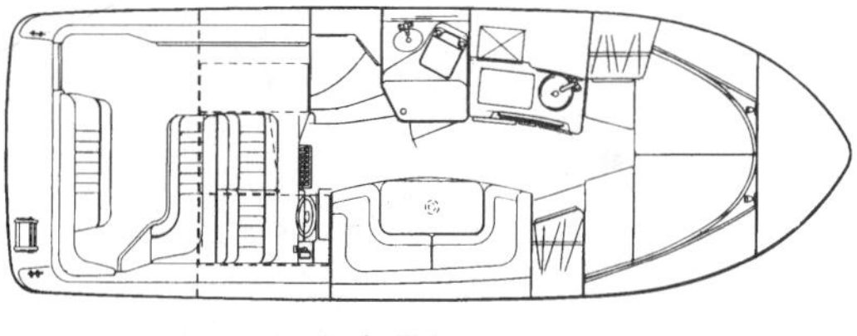

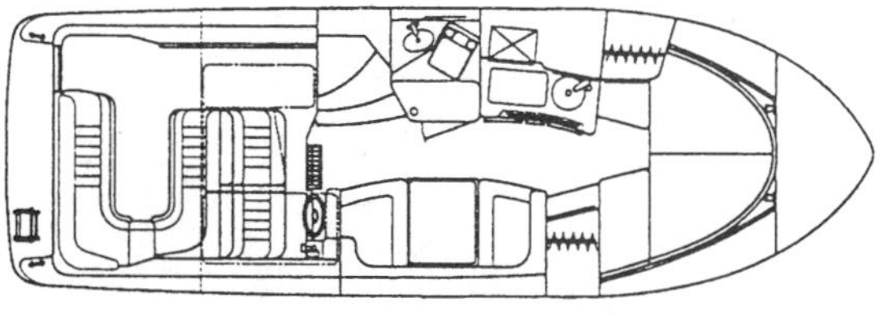

See Page 270 for Pricing Information

SEA RAY 300 WEEKENDER & SUNDANCER (1985–89)

SPECIFICATIONS

Length w/Pulpit	31'4"	Wgt., Sundancer	9,800#
Hull Length	29'8"	Water	40 gals.
Beam	11'0"	Fuel	140/200 gals.
Draft, Weekender	2'5"	Hull Type	Deep-V
Draft, Sundancer	2'11"	Deadrise Aft	NA
Wgt., Weekender	9,500#	Production	1985–89

Twins on the outside, the Sea Ray Weekender and Sundancer (called the SRV300 Weekender and Sundancer in 1985–87) are quite different boats when it comes to interior accommodations and power options. The Weekender is a straightforward express cruiser design with a single stateroom forward, a centerline companionway, berths for four, and inboard engines. The Sundancer, on the other hand, has a more spacious mid-cabin interior with a portside entry, berths for six and stern drive power. Both were built on a solid fiberglass, deep-V hull (the Weekender has prop pockets and side exhausts) and, while the styling is dated by today's standards, they were considered sporty-looking boats in the mid-1980s. The cabins were open and very comfortable with a full galley, convertible dinette, a large head and plenty of storage. The cockpit, too, is quite spacious with seating for a small crowd. A pair of 260-hp inboards will cruise the Weekender at 24 knots (32 top), and the Sundancer will cruise at 27 knots with twin 260-hp I/Os and reach 38 knots top. ❑

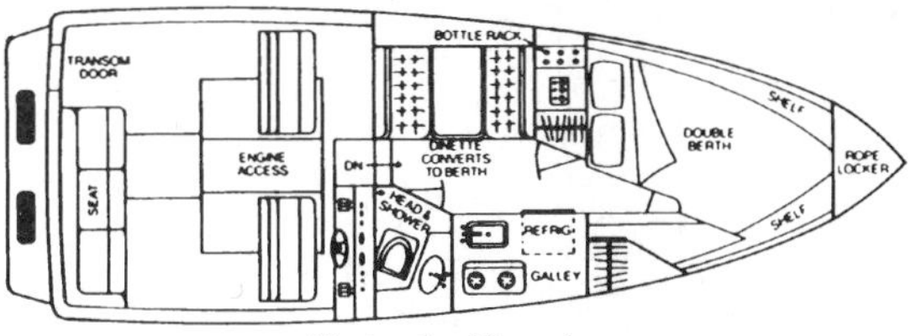

Weekender Floorplan

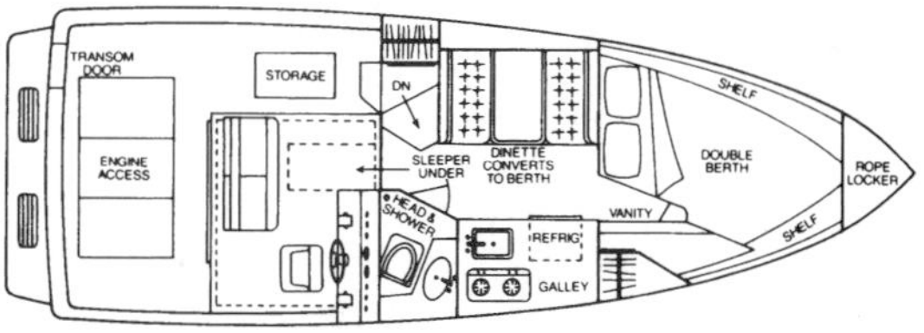

Sundancer Floorplan

See Page 270 for Pricing Information

SEA RAY 300 WEEKENDER

SPECIFICATIONS

Length w/Pulpit........31'11"	Water........................28 gals.
Hull Length..................29'9"	Fuel.........................200 gals.
Beam..............................10'6"	Hull Type...............Deep-V
Draft................................2'8"	Deadrise Aft....................21°
Weight........................7,800#	Designer..................Sea Ray
Clearance........................NA	Production.............1991–95

Introduced in 1991 as the 280 Weekender, the Sea Ray 300 Weekender (1992–95) is a very good-looking express cruiser with a sleek, low-profile appearance, a relatively small cabin, and king-sized cockpit accommodations. This is a boat that will appeal to those who enjoy the outdoors and are willing to sacrifice the sleep-six interior volume of a more conventional mid-cabin design. Inside, the 300 Weekender's layout is arranged with a wraparound settee/dinette/V-berth forward, a small galley, and a stand-up head with shower—basic accommodations for two adults. With the small cabin dimensions, the huge, single-level cockpit extends for well over half of the boat's length. Built on a deep-V hull with moderate beam and an integrated swim platform, the 300 Weekender came with a choice of inboard or stern drive power. Among several engine options, twin 5.7-litre V-drive inboards will cruise at 24 knots (32-33 top), and the 5.7-litre stern drives will cruise at about the same speed and reach 40 knots top. Note that inboard models have prop pockets and side exhausts. ❑

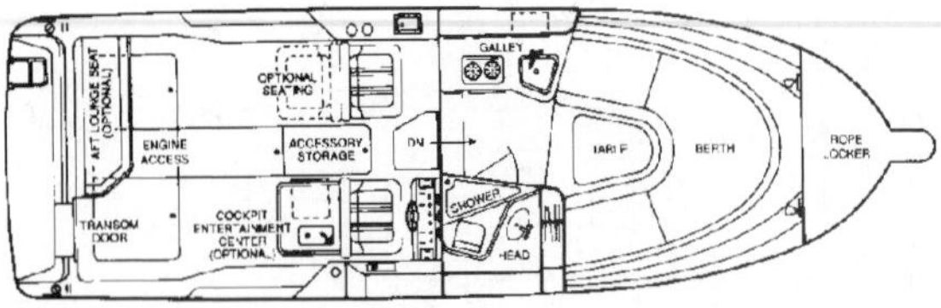

See Page 270 for Pricing Information

SEA RAY 300 SUNDANCER (EARLY)

SPECIFICATIONS

Length w/Pulpit........31'11"	Water........................35 gals.
Hull Length..................29'9"	Fuel.........................120 gals.
Beam..............................10'6"	Hull Type...............Deep-V
Draft................................2'8"	Deadrise Aft....................21°
Weight........................8,300#	Designer..................Sea Ray
Clearance........................8'8"	Production.............1992–93

The 300 Sundancer is a nice-looking family cruiser with better-than-average performance to go with her contemporary sport-boat styling. Sea Ray offered this model with two mid-cabin interiors: the one with the L-shaped settee to port is more open and has a larger galley, while the alternate layout has a big U-shaped settee/dinette for expanded entertaining capabilities. Topside, visibility from the elevated triple-wide helm seat is excellent. Guest seating is provided for six in the cockpit, and the bench seat at the transom folds away for access to the engine compartment. Additional features include an integral bow pulpit, sliding cabin windows, transom door, and cockpit refreshment center. Built on the standard Sea Ray deep-V hull, the 300 Sundancer was available with a choice of inboard or stern drive power. Among several engine options, twin 350-cid V-drive inboards will cruise at 19–20 knots (30 top), and the same motors with stern drives will cruise at 22 knots and reach 34 knots top. Note the limited fuel capacity. ❑

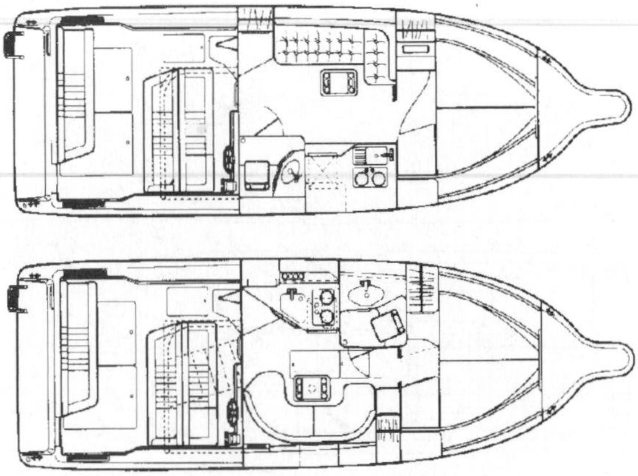

See Page 270 for Pricing Information

SEA RAY 300 SUNDANCER

SPECIFICATIONS

Length w/Pulpit	33'1"	Water	35 gals.
Hull Length	30'6"	Fuel	200 gals.
Beam	10'6"	Hull Type	Deep-V
Draft	2'11"	Deadrise Aft	21°
Weight	8,700#	Designer	Sea Ray
Clearance	8'8"	Production	1994–Current

With her oval portlights, low-profile arch, and sculptured hull lines, this latest version of Sea Ray's 300 Sundancer is easily one of the best-looking family sportboats in the market. She's built on the same balsa-cored hull as the previous 300 Sundancer model (1992–93), but with a longer hull length, a revised mid-cabin interior, additional (and badly needed) fuel capacity, and an all-new cockpit layout. Accommodations for six are provided below, along with a stand-up head with shower, a small galley area, and a convertible dinette with facing seats. Outside, the helm is elevated and a protected chart flat is built into the console.A filler converts the U-shaped cockpit seating aft of the helm into a large sunpad. Additional features include a walk-through transom, a double-wide helm seat and good engine access. The 300 Sundancer is available with a choice of inboard or stern drive power. Among several engine options, twin 250-hp MerCruiser V-drive inboards will cruise at 19–20 knots (30 top), and the stern drive versions of the same engines will cruise at around 22 knots and reach 34 knots top. ❑

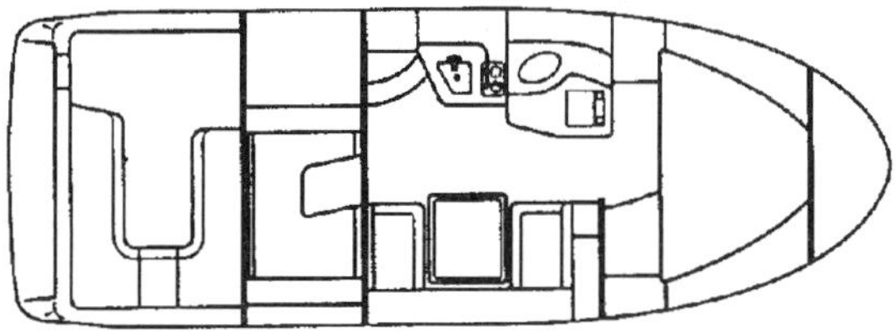

See Page 270 for Pricing Information

SEA RAY 300 SEDAN BRIDGE

SPECIFICATIONS

Length	29'1"	Fuel	140 gals.
Beam	11'0"	Cockpit	60 sq. ft.
Draft	2'5"	Hull Type	Deep-V
Weight	10,500#	Deadrise Aft	NA
Clearance	NA	Designer	Sea Ray
Water	40 gals.	Production	1985–87

The Sea Ray 300 Sedan Bridge is a wide-beam flybridge cruiser with a well-balanced combination of comfort and performance. Designed primarily for the family market, she features an efficient and practical floorplan with overnight accommodations for as many as six. An offset double bed is fitted in the forward stateroom in place of the normal V-berths, and both the dinette and salon sofa convert to double berths. Most were sold with the optional lower helm. Note that the interior is laid out a step down from the cockpit level, and the engines are located aft, under the cockpit, rather than beneath the salon sole. Three lift-out hatches in the cockpit provide good access to the engine compartment, and a transom door and swim platform were standard. Topside, the flybridge is arranged cruising-style with the helm forward and guest seating aft. Note the side-dumping exhausts. Twin 260-hp MerCruiser inboard gas engines (with V-drives) will cruise the 300 Sedan Bridge around 21 knots, and the top speed is 28–29 knots. ❑

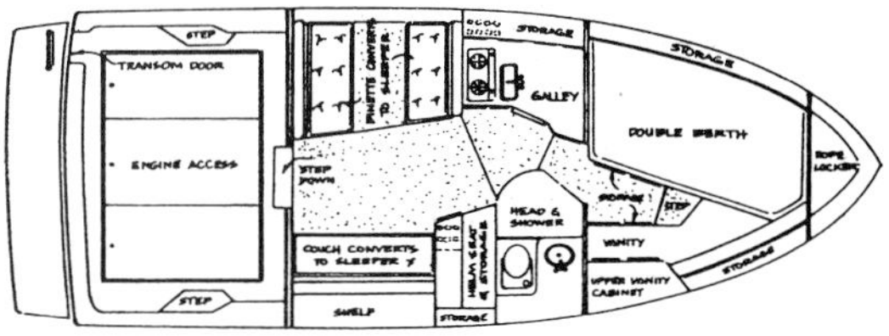

See Page 270 for Pricing Information

SEA RAY 305/300 SEDAN BRIDGE

SPECIFICATIONS

Length	29'10"	Fuel	200 gals.
Beam	12'0"	Cockpit	40 sq. ft.
Draft	2'6"	Hull Type	Deep-V
Weight	11,500#	Deadrise Aft	NA
Clearance	NA	Designer	Sea Ray
Water	60 gals.	Production	1988–89

Not remembered for her spectacular styling, the 300 Sedan Bridge (originally called the 305 Sedan Bridge in 1988) is long on interior accommodations but short of sex appeal. (Indeed, her ungainly profile probably had a lot to do with her unusually brief two-year production run.) Built on a wide-beam deep-V hull with propeller pockets, the interior accommodations are very spacious for a boat this size. With a mid-cabin stateroom tucked beneath the dinette, the 300 Sedan Bridge can boast of two private staterooms in addition to a roomy salon with a full-size galley. The athwartships double-berth arrangement in the forward stateroom is innovative in its use of space, and the concealed galley is particularly appealing. The head is located aft in the salon, just inside the companionway door, where access from the outside is easiest. The cockpit itself is very small, but the flybridge (with its overhang) is exceptionally large. Standard 260-hp MerCruiser engines (with V-drives) will cruise the 300 Sedan Bridge around 22 knots and have a top speed of 29 knots. ❑

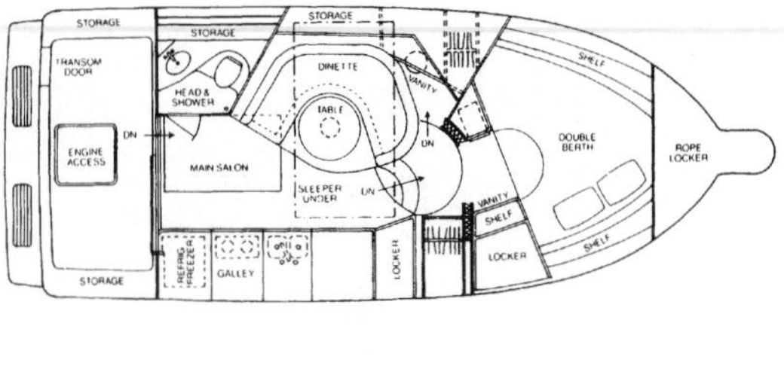

See Page 270 for Pricing Information

SEA RAY 310 AMBERJACK LAGUNA 31

SPECIFICATIONS

Length	31'2"	Water	40 gals.
Beam	11'5"	Fuel	296 gals.
Draft	3'1"	Hull Type	Deep-V
Weight	10,500#	Deadrise Aft	18°
Cockpit	57 sq. ft.	Designer	Sea Ray
Clearance	NA	Production	1991–94

Sportboat enthusiasts will find much to like in the Sea Ray 310 Amberjack, a good-looking dayboat with the aggressive low-profile silhouette of a small Bertram or Blackfin. She's built on a deep-V hull with cored hullsides, a wide beam, prop pockets, and 18 degrees of transom deadrise. The Amberjack's original design emphasis was in the large and well-organized cockpit. In 1994, Sea Ray engineers replaced the dinette opposite the helm with an elevated lounge area. The cockpit can be fitted with in-deck fish boxes, rod holders, and a transom livewell. While cabin space is at a premium, the 310 AJ manages to include overnight berths for two plus a stand-up head with shower, small galley, and convertible dinette. The sidedecks are a foot wide, and the motors are accessed via engine boxes. A good performer with twin 454-cid MerCruiser gas engines, she'll cruise at an easy 24 knots and reach 31–32 knots top. Note that she was marketed as the Sea Ray 31 Laguna during the 1993 model year. ❑

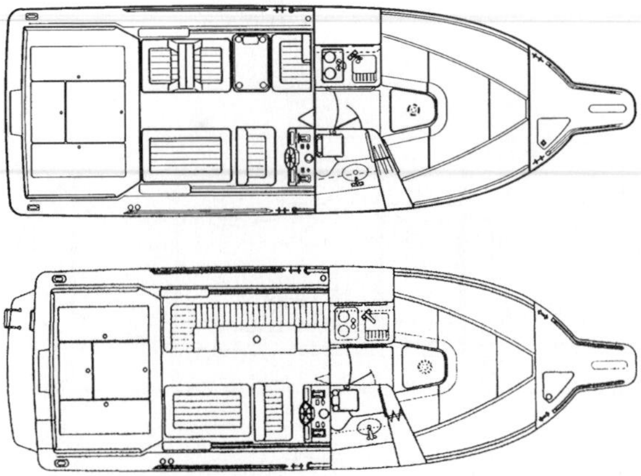

See Page 270 for Pricing Information

SEA RAY 310 SPORT BRIDGE

SPECIFICATIONS

Length w/Pulpit..........33'8"	Cockpit....................57 sq. ft.
Hull Length ....31'2"	Water........................40 gals.
Beam..............................11'5"	Fuel ....296 gals.
Draft ....3'1"	Hull Type ....Deep-V
Weight ....11,500#	Deadrise Aft...................18°
Clearance ....9'6"	Production 1992–93

A great-looking boat with aggressive styling and a low-profile appearance, the 310 Sport Bridge is basically a 310 Amberjack with a flybridge and semi-enclosed lower helm. She's built on an easy-riding deep-V hull with a wide beam, side-dumping exhausts and prop pockets. With no salon bulkhead, the lower helm is wide open to the huge cockpit, which consumes well over half of the boat's hull length. There's plenty of guest seating, including a sunpad and dinette, and the cockpit can be fitted with in-deck storage boxes, rod holders, and a transom livewell. While cabin space is at a premium, the 310 manages to include overnight berths for two plus a stand-up head with shower, small galley, and convertible dinette. The bridge is small, with seating for two. Hinged motor boxes provide good access to the engines, and the sidedecks are a foot wide. Twin 454-cid gas engines will cruise at 23 knots (30–31 knots top), and optional 291-hp Cummins diesels will cruise around 27 knots (31 knots top). ❑

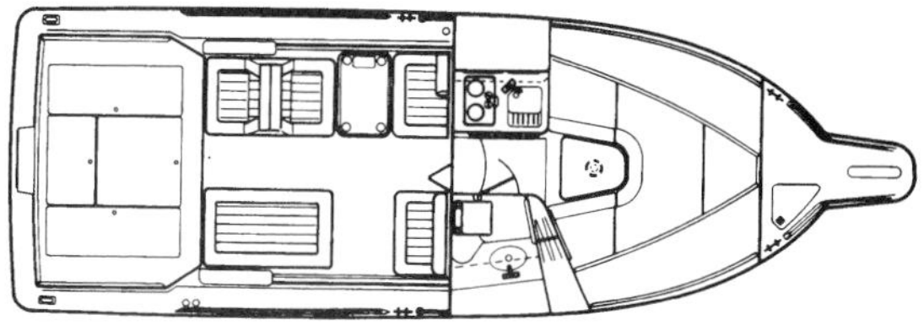

See Page 270 for Pricing Information

SEA RAY 310 SUN SPORT

SPECIFICATIONS

Length ....31'2"	Fuel ....160 gals.
Beam................................9'6"	Cockpit............................NA
Draft ....3'1"	Hull Type ....Deep-V
Weight ....8,200#	Deadrise Aft...................22°
Clearance ....NA	Designer ....Sea Ray
Water ....20 gals.	Production 1991–95

With her bold European styling and sleek profile, the 310 Sun Sport looks very much like a genuine Mediterranean-bred sportboat. She's a distinctive boat with her reversed arch and colorful hull graphics, and the stylish aluminum-framed wraparound windshield adds much to her appeal. The Sun Sport is built on a lightweight and relatively narrow hull (compared with other express boats her size), and her low freeboard results in only marginal cabin headroom. Because she's really an outdoor boat rather than a family cruiser, the accommodations below are basic. The big U-shaped dinette (which can seat up to six) converts into a double bed, and there's a mini-berth/storage forward of the dinette area. Outside, the cockpit provides circular seating aft of the helm, and a full-length sun pad is located over the engine compartment. Note that the original tubular arch was replaced with a fiberglass arch in 1993. Performance is excellent: she'll cruise at 30 knots with twin 454 MerCruiser I/Os and reach 46–47 knots top. ❑

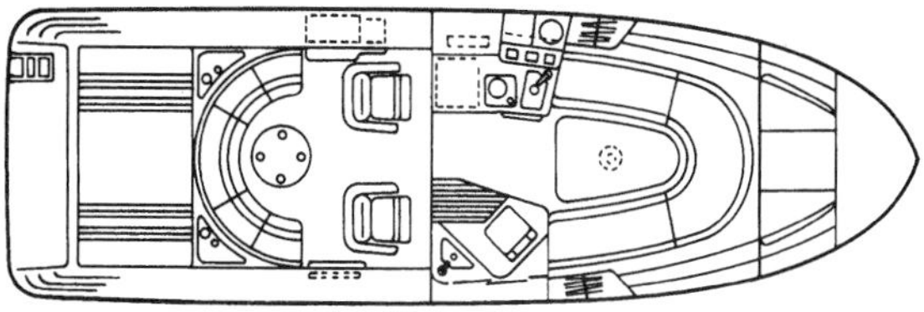

See Page 270 for Pricing Information

SEA RAY 310/330 EXPRESS CRUISER

1990–93

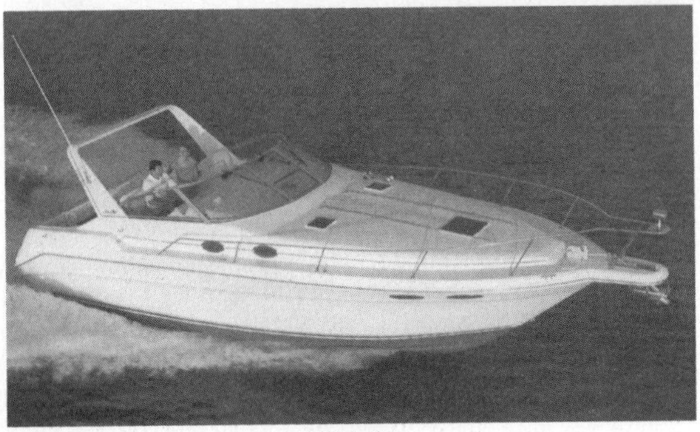

1994–95

SPECIFICATIONS

Length w/Pulpit..........35'4"	Water........................40 gals.
Hull Length................32'10"	Fuel.........................200 gals.
Beam..............................11'5"	Hull Type................Deep-V
Draft, Inboard................2'3"	Deadrise Aft...................17°
Draft, I/Os.......................3'0"	Designer.................Sea Ray
Weight......................10,000#	Production.............1990–95

Originally called the 310 Express Cruiser (1990–91), the Sea Ray 330 EC is a good-looking family sportboat with crisp styling and a surprisingly roomy interior. She's built on a fully-cored hull with moderate beam, an integral swim platform and bow pulpit and—inboard models only—prop pockets and side exhausts. On the outside she looks the same as her sistership, the 310/330 Sundancer, but the interiors are entirely different. Lacking a mid-cabin, the wide-open salon of the EC makes for a more practical dayboat layout. The long starboard-side sofa offers increased entertainment space, and the wider entryway is a plus compared to the Sundancer's narrow passageway. The cockpit seating is also different with double helm and companion seats and a little more free space for moving around. Twin 5.7-litre stern drives were standard, but most of these boats were sold with the 7.4-litre gas inboards. A good performer, she'll cruise at 24–25 knots and reach a top speed of about 32 knots. Note that oval ports replaced the original sliding cabin windows in 1994. ❑

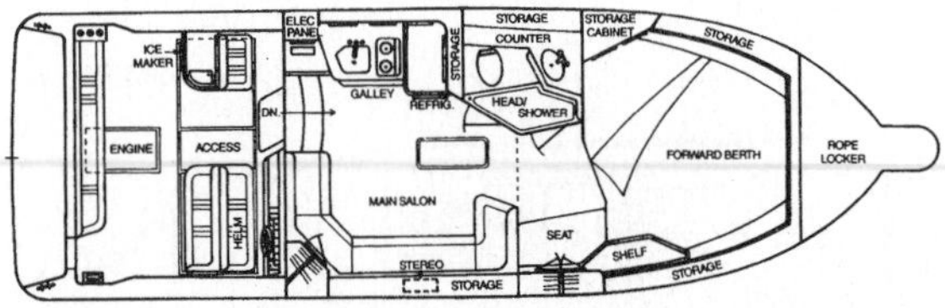

See Page 270 for Pricing Information

SEA RAY 310/330 SUNDANCER

1990–93

1994–Current

SPECIFICATIONS

Length w/Pulpit..........35'4"	Water........................40 gals.
Hull Length................32'10"	Fuel.........................180 gals.
Beam..............................11'5"	Hull Type................Deep-V
Draft, Inboards...............2'3"	Deadrise Aft....................17°
Draft, I/Os......................3'0"	Designer..................Sea Ray
Weight......................10,000#	Production....1990–Current

A popular model, the Sea Ray 330 Sundancer (she was called the 310 Sundancer from 1990–91) is nearly identical on the outside to her sistership, the 310/330 Express Cruiser. She's built on a fully-cored deep-V hull with moderate beam, an integral swim platform, and prop pockets for reduced shaft angles. While she has the same profile as the 310/330 Express Cruiser, the Sundancer's more expansive mid-cabin floorplan provides overnight accommodations for an extra couple. (Note that the layout was updated in 1992.) Outside, the elevated triple-wide helm seat provides excellent visibility in all directions. A fold-away bench seat at the transom facilitates engine access, and a wet bar and transom door are standard. While stern drives are available, most have been delivered with V-drive inboards. Twin 7.4-litre MerCruisers will cruise the Sea Ray 310/330 Sundancer at 23–24 knots and reach a top speed of around 31 knots. In 1994, Sea Ray replaced the sliding cabin windows with more stylish oval ports. ❑

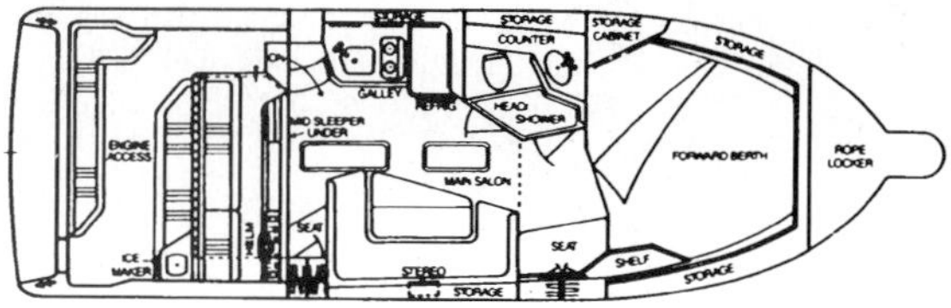

310 Floorplan (1990–91)

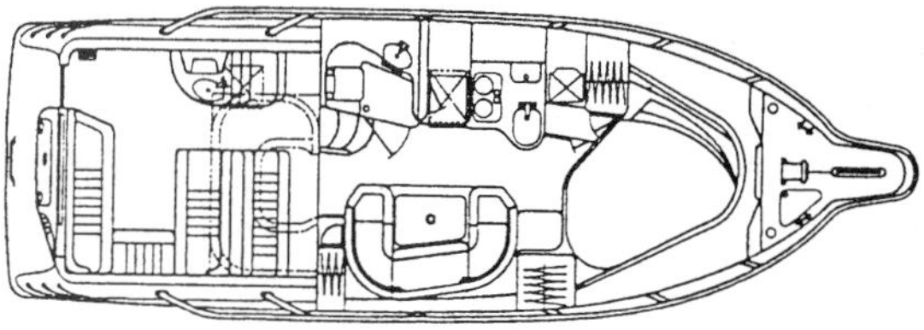

330 Floorplan (1992–Current)

See Page 270 for Pricing Information

SEA RAY 340 SEDAN BRIDGE

SPECIFICATIONS

Length	33'7"	Fuel	204 gals.
Beam	11'11"	Cockpit	50 sq. ft.
Draft	2'6"	Hull Type	Deep-V
Weight	11,400#	Deadrise Aft	21°
Clearance	NA	Designer	Sea Ray
Water	80 gals.	Production	1983–87

The 340 Sedan Bridge is a capable family cruiser with a conservative profile and comfortable cabin accommodations. She was built on a solid fiberglass deep-V hull with a fairly wide beam and prop pockets—the same hull used for the popular 340 Express Cruiser. The step-down interior is dominated by an attractive drum-shaped bottle-and-glass cabinet with circular tambour doors and a grab rail. Although optional, most 340 Sedans were sold with the lower helm. The toilet is located in the shower stall of the head—a space-saving idea later seen in other Sea Ray models. Large wrap-around cabin windows give the interior a notably spacious appearance, and most will find the layout to be functional and well-suited for family cruising. Outside, the hatch in the cockpit sole provides access to the engines, and a transom door and swim platform were standard equipment. Popular 350-hp gas engines (with V-drives) will cruise the Sea Ray 340 Sedan Bridge at 20–21 knots with a top speed of around 30 knots. ❑

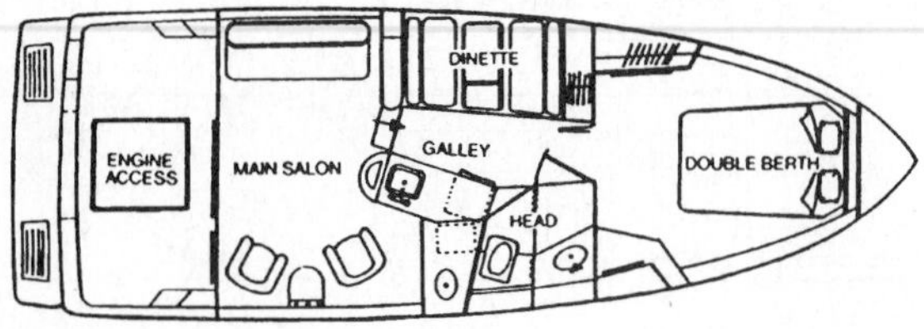

See Page 270 for Pricing Information

SEA RAY 345/340 SEDAN BRIDGE

SPECIFICATIONS

Length	33'9"	Fuel	250 gals.
Beam	12'6"	Cockpit	44 sq. ft.
Draft	3'9"	Hull Type	Deep-V
Weight	16,500#	Deadrise Aft	NA
Clearance	NA	Designer	Sea Ray
Water	100 gals.	Production	1988–89

Lasting only two years in production, Sea Ray introduced this model as the 345 Sedan Bridge in 1989 and changed the name to 340 Sedan Bridge the following year. Clearly, this was not one of Sea Ray's better-looking boats. While the interior is big for a 34-foot sedan, the oversized flybridge—with its exaggerated flybridge overhang—and the small cockpit give her a chunky, overfed appearance that severely limited her appeal. She was built on a solid fiberglass deep-V hull with prop pockets and a notably wide beam. Inside, the unusual two-stateroom floorplan will sleep six and includes a private mid-cabin below theraised dinette with partial standing headroom. Note that the galley is aft in the salon—an unusual layout in a sedan-style boat but a great convenience to those in the cockpit. Additional features include a separate stall shower in the head, fairly wide sidedecks, a transom door, and a swim platform with boarding ladder. Standard 340-hp MerCruiser gas engines will cruise the Sea Ray 345/340 Sedan Bridge around 21–22 knots and deliver 30 knots wide open. ❑

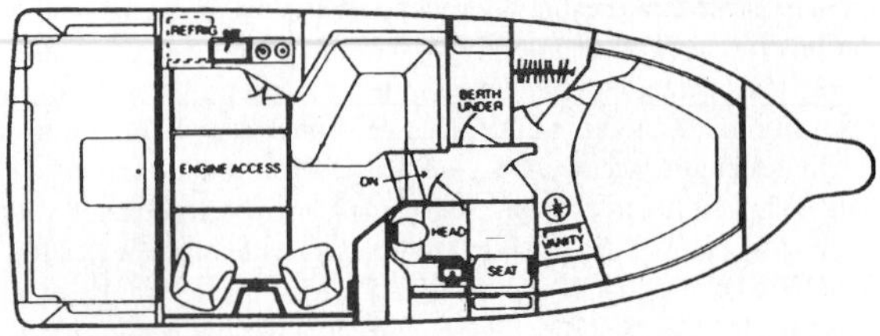

See Page 270 for Pricing Information

SEA RAY 340 EXPRESS CRUISER

SPECIFICATIONS

Length ....33'7"	Fuel ....204/250 gals.
Beam ....11'11"	Cockpit ....NA
Draft ....2'5"	Hull Type ....Deep-V
Weight ....10,100#	Deadrise Aft ....21°
Clearance ....NA	Designer ....Sea Ray
Water ....52 gals.	Production 1984–89

The 340 Express Cruiser (and her sistership, the 340 Sundancer) proved to be one of Sea Ray's most popular models. She was built on a solid fiberglass deep-V hull with a relatively wide beam, a well-flared entry and prop pockets to reduce the shaft angles. The once-contemporary styling of the 340 Express is somewhat dated compared to many of the newer sportboat designs now on the market. Aimed at the family sportboat market, she benefited from several production updates during her lifetime. The galley and dinette were rearranged in 1986, and the original island berth in the stateroom was dropped in the 1988 models in favor of a full-width bed and (optional) built-in entertainment center. The fuel capacity was increased in 1987. Standard features included a swim platform, transom door, side exhausts and sliding cabin windows that lead. A good-running boat, standard 340-hp gas engines will cruise the Sea Ray 340 at 24 knots and reach about 32 knots wide open. Note that the Sea Ray 340 Sport Fisherman (1984–86) is the same boat as the 340 EC with the addition of a flybridge. ❑

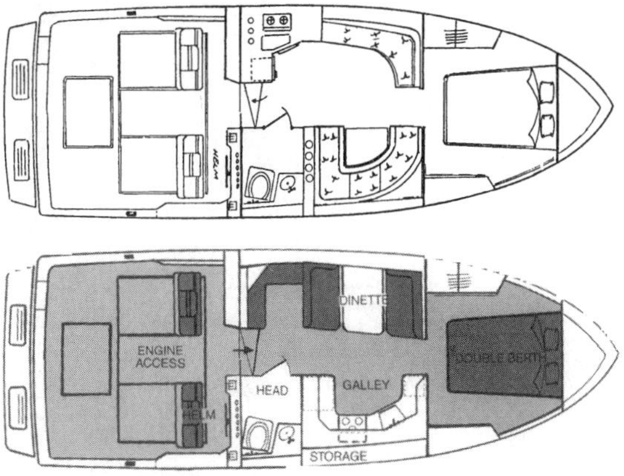

See Page 271 for Pricing Information

SEA RAY 340 SUNDANCER

SPECIFICATIONS

Length ....33'7"	Fuel ....172 gals.
Beam ....11'11"	Cockpit ....NA
Draft ....2'5"	Hull Type ....Deep-V
Weight ....10,500#	Deadrise Aft ....21°
Clearance ....NA	Designer ....Sea Ray
Water ....52 gals.	Production 1984–89

The Sea Ray 340 Sundancer has the same hull and exterior profile as the 340 Express Cruiser (EC), the difference being that the Sundancer has a separate mid-cabin located beneath the bridgedeck. The additional interior space is made possible by moving the engines further aft under the cockpit and using V-drives. The Sundancer's bigger layout made her a better-selling model than the 340 EC, and that popularity continues in today's second-hand brokerage market. Inside, the forward stateroom and mid-cabin are fitted with double berths, but privacy is limited to a couple of draw curtains. The Sundancer's cockpit is quite roomy and includes a companion seat next to the helm, transom door, bench seating aft, and a swim platform. Removable hatches in the cockpit sole provide good access to the motors. A good-running boat, standard 454-cid gas engines will cruise the Sea Ray 340 Sundancer at 23 knots and deliver a top speed in the neighborhood of 32 knots. Note that with only 172 gallons of fuel capacity, the cruising range is very limited. ❑

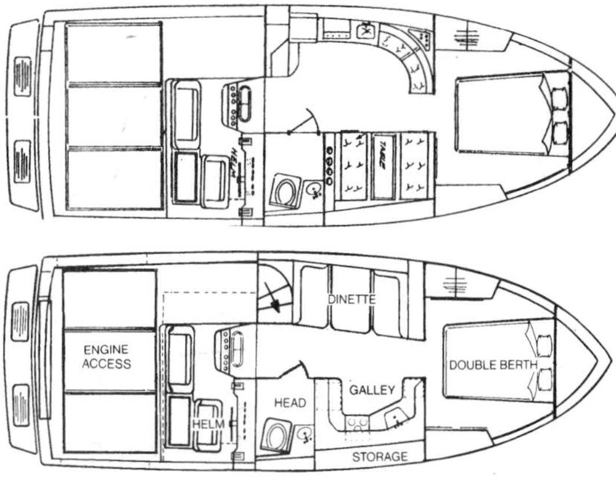

See Page 271 for Pricing Information

SEA RAY 350 EXPRESS BRIDGE

SPECIFICATIONS

Length	35'4"	Fuel	200 gals.
Beam	11'5"	Cockpit	NA
Draft	3'1"	Hull Type	Deep-V
Weight	11,500#	Deadrise Aft	18°
Clearance	NA	Designer	Sea Ray
Water	60 gals.	Production	1992–93

Express Bridge boats have become popular in recent years because of their sunken, full-width interiors (no sidedecks) and easy bridge access (molded steps rather than a ladder). Like others of her type, the 350 Express Bridge has an expansive and wide-open interior arranged on a single level with facing semi-circular settees dominating the salon and a single stateroom forward. While the layout is indeed cavernous for a 35-footer, the lack of a separate stall shower in the head is notable. The cockpit is arranged with built-in bench seating at the transom. Lacking sidedecks, a cut-out in the flybridge coaming provides easy foredeck access. Interestingly, the cabin windows are larger than those found in other express bridge models, and the interior seems less confining. Small 260-hp stern drives were standard in the 350 Express Bridge—a poor choice in our opinion for a boat this size. Optional 454-cid gas inboards (with V-drives) will cruise around 22–23 knots and reach close to 32 knots wide open. ❑

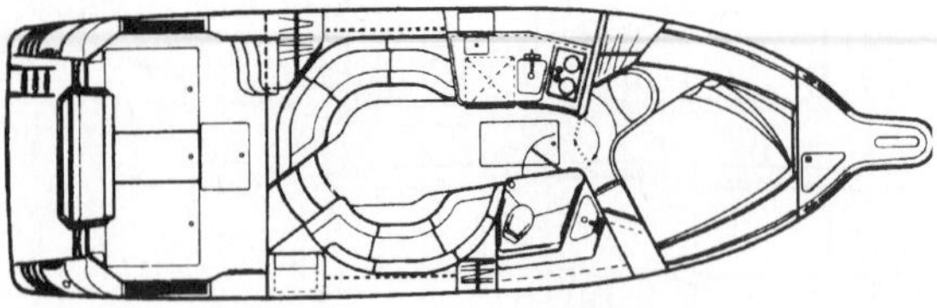

See Page 271 for Pricing Information

SEA RAY 355T SEDAN

SPECIFICATIONS

Length	36'3"	Fuel	270 gals.
Beam	12'6"	Cockpit	36 sq. ft.
Draft	2'11"	Hull Type	Modified-V
Weight	13,000#	Deadrise Aft	9°
Clearance	10'3"	Designer	Sea Ray
Water	120 gals.	Production	1982–83

The Sea Ray 355T is an odd-looking family cruiser with a spacious interior and the largest master stateroom seen in any sedan-style boat under 40 feet. She was built on a solid fiberglass hull with prop pockets, side exhausts, and a shallow keel below. With her stepped sheer and Eurostyle cabin windows, the 355T has an unusual and distinctive profile. Rather than providing the usual two-stateroom layout in a boat this size, Sea Ray opted for a more open single-stateroom floorplan. As noted, the master stateroom is enormous with a walkaround island berth, lots of dressing space, and a large hanging locker. A serving counter separates the step-down galley from the salon, and the optional lower helm is to port rather than starboard. The carpeted overhead and cheap teak-and-mica interior woodwork are obviously dated by current decor standards. Outside, the flybridge is very roomy, and the cockpit is tiny. Single and twin engines—gas and diesel—were offered. With the popular 135-hp Perkins diesels, she'll cruise economically at 10–11 knots. ❑

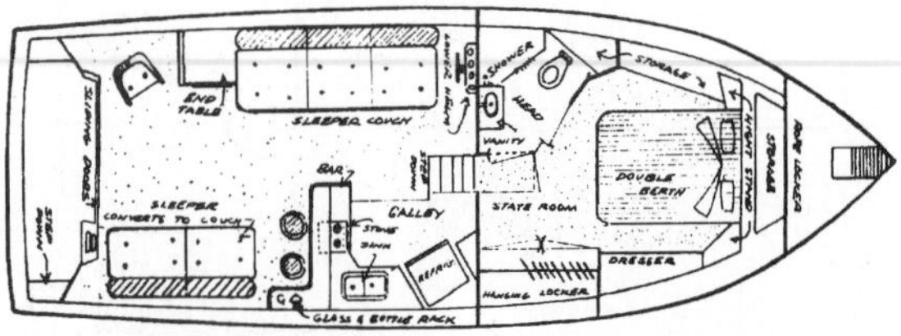

See Page 271 for Pricing Information

SEA RAY 360 EXPRESS CRUISER

SPECIFICATIONS

Length	36'6"	Water	100 gals.
Beam	13'11"	Fuel	300 gals.
Draft	2'7"	Hull Type	Deep-V
Weight	17,900#	Deadrise Aft	NA
Clearance	9'7"	Designer	Sea Ray
Cockpit	NA	Production	1979–83

An innovative and unusual design, the 360 Express Cruiser is distinguished by her unique T-shaped hardtop and spoiler section. Supported by the windshield, the forward end of the top provides wind protection while underway. To get all-weather protection, the slots in the T-top can be closed with clear snap-in vinyl inserts or Plexiglas panels. She was equally innovative below, where angled bulkheads give the staterooms and head compartment unusual shapes—a notable departure from the rigid, squared-off interiors found in most boats of the early 1980s. The salon is quite spacious thanks to her extra-wide beam. She'll sleep up to six, and the head compartment is fitted with a separate stall shower. Outside, the cockpit is very large with seating for eight to ten people. A teak pulpit and swim platform were standard, and three in-deck hatches provide good access to the motors. No racehorse, twin 454-cid gas engines will cruise the 360 Express Cruiser around 17 knots and deliver a top speed of 26–27 knots. ❑

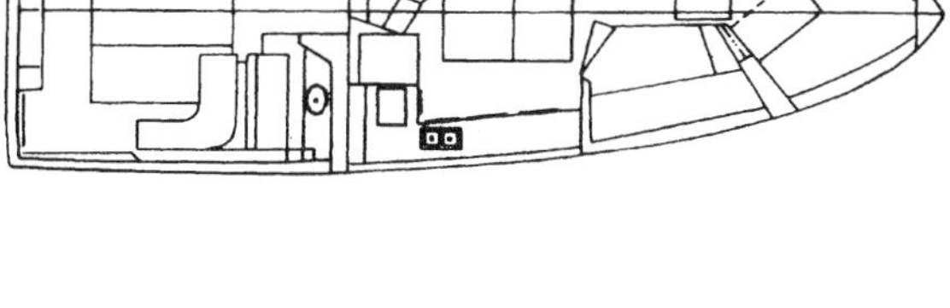

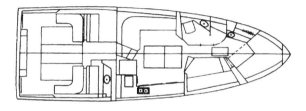

See Page 271 for Pricing Information

SEA RAY 350/370 EXPRESS CRUISER

1990–93

1994–95

SPECIFICATIONS

Length w/Pulpit........36'10"	Fuel........................250 gals.
Hull Length ....36'10"	Waste.......................20 gals.
Beam..............................12'4"	Hull Type ....Deep-V
Draft ....2'5"	Deadrise Aft...................21°
Weight ....13,100#	Designer ....Sea Ray
Water........................70 gals.	Production 1990–95

Called the 350 Express Cruiser (EC) until 1992, Sea Ray's 370 EC is a modern family cruiser with contemporary sportboat lines and a very spacious interior layout. She's built on a good-running deep-V hull with a fairly wide beam, prop pockets, and side-dumping exhausts. While she has the same profile as the 370 Sundancer, the EC has a larger salon with an extended U-shaped settee and a bigger galley. There's a stall shower in the head, and a built-in TV can be pulled out and viewed from the salon to the forward cabin. On the downside, only a curtain provides privacy in the stateroom. Additional features include good interior headroom throughout, an integral bow pulpit and swim platform, cockpit wet bar, side-dumping exhausts and a fold-away transom seat. Standard 310-hp 7.4-litre MerCruiser inboard engines will cruise the Sea Ray 370 Express Cruiser around 20 knots and reach a top speed of 28–29 knots. Note that in 1994, Sea Ray redesigned the helm console and replaced the original sliding cabin windows with stylish oval portlights. ❑

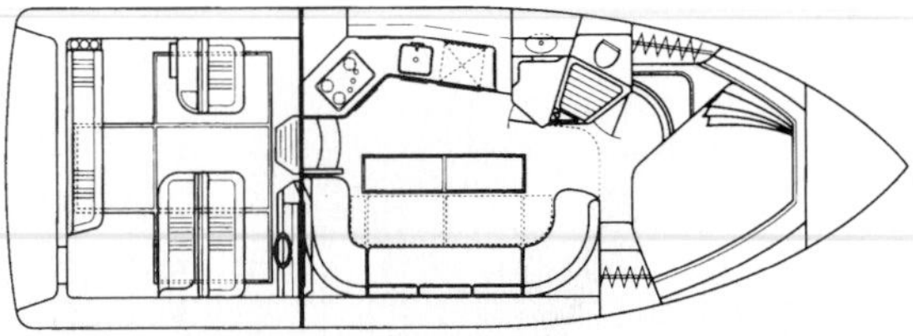

See Page 271 for Pricing Information

SEA RAY 350/370 SUNDANCER

1990–93

1994

SPECIFICATIONS

Length w/Platform.......39'5"	Water ....70 gals.
Hull Length ....36'10"	Fuel ....250 gals.
Beam..............................12'4"	Hull Type ....Deep-V
Draft ....2'5"	Deadrise Aft....................21°
Weight ....13,500#	Designer ....Sea Ray
Clearance.......................NA	Production 1990–94

Called the 350 Sundancer until 1992, the Sea Ray 370 is an upscale family cruiser with modern sportboat lines and a mid-cabin interior layout. While she has the same exterior profile as the 370 Express Cruiser, the Sundancer has a more compact salon to make room for the mid-cabin stateroom. There's a separate stall shower in the head, and a built-in TV can be pulled out and viewed from the salon or the forward cabin. On the downside, only draw curtains provide privacy for the staterooms. Unlike the EC model, the Sundancer is driven with V-drives, and access to the engines is further aft in the cockpit. (Note that stern drives were also available.) Additional features include good interior headroom, an integral pulpit and swim platform, wet bar, and transom door. Standard 454-cid MerCruiser gas inboards will cruise the 370 Sundancer around 20 knots and reach a top speed of 29 knots. In 1994, Sea Ray added U-shaped cockpit seating and replaced the original sliding cabin windows with oval portlights. ❑

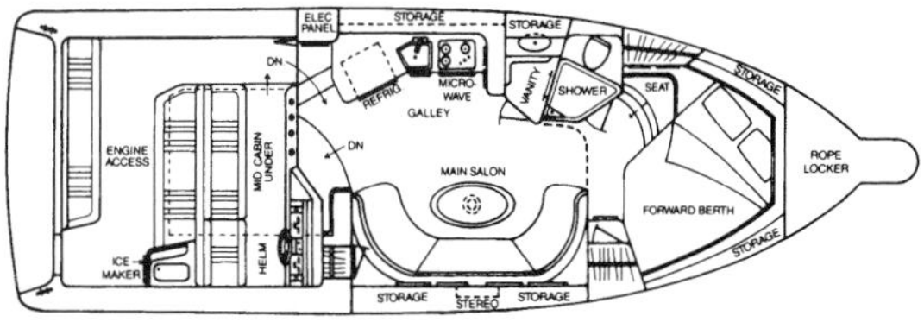

See Page 271 for Pricing Information

SEA RAY 370 SEDAN BRIDGE

SPECIFICATIONS

Length w/Platform.....40'10"	Fuel ....250 gals.
Hull Length ....36'10"	Waste ....20 gals
Beam..............................12'4"	Hull Type ....Deep-V
Draft ....2'7"	Deadrise Aft...................21°
Weight ....14,600#	Designer ....Sea Ray
Water ....70 gals.	Production 1991–Current

With her long foredeck and relatively small cockpit the 370 Sedan Bridge is a maxi-volume family sedan with a conservative profile and spacious interior layout. She's built on the same hull used in the 370 EC and Sundancer models—a deep-V affair with prop pockets, moderate beam, and side-dumping exhausts. Her two-stateroom, galley-down floorplan features an expansive salon (for a 37-footer) with a full-length settee, removable dinette table, breakfast bar, and large wraparound cabin windows. There's an offset double berth in the master stateroom forward, and the portside guest cabin has another double berth extending below the salon sole. The cockpit is too small for any serious fishing and comes with a transom door, coaming padding, and optional bench seating. Note that the helm console is all the way forward on the flybridge with L-shaped lounge seating aft. Additional features include an arch, swim platform, and integral bow pulpit. Standard 454-cid gas engines will cruise the 370 Sedan Bridge at 19 knots and deliver a top speed of around 28 knots. ❑

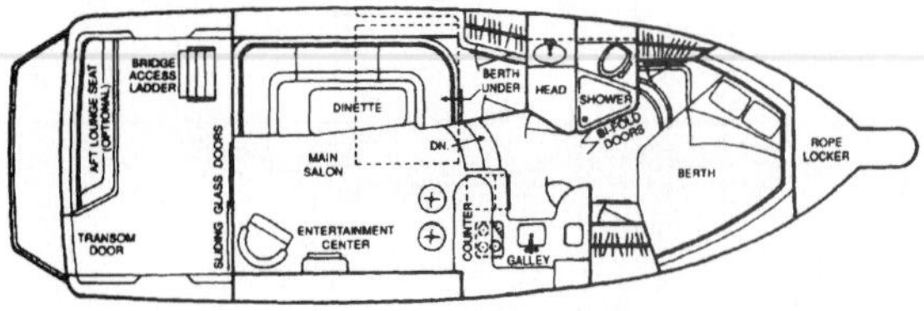

See Page 271 for Pricing Information

SEA RAY 370 SUNDANCER

SPECIFICATIONS

Length ....37'6"	Waste ....28 gals.
Beam.............................12'7"	Clearance ....NA
Draft ....2'8"	Hull Type ....Deep-V
Weight.....................15,400#	Deadrise Aft...................20°
Fuel ....275 gals.	Designer ....Sea Ray
Water ....70 gals.	Production 1995–Current

It would be difficult to find a better-looking mid-size family cruiser than Sea Ray's new 370 Sundancer. Indeed, with her rakish profile (note the reverse arch, oval ports, and the absence of a bow pulpit), this Sea Ray closely resembles the sleek styling of a pure-bred Mediterranean sportboat. While all Sundancer models employ mid-cabin floorplans, the interior of the 370 seems unusually expansive for a 37-footer. There are double berths in both sleeping areas, and the curving, high-gloss galley—with its breakfast bar and sculptured overhead—is an eye-catching display of high-style design. The dinette table is removable, and the head compartment has a separate stall shower. The 370's interior is large because the cabin bulkhead is set well aft resulting in a cockpit of somewhat limited (but still adaquate) dimensions. Additional features include an underwater exhaust system, an unusual two-tier swim platform, U-shaped cockpit seating that converts into a sunpad and very secure walkarounds. Twin V-drive 310-hp gas inboards will cruise at 19 knots and reach a top speed of 30 knots. Diesels to 300 hp are optional.❑

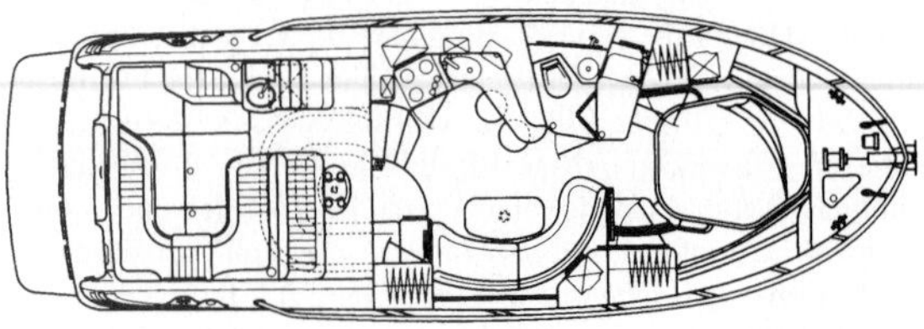

See Page 271 for Pricing Information

SEA RAY 380 SUN SPORT

SPECIFICATIONS

Length	38'5"	Water	40 gals.
Beam	11'0"	Fuel	200 gals.
Draft, Up	1'11"	Hull Type	Deep-V
Draft, Down	3'0"	Deadrise Aft	21°
Weight	11,200#	Designer	J. Michalak
Clearance	NA	Production	1990–Current

One of Sea Ray's best-looking boats, the 380 Sun Sport (originally called the 370 Sun Sport) closely resembles the expensive, high-style European go-fast boats typically found in the Mediterranean. Indeed, with her rakish profile, sexy graphics, and expansive cockpit accommodations her only mission in life is fun in the sun. Note the absence of a molded bow pulpit—an evolving trend in modern sportboat design. Built on a fully cored deep-V hull with a narrow beam, the 380's layout is evenly divided between an expansive cockpit and a stylish interior. Inside, a huge semi-circular dinette/settee faces aft, and a small galley and head are on opposite sides of the entryway. Clearly designed for daytime entertaining, the interior accommodations are secondary in this layout. The cockpit is arranged with another semi-circular lounge with a built-in wet bar, and the sun pad is raised hydraulically for access to the engines. A fast ride with 454-cid stern drives, the 380 Sun Sport cruises at 25 knots and delivers a top speed of about 40 knots. ❑

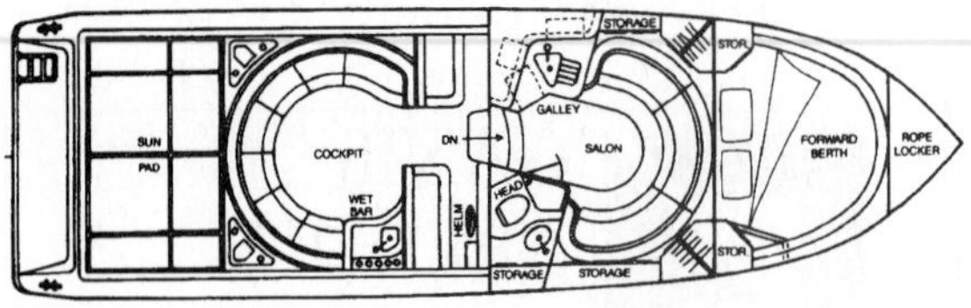

See Page 271 for Pricing Information

SEA RAY 390 EXPRESS CRUISER

SPECIFICATIONS

Length	39'0"	Fuel	300 gals.
Beam	13'11"	Cockpit	NA
Draft	2'4"	Hull Type	Deep-V
Weight	16,400#	Deadrise Aft	19°
Clearance	NA	Designer	Sea Ray
Water	100 gals.	Production	1984–91

The 390 Express Cruiser turned out to be one of the most popular boats ever built by Sea Ray. First of the big production express boats when she came out in 1984, her sleek lines and European styling, while tame by today's design standards, made a lasting impression on the mid-1980's sportboat market. Inside, her expansive two-stateroom interior is arranged with a queen berth forward and a combined galley-and-breakfast bar facing the curved settee in the salon. The guest stateroom is unique: it's separated from the salon by a retractable mirrored bulkhead. Slide it away, convert the bunk berths into a sofa, and the area actually becomes a part of the main cabin. The 390's interior was updated twice over the years changing from the original wood-grain mica to teak in 1986, and to a white-mica/teak-trim decor in 1988. (The sliding cabin windows are prone to leaking.) Outside, the spacious cockpit provides lounge seating for as many as eight passengers. Twin 340-hp inboard MerCruisers will cruise the 340 EC at 17–18 knots (about 28 knots top), and optional 375-hp Cats will cruise at 25 knots (29 knots wide open). ❑

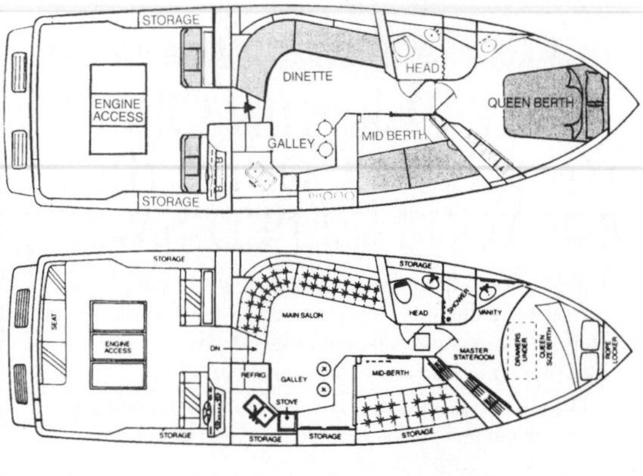

See Page 271 for Pricing Information

SEA RAY 400 EXPRESS CRUISER

SPECIFICATIONS

Length w/Pulpit	43'0"	Water	100 gals.
Hull Length	40'4"	Fuel	300 gals.
Beam	13'0"	Hull Type	Deep-V
Draft	3'3"	Deadrise Aft	19°
Weight	16,100#	Designer	Sea Ray
Clearance	NA	Production	1992–Current

The 400 Express Cruiser (EC) is the long-awaited replacement for Sea Ray's hugely popular 390 EC. With her stylish windshield, integral swim platform, and sleek hull profile, the 400 EC is truly a handsome boat and a big step up from her predecessor in appearance. It's interesting to note that the new hull (solid fiberglass with prop pockets, side exhausts, and 19 degrees of deadrise aft) is narrower by a foot than the 390's, and interior and cockpit dimensions are reduced accordingly. The good news is that the 400 EC basically retains the 390's innovative two-stateroom floorplan, albeit completely updated and restyled. A sliding wall partition opens the guest cabin's convertible settee to the salon for additional seating during the day—a practical design feature. Outside, the cockpit is fitted with an elevated helm, wet bar, and plenty of guest seating. An optional bolt-on extended platform attachment with fender storage is available. No racehorse with standard 310-hp gas engines (17 knots cruise/26–27 knots top), optional Cat 3116 diesels (350-hp) deliver 24 knots at cruise and a top speed of about 29 knots. ❑

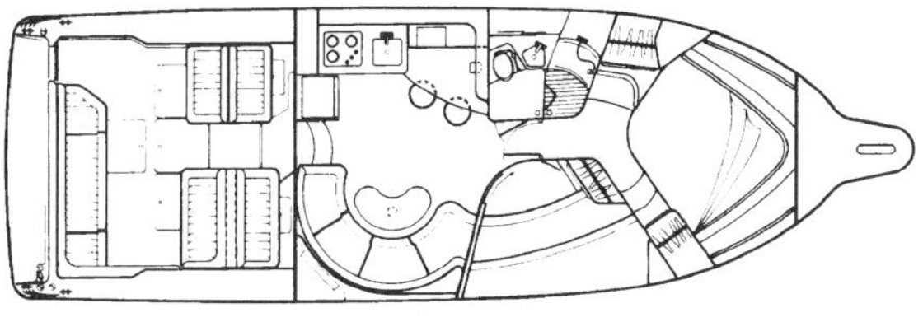

See Page 271 for Pricing Information

SEA RAY 420/440 SUNDANCER

SPECIFICATIONS

Length w/Pulpit	47'1"	Water	100 gals.
Hull Length	44'0"	Fuel	400 gals.
Beam	13'11"	Waste	28 gals.
Draft	3'3"	Hull Type	Deep-V
Weight	20,000#	Deadrise Aft	19°
Clearance	NA	Production	1989–95

Introduced in late 1989 as the 420 Sundancer, Sea Ray made some hull changes and reintroduced this boat in 1992 as the 440 Sundancer. She's built on a solid fiberglass bottom with cored hullsides and 19 degrees of deadrise aft—basically the same hull used in the long-running 390 EC model, only longer. Note that the 440's hull has prop pockets while the original 420 hull did not. A good-looking boat with a muscular profile (the long foredeck and low-profile arch add much to her rakish appearance), the Sundancer's wide-open interior is a blend of curved bulkheads, white Formica cabinetry, and light oak woodwork. Offering complete privacy for two couples, a unique wraparound door closes off the mid-cabin at night. Outside, the cockpit is arranged with a triple-wide elevated helm seat and facing settees aft. Additional features include an integral pulpit and swim platform, and side-dumping exhausts. Originally powered with 330-hp gas inboards (17 knots cruise/26 top), 300-hp Cat (or Cummins) diesels were standard in later years (20 knots cruise/24 top). Optional 425-hp Cats will cruise around 24 knots. In 1994, Sea Ray replaced the original sliding cabin windows with oval ports. ❑

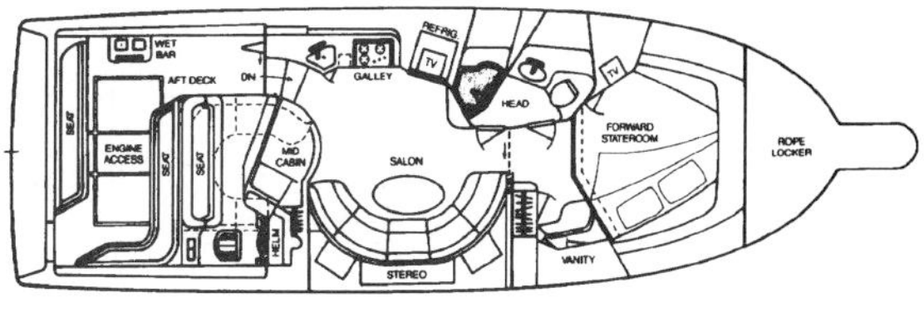

See Page 271 for Pricing Information

SEA RAY 440 EXPRESS BRIDGE

SPECIFICATIONS

Length w/Pulpit..........49'2"	Water......................100 gals.
Hull Length..................44'0"	Fuel.........................400 gals.
Beam............................13'11"	Waste........................60 gals.
Draft................................3'3"	Hull Type................Deep-V
Weight......................26,600#	Deadrise Aft....................19°
Clearance........................NA	Production....1993–Current

Hands down, the 440 Express Bridge has one of the most expansive interior layouts of any similar boat in her class. Like all of the so-called express bridge designs, with their space-saving V-drive power systems and low deckhouse profiles, the 440's sunken salon utilizes the entire width of the hull to create a huge, wide-open floorplan laid out on a single level. With the engines aft below the cockpit, there's even room for an innovative mid-cabin stateroom under the molded cockpit bridge steps—something not seen in other express bridge models. Built on a fully cored deep-V hull with moderate beam and prop pockets to reduce the shaft angles, the 440's huge, party-time flybridge is arranged with the wraparound helm console/settee on the centerline and additional bench seating forward. A pass-thru in the bridge coaming provides access to the foredeck (and its built-in seating), and the walkways are well-secured with raised bulwarks. Optional 375-hp Cats will cruise the 440 Sedan Bridge at 22 knots and deliver a top speed of 26–27 knots.❑

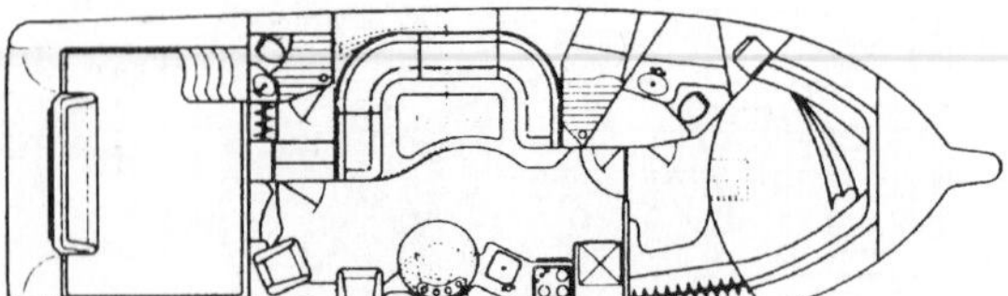

See Page 271 for Pricing Information

SEA RAY 450 SUNDANCER

SPECIFICATIONS

Length w/Pulpit..........48'1"	Water......................100 gals.
Hull Length..................45'6"	Waste........................60 gals.
Beam............................13'11"	Clearance......................12'0"
Draft................................3'7"	Hull Type................Deep-V
Weight......................22,500#	Deadrise Aft....................19°
Fuel.........................400 gals.	Production....1995–Current

Introduced in mid-1995 as a replacement for the 440 Sundancer, the exterior styling of the Sea Ray 450 Sundancer is more rakish than her predecessor and, while the beam is the same, the 450 is built on a fully cored hull with prop pockets and a sharper entry. (Note the optional bolt-on swim platform in the picture above.) Inside, the luxurious accommodations are dominated by a huge wraparound settee in the salon across from an equally large galley with a built-in breakfast bar. Privacy doors separate both staterooms from the main cabin, and there are *two* head compartments with a separate stall shower forward. In the cockpit, circular seating and aft-facing benches create an impressive open-air entertainment platform with a wet bar, triple-wide helm seat, and transom door standard. A gas-assist hatch in the cockpit sole provides good access to the engine compartment. A split exhaust system sends most of the exhaust underwater and the rest through side exhausts in the hull. Optional 375-hp V-drive Cat diesels will cruise the Sea Ray 450 at a fast 27–28 knots (30+ knots top). ❑

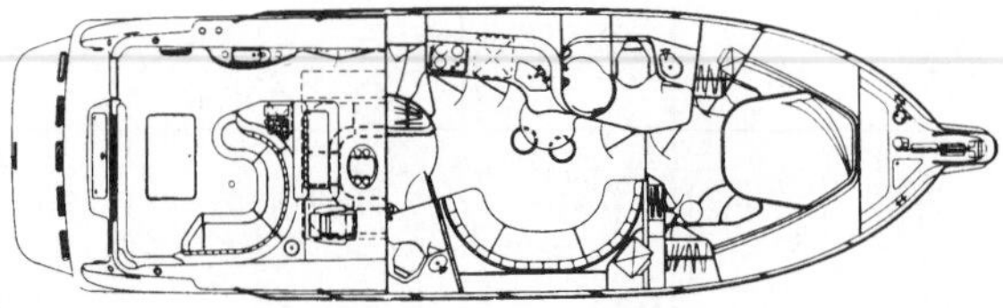

See page 271 for Pricing Information

SEA RAY 460 EXPRESS CRUISER

SPECIFICATIONS

Length	45'6"	Fuel	420 gals.
Beam	14'11"	Cockpit	NA
Draft	3'2"	Hull Type	Deep-V
Weight	25,000#	Deadrise Aft	17°
Clearance	9'9"	Designer	Sea Ray
Water	150 gals.	Production	1985–89

In the mid-1980s, the Sea Ray 460 EC reigned supreme as the largest *full-production* express cruiser on the market. With her then-aggressive low profile hull, long foredeck, and Euro-style reversed arch, her appeal was such that she soon became a very good-selling model for Sea Ray. The hull is a modified deep-V with prop pockets and solid fiberglass construction. Originally offered with either a one- or two-stateroom floorplan, Sea Ray settled on a spacious single-stateroom arrangement in 1988 with an absolutely huge main salon. This is an elaborate interior with wraparound suede sofas, overhead track lighting, high-pressure laminate counters and cabinetry, and no teak anywhere. Outside, the bi-level cockpit is massive with seating for a small crowd. Notable features include a flush cockpit sole, wide sidedecks, teak covering boards, transom door and side-dumping exhausts. Twin 375-hp Caterpillar diesels were standard and provide about 20 knots at cruise (23–24 knots top). With the optional 550-hp 6V92 Detroits, the Sea Ray 390 EC will cruise at a fast 27 knots and reach a top speed of 30 knots. ❑

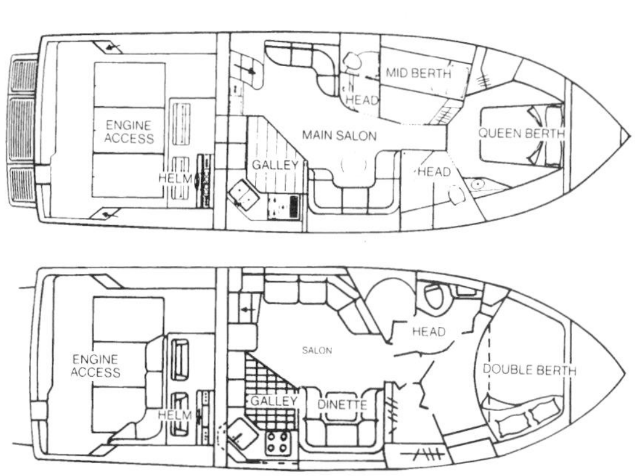

See Page 271 for Pricing Information

SEA RAY 480/500 SUNDANCER

SPECIFICATIONS

Length w/Pulpit	54'6"	Fuel	500 gals.
Hull Length	50'1"	Waste	40 gals.
Beam	15'0"	Clearance	NA
Draft	4'0"	Hull Type	Deep-V
Weight	32,100#	Deadrise Aft	17°
Water	150 gals.	Production	1990–Current

A great-looking boat, the 500 Sundancer (originally called the 480 Sundancer during 1990–91) is one of the largest production express cruisers on the market. With her long foredeck and sleek profile, the 500 is a crowd-stopper at any dock. Her sheer size is impressive enough, but it's the extravagant high-style interior that causes first-time viewers to catch their breath. Here, laid out on a single level and presenting a panorama of curved bulkheads and designer furnishings, the accommodations rival those found in a small motor yacht. There are two private staterooms, two heads (each with a stall shower), a plush U-shaped sofa below the bridgedeck, and a wide-open salon with good headroom throughout. The cockpit—with its raised helm, wet bar, and built-in lounge seating—can seat a small crowd. Standard 485-hp 6-71 diesels (with V-drives) will cruise the 500 Sundancer at 23–24 knots, and optional 735-hp 8V92s will deliver a fast 29 knots at cruise and 32 knots wide open. Note that oval ports replaced the original sliding cabin windows beginning in 1994 models. ❑

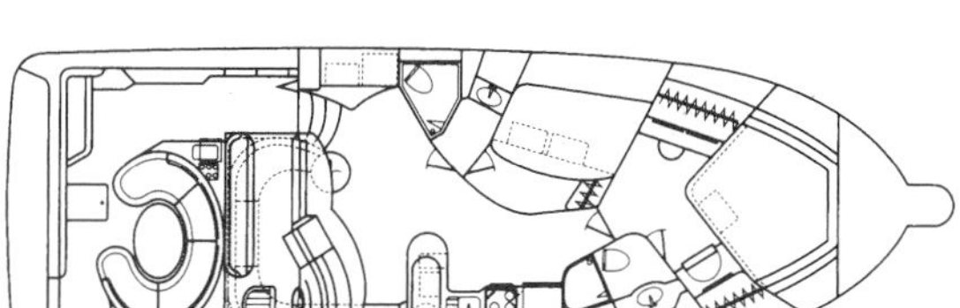

See Page 271 for Pricing Information

SEA RAY 600/630 SUPER SUN SPORT
630 SUNDANCER

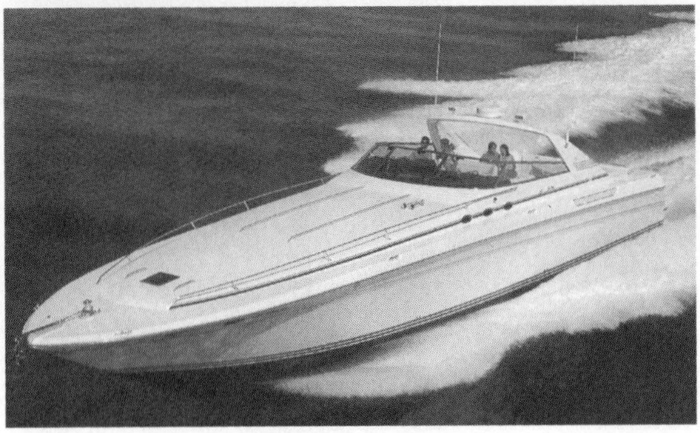

SPECIFICATIONS

Length w/Platform.....64'6"	Water......................200 gals.
Hull Length ....62'6"	Fuel.........................800 gals.
Beam.............................15'9"	Hull Type ....Deep-V
Draft ....5'0"	Deadrise Aft....................19°
Weight ....52,000#	Designer ....Sea Ray
Clearance ....12'9"	Production 1991–Current

One of the largest full-production express cruisers in the business, the 630 Super Sun Sport is a completely impressive boat with a stunning profile (note the long foredeck, low-profile bow rails and the absence of a bow pulpit) and the accommodations of a small motor yacht. She's built on a fully cored, deep-V hull with moderate beam and prop pockets. Inside, the massive salon is dominated by sculptured overhead panels and a long contoured leather sofa. The standard layout includes one stateroom and two heads, however an alternate floorplan replaces the dinette with a second stateroom for improved cruising capabilities. Note the innovative crew quarters hidden beneath the transom and accessed via the cockpit sunpad. Additional features include a reverse arch, two transom doors, circular lounge seating in the cockpit, and a well-arranged engine room with push-button access. A great performer with standard 1,080-hp 12V92s, the 630 Sun Sport will cruise at 30–31 knots (at about 100 gph!) and reach a top speed of 34 knots. The 630 Sundancer (1995–Current) is basically the same boat with Arneson Surface Drives, reduced draft, and about 10-knot-faster speeds. ❑

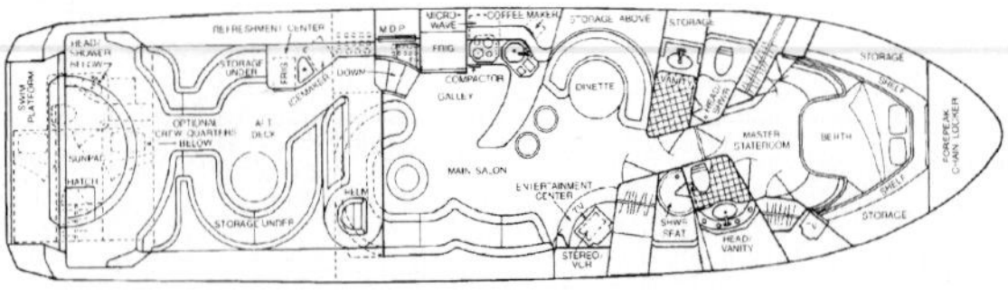

See Page 272 for Pricing Information

SHANNON 36 VOYAGER

SPECIFICATIONS

Length w/Pulpit..........38'3"	Water......................150 gals.
Hull Length ....35'7"	Fuel.........................325 gals.
Beam..............................13'3"	Hull Type ....Modified-V
Draft ....3'0"	Deadrise Aft....................13°
Weight......................17,500#	Designer............W. Schultz
Clearance ....12'6"	Production 1991–Current

While she may look like a trawler, the Shannon 36 is built on a planing hull with the power to cruise efficiently at faster speeds than traditional, semi-displacement trawlers (Grand Banks, Inland Gypsy, etc.). The modified-V hull of the Shannon, which is fully cored and very light, is quick to plane, and her fine entry and well-flared bow make for a comfortable, dry ride in a chop. The two-stateroom, galley-up teak interior features a lower helm station and built-in dinette in the salon, a sit-down shower in the head, and a queen bed in the forward stateroom. A hatch in the salon sole provides access to the engines. Like all trawler-style boats, the Shannon's salon dimensions are limited thanks to her wide sidedecks. The cockpit is very large with room for a small crowd. Topside, the flybridge will seat six and includes and wet bar and cocktail table. Built on a semi-custom basis, a pair of 300-hp Cat 3116 diesels will provide a cruising speed of 16 knots (at 16 gph) and a top speed of 18–19 knots. ❑

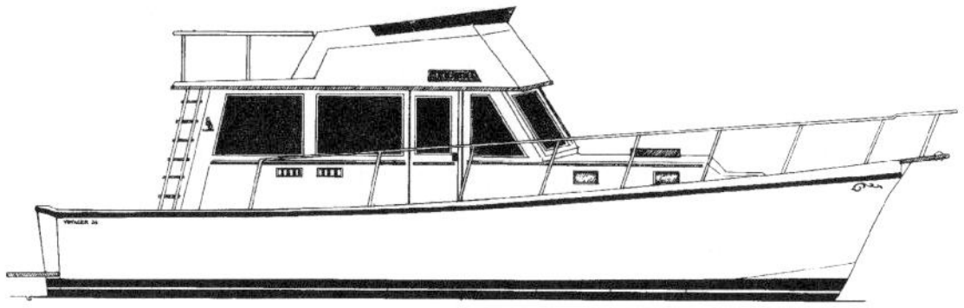

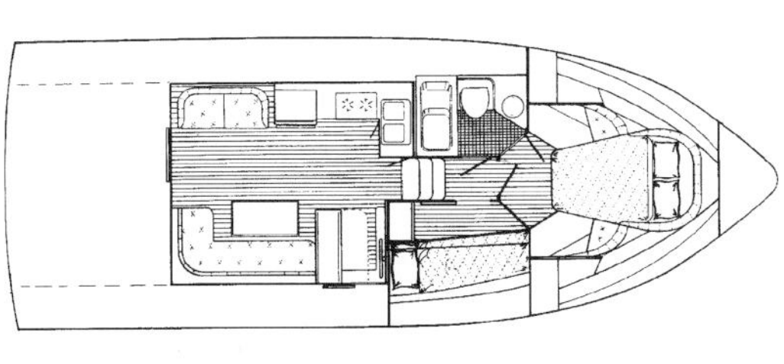

See Page 272 for Pricing Information

SILHOUETTE 42

SPECIFICATIONS

Length ....41'10"	Water......................150 gals.
LWL..............................37'6"	Fuel.........................400 gals.
Beam..............................14'6"	Cockpit...........................NA
Draft ....3'2"	Hull Type ....Modified-V
Weight......................28,000#	Designer................J. Krogen
Clearance ....NA	Production 1987–91

The Silhouette 42 is truly an exceptional design. If her profile is unusual, the Silhouette manages to offer a unique interior layout with more living space than one might expect in a boat this size. She was built in Taiwan by Chien Hwa on a PVC-cored, modified-V hull. While she incorporates several unusual features, it's the semi-enclosed pilothouse/sundeck and the wide-open master stateroom (with its private cockpit) that attract the most attention. A real surprise is the hydraulically operated stern gate which drops to create a practically wide-open transom and swim platform. Inside, a breakfast bar separates the spacious main salon from the galley below, and both staterooms feature double berths and stall showers. The interior is finished with light ash (or teak) woodwork and mica veneers. With standard Caterpillar 375-hp diesels, the Silhouette 42 will cruise around 21 knots and reach a top speed of 25–26 knots. A total of twelve of these boats were built before production was discontinued in 1991. ❑

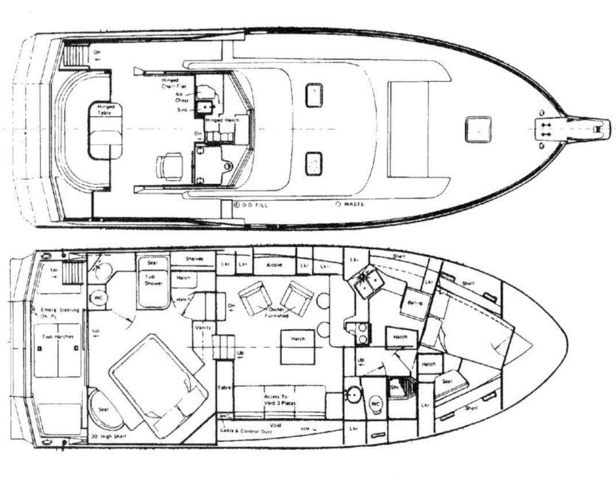

See Page 272 for Pricing Information

SILVERTON 271 EXPRESS

SPECIFICATIONS

Length w/Pulpit	29'9"	Fuel	109 gals.
Hull Length	27'10"	Water	30 gals.
Beam	8'6"	Clearance	NA
Draft, Up	1'8"	Hull Type	Modified-V
Draft, Down	3'1"	Deadrise Aft	14°
Weight	7,643#	Production	1995–Current

The smallest boat ever built by Silverton, the 271 Express is a maxi-cube, *trailerable* family cruiser with a stand-up interior and an affordable price tag. (Trailerable, yes, but with an over-the-road weight approaching 9,000 lbs. including trailer, it'll take a one-ton vehicle to do the job.) Built on a solid fiberglass hull with moderate transom deadrise, the 271 Express is a big boat on the inside thanks to her high-profile foredeck. The mid-cabin floorplan is arranged with double berths fore and aft, a complete galley, removable dinette, and an enclosed head with shower. The cabin headroom is an honest 6 feet, 2 inches—no easy design achievement in a 27-footer. A wraparound settee is opposite the helm, and the integral swim platform has a hot and cold shower, swim ladder and storage for fenders and electrical cords and assorted gear. Lacking sidedecks, a walk-through windshield provides access to the foredeck. The standard 5.7-litre MerCruiser stern drive will cruise the Silverton 271 Express at 15 knots (26 knots top), and the optional 7.4 litre motor delivers 18–19 knots at cruise and 30 knots wide open. ❑

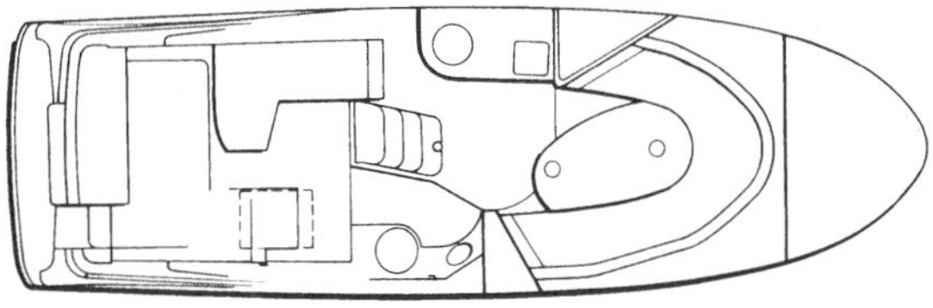

See Page 272 for Pricing Information

SILVERTON 28 SEDAN

SPECIFICATIONS

Length	28'0"	Fuel	130 gals.
Beam	10'6"	Cockpit	90 sq. ft.
Draft	2'8"	Hull Type	Modified-V
Weight	9,500#	Deadrise Aft	NA
Clearance	9'6"	Designer	Silverton
Water	37 gals.	Production	1975–78

A low price and generous interior accommodations made the Silverton 28 Sedan a fairly popular boat in the mid-1970s. Compared with most small flybridge designs of her era, the Silverton 28 has a notably low profile and her lines are quite aggressive. Inside, the step-down floorplan is arranged on a single level, with both the galley and head aft, just inside the salon door. A lower helm was standard, and the dinette converts into a double berth in the normal fashion. This is not the most expansive interior to be found in a 28-footer but practical nonetheless and certainly adequate for weekend family cruising. The cockpit is surprisingly large, with plenty of room for some light-tackle fishing activities or a few deck chairs. Removable hatches in the cockpit sole provide very good access to the engines and V-drives. Among several power options offered (including single-screw installations), the twin 225-hp Chryslers will cruise the Silverton 28 Sedan at 21 knots and reach about 30 knots wide open. Note the limited fuel capacity. ❑

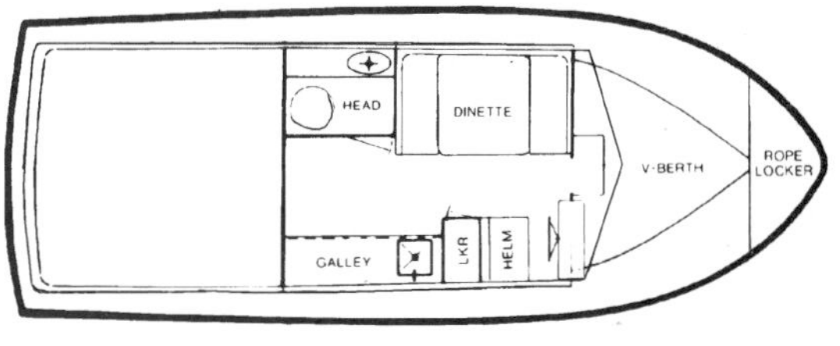

See Page 272 for Pricing Information

SILVERTON 29 SPORTCRUISER

SPECIFICATIONS

Length	29'2"	Fuel	150 gals.
Beam	10'10"	Cockpit	50 sq. ft.
Draft	1'7"	Hull Type	Modified-V
Weight	7,800#	Deadrise Aft	NA
Clearance	8'2"	Designer	M. Peters
Water	40 gals.	Production	1985–87

No award-winner when it comes to sex appeal, the Silverton 29 Sportcruiser is a surprisingly spacious family cruiser with a very unusual two-stateroom interior and a huge (for a 29-footer) flybridge. Hull construction is solid fiberglass and—with the engines located under the cockpit sole—prop pockets (and not V-drives) are used to reduce the shaft angles. If her conservative lines are dated, the Sportcruiser's single-level floorplan was still a relatively new concept in the mid-1980s. What really separates her from other boats, however, is the layout. There's a second stateroom aft of the dinette with an athwartships bed, night stand, and a sliding privacy door. This completely unusual arrangement results in a tight salon and moving-around space is at a premium. Topside, the flybridge is among the largest to be found in a boat this size with room for a crowd. Twin 195-hp Crusader (V6) gas engines will cruise the Silverton 29 Sportcruiser at a very satisfactory 17–18 knots (about 25 knots top) while burning only 12 gph—very impressive economy indeed. ❑

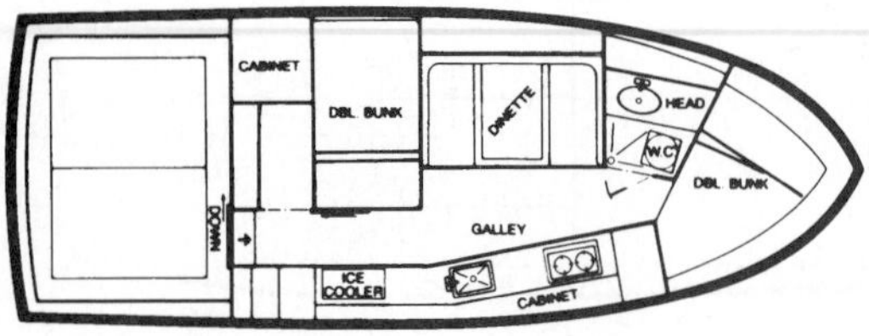

See Page 272 for Pricing Information

SILVERTON 30X EXPRESS

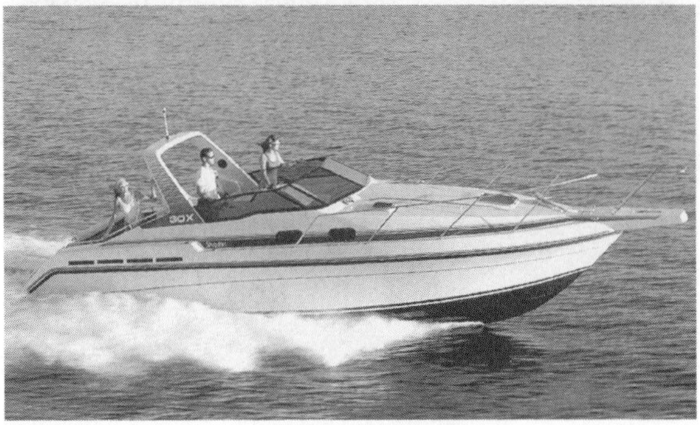

SPECIFICATIONS

Length	30'8"	Fuel	185 gals.
Beam	10'10"	Cockpit	NA
Draft	3'0"	Hull Type	Modified-V
Weight	9,100#	Designer	M. Peters
Clearance	8'5"	Deadrise Aft	NA
Water	37 gals.	Production	1988–89

The 30X was second in a series of sportboat designs introduced by Silverton a few years ago beginning with the original 34X model in 1987. In spite of her shorter length, the addition of an integral swim platform made the 30X a better-looking boat than her predecessor. Designed as a weekend family cruiser, the interior layout is fairly conventional with facing settees in the salon, a compact head and galley, and an offset double berth forward. (Note that she is not a mid-cabin design like most of the competition.) The decor is a blend of pastel fabrics and textured wall coverings, and there's no teak in sight. Outside, a companion seat to port and bench seating along the transom will seat five or six guests. Additional features include four opening ports, a radar arch, and transom door. The performance of the 30X is quite good. With standard 270-hp gas engines, she'll cruise about 24 knots and reach a top speed of 31–32 knots. Note that she remained in production for only two years. ❑

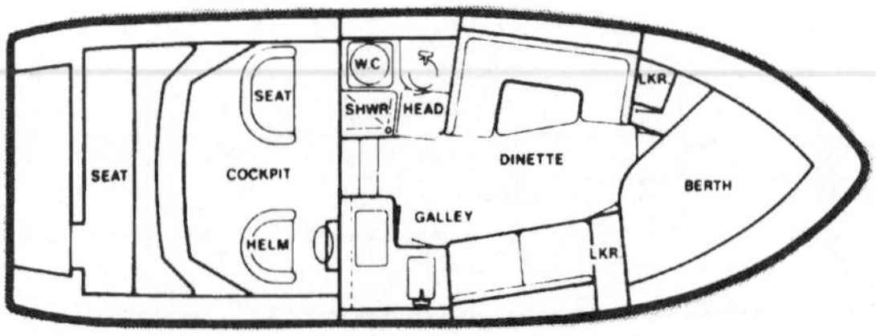

See Page 272 for Pricing Information

SILVERTON 31 CONV. (EARLY)

1977–81

1982–87

SPECIFICATIONS

Length ....31'0"	Fuel ....220 gals.
Beam ....11'11"	Cockpit ....82 sq. ft.
Draft ....2'11"	Hull Type ....Modified-V
Weight ....11,400#	Deadrise Aft ....NA
Clearance ....10'8"	Designer ....Silverton
Water ....40 gals.	Production 1977–87

A popular boat for many years, the appeal of the Silverton 31 Convertible (production ran for a full decade) had much to do with her roomy accommodations, attractive design, and affordable price tag. Compared with other convertibles and family sedans of her size, the Silverton 31 gets high marks for a spacious salon area (a rare luxury in a boat this small) with enough room to comfortably seat several guests without being cramped. Her large cockpit provides a good platform for swimming and casual fishing activities. On the downside, the flybridge is notably small with seating for three. The Silverton 31 Convertible received a major styling update in 1982, when the deckhouse was redesigned with a much-improved profile. Light oak interior woodwork was added in the 1985 model. Throughout her long production run the Silverton 31 Convertible retained the same basic interior floorplan with the galley and head forward and down from the salon. Among several engine options, a pair of 220-hp V-drive gas inboards will cruise the Silverton 31 Convertible around 17–18 knots and a top speed of about 27 knots. ❑

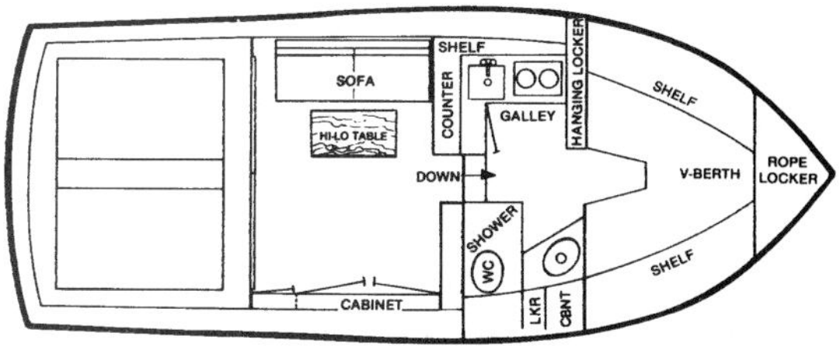

See Page 272 for Pricing Information

SILVERTON 31 CONVERTIBLE

SPECIFICATIONS

Length	31'2"	Water	84 gals.
Beam	11'8"	Fuel	250 gals.
Draft	3'0"	Hull Type	Modified-V
Weight	11,000#	Deadrise Aft	NA
Clearance	11'9"	Designer	Silverton
Cockpit	48 sq. ft.	Production	1991–95

The Silverton 31 is certainly one of the roomiest flybridge sedans in her size range and one of the least expensive as well. Introduced as the Silverton 31 Mid-Cabin in 1991, the original floorplan featured a small stateroom off the galley beneath the salon settee. In 1992, a second configuration (the 31 Convertible) eliminated the mid-cabin in favor of a larger galley. Of the two floorplans, the Convertible has the larger and more appealing salon. The Mid-Cabin's elevated dinette provides some needed headroom for the small stateroom below (accessed from a door in the galley) but robs the salon of some of its wide-open appeal. Either way, the spacious interior dimensions are a genuine surprise in a 31-foot boat. Both models have a pedestal island berth in the master stateroom, and a stall shower is included in the head. With such generous interior accommodations, it's no surprise that the cockpit is small. Standard 235-hp gas engines will cruise the Silverton 31 at a respectable 18-19 knots and deliver a top speed of about 26 knots. ❑

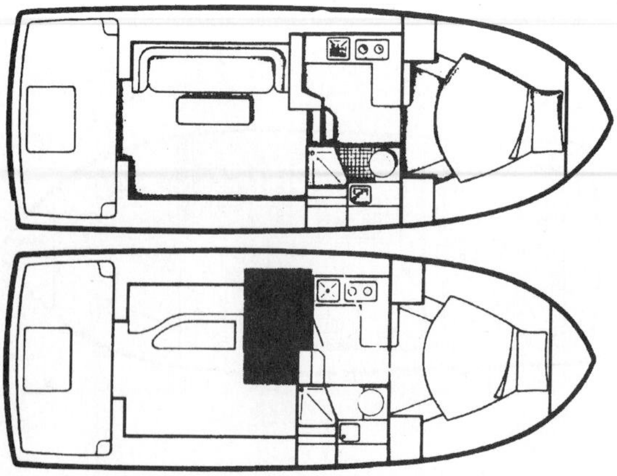

See Page 272 for Pricing Information

SILVERTON 31 GULFSTREAM

SPECIFICATIONS

Length	31'0"	Fuel	250 gals.
Beam	11'11"	Cockpit	115 sq. ft.
Draft	2'11"	Hull Type	Modified-V
Weight	9,500#	Deadrise Aft	NA
Clearance	NA	Designer	Bob Rioux
Water	40 gals.	Production	1979–86

When the Silverton 31 Gulfstream was introduced in 1979, she represented a dramatic break from Silverton's past market reliance on flybridge convertibles and family cruisers. Built on a solid fiberglass hull with a relatively wide beam, the 31 Gulfstream will appeal to those seeking an inexpensive dayboat with plenty of cockpit space and rather basic cabin accommodations. Indeed, she's a conservative design when measured against today's Eurostyle sportboats, although she was a popular boat for Silverton in the early 1980s. Inside, there are berths for four adults, along with a stand-up head and a compact galley. The Gulfstream was never offered with a radar arch or a curved windshield, but she does have a surprisingly big cockpit capable of accommodating a number of guests without being crowded. Twin 270-hp Crusaders were standard (18–19 knots cruise/28 top) with big-block 350-hp gas engines (around 24 knots cruise/32–33 knots top) offered as an option. Interestingly, V-drives were used through the 1982 model year, and in 1983 she was redesigned with straight inboards. ❑

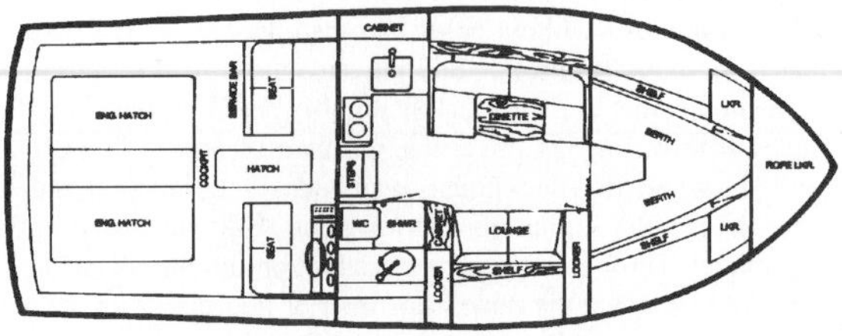

See Page 272 for Pricing Information

SILVERTON 310 EXPRESS

SPECIFICATIONS

Length ....31'10"	Fuel ....150 gals.
Beam ....11'6"	Waste ....35 gals.
Draft ....2'2"	Hull Type ....Modified-V
Weight ....9,500#	Deadrise Aft ....14°
Clearance ....9'1"	Designer ....Silverton
Water ....60 gals.	Production 1994–Current

A glitzy boat with her splashy hull graphics and a sculptured profile, the Silverton 310 Express is an affordably-priced mid-cabin family cruiser with a big interior and very good performance. Like all Silverton boats, the 310's hull is solid fiberglass, and her 11-foot, 6-inch beam is reasonably wide for a 30-footer. Going below, the entryway steps are suspended by aluminum weldments, and the open design makes the aft cabin—tucked below the cockpit—seem unusually spacious. There are berths for six, and the opening ports and deck hatches provide excellent cabin ventilation. The cockpit is arranged with three seating areas (including a double-wide helm seat that tilts up for use as a bolster), and the cockpit table can be converted into a sun pad. Additional features include a walk-thru windshield, privacy curtains for both staterooms, a fold-away transom seat, cockpit wet bar and fender racks built into the swim platform. Standard 230-hp 5.7-litre MerCruiser stern drives will cruise the 310 Express at 19-20 knots (35 knots top), and optional 300-hp 7.4-litre engines will deliver a 25-knot cruising speed and a top speed of around 36–37 knots. ❑

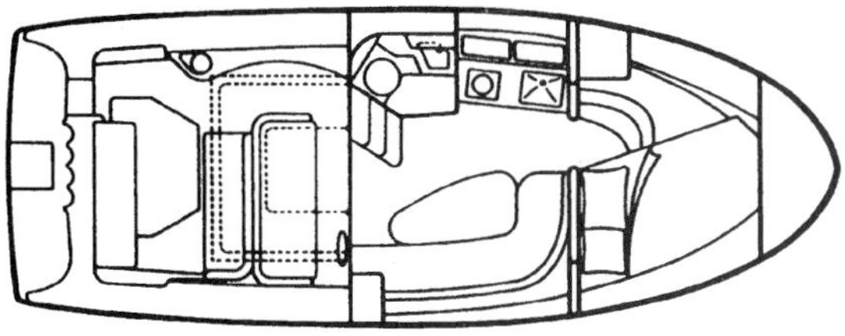

See Page 272 for Pricing Information

SILVERTON 312 SEDAN CRUISER

SPECIFICATIONS

Length w/Pulpit ....31'10"	Water ....60 gals.
Hull Length ....28'0"	Fuel ....150 gals.
Beam ....11'6"	Cockpit ....NA
Draft ....2'4"	Hull Type ....Modified-V
Weight ....10,500#	Deadrise Aft ....14°
Clearance ....10'6"	Production 1994–Current

One of the few Silvertons designed with stern drives, the 312 Sedan (originally called the 302 Sedan) is a budget-priced family cruiser with a stylish profile and a big interior. Hull construction is solid fiberglass, and her integral swim platform, rakish flybridge, and attractive hull graphics add much to her visual appeal. Below, the 312 has a rather unusual layout. The floorplan diagram (below) gives the appearance of a two-stateroom layout. Going aboard, however, reveals that the second stateroom is actually a pair of stacked bunk berths in the passageway across from the head. These berths extend below the salon settee and can be curtained-off at night for privacy. The salon—with its elevated dinette and wraparound windows—is surprisingly roomy, and the cherry wood cabinetry is a nice touch. Additional features include full-size dinette, a big flybridge with molded steps leading up from the cockpit, and fender racks built into the swim platform. Twin 190-hp MerCruiser I/Os will cruise the 312 Sedan at 17 knots and reach a top speed of around 29–30 knots. ❑

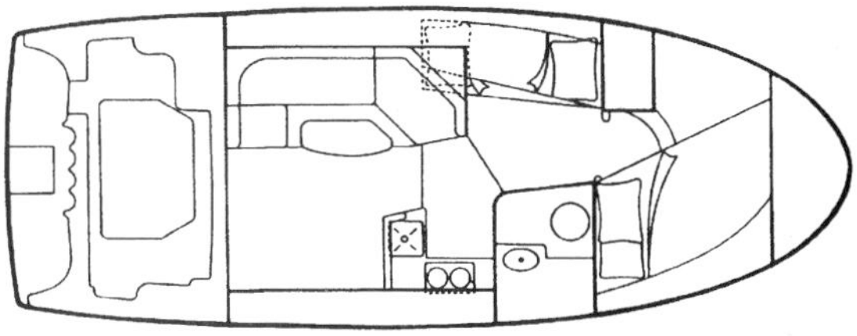

See Page 272 for Pricing Information

SILVERTON 33 SPORT SEDAN

SPECIFICATIONS

Length ....33'8"	Fuel ....220 gals.
Beam ....12'6"	Cockpit ....86 sq. ft.
Draft ....2'10"	Hull Type ....Modified-V
Weight ....12,000#	Deadrise Aft ....14°
Clearance ....11'1"	Designer ....J. Fielding
Water ....40 gals.	Production 1973–76

The 33 Sport Sedan was the top-of-the-line cruiser for Silverton back in the early 1970s. Because of her low price and durable construction, she turned out to be a fairly popular boat in her day, and used models are often encountered on the brokerage market. The hull, flybridge, and cockpit liner are constructed of molded fiberglass, while the deck and superstructure are marine plywood with a glass overlay. The 33 Sport Sedan will sleep up to six in two cabins—two forward in the V-berth and the others on the convertible dinette and fold-out settee. A lower helm was standard, and the cabin floor is a step down from the cockpit level. Both the head and galley are aft in the salon, where they're easily reached from outside. Large hatches in the cockpit sole provide good access to the engines (and V-drives), and the cockpit dimensions are surprisingly spacious. Twin 225-hp Chrysler gas engines deliver a cruising speed of around 19 knots and a top speed in the neighborhood of 28–29 knots. ❑

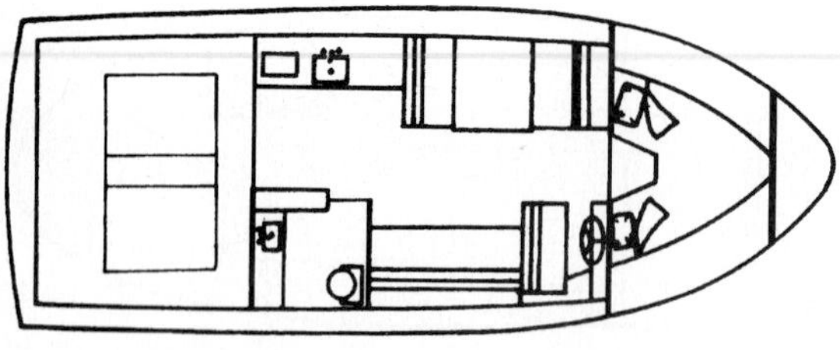

See Page 272 for Pricing Information

SILVERTON 34 SEDAN

SPECIFICATIONS

Length ....34'0"	Fuel ....220 gals.
Beam ....12'6"	Cockpit ....100 sq. ft.
Draft ....3'1"	Hull Type ....Modified-V
Weight ....12,500#	Deadrise Aft ....15°
Clearance ....11'6"	Designer ....Silverton
Water ....40 gals.	Production 1977–81

The Silverton 34 Sedan was conceived as a stylish (for the late 1970s) family cruiser with big-boat accommodations and an affordable price tag. She's built on a solid fiberglass hull with moderate beam, a fairly flat sheer, and considerable flare at the bow. Inside, the interior is arranged on a single level (no steps leading down to the forward stateroom), which creates the impression of a large and very open cabin. The inside helm was a standard feature, and the visibility is quite good considering the lowered salon level. Both the galley and head are located aft, just inside the salon door, where they're within easy reach of those outside. The cockpit is a step up from the salon level and measures a good 10'x10'—large for a 34-foot boat. Hatches in the cockpit sole provide good access to the motors and V-drive units. Chrysler 250-hp gas engines were standard with 270-hp Crusaders offered as options. Cruising speeds for both are in the neighborhood of 17 knots and top speeds are around 26–27 knots. ❑

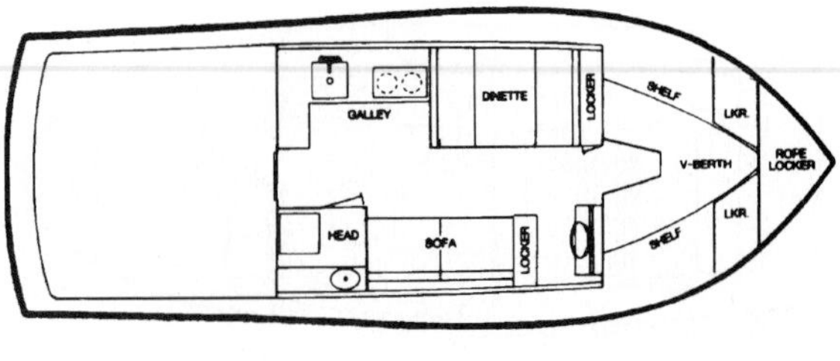

See Page 272 for Pricing Information

SILVERTON 34 CONV. (1978–88)

1978–82

1983–88

SPECIFICATIONS

Length	34'0"	Fuel	250 gals.
Beam	12'6"	Cockpit	70 sq. ft.
Draft	3'1"	Hull Type	Modified-V
Weight	12,500#	Deadrise Aft	15°
Clearance	13'3"	Designer	J. Fielding
Water	40 gals.	Production	1978–88

After a decade in production, the 34 Convertible proved to be Silverton's most popular boat ever. She's constructed on a solid fiberglass hull with average beam and moderate transom deadrise. In her original form, the 34 Convertible presents a somewhat conservative appearance—a white fiberglass cruiser with a sturdy, plain-Jane profile. That changed in 1983, when Silverton redesigned this boat by adding a more modern new deck and superstructure and eliminating the V-drives of previous years in favor of a conventional straight-drive engine installation. In 1985, a stall shower and double berth were added below along with a new light oak interior. With the dinette and sofa converted, there are overnight berths for up to six. Topside, the flybridge is on the small side. Several engine options were offered over the years, with the 270-hp Crusaders being among the most frequently seen in used models. A good performer, the Silverton 34 will cruise around 18 knots with a top speed of 27–28 knots. Note that the fuel capacity was increased from 220 to 250 gallons in 1983. ❑

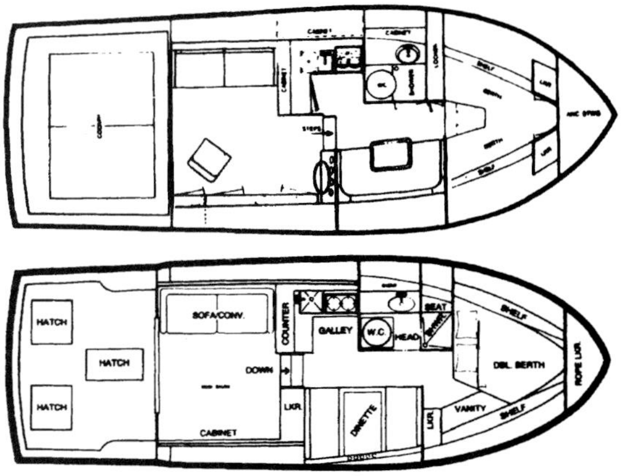

See Page 272 for Pricing Information

SILVERTON 34 CONV. (1989–90)

SPECIFICATIONS

Length	34'6"	Fuel	300 gals.
Beam	12'7"	Cockpit	56 sq. ft.
Draft	3'2"	Hull Type	Modified-V
Weight	13,500#	Deadrise Aft	17°
Clearance	13'5"	Designer	M. Peters
Water	40 gals.	Production	1989–90

Introduced in 1989 as a replacement for the Silverton's previous 34 Convertibles (previous page), this new, more rakish Silverton 34 lasted only two years in production before being replaced herself with an updated model in 1991. She was built on a deeper Vee hull than her predecessor with additional fuel capacity and an improved bottom design for better overall performance. Like all Silverton boats, hull construction is solid fiberglass. With her extended deckhouse and small cockpit, it's clear she was designed with family cruising in mind rather than fishing. The galley-and-dinette-down floorplan has a single stateroom, and the salon is finished out with pastel fabrics and oak woodwork. Full wraparound cabin windows make the interior seem wide open and very comfortable. Unlike the earlier Silverton 34 Convertibles, a lower helm was not standard. If the cockpit is on the small side, the flybridge — with the helm forward — is big for a 34-footer. Additional features include a transom door, swim platform and pulpit. Standard 350-hp Crusader inboards will cruise the Silverton 34 at 19–20 knots and reach a top speed of about 29 knots. ❑

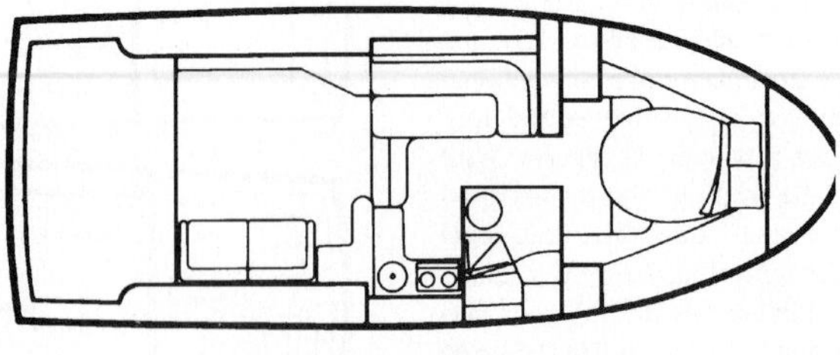

See Page 272 for Pricing Information

SILVERTON 34 CONV. (1991–95)

1991–1994

1995–95

SPECIFICATIONS

Length	34'6"	Fuel	300 gals.
Beam	12'10"	Waste	28 gals.
Draft	2'11"	Cockpit	56 sq. ft.
Weight	13,500#	Hull Type	Modified-V
Clearance	13'5"	Deadrise Aft	17°
Water	40 gals.	Production	1991–95

The Silverton 34 Convertible has always been a popular move-up cruiser for famalies graduating from 27- to 30-foot I/Os seeking the versatility of an inboard flybridge model. After building more than a thousand 34 Convertibles since 1978, Silverton introduced an updated version of this venerable boat in 1991 (photo above, top) with an all-new profile on the outside and an enlarged galley and stateroom on the inside. Hull construction is solid fiberglass, and her modified deep-V hull is a surprisingly easy ride when the seas pick up. While a single-stateroom layout was standard, an optional two-stateroom, dinette-up layout was also available. The sidedecks were also slightly widened in the new 34, and the non-skid patterns became a part of the mold rather than painted on. Additional features include a stall shower in the head, cockpit steps, side exhausts and a swim platform. Note that in 1995, a stylish new flybridge added much to her already-rakish profile. Standard 350-hp Crusader inboards will cruise the Silverton 34 at 19–20 knots and reach a top speed of about 29 knots. ❑

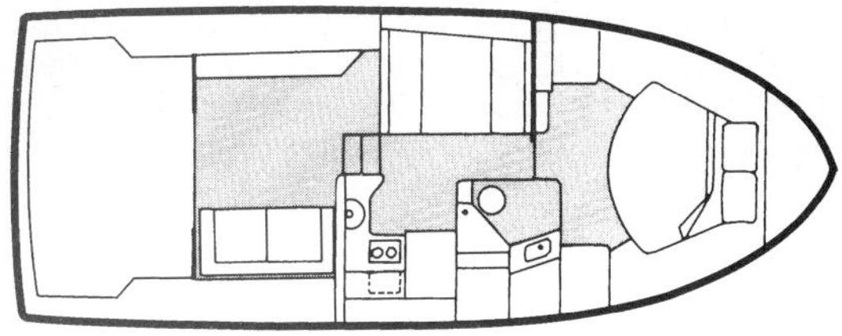

Standard Layout

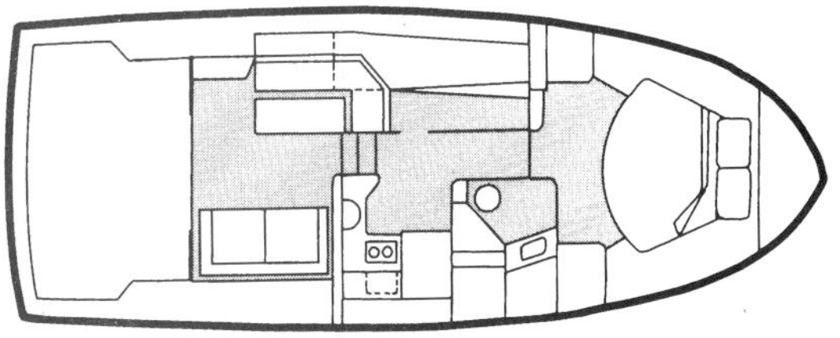

Two-Stateroom Layout (Optional)

See Page 272 for Pricing Information

SILVERTON 34X EXPRESS

SPECIFICATIONS

Length .... 34'6"	Fuel .... 250 gals.
Beam .... 12'7"	Cockpit .... 62 sq. ft.
Draft .... 3'8"	Hull Type .... Modified-V
Weight .... 11,000#	Deadrise Aft .... 17°
Clearance .... 12'7"	Designer .... M. Peters
Water .... 40 gals.	Production 1987–89

With her bolt-on swim platform, colorful hull graphics, and squared-off windshield, the original Silverton 34X looks a little dated by today's sportboat standards. She was built on a solid fiberglass hull with moderate beam and a relatively steep 17 degrees of transom deadrise. Inside, the mid-cabin floorplan is arranged with a big L-shaped settee to port and double berths in both staterooms. The aft cabin has a door for privacy, while the forward stateroom has only a curtain. Note that there's a stall shower in the head compartment. The cockpit provides plenty of outdoor seating space for guests, and a cut-out in the transom allows for easier boarding. Visibility from the raised helm position is excellent. A sunpad is fitted on the foredeck, although getting forward is difficult thanks to the narrow sidedecks. Hinged hatches in the cockpit sole provide good access to the engines and V-drives. A good-running boat in a chop, twin 350-hp Crusaders will cruise the Silverton 34X around 22 knots and reach a top speed of 30+ knots. ❑

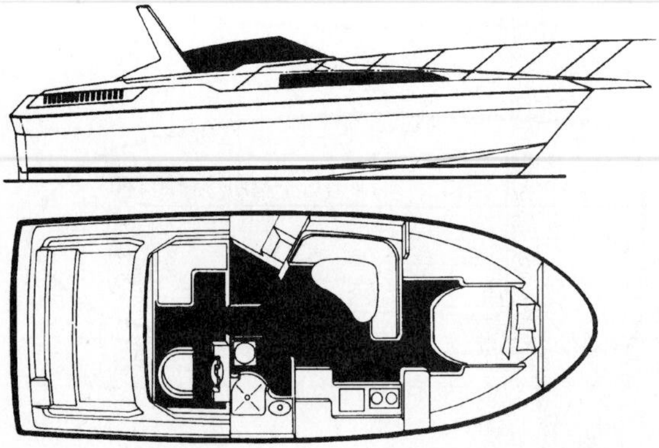

SILVERTON 34 EXPRESS

SPECIFICATIONS

Length .... 34'3"	Fuel .... 254 gals.
Beam .... 12'8"	Cockpit .... 62 sq. ft.
Draft .... 3'1"	Hull Type .... Modified-V
Weight .... 16,500#	Deadrise Aft .... 17°
Clearance .... 9'3"	Designer .... M. Peters
Water .... 47 gals.	Production 1990–94

The Silverton 34 Express is an affordably priced family cruiser with a modern sportboat profile to go with her spacious mid-cabin floorplan. (Indeed, it's only the absence of a curved windshield that keeps the 34 from being one of the more attractive express cruisers on the market.) Like all Silverton boats, hull construction is good old-fashioned solid fiberglass—only the decks are cored. Inside, the floorplan is arranged very similar to the earlier Silverton 34X (the boat she replaced in the fleet) with berths for six and a separate stall shower in the head. Only a privacy curtain divides the forward stateroom from the salon while a door closes off the mid-cabin. The bi-level cockpit features an L-shaped lounge opposite the helm, bench seating at the transom, and an aft deck wet bar. Additional features include a hydraulically operated engine access hatch, foredeck sunpad, radar arch, and transom door. Twin 454-cid gas engines (with V-drives) will cruise the Silverton 34 Express at 21 knots and deliver a top speed of 27–28 knots. ❑

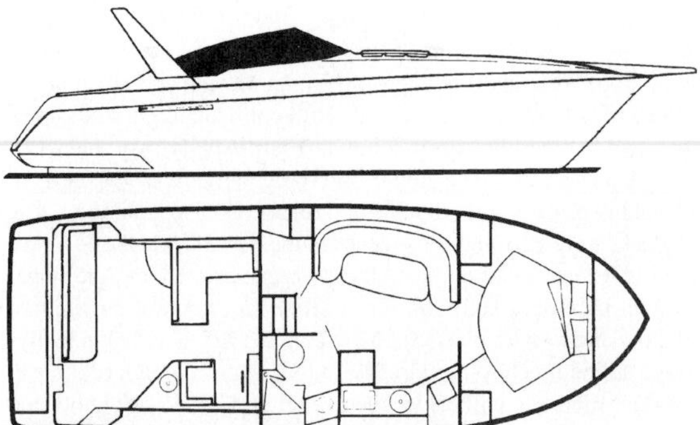

See Page 272 for Pricing Information

SILVERTON 361 EXPRESS

SPECIFICATIONS

Length	36'1"	Waste	40 gals.
Beam	12'11"	Clearance	11'0"
Draft	3'0"	Hull Type	Modified-V
Weight	14,314#	Deadrise Aft	14°
Fuel	300 gals.	Designer	Silverton
Water	100 gals.	Production	1995–Current

The gently curved lines, swept-back arch and vivid hull graphics of the Silverton 361 Express will appeal to those buyers seeking a stylish family cruiser at an affordable price. She's built on a solid fiberglass hull with a wide beam, prop pockets, and a handsome integrated swim platform. The mid-cabin floorplan of the 361 Express is arranged with double berths fore and aft, a full galley, and a circular dinette that converts into a double berth. There are privacy doors for both staterooms—a convenience seldom found in mid-cabin cruisers this size—and all of the galley cabinetry is cherry wood. There's comfortable seating in the cockpit for six, and the transom has built-in storage area and a hot-and-cold water shower. Lacking any sidedecks, a walk-through windshield provides access to the foredeck sun pad. Note the sporty air intake vents in the hullsides. Twin 320-hp Crusader gas inboards (with V-drives) will cruise the Silverton 361 Express at 22 knots and reach a top speed of around 32 knots. Note that stern drive power is available. ❑

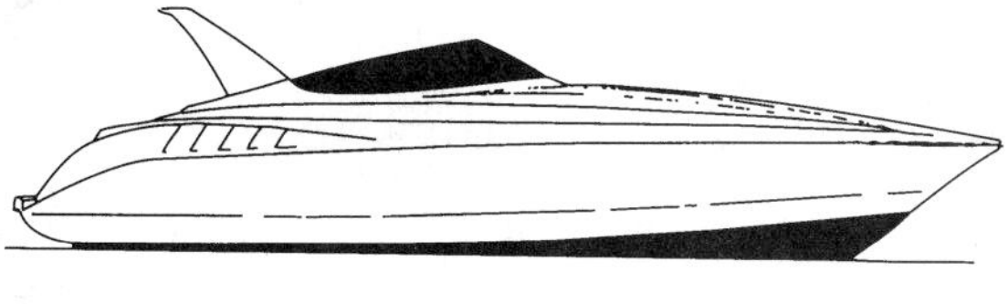

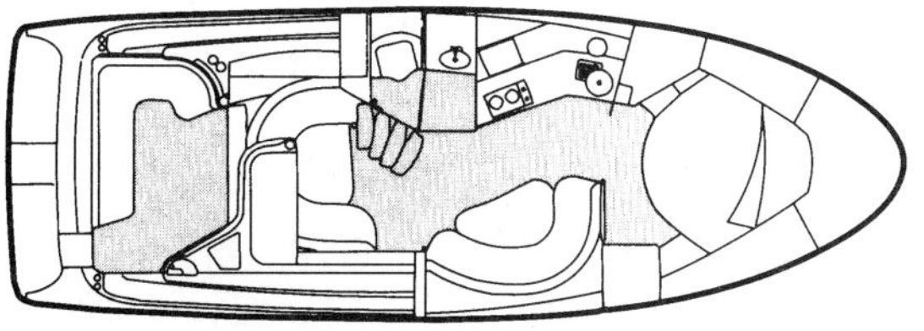

See Page 272 for Pricing Information

SILVERTON 362 SEDAN CRUISER

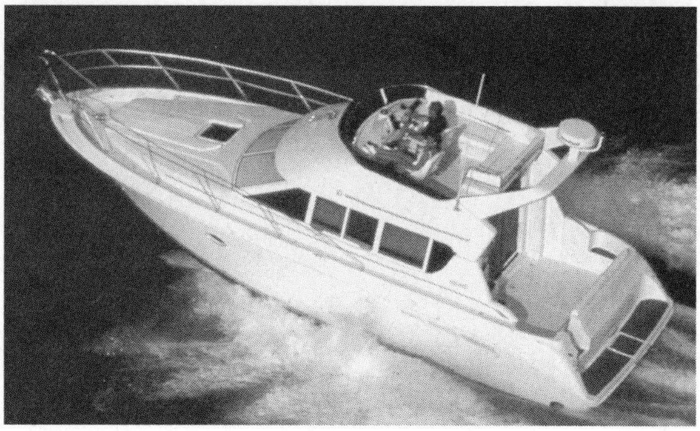

SPECIFICATIONS

Length	36'1"	Fuel	300 gals.
Beam	12'11"	Waste	40 gals.
Draft	3'0"	Hull Type	Modified-V
Weight	15,058#	Deadrise Aft	17°
Clearance	13'0"	Designer	Silverton
Water	100 gals.	Production	1994–Current

A good-looking boat with an attractive deckhouse profile, the Silverton 362 is an affordably priced family cruiser with a lot of living space packed into her 36-foot hull. She's built on a solid fiberglass hull with a wide beam and a relatively steep 17 degrees of transom deadrise. The two-stateroom floorplan is arranged with a mid-level galley and an island berth in the forward stateroom. The guest stateroom (which extends beneath the salon settee) has two single berths that convert into a queen berth with a filler. Note the split head/shower compartments—a great idea that allows someone to take a shower without tying up the head. With her spacious interior dimensions, it's no surprise that the 362's cockpit is on the small side. Two hatches in the sole provide easy access to the engines, and molded steps lead up to the oversize flybridge with its wrap-around lounge seating. Additional features include excellent cabin headroom, side exhausts, and fold-down bench seating at the transom. Twin 315-hp V-drive Crusaders gas inboards will cruise at 18 knots and deliver 28–29 knots top. ❑

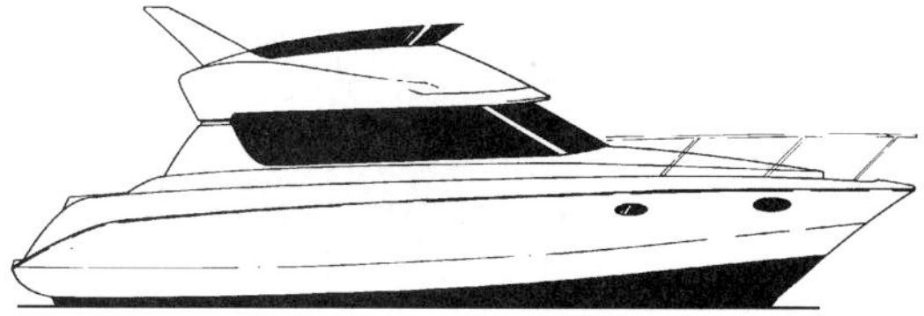

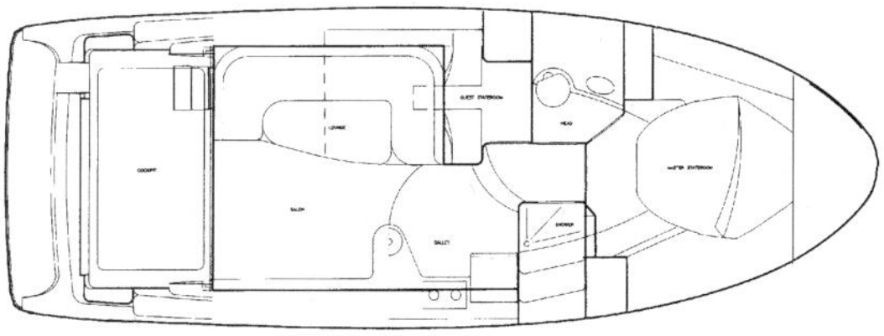

See Page 273 for Pricing Information

SILVERTON 37 CONV. (EARLY)

SPECIFICATIONS

Length	37'0"	Fuel	300 gals.
Beam	14'0"	Cockpit	75 sq. ft.
Draft	3'7"	Hull Type	Modified-V
Weight	20,000#	Deadrise Aft	14°
Clearance	12'6"	Designer	Bob Rioux
Water	100 gals.	Production	1980–89

Clean lines, excellent versatility, and an attractive price combined to made the Silverton 37 Convertible one of the most popular boats in her class during the past decade. Unlike many other convertibles this size, the Silverton 37 has a single-stateroom floorplan with a full-size dinette in place of a second stateroom. The salon is completely open to the galley in this layout, and the 360-degree wraparound windows make the salon seem unusually spacious and inviting. There's a stall shower in the head, and light oak paneling is applied throughout the interior. (Teak woodwork is found in pre-1985 models.) The cockpit is large enough for a couple of anglers, and the flybridge is arranged with guest seating forward of the helm. Twin 200-hp Perkins diesels were standard in early models, but the majority of Silverton 37s were powered with twin 350-hp Crusader gas engines. The cruising speed is 18–19 knots, and the top speed is around 29 knots. Note that Silverton engineers replaced the original V-drive engine installations with straight-drives in 1981. ❑

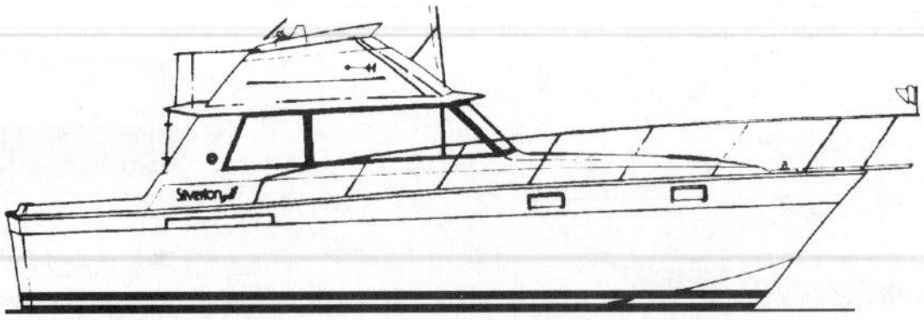

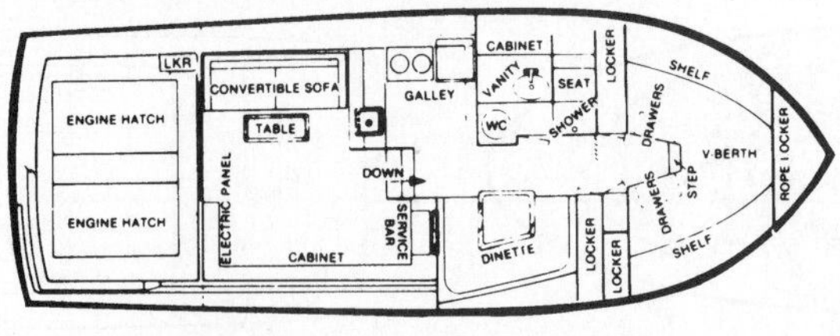

See Page 273 for Pricing Information

SILVERTON 37 CONVERTIBLE

SPECIFICATIONS

Length w/Pulpit	41'3"	Water	100 gals.
Hull Length	37'4"	Fuel	375 gals.
Beam	13'11"	Waste	40 gals.
Draft	3'7"	Hull Type	Modified-V
Weight	21,852#	Deadrise Aft	17°
Clearance	18'2"	Production	1990–Current

With her rakish lines and a budget-level price, the newest Silverton 37 (the original 37 Convertible ran from 1980 to 1989) is simply a lot of boat for the money. She's built on a solid fiberglass modified-V hull with a wide beam and a fairly steep 17 degrees of transom deadrise. The original single-stateroom floorplan had the galley and dinette down and a centerline queen berth forward. In 1993, Silverton engineers redesigned the interior with a larger salon while also offering an optional two-stateroom layout (at the expense of the dinette). While the Silverton 37 is more family cruiser than fishboat, the cockpit is still roomy enough for a couple of light-tackle anglers and features an in-deck fish box, padded coaming, and a transom door. The flybridge seats six with bench seating forward of the helm, and the well-planned console has space for flush-mounting electronics. Additional features include wide sidedecks, a separate stall shower in the head, and side-dumping exhausts. No racehorse, standard 454-cid gas engines (320-hp) will cruise the 37 Convertible at 15–16 knots with a top speed of about 25 knots. ❑

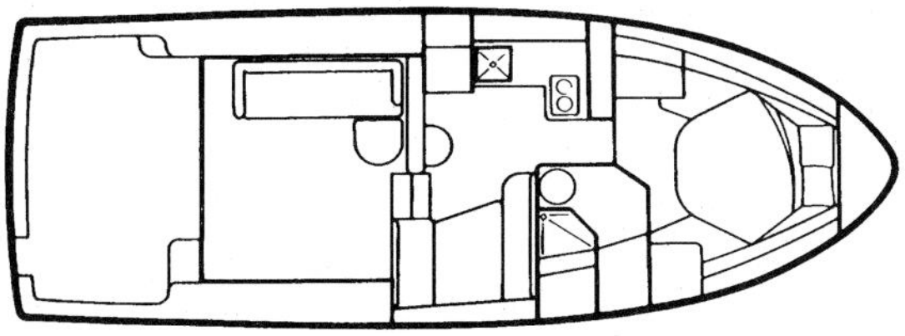

Single-Stateroom Floorplan (1989–92)

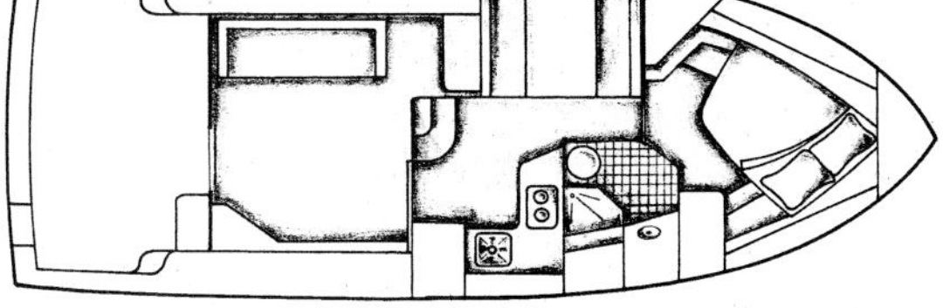

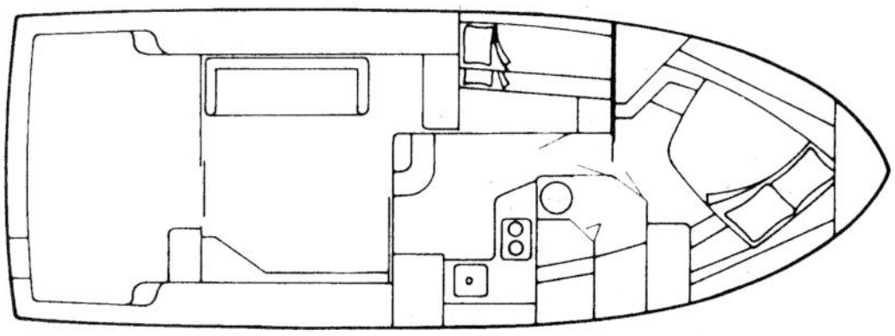

Single & Two-Stateroom Floorplans (1993–Current)

See Page 273 for Pricing Information

SILVERTON 38 EXPRESS

SPECIFICATIONS

Length	37'7"	Fuel	300 gals.
Beam	13'11"	Cockpit	NA
Draft	3'7"	Hull Type	Modified-V
Weight	21,000#	Deadrise Aft	17°
Clearance	9'9"	Designer	M. Peters
Water	110 gals.	Production	1990–94

Introduced as the 38X in 1990, the Silverton 38 Express is a wide-body family cruiser with modern styling, a big cockpit, and a traditional mid-cabin layout. She's built on the same hull used for the 37 Convertible—a solid fiberglass modified-V with a wide beam and plenty of transom deadrise. Below, the floorplan is arranged with double berths in both staterooms, a big U-shaped dinette, and a roomy head with a separate stall shower. A cluster of six overhead skylights provide excellent cabin lighting, and the liberal use of mirrors makes the interior seem unusually spacious. Sold with a long list of standard equipment, the 38 Express has a well-arranged bi-level cockpit with a companion seat and sun lounge opposite the helm. A wet bar and ice maker were standard, and a walk-through transom door opens to the integral swim platform. Twin 502-cid Crusader gas engines (with V-drives) will cruise the 38 Express at 22–23 knots and deliver a top speed of around 30 knots. Note that 425-hp Cats were optional. ❑

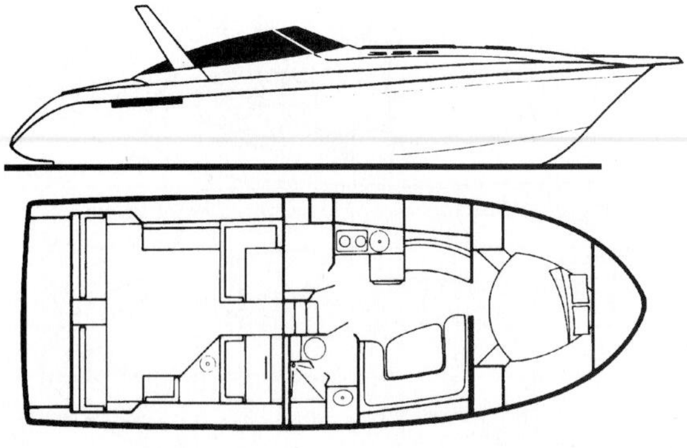

See Page 273 for Pricing Information

SILVERTON 40 CONVERTIBLE

SPECIFICATIONS

Length	40'0"	Fuel	300 gals.
Beam	14'0"	Cockpit	79 sq. ft.
Draft	3'0"	Hull Type	Modified-V
Weight	23,000#	Deadrise Aft	NA
Clearance	13'6"	Designer	Bob Rioux
Water	100 gals.	Production	1985–90

A conservatively styled boat with a distinctive profile (note the stepped sheer), the Silverton 40 Convertible was one of the lowest-priced sedan cruisers available in her class during the late 1980s. She was clearly designed to appeal to the weekend cruiser market and came equipped with just about everything required for immediate use. During the first few years of production her two-stateroom floorplan was arranged with the galley and dinette forward in the salon—a layout that required the galley sole to be sunken in order to have any headroom. In 1989, the interior was redesigned with the galley and dinette down in the conventional manner. Both floorplans included a separate stall shower in the head. Notably, an inside helm was never offered. Outside, the cockpit is large enough for a couple of anglers, and the wide sidedecks make for easy foredeck access. No racehorse with the standard 350-hp Crusader gas engines, the Silverton 40 will cruise at 15–16 knots and reach a top speed of 25 knots. Note that Cat diesels were optional. ❑

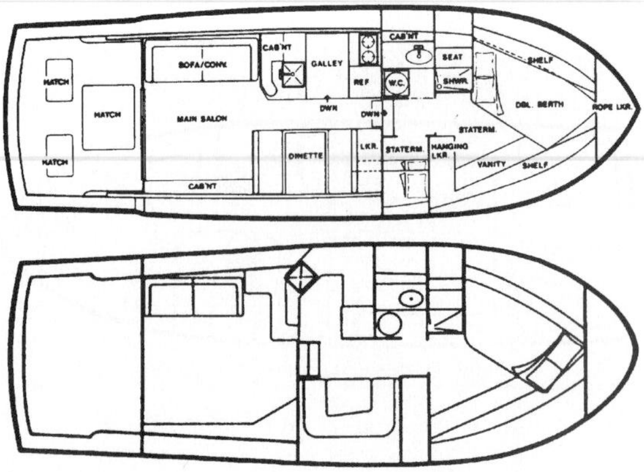

See Page 273 for Pricing Information

SILVERTON 41 CONVERTIBLE

SPECIFICATIONS

Length w/Pulpit	46'3"	Water	200 gals.
Hull Length	41'3"	Fuel	516 gals.
Beam	14'10"	Waste	40 gals.
Draft	3'7"	Hull Type	Modified-V
Weight	27,000#	Deadrise Aft	17°
Clearance	15'5"	Production	1991–Current

The Silverton 41 Convertible is a moderately priced sedan cruiser with a clean-cut profile and a practical two-stateroom interior layout. With her long foredeck, step-down sheer, and raked bridge, the 41 has the look of a sportfisherman (although Silvertons have never been noted for building tournament-level boats). The cockpit is large enough for a fighting chair, and there's a good-size fish box below the sole. Inside, wraparound cabin windows provide excellent natural lighting. The light oak interior is arranged with the galley and (big) dinette down from the salon level, a double-entry head with a stall shower, over/under single berths in the guest cabin, and an island berth in the master stateroom. Additional features include a reasonably spacious flybridge with plenty of seating, side exhausts, transom door, and swim platform. A good-selling model, standard 502-cid gas engines will cruise the Silverton 41 Convertible at 19–20 knots (about 28 knots top), and the optional 425-hp Caterpillar diesels will cruise at 24–25 knots and reach 28 knots wide open. ❑

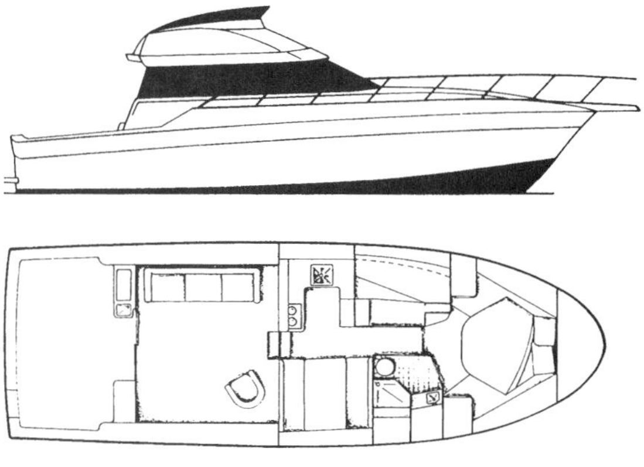

See Page 273 for Pricing Information

TEMPEST 42 SPORT YACHT

SPECIFICATIONS

Length	42'0"	Fuel	375 gals.
Beam	12'6"	Cockpit	NA
Draft	2'10"	Hull Type	Deep-V
Weight	19,000#	Deadrise Aft	21°
Clearance	NA	Designer	Baglietto
Water	75 gals.	Production	1988–92

The Italian profile of the Tempest 42 is more than just skin deep; she was originally designed and built for the Mediterranean market by Baglietto, the Italian motor yacht builder. Tempest purchased the molds in 1988 and quickly redesigned the bottom, revised the interior layout, and added Tempest's unique "T-Torque" fixed-drive system. The 42 was a limited production boat, and fewer than a dozen were built. Perhaps the most attractive feature of the 42 is her sculptured cockpit with curved lounge seating, circular sunpad, and gorgeous helm console. There's one basic interior layout, and the decor is high-style Italian with plenty of off-white laminates, rich fabrics, and designer furnishings and appliances. Additional features include an open transom, reverse radar arch, hand rails for the swim platform (nice touch), and the notable lack of any foredeck rails or a bow pulpit. The Tempest 42 Sport Yacht is a real performer. With standard 375-hp Cat diesels, she'll cruise easily at 33 knots and reach a top speed of about 37 knots. Larger GM 6V92TAs were optional. ❑

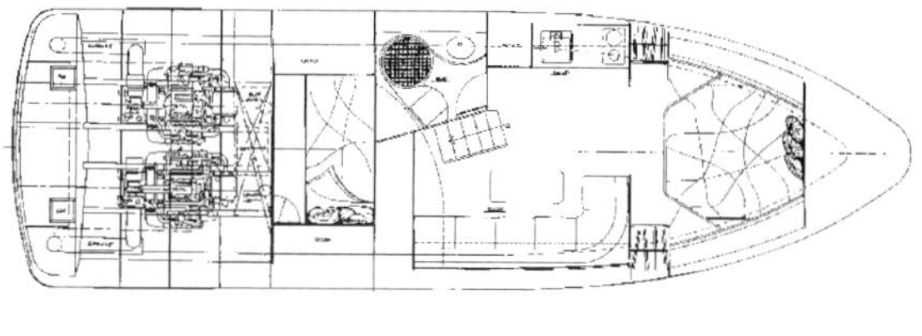

See Page 273 for Pricing Information

TEMPEST 60 SPORT YACHT

SPECIFICATIONS

Length ....60'0"	Water......................250 gals.
Length WL......................NA	Fuel ....1,000 gals.
Beam.............................15'9"	Hull Type ....Modified-V
Draft ....3'6"	Deadrise Aft....................21°
Weight......................50,000#	Designer ....P. Scanu
Clearance........................NA	Production 1988–92

The Tempest 60 was a limited production high-performance sportboat with a thoroughly European profile and an upscale price tag. Fully half of her length is given over to a huge bi-level cockpit which includes a collapsible sun lounge, fore and aft bench seating, and wet bar. Her space-age helm console—with retractable electronics pod and single-level controls—is impressive. The high-style interior of the Tempest is a striking blend of mirrored walls, lacquered cabinetry, indirect lighting and suede wall coverings. While the interior dimensions are modest for a 60-footer, the master stateroom (aft, under the bridgedeck) is quite large and features a bathtub in the head. The guest stateroom is forward, and there's a third sleeping area in a small compartment abaft the engine room. With Tempest's unique "T-Torque" drive system, the shafts (fixed at an 8-degree down-angle) extend through the transom. The Tempest 60 performs well at speed (when the props are partially exposed) and in shallow water. Standard 1,050-hp Cats provide an exhilarating 35-knot cruising speed and 40+ knots top. ❑

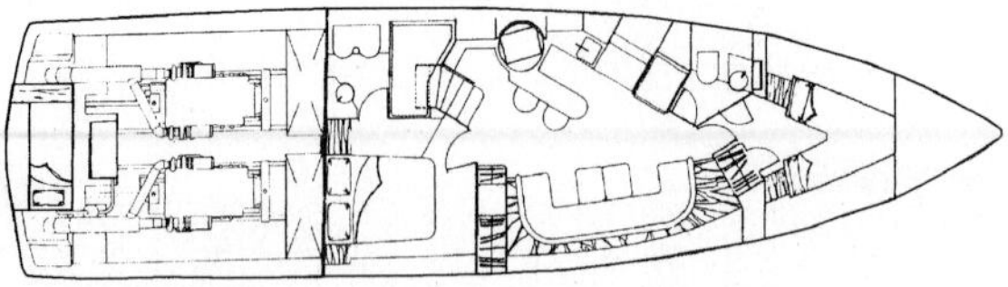

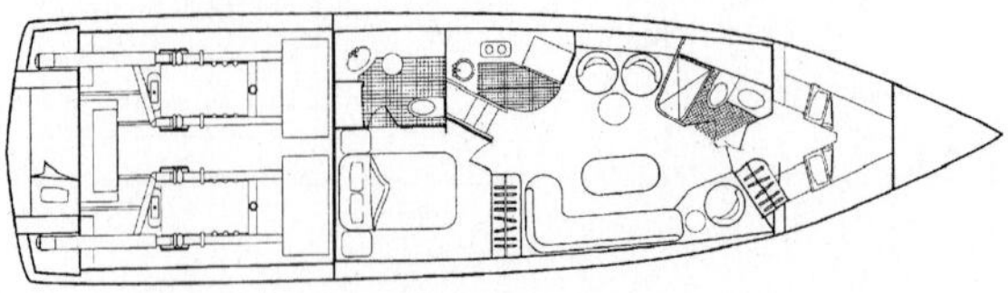

See Page 273 for Pricing Information

THOMPSON 3100 SANTA CRUZ

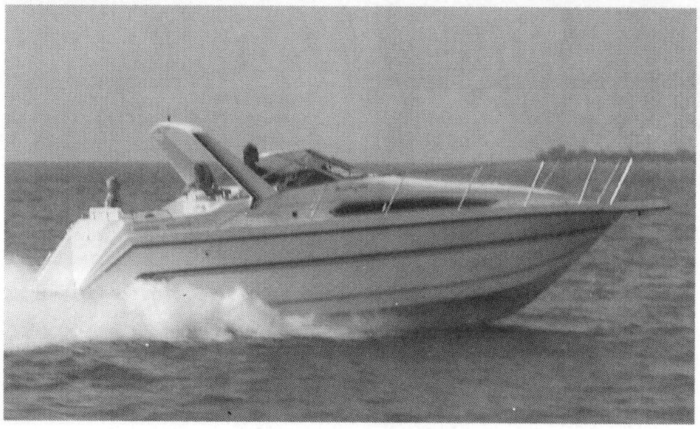

SPECIFICATIONS

Length w/Pulpit..........33'0"	Water........................42 gals.
Hull Length..................31'9"	Clearance w/Arch.........8'2"
Beam.............................11'4"	Hull Type................Deep-V
Draft...............................2'7"	Deadrise Aft....................18°
Weight......................11,200#	Designer.............Thompson
Fuel.........................208 gals.	Production....1991–Current

The Thompson 3100 Santa Cruz (note that she was called the 310 Santa Cruz when she was introduced in 1991) is an affordably priced mid-cabin family express with contemporary lines, a very roomy interior and twin stern drive power. She's constructed on a solid fiberglass hull with a wide beam and a relatively steep 18 degrees of deadrise at the transom. The interior of the Santa Cruz, with its wide beam and excellent headroom, is big for a 31-footer because the cabin bulkhead is set well aft into what might be considered the cockpit area in other boats her size. There are double berths fore and aft (each with a privacy curtain) as well as a complete galley, an enclosed head with a sit-down shower, and a convertible dinette. Outside, the flush cockpit has a double-wide seat at the helm and bench seating for three at the transom. Since there's no windshield walk-through, passangers must use the narrow walkarounds to reach the bow. A good performer, twin 250-hp 5.7-litre Volvo I/Os will cruise the Thompson 3100 at 25 knots and reach a top speed of nearly 40 knots. ❑

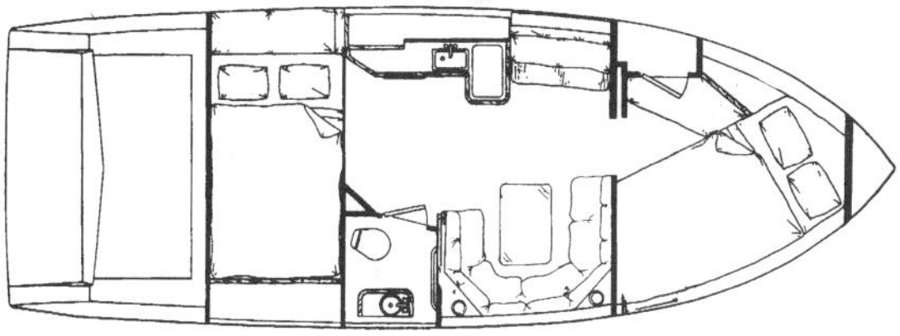

See Page 273 for Pricing Information

THUNDERCRAFT 280 EXPRESS

SPECIFICATIONS

Length w/Pulpit..........30'0"	Water........................20 gals.
Hull Length..................28'0"	Fuel...........................90 gals.
Beam.............................10'0"	Hull Type................Deep-V
Draft...............................2'9"	Deadrise Aft....................19°
Weight........................7,210#	Designer.........Thundercraft
Clearance........................9'2"	Production..............1989–95

A popular model during her seven-year production run, the Thundercraft 280 Express is a well-arranged mid-cabin cruiser with a modern sportboat profile on the outside and family-size accommodations below. She's built in Quebec on a solid fiberglass hull with moderate beam and relatively high freeboard for standing headroom in the cabin. Inside, there are berths for six (with the dinette converted), and both fore and aft sleeping areas have privacy curtains. Storage is quite good—better than many other family cruisers her size—and the hardware, furnishings and fabrics are all of good quality. Outside, her wraparound windshield and integral swim platform give the Thundercraft 280 a modern sportboat appearance. Lounge seating is provided for six in the cockpit and narrow sidedecks provide access to the sun pad on the foredeck. A good-running boat, twin 175-hp MerCruiser V-6 stern drives (standard) will cruise the 280 Express at 22–23 knots and deliver a top speed of 35 knots. Range, with just 90 gallons of fuel, is very limited. ❑

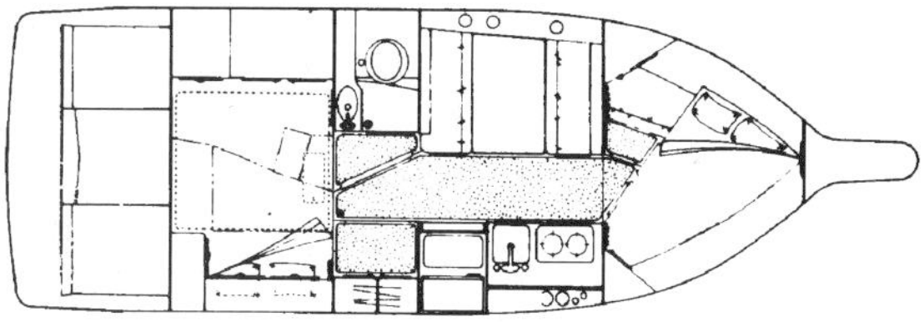

See Page 273 for Pricing Information

THUNDERCRAFT 350 EXPRESS

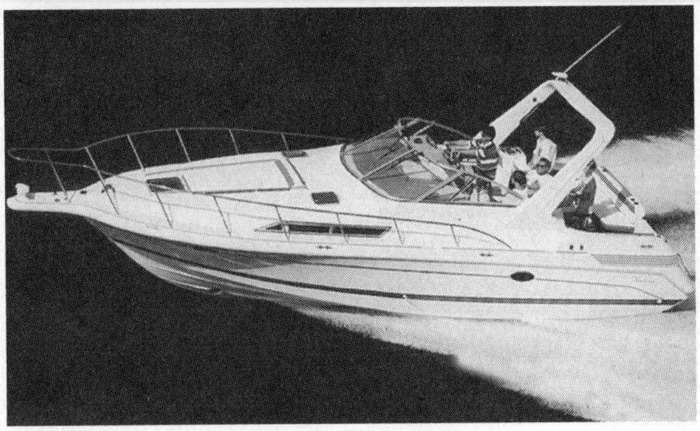

SPECIFICATIONS

Length w/Pulpit........36'10"	Water........................32 gals.
Hull Length.................35'0"	Fuel.........................210 gals.
Beam.............................12'0"	Hull Type................Deep-V
Draft...............................3'2"	Deadrise Aft....................20°
Weight......................11,904#	Designer.........Thundercraft
Clearance.......................9'2"	Production.............1993–95

The Thundercraft 350 Express is a good-quality Canadian cruiser with a modern sportboat profile and a roomy mid-cabin interior. Built on a fully cored hull, her wraparound windshield and integral swim platform add much to her appearance. However, the use of stern drives may raise a few eyebrows since inboards are generally preferred in a boat this size. Below, a single-piece inner liner saves money in building out the interior (while adding strength to the boat) and creates a more open and spacious feeling in the cabin. Although the decor is somewhat conservative, the detailing is above average, and the fabrics and hardware are first rate. Outside, an L-shaped lounge is opposite the helm on the bridgedeck, and the fold-down bench seat at the transom is removable. Additional features include fender storage in the transom, foredeck sunpad, and a stylish helm console. The 210-gallon fuel capacity is light for a 35-footer. Standard 330-hp 7.4-litre MerCruiser I/Os will cruise at an easy 22 knots and reach about 35 knots top. ❑

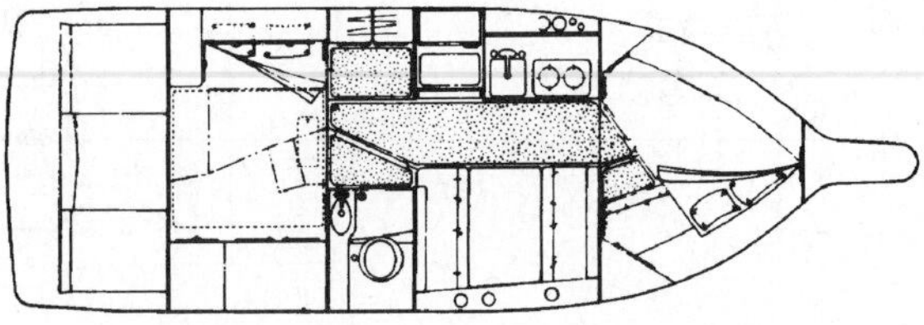

See Page 273 for Pricing Information

TIARA 250 SPORTBOAT

SPECIFICATIONS

Length	25'0"	Clearance	5'11"
Beam	8'11"	Cockpit Length	10'4"
Draft	2'8"	Hull Type	Deep-V
Weight	4,800#	Deadrise Aft	20°
Fuel	85 gals.	Designer	Tiara
Water	12 gals.	Production	1991–93

Those seeking a stylish, top-quality runabout would do well to keep their eyes open for a used Tiara 250 Sportboat. Hands down, this is one of the best looking dayboats around with a practical layout and a host of innovative features. She's built on a solid fiberglass, deep-V hull with a relatively wide beam and a fully integrated swim platform. More sportboat than cruiser, the 250's styling includes a beautifully curved windshield, no pulpit, and a sleek, low-profile appearance. The cuddy cabin contains a V-berth/dinette forward in addition to a compact galley. A slide-out portable toilet is concealed beneath the cockpit step in the cabin. There's sitting headroom below and generous storage in an otherwise small cabin. The single-level cockpit is the focal point in this design with wide-open spaces and lounge seating for a crowd. Note that there are lockable stowage compartments in the swim platform. Not an inexpensive boat when she was new, a single 7.4-litre MerCruiser stern drive will cruise the 250 Sportboat at a brisk 25 knots (about 38 knots top.) ❑

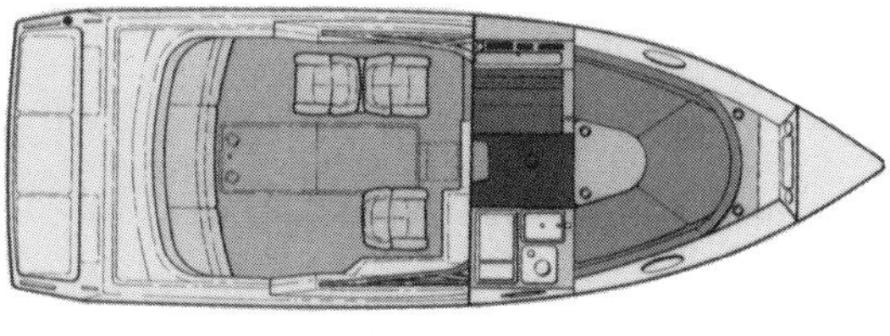

See Page 273 for Pricing Information

TIARA 260 SPORTBOAT

SPECIFICATIONS

Length	26'0"	Clearance	6'8"
Beam	8'9"	Cockpit Length	9'0"
Draft	2'8"	Hull Type	Deep-V
Weight	5,200#	Deadrise Aft	20°
Fuel	100 gals.	Designer	Tiara
Water	20 gals.	Production	1991–93

Like her smaller sistership (the 250 Sportboat), the Tiara 260 is a four-star combination of outstanding styling, superb craftmanship, and excellent use of interior space. Where other mid-cabin boats her size look bulky and often topheavy, Tiara designers gave up some interior headroom (which is still 5 feet, 10 inches) in exchange for a lower foredeck profile. The result is a great-looking boat that stands out prominently in a crowd of me-too small day cruisers. The stylish and well-finished interior features berths for four as well as a small galley, plenty of storage, and an enclosed head with sink and shower. The cockpit has a curved lounge opposite the helm, a nice instrument console, and bench seating aft with engine access under. A fresh water shower and stowage compartments are found in the swim platform. Hull construction is solid fiberglass and, at just over 5,000 lbs., the Tiara 260's brisk performance is surprising with just a single engine. The cruising speed with a 7.4-litre MerCruiser stern drive is 23–24 knots, and the top speed is about 36 knots. ❑

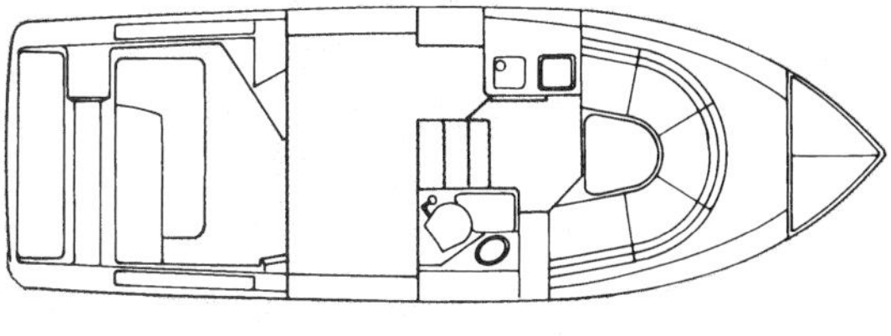

See Page 273 for Pricing Information

TIARA 2700 CONTINENTAL

SPECIFICATIONS

Length	27'6"	Clearance	7'0"
Beam	9'10"	Cockpit Length	11'0"
Hull Draft	2'8"	Hull Type	Deep-V
Weight	7,400#	Deadrise Aft	20°
Fuel	137 gals.	Designer	L. Slikkers
Water	24 gals.	Production	1982–87

The 2700 Continental was one of the first express cruisers ever built by Tiara, a company whose reputation was made for its series of high-quality saltwater fishing boats. Hull construction is solid fiberglass, and her deep-V bottom and relatively wide beam provide a stable and comfortable ride in a chop. Although dated by today's sportboat standards, the 2700 was a very contemporary boat back in the mid-1980s. Indeed, her oval ports and the absence of a bow pulpit were clearly ahead of their time. Below decks, the plush interior is arranged with a V-berth/dinette forward and a double berth in the private aft cabin—comfortable accommodations for four adults. The cabin furnishings and fixtures are top quality, and there's near-standing headroom in the head and galley. Additional features included a double-wide helm seat, a beautifully crafted aluminum windshield, bench seating at the transom, a swim platform and good access to the engines. Twin 260-hp MerCruiser stern drives will cruise the Tiara 2700 Continental at 24–25 knots and deliver a top speed of 36+ knots. ❑

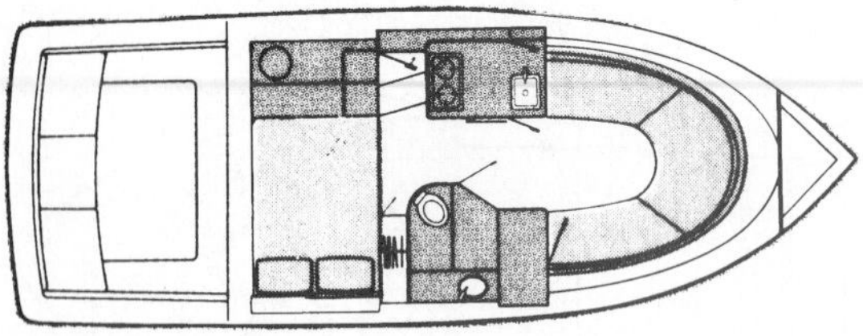

See Page 273 for Pricing Information

TIARA 2700 OPEN

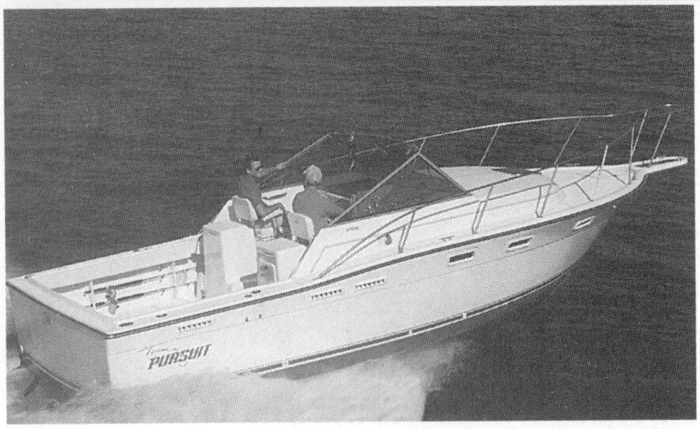

SPECIFICATIONS

Length w/Pulpit	29'5"	Water	20 gals.
Hull Length	27'0"	Fuel	240 gals.
Beam	10'0"	Hull Type	Deep-V
Draft	2'0"	Deadrise Aft	22°
Weight	7,500#	Designer	L. Slikkers
Clearance	7'0"	Production	1988–93

The Tiara 2700 Open is essentially the same boat as the Pursiut 2700 (1983–1993) without the Pursuit's fishing package, i.e. tackle centers. She's built on a deep-V hull with moderate beam, balsa-cored hullsides and a steep 22 degrees of deadrise at the transom—a good offshore design with proven handling characteristics. The popularity of this boat has much to do with her built-in versatility. As a fisherman, her spacious single-level cockpit is completely uncluttered and large enough for a mounted chair. As a family cruiser, the 2700 Open offers the advantages of inboard power (most of her competitors have outboards) and a proven offshore hull to go with her upscale interior. The interior is well arranged with V-berths/dinette forward, a compact galley and a stand-up head with shower. The detailing is excellent. Additional features include engine boxes, wide side decks, pulpit and swim platform. Resale values are above average and a measure of this boat's overall quality. Standard 350-cid gas engines will cruise the Tiara 2700 around 23 knots with a top speed of 30–31 knots. ❑

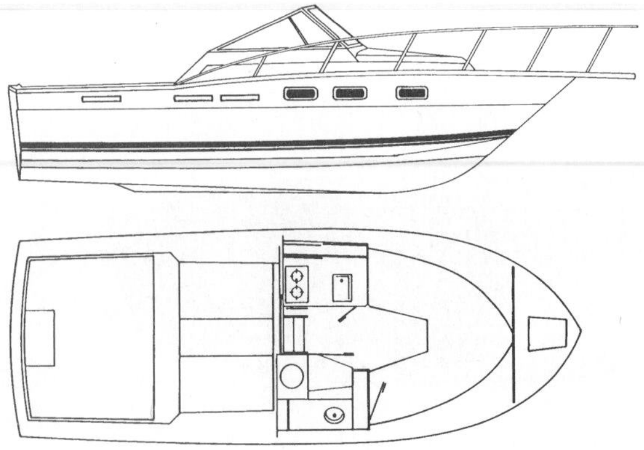

See Page 273 for Pricing Information

TIARA 270 SPORTBOAT

SPECIFICATIONS

Length w/Pulpit .... 31'7"	Water .... 30 gals.
Hull Length .... 29'8"	Clearance w/Arch .... 8'8"
Beam .... 10'7"	Hull Type .... Deep-V
Hull Draft .... 1'10"	Deadrise Aft .... 20°
Weight .... 8,000#	Designer .... Tiara
Fuel .... 126 gals.	Production 1991–93

Still beautiful today in spite of the fact that she's been out of production for several years, the Euro-styling of the Tiara 270 Sportboat is reflected in her graceful profile, her integrated transom platform and bow pulpit, and the sculptured oval hull ports. She's built on a beamy, deep-V hull and, while there's 6 feet, 4 inches of headroom below, the 270 Sportboat manages to avoid the topheavy look of many other maxi-cube express boats her size. The mid-cabin floorplan will sleep five (note the athwartship berth just forward of the circular dinette) and includes a small galley and an enclosed stand-up head and shower. The high-end fabrics and quality furnishings found in the 270 are typical of a Tiara product, and the interior is very fashionable indeed. The cockpit has a curved lounge for four opposite the helm and bench seating aft. Additional features include wide walkarounds, a wide swim platform, radar arch and anchor locker. Among several stern drive engine options, twin 230-hp 5.7-litre MerCruisers will cruise at 25 knots and reach 40+ knots wide open. ❑

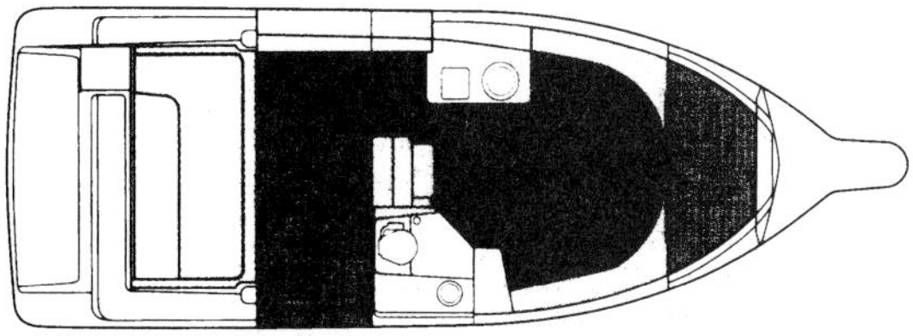

See Page 273 for Pricing Information

TIARA 2900 OPEN

SPECIFICATIONS

Length w/Pulpit .... 30'9"	Water .... 30 gals.
Hull Length .... 28'9"	Fuel .... 200 gals.
Beam .... 11'4"	Cockpit .... 60 sq. ft.
Hull Draft .... 2'2"	Hull Type .... Deep-V
Weight .... 10,000#	Deadrise Aft .... 19°
Clearance .... 7'8"	Production 1993–Current

With her conservative styling and quality construction, the Tiara 2900 Open will appeal to those looking for an upscale express cruiser with genuine offshore capabilities. She's built on a proven deep-V hull design with cored hullsides, a wide beam, and a relatively steep 19 degrees of deadrise at the transom. Note the lack of an integrated swim platform—the 2900 retains a traditional full-height transom configuration with a bolt-on platform. Unlike most other contemporary family sportboats, the 2900 does not have a mid-cabin interior layout (but neither does she require the V-drives found in mid-cabin designs to deliver the power). The cabin appointments are lush indeed, and the level of finish is excellent. Additional features include hide-away bench seating at the transom, a hinged helm console, molded pulpit, and a transom door. The bridge deck can be raised hydraulically for engine access. Standard 260-hp gas inboards will cruise the 2900 Open at 18 knots (about 30 knots top), and optional 170-hp Yanmar diesels will cruise efficiently at 25 knots (29–30 top). ❑

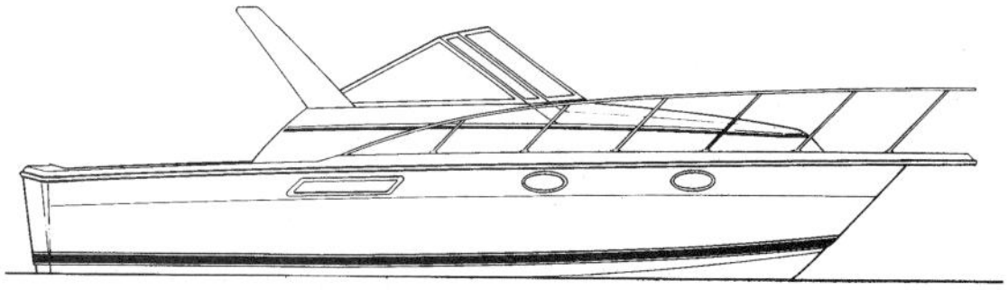

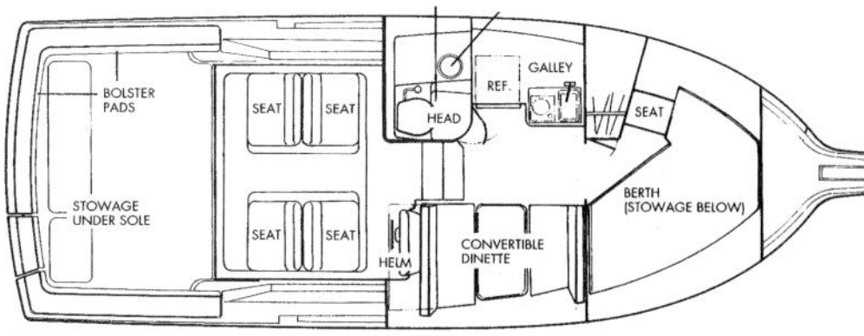

See Page 273 for Pricing Information

TIARA 3100 OPEN (EARLY)

SPECIFICATIONS

Length ....31'3"	Fuel, Std. ....196 gals.
Beam ....12'0"	Cockpit ....144 sq. ft.
Draft ....2'9"	Hull Type ....Modified-V
Weight ....10,500#	Deadrise Aft ....16°
Clearance ....7'6"	Designer ....L. Slikkers
Water ....36 gals.	Production 1979–92

Originally called the 3100 Pursuit, the Tiara 3100 Open has long been a popular model with family cruisers and anglers alike. After more than a decade in production she remained basically unchanged, until she was replaced with an all-new 3100 Open model in 1992. Her popularity derives from her large cockpit and good offshore handling along with the realization that she's a well-engineered boat built to high standards. The addition of the optional radar arch, swim platform, and bench seating in the cockpit transforms the 3100 into a conservative but good-looking family sportboat with genuine eye appeal. Although more than half of her overall length is committed to the cockpit, the interior accommodations are plush if somewhat compact. Built on a rugged modified-V hull, standard 454 gas engines will cruise at 22–23 knots and reach a top speed of around 32 knots. GM 8.2 diesels (300-hp) were a popular option (22–23 knots cruise). Note that the Tiara 3100 FB Convertible model is the same boat with a flybridge. ❑

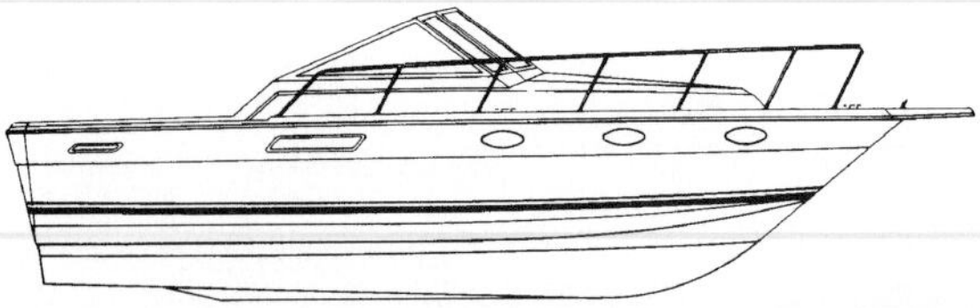

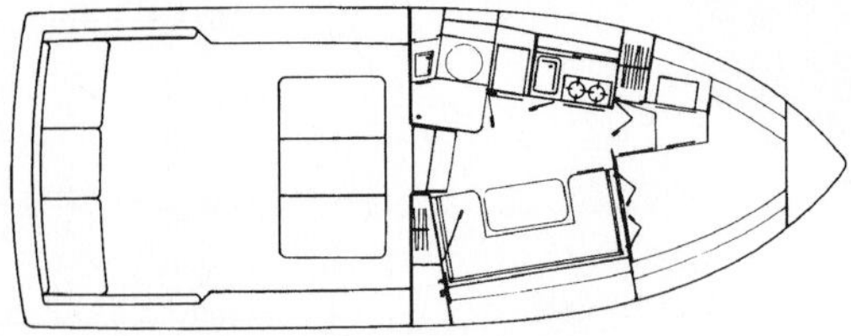

See Page 274 for Pricing Information

TIARA 3100 OPEN

SPECIFICATIONS

Length w/Pulpit	33'10"
Hull Length	31'3"
Beam	12'0"
Draft	2'9"
Weight	11,500#
Clearance w/Arch	8'7"
Cockpit	NA
Water	38 gals.
Fuel	246 gals.
Hull Type	Deep-V
Deadrise Aft	18°
Production	1992–Current

The new Tiara 3100 Open is a complete update of the original 3100 Open model. Her reworked hull features a sharper entry, additional transom deadrise (18 degrees vs. 16 degrees), greater bow flare for a dryer ride, and prop pockets for shallow draft. The 3100 also has a new bi-level cockpit layout which allows for the installation of optional Volvo, Cat, or Cummins diesels in an enlarged engine compartment. Tiara has always been a conservative builder, and it's no surprise that the new 3100 looks a lot like the original—basically a no-glitz express with good-quality construction, systems, and hardware. The slightly enlarged interior of the 3100 has more headroom than before, and there's also a bigger U-shaped dinette. Additional updates include increased fuel, a tilt-away helm console, recessed trim tabs, and an in-deck fish box and livewell in the cockpit. A transom door became standard in 1994. Standard 454-cid gas engines will cruise at 20–21 knots (29 knots top), and 291-hp 3116 Cat diesels will cruise efficiently at 25 knots (30 knots wide open). ❑

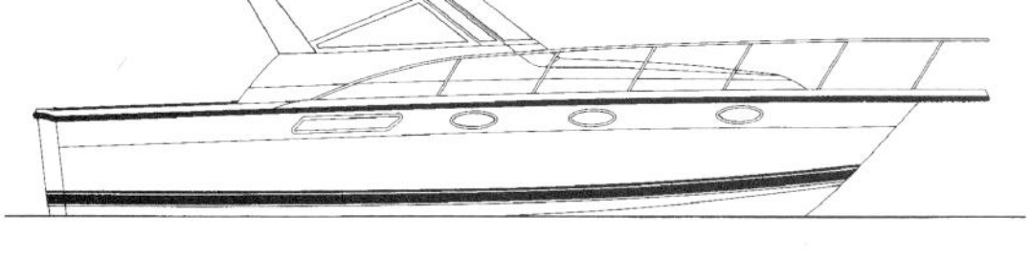

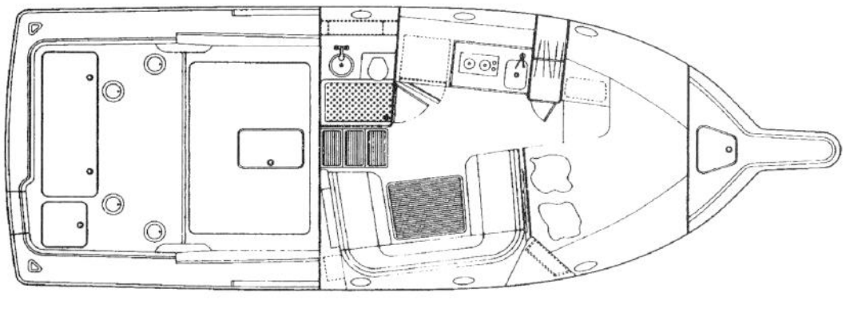

See Page 274 for Pricing Information

TIARA 3100 CONVERTIBLE

SPECIFICATIONS

Length	31'3"
Beam	12'0"
Draft	2'11"
Weight	13,200#
Clearance	12'2"
Water	36 gals.
Fuel, Std.	206 gals.
Fuel, Opt.	286 gals.
Cockpit	NA
Hull Type	Modified-V
Deadrise Aft	16°
Production	1982–92

The Tiara 3100 is an upscale flybridge cruiser with attractive lines and good overall performance. She was originally introduced in 1982 as the 3100 Continental, a designation that lasted through 1986. Built on the same hull used for the original 3100 Open, the Convertible offers the added comforts of a salon and an enclosed lower helm along with the ability to sleep six persons overnight. The stylish interior is an attractive blend of quality fabrics and teak trim with off-white mica cabinets featured in the galley. This is, in fact, one of the more appealing layouts to be found in any 31-foot convertible, and most will find it well-suited to the demands of family cruising. Additional features include a good-size cockpit, wide sidedecks, a molded bow pulpit, and decent engine access. The relatively small flybridge has bench seating forward of the helm console for three guests. Standard 454-cid gas engines will cruise the Tiara 3100 Convertible at 20 knots with a top speed of about 29 knots. ❑

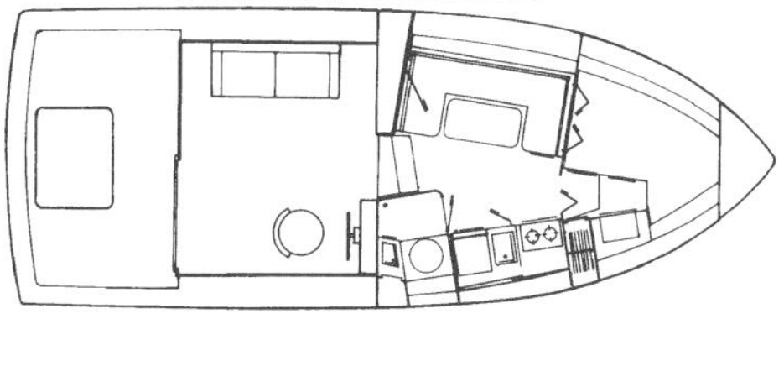

See Page 274 for Pricing Information

TIARA 3300 OPEN

SPECIFICATIONS

Length w/Pulpit..........35'8"	Water ....46 gals.
Hull Length ....32'10"	Fuel ....295 gals.
Beam..............................12'6"	Cockpit.................117 sq. ft.
Draft ....2'3"	Hull Type ....Modified-V
Weight......................11,500#	Deadrise Aft ....14°
Clearance ....8'8"	Production 1988–Current

Tiara's 3300 Open is a stylish family cruiser whose conservative design and top quality construction have made her an attractive alternative to the built-in glitz of competitive models in this size range. She's built on a rugged modified-V hull with a shallow skeg and balsa coring in the hullsides. Unlike the Tiara 3100 Open, the 3300 was not designed as a dedicated fisherman. Instead, she's more at home in the family cruiser role where her plush interior and sport-boat profile are most appreciated. Her well-designed interior features overnight berths for six in a cabin of unusual elegance and luxury. The interior is finished with grain-matched teak joinerwork, and the galley features white Formica cabinetry. In spite of her generous interior dimensions, the 3300 still manages to provide an excellent fishing cockpit with a transom door, inwale padding, and cockpit washdown as standard equipment. Standard 454-cid gas engines will cruise the Tiara 3300 Open at 22 knots (32 knots top), and optional 300-hp GM 8.2 diesels will cruise at about 24 knots. ❑

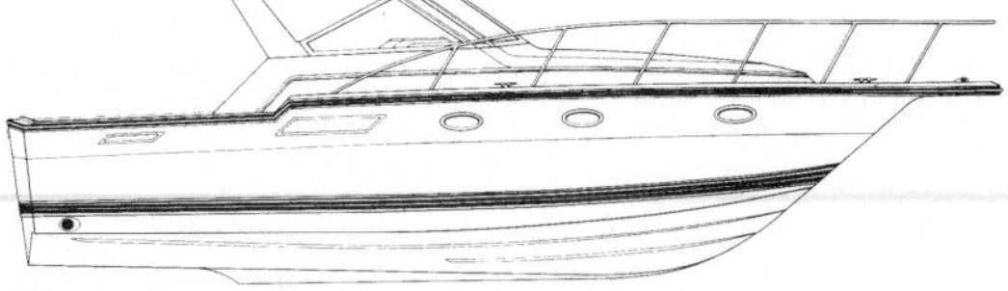

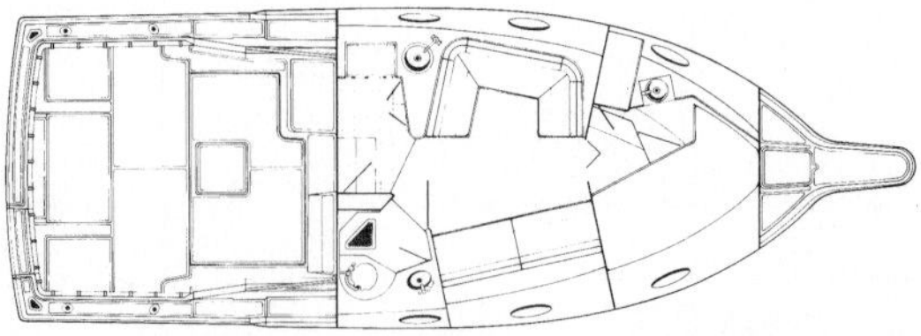

See Page 274 for Pricing Information

TIARA 3500 EXPRESS

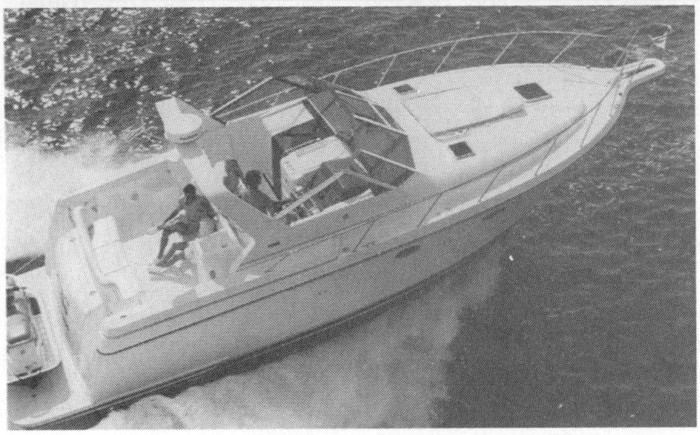

SPECIFICATIONS

Length w/Pulpit	38'10"	Water	124 gals.
Hull Length	35'8"	Clearance w/Arch	9'10"
Beam	13'9"	Cockpit	105 sq. ft.
Draft	2'10"	Hull Type	Deep-V
Weight	19,800#	Deadrise Aft	18°
Fuel	354 gals.	Production	1995–Current

A scaled-down version of Tiara's popular 4000 Open, the 3500 Express is a high-style family cruiser with impressive accommodations and an upscale price tag. She's heavily built on a beamy, deep-V hull with a shallow keel and prop pockets to reduce the draft. The interior is huge for a 35-footer thanks to the super-wide beam. The big lounge next to the cockpit steps can be converted into a private stateroom at night, and both sleeping areas have folding privacy doors instead of curtains. A removable pestal seat allows the dinette to seat five and a night-time lighting system activates when you step on the top companionway step. All in all, this is easily the nicest interior to be found in a production express cruiser this size. Additional features include a teak cabin sole, a huge storage trunk built into the transom, single-level cockpit seating for eight, and an optional 4-foot swim platform for stowing an inflatable (or water toy). Twin 355-hp V-drive inboards will cruise the Tiara 3500 at 17 knots (26 top), and 407-hp Cummins diesels cruise at 27–28 knots and reach a top speed of 32 knots. ❑

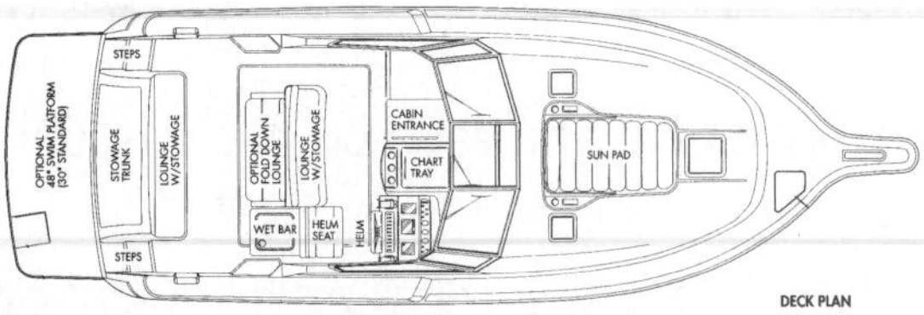

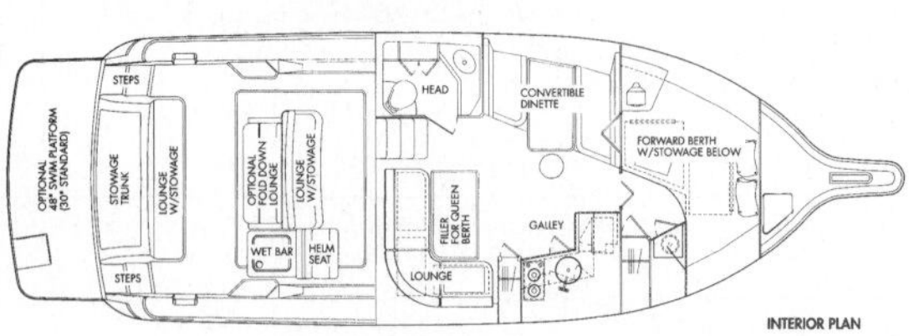

See Page 274 for Pricing Information

TIARA 3600 OPEN

SPECIFICATIONS

Length w/Pulpit	36'8"	Water	85 gals.
Hull Length	36'8"	Fuel	396 gals.
Beam	13'9"	Cockpit	NA
Draft	2'11"	Hull Type	Modified-V
Weight	16,500#	Deadrise Aft	14°
Clearance	9'7"	Production	1985–Current

A hugely popular boat, the 3600 Open is a wide-beamed express-cruiser with conservative lines, top-shelf construction, and very upscale interior accommodations. What sets the 3600 apart from much of the competition is her qualified ability to be transformed from a stylish family cruiser into a tournament-level fisherman. (Indeed, during 1985–86 she was called the Pursuit 3600.) The spacious bi-level cockpit is fitted with an in-deck big fish box on the centerline along with two circulating livewells, rod storage and a transom door. The interior accommodations are finished with traditional teak cabinetry and designer fabrics throughout. An island berth is forward in the original floorplan and an alternate layout (new in 1989) has a settee opposite the dinette and overnight berths for six but no stall shower. The bridgedeck has a hydraulic lift for engine access. Standard 454-cid gas engines will cruise at 20 knots and reach about 29 knots top. Optional 375-hp Cats offer cruising speeds at a respectable 26 knots and reach 32+ knots wide open. Note that she can be a wet ride in a chop. ❑

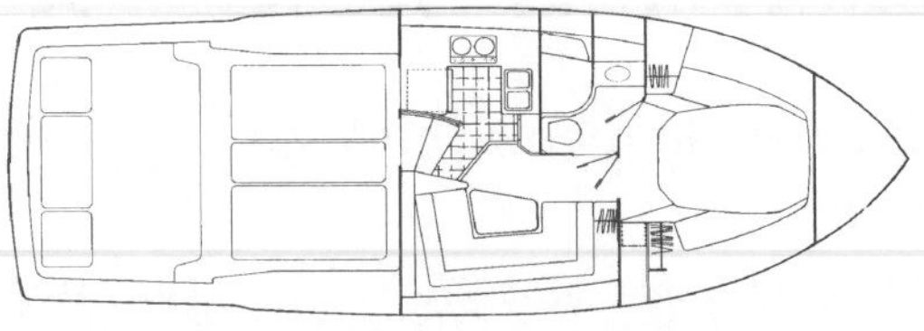

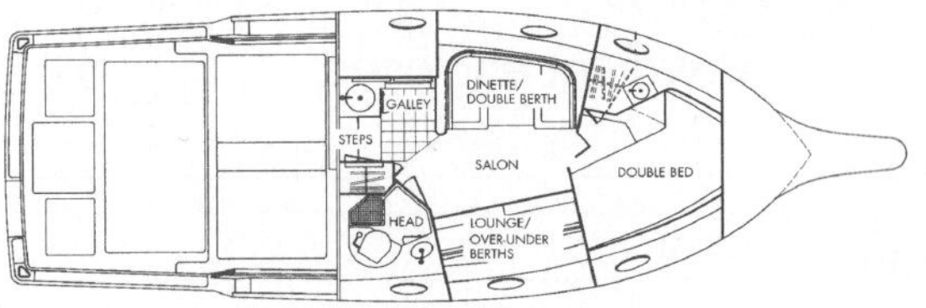

See Page 274 for Pricing Information

TIARA 3600 CONVERTIBLE

SPECIFICATIONS

Length w/Pulpit	39'8"	Water	85 gals.
Hull Length	36'8"	Fuel	396 gals.
Beam	13'9"	Cockpit	NA
Draft	3'0"	Hull Type	Modified-V
Weight	18,300#	Deadrise Aft	14°
Clearance	12'6"	Production	1987–Current

The Tiara 3600 Convertible is a good-looking flybridge sedan with an upscale and comfortable interior to go with her attractive lines. She's built on the same hull used for the 3600 Open, a proven offshore design with cored hullsides and relatively wide beam. The tooling is excellent—typical of the quality you get in a Tiara boat. Inside, a lower helm is optional, and the light-grain interior woodwork and decorator fabrics are impressive. Two floorplans are available: a two-stateroom arrangement, or a single-stateroom floorplan with a dinette. Both have a mid-level galley and include a stall shower in the head. The cockpit is equipped with a transom door and gate, and wide walkaround decks provide safe access to the bow. The cockpit isn't notably roomy and makes no allowance for the addition of tackle centers—a matter of no real consequence to family cruisers but a definite drawback for anglers. Standard 454-cid gas engines cruise the Tiara 3600 at 19-20 knots and reach 28 knots wide open. Optional Cat 375-hp diesels cruise at 25 knots and deliver a top speed of 29–30 knots. ❑

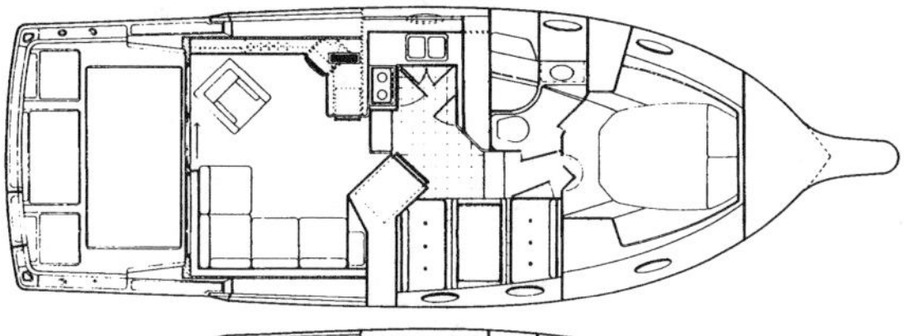

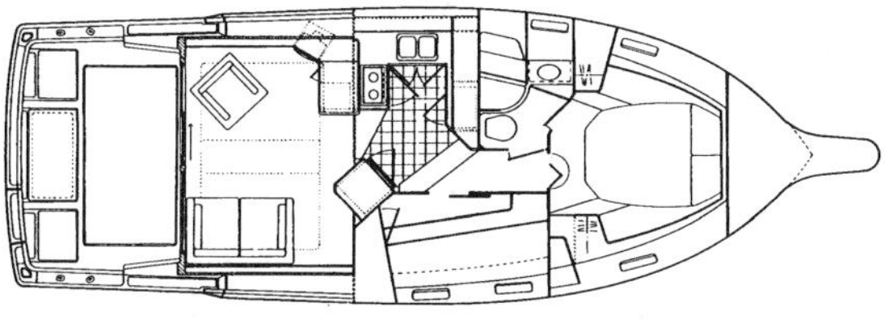

See Page 274 for Pricing Information

TIARA 3700 OPEN

SPECIFICATIONS

Length w/Pulpit	39'8"	Water	98 gals.
Hull Length	37'1"	Waste	40 gals.
Beam	14'2"	Windshield Clearance	9'9"
Draft	3'9"	Hull Type	Deep-V
Weight	21,000#	Deadrise Aft	18°
Fuel	411 gals.	Production	1995–Current

Designed as the replacement boat for the long-running 3600 Open, the Tiara 3700 retains the same conservative profile as her predecessor and for good reason. Like the 3600, this is a true dual-purpose boat with the plush interior accommodations demanded by upscale family cruisers and the hull and cockpit layout of a serious sportfishing machine. She features considerably more beam and deadrise than the 3600, and is a measurably better rough-water performer. The very upscale (plush, actually) interior of the 3700 Open is arranged with a single stateroom forward, a huge U-shaped dinette, a double-entry head with a stall shower, good storage and a surprisingly roomy galley. As usual in a Tiara boat, the joinerwork, appliances, fabrics and hardware are first-rate throughout. Outside, a wraparound lounge is opposite the helm, and the cockpit can easily handle a full-size fighting chair. The entire bridgedeck lifts electrically for complete access to the motors. Standard 435-hp Cat (or 420-hp Cummins) diesels will cruise the Tiara 3700 at 23–24 knots and reach a top speed of 29 knots. ❑

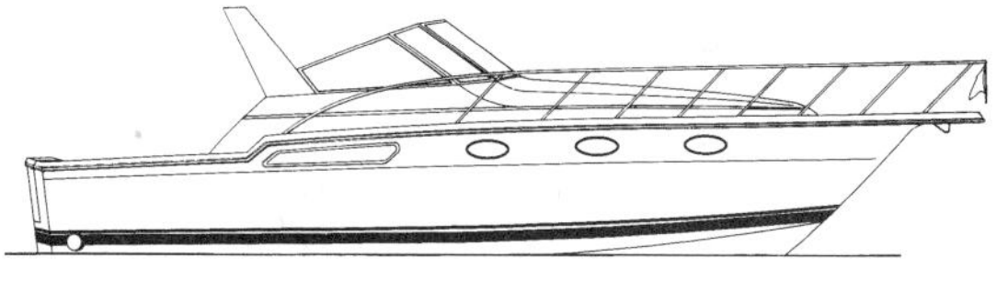

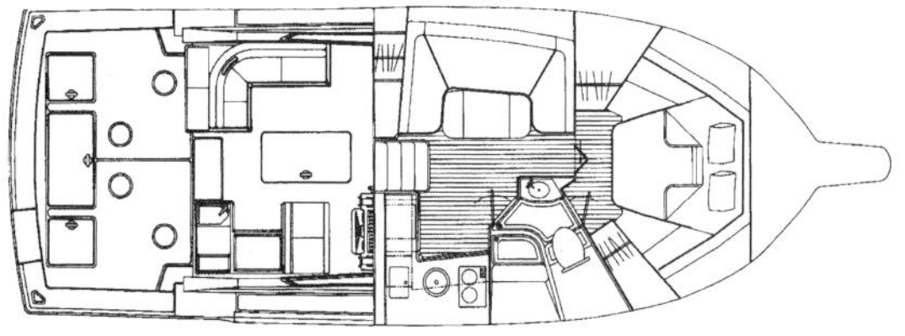

See Page 274 for Pricing Information

TIARA 4000 OPEN

SPECIFICATIONS

Length w/Pulpit..........43'6"	Water.....................160 gals.
Hull Length ....40'6"	Fuel........................444 gals.
Beam..............................14'6"	Cockpit ....120 sq. ft.
Draft ....3'0"	Hull Type ....Deep-V
Weight.....................25,000#	Deadrise Aft...................18°
Clearance ....10'2"	Production 1994–Current

A completely innovative express cruiser, the 4000 Open is the first mid-cabin design from Tiara. Indeed, there's so much that's unique about her that it's fair to say she has no competition among production sportboats. Features abound: built into the transom is a mini-garage for storing bicycles, outboard motors, or even a personal watercraft. Flip a switch and two fiberglass panels are raised from the cockpit sole, fitting between the facing settees to create a table or a sun lounge. The optional entended swim platform (designed to stow an inflatable) will appeal to serious cruisers but adds little to the boat's visual appeal. The mid-cabin layout is huge with the kind of accommodations normally expected in a motor yacht. Note that there are two heads—unusual in an express boat. The long U-shaped lounge in the salon is big enough to seat eight people, and headroom in the aft stateroom dressing area is excellent. Hydraulically activated rams lift the cockpit deck for access to the engines. A good performer, 400-hp Cummins diesels (or 435-hp Cats) will cruise the Tiara 4000 at 23–24 knots (about 27 knots top). ❑

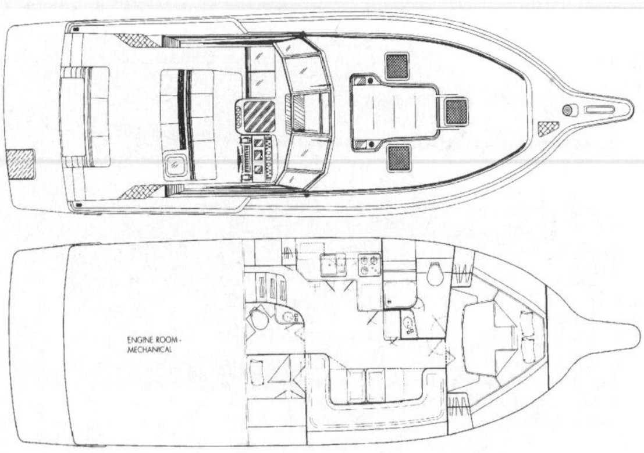

See Page 274 for Pricing Information

TIARA 4300 OPEN

SPECIFICATIONS

Length w/Pulpit..........46'7"	Cockpit.................167 sq. ft.
Hull Length ....43'2"	Water.....................150 gals.
Beam..............................15'2"	Fuel........................525 gals.
Draft ....4'0"	Hull Type ....Modified-V
Weight ....28,000#	Deadrise Aft...................16°
Clearance ....10'4"	Production 1991–Current

Conservatively styled (note the absence of an integrated swim platform) and elegantly appointed, the Tiara 4300 Open is one of the larger—and more expensive—production sportboats available in today's market. Built on the same wide-beam hull used in the 4300 Convertible, she's aimed at the market for upscale express cruisers, although she can easily be converted into a serious fishing platform. The belowdeck accommodations are plush, with light ash woodwork, leather upholstery, a teak and holly cabin sole, hydraulically operated dinette, and a spacious master stateroom with a walkaround island berth and built-in TV. Outside, the huge bi-level cockpit—reinforced for a mounted chair—provides seating for ten with in-deck storage compartments, cockpit steps, and a transom door with gate. Additional features include a superb helm console with room for flush-mounting an array of electronics, wide walkarounds, excellent engine room access, and hide-away bench seating at the transom. A surprisingly fast boat with 535-hp 6V92s, she'll cruise around 27 knots and reach 30 knots wide open. ❑

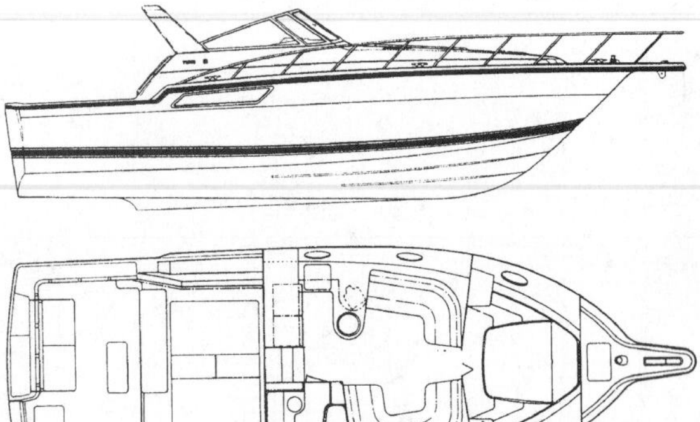

See Page 274 for Pricing Information

TOLLYCRAFT 26 SEDAN

SPECIFICATIONS

Length	26'8"	Fuel	140 gals.
Beam	10'0"	Cockpit	49 sq. ft.
Draft	2'10"	Hull Type	Modified-V
Weight	9,000#	Deadrise Aft	NA
Clearance	10'0"	Designer	Ed Monk
Water	33 gals.	Production	1973–85

Tollycraft's all-time best-selling boat, the 26 Sedan attracted a loyal following over the years due to her roomy interior and rugged all-fiberglass construction. At 9,000 lbs., the Tollycraft 26 is no lightweight for her size, and she has the ride of a bigger boat. Inside, the straightforward cabin accommodations are practical, if somewhat Spartan. Note that the decor was updated from wood-grain mica to teak in 1982. With the dinette converted, there are berths for four adults. There's a stand-up head, and visibility from the lower helm is excellent. The cabin windows in the 26 Sedan are very large, and the interior is surprisingly open for such a small boat. There's seating for five on the flybridge—far too much up-top weight for a small boat to carry for long with any degree of safety. Most Tollycraft 26s were equipped with a single 270-hp inboard gas engine with a V-drive (stern drives were also offered). The cruising speed is around 18 knots, and the top speed is 24–25 knots. ❑

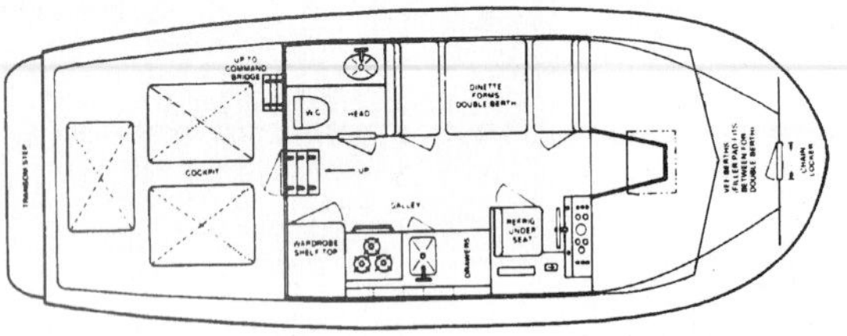

See Page 274 for Pricing Information

TOLLYCRAFT 30 SEDAN

SPECIFICATIONS

Length	29'11"	Fuel	200 gals.
Beam	11'9"	Cockpit	NA
Draft	2'6"	Hull Type	Modified-V
Weight	13,500#	Deadrise Aft	NA
Clearance	11'8"	Designer	Ed Monk
Water	58 gals.	Production	1977–84

The Tollycraft 30 Sedan may come up a little short on sex appeal, but she's certainly long on interior volume and living space. The house and flybridge are exceptionally large for a 30-footer and—at 13,500 lbs.—she's a heavy boat for her size. By building on a wide-beam hull and extending the salon bulkhead well into the cockpit, Tollycraft designers were able to create a spacious and very open interior with berths for as many as five. Storage space is impressive and includes a full wardrobe locker opposite the head. The interior decor was updated from simulated teak mica to real teak in 1982, and the woodwork and cabinetry are well-crafted throughout. As with all Tollycraft designs, the sidedecks are wide, and extra-large cabin windows provide plenty of natural lighting as well as good lower-helm visibility. With her big interior, the cockpit dimensions are very compact. Most Tollycraft 30 Sedans were built with twin 270-hp Crusader gas engines. The cruising speed is 23–24 knots, and the top speed is about 30 knots. ❑

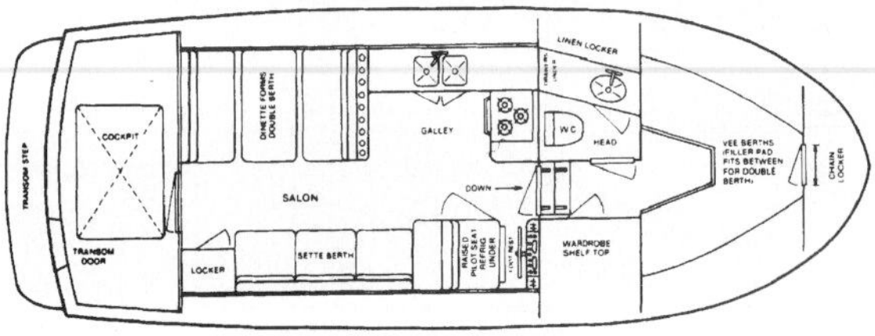

See Page 274 for Pricing Information

TOLLYCRAFT 30 SPORT CRUISER

SPECIFICATIONS

Length	30'6"	Fuel	150/198 gals.
Beam	11'6"	Cockpit	45 sq. ft.
Draft	2'7"	Hull Type	Modified-V
Weight	11,500#	Deadrise Aft	10°
Clearance	11'8"	Designer	Ed Monk
Water	42 gals.	Production	1985–92

A good-looking boat with a rakish profile (note the radar arch and integral swim platform), the Tollycraft 30 is an appealing combination of modern styling, quality construction and dependable performance. Inside, the accommodations are impressive for a 30-footer and include a U-shaped dinette, a surprisingly roomy galley, and a stand-up head with shower. The solid teak cabinetry and upscale fabrics are impressive, and the Sport Cruiser's interior has a decidedly upscale appearance. Outside, there's room in the cockpit for a couple of anglers, and hatches in the cockpit sole provide good access to the engines and V-drives. The helm console is forward on the flybridge with guest seating aft. (The flybridge is one of the largest yet seen on a boat this size.) On the downside, the sidedecks are very narrow, and storage space is at a premium. Built on Tollycraft's efficient Quadra-Lift hull, standard 260-hp MerCruiser gas engines cruise the 30 Sport Cruiser around 25 knots and reach 31–32 knots top. (The fuel capacity was increased in 1988.) ❑

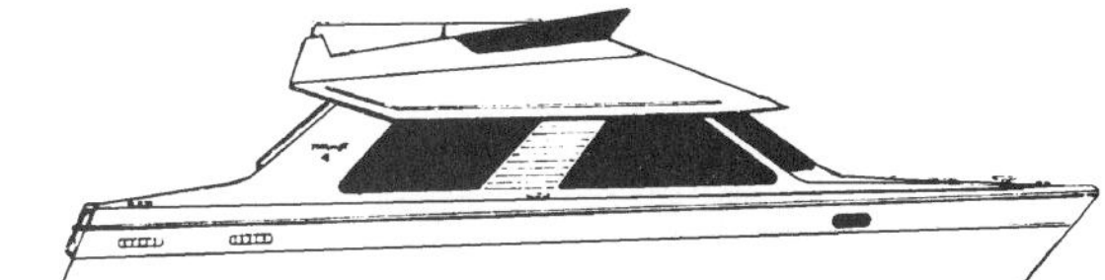

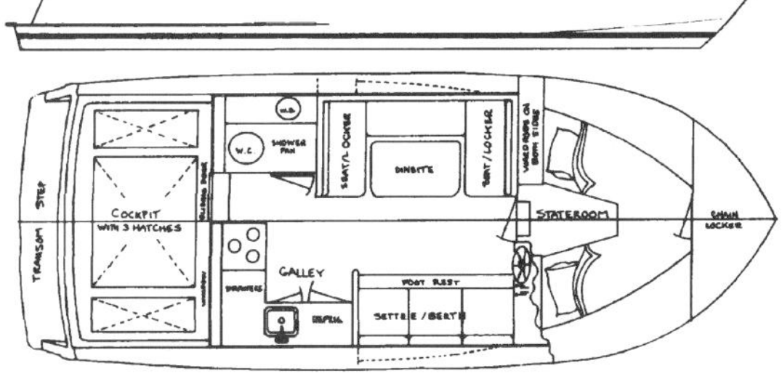

See Page 275 for Pricing Information

TOLLYCRAFT 34 SEDAN

SPECIFICATIONS

Length	33'7"	Fuel	160 gals.
Beam	12'3"	Cockpit	NA
Draft	2'6"	Hull Type	Modified-V
Weight	15,000#	Deadrise Aft	16°
Clearance	NA	Designer	Ed Monk
Water	50 gals.	Production	1972–80

The Tollycraft 34 Sedan was a popular and well-built family cruiser with a conservative profile and a practical interior layout. Hull construction is solid fiberglass, and V-drives were used to move the engines aft and maximize the interior space. Note that the salon, galley and dinette are all on the same level. This floorplan arrangement—accented with the wraparound cabin windows and good headroom—provides for an unusually open and bright interior. A lower station with full instrumentation was standard. Additional features include a stall shower in the head, a huge clothes locker forward, and berths for up to six. Mahogany woodwork was used until the 1977 models, when a simulated woodgrain mica became standard. Outside, the sidedecks are quite wide, and the helm console is forward on the flybridge with guest seating aft. The cruising speed is around 20 knots with standard 270-hp Crusader gas engines, and the top speed is 27–28 knots. Still a popular boat on the West Coast markets, the Tollycraft 34 has a reputation for economical and dependable operation. ❑

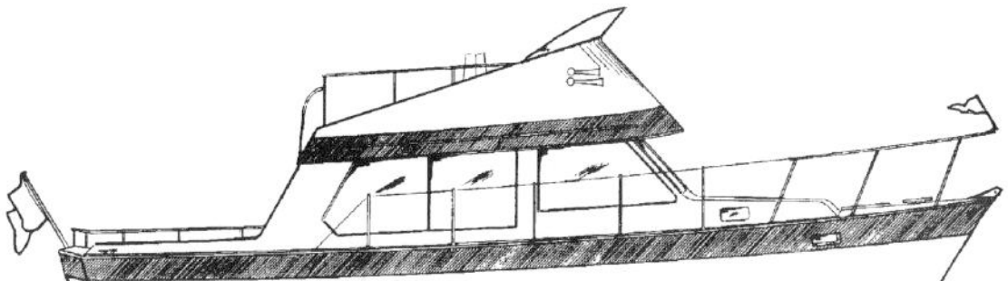

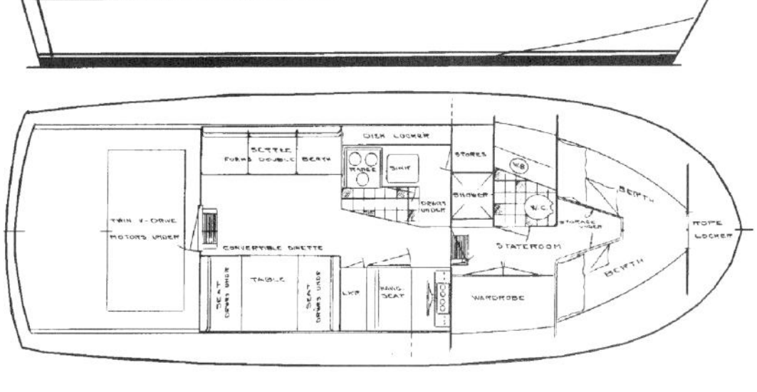

See Page 275 for Pricing Information

TOLLYCRAFT 34 CONV. SEDAN

SPECIFICATIONS

Length ....34'0"	Fuel ....200 gals.
Beam.............................12'6"	Cockpit ....72 sq. ft.
Draft ....2'10"	Hull Type ....Modified-V
Weight......................17,000#	Deadrise Aft....................12°
Clearance ....12'2"	Designer................Ed Monk
Water ....100 gals.	Production 1981–1986

Although out of production for nearly a decade, the Tollycraft 34 Convertible Sedan continues to be a popular boat on West Coast markets thanks to her modern styling, a practical interior layout, and better-than-average construction and finish work. The hull is solid fiberglass, and her 12-foot, 6-inch beam is relatively wide for a boat this size. Inside, the floorplan is arranged with the galley down, which results in a spacious salon. A lower helm was standard, and solid teak woodwork replaced the pseudo-teak veneers used through 1991. Note that a tournament-style flybridge option became available in 1985 for the East Coast market, and the simulated teak non-skid deck surface was dropped the same year. Additional features include a good-size cockpit with transom door and swim platform, wide sidedecks, good access to the motors, and a separate stall shower in the head. A good-running boat in a variety of sea conditions, standard 270-hp Crusader gas engines will cruise the Tollycraft 34 Convertible at 18–19 knots and reach a top speed of around 26 knots. ❑

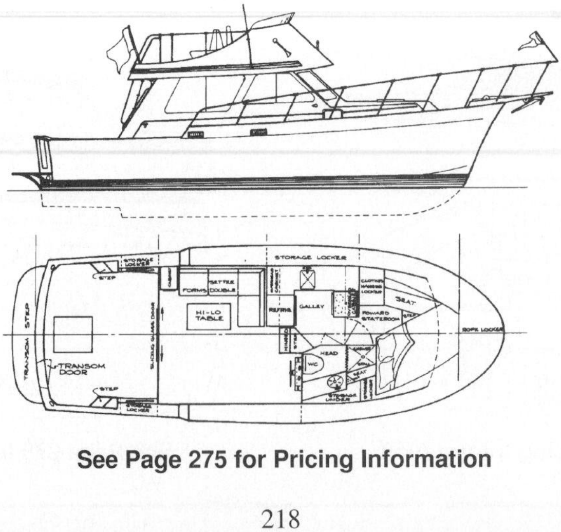

See Page 275 for Pricing Information

TOLLYCRAFT 34 SPORT SEDAN

SPECIFICATIONS

Length	34'0"	Fuel	200/296 gals.
Beam	12'6"	Cockpit	72 sq. ft.
Draft	2'10"	Hull Type	Modified-V
Weight	17,000#	Deadrise Aft	13°
Clearance	13'11"	Designer	Ed Monk
Water	77/116 gals.	Production	1987–93

The Tollycraft 34 Sport Sedan is a versatile and good-looking boat equally at home as a weekend fisherman or family cruiser. Built on an efficient Quadra-Lift hull with solid fiberglass construction and a relatively wide beam, the 34 Sport Sedan features a surprisingly open (and well-appointed) floorplan with two full staterooms—no small achievement in a 34-foot boat. A lower helm was standard, and there's a separate stall shower in the head in addition to a fair amount of storage space. The teak interior woodwork and upscale fabrics are impressive. Outside, an insulated fish box is built into the cockpit sole, and molded steps provide easy access to the wide sidedecks. Two flybridge designs were offered: a helm-aft arrangement with guest seating forward for East Coast buyers, and a helm-forward layout with guest seating aft for the Pacific market. Standard 454-cid gas engines will cruise the Tollycraft 34 Sport Sedan at 20 knots and reach top speeds in the neighborhood of 28–29 knots. Fuel and water were increased in the 1988 models. ❑

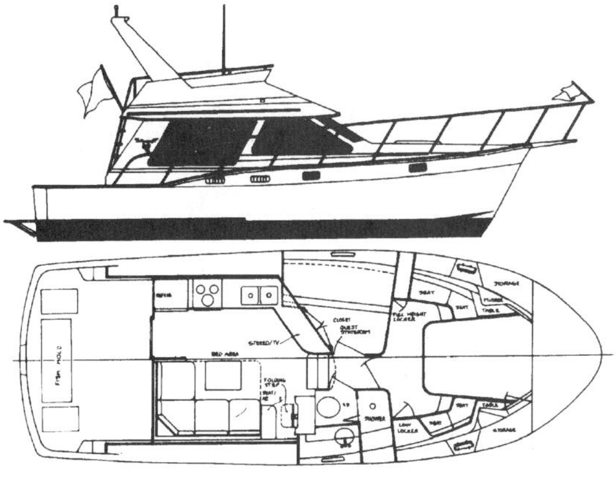

See Page 275 for Pricing Information

TOLLYCRAFT 37 CONVERTIBLE

SPECIFICATIONS

Length	37'4"	Fuel	300 gals.
Beam	13'2"	Cockpit	89 sq. ft.
Draft	3'0"	Hull Type	Modified-V
Weight	22,000#	Deadrise Aft	NA
Clearance	12'6"	Designer	Ed Monk
Water	140 gals.	Production	1974–85

The Tollycraft 37 Convertible is one of those rare boats whose good reputation has grown over the years. Introduced in 1974, she enjoyed a long production run and remains popular today because of her sturdy construction, practical layout, and low maintenance demands. Showing a distinctive West Coast profile, her relatively heavy displacement and a sharp entry allow the Tollycraft 37 to handle adverse sea conditions with confidence. Two interior layouts were offered with the galley-up floorplan having an extra guest stateroom forward in place of the dinette. Early models were fitted with a wood-grain mica decor; a more appealing full teak interior became standard in 1977. Note that the exterior deck surfaces were given Tollycraft's simulated-teak non-skid treatment. With nearly 90 sq. ft. of space, the cockpit is large enough for a couple of anglers and their gear. Twin 454-cid gas engines will cruise the 37 Convertible at 20–21 knots (about 30 knots top) while optional 210-hp Cat diesels cruise efficiently at 16–17 knots with a top speed of around 21 knots. ❑

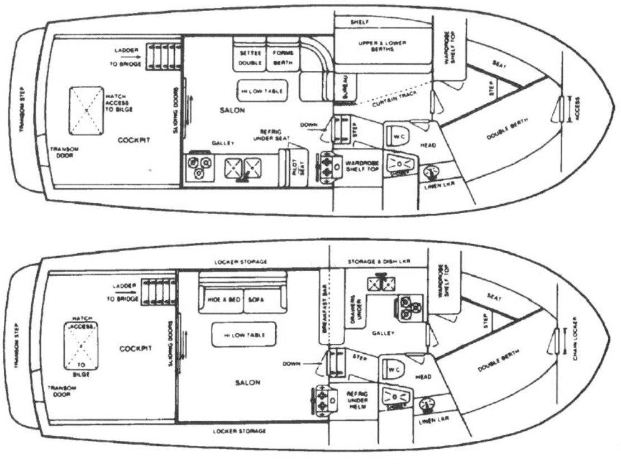

See Page 275 for Pricing Information

TROJAN 26 EXPRESS

SPECIFICATIONS

Length	26'4"	Fuel, Single	75 gals.
Beam	10'2"	Fuel, Twins	100 gals.
Draft	2'3"	Cockpit	NA
Weight	6,000#	Hull Type	Modified-V
Clearance	9'0"	Deadrise Aft	NA
Water	20 gals.	Production	1975–83

A popular boat with both weekend cruisers and light tackle fishermen, the Trojan 26 Express is an affordable cruiser with a surprisingly roomy interior. Indeed, more than half of the boat's hull length is devoted to cabin space, so it's hardly surprising that the cockpit dimensions are somewhat compact. Inside, the wide beam of the Trojan 26 is evident in the roomy (for a 26-footer) layout, which includes a complete galley, convertible dinette, adult-size V-berths, and a stand-up head compartment. With overnight berths for four and decent storage, the accommodations are more than adequate for a boat this size. A helm and companion seat are provided in the cockpit, and a hatch in the cockpit sole provides good access to the engine compartment. Additional features include opening windshield vents, wide sidedecks, and various hull graphics. A good-running boat with just a single 230-hp gas inboard, the Trojan 26 Express will cruise efficiently at 14–15 knots and reach a top speed of around 25 knots. Note that a flybridge was a popular option. ❑

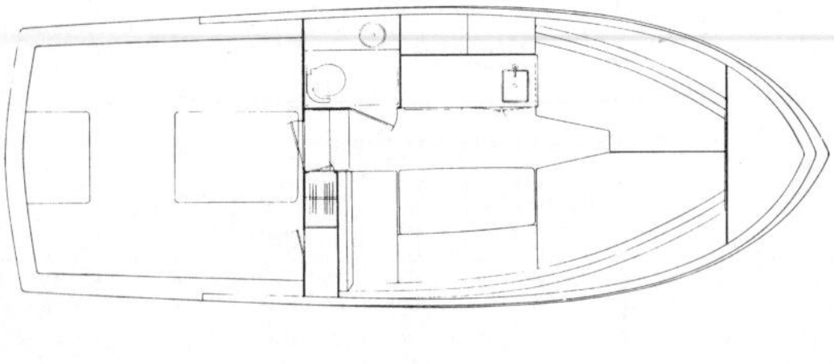

See Page 275 for Pricing Information

TROJAN 28 SEDAN

SPECIFICATIONS

Length	28'2"	Water	60 gals.
LWL	23'11"	Fuel	100 gals.
Beam	12'3"	Cockpit	12°
Draft	2'0"	Hull Type	Modified-V
Weight	7,700#	Designer	Trojan
Clearance	11'6"	Production	1976–79

The Trojan 28 Sedan is a big boat for her length. Indeed, her 12-foot, 3-inch beam would be considered normal for most 32-footers. The use of V-drives allows the cabin level to be lower than the cockpit sole, which results in an attractive, somewhat low-profile appearance. Inside, there are berths for seven—five in the salon (the settee backrests fold up and the dinette converts). The 28's somewhat cramped salon is packed with a lower helm and the galley in addition to the facing settees. The head compartment is a tight fit. While the cockpit is small, the large flybridge can accommodate as many as five people. (That much weight on the flybridge of any 28-foot boat, regardless of beam, will have a substantial effect on the stability and handling characteristics, and this model is no exception.) Note that the standard fuel tankage is only 100 gallons (an additional 50 gallons was optional), and the cabin windows are made of plastic. Twin 225-hp Chrysler inboards will cruise around 20 knots. The top speed is around 27–28 knots. ❑

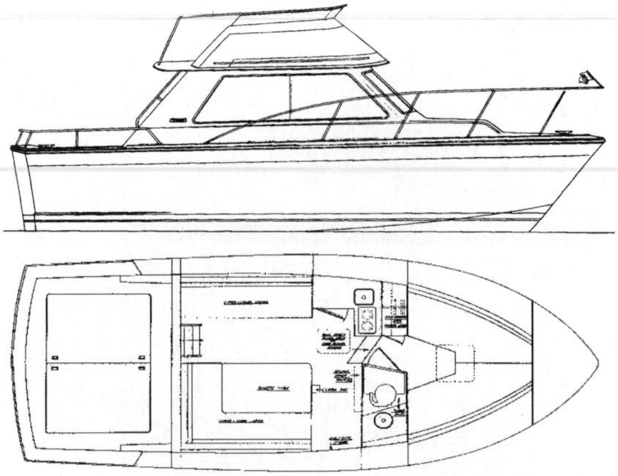

See Page 275 for Pricing Information

TROJAN 8.6 METER MID-CABIN

SPECIFICATIONS

Length ....28'8"	Fuel ....140 gals.
Beam ....10'6"	Cockpit ....NA
Draft, drives down ....2'2"	Hull Type ....Modified-V
Weight ....9,500#	Deadrise Aft ....14°
Clearance ....8'7"	Designer ....H. Schoell
Water ....40 gals.	Production 1987–90

The Trojan 8.6 Meter Mid-Cabin is a conservative mid-cabin family cruiser with expansive interior accommodations (for a 29-footer) and good performance. Hull construction is solid fiberglass, and her Delta-Conic hull design insures a stable (if sometimes stiff) ride in most conditions. The floorplan of the 8.6 is arranged with double berths in both staterooms, a full-size convertible dinette, a complete galley, and a small head—a practical layout taking full advantage of the relatively wide beam. The cockpit is set up with a triple-wide elevated helm seat, removable bench seating at the transom, and a transom cut-out for easier access to the swim platform. Access to the engines is somewhat tight. An affordable boat when she was new, the absence of a modern Eurostyle wraparound windshield and integral swim platform gives her a very conservative appearance compared to most the competition. Standard 260-hp stern drives will cruise the Trojan 8.6 Mid-Cabin Express at a brisk 25 knots and reach a top speed of about 37 knots.

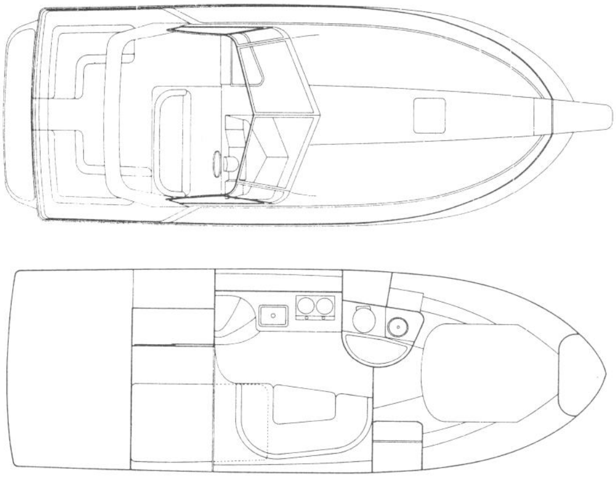

See Page 275 for Pricing Information

TROJAN 30 SPORT CRUISER

SPECIFICATIONS

Length ....30'2"	Fuel ....160 gals.
Beam ....11'1"	Cockpit ....80 sq. ft.
Draft ....2'2"	Hull Type ....Modified-V
Weight ....8,100#	Deadrise Aft ....12°
Clearance ....9'5"	Designer ....Trojan
Water ....33 gals.	Production 1973–79

When she was introduced in 1973 the Trojan 30 Sport Cruiser was something of a radical design. Trojan ads began by saying, "Don't laugh. The more serious you are about fishing, the less strange she looks." The Sport Cruiser was built on a solid fiberglass hull with a fairly wide beam and moderate transom deadrise. With her large bi-level cockpit and big tournament-style flybridge, the Sport Cruiser can indeed be fished, but, with a 160-gallon fuel supply, she's not heading out too far. (Early models had only 100 gallons of fuel.) The cabin layout sleeps six and includes a convertible dinette and settee, V-berths forward, and a small galley area. The head compartment is located just inside the salon door for easy outside access. The teak cabinetry and woodwork is nice, but storage space is limited, both in the cabin and the cockpit. A good-running boat, twin 225-hp Chrysler gas engines (318-cid inboards) will cruise the Sport Cruiser at 20 knots and deliver a top speed in the neighborhood of 27 knots. ❑

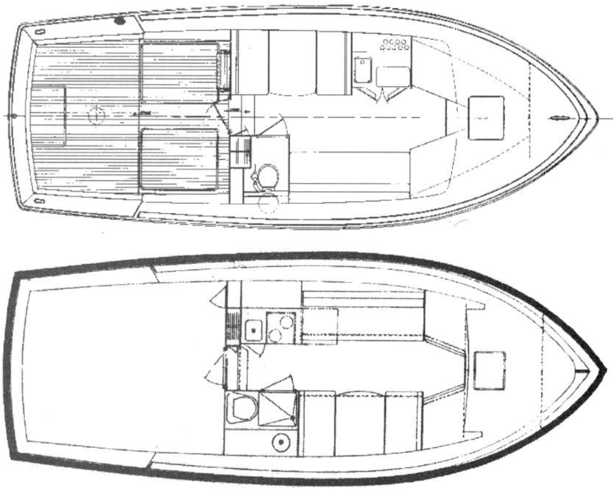

See Page 275 for Pricing Information

TROJAN 30 FB EXPRESS

SPECIFICATIONS

Length.....30'0"	Fuel.....100/160 gals.
Beam.....11'0"	Cockpit.....NA
Draft.....2'1"	Hull Type.....Modified-V
Weight.....8,100#	Deadrise Aft.....12°
Clearance.....11'9"	Designer.....Trojan
Water.....33 gals.	Production.....1975–79

The Trojan 30 Flybridge Express was a moderately priced cruiser designed to appeal to the family market. These were fairly basic boats with an open lower helm and practical cabin accommodations with berths for six. Early models carried only 100 gallons of fuel, which severely limited the cruising range. In 1978, a number of design changes were made, including the removal of the molded foredeck seating in favor of front windows to brighten up the interior. The head was also relocated and enlarged and a built-in stove was added in the galley. The cockpit is roomy enough for weekend fishing activities, and the small flybridge has seating for three. Engine access is via removable hatches in the cockpit sole. A choice of single or twin gas engines was offered. With the popular 225-hp Chrysler gas inboards, the Trojan 30 FB Express can be expected to cruise around 20 knots with a top speed of about 27 knots. The larger 250-hp Chryslers will add one or two knots to those speeds. Note that a hardtop model was also offered. ❑

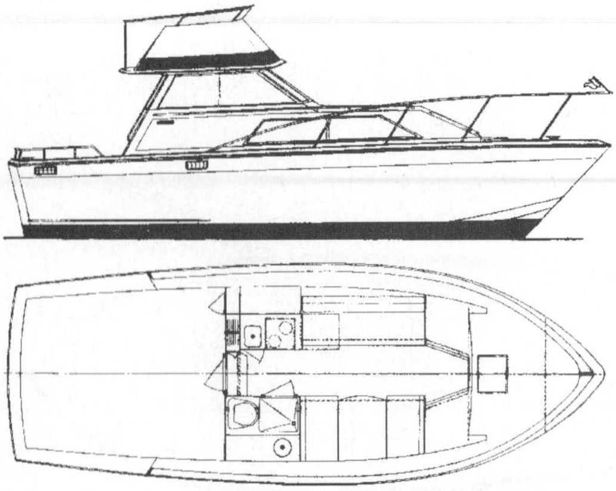

See Page 275 for Pricing Information

TROJAN 32 FB SEDAN

SPECIFICATIONS

Length.....32'0"	Fuel.....120/220 gals.
Beam.....13'0"	Cockpit.....60 sq. ft.
Draft.....2'6"	Hull Type.....Modified-V
Weight.....12,000#	Deadrise Aft.....8°
Clearance.....12'6"	Designer.....Trojan
Water.....40 gals.	Production.....1973–92

There were more Trojan 32s built (over 2,700 in all) than any other production fiberglass boat over 30 feet in the business. Her appeal was a straightforward combination of an affordable price, contemporary design, roomy cabin accommodations, and low operating costs. Several versions of the Trojan 32 were offered over the years, including Hardtop and Express models, a Flybridge Express (with an open lower helm), and the very popular Flybridge Sedan pictured above. All were built on a low-deadrise modified-V hull with moderate beam and solid fiberglass construction. Surprisingly, the basic interior and exterior design of the Trojan 32 never changed much except for periodic decor and hardware updates. A lower helm was standard, and wraparound cabin windows give the interior a bright and wide-open appearance. A stable and good-running boat, cruising speed with 250-hp Chrysler engines is approximately 18–19 knots, and the top speed is around 25 knots. Add 1–2 knots for more recent models equipped with the 270-hp Crusaders. The once-optional 220-gallon fuel capacity became standard in 1984. ❑

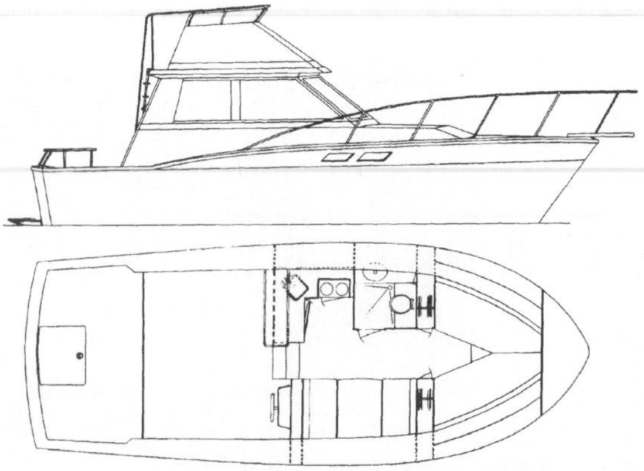

See Page 275 for Pricing Information

TROJAN 10 METER EXPRESS

SPECIFICATIONS

Length ....33'0"	Fuel ....242 gals.
Beam ....13'0"	Cockpit ....NA
Draft ....2'0"	Hull Type ....Modified-V
Weight ....11,250#	Deadrise Aft ....9°
Clearance ....9'4"	Designer ....H. Schoell
Water ....40 gals.	Production 1981–89

First of Trojan's popular Euro-style International series, the 10 Meter Express was something of a breakthrough design when she was introduced in 1981. Boldly styled and featuring all-new modular construction, the "experts" had a field day with this boat, calling her too wide and too glitzy for the conservative American market. Nevertheless, she quickly captured the public's imagination and soon became a marketing success. Hull construction is solid fiberglass, and she rides on a beamy DeltaConic hull with moderate transom deadrise. Below, the original, somewhat gaudy interior was toned down in later years, but her Mediterranean styling, curved bulkheads, and distinctive decor were soon copied by other manufacturers. Notable features include electrically operated sliding doors to the head and forward cabin, a big bi-level cockpit with an offset companionway, teak covering boards, side-dumping exhausts, and a curved cockpit windshield. Engine access is good compared with other express boats this size. Standard 454-cid gas engines cruise the Trojan 10 Meter at 19–20 knots with a top speed of around 28 knots. ❑

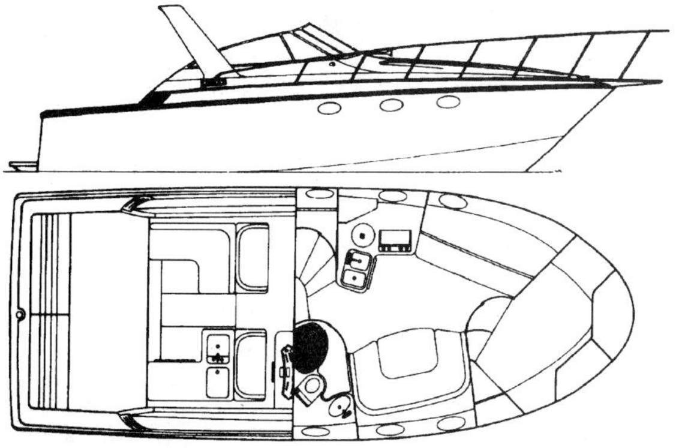

See Page 275 for Pricing Information

TROJAN 10 METER SEDAN

SPECIFICATIONS

Length ....33'0"	Fuel ....242 gals.
Beam ....13'0"	Cockpit ....60 sq. ft.
Draft ....2'0"	Hull Type ....Modified-V
Weight ....14,250#	Deadrise Aft ....9°
Clearance ....12'2"	Designer ....H. Schoell
Water ....40/55 gals.	Production 1982–89

A good-looking boat in spite of the graphics found on the early models, the Trojan 10 Meter is a beamy family cruiser with a lot of living space packed into her 33-foot length. Hull construction is solid fiberglass, and she's built on an easy-riding DeltaConic hull bottom with moderate transom deadrise and wide chine flats. The original floorplan of the 10 Meter Sedan was a disappointment—an offset companionway (very unusual in a convertible) all but isolated the salon from the lower level dinette and galley. A revised floorplan (introduced in 1984) had a more open layout with an island berth forward and a serving counter overlooking the galley. Outside, the cockpit is large enough for some modest fishing pursuits. The flybridge, on the other hand, is small for a 33-footer. Additional features include a standard lower helm in pre-1987 models, good engine access and reasonably wide sidedecks. With standard 454-cid Crusader gas engines, the cruising speed of the Trojan 10 Meter Sedan is 18 knots, and the top speed is around 27–28 knots. ❑

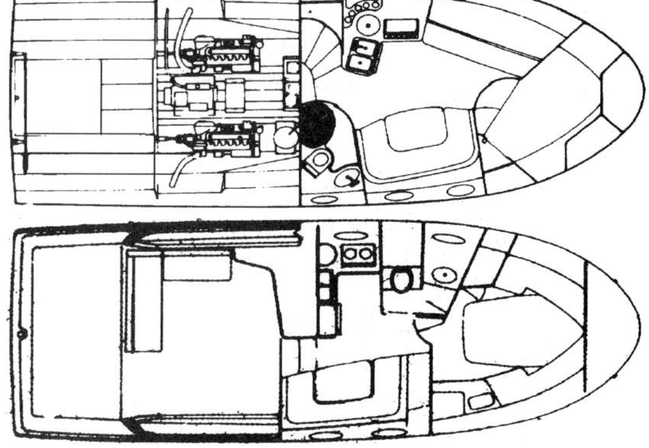

See Page 275 for Pricing Information

TROJAN 10 METER MID-CABIN

SPECIFICATIONS

Length ....33'0"	Fuel ....250 gals.
Beam..............................13'0"	Cockpit............................NA
Draft ....2'0"	Hull Type ....Modified-V
Weight.......................12,500#	Deadrise Aft......................9°
Clearance w/Arch ....9'4"	Designer ....H. Schoell
Water ....55 gals.	Production 1986–92

While she has the same exterior profile as the 10 Meter Express, the 10 Meter Mid-Cabin has an elevated bridgedeck to accommodate a private aft cabin tucked beneath the helm. Like all of Trojan's 10 Meter designs, she's a beamy boat for her length, with plenty of interior volume and cockpit space. Hull construction is solid fiberglass, and Trojan ads made much of her Delta-Conic hull—a somewhat unique bottom design that provides a stable and reasonably comfortable ride in most conditions. Inside, the mid-cabin floorplan is arranged with double berths in both staterooms. There's also a shower stall in the head compartment and adequate storage space throughout the cabin. The bi-level cockpit is very spacious, and hatches in the sole provide good access to the motors. A new Euro-style instrument panel was added in 1989 along with a sportier bolt-on swim platform and white powder-coated deck rails—very appealing. With the standard 454-cid gas engines, the 10 Meter Mid-Cabin will cruise at 17–18 knots with a top speed of around 26 knots.
❑

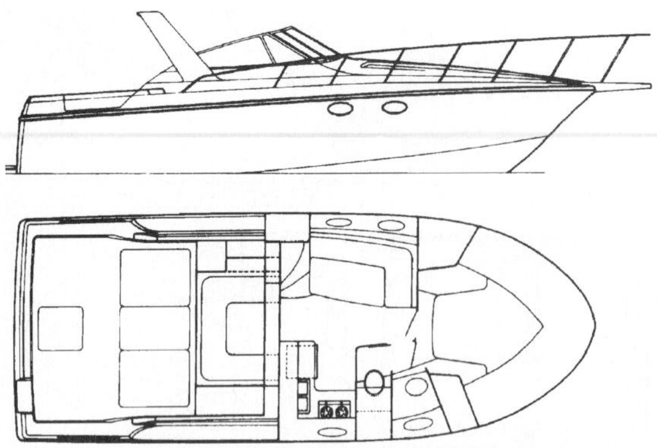

See Page 276 for Pricing Information

TROJAN 10.8 METER CONV.

SPECIFICATIONS

Length ....35'4"	Fuel ....325 gals.
Beam..............................13'0"	Cockpit....................87 sq. ft.
Draft ....2'4"	Hull Type ....Modified-V
Weight.......................15,000#	Deadrise Aft......................9°
Clearance ....12'2"	Designer ....H. Schoell
Water ....55 gals.	Production 1986–92

The 10.8 Meter Convertible is essentially a stretched version of the Trojan's earlier 10 Meter Sedan model. The deck plans and interior layouts are essentially the same in both boats, the difference being the larger cockpit and additional fuel capacity of the 10.8 Meter. Although not designed as a sportfishing boat, a transom door and tackle center were standard, and the cockpit is large enough for a couple of anglers. Indeed, the added cockpit space is a big improvement over her predecessor and makes the 10.8 Meter a more versatile family cruiser. The original single-stateroom floorplan has a dinette opposite the galley, and an alternate two-stateroom arrangement (introduced in 1989) eliminates the dinette. A beamy boat, the cabin dimensions are quite generous, but the engine room below the salon sole is a tight fit. Topside, the flybridge is on the small side for a boat of this size with guest seating forward of the helm. Standard 454-cid gas engines will cruise at 17–18 knots and reach around 26 knots wide open. ❑

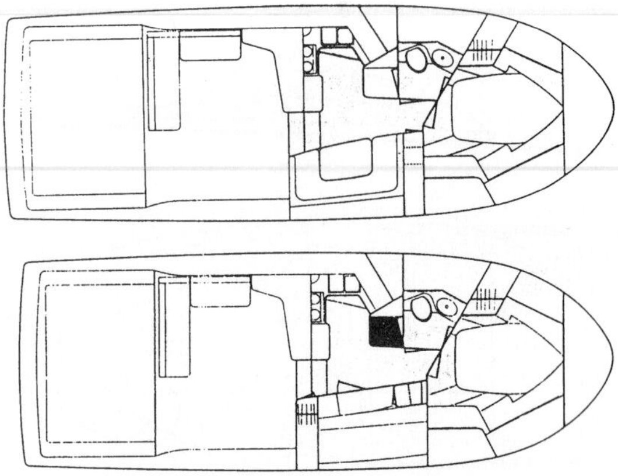

See Page 276 for Pricing Information

TROJAN 10.8 METER EXPRESS

SPECIFICATIONS

Length w/Pulpit	39'4"	Water	91 gals.
Hull Length	35'5"	Fuel	280 gals.
Beam	13'2"	Hull Type	Deep-V
Draft	3'7"	Deadrise Aft	20°
Weight	19,572#	Designer	Trojan
Clearance	11'0"	Production	1991–92

A very appealing design with plenty of eye appeal, the 10.8 Meter Mid Cabin was introduced in 1991 by Trojan just before the company declared bankruptcy. (Trojan's assets—including the name—were acquired by Irwin Jacobs, owner of Hatteras, Wellcraft, Carver, etc., and in 1993 this boat was reintroduced as the Trojan 370 Express.) She was constructed on a solid fiberglass deep-V hull with a relatively wide beam for her length. Note that unlike other Trojan express cruisers, the 10.8 does not employ a Delta-Conic hull bottom. The mid-cabin floorplan is very spacious for a 35-footer with double berths fore and aft, a good-size galley, full dinette and a separate stall shower in the head. A draw curtain provides privacy aft while the forward stateroom has a door—a definate plus. Outside, there's plenty of room for a crowd in the bi-level cockpit, and the entire deck aft of the helm can be hydraulically raised for access to the engines and V-drives. Among several engine options, big-block 502-cid gas inboards will cruise the 370 Express at 18 knots and reach a top speed of about 28 knots. ❑

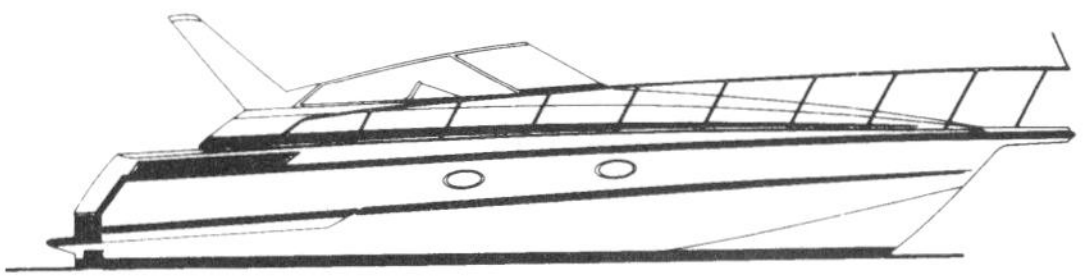

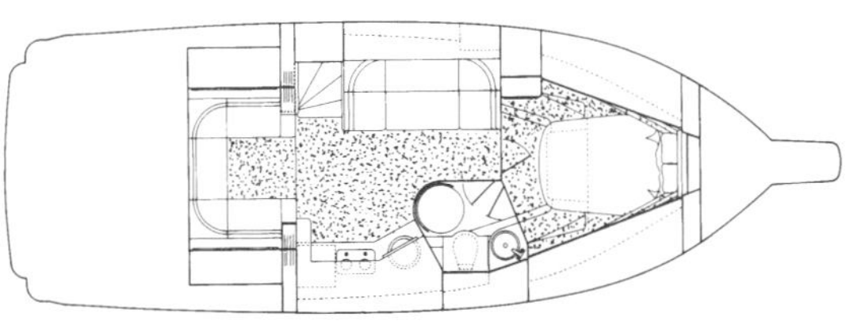

See Page 276 for Pricing Information

TROJAN 350 EXPRESS

SPECIFICATIONS

Length w/Pulpit	37'8"	Waste	30 gals.
Beam	12'0"	Clearance w/Arch	9'8"
Draft	2'10"	Hull Type	Modified-V
Weight	16,403#	Deadrise Aft	16.5°
Fuel	220 gals.	Designer	F. DeSimoni
Water	60 gals.	Production	1995–Current

Whether one likes the styling of the winged electronics arch or not, it can hardly be denied that the Trojan 350 is an eye-catching boat. Indeed, this Italian-designed express cruiser incorporates a number of innovative features including what may well be one of the most stylish integral swim platforms in the business. She's built on a modified-V hull with a relatively sharp 16.5 degrees of deadrise at the transom, moderate beam, and prop pockets to reduce the shaft angles. The 350's mid-cabin interior is arranged in the conventional manner with double berths in both staterooms and a convertible dinette. The sleeping areas are separated from the salon by a curtain forward and a bi-fold door aft, and the galley is somewhat larger than that found in other express boats this size. Outside, a bi-level cockpit has a triple-wide helm seat together with a built-in wet bar and lounge seating aft. No lightweight, twin V-drive 320-hp Crusader inboards will cruise the Trojan 350 at 15–16 knots and deliver a top speed of 27 knots. ❑

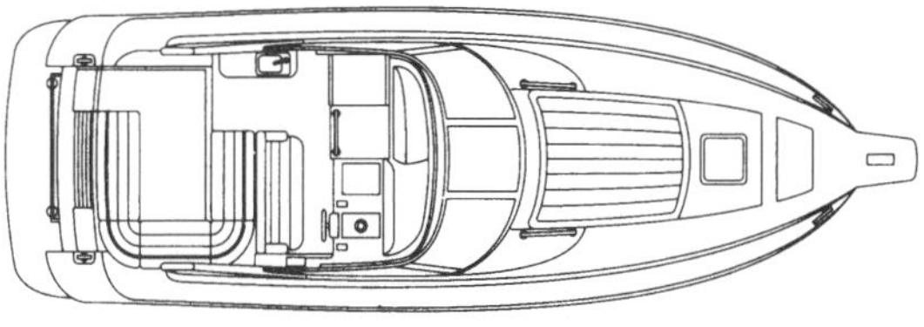

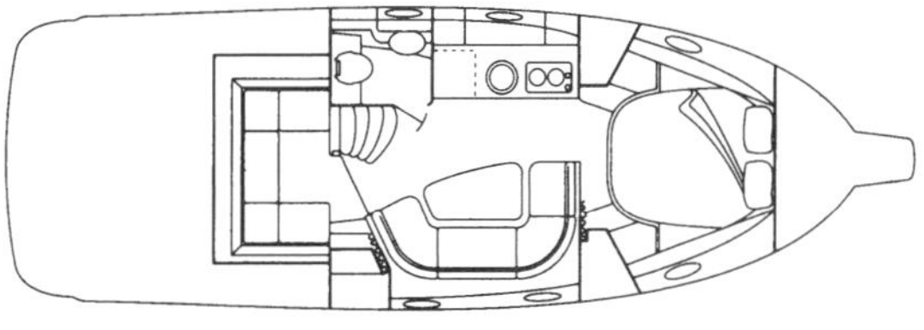

See Page 276 for Pricing Information

TROJAN 36 CONVERTIBLE

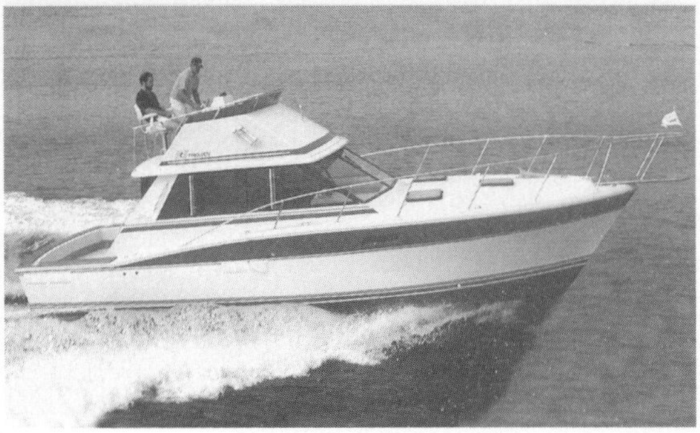

SPECIFICATIONS

Length ....36'0"	Fuel.................250/350 gals.
Beam..............................13'0"	Cockpit...................75 sq. ft.
Draft ....2'11"	Hull Type ....Modified-V
Weight......................16,000#	Deadrise Aft.....................9°
Clearance ....13'0"	Designer....................Trojan
Water ....80 gals.	Production 1972–89

One of the most popular production boats ever designed, the Trojan 36 Convertible is an affordable blend of traditional styling, comfortable accommodations, and good all-round performance. She was built on an easy-riding modified-V hull with moderate beam, nearly flat aftersections, and solid fiberglass construction. The original two-stateroom floorplan featured a mid-level galley opposite the lower helm. The head compartment was redesigned in 1981, with a separate stall shower, and in 1982 an new single-stateroom dinette layout became available. Outside, the cockpit is big enough for some light-tackle fishing, and the tournament-style flybridge provides seating for up to five. A teak cockpit sole was standard through 1976. Up until the last few years of production the standard fuel capacity was only 250 gallons with an extra 100 gallons optional. A variety of gas and diesel engine options were offered over the years. Among the most popular, twin 350-hp Crusaders will cruise the 36 Convertible at 19 knots and deliver a top speed of around 27–28 knots. ❑

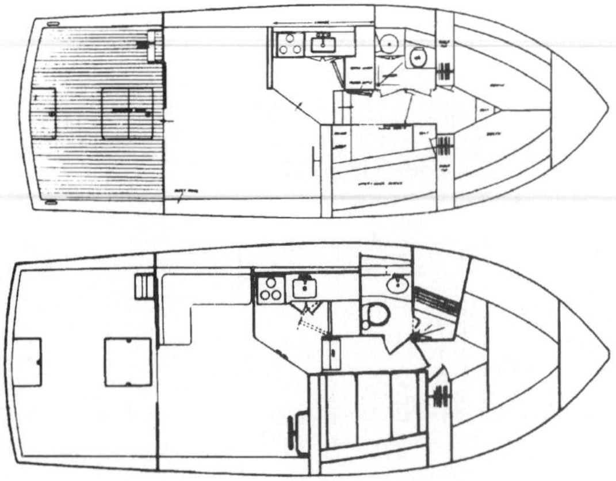

See Page 276 for Pricing Information

TROJAN 11 METER EXPRESS (EARLY)

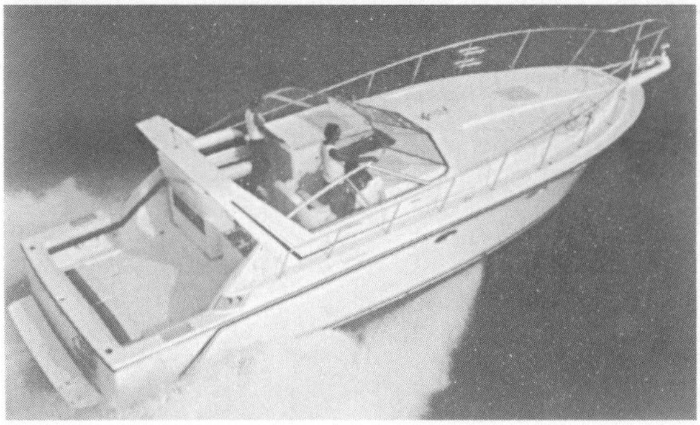

SPECIFICATIONS

Length ....37'6"	Fuel ....350 gals.
Beam..............................14'0"	Cockpit............................NA
Draft ....3'3"	Hull Type ....Modified-V
Weight......................16,800#	Deadrise Aft....................14°
Clearance ....9'4"	Designer ....H. Schoell
Water ....100 gals.	Production 1983–89

While she's obviously dated by today's crop of high-style family sportboats, the Trojan 11 Meter was considered a radical design when she was introduced back in 1983. With her dramatic hull graphics (toned down in later years) and her super-wide 14-foot beam, she attracted attention for her huge cockpit and wide-open Euro-style interior. Like all of the early Trojan express boats, the 11 Meter rides on a Delta-Conic hull bottom, and it's notable that the entire hull—including the bottom—is cored. Below, the interior is a blend of rounded corners, indirect lighting, and bright-colored laminates. The curved doors to the stateroom and head are pneumatic—push a button, and they automatically open or close. Outside, the bi-level cockpit is arranged with a double-wide helm seat and portside lounge seating. Crusader 454-cid gas engines were standard in the 11 Meter Express (18 knots cruise/27 knots top) with 375-hp Cat diesels (24 knots cruise/28 knots top) and 485-hp 6-71s (29 knots cruise/32 knots top) offered as options. ❑

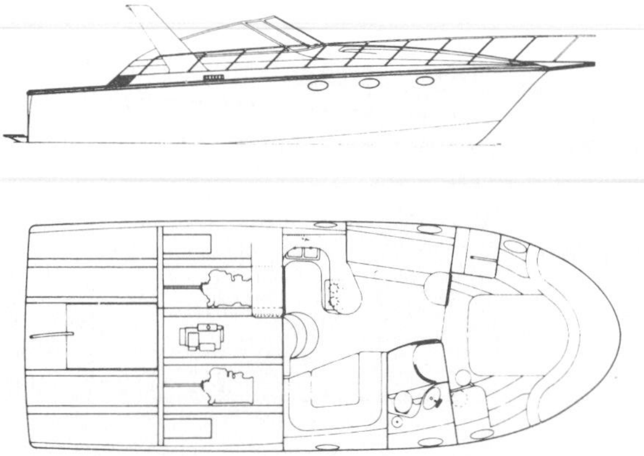

See Page 276 for Pricing Information

TROJAN 11 METER EXPRESS

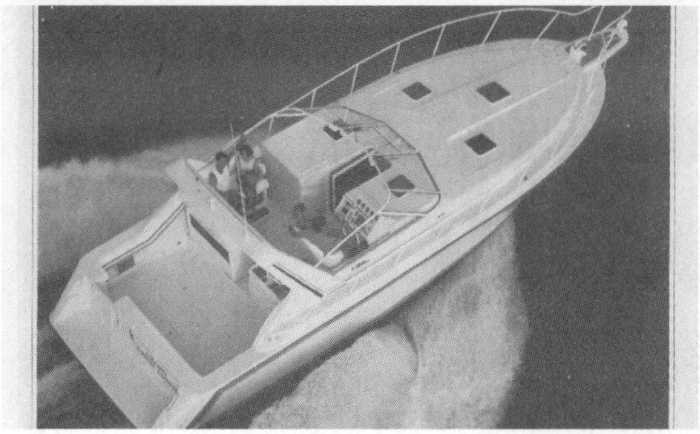

SPECIFICATIONS

Length	37'6"	Fuel	350 gals.
Beam	14'0"	Cockpit	NA
Draft	3'3"	Hull Type	Modified-V
Weight	16,800#	Deadrise Aft	14°
Clearance	9'4"	Designer	H. Schoell
Water	100 gals.	Production	1990–92

While she's built on the original 11 Meter Express hull, the second Trojan 11 Meter Express is a dramatically restyled and updated boat compared with her predecessor. Perhaps most notably, the cabin layout was a clear departure from those of other express cruisers this size. Not a mid-cabin design like most of her competition, the 11 Meter has a portside master stateroom with private access to a roomy head compartment. Guests can sleep in the (non-private) lounge/dinette area forward, which otherwise serves as a big entertaining and/or dining area. The 11 Meter's layout is unique and manages to provide a great owner's cabin but at the expense of the salon dimensions. Features include an integral swim platform, fold-away stern seat, a spacious cockpit, and a walk-through transom door. A pair of 360-hp (502-cid) gas engines will cruise at 18 knots and reach a top speed of around 27–28 knots. Diesel options include 425-hp Cats (24 knots cruise/28 knots top) and 485-hp 6-71TIs (29 knots cruise/32 knots wide open). ❑

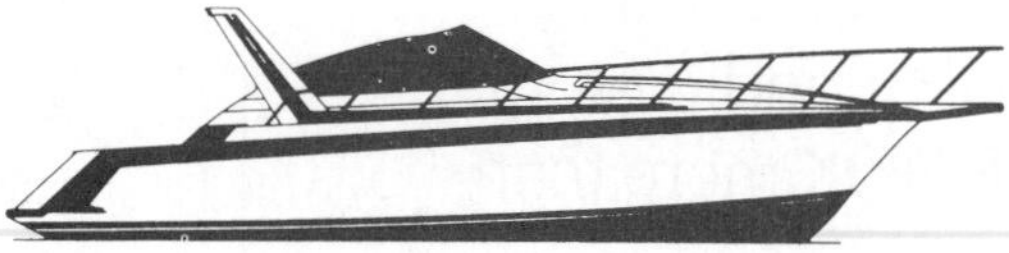

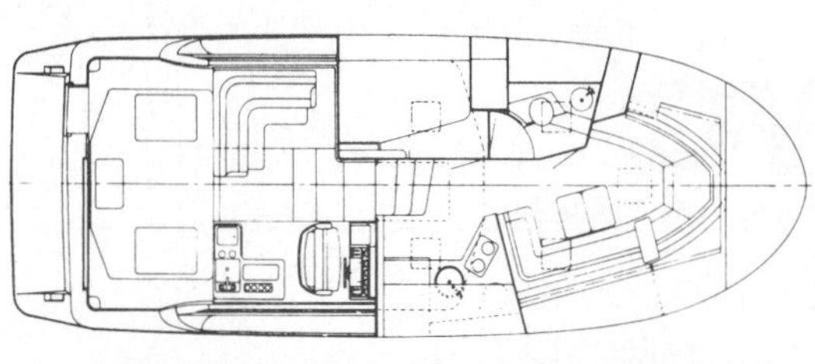

See Page 276 for Pricing Information

TROJAN 11 METER SEDAN

SPECIFICATIONS

Length	37'6"	Fuel	350 gals.
Beam	14'0"	Cockpit	NA
Draft	3'5"	Hull Type	Modified-V
Weight	18,000#	Deadrise Aft	14°
Clearance	12'6"	Designer	H. Schoell
Water	100 gals.	Production	1985–88

Aside from her dramatic (and unattractive) hull graphics, the most notable feature of the Trojan 14 Meter Sedan is her unusually wide beam. Indeed, it's fair to say that she has more interior volume than just about any other boat in her class. Built on a fully cored modified-V (Delta-Conic) hull with wide chine flats and side exhausts, the 11 Meter Sedan was one of the early Med-style convertibles introduced into the American market. Her single-stateroom floorplan includes a spacious and wide-open salon with a serving counter overlooking the galley. A lower helm was optional. Notable features include teak covering boards in the cockpit, a tournament-style flybridge with guest seating forward of the helm, excellent storage, and a separate stall shower in the head compartment. With standard 454-cid Crusader gas engines, the Trojan 11 Meter Sedan will cruise at around 18 knots and reach a top speed of 27–28 knots. Caterpillar 375-hp diesels were a popular option: they'll cruise around 23 knots and reach 26–27 knots top. ❑

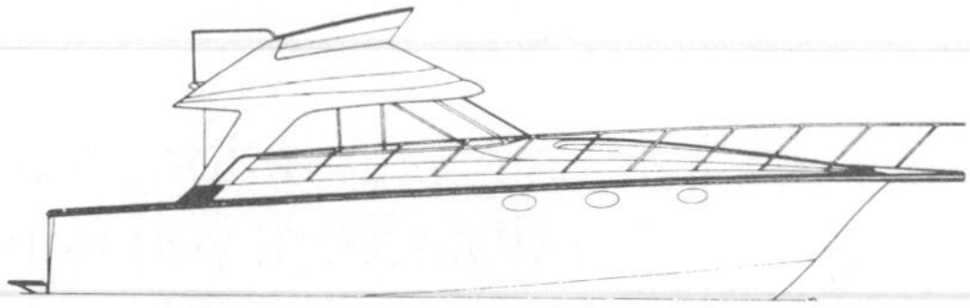

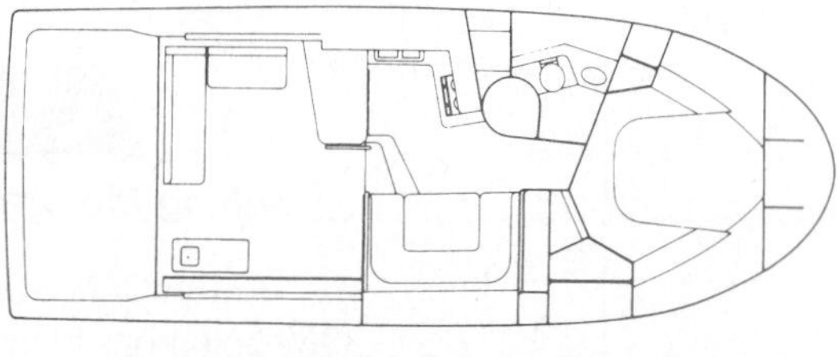

See Page 276 for Pricing Information

TROJAN 370/390 EXPRESS

SPECIFICATIONS

Length w/Pulpit ....39'4"	Water ....91 gals.
Hull Length..................35'5"	Fuel.........................280 gals.
Beam ....13'6"	Hull Type ....Deep-V
Draft ....3'7"	Deadrise Aft ....20°
Weight ....19,572#	Designer ....Trojan
Clearance......................11'0"	Production.......1993–Current

Today's new Trojan 390 Express is basically the 10.8 Meter Mid Cabin model introduced in 1991 by the original Trojan Company just before they declared bankruptcy. Trojan's assets—including the name—were acquired by Irwin Jacobs (owner of Hatteras, Wellcraft, Carver, etc.) and in 1993 the boat was reintroduced as the Trojan 370 Express. (Note that she was called the 370 Express for 1993–94.) Built at the Carver plant in Wisconsin, she rides on a solid fiberglass deep-V hull with a relatively wide beam. Inside, the mid-cabin floorplan remains much like the original layout although the galley has been improved with added counter space (at the expense of the 10.8's stall shower). The cockpit layout and helm console have been updated as well. For access to the engines and V-drives, the entire deck aft of the helm can be hydraulically raised. Among several engine options, big-block 502-cid gas inboards will cruise the 370 Express at 18 knots and reach a top speed of about 28 knots. ❑

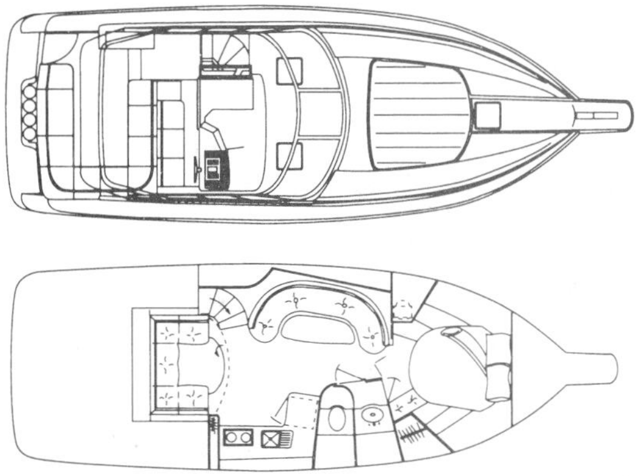

See Page 276 for Pricing Information

TROJAN 12 METER EXPRESS

SPECIFICATIONS

Length ....39'9"	Fuel ....325 gals.
Beam ....14'3"	Cockpit.............................NA
Draft ....3'8"	Hull Type ....Modified-V
Weight......................18,000#	Deadrise Aft....................12°
Clearance.........................NA	Designer..............H. Schoell
Water ....95 gals.	Production 1989–92

Still a great-looking boat with plenty of sex appeal, the Trojan 12 Meter Express set the standards for most of today's sportboat designs when she was introduced back in 1989. She's built on a fully cored Delta-Conic hull form with prop pockets and—with over 14 feet of beam—the 12 Meter Express is a big boat inside for her length. Below, the wide open floorplan features an abundance of curved bulkheads, indirect lighting, and upscale fabrics and hardware. An accordion-style privacy curtain (hidden in a small bulkhead door) converts the portside settee into a unique private stateroom. The cockpit is a piece of work: plenty of lounge seating fore and aft, good access to the motors below the bridgedeck, a space-age helm console, and a hydraulically operated in-deck storage well for an inflatable. The powder-coated all-white deck hardware and bow rails are especially attractive. With optional 485-hp 6-71s, the Trojan 12 Meter Express will cruise at a fast 26–27 knots and reach a top speed of around 30 knots. ❑

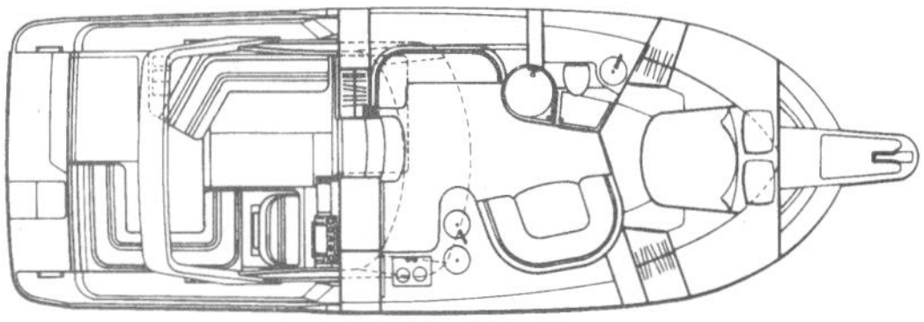

See Page 276 for Pricing Information

TROJAN 13 METER EXPRESS

SPECIFICATIONS

Length	43'0"	Fuel	510 gals.
Beam	16'3"	Cockpit	NA
Draft	3'2"	Hull Type	Modified-V
Weight	24,000#	Deadrise Aft	12°
Clearance	10'1"	Designer	H. Schoell
Water	175 gals.	Production	1984–90

The most compelling feature of the Trojan 13 Meter Express is her massive beam—the cockpit and cabin proportions in this boat are truly immense. Indeed, the 13 Meter is so wide that she'll be a tight fit in many 45-foot slips. She's built on a fully cored, low-deadrise hull with broad chine flats and side-dumping exhausts. Inside, her spacious two-stateroom floorplan is a blend of designer fabrics, curved bulkheads, and white Formica surfaces. The forward stateroom is huge, and the dinette table can be electrically lowered—a nice touch. Additional features include push-button pneumatic sliding cabin doors, a stylish helm console, good access to the engines, and a convention-size cockpit with plenty of lounge seating. Visibility from the raised helm position is excellent, and a center section of the windshield can be opened for ventilation. Optional 735-hp 8V92 diesels will provide an honest 30-knot cruising speed and a top speed of 32+ knots. Note that the short-lived Trojan 13 Meter Sedan; Trojan 13 Meter Sedan (with the same lower-level floorplan) ran from 1986–87. ❑

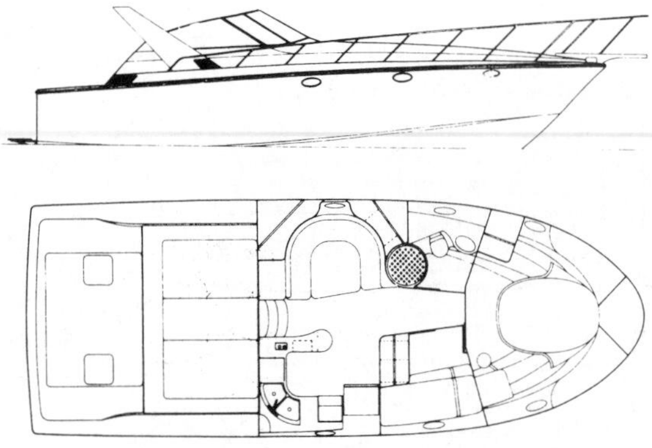

See Page 276 for Pricing Information

UNIFLITE 26 SEDAN

SPECIFICATIONS

Length	26'2"	Fuel	130 gals.
Beam	9'11"	Cockpit	50 sq. ft.
Draft	2'8"	Hull Type	Modified-V
Weight	7,000#	Deadrise Aft	NA
Clearance	9'0"	Designer	Uniflite
Water	50 gals.	Production	1978–83

Still a good-looking small cruiser in spite of her age, the Uniflite 26 Sedan is one of a handful of flybridge boats under 28 feet in length. (If it weren't for her wide beam, it would be impossible for the 26 Sedan to handle the added weight of a flybridge without becoming dangerously unstable.) Like all Uniflite models, hull construction was solid fiberglass, and fire-retardant resins were used in the laminate. Perhaps her most unusual feature is found in the forward cabin, where an offset double berth replaced the usual V-berth arrangement. Also unusual was the portside location of the lower helm. There's a shower in the head, and storage is better than average for a boat this size. The cockpit includes molded steps and in-deck storage bins. Topside, the flybridge is fitted with a double-wide helm seat and L-shaped lounge seating. Additional features include a teak interior, a surprisingly roomy galley, good engine access, and decent sidedecks. Among several power options, a single 270-hp Crusader inboard cruises at 15 knots (about 23 knots top). ❑

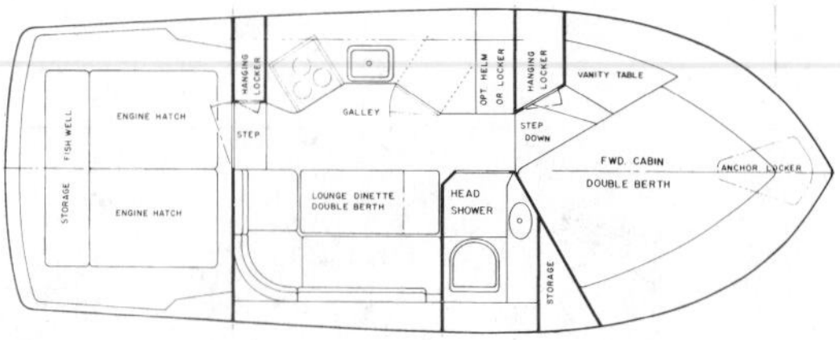

See Page 276 for Pricing Information

UNIFLITE 28 MEGA

SPECIFICATIONS

Length	28'2"	Fuel	140 gals.
Beam	10'10"	Cockpit	NA
Draft	2'10"	Hull Type	Modified-V
Weight	10,500#	Deadrise Aft	NA
Clearance	10'0"	Designer	Uniflite
Water	50 gals.	Production	1977–84

The Uniflite 28 Mega is a well-built family cruiser with attractive lines and surprisingly roomy cabin accommodations. With her wide 11-foot beam, the Mega delivers a big salon complete with an L-shaped dinette and a facing settee. Most were sold with a port-side lower helm. The wraparound cabin windows provide good all-round visibility, and the traditional teak interior woodwork is well-crafted. The galley in the Mega 28 is two steps down from the salon level, opposite the small head (with shower). Outside, the cockpit area is on the small side but large enough for a couple of folding chairs. Access to the engines and V-drives is via removable hatches in the cockpit sole. Seating for five is provided on the bridge (although a prudent helmsman is unlikely to want that much weight topside in a boat this size except in very calm water). Like many Uniflites of her era, gelcoat blisters are a common problem. Twin 220-hp Crusaders cruise the Uniflite 28 Mega at 20 knots with a top speed of around 27 knots. ❑

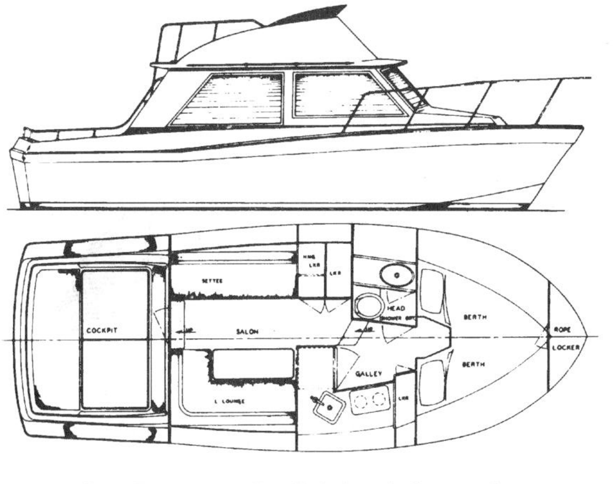

See Page 276 for Pricing Information

UNIFLITE 32 SPORT SEDAN

SPECIFICATIONS

Length	31'8"	Fuel	200 gals.
Beam	11'11"	Cockpit	NA
Draft	2'8"	Hull Type	Modified-V
Weight	15,000#	Deadrise Aft	15°
Clearance	11'0"	Designer	Uniflite
Water	75 gals.	Production	1975–84

A popular boat, the Uniflite 32 Sport Sedan was clearly designed with family cruising in mind. She was built on a solid fiberglass hull with a relatively wide beam and moderate transom deadrise. Like all Uniflites, the styling was conservative even by 1975 standards (when she was introduced), and today she looks like a museum piece when compared to her more modern counterparts. Nonetheless, the cabin accommodations are quite expansive for a boat of this size, with both the head and galley conveniently located just inside the companionway door, where they're easily accessed from outside. The cockpit is very spacious with enough room for some light-tackle fishing activities. Topside, the flybridge is arranged with the helm forward and lounge seating aft. Throughout, construction is on the heavy side, and quality is above average. Powered with twin 270-hp Crusaders with V-drives, the Uniflite 32 will cruise around 19 knots and top out at 27–28 knots. Trim tabs are required to keep her running angles down at planing speeds as her tendency is to otherwise run bow-high. ❑

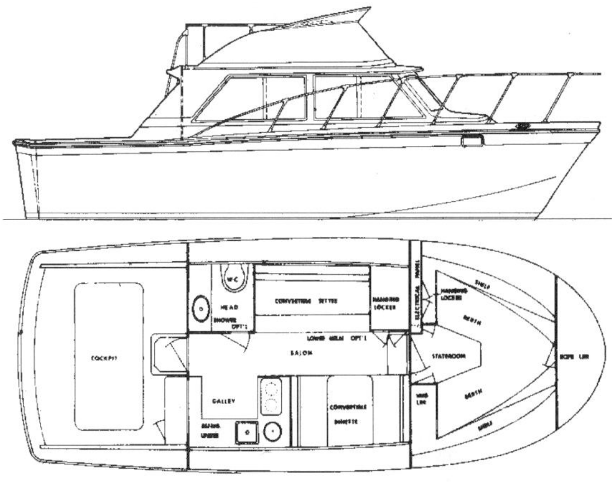

See Page 276 for Pricing Information

VIKING SPORT CRUISER V38 SC

SPECIFICATIONS

Length Overall	40'2"	Water	121 gals.
Hull Length	38'7"	Clearance	NA
Beam	12'8"	Hull Type	Deep-V
Draft	2'10"	Deadrise Aft	19°
Weight	21,280#	Designer	B. Olesinski
Fuel	230 gals.	Production	1995–Current

A great-looking boat with terrific lines, the Viking 38 Sport Cruiser is an English-built import for those seeking the look and feel of a true European family cruiser. She rides on a solid fiberglass modified-V hull with moderate beam, prop pockets (to reduce shaft angles), and an integrated swim platform. The interior layout is basically a scaled-down version of the larger 42 Sport Cruiser (next page) with two-staterooms and heads, an elevated lower helm, and a relatively small salon with facing settees. Large wraparound windows and good cabin headroom make the salon seem larger than it really is, and the interior furnishings and appliances are top-quality throughout. There's plenty of seating space in the cockpit (which is mostly shaded by a flybridge overhand), and molded steps at the corners lead up to wide sidedecks. Topside, the helm is forward on the bridge with guest seating aft. Among several diesel engine options, a pair of 355-hp Cats will cruise the 38 Sport Cruiser at 24–25 knots and deliver a top speed in the neighborhood of 30 knots. ❑

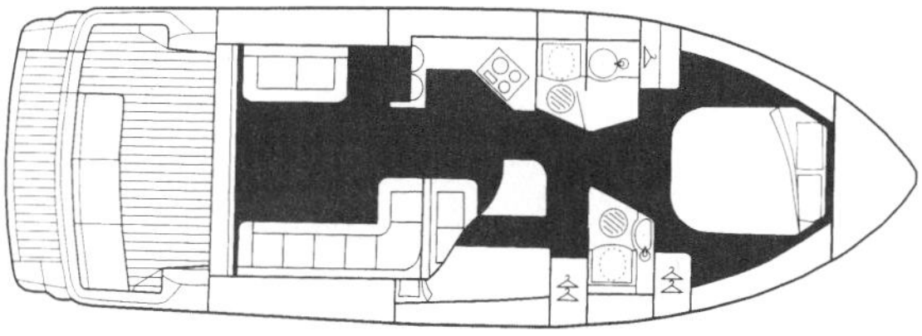

See Page 276 for Pricing Information

VIKING SPORT CRUISER V39 EX

SPECIFICATIONS

Length Overall	40'3"	Water	88 gals.
Hull Length	38'11"	Clearance	NA
Beam	12'3"	Hull Type	Deep-V
Draft	3'0"	Deadrise Aft	19°
Weight	16,800#	Designer	B. Olesinski
Fuel	192 gals.	Production	1995–Current

The Viking 39 Express is a pure-bred Mediterranean performance cruiser with the sleek styling and upscale accommodations European buyers have come to expect in a modern sportboat design. Built in England on an easy-riding deep-V hull with moderate beam, the Viking 39's spacious two-stateroom interior is arranged around a comfortable salon with a big U-shapped settee/dinette opposite a large and well-equipped galley. Privacy doors separate both staterooms from the main cabin, and the aft guest cabin comes with twin single berths as well as a hidden wash basin. There's a separate shower stall in the double-entry head, and the lacquered woodwork and plush furnishings are impressive. Outside, the spacious cockpit and elevated helm deck provide seating for a small crowd. Additional features include wide sidedecks, cockpit wet bar, foredeck sun pad, and a reversed radar arch. Gas or diesel stern drive power is available. Twin 270-hp MerCruiser diesels will cruise the Viking 39 Express at 30+ knots and reach about 36 knots wide open. ❑

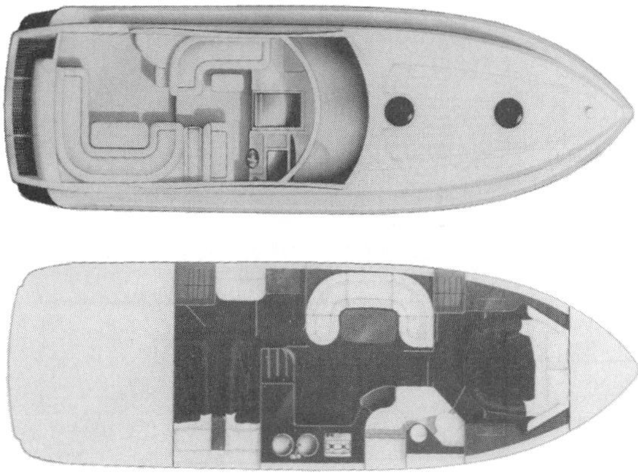

See Page 277 for Pricing Information

VIKING SPORT CRUISER V42 SC

SPECIFICATIONS

Length Overall...........42'10"	Water......................128 gals.
Hull Length..................41'9"	Clearance........................NA
Beam..............................13'8"	Hull Type...............Deep–V
Draft................................3'3"	Deadrise Aft...................19°
Weight......................23,520#	Designer...........B. Olesinski
Fuel........................360 gals.	Production....1995–Current

Introduced into the American market in mid-1995, the Viking 42 Sport Cruiser is a well-constructed flybridge sedan for those who enjoy the distinctive look and feel of a fine European yacht. She's built on a solid fiberglass hull with moderate beam, prop pockets, and a fully integrated swim platform. Below decks, the interior of the 42 Sport Cruiser is a big departure from most American boats. The two-stateroom layout is arranged with the galley down, just across from an *elevated* lower helm station. Not only does this result in excellent helm visability, it also provides the space for a second head. The salon and cockpit are on the same level and, with the galley open to the salon, the layout seems open and very comfortable. The cockpit, shaded by the extended flybridge overhang, is fitted with lounge seating and a transom door, and the flybridge (accessed by steps, not a ladder) has the helm console forward. A good-running boat with a comfortable ride, twin 355-hp Cat diesels will cruise at 23 knots with a top speed of about 28 knots. ❑

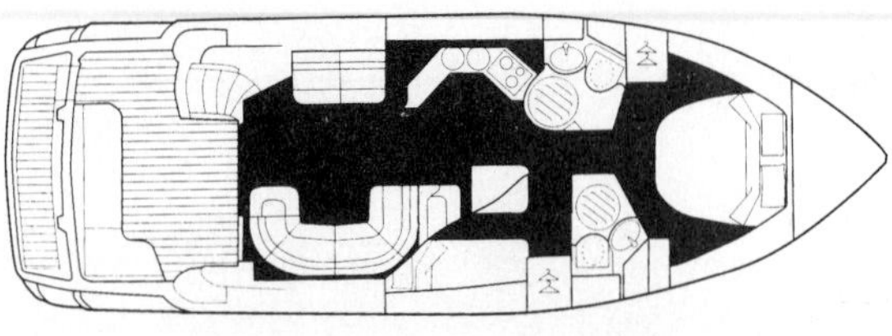

See Page 277 for Pricing Information

VIKING SPORT CRUISER V45 SC

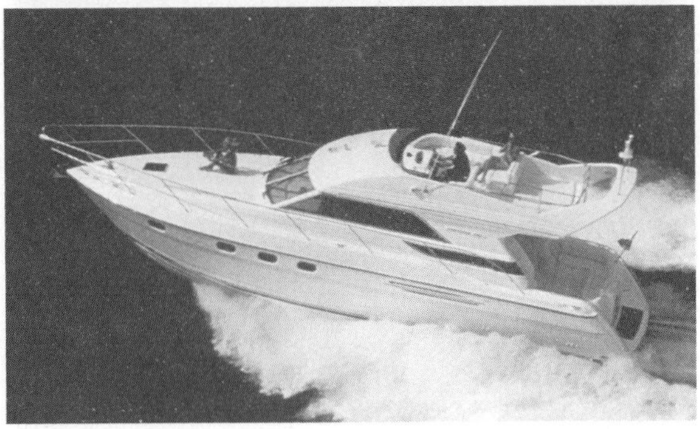

SPECIFICATIONS

Length Overall.............47'4"	Water......................128 gals.
Hull Length..................45'1"	Clearance........................NA
Beam............................13'10"	Hull Type...............Deep-V
Draft................................3'4"	Deadrise Aft...................19°
Weight......................28,000#	Designer...........B. Olesinski
Fuel........................372 gals.	Production....1995–Current

The Viking 45 Sport Cruiser combines the rakish good looks of a Euro-style flybridge sedan with the interior accommodations of a much larger boat. Built in England, her solid fiberglass modified-V hull (with prop pockets to reduce the shaft angles) is fairly light for a boat this size. The three-stateroom floorplan has the galley forward, a step down from the salon level and opposite the elevated lower helm. A huge wraparound settee dominates the spacious salon where unique lower-level windows allow guests a view of the outdoors while seated. Visibility from the lower helm is very good, and cabin headroom is about 6 feet, 4 inches throughout. The cockpit of the 45 Sport Sedan, with built-in lounge seating and a transom door, is well sheltered by the bridge overhang. Additional features include a huge flybridge with seating for a crowd, foredeck sunpads, a double-wide seat at the lower helm, and wide walkarounds. The engine room is a tight fit. An good performer, twin 425-hp Cat diesels will cruise at a respectable 25 knots (about 32 knots top). ❑

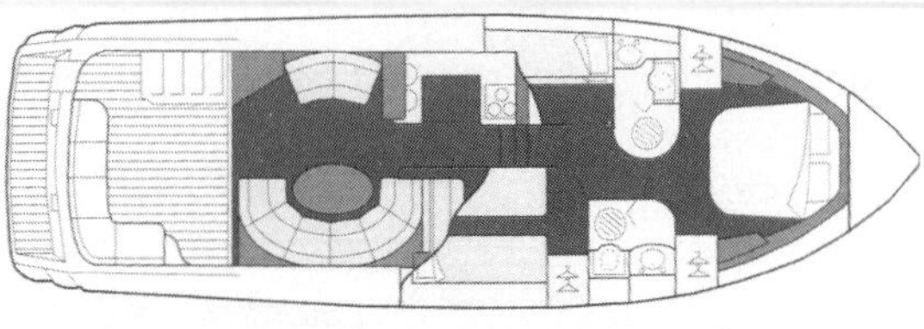

See Page 277 for Pricing Information

VIKING SPORT CRUISER V52 EX

SPECIFICATIONS

Length Overall	53'8"	Water	106 gals.
Hull Length	52'4"	Clearance	NA
Beam	14'0"	Hull Type	Deep-V
Draft	3'6"	Deadrise Aft	19°
Weight	32,032#	Designer	B. Olesinski
Fuel	540 gals.	Production	1995–Current

While the demand for 50-foot-plus express cruisers is limited by the number of buyers who can afford such toys, there's little doubt that this is one of the most dynamic market segments in today's boating industry. The 52 Express is one of the latest models to join the fray—a U.K.-built sportster imported into the American market by Viking Yachts. Long and lean, she's a high-performance Mediterranean sportboat with elegant styling, an enormous cockpit, and an innovative three-stateroom interior. While the accommodations below are spacious and well arranged (note the identical mid-cabin staterooms), more than half of the hull length is devoted to cockpit space including a huge sun pad aft with dinghy storage (i.e., a garage) below with its own hydraulic lift system. The straight-drive engines are located below the cockpit sole where a centerline hatch provides access to the engine room. Built on a narrow deep-V hull with prop pockets, the Viking 52 Express is a good performer with 600-hp MAN diesels. She'll cruise at a fast 30 knots and reach a top speed of 34–35 knots. ❑

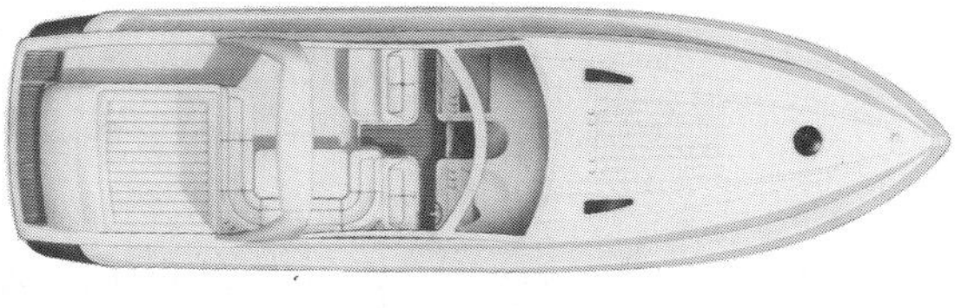

See Page 277 for Pricing Information

VIKING 35 CONVERTIBLE

1975–84

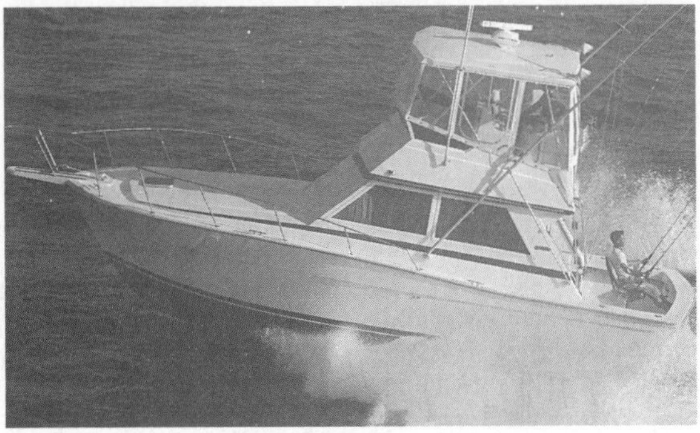

1985–92

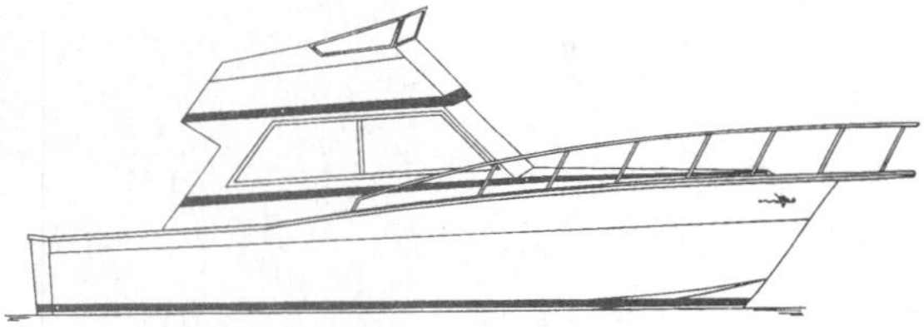

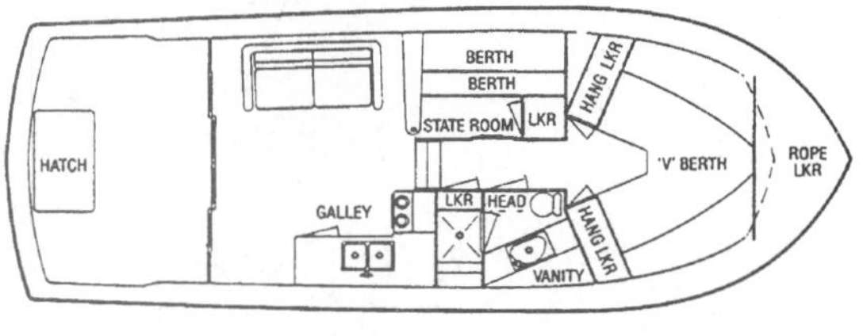

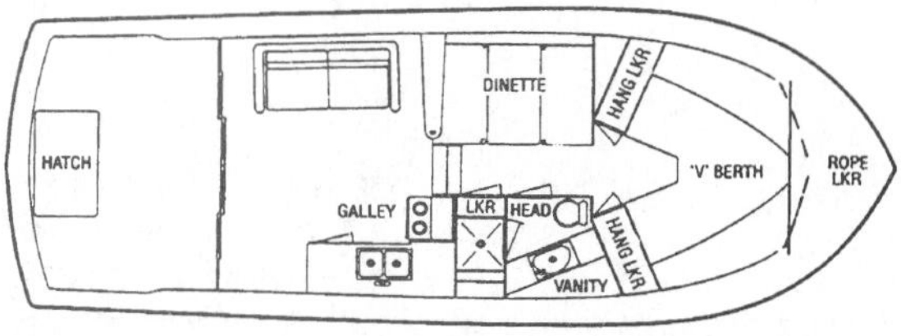

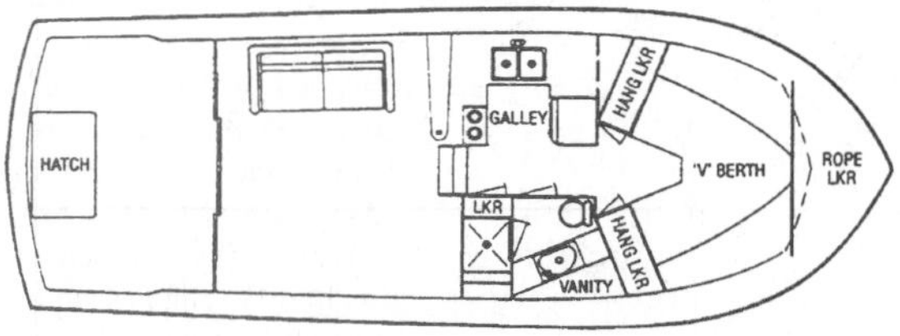

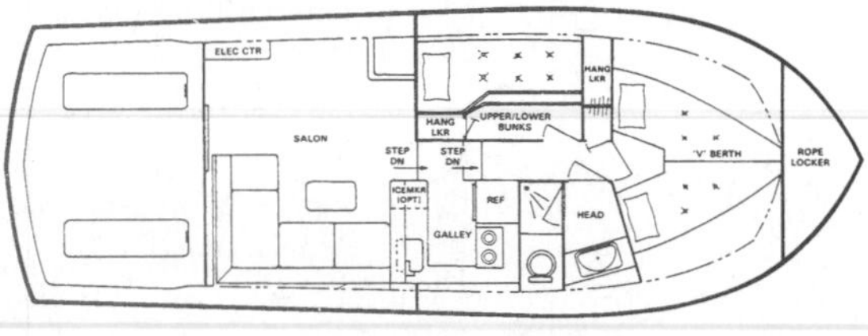

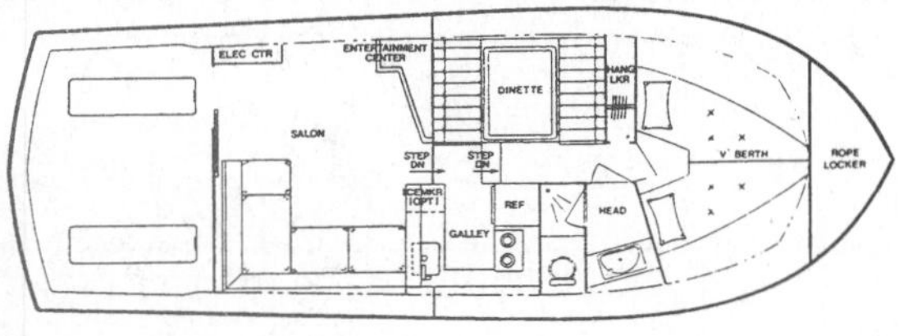

SPECIFICATIONS

Length	35'0"	Fuel	275/300 gals.
Beam	13'1"	Cockpit	80 sq. ft.
Draft	2'5"	Hull Type	Modified-V
Weight	20,000#	Deadrise Aft	15.5°
Clearance	12'4"	Designer	Viking
Water	75 gals.	Production	1975–92

A popular and durable family convertible, the Viking 35 has been recognized as a successful design since her introduction in 1975. She combines the essential elements of modern convertible styling with an attractive interior layout, superior construction, and proven offshore capabilities. Built on a beefed-up modified-V hull with 15.5 degrees of deadrise aft, the hullsides are balsa-cored for weight reduction and strength. She was extensively redesigned and updated in 1985 with a solid front windshield, a completely restyled flybridge, and a luxurious teak interior with a choice of one or two staterooms. (The original wood-grain mica interior was replaced with teak in 1980.) Also in 1985, the generator was relocated from beneath the cockpit to the engine room. With her uncluttered cockpit and comfortable interior, the Viking 35 can easily double as a weekend family cruiser. A stiff ride in a chop, 454-cid gas engines will cruise at 18–19 knots with a top speed of nearly 30 knots. Cat 375-hp diesels provide a cruising speed of 24–25 knots and 28 knots top. ❑

See Page 277 for Pricing Information

VIKING 43 EXPRESS & OPEN FISHERMAN

43 Express

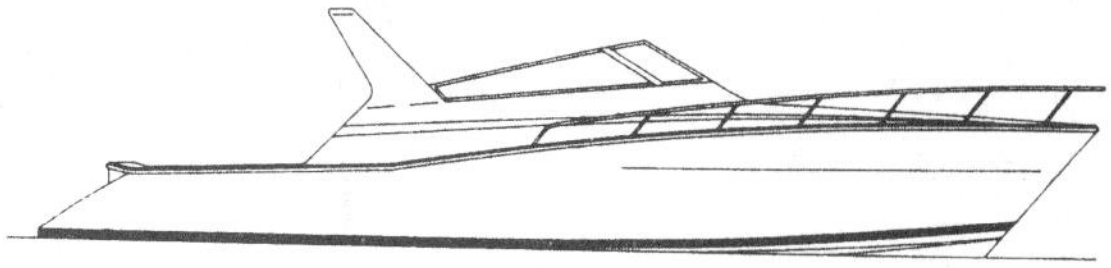

43 Open Sportfish

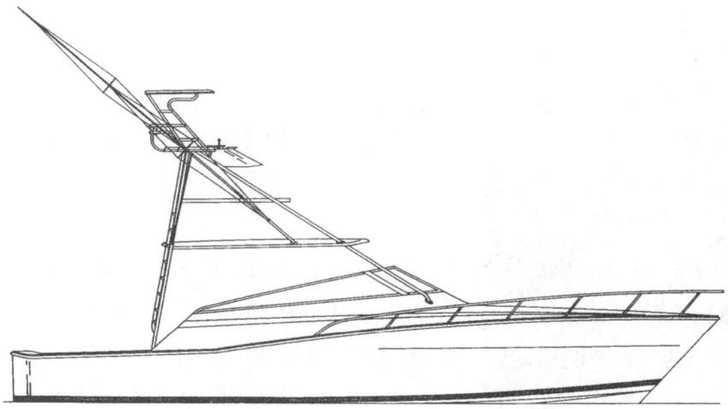

SPECIFICATIONS

Length	43'0"	Fuel	525 gals.
Beam	15'3"	Cockpit	116 sq. ft.
Draft	4'3"	Hull Type	Modified-V
Weight	34,500#	Deadrise Aft	15.5°
Clearance	8'6"	Designer	B. Wilson
Water	115 gals.	Production	1994–Current

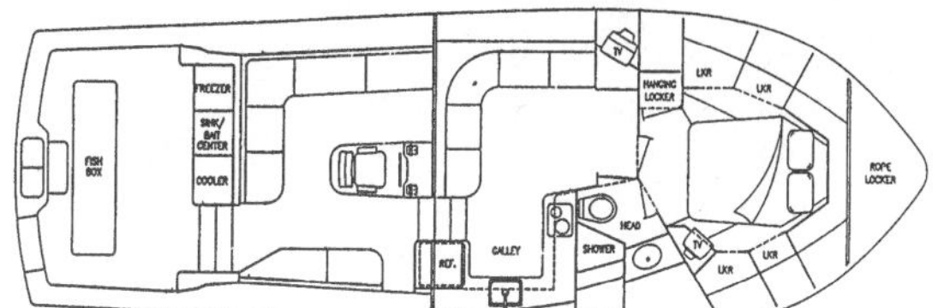

Standard Floorplan

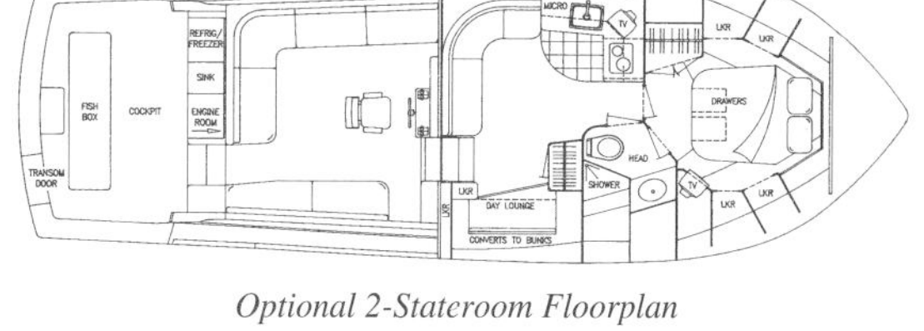

Optional 2-Stateroom Floorplan

Built on the Viking 43 Convertible hull, the 43 Express/Open Fisherman is one of the larger full-production boats of her type on the market. Both versions of this model share the same single-stateroom floorplan (an optional two-stateroom layout is available), and the only notable difference between the two is the bolt-on swim platform and radar arch of the Express. The deck plan is somewhat unusual: the helm is centered on the raised bridgedeck (visibility forward is excellent), and the steps leading down to the cockpit are offset to starboard. This permits a full set of in-line tackle centers and a centerline access door to the spacious engine room. A fish box is built into the cockpit sole, and a transom door and transom livewell are standard. Inside, the plush interior features a wide open salon/galley area along with a big stateroom forward and plenty of storage—an excellent day boat layout. Standard 550-hp 6V92s will cruise at 28 knots with a top speed of 32 knots. Optional 600-hp MANs became available in 1995, and 625-hp 6V92s became optional in 1996. ❑

See Page 277 for Pricing Information

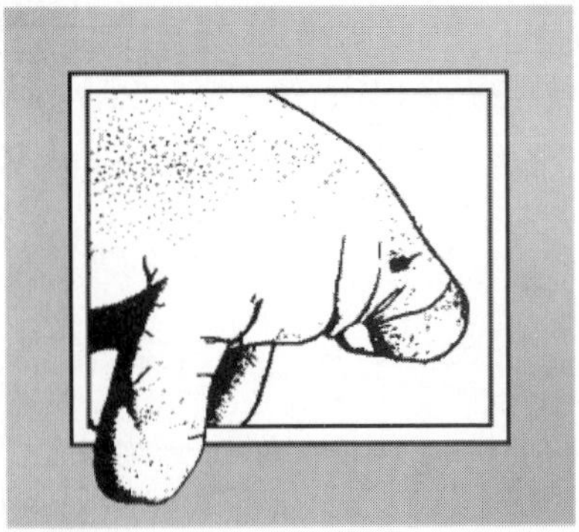

Get Your M.A. (Manatee Awareness) Degree In Recreational Watersports:

Tips To Protect Manatees

There are many things YOU can do to protect manatees from a watercraft collision or other human-related injuries:

- ✤ Wearing polarized sunglasses can help eliminate the glare of the sun and helps boaters to see below the water's surface.

- ✤ Stay in deep water channels when boating. Avoid boating over seagrass beds and shallow areas where manatees might be feeding (but be aware that manatees also use deep water channels when traveling).

- ✤ Look for a snout, back, tail, or flipper breaking the surface of the water, or a swirl or a flat spot on the water that is created by the motion of the manatee's paddle-shaped tail when it dives or swims.

- ✤ If you see a manatee when operating a powerboat, remain a safe distance away — 50 feet is suggested. If you want to observe the manatee, cut the motor, but do not drift over the animal.

- ✤ If you like to jet-ski, water-ski, or participate in high-speed water sports, choose areas that manatees do not, or cannot frequent, such as a landlocked lake.

- ✤ Obey posted speed zone signs and keep away from posted manatee sanctuaries.

- ✤ Keep your litter on board your vessel. Recycle it or throw it in a trash container when you get back on shore.

- ✤ Discard monofilament line or hooks properly. Discarding monofilament line into or onto the waters of the state of Florida is against the law.

- ✤ Look, but don't touch manatees. If manatees become accustomed to being around people, it can alter their behavior in the wild, perhaps causing them to lose their natural fear of boats and humans, and this may make them susceptible to harm. Passive observation is the best way to interact with manatees and all wildlife.

- ✤ Resist the urge to feed manatees or give them water. Remember, passive observation!

- ✤ When swimming or diving, the key words are ________ ____________ (right! passive observation). You may not know it, but your presence might accidentally separate a mother manatee and calf or keep a manatee away from its warm water source — both of which are potentially life-threatening situations.

- ✤ Call the Manatee Hotline at 1-800-DIAL-FMP if you happen to spot an injured, dead, tagged, or orphaned manatee, or if you see a manatee that is being harassed.

Save the Manatee® Club
500 N. Maitland Avenue • Maitland, FL 32751
1 - 800 - 432 - JOIN

WELLCRAFT 2600 EXPRESS

SPECIFICATIONS

Length w/Pulpit..........28'7"	Water........................20 gals.
Hull Length..................26'1"	Fuel.........................100 gals.
Beam................................9'8"	Hull Type................Deep-V
Draft, drive down..........3'0"	Deadrise Aft....................18°
Weight........................7,200#	Designer................Wellcraft
Clearance........................7'0"	Production.............1991–92

The Wellcraft 2600 Express is a straightforward family cruiser with an attractive (if conservative) profile and a roomy interior. Her old-fashioned trunk cabin foredeck and traditional (not curved) windshield make the 2600 something of a throwback to the days when Euro-styling trends were less conspicuous in the marketplace. The accommodations are quite generous for a 26-footer, with berths for five and a large head with shower. Storage is adequate, and the large cabin windows provide a good deal of natural lighting inside. Outside, the single-level cockpit is arranged with a fold-away bench seat at the transom in addition to a helm and companion seat. Additional features include a bow pulpit, an integral swim platform with a walk-thru transom door, good engine access, and a completely flush cockpit deck. Typical of most small cruisers, the walkarounds are extremely narrow. A economical performer with a single 330-hp MerCruiser stern drive, the 2600 Express will cruise at 20 knots and reach 30–31 knots top. (Twin I/Os were also available.) Production lasted for only two years. ❑

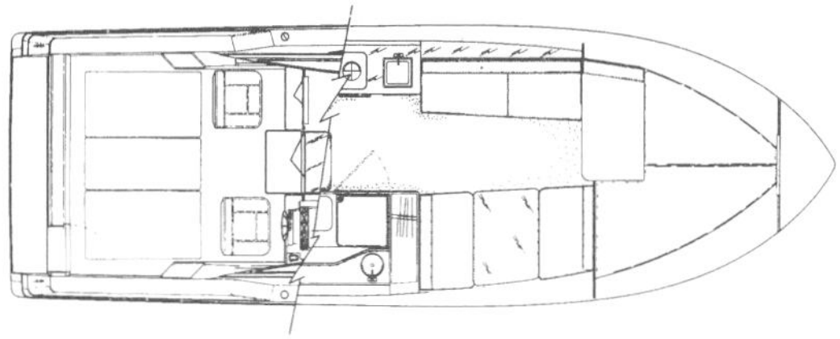

See Page 277 for Pricing Information

WELLCRAFT 2700 MARTINIQUE

SPECIFICATIONS

Length w/Pulpit..........28'4"	Bridge Clearance...........7'5"
Hull Length..................26'6"	Water........................22 gals.
Beam................................9'6"	Fuel.........................100 gals.
Draft, Up.......................1'10"	Hull Type.........Modified-V
Draft, Down..................3'1"	Deadrise Aft....................17°
Weight........................6,950#	Production....1994–Current

A new model for Wellcraft in 1994, the 2700 Martinique is an attractively priced family cruiser with a modern profile, roomy cockpit dimensions, and berths for six. Notably, the 2700 Martinique's emphasis on cockpit space results in a somewhat compact cabin—a trade-off that many experienced weekend cruisers will certainly applaud. Besides, the Martinique's mid-cabin accommodations are more than adequate and include a full galley (with some very useful counter space), a small dinette, stand-up head with shower, and good headroom. Not surprisingly, storage space is scarce. Visibility from the elevated helm is excellent. Cockpit seating includes a triple-wide helm seat and aft-facing guest seat (that slides out of the way), plus an L-shaped bench seat aft. A built-in ladder, walk-thru transom door, and transom shower are standard in the integral swim platform. Lacking sidedecks, access to the foredeck is via a walk-thru in the windshield. A single 300-hp MerCruiser 7.4-litre stern drive will cruise the 2700 Martinique at 21 knots (about 33 knots top), and the Volvo 7.4-litre Duoprop runs a few knots faster. ❑

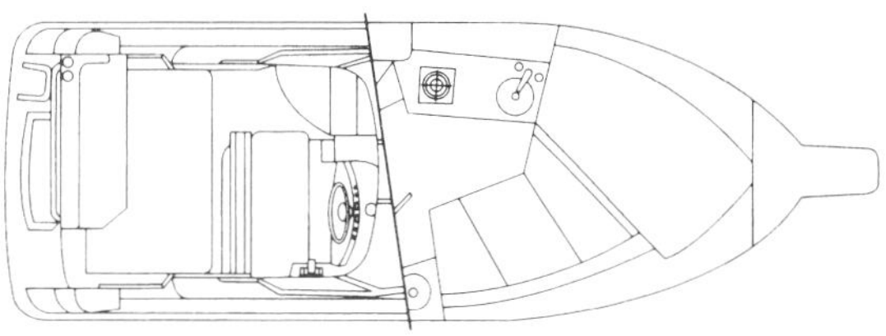

See Page 277 for Pricing Information

WELLCRAFT 2800 MONTE CARLO

SPECIFICATIONS

Length ....27'7"	Water ....28 gals.
Beam ....9'11"	Fuel ....115 gals.
Draft, Up ....1'9"	Hull Type ....Modified-V
Draft, Down ....2'9"	Deadrise Aft ....16°
Weight ....7,200#	Designer ....Wellcraft
Clearance ....NA	Production 1986–89

Dramatic styling (for the late 1980s), an affordable price tag, and a roomy mid-cabin floorplan made the 2800 Monte Carlo one of the more popular models in the Wellcraft fleet a few years back. Hull construction is solid fiberglass, and she rides on a conventional modified-V bottom with moderate deadrise at the transom. The liberal hull graphics (which were often quite colorful) are the most distinguishing feature of the Monte Carlo. Below, there are overnight accommodations for up to six. The absence of interior bulkheads results in a wide-open cabin with privacy curtains fore and aft, a compact galley, and a stand-up head with shower. The aft cabin has near-standing headroom as well—unusual in such a small boat. The cockpit is large enough for several guests and includes molded steps port and starboard, a transom cut-out, a double-wide helm seat, and removable bench seating at the transom. A radar arch was optional. Twin 260-hp stern drives cruise the 2800 Monte Carlo at an easy 25 knots and deliver a 35-knot top speed. ❑

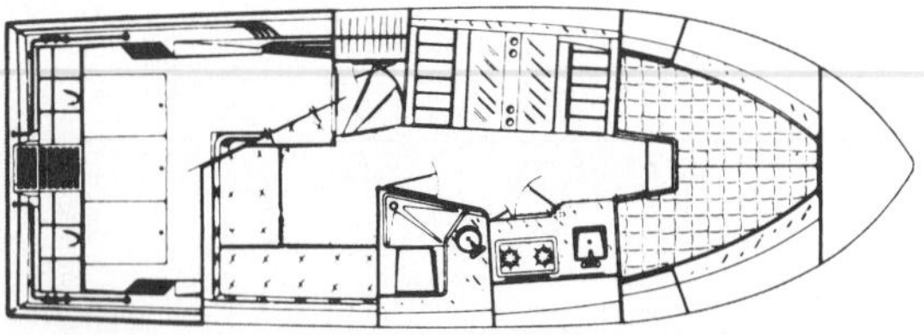

See Page 277 for Pricing Information

WELLCRAFT 287 PRIMA

SPECIFICATIONS

Length w/Pulpit ....28'7"	Water ....20 gals.
Hull Length ....26'1"	Fuel ....100 gals.
Beam ....9'8"	Hull Type ....Deep-V
Draft ....3'0"	Deadrise Aft ....18°
Weight ....7,200#	Designer ....Wellcraft
Clearance ....7'0"	Production 1990–93

The Wellcraft 287 Prima is a maxi-cube family cruiser with a nice profile (note the elevated foredeck) and good all-around performance characteristics. Sharing her hull with Wellcraft's 2600 Coastal fishing boat, she's constructed on a solid fiberglass deep-V hull with moderate beam and 19 degrees of transom deadrise. Inside, Prima's full-width mid-cabin floorplan will sleep five with privacy curtains separating the fore and aft sleeping areas from the rest of the cabin. There's a flexible shower in the head compartment, and the absence of interior bulkheads results in a wide-open and very inviting layout. The cockpit is arranged with a raised double-wide helm seat and bench seating aft. Engine access is via removable hatches in the cockpit sole. Additional features include a center-opening windshield for easy access to the foredeck sunpad, an integral swim platform, and distinctive oval ports in the hullsides. Twin 155-hp MerCruiser V-6 stern drives will cruise at 21–22 knots (31 knots top), and a Volvo 300-hp V-8 will cruise at an efficient 24 knots (about 36 top). ❑

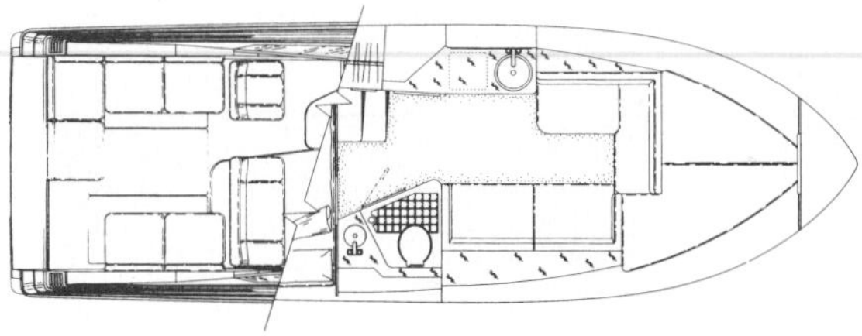

See Page 277 for Pricing Information

WELLCRAFT 2900 EXPRESS

SPECIFICATIONS

Length	28'8"
Beam	10'8"
Draft	2'6"
Weight	9,000#
Clearance	7'4"
Water	28 gals.
Fuel	120 gals.
Cockpit	NA
Hull Type	Modified-V
Deadrise Aft	16°
Designer	B. Collier
Production	1980–87

The 2900 Express pictured above was originally called the Wellcraft 288 Suncruiser at her introduction back in 1980. She was designed as an inexpensive family cruiser with conservative lines, a spacious cockpit layout, and comfortable accommodations below for four. The original 288 Suncruiser was dropped from production in 1983 when the re-styled 2900 Express took her place. Aside from the hull graphics and several miscellaneous decor and hardware updates, she's basically the same boat as her predecessor. Further changes were made in 1985, with the addition of new interior fabrics and modern high-gloss mica laminates. The 2900 was built on a solid fiberglass hull with 16 degrees of deadrise at the transom—the same hull later used for the Wellcraft 2900 Sport Bridge model. The relatively wide beam provides a comfortable and open floorplan with a full galley and convertible dinette and a stand-up head with shower. Twin 230-hp MerCruiser gas engines will cruise the 2900 Express at an economical 19–20 knots and reach 29 knots at full throttle. Note the very limited fuel capacity. ❑

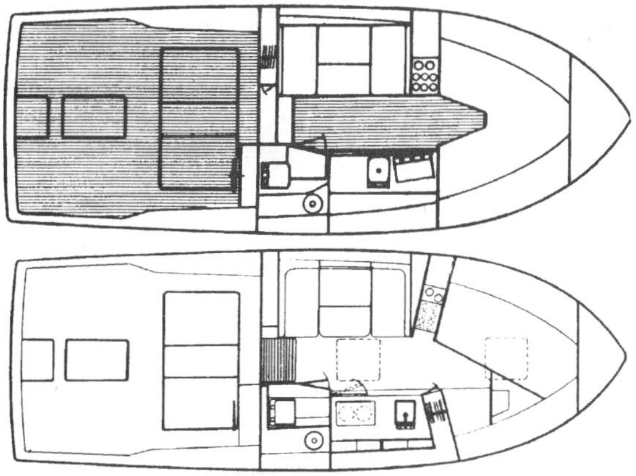

See Page 277 for Pricing Information

WELLCRAFT 3000 MONACO

SPECIFICATIONS

Length w/Pulpit	30'2"
Hull Length	28'2"
Beam	10'8"
Draft, drive up	1'11"
Draft, drive down	3'0"
Weight	9,800#
Clearance	7'6"
Water	31 gals.
Fuel	120 gals.
Hull Type	Modified-V
Deadrise Aft	16°
Production	1989–1992

The Wellcraft 3000 Monaco is a maxi-cube mid-cabin family cruiser with a raised foredeck profile (the wraparound black stripe is actually a window) and comfortable accommodations. Hull construction is solid fiberglass, and her 10-foot, 8-inch beam—once considered wide for a 28-footer—is about average for a modern sportboat design. Inside, the full-width interior of the Monaco is unusually bright and open (thanks in part to the wraparound deck window) with very good headroom. The small aft cabin is arranged with facing settees, and draw curtains separate both sleeping areas from the main cabin. The bi-level cockpit includes an L-shaped settee opposite the helm and removable bench seating aft. The companionway is to port and—lacking sidedecks—a molded centerline step provides access to the center-opening windshield. The somewhat useless fold-away instrument panel found on the 1989 Monaco was eliminated in 1990.) Engine access is very good. Twin 260-hp MerCruiser I/Os (standard) will cruise the Monaco at a brisk 25 knots and reach a top speed of about 35 knots. ❑

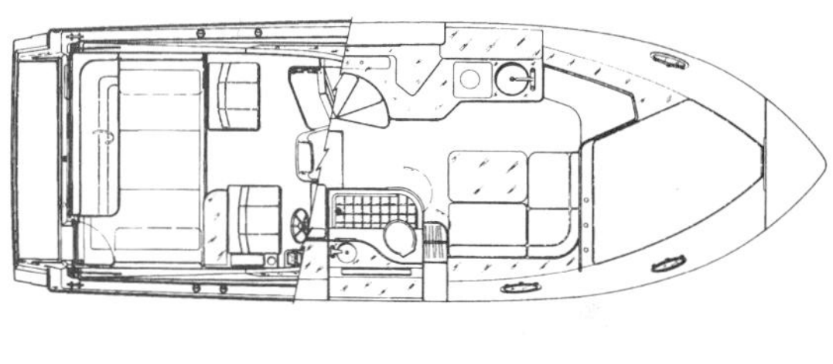

See Page 277 for Pricing Information

WELLCRAFT 3100 EXPRESS

SPECIFICATIONS

Length	31'3"	Fuel	160 gals.
Beam	11'6"	Cockpit	NA
Draft	2'11"	Hull Type	Deep-V
Weight	10,200#	Deadrise Aft	19°
Clearance	8'1"	Designer	Wellcraft
Water	28 gals.	Production	1979–85

The Wellcraft 3100 Express evolved from the original Wellcraft 310 Suncruiser introduced back in 1979. Conservatively styled by today's standards, she was built on a deep-V hull form with a steep 19 degrees of deadrise at the transom. The profile of the 3100 Express shows considerable freeboard resulting in a full 6 feet, 5 inches of headroom in the main cabin. Teak trim and attractive fabrics are used throughout, and overnight berths are provided for as many as six. Always a comfortable layout, a new Eurostyle interior was installed in the 1985 models with curved bulkheads and shiny off-white mica surfaces. Removable hatches in the cockpit sole access the engines and V-drives, which are somewhat close together due to the outboard fuel tanks. Performance with the optional 454-cid big-block gas engines (350-hp) is around 22 knots at cruise and 31+ knots wide open. Trim tabs are usually required for the 3100 Express to obtain proper running angles. Note that Wellcraft's 310 FB Cruiser was essentially the same boat with the addition of a flybridge and a salon bulkhead. ❑

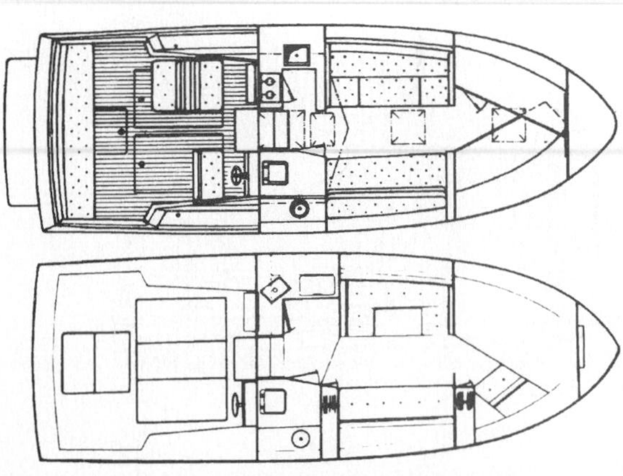

See Page 277 for Pricing Information

WELLCRAFT 310 FB SEDAN

SPECIFICATIONS

Length	31'3"	Fuel	200 gals.
Beam	11'6"	Cockpit	NA
Draft	2'11"	Hull Type	Deep-V
Weight	11,200#	Deadrise Aft	19°
Clearance	11'0"	Designer	R. Cole
Water	50 gals.	Production	1981–83

The Wellcraft 310 Flybridge is a straightforward sedan cruiser with a raised-foredeck profile and a comfortable interior. Notably, her deep-V hull gives the 310 above-average seakeeping characteristics and the ability to run well in a chop. Belowdecks, the galley-down floorplan results in a fairly expansive salon with enough floor space for a sofa and chairs and the choice of an optional wet bar or inside helm station to starboard. The wraparound cabin windows and sliding glass door give the interior a wide-open and spacious appearance. While the 310's cockpit isn't designed for any serious fishing activities, it's still adequate for a couple of light tackle anglers. Topside, the helm is forward on the bridge with bench seating aft. Additional features include fairly wide sidedecks, teak covering boards in the cockpit, and a teak bow pulpit. A variety of gas and diesel engine options were available in the 310 Sedan. Among them, the popular 235-hp MerCruisers (with V-drives) will cruise at 18 knots and reach 24–25 knots top. ❑

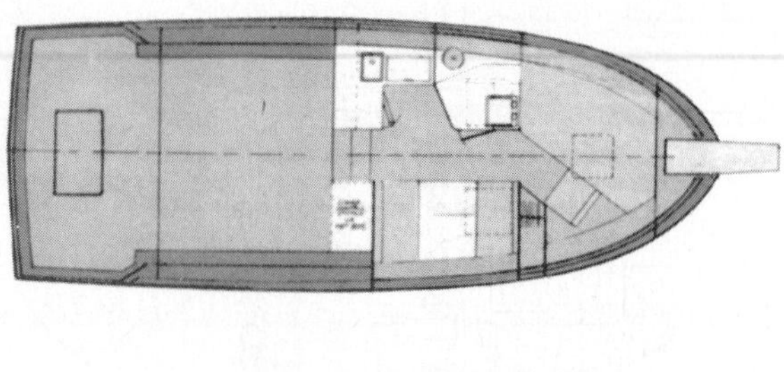

See Page 277 for Pricing Information

WELLCRAFT 3200 SEDAN BRIDGE

SPECIFICATIONS

Length ....32'0"	Fuel ....290 gals.
Beam ....11'6"	Cockpit ....70 sq. ft.
Draft ....3'0"	Hull Type ....Modified-V
Weight ....14,200#	Deadrise Aft ....14°
Clearance ....NA	Designer ....B. Collier
Water ....80 gals.	Production 1985–86

Sharing the same hull as the well-regarded 3200 Coastal fishboat, the 3200 Sedan Bridge is basically the same boat as the Coastal with the addition of a flybridge and an enclosed salon. (Notably, she enjoyed only a short production run before being phased out of the Wellcraft line-up for 1987.) Inside, the galley-down floorplan is arranged with V-berths forward and a full-size dinette opposite the galley and head compartment. With 360-degree wraparound cabin windows, the salon seems particularly open and bright. A lower helm was a popular option, and the interior is completely finished with teak paneling and trim. With some 70 sq. ft. of space, the cockpit is large enough for some serious fishing. A transom door and in-deck storage were standard. Topside, the flybridge is big for a 32-footer with guest seating forward of the helm console. Twin 454-cid gas engines will cruise the 3200 Sedan Bridge around 19 knots and reach a top speed of 27–28 knots. ❑

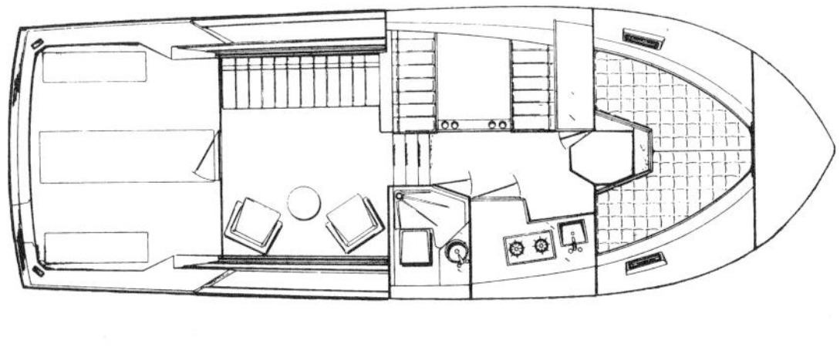

See Page 277 for Pricing Information

WELLCRAFT 3200 ST. TROPEZ

SPECIFICATIONS

Length ....31'8"	Fuel ....180 gals.
Beam ....11'8"	Cockpit ....NA
Draft ....2'10"	Hull Type ....Modified-V
Weight ....10,300#	Deadrise Aft ....16°
Clearance ....8'5"	Designer ....B. Collier
Water ....40 gals.	Production 1985–93

One of the most popular Wellcraft designs ever, the St. Tropez was scheduled to go out of production in 1990 with the introduction of the new 3300 St. Tropez model. She stayed around for a couple of more years, however, not retiring from the fleet until 1994. Secret to her success was a stylish profile and a surprisingly spacious interior for a boat her size—a layout made possible by Wellcraft's use of an integral cabin liner which eliminates any structural bulkheads. There are berths for five and a big L-shaped galley aft, opposite a roomy head compartment. Outside, the cockpit is large enough for a small crowd. A bolt-on swim platform was added in 1988 and upgrades in 1991 included reduced hull graphics and a stylish white-on-white helm. Standard 260-hp MerCruiser gas engines (using V-drives) will cruise the St. Tropez around 20–21 knots with a top speed of 29 knots, and optional 340-hp big-block Mercs will cruise at a fast 25 knots (about 35 knots top). ❑

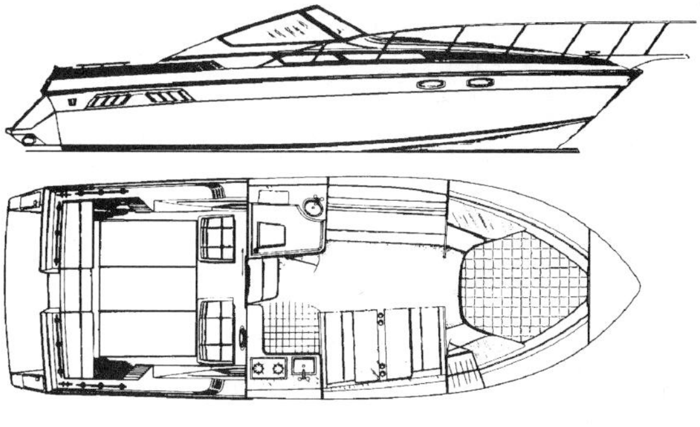

See Page 277 for Pricing Information

WELLCRAFT 3200 MARTINIQUE

SPECIFICATIONS

Length w/Pulpit	34'5"	Water	37 gals.
Hull Length	32'0"	Fuel	162 gals.
Beam	11'2"	Hull Type	Modified-V
Draft	3'1"	Deadrise Aft	16°
Weight	10,300#	Designer	Wellcraft
Clearance	8'0"	Production	1994–Current

The 3200 Martinique is a maxi-volume family cruiser with an attractive profile (in spite of her sloping foredeck) and a conventional mid-cabin floorplan. She's built on a solid fiberglass modified-V hull with moderate beam and transom deadrise. The interior of the Martinique will sleep six and includes a roomy galley (with good storage and counter space), a stand-up head with shower, and a low-overhead aft cabin with a dinette that converts into a big double bed. Draw curtains are used for privacy in the fore and aft sleeping areas, and translucent deck hatches and decent-sized cabin windows combine to provide a good deal of natural lighting below. Outside, the Martinique's bi-level cockpit features a triple-wide helm seat, an aft-facing bench seat, a walk-thru windshield and L-shaped lounge seating aft. A transom door and shower are standard. Twin Volvo 310-hp stern drives will cruise the 3200 Martinique at 25 knots (about 36 knots top), and a pair of inboard 320-hp V-drive MerCruisers will cruise at 23 knots and reach a top speed of 33–34 knots. ❏

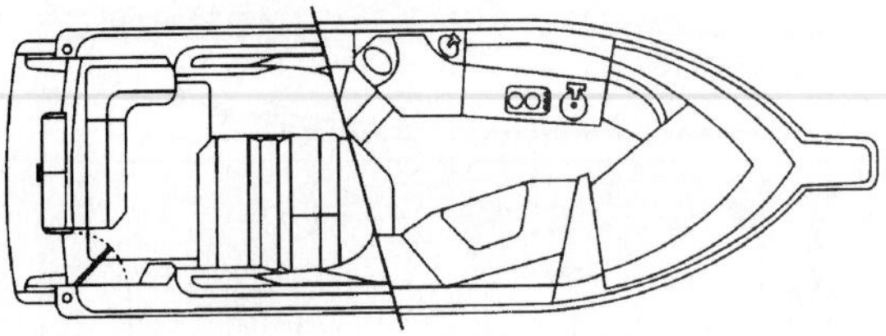

See Page 277 for Pricing Information

WELLCRAFT 33 ST. TROPEZ

SPECIFICATIONS

Length w/Pulpit	33'7"	Water	40 gals.
Hull Length	31'5"	Fuel	180 gals.
Beam	11'8"	Hull Type	Modified-V
Draft	3'1"	Deadrise Aft	16°
Weight	11,200#	Designer	B. Collier
Clearance	9'0"	Production	1990–92

Not to be confused with the original (and hugely popular) 3200 St. Tropez, the 33 St. Tropez lasted only three years in production before being retired from the Wellcraft fleet in 1993. She was built on a solid fiberglass hull with moderate beam and a fairly steep 16 degrees of transom deadrise—the same good-running hull used in the production of the 3200 St. Tropez. Belowdecks, the centerline island berth found in the original floorplan was replaced in 1991 with an offset double berth and extended portside seating. Tinted cabin windows (disguised as a black wraparound stripe on the outside), oval portlights, and translucent deck hatches provide good natural lighting below. While the layout is very similar to the original St. Tropez, the elevated cabintop of the 33 adds interior headroom and some noticeable height to her exterior profile. The cockpit is arranged with plenty of guest seating and a walk-through windshield provides access to the foredeck. Twin 260-hp gas engines (with V-drives) will cruise at 20 knots with a top speed of around 29 knots. ❏

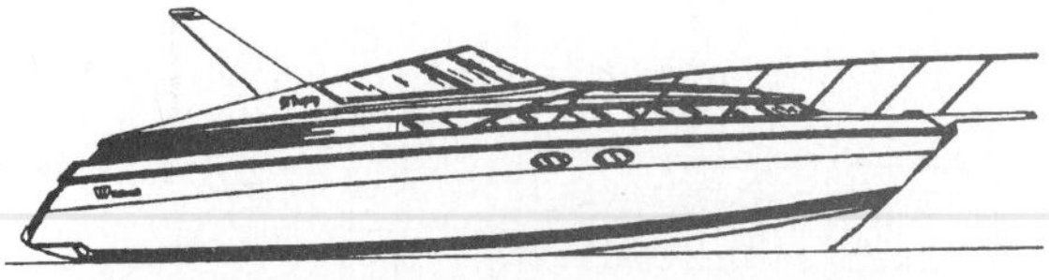

See Page 277 for Pricing Information

WELLCRAFT 3400 GRAN SPORT

SPECIFICATIONS

Length w/Pulpit..........35'5"	Water........................75 gals.
Length...........................33'7"	Fuel.........................270 gals.
Beam..............................12'6"	Hull Type.........Modified-V
Draft................................3'0"	Deadrise Aft.....................16°
Weight......................13,400#	Designer...............B. Collier
Clearance........................9'4"	Production.............1984–92

A popular model for many years, the Wellcraft 34 Gran Sport is built on an easy-riding modified-V hull with average beam and 16 degrees of deadrise at the transom. (Note that she was introduced in 1984 as the Wellcraft 3400 Express Cruiser.) Aside from her attractive lines, the chief attraction of the Gran Sport is her wide-open floorplan—a feature made possible by the absence of any structural interior bulkheads. The original floorplan (with an offset double berth forward) was replaced in 1990 with a more contemporary (and colorful) layout with a centerline companionway and an island bed forward. In 1988 a bolt-on swim platform was added along with side exhaust channels (quickly dropped in 1989 models), and in 1990 the Gran Sport was again updated on the outside with new hull graphics and a stylish white-on-white helm console. A good-running boat with plenty of cockpit seating, standard 454-cid gas engines will cruise the 3400 Gran Sport at 22 knots and reach a top speed of 30+ knots. ❑

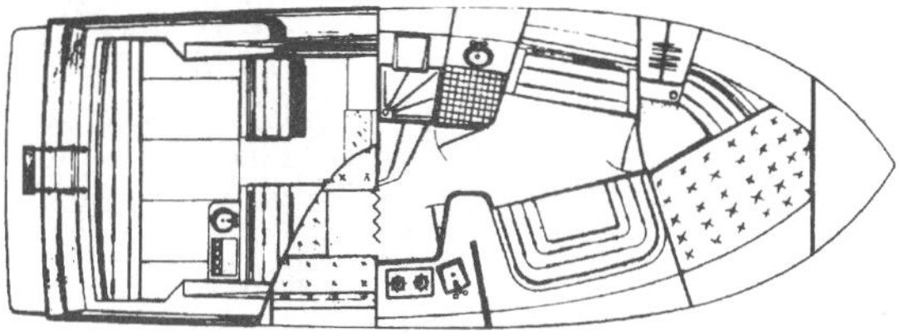

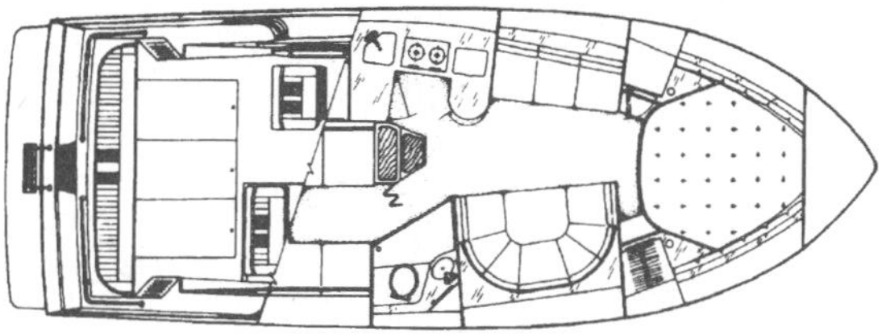

See Page 277 for Pricing Information

WELLCRAFT 34 TRIUMPH

SPECIFICATIONS

Length w/Pulpit.........36'9"	Water........................60 gals.
Length on Deck............34'0"	Fuel.........................256 gals.
Beam..............................12'6"	Cockpit....................60 sq. ft.
Draft................................3'0"	Hull Type.........Modified-V
Weight......................15,700#	Deadrise Aft.....................14°
Clearance........................9'9"	Production.............1990–93

When she was introduced in 1990, this maxi-volume family cruiser was presented to the public as the Triumph 34 Bridgedeck Sedan, the product of an all-new boatbuilding company closely associated with the Wellcraft factory. The Triumph operation (they had only two 34-foot models: the Bridgedeck pictured above and the mid-cabin Americus express) lasted just over a year before being absorbed into the Wellcraft fleet in 1991. The Triumph's low-profile appearance is the result of locating the engines aft, thereby lowering the salon sole and creating a wide-open single-level floorplan. Notable features include a unique pass-thru from the galley to the flybridge (very convenient) and a hidden privacy curtain and overhead track for use when the portside salon settee is converted into a double berth at night. Outside, both the cockpit and flybridge provide plenty of guest seating. No racehorse, Crusader 300-hp gas engines (with V-drives and side exhausts) will cruise the 34 Triumph at a sedate 15–16 knots and reach a top speed of 26 knots. ❑

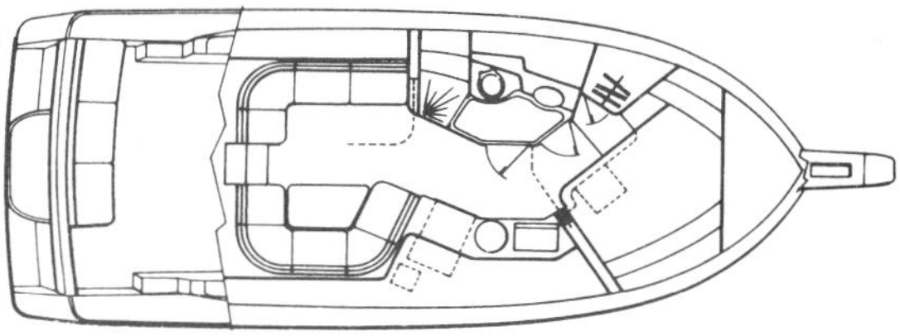

See Page 278 for Pricing Information

WELLCRAFT 3500 CORSAIR
3600 ST. TROPEZ

SPECIFICATIONS

Length w/Pulpit..........38'7"	Water........................76 gals.
Hull Length................33'10"	Clearance w/Arch.........9'9"
Beam..............................12'6"	Hull Type.........Modified-V
Draft...............................2'9"	Deadrise Aft....................16°
Weight......................14,400#	Designer................Wellcraft
Fuel.........................270 gals.	Production..............1992–93

The Wellcraft 3500 Corsair (called the 3600 St. Tropez in 1993) is a maxi-cube express cruiser with a rakish profile to go with her brisk performance. She's built on a relatively lightweight hull with a solid fiberglass bottom, and integral swim platform, and prop pockets. By eliminating the sidedecks, Wellcraft engineers were able to enlarge the interior dimensions, and the result is a wide-open and very expansive living area.Where many other express boats this size have mid-cabin floorplans, the Corsair/St. Tropez has a conventional layout with a single stateroom and berths for six. Note that the galley is recessed under the elevated helm station. There's a separate stall shower in the head, and the starboard settee converts into upper and lower bunks. There's plenty of cockpit seating (including fold-down aft-facing bench seating behind the helm and a triple-wide helm seat), and a windshield walk-through provides access to the foredeck. Twin 400-hp (502-cid) MerCruiser gas inboards (with V-drives and side exhausts) will cruise at about 20 knots and reach 30+ knots wide open. ❑

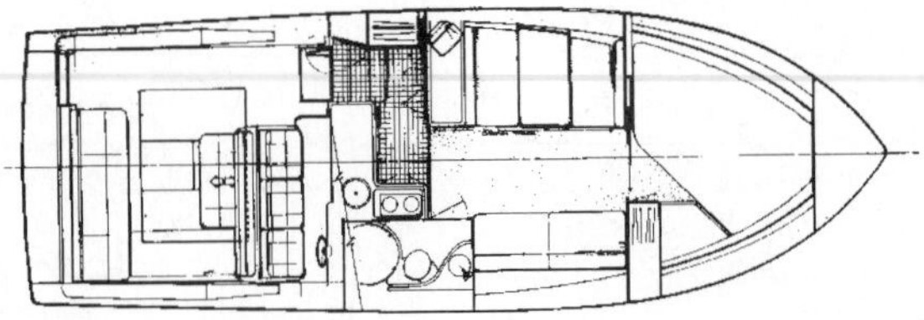

See Page 278 for Pricing Information

WELLCRAFT 3600 MARTINIQUE

SPECIFICATIONS

Length w/Pulpit..........38'0"	Water........................47 gals.
Hull Length.................35'6"	Fuel.........................264 gals.
Beam..............................12'6"	Hull Type.........Modified-V
Draft...............................2'9"	Deadrise Aft....................16°
Weight.....................14,000#	Designer................Wellcraft
Clearance w/Arch.......10'5"	Production....1994–Current

The 3600 Martinique is basically an updated version of the Wellcraft 3500 Corsair/3600 St. Tropez (see previous page) with an all-new floorplan and a rearranged cockpit with additional seating and a bigger helm console. She's built on a relatively lightweight hull with a solid fiberglass bottom, and integral swim platform, and prop pockets. By eliminating the sidedecks, Wellcraft engineers were able to enlarge the interior dimensions, and the result is a wide-open and very expansive living area.Where many other express boats this size have mid-cabin floorplans, the Martinique has a conventional layout with a single stateroom and berths for six. The wraparound dinette converts to a double berth in the normal fashion, and the portside settee converts into upper and lower bunks. Outside, there's plenty of cockpit seating (including fold-down aft-facing bench seating behind the helm and a triple-wide helm seat), and a windshield walk-through provides access to the foredeck. Twin 310-hp MerCruiser gas inboards (with V-drives and side exhausts) will cruise the Martinique at about 19 knots and reach 29–30 knots top. ❑

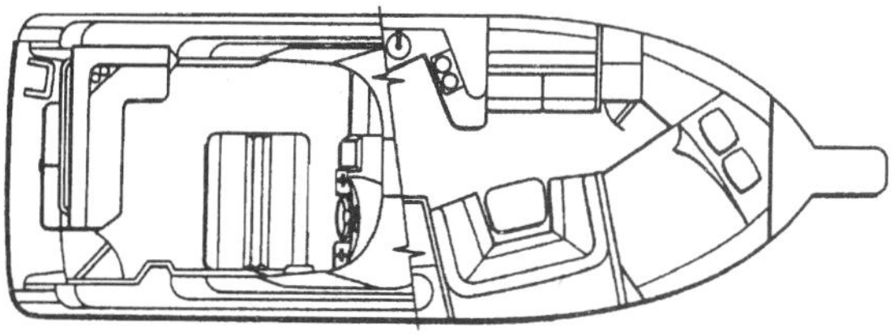

See Page 278 for Pricing Information

WELLCRAFT 37 CORSICA

SPECIFICATIONS

Length.........................36'11"	Fuel.........................300 gals.
Beam.............................13'6"	Cockpit............................NA
Draft...............................3'1"	Hull Type.........Modified-V
Weight......................16,800#	Deadrise Aft....................16°
Clearance........................9'9"	Designer................B. Collier
Water......................100 gals.	Production..............1989-91

Not among Wellcraft's more enduring designs (production lasted for only three years), the 37 Corsica is a straightforward express-style family cruiser with a roomy interior to go with her maxi-cube profile. The Corsica is built on a solid fiberglass hull with a relatively wide beam and an integral swim platform. The original mid-cabin layout was judged too confining, and Wellcraft designers introduced an all-new floorplan after the first 15 boats had been built. The small dinette found in the original floorplan was replaced by a wetbar and a serving counter—an unusual design since convertible dinettes are almost taken for granted in modern sportboats—and storage space was greatly improved. Outside, the cockpit is arranged with excellent seating accommodations including a double-wide helm seat, an L-shaped settee to port, and bench seating at the transom. A wet bar and walk-through transom door were standard. Additional features include wide sidedecks, excellent cabin headroom, and radar arch. An average performer even with big-block 502-cid V-drive gas engines, the Wellcraft 37 Corsica will cruise at 20 knots and reach a top speed of around 29 knots. ❑

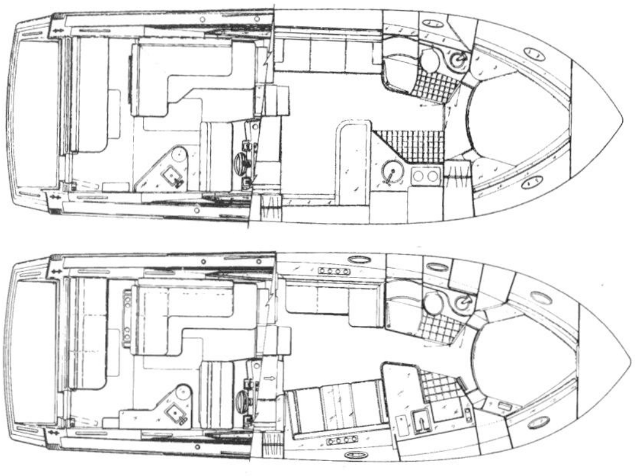

See Page 278 for Pricing Information

WELLCRAFT 43 PORTIFINO

SPECIFICATIONS

Hull Length ....42'10"	Fuel, Gas ....300 gals.
Beam ....14'6"	Fuel, Dsl. ....400 gals.
Draft ....3'0"	Hull Type ....Modified-V
Weight......................18,200#	Deadrise Aft....................14°
Clearance ....10'3"	Designer................B. Collier
Water ....100 gals.	Production 1987–Current

A good-selling boat since her introduction in 1987, the 43 Portifino is still one of the biggest full-production express cruisers available on the sportboat market. With her sleek low-profile appearance, stylish profile, and huge cockpit, the Portifino projects a powerful and very upscale appearance. She's constructed on a solid fiberglass modified-V hull with a wide beam, side exhausts, and prop pockets. The original single-stateroom floorplan was redesigned in 1992 to include a second stateroom and a dinette, but at the expense of the superb galley and breakfast bar found in earlier models. Outside, the Portifino's huge bi-level cockpit provides seating for a dozen. Note that hull graphics were reduced and the helm console upgraded in 1990. Engine access is excellent—the hatch in the bridgedeck reveals a ladder that leads down between the engines. With standard 454-cid gas engines, the 43 Portifino has a (barely respectable) cruising speed of 16 knots and a top speed of about 25 knots. Optional 375-hp Cat diesels will cruise about 23 knots and reach 27 knots wide open. ❑

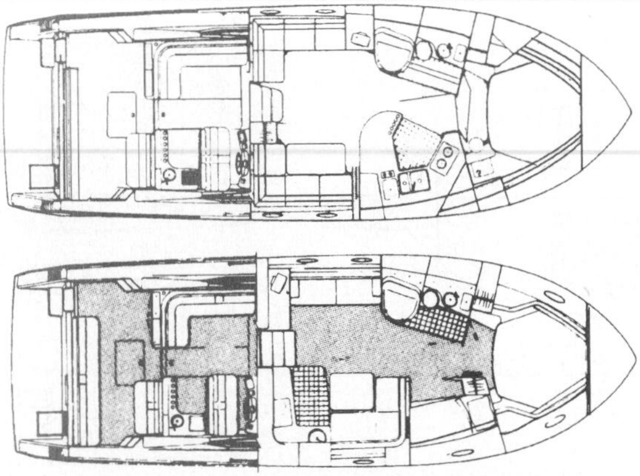

See Page 278 for Pricing Information

WILBUR 34 CRUISER

SPECIFICATIONS

Length	34'4"	Water	80 gals.
Length WL	32'3"	Fuel	200 gals.
Beam	12'0"	Cockpit	NA
Draft	3'8"	Hull Type	Semi-Disp.
Weight	15,000#	Designer	Ralph Ellis
Clearance	NA	Production	1982–Current

A fine example of Downeast styling and top-quality construction, the Wilbur 34 really can't be considered a production model since nearly all have been owner-customized to some extent. Actually, the 34 Cruiser pictured above is one of several 34-footers from Wilbur including hardtop, bass boat, and open express models. Hull construction is solid fiberglass, and her nearly plumb bow, sweeping sheer, and trunk cabin superstructure mark her as a classic New England design. The standard interior of the 34 Cruiser is arranged with the galley down and a single stateroom forward. A lower helm is a popular option, and the traditional teak interior is beautifully crafted throughout. Outside, the cockpit is large enough for serious fishing activities. Notable features include a prop-protecting keel, a very distinctive teak bow pulpit, opening ports, excellent dry storage, and wide sidedecks. A seaworthy and comfortable boat, a single 375-hp Cat diesel will cruise the Wilbur 34 around 17–18 knots with a top speed of 22 knots. Several smaller diesel engines are offered depending on speed requirements. ❑

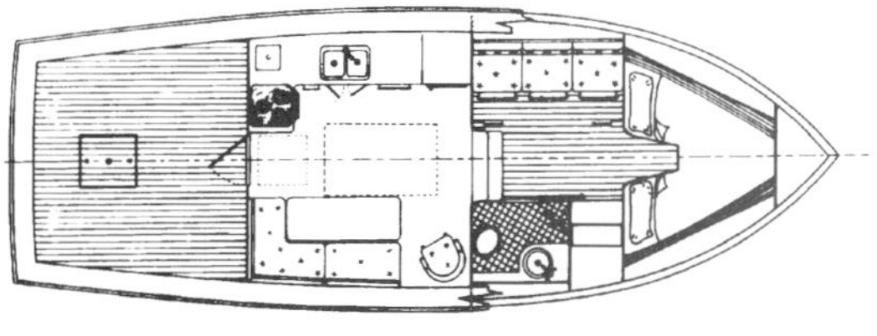

See Page 278 for Pricing Information

WILBUR 38 CRUISER

SPECIFICATIONS

Length	38'0"	Water	150 gals.
Length WL	35'7"	Fuel	500 gals.
Beam	13'0"	Cockpit	NA
Draft	4'0"	Hull Type	Semi-Disp.
Weight	22,500#	Designer	Ralph Ellis
Clearance	NA	Production	1980–Current

The Wilbur 38 is a traditional Downeast-style cruiser built in Manset, Maine. Her lobster boat heritage is reflected in the timeless beauty of her classic New England styling and the flexibility of her rugged, semi-displacement hull design. While not inexpensive, the Lee Wilbur yard is well-known for its commitment to top-quality engineering and above-average production standards. Each Wilbur 38 is built on a semi-custom basis, and the result is a yacht in which the elements of traditional styling are intimately matched with the interior priorities of her owner. There are several versions of the Wilbur 38 available, including three cruising models (one with an extended hardtop) and a flybridge fisherman with an enlarged cockpit and a slightly smaller salon. All feature truly elegant teak interior joinerwork and cabinetry, and virtually everything is created in-house at the Wilbur yard. A handsome boat with superb handling characteristics, a Wilbur 38 equipped with twin 375-hp Caterpillar diesels can be expected to cruise around 22 knots and reach 26 knots wide open. ❑

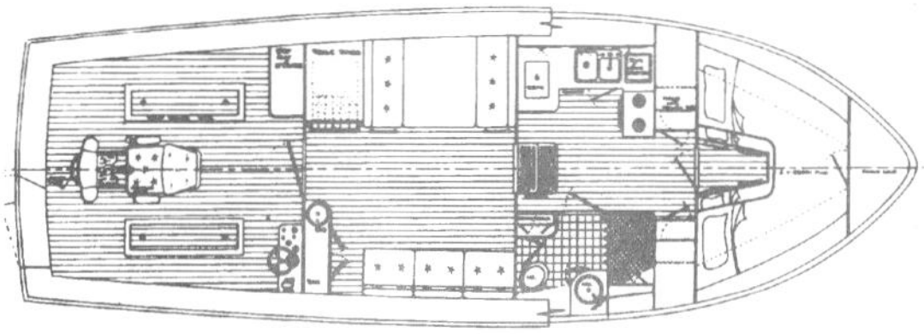

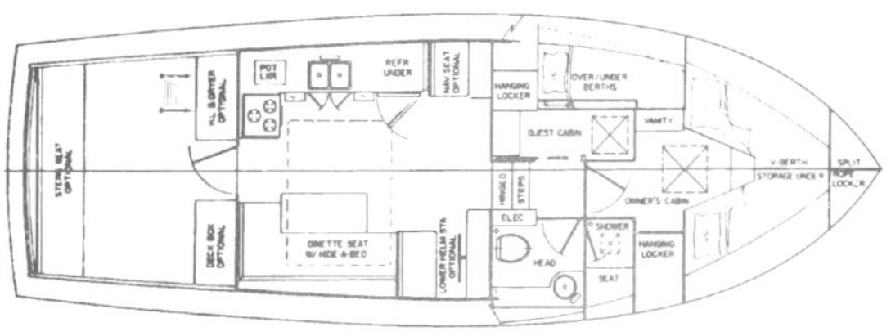

See Page 278 for Pricing Information

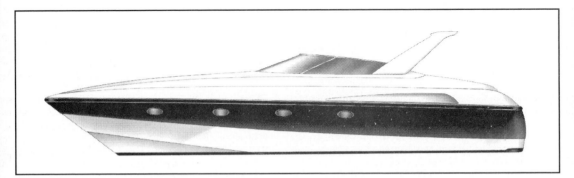

WINDY 31 SCIROCCO

SPECIFICATIONS

Length	30'7"	Clearance	10'10"
Beam	10'8"	Cockpit	NA
Draft	3'0"	Hull Type	Deep-V
Weight	10,000#	Deadrise Aft	20°
Fuel	130 US gals.	Designer	H. Johnsen
Water	53 US gals.	Production	1995–Current

The Windy 31 Scirocco is an extremely well-crafted sportcruiser from Norway with more flat-out sex appeal than just about any other boat in her class. Built on a solid fiberglass, deep-V hull with a fairly wide beam, the Scirocco's mid-cabin teak interior is designed to accommodate four adults in what can only be described as understated luxury. The floorplan is similiar to most mid-cabin layouts: the sofa/dinette forward converts into a double berth, and twin single berths are found in the aft (master) stateroom which also boasts direct access to the double-entry head. Six opening ports provide ventilation, and headroom is about 6 feet in the galley. The Scirocco's flush cockpit contains a huge U-shaped settee which provides comfortable seating for 6–8 people—with the teak table lowered, it converts into a big sunpad. Molded steps on the port side of the cockpit lead up to the sidedeck, and the wraparound stainless steel windshield is simply a work of art. Several gas and diesel I/O options are offered. Among them, twin 5.0-litre Volvo gas engines will cruise the Scirocco at 22–23 knots with a top speed of around 36 knots. ❑

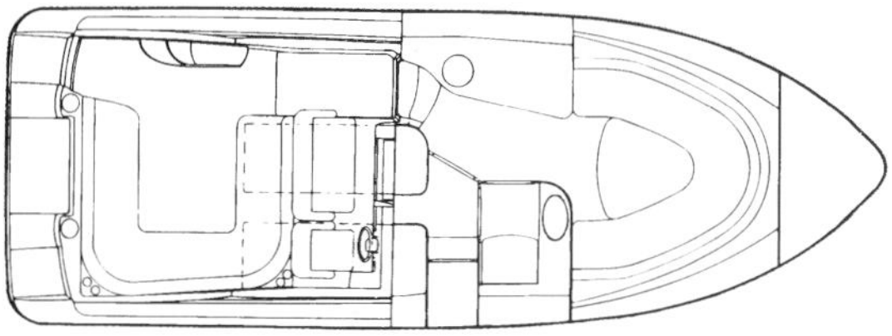

See Page 278 for Pricing Information

WINDY 33 MISTRAL

SPECIFICATIONS

Length	32'7"	Clearance	11'2"
Beam	11'6"	Cockpit	NA
Draft	2'10"	Hull Type	Deep-V
Weight	10,800#	Deadrise Aft	20°
Fuel	160 US gals.	Designer	H. Johnson
Water	53 US gals.	Production	1994–Current

Windy Boats is a small Norwegian builder with three decades of experience and a reputaion for quality in both design and construction. The 33 Mistral, which is now available in the U.S., is one of their newer models. Built on a solid fiberglass, deep-V hull with a relatively wide beam, she's a stylish and heavily-built Mediterranean sportcruiser with a superb accommodation plan and excellent overall performance. While many European designs of this type skimp on cabin dimensions in favor of cockpit space, the Mistral's beautifully crafted mid-cabin layout is surprisingly open and spacious. The master stateroom (with a privacy door—not a curtain) is forward and, with the dinette converted, there are berths for six including a double bed in the mid-cabin. The bi-level cockpit provides lounge seating for a small crowd and features a huge in-deck storage bin. The Windy's stainless steel windshield is pure sex appeal. A good-running boat in a chop, twin 230-hp Volvo diesels I/Os will cruise the 33 Mistral at a brisk 28–29 knots and deliver a top speed of 36 knots. ❑

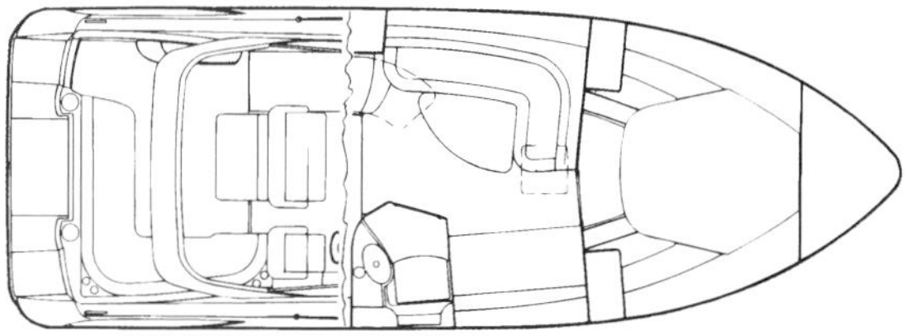

See Page 278 for Pricing Information

WINDY 36 GRAND MISTRAL

SPECIFICATIONS

Length	35'6"	Clearance	11'7"
Beam	11'6"	Cockpit	NA
Draft	NA	Hull Type	Deep-V
Weight	13,600#	Deadrise Aft	20°
Fuel	185 US gals.	Designer	H. Johnsen
Water	57 US gals.	Production	1995–Current

One of Windy's newest designs, the 36 Grand Mistral is an enlarged version of the popular Windy 33 Mistral with slightly enlarged cabin accommodations and additional cockpit seating. Built on a solid fiberglass, deep-V hull with moderate beam, the mid-cabin interior of the Grand Mistral is designed with private staterooms fore and aft, each with a double bed and generous storage space. Note that the aft stateroom has a stand-up dressing area and direct access to the head compartment. Cabin headroom is excellent throughout, and there are eight opening ports for ventilation. Outside, the flush cockpit is dominated by a big U-shaped lounge that can easily be converted into a sunpad. Molded steps ease access to the portside walkaround, and a transom door leads to the wide swim platform. Additional features include a teak cockpit sole, transom fender storage, a beautifully crafted stainless steel windshield, and a double-wide companion seat next to the bolster-type helm seat. Among several stern drive engine options, twin 230-hp Volvo diesels will cruise at 26–27 knots and deliver a top speed in the neighborhood of 33 knots. ❏

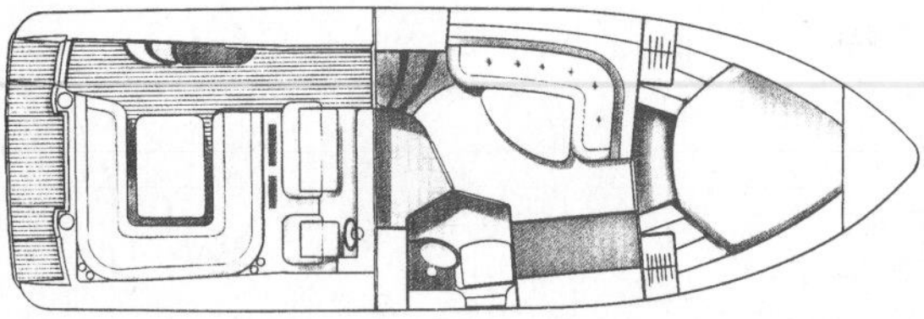

See Page 278 for Pricing Information

WINDY 38 GRAND SPORT

SPECIFICATIONS

Length	38'0"	Clearance	11'2"
Beam	11'5"	Cockpit	NA
Draft	NA	Hull Type	Deep-V
Weight	15,000#	Deadrise Aft	20°
Fuel	265 US gals.	Designer	H. Johnsen
Water	65 US gals.	Production	1994–Current

The Windy 38 Grand Sport (called the Windy 11600 when she was introduced in 1992) is a well-built Norwegian import with a stunning Mediterranean profile. She's built on a solid fiberglass, deep-V hull and, compared to many of her mega-beam U.S. counterpart, she has a relatively narrow beam for her size. Like most Med-style designs, the Grand Sport is a dedicated day boat as evidenced by her expansive cockpit with its huge three-person sunpad, built-in wet bar, ski lockers, and a big U-shaped settee/dinette abaft the helm. Below deck, the compact mid-cabin accommodations will sleep four with a sofa/dinette/double berth forward and an athwartship double bed aft. (Note that the aft cabin has direct access to the head and a partial standing headroom— a nice touch.) The teak woodwork and designer fabrics create a traditional and very upscale environment below. Additional features (there are many) include a teak cockpit sole, a completely sexy stainless steel windshield, and a hydraulic engine hatch. Among several stern drive engine options, twin 230-hp Volvo diesels will cruise the 38 Grand Sport around 25 knots (32 knots top). ❏

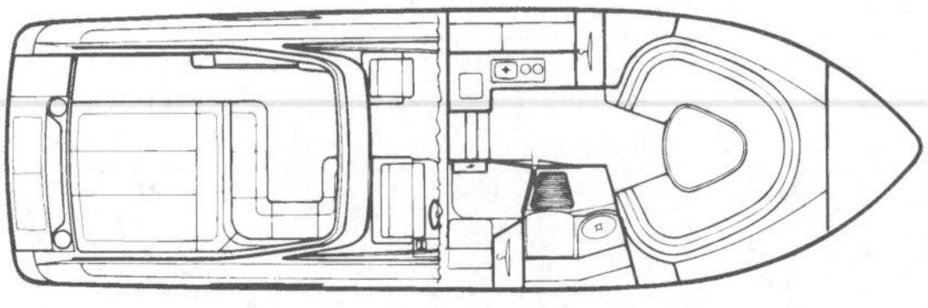

See Page 278 for Pricing Information

Notes

Notes

Notes

About These Prices...

❑ Values contained in the RETAIL HIGH-LOW PRICE GUIDE are intended to provide the reader with *general price estimates only* and are not meant to represent exact market values.

❑ The prices in this book reflect the market conditions projected by our staff to exist for 1996. Do not use these prices after December 31, 1996.

❑ We believe readers will find these prices to closely reflect real-world market conditions. Indeed, if you expect to purchase a boat in excellent condition for less than the published Retail High, you are likely to be very disappointed. In many cases—often depending on location, availability, condition or outfitting—a given model may sell at a price 10–15% *higher* than the published Retail High. On the other hand, a boat in particularly poor condition will almost certainly sell for less than the published Retail Low.

❑ The prices published in this guide apply to boats found on the East Coast, Florida, and the Gulf of Mexico. Prices in other regions must be adjusted as follows:

Great Lakes	+10–15%
Pacific Northwest	+10–15%
Inland Rivers & Lakes	+5–10%
California	+5–10%

❑ Those wishing to establish a consistent pattern for depreciation based on the prices in this book will be disappointed; we know of no such schedule. Rather, we have evaluated each model on its own merits and assigned values based on our research and experience.

❑ The *Retail High* is the average selling price of a clean, well-equipped and well-maintained boat with low-to-moderate engine hours. Boats with an exceptional equipment list—or those with unusually low hours—will often sell at a figure higher than the published Retail High.

❑ The *Retail Low* is the average selling price of a boat with below-average maintanance, poor equipment, high-time engines or excessive wear. High-time boats in poor condition will usually sell for less than the published Retail Low.

❑ The following abbreviations are used throughout the Price Guide:

S—single engine
T—twin engines
D—diesel engine(s)
G—gas engine(s)
IB—inboard engine(s)
I/O—inboard/outboard engine(s)
VD—V-drive(s)

Retail High-Low Price Guide

IMPORTANT!

Please note the use of asterisks in the price tables as follows:

* Outboard models only—Price is for a fully-rigged boat *without* motors.
**** Indicates pre-1975 model—Prices are not given for boats built before 1975.
****** Insufficient data— Not enough information to render a predicted value.

For information on how to apply these prices to boats in different regions, see "About These Prices" on the previous page.

Year	Power	Retail Low	Retail High
Albin 27 Cruiser			
1995	S/Diesel	64,458	72,262
1994	S/Diesel	58,230	65,281
1993	S/Diesel	54,645	61,261
1992	S/Diesel	50,442	56,549
1991	S/Diesel	47,079	52,779
1990	S/Diesel	42,035	47,124
1989	S/Diesel	36,990	41,469
1988	S/Diesel	32,874	37,699
1987	S/Diesel	30,408	34,872
1986	S/Diesel	27,943	32,044
1985	S/Diesel	25,477	29,217
1984	S/Diesel	23,833	27,332
1983	S/Diesel	23,309	26,730
Allmand 34 Classic			
1981	T/Gas	29,857	33,472
1980	T/Gas	28,151	31,559
1979	T/Gas	25,852	29,647
1978	T/Gas	24,184	27,734
1977	T/Gas	22,516	25,821
1976	T/Gas	20,848	23,908
1975	T/Gas	19,180	21,996
Atlantic 34 Sportsman			
1992	T/Gas	87,849	98,485
1992	T/Diesel	113,073	126,763
1991	T/Gas	77,411	86,784
1991	T/Diesel	103,505	116,037
1990	T/Gas	68,278	76,545
1990	T/Diesel	95,677	107,261
1989	T/Gas	61,755	69,232
1989	T/Diesel	89,153	99,948
1988	T/Gas	57,406	64,357
1988	T/Diesel	83,312	93,610
Bayliner 2556 Command Bridge			
1994	S/IO/Gas	34,440	38,610
1993	S/IO/Gas	31,857	35,714
1992	S/IO/Gas	29,274	32,818
1991	S/IO/Gas	26,691	29,923
1990	S/IO/Gas	24,108	27,027
1989	S/IO/Gas	21,525	24,131
1988	S/IO/Gas	18,942	21,236
1987	S/IO/Gas	17,220	19,305
1986	S/IO/Gas	15,498	17,374
Bayliner 2650/2655 Sunbridge			
1990	S/IO/Gas	23,247	26,062
1989	S/IO/Gas	20,664	23,166
1988	S/IO/Gas	18,081	20,270
Bayliner 2450/2455/2651/2655 Sunbridge			
1993	S/5.0L/IO	23,663	26,829
1992	S/5.0L/IO	21,380	24,240

Year	Power	Retail Low	Retail High
1991	S/5.0L/IO	19,792	22,440
1990	S/5.0L/IO	18,613	21,103
1989	S/5.0L/IO	17,547	19,894
1988	S/5.0L/IO	15,841	17,960
1987	S/5.0L/IO	13,604	15,424
1986	S/5.0L/IO	13,054	14,800
1985	S/5.0L/IO	12,217	13,852
1984	S/5.0L/IO	11,490	13,027

Bayliner 2655 Sunbridge

Year	Power	Retail Low	Retail High
1995	S/5.0L/IO	26,725	30,300
1994	S/5.0L/IO	24,340	27,596

Bayliner 2850 Command Bridge

Year	Power	Retail Low	Retail High
1989	S/IO/Gas	25,531	28,849
1988	S/IO/Gas	24,036	27,160
1987	S/IO/Gas	22,379	25,287
1986	S/IO/Gas	20,721	23,413
1985	S/IO/Gas	18,234	20,604
1984	S/IO/Gas	16,577	18,731
1983	S/IO/Gas	14,919	16,858

Bayliner 2850 Contessa SB

Year	Power	Retail Low	Retail High
1989	S/IO/Gas	23,929	27,131
1988	S/IO/Gas	21,454	24,324
1987	S/IO/Gas	19,804	22,453
1986	S/IO/Gas	18,153	20,582
1985	S/IO/Gas	16,503	18,711
1984	S/IO/Gas	15,678	17,775
1983	S/IO/Gas	14,853	16,840

Bayliner 2855 Sunbridge (Early)

Year	Power	Retail Low	Retail High
1993	S/IO/260	29,246	35,025
1992	S/IO/260	26,052	31,200
1991	S/IO/260	24,217	29,002

Bayliner 2855 Sunbridge

Year	Power	Retail Low	Retail High
1995	S/300/IO	40,293	45,171
1994	S/300/IO	33,565	38,056

Bayliner 2955 Sunbridge

Year	Power	Retail Low	Retail High
1990	S/IO	30,851	35,018
1990	T/IO	34,186	38,804
1989	S/IO	27,516	31,233
1989	T/IO	31,685	35,965
1988	S/IO	25,014	28,393
1988	T/IO	29,183	33,125

Bayliner 2958 Command Bridge

Year	Power	Retail Low	Retail High
1990	T/IO/Gas	37,129	42,144
1989	T/IO/Gas	34,654	39,335
1988	T/IO/Gas	32,179	36,525

Bayliner 3055 Sunbridge

Year	Power	Retail Low	Retail High
1994	S/IO/Gas	40,442	45,904
1994	T/IO/Gas	47,182	53,555
1993	S/IO/Gas	37,072	42,079
1993	T/IO/Gas	42,969	48,773
1992	S/IO/Gas	33,701	38,254
1992	T/IO/Gas	37,914	43,035
1991	S/IO/Gas	30,331	34,428
1991	T/IO/Gas	33,701	38,254

Bayliner 3058 Command Bridge (Early)

Year	Power	Retail Low	Retail High
1992	S/IO/Gas	40,002	45,405
1992	T/IO/Gas	44,084	50,039
1991	S/IO/Gas	37,553	42,625
1991	T/IO/Gas	41,635	47,259

Bayliner 3058 Command Bridge

Year	Power	Retail Low	Retail High
1993	T/IO/Gas	54,198	61,519
1992	T/IO/Gas	50,029	56,786

Bayliner 3255 Sunbridge

Year	Power	Retail Low	Retail High
1995	S/IO 300	67,257	76,255

Bayliner 3258 Command Bridge

Year	Power	Retail Low	Retail High
1995	S/IO 300	73,803	83,677

Bayliner 3288 Motor Yacht

Year	Power	Retail Low	Retail High
1995	T/Diesel	91,211	103,297
1994	T/Diesel	82,453	93,591
1993	T/Diesel	75,175	85,329
1992	T/Gas	57,533	65,304
1992	T/Diesel	66,705	75,715
1991	T/Gas	54,198	61,519
1991	T/Diesel	61,702	70,037
1990	T/Gas	51,696	58,679
1990	T/Diesel	58,367	66,251
1989	T/Gas	49,195	55,840
1989	T/Diesel	55,032	62,465
1988	T/Gas	47,527	53,947
1988	T/Diesel	52,530	59,626
1987	T/Gas	45,026	51,108
1987	T/Diesel	50,029	56,786
1986	T/Gas	42,524	48,268
1986	T/Diesel	47,527	53,947
1985	T/Gas	39,189	44,483
1985	T/Diesel	44,192	50,161
1984	T/Gas	35,854	40,697
1984	T/Diesel	40,857	46,376
1983	T/Gas	32,519	36,911
1983	T/Diesel	37,522	42,590
1982	T/Gas	29,183	33,125
1982	T/Diesel	34,186	38,804
1981	T/Gas	26,682	30,286
1981	T/Diesel	30,851	35,018

Bayliner 3350 Montego

Year	Power	Retail Low	Retail High
1978	T/Gas	25,848	29,340
1977	T/Gas	24,181	27,447
1976	T/Gas	22,513	25,554
1975	T/Gas	20,012	22,715

Bayliner 3450/3485/3785 Sunbridge

Year	Power	Retail Low	Retail High
1990	T/Gas	65,037	73,822
1989	T/Gas	55,032	62,465
1988	T/Gas	48,361	54,894
1987	T/Gas	41,691	47,322

Bayliner 3486 Convertible

Year	Power	Retail Low	Retail High
1989	T/Gas	62,536	70,983
1988	T/Gas	55,866	63,411
1987	T/Gas	50,029	56,786

Bayliner 3550 Bristol

Year	Power	Retail Low	Retail High
1981	T/Gas	40,023	45,429
1980	T/Gas	36,688	41,643
1979	T/Gas	33,353	37,858
1978	T/Gas	30,851	35,018

Bayliner 3250/3255/3555 Sunbridge

Year	Power	Retail Low	Retail High
1994	T/IO/Gas	68,373	77,608
1993	T/IO/Gas	60,868	69,090
1992	T/IO/Gas	53,364	60,572
1991	T/IO/Gas	49,195	55,840
1990	T/IO/Gas	45,026	51,108
1989	T/IO/Gas	36,688	41,643
1988	T/IO/Gas	34,186	38,804

Year	Power	Retail Low	Retail High

Bayliner 3688 Motor Yacht

Year	Power	Retail Low	Retail High
1994	T/Diesel	109,230	123,984
1993	T/Diesel	102,559	116,412
1992	T/Diesel	92,553	105,055

Bayliner 3888 Motor Yacht

Year	Power	Retail Low	Retail High
1994	T/Diesel	132,576	150,484
1993	T/Diesel	124,238	141,020
1992	T/Diesel	115,900	131,555
1991	T/Diesel	107,562	122,091
1990	T/Diesel	98,390	111,680
1989	T/Diesel	90,052	102,216
1988	T/Diesel	82,548	93,698
1987	T/Diesel	75,877	86,126
1986	T/Diesel	70,040	79,501
1985	T/Diesel	63,370	71,929
1984	T/Diesel	59,201	67,197
1983	T/Diesel	56,699	64,358

Bayliner 3988 Motor Yacht

Year	Power	Retail Low	Retail High
1995	T/Diesel	152,771	171,460

Bayliner 4050 Bodega

Year	Power	Retail Low	Retail High
1983	T/Gas	73,549	83,484
1982	T/Gas	66,716	75,727
1981	T/Gas	61,528	69,838
1980	T/Gas	57,040	64,744
1979	T/Gas	52,714	59,834
1978	T/Gas	48,523	55,077

Bayliner 4388 Mid-Cabin MY

Year	Power	Retail Low	Retail High
1994	T/Diesel	162,594	184,556
1993	T/Diesel	152,588	173,199
1992	T/Diesel	142,582	161,841
1991	T/Diesel	133,410	151,430

Bertram 28 Bahia Mar

Year	Power	Retail Low	Retail High
1992	T/Gas	80,139	89,842
1992	T/Diesel	95,745	107,337
1991	T/Gas	74,234	83,222
1991	T/Diesel	87,309	97,880
1990	T/Gas	67,907	76,129
1989	T/Gas	62,002	69,509
1988	T/Gas	55,253	61,943
1987	T/Gas	51,036	57,215
1986	T/Gas	49,349	55,323
1985	T/Gas	43,865	49,176

Bertram 28 Moppie

Year	Power	Retail Low	Retail High
1994	T/Gas	96,507	108,192
1993	T/Gas	89,269	100,078
1992	T/Gas	83,267	93,349
1991	T/Gas	73,825	82,763
1990	T/Gas	66,528	74,583
1989	T/Gas	60,948	68,328
1988	T/Gas	52,364	58,704
1987	T/Gas	41,204	46,193

Bertram 30 Moppie

Year	Power	Retail Low	Retail High
1995	T/Gas	119,278	133,720
1995	T/Diesel	153,255	171,811
1994	T/Gas	106,620	119,529
1994	T/Diesel	140,638	157,666

Bertram 31 Bahia Mar

Year	Power	Retail Low	Retail High
1981	T/Gas	36,483	40,900
1981	T/Diesel	44,638	50,043
1980	T/Gas	34,337	38,494
1980	T/Diesel	39,488	44,269
1979	T/Gas	31,762	35,607
1979	T/Diesel	36,054	40,419
1978	T/Gas	29,186	32,720
1978	T/Diesel	30,903	34,645
1977	T/Gas	26,182	29,352
1977	T/Diesel	28,328	31,758
1976	T/Gas	23,177	25,984
1976	T/Diesel	25,753	28,871
1975	T/Gas	20,602	23,097
1975	T/Diesel	22,319	25,021

Bertram 33 FB Cruiser

Year	Power	Retail Low	Retail High
1992	T/Gas	142,369	159,607
1992	T/Diesel	180,007	201,802
1991	T/Gas	127,193	142,593
1991	T/Diesel	162,109	181,736
1990	T/Gas	122,229	137,028
1990	T/Diesel	150,239	168,430
1989	T/Gas	116,287	130,366
1989	T/Diesel	135,809	152,253
1988	T/Gas	104,828	117,520
1988	T/Diesel	127,321	142,737
1987	T/Gas	95,915	107,529
1987	T/Diesel	118,833	133,221
1986	T/Gas	89,549	100,392
1986	T/Diesel	110,345	123,705
1985	T/Gas	81,910	91,827
1985	T/Diesel	101,857	114,190
1984	T/Gas	75,968	85,166
1984	T/Diesel	94,218	105,625
1983	T/Gas	70,027	78,505
1983	T/Diesel	86,579	97,061
1982	T/Gas	64,510	72,320
1982	T/Diesel	78,939	88,497
1981	T/Gas	59,841	67,086
1981	T/Diesel	72,149	80,884
1980	T/Gas	53,475	59,950
1980	T/Diesel	72,998	81,836
1979	T/Gas	46,685	52,337
1979	T/Diesel	63,661	71,368
1978	T/Gas	42,440	47,579
1978	T/Diesel	60,265	67,562
1977	T/Gas	39,045	43,773
1977	T/Diesel	56,021	62,804

Bertram 43 Moppie

Year	Power	Retail Low	Retail High
1995	550 DD	407,394	456,720
1995	600 MAN	425,725	477,270

Bertram 46 Moppie

Year	Power	Retail Low	Retail High
1995	T/Diesel	527,911	591,829
1994	T/Diesel	497,790	558,060
1993	T/Diesel	474,366	531,800

Blue Seas 31

Year	Power	Retail Low	Retail High
1991	S/Diesel	84,724	94,983
1990	S/Diesel	76,079	85,290
1989	S/Diesel	69,163	77,537
1988	S/Diesel	63,111	70,752

Brendan 32 Sedan

Year	Power	Retail Low	Retail High
1995	T/Diesel	151,426	169,760
1994	T/Diesel	135,852	152,300
1993	T/Diesel	122,483	137,313
1992	T/Diesel	110,738	124,146
1991	T/Diesel	100,671	112,860
1990	T/Diesel	92,282	103,455
1989	T/Diesel	84,732	94,990
1988	T/Diesel	77,181	86,526
1987	T/Diesel	70,470	79,002
1986	T/Diesel	66,275	74,300

Cabo 31

Year	Power	Retail Low	Retail High
1995	350 hp D	173,351	194,340

Cabo 35 Flybridge SF

Year	Power	Retail Low	Retail High
1995	375 hp D	251,859	282,353
1994	375 hp D	240,359	269,461
1993	375 hp D	231,956	260,040
1992	375 hp D	225,932	253,287

Cabo 35 Express SF

Year	Power	Retail Low	Retail High
1995	375 hp D	251,325	281,755
1994	375 hp D	238,373	267,234
1993	375 hp D	227,781	255,360

Californian 35 Convertible

Year	Power	Retail Low	Retail High
1987	T/Diesel	78,523	88,031
1986	T/Diesel	69,799	78,250
1985	T/Diesel	62,819	70,425

Californian 38 Convertible

Year	Power	Retail Low	Retail High
1987	T/Diesel	123,020	137,915
1986	T/Diesel	110,805	124,221
1985	T/Diesel	101,208	113,462
1984	T/Diesel	88,121	98,790

Californian 44 Veneti

Year	Power	Retail Low	Retail High
1989	T/Diesel	171,879	192,690
1988	T/Diesel	159,664	178,996

Camano 28

Year	Power	Retail Low	Retail High
1995	S/Diesel	106,817	119,750
1994	S/Diesel	98,758	110,716
1993	S/Diesel	92,694	103,917
1992	S/Diesel	87,496	98,090
1991	S/Diesel	82,299	92,263
1990	S/Diesel	77,967	87,407

Cape Dory 28 FB

Year	Power	Retail Low	Retail High
1995	S/Diesel	86,725	97,225
1994	S/Diesel	82,013	91,943
1993	S/Diesel	77,651	87,053
1992	S/Diesel	70,671	79,228
1991	S/Diesel	63,691	71,403
1990	S/Diesel	55,839	62,600
1989	S/Diesel	49,732	55,753
1988	S/Diesel	43,624	48,906
1987	S/Diesel	39,262	44,015
1986	S/Diesel	36,644	41,081
1985	S/Diesel	34,899	39,125

Cape Dory 30

Year	Power	Retail Low	Retail High
1995	T/Diesel	******	******
1991	T/Diesel	109,933	123,243
1990	T/Diesel	99,463	111,506

Cape Dory 33

Year	Power	Retail Low	Retail High
1995	T/Diesel	******	******
1992	T/Diesel	129,127	144,762
1991	T/Diesel	120,403	134,981
1990	T/Diesel	112,550	126,177
1989	T/Diesel	105,570	118,353
1988	T/Diesel	100,336	112,484

Cape Dory 36

Year	Power	Retail Low	Retail High
1990	T/Gas	130,000	145,740
1990	T/Diesel	151,812	170,193
1989	T/Gas	122,148	136,937
1989	T/Diesel	141,342	158,455
1988	T/Gas	113,423	127,156
1988	T/Diesel	134,362	150,630

Cape Dory 40 Explorer

Year	Power	Retail Low	Retail High
1995	T/Diesel	321,737	360,692
1994	T/Diesel	291,867	327,205
1993	T/Diesel	240,095	269,165
1992	T/Diesel	207,277	232,373

Carver 25 Allegra

Year	Power	Retail Low	Retail High
1990	T/IO/Gas	26,174	29,344
1989	T/IO/Gas	24,430	27,387

Carver 250 Mid-Cabin

Year	Power	Retail Low	Retail High
1995	S/IO 7.4L	35,387	39,672

Carver 26 Santa Cruz

Year	Power	Retail Low	Retail High
1987	S/IO 260	18,833	21,113
1986	S/IO 260	17,844	20,004
1985	S/IO 260	17,136	19,211
1984	S/IO 260	16,759	18,788
1983	S/IO 260	16,142	18,096
1982	S/IO 260	15,574	17,460
1981	S/IO 260	14,928	16,735
1980	S/IO 260	14,218	15,940

Carver 26 Monterey

Year	Power	Retail Low	Retail High
1984	S/IO 260	16,612	18,623
1983	S/IO 260	15,798	17,711
1982	S/IO 260	14,579	16,338
1981	S/IO 260	13,915	15,600

Carver 26 Montego

Year	Power	Retail Low	Retail High
1987	S/IO 260	16,612	20,539
1986	S/IO 260	15,798	19,800
1985	S/IO 260	17,109	19,180

Carver 26 Command Bridge 280 Sedan

Year	Power	Retail Low	Retail High
1995	T/IO/4.3L	55,760	62,511
1994	T/IO/4.3L	48,221	54,060
1993	T/IO/4.3L	43,992	49,318
1992	T/IO/4.3L	40,608	45,524
1991	T/IO/4.3L	38,070	42,679

Carver 27/530/300 Montego

Year	Power	Retail Low	Retail High
1993	T/IO/205	44,910	50,347
1992	T/IO/205	41,455	46,475
1991	T/IO/205	38,864	43,570
1990	T/IO/205	36,273	40,665
1989	T/IO/205	33,682	37,761
1988	T/IO/205	31,955	35,824
1987	T/IO/205	29,364	32,919
1986	T/IO/205	26,773	30,015

Carver 27/630/300 Santego

Year	Power	Retail Low	Retail High
1993	T/IO/205	50,955	57,125
1992	T/IO/205	45,774	51,316
1991	T/IO/205	42,319	47,443
1990	T/IO/205	39,728	44,538
1989	T/IO/205	36,273	40,665
1988	T/IO/205	34,546	38,729

Carver 2866 Santa Cruz

Year	Power	Retail Low	Retail High
1982	T/IO/Gas	21,812	24,453
1982	T/Gas	23,557	26,409
1981	T/IO/Gas	19,195	21,519
1981	T/Gas	20,940	23,475
1980	T/IO/Gas	17,058	19,562
1980	T/Gas	18,764	21,519
1979	T/IO/Gas	15,353	17,606
1979	T/Gas	17,058	19,562
1978	T/IO/Gas	14,500	16,628
1978	T/Gas	16,205	18,584
1977	T/IO/Gas	13,647	15,650
1977	T/Gas	15,353	17,606
1976	T/IO/Gas	12,794	14,672
1976	T/Gas	14,500	16,628

Carver 28 Mariner/Voyager

Year	Power	Retail Low	Retail High
1990	T/Gas	49,067	55,008
1989	T/Gas	43,146	48,369
1988	T/Gas	38,070	42,679
1987	T/Gas	35,532	39,834
1986	T/Gas	32,994	36,988

Year	Power	Retail Low	Retail High
1985	T/Gas	31,302	35,092
1984	T/Gas	30,537	34,234
1983	T/Gas	28,792	32,278

Carver 28 Riviera

Year	Power	Retail Low	Retail High
1989	T/Gas	37,430	41,962
1988	T/Gas	34,686	38,885
1987	T/Gas	32,148	36,040
1986	T/Gas	30,456	34,143
1985	T/Gas	28,764	32,246
1984	T/Gas	27,072	30,349
1983	T/Gas	25,380	28,453

Carver 28/300 Sedan

Year	Power	Retail Low	Retail High
1993	T/Gas	69,484	77,897
1992	T/Gas	64,461	72,266
1991	T/Gas	60,276	67,573

Carver 25 Montego/280 Express

Year	Power	Retail Low	Retail High
1995	S/IO/7.4L	45,353	50,844
1994	S/IO/7.4L	39,762	44,576
1993	S/IO/7.4L	37,224	41,730
1992	S/IO/7.4L	31,302	35,092
1991	S/IO/7.4L	28,764	32,246
1990	S/IO/7.4L	26,226	29,401
1989	S/IO/7.4L	24,534	27,504
1988	S/IO/7.4L	22,842	25,607

Carver 30 Allegra

Year	Power	Retail Low	Retail High
1990	T/IO/Gas	46,865	52,539
1989	T/IO/Gas	42,918	48,114

Carver 310 Santego

Year	Power	Retail Low	Retail High
1995	T/IO 4.3L	67,660	75852
1995	T/VD 5.7L	69,785	78234
1994	T/IO 4.3L	61,598	69,056
1994	T/VD 5.7L	63,956	71,699

Carver 310 Mid-Cabin Exp.

Year	Power	Retail Low	Retail High
1995	T/IO 275	76,422	85,675

Carver 32 Convertible

Year	Power	Retail Low	Retail High
1993	T/Gas	75,344	84,467
1992	T/Gas	68,647	76,959
1991	T/Gas	62,787	70,389
1990	T/Gas	56,090	62,881
1989	T/Gas	51,067	57,250
1988	T/Gas	48,555	54,434
1987	T/Gas	46,881	52,557

Year	Power	Retail Low	Retail High
1986	T/Gas	45,207	50,680
1985	T/Gas	42,695	47,865
1984	T/Gas	40,184	45,049

Carver 32/330 Mariner

Year	Power	Retail Low	Retail High
1995	T/Gas	93,207	108,380
1994	T/Gas	82,879	92,913
1993	T/Gas	77,019	86,344
1992	T/Gas	71,996	80,713
1991	T/Gas	66,136	74,143
1990	T/Gas	60,276	67,573
1989	T/Gas	55,253	61,942
1988	T/Gas	50,230	56,311
1987	T/Gas	46,044	51,619
1986	T/Gas	44,369	49,742
1985	T/Gas	41,858	46,926

Carver 32 Montego

Year	Power	Retail Low	Retail High
1991	T/Gas	61,371	68,801
1990	T/Gas	58,848	65,974
1989	T/Gas	56,326	63,146
1988	T/Gas	52,964	59,376
1987	T/Gas	48,760	54,664

Carver 320 Voyager

Year	Power	Retail Low	Retail High
1995	T/Gas	82,858	92,890
1994	T/Gas	70,321	78,836

Carver 33 Mariner

Year	Power	Retail Low	Retail High
1984	T/Gas	38,273	42,907
1983	T/Gas	36,533	40,956
1982	T/Gas	34,793	39,006
1981	T/Gas	31,462	36,081
1980	T/Gas	28,911	33,155
1979	T/Gas	26,934	30,888
1978	T/Gas	25,251	28,958
1977	T/Gas	24,334	27,906
1976	T/Gas	20,253	23,225
1975	T/Gas	19,372	22,216

Carver 33 Voyager

Year	Power	Retail Low	Retail High
1981	T/Gas	31,099	35,664
1980	T/Gas	28,946	33,195
1979	T/Gas	26,465	30,349
1978	T/Gas	24,811	28,453
1977	T/Gas	23,157	26,556

Carver 30/634/340 Santego

Year	Power	Retail Low	Retail High
1994	T/Gas	74,447	83,461

Year	Power	Retail Low	Retail High
1993	T/IO/Gas	64,564	72,381
1993	T/Gas	69,799	78,250
1992	T/IO/Gas	61,946	69,447
1992	T/Gas	65,436	73,359
1991	T/IO/Gas	58,456	65,534
1991	T/Gas	61,946	69,447
1990	T/IO/Gas	54,094	60,643
1990	T/Gas	57,584	64,556
1989	T/IO/Gas	50,604	56,731
1989	T/Gas	54,094	60,643
1988	T/IO/Gas	43,624	48,906
1988	T/Gas	47,114	52,818

Carver 34/350/370 Voyager

Year	Power	Retail Low	Retail High
1995	T/Gas	125,375	140,555
1995	T/Diesel	158,448	177,632
1994	T/Gas	109,060	122,265
1994	T/Diesel	135,235	151,609
1993	T/Gas	103,825	116,396
1993	T/Diesel	129,127	144,762
1992	T/Gas	99,463	111,506
1992	T/Diesel	121,275	135,959

Carver 36 Mariner

Year	Power	Retail Low	Retail High
1988	T/Gas	76,139	85,358
1987	T/Gas	71,909	80,616
1986	T/Gas	68,525	76,822
1985	T/Gas	65,987	73,977
1984	T/Gas	62,603	70,183

Carver 38 Santego

Year	Power	Retail Low	Retail High
1990	T/Gas	107,156	120,131
1989	T/Gas	102,081	114,440
1988	T/Gas	95,101	106,615

Carver 34/638/380 Santego

Year	Power	Retail Low	Retail High
1995	T/Gas	120,973	135,620
1994	T/Gas	110,825	124,243
1993	T/Gas	104,903	117,604
1992	T/Gas	98,981	110,965
1991	T/Gas	93,905	105,275
1990	T/Gas	90,521	101,481
1989	T/Gas	86,291	96,739

Carver 380 Express

Year	Power	Retail Low	Retail High
1994	T/Gas	105,143	117,873
1993	T/Gas	97,450	109,248
1992	T/Gas	93,176	104,457

Year	Power	Retail Low	Retail High
1991	T/Gas	89,756	100,624
1990	T/Gas	85,482	95,832

Celebrity 245/265 Sport Cruiser

Year	Power	Retail Low	Retail High
1995	S/IO/5.7L	30,942	34,688
1994	S/IO/5.7L	27,741	31,100
1993	S/IO/5.7L	26,577	29,795
1992	S/IO/5.7L	25,529	28,620

Celebrity 26 Crownline/ 268 /270

Year	Power	Retail Low	Retail High
1991	T/IO/5.7L	34,614	38,805
1990	T/IO/5.7L	31,467	35,277
1989	T/IO/5.7L	28,630	32,096
1988	T/IO/5.7L	26,426	29,625
1987	T/IO/5.7L	24,262	27,200

Celebrity 285/290/310 Sport Cruiser

Year	Power	Retail Low	Retail High
1995	T/IO/Gas	58,186	65,231
1994	T/IO/Gas	54,839	61,479
1993	T/IO/Gas	50,794	56,944
1992	T/IO/Gas	46,763	52,424
1991	T/IO/Gas	43,538	48,809
1990	T/IO/Gas	38,700	43,386
1989	T/IO/Gas	38,700	38,770

Chaparral Signature 26/27

Year	Power	Retail Low	Retail High
1995	S/IO/7.4L	39,852	44,577
1994	S/IO/7.4L	32,819	36,792
1993	S/IO/7.4L	30,537	34,234
1992	S/IO/7.4L	27,919	31,300

Chaparral Signature 28/29

Year	Power	Retail Low	Retail High
1995	S/IO/7.4L	54,626	61,240
1995	T/IO/4.3L	58,579	65,672
1994	S/IO/7.4L	50,528	56,646
1994	T/IO/4.3L	53,013	59,432
1993	S/IO/7.4L	43,073	48,288
1993	T/IO/4.3L	45,558	51,074
1992	S/IO/7.4L	37,275	41,788
1992	T/IO/4.3L	38,931	43,645
1991	S/IO/7.4L	33,133	37,145
1991	T/IO/4.3L	34,790	39,002

Chaparral Signature 30/31

Year	Power	Retail Low	Retail High
1995	S/IO/Gas	75,909	85,100
1994	T/IO/Gas	67,679	75,874

Year	Power	Retail Low	Retail High
1993	T/IO/Gas	59,219	66,389
1992	T/IO/Gas	53,297	59,750
1991	T/IO/Gas	47,375	53,112
1990	T/IO/Gas	42,300	47,421

Chaparral Laser 32

Year	Power	Retail Low	Retail High
1991	T/IO/Gas	56,418	63,249
1990	T/IO/Gas	50,434	56,541
1989	T/IO/Gas	45,306	50,791
1988	T/IO/Gas	41,031	45,999

Chris Craft 25 Catalina

Year	Power	Retail Low	Retail High
1986	S/Gas	18,137	20,333
1985	S/Gas	16,409	18,396
1984	S/Gas	14,682	16,460
1983	S/Gas	13,818	15,492
1982	S/Gas	12,955	14,523
1981	S/Gas	12,091	13,555
1980	S/Gas	11,227	12,587
1979	S/Gas	10,364	11,619
1978	S/Gas	9,500	10,650
1977	S/Gas	8,637	9,682
1976	S/Gas	7,773	8,714
1975	S/Gas	7,773	8,714

Chris Craft 262 Amerosport

Year	Power	Retail Low	Retail High
1990	S/IO/Gas	26,554	29,769
1989	S/IO/Gas	23,984	26,888
1988	S/IO/Gas	22,271	24,968

Chris Craft 262/26 Crowne

Year	Power	Retail Low	Retail High
1995	S/IO/5.0L	30,631	34,340
1994	S/IO/5.0L	28,424	31,866
1993	S/IO/5.0L	25,728	28,843

Chris Craft 258/268/27 Concept

Year	Power	Retail Low	Retail High
1995	S/IO/Gas	34,679	38,878
1994	S/IO/Gas	31,812	35,664
1993	S/IO/Gas	28,463	31,910
1992	S/IO/Gas	25,952	29,094

Chris Craft 28 Catalina

Year	Power	Retail Low	Retail High
1985	S/Gas	21,282	23,859
1985	T/Gas	24,687	27,676
1984	S/Gas	19,580	21,950
1984	T/Gas	22,985	25,768
1983	S/Gas	17,877	20,042
1983	T/Gas	21,282	23,859

Year	Power	Retail Low	Retail High
1982	S/Gas	17,026	19,087
1982	T/Gas	20,431	22,905
1981	S/Gas	16,174	18,133
1981	T/Gas	18,728	20,996
1980	S/Gas	15,066	17,178
1980	T/Gas	17,576	20,042
1979	S/Gas	14,229	16,224
1979	T/Gas	16,739	19,087
1978	S/Gas	13,392	15,270
1978	T/Gas	15,903	18,133

Chris Craft 284 Amerosport

Year	Power	Retail Low	Retail High
1990	T/IO/Gas	34,012	38,130
1989	T/IO/Gas	31,922	35,788
1988	T/IO/Gas	29,334	32,886
1987	T/IO/Gas	27,609	30,951

Chris Craft 292 Sunbridge

Year	Power	Retail Low	Retail High
1989	T/Gas	34,903	39,129
1988	T/Gas	32,349	36,266
1987	T/Gas	30,646	34,357
1986	T/Gas	28,944	32,448

Chris Craft 302 Crowne

Year	Power	Retail Low	Retail High
1995	T/IO/Gas	60,567	67,900
1994	T/IO/Gas	54,415	61,004
1993	T/IO/Gas	50,230	56,311
1992	T/IO/Gas	46,881	52,557
1991	T/IO/Gas	42,695	47,865

Chris Craft 310 Catalina

Year	Power	Retail Low	Retail High
1981	T/Gas	27,262	31,300
1980	T/Gas	25,558	29,344
1979	T/Gas	23,854	27,387

Chris 320/322 Amerosport Express

Year	Power	Retail Low	Retail High
1990	T/270G	49,876	56,549
1990	T/350G	55,695	63,146
1989	T/270G	46,551	52,779
1989	T/350G	51,539	58,434
1988	T/270G	44,057	49,951
1988	T/350G	49,045	55,606
1987	T/270G	40,732	46,182
1987	T/350G	44,888	50,894

Chris 320 Amerosport Sedan

Year	Power	Retail Low	Retail High
1990	T/270G	54,600	61,905

Year	Power	Retail Low	Retail High
1990	T/350G	60,480	68,571
1989	T/270G	48,720	55,238
1989	T/350G	54,600	61,905
1988	T/270G	45,360	51,429
1988	T/350G	50,400	57,143
1987	T/270G	41,160	46,667
1987	T/350G	45,360	51,429

Chris Craft 322/30 and 340/34 Crowne

Year	Power	Retail Low	Retail High
1995	T/IO/5.7L	70,504	79,040
1995	T/IB/7.4L	78,594	88,110
1994	T/IO/5.7L	65,393	73,311
1994	T/IB/7.4L	72,580	81,368
1993	T/IO/5.7L	61,218	68,630
1993	T/IB/7.4L	66,905	75,006

Chris Craft 33 Corinthian

Year	Power	Retail Low	Retail High
1980	T/Gas	32,131	36,680
1979	T/Gas	29,660	33,858
1978	T/Gas	27,188	31,036
1977	T/Gas	25,540	29,156
1976	T/Gas	23,892	27,274
1975	T/Gas	23,069	26,334

Chris Craft 33 Catalina

Year	Power	Retail Low	Retail High
1980	T/Gas	32,436	37,027
1979	T/Gas	29,941	34,179
1978	T/Gas	28,277	32,280
1977	T/Gas	26,614	30,381
1976	T/Gas	24,950	28,482
1975	T/Gas	23,287	26,583

Chris Craft 332 Express

Year	Power	Retail Low	Retail High
1986	T/260G	45,305	51,020
1986	T/340G	50,248	56,585
1985	T/260G	42,011	47,309
1985	T/340G	46,953	52,875
1984	T/260G	38,716	43,599
1984	T/340G	42,834	48,237
1983	T/260G	35,421	39,888
1983	T/340G	39,539	44,526
1982	T/260G	33,773	38,033
1982	T/340G	37,892	42,671
1981	T/260G	32,126	36,178
1981	T/340G	36,244	40,816

Chris Craft 333 Sedan

Year	Power	Retail Low	Retail High
1987	T/Gas	56,987	64,758
1986	T/Gas	53,683	61,004
1985	T/Gas	50,380	57,250
1984	T/Gas	46,250	52,557
1983	T/Gas	42,947	48,803
1982	T/Gas	39,643	45,049
1981	T/Gas	38,817	44,110

Chris Craft 336 Mid-Cabin

Year	Power	Retail Low	Retail High
1986	T/260G	49,170	55,123
1986	T/340G	54,256	60,826
1985	T/260G	45,779	51,322
1985	T/340G	50,865	57,024
1984	T/260G	41,540	46,570
1984	T/340G	45,779	51,322

Chris Craft 360 Express

Year	Power	Retail Low	Retail High
1992	T/Gas	107,109	120,077
1991	T/Gas	96,781	108,499
1990	T/Gas	88,365	99,064
1989	T/Gas	80,791	90,573
1988	T/Gas	75,742	84,912

Chris Craft 360 Sport Sedan

Year	Power	Retail Low	Retail High
1986	T/Gas	76,400	85,650
1986	T/Diesel	99,577	111,634
1985	T/Gas	70,391	78,914
1985	T/Diesel	91,851	102,973
1984	T/Gas	66,957	75,064
1984	T/Diesel	87,989	98,642
1983	T/Gas	62,665	70,252
1983	T/Diesel	82,409	92,387
1982	T/Gas	57,085	63,997
1982	T/Diesel	78,975	88,537
1981	T/Gas	55,368	62,072
1981	T/Diesel	70,820	79,395
1980	T/Gas	50,647	56,779
1980	T/Diesel	64,811	72,658
1979	T/Gas	47,213	52,930
1979	T/Diesel	60,519	67,846
1978	T/Gas	42,063	47,156
1978	T/Diesel	53,222	59,666
1977	T/Gas	38,629	43,306
1977	T/Diesel	49,789	55,817
1976	T/Gas	34,766	38,976
1976	T/Diesel	43,350	48,599
1975	T/Gas	31,333	35,126
1975	T/Diesel	38,629	43,306

Chris Craft 380 Continental

Year	Power	Retail Low	Retail High
1995	T/Gas	121,914	136,675
1994	T/Gas	108,831	122,008
1993	T/Gas	101,296	113,561

Chris 412 Amerosport Express

Year	Power	Retail Low	Retail High
1990	T/Gas	114,212	129,934
1990	T/Diesel	142,556	162,180
1989	T/Gas	108,376	123,295
1989	T/Diesel	131,718	149,850
1988	T/Gas	99,206	112,862
1988	T/Diesel	121,715	138,469
1987	T/Gas	91,703	104,326
1987	T/Diesel	112,544	128,037

Chris Craft 421 Continental

Year	Power	Retail Low	Retail High
1995	T/Gas	161,446	180,993
1995	T/Diesel	207,212	232,301
1994	T/Gas	143,818	161,231
1994	T/Diesel	189,502	212,446
1993	T/Gas	134,513	150,799
1993	T/Diesel	177,658	199,168

Cruisers 2420 Aria

Year	Power	Retail Low	Retail High
1995	S/IO/5.7L	29,610	33,270
1994	S/IO/5.7L	24,085	27,062

Cruisers 2470 Rogue

Year	Power	Retail Low	Retail High
1995	S/IO/5.7L	31,693	35,610
1994	S/IO/5.7L	26,284	29,533

Cruisers 2660 Vee Sport

Year	Power	Retail Low	Retail High
1991	T/IO/Gas	37,803	42,813
1990	T/IO/Gas	33,603	38,056
1989	T/IO/Gas	30,243	34,250
1988	T/IO/Gas	27,723	31,396
1987	T/IO/Gas	26,042	29,493
1986	T/IO/Gas	24,362	27,590
1985	T/IO/Gas	22,682	25,688
1984	T/IO/Gas	21,842	24,736
1983	T/IO/Gas	20,769	23,785
1982	T/IO/Gas	20,146	23,071
1981	T/IO/Gas	19,306	22,110
1980	T/IO/Gas	18,467	21,148
1979	T/IO/Gas	17,627	20,187

Cruisers 2670 Rogue

Year	Power	Retail Low	Retail High
1995	S/IO/7.4L	40,670	45,645

Year	Power	Retail Low	Retail High
1994	S/IO/7.4L	37,968	42,853
1993	S/IO/7.4L	35,492	40,058
1992	S/IO/7.4L	33,016	37,264
1991	S/IO/7.4L	30,539	34,469

Cruisers 2870 Holiday & 2870/2970 Rogue

Year	Power	Retail Low	Retail High
1995	T/IO/5.7L	55,488	61,998
1994	T/IO/5.7L	50,519	56,827
1993	T/IO/5.7L	47,216	53,112
1992	T/IO/5.7L	43,844	49,318
1991	T/IO/5.7L	40,471	45,524
1990	T/IO/5.7L	37,098	41,730

Cruisers 296 Avanti Vee

Year	Power	Retail Low	Retail High
1987	T/Gas	34,794	39,007
1986	T/Gas	32,248	36,153
1985	T/Gas	30,551	34,250
1984	T/Gas	28,854	32,347

Cruisers 2970 Esprit

Year	Power	Retail Low	Retail High
1991	T/Gas	47,771	53,555
1990	T/Gas	43,506	48,773
1989	T/Gas	40,094	44,948
1988	T/Gas	36,681	41,123
1987	T/Gas	34,975	39,210
1986	T/Gas	33,269	37,297

Cruisers 288/298 Villa Vee

Year	Power	Retail Low	Retail High
1990	T/Gas	47,161	52,871
1989	T/Gas	42,874	48,064
1988	T/Gas	39,444	44,219
1987	T/Gas	36,871	41,335
1986	T/Gas	35,156	39,413
1985	T/Gas	33,441	37,490
1984	T/Gas	31,726	35,568
1983	T/Gas	29,507	33,645
1982	T/Gas	27,821	31,723
1981	T/Gas	25,837	29,800
1980	T/Gas	24,170	27,877
1979	T/Gas	22,503	25,955
1978	T/Gas	20,836	24,032

Cruisers 3020/3120 Aria

Year	Power	Retail Low	Retail High
1995	T/IO/5.7L	67,137	75,350
1994	T/IO/Gas	61,554	69,084
1993	T/IO/Gas	56,563	63,483
1992	T/IO/Gas	51,572	57,881

Cruisers 3070 Rogue

Year	Power	Retail Low	Retail High
1994	T/IO/Gas	62,819	70,425
1993	T/IO/Gas	57,584	64,556
1992	T/IO/Gas	53,221	59,665
1991	T/IO/Gas	48,859	54,775
1990	T/IO/Gas	45,369	50,862

Cruisers 3175 Rogue

Year	Power	Retail Low	Retail High
1995	T/IO/5.7L	67,827	76,125

Cruisers 3260/3270 Esprit

Year	Power	Retail Low	Retail High
1994	T/Gas	68,382	76,662
1993	T/Gas	61,628	69,090
1992	T/Gas	56,563	63,411
1991	T/Gas	52,342	58,679
1990	T/Gas	48,965	54,894
1989	T/Gas	45,588	51,108
1988	T/Gas	42,211	47,322

Cruisers 336 Ultra Vee

Year	Power	Retail Low	Retail High
1988	T/260G	48,589	54,472
1988	T/350G	52,572	58,937
1987	T/260G	44,606	50,007
1987	T/350G	48,589	54,472
1986	T/260G	40,623	45,542
1986	T/350G	43,810	49,114
1985	T/260G	38,234	42,863
1985	T/350G	41,420	46,435
1984	T/260G	35,844	40,184
1984	T/350G	39,030	43,756
1983	T/260G	34,251	38,398
1983	T/350G	37,437	41,970

Cruisers 3370 Esprit

Year	Power	Retail Low	Retail High
1994	T/Gas	79,774	89,433
1993	T/Gas	75,619	84,775
1992	T/Gas	71,464	80,117
1991	T/Gas	68,140	76,390
1990	T/Gas	64,816	72,664
1989	T/Gas	60,661	68,006
1988	T/Gas	56,507	63,348
1987	T/Gas	52,352	58,690
1986	T/Gas	47,366	53,101

Cruisers 3380 Esprit

Year	Power	Retail Low	Retail High
1994	T/Gas	90,332	101,269
1993	T/Gas	86,111	96,537
1992	T/Gas	80,201	89,912
1991	T/Gas	75,136	84,233
1990	T/Gas	70,071	78,555
1989	T/Gas	64,161	71,929
1988	T/Gas	59,096	66,251
1987	T/Gas	54,875	61,519
1986	T/Gas	51,498	57,733
1985	T/Gas	48,121	53,947

Cruisers 3570 Express

Year	Power	Retail Low	Retail High
1995	T/7.4L	105,321	117,941

Cruisers 3670/3675/3775 Esprit

Year	Power	Retail Low	Retail High
1995	T/7.4L	118,462	132,656
1994	T/7.4L	112,893	126,562
1993	T/7.4L	107,310	120,303
1992	T/7.4L	101,403	113,681
1991	T/7.4L	93,023	104,286
1990	T/7.4L	85,480	95,830
1989	T/7.4L	77,938	87,374

Cruisers 4280/4285 Exp. Bridge

Year	Power	Retail Low	Retail High
1995	T/Diesel	263,698	296,290
1994	T/Diesel	221,613	248,445
1993	T/Diesel	200,706	225,007
1992	T/Gas	146,348	164,068
1992	T/Diesel	183,981	206,257
1991	T/Gas	137,986	154,692
1991	T/Diesel	171,437	192,194
1990	T/Gas	129,623	145,317
1990	T/Diesel	160,570	180,012

Doral 270 Prestancia

Year	Power	Retail Low	Retail High
1995	S/IO/5.7L	45,418	51,262
1994	T/IO/4.3L	41,752	47,124
1993	T/IO/4.3L	38,156	43,065
1992	T/IO/4.3L	36,077	40,719
1991	T/IO/4.3L	32,870	37,099
1990	T/IO/4.3L	30,465	34,385
1989	T/IO/4.3L	28,861	32,575

Doral 300 Prestancia

Year	Power	Retail Low	Retail High
1995	T/IO/5.7L	69,447	78,383
1994	T/IO/5.7L	60,445	68,223
1993	T/IO/5.7L	53,270	60,125
1992	T/IO/5.7L	48,197	54,399
1991	T/IO/5.7L	44,815	50,581
1990	T/IO/5.7L	42,278	47,718

Year	Power	Retail Low	Retail High
1989	T/IO/5.7L	39,741	44,855

Doral 350 Boca Grande

Year	Power	Retail Low	Retail High
1992	T/Gas	90,117	101,713
1991	T/Gas	82,744	93,391
1990	T/Gas	77,009	86,918

Duffy 35 Sport Cruiser

Year	Power	Retail Low	Retail High
1995	S/Diesel	218,329	244,764
1994	S/Diesel	198,640	222,691
1993	S/Diesel	187,413	210,104
1992	S/Diesel	167,549	187,835
1991	S/Diesel	152,866	171,375
1990	S/Diesel	138,184	154,915
1989	S/Diesel	128,684	144,265
1988	S/Diesel	120,048	134,583
1987	S/Diesel	111,411	124,900
1986	S/Diesel	103,638	116,186
1985	S/Diesel	95,002	106,504
1984	S/Diesel	88,299	98,990
1983	S/Diesel	79,380	88,991

Duffy 42 Sport Cruiser

Year	Power	Retail Low	Retail High
1995	S/375D	350,130	392,522
1994	S/375D	320,805	359,647
1993	S/375D	289,784	324,870
1992	S/375D	264,140	296,121
1991	S/375D	238,495	267,371
1990	S/375D	221,399	248,205
1989	S/375D	205,157	229,997
1988	S/375D	192,335	215,622
1987	S/375D	180,367	202,206
1986	S/375D	171,007	191,712
1985	S/375D	157,919	177,040

Dyer 29

Year	Power	Retail Low	Retail High
1995	S/Gas	84,725	94,983
1994	S/Gas	75,213	84,319
1993	S/Gas	65,695	73,649
1992	S/Gas	58,869	65,997
1991	S/Gas	52,044	58,345
1990	S/Gas	47,778	53,563
1989	S/Gas	41,806	46,868
1988	S/Gas	37,540	42,085
1987	S/Gas	35,518	39,818
1986	S/Gas	32,053	35,934
1985	S/Gas	28,588	32,049
1984	S/Gas	25,122	28,164
1983	S/Gas	21,657	24,280
1982	S/Gas	20,791	23,308
1981	S/Gas	19,925	22,337
1980	S/Gas	19,058	21,366
1979	S/Gas	18,192	20,395
1978	S/Gas	17,326	19,424
1977	S/Gas	16,775	18,806
1976	S/Gas	15,892	17,816
1975	S/Gas	15,009	16,827

Egg Harbor 33 Sedan

Year	Power	Retail Low	Retail High
1981	T/Gas	46,206	51,801
1981	T/Diesel	60,889	68,261
1980	T/Gas	44,047	49,380
1980	T/Diesel	51,388	57,610
1979	T/Gas	41,024	45,991
1979	T/Diesel	47,934	53,737
1978	T/Gas	37,138	41,634
1978	T/Diesel	48,366	54,221
1977	T/Gas	34,979	39,214
1977	T/Diesel	44,479	49,864
1976	T/Gas	31,524	35,341
1976	T/Diesel	40,592	45,507
1975	T/Gas	28,501	31,952
1975	T/Diesel	38,001	42,603

Ellis 32 Cruiser

Year	Power	Retail Low	Retail High
1995	S/Diesel	148,473	166,450
1994	S/Diesel	133,663	149,846
1993	S/Diesel	121,132	135,798
1992	S/Diesel	111,943	125,496
1991	S/Diesel	99,412	111,448

Excel 26 SE

Year	Power	Retail Low	Retail High
1995	S/IO/5.7L	29,802	33,410
1994	S/IO/5.7L	26,100	29,261

Fexas 42 Sport Sedan

Year	Power	Retail Low	Retail High
1990	T/Diesel	182,646	204,989
1989	T/Diesel	161,772	181,562
1988	T/Diesel	147,000	164,984
1987	T/Diesel	136,759	153,490
1986	T/Diesel	129,923	145,817
1985	T/Diesel	123,845	138,996
1984	T/Diesel	120,979	135,778
1983	T/Diesel	116,877	131,175
1982	T/Diesel	114,204	128,175

Formula 26 PC

Year	Power	Retail Low	Retail High
1993	T/IO/5.7L	47,808	54,266
1992	T/IO/5.7L	44,144	50,107
1991	T/IO/5.7L	40,797	46,308
1990	T/IO/5.7L	38,694	43,920
1989	T/IO/5.7L	35,122	39,866
1988	T/IO/5.7L	30,765	34,920

Formula 27 PC

Year	Power	Retail Low	Retail High
1995	T/IO/4.3L	69,264	78,620
1994	T/IO/4.3L	60,160	68,286

Formula 28 PC

Year	Power	Retail Low	Retail High
1987	T/IO/Gas	32,550	36,491
1986	T/IO/Gas	30,537	34,234
1985	T/IO/Gas	27,919	31,300

Formula 29 PC

Year	Power	Retail Low	Retail High
1992	T/IO/Gas	63,387	71,062
1991	T/IO/Gas	58,248	65,300
1990	T/IO/Gas	53,965	60,499
1989	T/IO/Gas	48,825	54,737
1988	T/IO/Gas	45,399	50,896

Formula 31 SC Express

Year	Power	Retail Low	Retail High
1984	T/Gas	44,634	50,039
1983	T/Gas	38,626	43,303
1982	T/Gas	35,193	39,453
1981	T/Gas	32,617	36,567

Formula 31 PC

Year	Power	Retail Low	Retail High
1995	T/IO/Gas	107,544	120,565
1994	T/IO/Gas	94,030	105,415
1993	T/IO/Gas	84,627	94,874

Formula 34 PC

Year	Power	Retail Low	Retail High
1995	T/IO/Gas	133,220	149,350
1995	T/Gas	136,554	153,088
1994	T/IO/Gas	113,423	127,156
1994	T/Gas	117,785	132,046
1993	T/IO/Gas	99,463	111,506
1992	T/IO/Gas	89,866	100,746
1991	T/IO/Gas	82,886	92,921

Formula 35 PC

Year	Power	Retail Low	Retail High
1989	T/Gas	76,503	85,766
1988	T/Gas	68,937	77,283
1987	T/Gas	64,041	71,795
1986	T/Gas	58,848	65,974

Formula 36 PC

Year	Power	Retail Low	Retail High
1995	T/Gas	160,876	180,354
1994	T/Gas	145,510	163,128
1993	T/Gas	126,899	142,263
1992	T/Gas	109,979	123,295
1991	T/Gas	96,443	108,120
1990	T/Gas	87,137	97,687

Four Winns 258 Vista

Year	Power	Retail Low	Retail High
1995	S/IO/5.7L	32,207	36,147

Four Winns 265 Vista

Year	Power	Retail Low	Retail High
1993	S/IO/5.7L	32,697	36,821
1993	T/IO/4.3L	34,872	39,270
1992	S/IO/5.7L	30,069	33,862
1992	T/IO/4.3L	31,923	35,949
1991	S/IO/5.7L	27,354	30,804
1991	T/IO/4.3L	29,088	32,757
1990	S/IO/5.7L	23,734	26,727
1990	T/IO/4.3L	24,793	27,920

Four Winns 275/278 Vista

Year	Power	Retail Low	Retail High
1995	T/IO/5.0L	44,595	50,390
1994	T/IO/5.0L	39,197	44,290

Four Winns 285 Express

Year	Power	Retail Low	Retail High
1993	T/IO/Gas	50,118	56,887
1992	T/IO/Gas	43,545	49,427
1991	T/IO/Gas	40,259	45,696
1990	T/IO/Gas	36,972	41,966
1989	T/IO/Gas	35,329	40,101
1988	T/IO/Gas	33,686	38,236

Four Winns 315/325 Express

Year	Power	Retail Low	Retail High
1993	T/IO/Gas	62,906	71,403
1993	T/Gas	67,872	77,040
1992	T/IO/Gas	55,456	62,947
1992	T/Gas	60,423	68,584
1991	T/IO/Gas	48,835	55,431
1991	T/Gas	53,801	61,068
1990	T/IO/Gas	46,352	52,613
1989	T/IO/Gas	42,524	48,268
1988	T/IO/Gas	40,023	45,429

Four Winns 365 Express

Year	Power	Retail Low	Retail High
1994	T/Gas	111,741	126,834
1993	T/Gas	102,636	116,499
1992	T/Gas	94,359	107,104
1991	T/Gas	86,082	97,709

Hatteras 36 Sedan Cruiser

Year	Power	Retail Low	Retail High
1987	T/Gas	105,570	118,353
1987	T/Diesel	143,087	160,412
1986	T/Gas	96,846	108,571
1986	T/Diesel	130,872	146,718

Hatteras 39 Sport Express

Year	Power	Retail Low	Retail High
1995	T/465D	315,131	353,286

Hinckley 39/42 Talaria

Year	Power	Retail Low	Retail High
1995	S/Diesel	405,095	452,620
1994	S/Diesel	374,363	418,283
1993	S/Diesel	348,207	389,058
1992	S/Diesel	312,580	349,251
1991	S/Diesel	271,990	303,900

Larson 250 Cabrio

Year	Power	Retail Low	Retail High
1995	S/IO/7.4L	30,437	34,353
1994	S/IO/7.4L	27,126	30,616

Larson 260 Cabrio

Year	Power	Retail Low	Retail High
1993	S/IO/Gas	29,799	33,407
1992	S/IO/Gas	27,353	30,665

Larson 270 Cabrio

Year	Power	Retail Low	Retail High
1993	S/IO/Gas	38,145	42,956
1993	T/IO/Gas	42,203	47,526
1992	S/IO/Gas	34,899	39,301
1992	T/IO/Gas	38,957	43,870
1991	S/IO/Gas	31,653	35,645
1991	T/IO/Gas	34,899	39,301
1990	S/IO/Gas	29,218	32,903
1990	T/IO/Gas	32,464	36,559
1989	S/IO/Gas	27,595	31,075
1989	T/IO/Gas	30,841	34,731

Larson 280 Cabrio

Year	Power	Retail Low	Retail High
1995	S/IO/7.4L	45,580	51,099
1994	S/IO/7.4L	41,328	46,332

Larson 300/310 Cabrio

Year	Power	Retail Low	Retail High
1995	T/IO/5.7L	62,327	69,873
1994	T/IO/5.7L	55,793	62,548
1993	T/IO/5.7L	50,420	56,525
1992	T/IO/5.7L	47,114	52,818
1991	T/IO/5.7L	43,681	48,969

Limestone 24

Year	Power	Retail Low	Retail High
1995	S/Gas	******	******

Little Harbor 36/40

Year	Power	Retail Low	Retail High
1995	T/Diesel	406,217	455,400
1994	T/Diesel	364,915	409,098
1993	T/Diesel	305,510	342,500
1992	T/Diesel	254,592	285,417
1991	T/Diesel	233,376	261,632
1990	T/Diesel	212,160	237,848

Luhrs Alura 30

Year	Power	Retail Low	Retail High
1990	S/Gas	31,697	35,535
1989	S/Gas	27,842	31,213
1988	S/Gas	25,272	28,332
1987	S/Gas	21,417	24,010

Luhrs 3400 Motor Yacht

Year	Power	Retail Low	Retail High
1992	T/Gas	79,859	89,528
1991	T/Gas	70,708	79,269
1990	T/Gas	62,390	69,944

Luhrs 3420 Motor Yacht

Year	Power	Retail Low	Retail High
1993	T/Gas	84,850	95,123
1992	T/Gas	79,859	89,528
1991	T/Gas	70,708	79,269

Luhrs Alura 35

Year	Power	Retail Low	Retail High
1989	T/Gas	54,492	61,089
1989	T/Diesel	68,115	76,362
1988	T/Gas	51,191	57,389
1988	T/Diesel	62,282	69,823

Mainship 31 Sedan Bridge

Year	Power	Retail Low	Retail High
1995	T/Gas	88,544	99,265
1994	T/Gas	82,508	92,498

Mainship 34 Sedan

Year	Power	Retail Low	Retail High
1982	S/Diesel	39,604	44,902
1981	S/Diesel	37,547	42,570
1980	S/Diesel	35,416	40,154
1979	S/Diesel	34,569	39,194
1978	S/Diesel	33,617	38,115

Mainship 34 II

Year	Power	Retail Low	Retail High
1982	S/Diesel	35,156	39,859
1981	S/Diesel	33,441	37,915
1980	S/Diesel	32,243	36,557

Mainship 34 III

Year	Power	Retail Low	Retail High
1988	S/Diesel	54,633	61,247
1987	S/Diesel	52,031	58,331
1986	S/Diesel	49,430	55,414

Year	Power	Retail Low	Retail High
1985	S/Diesel	46,828	52,498
1984	S/Diesel	45,094	50,553
1983	S/Diesel	42,492	47,637

Mainship 35 Convertible

Year	Power	Retail Low	Retail High
1994	T/Gas	101,487	113,775
1993	T/Gas	94,998	106,500
1992	T/Gas	86,591	97,075
1991	T/Gas	79,025	88,593
1990	T/Gas	72,300	81,053
1989	T/Gas	66,263	74,286
1988	T/Gas	61,166	68,571

Mainship 36 Sedan

Year	Power	Retail Low	Retail High
1988	T/Gas	67,112	75,238
1987	T/Gas	59,467	66,667
1986	T/Gas	54,369	60,952

Mainship 35 Open & 36 Express

Year	Power	Retail Low	Retail High
1994	T/Gas	99,823	111,910
1993	T/Gas	90,673	101,651
1992	T/Gas	84,018	94,191
1991	T/Gas	77,363	86,730
1990	T/Gas	72,372	81,134

Mainship 35 Open Bridge & 36 Sedan Bridge

Year	Power	Retail Low	Retail High
1992	T/Gas	91,019	102,039
1991	T/Gas	81,090	90,908
1990	T/Gas	74,470	83,487

Mainship 39 Express

Year	Power	Retail Low	Retail High
1994	T/Gas	131,676	147,619
1993	T/Gas	118,933	133,333
1992	T/Gas	109,588	122,857
1991	T/Gas	101,943	114,286
1990	T/Gas	95,147	106,667
1989	T/Gas	89,014	99,792

Mainship 40 Sedan Bridge

Year	Power	Retail Low	Retail High
1995	T/Gas	140,668	157,700
1994	T/Gas	127,428	142,857
1993	T/Gas	117,593	131,830

Mainship 41 Grand Salon

Year	Power	Retail Low	Retail High
1990	T/Gas	103,027	115,502
1990	T/Diesel	134,532	150,820
1989	T/Gas	93,195	104,479
1989	T/Diesel	120,908	135,547

Mainship 41 Convertible

Year	Power	Retail Low	Retail High
1992	T/Gas	131,539	147,465
1992	T/Diesel	170,577	191,229
1991	T/Gas	121,356	136,049
1991	T/Diesel	153,604	172,202
1990	T/Gas	112,020	125,583
1990	T/Diesel	143,198	160,535
1989	T/Gas	105,418	118,181
1989	T/Diesel	133,765	149,961

Mares 38 Cat

Year	Power	Retail Low	Retail High
1995	T/IO/Gas	164,404	188,537
1994	T/IO/Gas	137,987	158,242

Mares 54 Cat

Year	Power	Retail Low	Retail High
1995	T/8V92	694,896	789,654
1994	T/8V92	615,764	699,732

Marinette 32 Sedan

Year	Power	Retail Low	Retail High
1990	T/Gas	59,131	66,290
1989	T/Gas	55,846	62,608
1988	T/Gas	53,382	59,846
1987	T/Gas	50,918	57,083
1986	T/Gas	48,455	54,321
1985	T/Gas	45,991	51,559
1984	T/Gas	43,527	48,797
1983	T/Gas	41,063	46,035
1982	T/Gas	37,778	42,352
1981	T/Gas	34,804	39,917
1980	T/Gas	31,492	36,115
1979	T/Gas	28,177	32,314
1978	T/Gas	25,691	29,462
1977	T/Gas	23,205	26,611
1976	T/Gas	20,719	23,760

Maxum 2700 SCR

Year	Power	Retail Low	Retail High
1995	T/IO/5.7L	39,329	44,091
1994	T/IO/5.7L	35,403	39,690
1993	T/IO/5.7L	31,898	35,760

Maxum 3200 SCR

Year	Power	Retail Low	Retail High
1995	T/IO/5.7L	63,517	71,207
1994	T/IO/5.7L	54,094	60,644

Mediterranean 38 Conv.

Year	Power	Retail Low	Retail High
1995	T/Diesel	231,902	259,980
1994	T/Diesel	209,624	235,004
1993	T/Diesel	189,212	212,121
1992	T/Diesel	177,568	199,067
1991	T/Diesel	164,469	184,382
1990	T/Diesel	150,399	168,609
1989	T/Diesel	139,241	156,099
1988	T/Diesel	132,448	148,485
1987	T/Diesel	124,686	139,782
1986	T/Diesel	120,512	135,103
1985	T/Diesel	117,592	131,830

Midnight Lace 40 Express

Year	Power	Retail Low	Retail High
1994	T/Diesel	241,231	270,438
1993	T/Diesel	218,334	244,770
1992	T/Diesel	202,798	227,352
1991	T/Diesel	188,896	211,767

Midnight Lace 44 Express

Year	Power	Retail Low	Retail High
1989	T/Diesel	177,704	201,479
1988	T/Diesel	163,588	185,474
1987	T/Diesel	153,623	174,176
1986	T/Diesel	144,489	163,819
1985	T/Diesel	137,015	155,346
1984	T/Diesel	132,033	149,697
1983	T/Diesel	127,050	144,048
1982	T/Diesel	124,635	141,310
1981	T/Diesel	120,779	136,938
1980	T/Diesel	119,940	135,986
1979	T/Diesel	118,054	133,848
1978	T/Diesel	113,513	128,700

Midnight Lace 52 Express

Year	Power	Retail Low	Retail High
1989	T/Diesel	241,040	273,288
1988	T/Diesel	223,216	253,080
1987	T/Diesel	210,485	238,645
1986	T/Diesel	196,057	222,287
1985	T/Diesel	185,872	210,739
1984	T/Diesel	179,082	203,041
1983	T/Diesel	173,990	197,267
1982	T/Diesel	167,200	189,569

Monterey 236/246/256 Cruiser

Year	Power	Retail Low	Retail High
1995	S/IO/5.7L	30,234	33,895
1994	S/IO/5.7L	27,340	30,650
1993	S/IO/5.7L	25,160	28,206
1992	S/IO/5.7L	23,294	26,114

Monterey 265/276 Cruiser

Year	Power	Retail Low	Retail High
1995	S/IO/7.4L	41,882	46,953
1994	S/IO/7.4L	37,067	41,555
1993	S/IO/7.4L	33,414	37,460

Monterey 286/296 Cruiser

Year	Power	Retail Low	Retail High
1995	T/IO/4.3L	53,790	60,303
1994	T/IO/4.3L	49,638	55,648
1993	T/IO/4.3L	44,032	49,363

Nauset 35 Sport Cruiser

Year	Power	Retail Low	Retail High
1994	S/Diesel	150,124	168,300
1989	S/Diesel	85,659	96,030
1984	S/Diesel	57,400	64,350

Ocean 35 Sport Cruiser

Year	Power	Retail Low	Retail High
1993	T/Diesel	149,843	167,986
1992	T/Gas	118,880	133,273
1992	T/Diesel	138,201	154,934
1991	T/Gas	102,387	114,783
1991	T/Diesel	123,875	138,874
1990	T/Gas	96,909	108,643
1990	T/Diesel	117,977	132,261

Ocean Alexander 42/46 Sedan

Year	Power	Retail Low	Retail High
1994	T/250D	240,339	269,438
1994	T/375D	258,142	289,397
1993	T/250D	223,426	250,478
1993	T/375D	240,339	269,438
1992	T/250D	210,074	235,509
1992	T/375D	226,097	253,472
1991	T/250D	199,392	223,534
1991	T/375D	214,525	240,499
1990	T/250D	190,491	213,555
1990	T/375D	203,843	228,524
1989	T/250D	181,590	203,576
1989	T/375D	194,942	218,544
1988	T/250D	174,468	195,592
1988	T/375D	186,930	209,563

Phoenix 27 Weekender

Year	Power	Retail Low	Retail High
1994	O/B*	45,290	50,774
1994	T/Gas	69,387	77,788
1994	T/Diesel	88,934	99,701
1993	O/B*	41,996	47,081
1993	T/Gas	63,380	71,054
1993	T/Diesel	79,875	89,547
1992	O/B*	38,703	43,389
1992	T/Gas	58,660	65,762
1992	T/Diesel	72,464	81,238
1991	O/B*	32,115	36,003
1991	T/Gas	54,348	60,929
1991	T/Diesel	63,406	71,083
1990	O/B*	27,998	31,387
1990	T/Gas	47,761	53,543
1990	T/Diesel	58,877	66,006
1989	O/B*	24,704	27,695
1989	T/Gas	42,820	48,004
1989	T/Diesel	53,525	60,005
1988	O/B*	23,057	25,848
1988	T/Gas	38,291	42,927
1988	T/Diesel	49,408	55,390
1987	O/B*	21,822	24,464
1987	T/Gas	35,409	39,696
1987	T/Diesel	46,937	52,620
1986	O/B*	20,586	23,079
1986	T/Gas	32,938	36,926
1986	T/Diesel	44,055	49,389
1985	O/B*	18,940	21,233
1985	T/Gas	31,291	35,080
1985	T/Diesel	41,173	46,158
1984	O/B*	17,293	19,386
1984	T/Gas	28,821	32,311
1984	T/Diesel	38,703	43,389
1983	O/B*	15,646	17,540
1983	T/Gas	26,351	29,541
1983	T/Diesel	35,409	39,696
1982	O/B*	13,999	15,694
1982	T/Gas	24,704	27,695
1982	T/Diesel	32,115	36,003
1981	O/B*	12,075	13,847
1981	T/Gas	22,137	25,387
1981	T/Diesel	27,975	32,081
1980	O/B*	11,509	13,199
1980	T/Gas	20,552	23,569
1980	T/Diesel	25,896	29,697
1979	O/B*	10,687	12,256
1979	T/Gas	19,730	22,626
1979	T/Diesel	24,252	27,811

Phoenix 27 Tournament

Year	Power	Retail Low	Retail High
1995	T/Gas	73,391	82,277
1995	T/Diesel	93,874	105,240
1994	T/Gas	67,835	76,048
1994	T/Diesel	88,115	98,784
1993	T/Gas	64,878	72,733
1993	T/Diesel	84,426	94,648
1992	T/Gas	61,502	68,949
1992	T/Diesel	79,285	88,884
1991	T/Gas	57,100	64,014
1991	T/Diesel	71,174	79,792
1990	T/Gas	47,852	53,645
1990	T/Diesel	61,925	69,423

Phoenix Blackhawk 909

Year	Power	Retail Low	Retail High
1994	T/Gas	94,578	106,029
1994	T/Diesel	112,858	126,522
1993	T/Gas	86,630	97,119
1993	T/Diesel	104,115	116,721
1992	T/Gas	79,477	89,100
1992	T/Diesel	95,373	106,920
1991	T/Gas	71,529	80,190
1991	T/Diesel	86,630	97,119
1990	T/Gas	63,582	71,280
1990	T/Diesel	78,682	88,209
1989	T/Gas	56,429	63,261
1989	T/Diesel	70,735	79,299
1988	T/Gas	50,071	56,133
1988	T/Diesel	63,582	71,280
1987	T/Gas	45,302	50,787
1987	T/Diesel	56,429	63,261
1986	T/Gas	40,533	45,441
1986	T/Diesel	51,660	57,915
1985	T/Gas	35,765	40,095
1985	T/Diesel	46,892	52,569

Portsmouth 30 Cruiser

Year	Power	Retail Low	Retail High
1992	S/Diesel	59,982	67,320
1991	S/Diesel	52,043	58,410
1990	S/Diesel	45,869	51,480
1989	S/Diesel	40,488	45,441

President 35 Sedan

Year	Power	Retail Low	Retail High
1992	T/Diesel	128,859	144,461
1991	T/Diesel	119,788	134,292
1990	T/Diesel	108,974	122,168
1989	T/Diesel	98,160	110,044
1988	T/Diesel	85,751	96,133
1987	T/Diesel	74,822	83,881

Regal Valanti 252/256; Commodore 256

Year	Power	Retail Low	Retail High
1995	S/IO/5.7L	34,454	38,625
1994	S/IO/5.7L	30,418	34,101
1993	S/IO/5.7L	27,481	30,808

Regal 265/270/276

Year	Power	Retail Low	Retail High
1993	S/IO/7.4L	37,434	41,966
1992	S/IO/7.4L	34,938	39,168
1991	S/IO/7.4L	32,443	36,371
1990	S/IO/7.4L	30,779	34,505

Regal Commodore 272

Year	Power	Retail Low	Retail High
1995	S/IO/7.4L	46,218	51,814
1995	T/IO/4.3L	49,619	55,627
1994	S/IO/7.4L	39,023	43,748
1994	T/IO/4.3L	42,476	47,619
1993	S/IO/7.4L	37,289	41,804
1993	T/IO/4.3L	38,672	43,354
1992	S/IO/7.4L	34,687	38,887
1992	T/IO/4.3L	36,422	40,832
1991	S/IO/7.4L	31,441	35,248
1991	T/IO/4.3L	32,543	36,483

Regal Ventura 8.3

Year	Power	Retail Low	Retail High
1995	S/IO/7.4L	37,607	42,160
1994	S/IO/7.4L	33,274	37,303
1993	S/IO/7.4L	31,219	34,998

Regal 277XL/280/290/300

Year	Power	Retail Low	Retail High
1994	T/IO/5.7L	61,577	69,032
1993	T/IO/5.7L	55,672	62,413
1992	T/IO/5.7L	53,142	59,576
1991	T/IO/5.7L	48,924	54,848
1990	T/IO/5.7L	46,393	52,011
1989	T/IO/5.7L	39,645	44,445
1988	T/IO/5.7L	37,115	41,609
1987	T/IO/5.7L	31,210	34,989
1986	T/IO/5.7L	28,680	32,152
1985	T/IO/5.7L	25,563	29,315
1984	T/IO/5.7L	23,737	27,221
1983	T/IO/5.7L	22,041	25,277
1982	T/IO/5.7L	20,346	23,332

Regal Commodore 292

Year	Power	Retail Low	Retail High
1995	T/IO/5.7L	70,191	78,690

Regal Commodore 320

Year	Power	Retail Low	Retail High
1992	T/IO/5.7L	66,161	74,172
1991	T/IO/5.7L	61,865	69,355
1990	T/IO/5.7L	57,569	64,539
1989	T/IO/5.7L	53,273	59,723
1988	T/IO/5.7L	48,976	54,906

Regal Ventura 9.8 & Commodore 322

Year	Power	Retail Low	Retail High
1995	T/IO/7.4L	84,740	95,000
1994	T/IO/7.4L	75,894	85,083
1993	T/IO/7.4L	68,350	76,626

Regal 360/380/400/402

Year	Power	Retail Low	Retail High
1995	T/IO/7.4L	144,791	162,322
1994	T/IO/7.4L	130,862	146,706
1993	T/IO/7.4L	121,809	136,557
1992	T/IO/7.4L	116,047	130,098
1991	T/IO/7.4L	97,941	109,799
1990	T/IO/7.4L	88,887	99,649
1989	T/IO/7.4L	81,480	91,345
1988	T/IO/7.4L	74,073	83,041
1987	T/IO/7.4L	66,665	74,737
1986	T/IO/7.4L	60,081	67,356
1985	T/IO/7.4L	54,320	60,897

Rinker 260/265 Fiesta Vee

Year	Power	Retail Low	Retail High
1995	S/IO/7.4L	30,543	34,434
1994	S/IO/7.4L	26,548	29,930
1993	S/IO/7.4L	24,038	27,100
1992	S/IO/7.4L	22,045	24,854
1991	S/IO/7.4L	19,407	21,879

Rinker 280 Fiesta Vee

Year	Power	Retail Low	Retail High
1995	T/IO/5.7L	46,929	52,908
1994	T/IO/5.7L	41,528	46,819
1993	T/IO/5.7L	37,056	41,777

Rinker 300 Fiesta Vee

Year	Power	Retail Low	Retail High
1995	T/IO/5.7L	58,130	65,535
1994	T/IO/5.7L	53,318	60,111
1993	T/IO/5.7L	48,930	55,163
1992	T/IO/5.7L	44,754	50,456
1991	T/IO/5.7L	40,731	45,920
1990	T/IO/5.7L	36,343	40,973

Sabreline 34

Year	Power	Retail Low	Retail High
1995	T/Diesel	203,705	228,113
1994	T/Diesel	188,364	210,934
1993	T/Diesel	176,099	197,199
1992	T/Diesel	166,922	186,923
1991	T/Diesel	157,207	176,044

Sea Ray 250 Sundancer (Early)

Year	Power	Retail Low	Retail High
1991	S/IO/5.7L	26,366	29,961
1990	S/IO/5.7L	23,628	26,850
1989	S/IO/5.7L	21,915	24,903

Sea Ray 250 Sundancer

Year	Power	Retail Low	Retail High
1995	S/IO/5.7L	38,999	44,317

Sea Ray 250 EC

Year	Power	Retail Low	Retail High
1994	S/IO/5.7L	31,701	36,024
1994	S/IO/7.4L	33,911	38,535
1993	S/IO/5.7L	28,952	32,900
1993	S/IO/7.4L	30,907	35,122

Sea Ray 260 Cuddy

Year	Power	Retail Low	Retail High
1991	S/IO/5.7L	25,319	28,772
1990	S/IO/5.7L	22,927	26,053
1989	S/IO/5.7L	22,076	25,086

Sea Ray 260 Overnighter

Year	Power	Retail Low	Retail High
1991	S/IO/5.7L	26,534	30,152
1990	S/IO/5.7L	24,317	27,633
1989	S/IO/5.7L	22,970	26,102

Sea Ray 268 Sundancer

Year	Power	Retail Low	Retail High
1989	S/IO/7.4L	26,581	30,206
1988	S/IO/7.4L	23,734	26,970
1987	S/IO/7.4L	21,428	24,350
1986	S/IO/7.4L	20,296	23,064

Sea Ray 270 Amberjack

Year	Power	Retail Low	Retail High
1990	175 I/O	31,762	35,607
1990	260 I/O	36,483	40,900
1989	175 I/O	30,045	33,683
1989	260 I/O	33,479	37,532
1988	175 I/O	27,040	30,314
1988	260 I/O	30,474	34,164
1987	175 I/O	24,036	26,946
1987	260 I/O	26,182	29,352
1986	175 I/O	21,890	24,540
1986	260 I/O	24,465	27,427

Sea Ray 270 Sundancer

Year	Power	Retail Low	Retail High
1988	T/IO/Gas	32,953	36,943
1987	T/IO/Gas	30,351	34,026
1986	T/IO/Gas	27,750	31,110
1985	T/IO/Gas	26,016	29,165
1984	T/IO/Gas	24,281	27,221
1983	T/IO/Gas	23,414	26,249
1982	T/IO/Gas	22,547	25,277

Year	Power	Retail Low	Retail High
Sea Ray 270 Sundancer (1992–93)			
1993	S/IO/Gas	37,289	41,804
1993	T/IO/Gas	39,890	44,720
1992	S/IO/Gas	34,687	38,887
1992	T/IO/Gas	36,422	40,832
Sea Ray 270 Sundancer			
1995	S/IO/7.4L	46,834	52505
1994	S/IO/7.4L	39,890	44,720
Sea Ray 280 Sundancer			
1991	T/IO/Gas	45,094	50,553
1990	T/IO/Gas	40,758	45,692
1989	T/IO/Gas	36,422	40,832
Sea Ray 270/290 Sundancer			
1993	S/IO/7.4L	40,699	45,832
1993	T/IO/4.3L	42,615	47,990
1992	S/IO/7.4L	35,520	40,000
1992	T/IO/4.3L	36,959	41,620
1991	S/IO/7.4L	31,291	35,238
1991	T/IO/4.3L	32,297	36,370
1990	S/IO/7.4L	27,063	30,476
1990	T/IO/4.3L	28,214	31,772
Sea Ray 290 Sundancer			
1995	S/IO/7.4L	57,946	64,962
1995	T/IO/4.3L	59,889	67,140
1994	S/IO/7.4L	48,259	54,102
1994	T/IO/4.3L	50,122	56,190
Sea Ray 300 Weekender/Sundancer			
1989	T/IO/Gas	41,107	46,084
1989	T/Gas	42,785	47,966
1988	T/IO/Gas	38,229	42,857
1988	T/Gas	39,928	44,762
1987	T/IO/Gas	35,680	40,000
1987	T/Gas	37,806	42,384
1986	T/IO/Gas	33,981	38,095
1986	T/Gas	35,680	40,000
1985	T/IO/Gas	32,651	36,604
1985	T/Gas	34,369	38,531
Sea Ray 300 Weekender			
1995	T/IO/5.7L	69,421	77,826
1995	T/VD/5.7L	73,709	82,633
1994	T/IO/5.7L	55,901	62,669
1994	T/VD/5.7L	59,507	66,712
1993	T/IO/5.7L	51,393	57,615
1993	T/VD/5.7L	54,999	61,658
1992	T/IO/5.7L	47,344	53,076
1992	T/VD/5.7L	50,075	56,138
1991	T/IO/5.7L	40,931	45,886
1991	T/VD/5.7L	42,750	47,926
Sea Ray 300 Sundancer (Early)			
1993	T/IO/5.7L	52,944	59,354
1993	T/VD/5.7L	55,486	62,204
1992	T/IO/5.7L	49,528	55,525
1992	T/VD/5.7L	51,411	57,636
Sea Ray 300 Sundancer			
1995	T/IO/Gas	77,075	86,407
1995	T/Gas	79,566	89,200
1994	T/IO/Gas	62,072	69,587
1994	T/Gas	65,569	73,508
Sea Ray 300 Sedan Bridge			
1987	T/Gas	39,042	44,265
1986	T/Gas	36,495	41,378
1985	T/Gas	33,949	38,491
Sea Ray 305/300 Sedan Bridge			
1989	T/Gas	52,123	58,434
1988	T/Gas	47,079	52,779
Sea Ray 310 Amberjack			
1994	T/Gas	79,225	88,817
1994	T/Diesel	117,571	131,806
1993	T/Gas	74,221	83,208
1993	T/Diesel	106,962	119,913
1992	T/Gas	66,299	74,326
1992	T/Diesel	94,504	105,946
1991	T/Gas	59,210	66,379
1991	T/Diesel	86,731	97,232
Sea Ray 310 Sport Bridge			
1993	T/Gas	81,332	91,179
1993	T/Diesel	104,468	117,117
1992	T/Gas	72,404	81,170
1992	T/Diesel	96,432	108,108
Sea Ray 310 Sun Sport			
1995	T/IO/7.4L	80,300	90,022
1994	T/IO/7.4L	70,510	79,048
1993	T/IO/7.4L	63,714	71,428
1992	T/IO/7.4L	58,617	65,714
1991	T/IO/7.4L	54,369	60,952
Sea Ray 310/330 Express Cruiser			
1995	T/IO/7.4L	87,196	97,753
1995	T/IB/7.4L	88,499	99,214
1994	T/IO/7.4L	76,535	85,801
1994	T/IB/7.4L	78,163	87,627
1993	T/IO/7.4L	70,835	79,412
1993	T/IB/7.4L	73,278	82,150
1992	T/IO/7.4L	65,136	73,022
1992	T/IB/7.4L	68,393	76,674
1991	T/IO/7.4L	59,437	66,633
1991	T/IB/7.4L	64,322	72,110
1990	T/IO/7.4L	52,923	59,331
1990	T/IB/7.4L	59,437	66,633
Sea Ray 310/330 Sundancer			
1995	T/IO/7.4L	98,984	110,969
1995	T/VD/7.4L	100,261	112,400
1994	T/IO/7.4L	84,910	95,190
1994	T/VD/7.4L	86,591	97,075
1993	T/IO/7.4L	76,503	85,766
1993	T/VD/7.4L	79,025	88,593
1992	T/IO/7.4L	69,777	78,226
1992	T/VD/7.4L	74,822	83,881
1991	T/IO/7.4L	63,893	71,628
1991	T/VD/7.4L	69,777	78,226
1990	T/IO/7.4L	57,167	64,089
1990	T/VD/7.4L	63,052	70,686
Sea Ray 340 Sedan Bridge			
1987	T/340G	55,322	62,021
1986	T/340G	51,970	58,262
1985	T/340G	48,617	54,503
1984	T/340G	46,102	51,684
1983	T/340G	43,587	48,865
Sea Ray 345/340 Sedan Bridge			
1989	T/Gas	72,065	80,790
1988	T/Gas	63,221	70,876

PRICE GUIDE

Sea Ray 340 Express Cruiser

Year	Power	Retail Low	Retail High
1989	T/340G	64,447	72,250
1988	T/340G	57,859	64,865
1987	T/340G	52,617	58,988
1986	T/340G	47,416	53,157
1985	T/340G	43,257	48,494
1984	T/340G	39,929	44,764

Sea Ray 340 Sundancer

Year	Power	Retail Low	Retail High
1989	T/340G	69,135	77,505
1988	T/340G	60,904	68,278
1987	T/340G	55,486	62,204
1986	T/340G	49,601	55,606
1985	T/340G	46,238	51,836
1984	T/340G	42,875	48,066

Sea Ray 350 Express Bridge

Year	Power	Retail Low	Retail High
1993	T/Gas	84,598	94,840
1992	T/Gas	75,474	84,613

Sea Ray 355T Sedan

Year	Power	Retail Low	Retail High
1983	T/Gas	40,761	45,696
1983	T/Diesel	46,238	51,836
1982	T/Gas	37,434	41,966
1982	T/Diesel	42,875	48,066

Sea Ray 360 Express Cruiser

Year	Power	Retail Low	Retail High
1983	T/350G	47,951	53,757
1982	T/350G	44,644	50,049
1981	T/350G	42,164	47,269
1980	T/350G	39,683	44,488
1979	T/350G	37,203	41,708

Sea Ray 350/370 Express Cruiser

Year	Power	Retail Low	Retail High
1995	T/IB/7.4L	122,459	137,286
1994	T/IB/7.4L	101,775	114,098
1993	T/IB/7.4L	92,194	103,356
1992	T/IB/7.4L	85,835	96,228
1991	T/IB/7.4L	80,272	89,991
1990	T/IB/7.4L	72,218	80,962

Sea Ray 350/370 Sundancer

Year	Power	Retail Low	Retail High
1994	T/IO/7.4L	112,039	125,604
1994	T/VD/7.4L	117,224	131,418
1993	T/IO/7.4L	96,496	108,179
1993	T/VD/7.4L	99,108	111,108
1992	T/IO/7.4L	89,841	100,719
1992	T/VD/7.4L	92,194	103,356
1991	T/IO/7.4L	83,840	93,991
1991	T/VD/7.4L	85,518	95,873
1990	T/IO/7.4L	75,705	84,871
1990	T/VD/7.4L	77,464	86,843

Sea Ray 370 Sedan Bridge

Year	Power	Retail Low	Retail High
1995	T/Gas	134,018	150,244
1995	T/Diesel	169,765	190,320
1994	T/Gas	122,218	137,016
1994	T/Diesel	157,630	176,715
1993	T/Gas	109,414	122,661
1993	T/Diesel	140,630	157,658
1992	T/Gas	97,691	109,519
1992	T/Diesel	126,828	142,184
1991	T/Gas	89,875	100,757
1991	T/Diesel	118,474	132,818

Sea Ray 370 Sundancer

Year	Power	Retail Low	Retail High
1995	T/IO/7.4L	161,729	181,311

Sea Ray 380 Sun Sport

Year	Power	Retail Low	Retail High
1995	T/IO/7.4L	136,718	153,271
1994	T/IO/7.4L	118,956	133,359
1993	T/IO/7.4L	106,478	119,370
1992	T/IO/7.4L	97,328	109,112
1991	T/IO/7.4L	86,514	96,988
1990	T/IO/7.4L	74,868	83,932

Sea Ray 390 Express Cruiser

Year	Power	Retail Low	Retail High
1991	T/Gas	103,550	116,087
1991	T/Diesel	133,818	150,021
1990	T/Gas	96,381	108,051
1990	T/Diesel	122,667	137,519
1989	T/Gas	87,619	98,228
1989	T/Diesel	113,905	127,696
1988	T/Gas	84,952	95,238
1988	T/Diesel	110,438	123,809
1987	T/Gas	76,503	85,766
1987	T/Diesel	99,202	111,213
1986	T/Gas	70,618	79,168
1986	T/Diesel	91,635	102,730
1985	T/Gas	66,415	74,456
1985	T/Diesel	84,910	95,190
1984	T/Gas	62,211	69,744
1984	T/Diesel	78,184	87,651

Sea Ray 400 Express Cruiser

Year	Power	Retail Low	Retail High
1995	T/Gas	159,100	178,363
1995	T/Diesel	198,083	222,066
1994	T/Gas	140,587	157,609
1994	T/Diesel	177,584	199,085
1993	T/Gas	130,721	146,549
1993	T/Diesel	161,963	181,573
1992	T/Gas	118,389	132,723
1992	T/Diesel	147,164	164,983

Sea Ray 420/440 Sundancer

Year	Power	Retail Low	Retail High
1995	T/375D	259,047	290,411
1994	T/375D	238,750	267,656
1993	T/375D	223,672	250,754
1992	T/375D	202,802	227,356
1991	T/375D	182,854	204,993
1990	T/375D	166,317	186,454
1989	T/375D	155,397	174,212

Sea Ray 440 Express Bridge

Year	Power	Retail Low	Retail High
1995	T/Diesel	285,680	320,269
1994	T/Diesel	242,119	271,434
1993	T/Diesel	222,218	249,124

Sea Ray 450 Sundancer

Year	Power	Retail Low	Retail High
1995	T/375 D	******	******

Sea Ray 460 Express Cruiser

Year	Power	Retail Low	Retail High
1989	T/375D	179,682	201,437
1989	T/550D	200,053	224,275
1988	T/375D	166,019	186,120
1988	T/550D	183,451	205,663
1987	T/375D	151,907	170,300
1987	T/550D	166,019	186,120
1986	T/375D	142,776	160,063
1986	T/550D	154,875	173,626
1985	T/375D	138,184	154,915
1985	T/550D	149,205	167,270

Sea Ray 480/500 Sundancer

Year	Power	Retail Low	Retail High
1995	T/485D	409,803	459,420
1995	T/735D	471,244	528,300

Year	Power	Retail Low	Retail High
1994	T/485D	363,221	407,199
1994	T/735D	424,429	475,818
1993	T/485D	312,483	350,317
1993	T/735D	368,859	413,519
1992	T/485D	282,685	316,911
1992	T/735D	335,839	376,501
1991	T/485D	256,913	288,019
1991	T/735D	308,456	345,803
1990	T/485D	240,000	269,058
1990	T/735D	286,711	321,425

Sea Ray 600/630 Super Sun Sport

Year	Power	Retail Low	Retail High
1995	T/1040 D.	970,519	1,088,026
1994	T/1040 D.	903,688	1,013,103
1993	T/1040 D.	840,180	941,906
1992	T/1040 D.	780,201	874,665
1991	T/1040 D.	750,339	841,187

Shannon 36 Voyager

Year	Power	Retail Low	Retail High
1995	T/Diesel	266,419	298,676
1994	T/Diesel	220,638	247,352
1993	T/Diesel	195,470	219,136
1992	T/Diesel	176,174	197,505
1991	T/Diesel	161,913	181,516

Silhouette 42

Year	Power	Retail Low	Retail High
1991	T/Diesel	174,691	195,842
1990	T/Diesel	159,717	179,055
1989	T/Diesel	147,239	165,067
1988	T/Diesel	136,425	152,943
1987	T/Diesel	127,275	142,685

Silverton 271 Express

Year	Power	Retail Low	Retail High
1995	S/IO/5.7L	38,231	42,860

Silverton 28 Sedan

Year	Power	Retail Low	Retail High
1978	T/Gas	13,938	16,359
1977	T/Gas	13,118	15,396
1976	T/Gas	12,298	14,434
1975	T/Gas	11,478	13,472

Silverton 29 Sportcruiser

Year	Power	Retail Low	Retail High
1987	T/Gas	31,432	35,238
1986	T/Gas	28,884	32,381
1985	T/Gas	26,335	29,524

Silverton 30X Express

Year	Power	Retail Low	Retail High
1989	T/Gas	41,194	46,182
1988	T/Gas	38,672	43,354

Silverton 31 Conv. (Early)

Year	Power	Retail Low	Retail High
1987	T/Gas	39,104	43,838
1986	T/Gas	36,581	41,010
1985	T/Gas	34,058	38,182
1984	T/Gas	32,376	36,296
1983	T/Gas	30,694	34,411
1982	T/Gas	28,172	31,582
1981	T/Gas	25,599	29,697
1980	T/Gas	23,161	26,869
1979	T/Gas	21,535	24,983
1978	T/Gas	20,316	23,569
1977	T/Gas	19,504	22,626

Silverton 31 Convertible

Year	Power	Retail Low	Retail High
1995	T/5.7L	79,550	92,285
1994	T/5.7L	71,604	80,273
1993	T/5.7L	66,665	74,737
1992	T/5.7L	59,258	66,433

Silverton 31 Gulfstream

Year	Power	Retail Low	Retail High
1986	T/270G	34,334	38,491
1986	T/350G	38,626	43,303
1985	T/270G	31,759	35,604
1985	T/350G	36,051	40,416
1984	T/270G	30,042	33,680
1984	T/350G	33,476	37,529
1983	T/270G	29,484	33,054
1983	T/350G	32,086	35,971
1982	T/270G	28,296	32,082
1982	T/350G	30,869	34,998
1981	T/270G	26,581	30,138
1981	T/350G	30,011	34,026
1980	T/270G	22,889	26,249
1980	T/350G	27,975	32,082
1979	T/270G	22,041	25,277
1979	T/350G	26,280	30,138

Silverton 310 Express

Year	Power	Retail Low	Retail High
1995	T/IO/7.4L	71,946	80,657
1994	T/IO/7.4L	62,390	69,944

Silverton 312 Sedan Cruiser

Year	Power	Retail Low	Retail High
1995	T/IO/5.0L	62,266	69,805
1994	T/IO/5.0L	56,994	63,895

Silverton 33 Sport Sedan

Year	Power	Retail Low	Retail High
1976	T/Gas	21,123	24,504
1975	T/Gas	18,686	21,677

Silverton 34 Sedan

Year	Power	Retail Low	Retail High
1981	T/Gas	32,921	36,907
1980	T/Gas	30,111	34,139
1979	T/Gas	27,042	31,371
1978	T/Gas	23,861	27,680
1977	T/Gas	21,474	24,912

Silverton 34 Convertible (1978–88)

Year	Power	Retail Low	Retail High
1988	T/Gas	54,320	60,897
1987	T/Gas	51,028	57,206
1986	T/Gas	47,416	53,157
1985	T/Gas	45,025	50,476
1984	T/Gas	41,627	46,667
1983	T/Gas	37,379	41,905
1982	T/Gas	35,555	39,859
1981	T/Gas	32,261	36,996
1980	T/Gas	30,232	34,670
1979	T/Gas	28,454	32,630
1978	T/Gas	26,675	30,591

Silverton 34 Convertible (1989–90)

Year	Power	Retail Low	Retail High
1990	T/Gas	64,053	71,809
1989	T/Gas	56,567	63,415

Silverton 34 Convertible (1991–95)

Year	Power	Retail Low	Retail High
1995	T/Gas	103,153	115,642
1994	T/Gas	100,883	113,098
1993	T/Gas	93,317	104,615
1992	T/Gas	84,910	95,190
1991	T/Gas	78,725	88,257

Silverton 34X Express

Year	Power	Retail Low	Retail High
1989	T/Gas	57,167	64,089
1988	T/Gas	52,964	59,376
1987	T/Gas	50,442	56,549

Silverton 34 Express

Year	Power	Retail Low	Retail High
1994	T/Gas	97,941	109,799
1993	T/Gas	88,105	98,772
1992	T/Gas	78,488	87,991
1991	T/Gas	71,450	80,101
1990	T/Gas	64,535	72,349

Silverton 361 Express

Year	Power	Retail Low	Retail High
1995	T/Gas	108,830	122,007

Silverton 362 Sedan Cruiser

Year	Power	Retail Low	Retail High
1995	T/Gas	112,190	125,773
1994	T/Gas	97,328	109,112

Silverton 37 Conv. (Early)

Year	Power	Retail Low	Retail High
1989	T/Gas	77,226	86,576
1989	T/Diesel	98,442	110,361
1988	T/Gas	72,983	81,820
1988	T/Diesel	89,107	99,896
1987	T/Gas	66,025	74,019
1987	T/Diesel	83,175	93,245
1986	T/Gas	61,738	69,213
1986	T/Diesel	77,172	86,516
1985	T/Gas	58,308	65,368
1985	T/Diesel	72,028	80,748
1984	T/Gas	54,021	60,561
1984	T/Diesel	66,883	74,981
1983	T/Gas	51,448	57,677
1982	T/Gas	49,733	55,755
1981	T/Gas	48,018	53,832
1980	T/Gas	46,303	51,910

Silverton 37 Convertible

Year	Power	Retail Low	Retail High
1995	T/7.4L	135,475	151,878
1995	T/375 D.	176,898	198,316
1994	T/7.4L	124,699	139,797
1994	T/375 D.	159,281	178,566
1993	T/7.4L	119,711	134,205
1993	T/375 D.	149,639	167,756
1992	T/7.4L	109,735	123,021
1992	T/375 D.	139,663	156,573
1991	T/7.4L	94,730	106,200
1991	T/375 D.	127,844	143,323
1990	T/7.4L	85,509	95,862

Silverton 38X Express

Year	Power	Retail Low	Retail High
1994	T/Gas	122,024	136,798
1994	T/Diesel	172,274	193,132
1993	T/Gas	111,824	125,364
1993	T/Diesel	153,241	171,795
1992	T/Gas	103,151	115,640
1992	T/Diesel	138,089	154,808
1991	T/Gas	99,726	111,801
1991	T/Diesel	130,078	145,827
1990	T/Gas	91,922	103,051
1990	T/Diesel	117,937	132,216

Silverton 40 Convertible

Year	Power	Retail Low	Retail High
1990	T/Gas	107,239	120,223
1990	T/Diesel	131,797	147,755
1989	T/Gas	98,234	110,128
1989	T/Diesel	122,792	137,660
1988	T/Gas	90,048	100,950
1988	T/Diesel	111,332	124,811
1987	T/Gas	81,043	90,855
1987	T/Diesel	99,052	111,045
1986	T/Gas	72,038	80,760
1986	T/Diesel	88,410	99,115
1985	T/Gas	63,852	71,583
1985	T/Diesel	78,587	88,102

Silverton 41 Convertible

Year	Power	Retail Low	Retail High
1995	T/Gas	179,002	200,675
1995	T/435D	225,563	252,873
1994	T/Gas	168,188	188,552
1994	T/425D	208,554	233,804
1993	T/Gas	158,809	178,037
1993	T/375D	199,046	223,146
1992	T/Gas	145,074	162,639
1992	T/375D	183,469	205,682
1991	T/Gas	133,056	149,166
1991	T/375D	163,101	182,848

Tempest 42 Sport Yacht

Year	Power	Retail Low	Retail High
1992	T/Diesel	228,188	255,816
1991	T/Diesel	207,215	232,304
1990	T/Diesel	192,114	215,374
1989	T/Diesel	176,174	197,505
1988	T/Diesel	164,429	184,338

Tempest 60 Sport Yacht

Year	Power	Retail Low	Retail High
1992	T/Diesel	901,845	1,011,038
1990	T/Diesel	729,866	818,235
1988	T/Diesel	587,248	658,350

Thompson 3100 Santa Cruz

Year	Power	Retail Low	Retail High
1995	T/IO/5.7L	66,597	74,660
1994	T/IO/5.7L	54,623	61,236
1993	T/IO/5.7L	48,899	54,820
1992	T/IO/5.7L	45,115	50,577
1991	T/IO/5.7L	42,602	47,760

Thundercraft 280 Express

Year	Power	Retail Low	Retail High
1995	T/IO/4.3L	57,019	63923
1994	T/IO/4.3L	50,865	57,024
1993	T/IO/4.3L	47,819	53,608
1992	T/IO/4.3L	44,463	49,846
1991	T/IO/4.3L	41,946	47,025
1990	T/IO/4.3L	39,430	44,204
1989	T/IO/4.3L	37,752	42,322

Thundercraft 350 Express

Year	Power	Retail Low	Retail High
1995	T/IO/7.4L	100,395	112550
1994	T/IO/7.4L	86,409	96,872
1993	T/IO/7.4L	78,859	88,407

Tiara 250 Sportboat

Year	Power	Retail Low	Retail High
1993	S/IO/7.4L	35,582	39,890
1992	S/IO/7.4L	32,045	35,925
1991	S/IO/7.4L	28,868	32,363

Tiara 260 Sportboat

Year	Power	Retail Low	Retail High
1993	S/IO/7.4L	39,492	44,274
1992	S/IO/7.4L	36,304	40,700
1991	S/IO/7.4L	33,135	37,147

Tiara 2700 Continental

Year	Power	Retail Low	Retail High
1987	T/IO/5.7L	35,649	39,965
1986	T/IO/5.7L	34,173	38,310
1985	T/IO/5.7L	32,537	36,477
1984	T/IO/5.7L	30,417	34,100
1983	T/IO/5.7L	28,321	31,750
1982	T/IO/5.7L	25,823	28,949

Tiara 2700 Open

Year	Power	Retail Low	Retail High
1993	T/Gas	64,079	71,838
1992	T/Gas	55,757	62,508
1991	T/Gas	49,516	55,511
1990	T/Gas	46,603	52,246
1989	T/Gas	42,858	48,047
1988	T/Gas	40,362	45,249
1987	T/Gas	37,449	41,983
1986	T/Gas	35,369	39,651
1985	T/Gas	33,288	37,318
1984	T/Gas	31,208	34,986
1983	T/Gas	28,889	32,387
1982	T/Gas	26,611	29,833

Tiara 270 Sportboat

Year	Power	Retail Low	Retail High
1993	T/IO/5.7L	61,023	68,411
1992	T/IO/5.7L	56,334	63,155
1991	T/IO/5.7L	52,604	58,973

Tiara 2900 Open

Year	Power	Retail Low	Retail High
1995	T/Gas	91,013	102,032
1994	T/Gas	79,474	89,097

Year	Power	Retail Low	Retail High
1993	T/Gas	73,542	82,446

Tiara 3100 Open (Early)

Year	Power	Retail Low	Retail High
1992	T/Gas	88,847	99,604
1992	T/Diesel	113,357	127,081
1991	T/Gas	77,258	86,612
1991	T/Diesel	106,473	119,364
1990	T/Gas	71,678	80,357
1990	T/Diesel	97,242	109,015
1989	T/Gas	66,099	74,102
1989	T/Diesel	86,524	97,000
1988	T/Gas	60,519	67,846
1988	T/Diesel	77,254	86,608
1987	T/Gas	59,231	66,403
1987	T/Diesel	69,532	77,951
1986	T/Gas	53,652	60,148
1986	T/Diesel	64,382	72,177
1985	T/Gas	50,194	56,272
1985	T/Diesel	59,661	66,884
1984	T/Gas	48,072	53,892
1984	T/Diesel	51,506	57,742
1983	T/Gas	37,771	42,344
1983	T/Diesel	42,921	48,118
1982	T/Gas	35,195	39,457
1981	T/Gas	31,333	35,126
1980	T/Gas	28,253	31,674
1979	T/Gas	26,190	29,694

Tiara 3100 Open

Year	Power	Retail Low	Retail High
1995	T/Gas	125,085	140,230
1995	T/Diesel	160,087	179,470
1994	T/Gas	116,227	130,299
1994	T/Diesel	146,761	164,530
1993	T/Gas	104,885	117,584
1993	T/Diesel	142,556	159,816
1992	T/Gas	95,289	106,826
1992	T/Diesel	134,806	151,128

Tiara 3100 Convertible

Year	Power	Retail Low	Retail High
1992	T/Gas	95,285	106,822
1991	T/Gas	87,130	97,680
1990	T/Gas	81,550	91,424
1989	T/Gas	73,825	82,763
1988	T/Gas	70,391	78,914
1987	T/Gas	67,816	76,026
1986	T/Gas	61,377	68,809
1985	T/Gas	58,802	65,922
1984	T/Gas	54,939	61,591
1983	T/Gas	51,076	57,260
1982	T/Gas	46,784	52,449

Tiara 3300 Open

Year	Power	Retail Low	Retail High
1995	T/Gas	128,133	143,647
1995	T/Diesel	164,316	184,211
1994	T/Gas	115,887	129,919
1994	T/Diesel	151,083	169,375
1993	T/Gas	107,732	120,776
1993	T/Diesel	139,923	156,865
1992	T/Gas	104,896	117,596
1992	T/Diesel	126,188	141,467
1991	T/Gas	91,422	102,491
1991	T/Diesel	115,029	128,956
1990	T/Gas	84,555	94,792
1990	T/Diesel	107,303	120,295
1989	T/Gas	78,546	88,056
1989	T/Diesel	100,007	112,115
1988	T/Gas	72,262	81,012
1988	T/Diesel	89,138	99,931

Tiara 3500 Express

Year	Power	Retail Low	Retail High
1995	T/435D	234,040	262,377

Tiara 3600 Open

Year	Power	Retail Low	Retail High
1995	T/Gas	173,935	194,994
1995	T/Diesel	222,831	249,811
1994	T/Gas	156,233	175,150
1994	T/Diesel	210,314	235,778
1993	T/Gas	155,804	174,668
1993	T/Diesel	197,438	221,343
1992	T/Gas	139,096	155,938
1992	T/Diesel	184,124	206,417
1991	T/Gas	127,505	142,943
1991	T/Diesel	168,521	188,924
1990	T/Gas	117,251	131,447
1990	T/Diesel	157,821	176,929
1989	T/Gas	107,889	120,952
1989	T/Diesel	145,338	162,935
1988	T/Gas	99,864	111,955
1988	T/Diesel	132,855	148,940
1987	T/Gas	93,623	104,958
1987	T/Diesel	117,950	132,231
1986	T/Gas	86,966	97,495
1986	T/Diesel	115,660	129,664
1985	T/Gas	81,668	91,556
1985	T/Diesel	105,948	118,776

Tiara 3600 Convertible

Year	Power	Retail Low	Retail High
1995	T/Gas	196,964	220,812
1995	T/Diesel	244,463	274,062
1994	T/Gas	174,134	195,218
1994	T/Diesel	232,701	260,875
1993	T/Gas	173,436	194,435
1993	T/Diesel	220,063	246,708
1992	T/Gas	148,597	166,589
1992	T/Diesel	193,481	216,907
1991	T/Gas	135,088	151,444
1991	T/Diesel	176,922	198,343
1990	T/Gas	122,755	137,617
1990	T/Diesel	161,813	181,405
1989	T/Gas	113,312	127,032
1989	T/Diesel	151,083	169,375
1988	T/Gas	105,972	119,070
1988	T/Diesel	140,424	157,780
1987	T/Gas	100,303	112,700
1987	T/Diesel	133,447	149,940

Tiara 3700 Open

Year	Power	Retail Low	Retail High
1995	T/Diesel	273,732	303,511

Tiara 4000 Open

Year	Power	Retail Low	Retail High
1995	T/Diesel	330,593	370,620
1994	T/Diesel	302,649	339,293

Tiara 4300 Open

Year	Power	Retail Low	Retail High
1995	T/Diesel	376,745	422,360
1994	T/Diesel	343,370	384,944
1993	T/Diesel	327,918	367,622
1992	T/Diesel	311,513	349,230
1991	T/Diesel	292,723	328,165

Tollycraft 26 Sedan

Year	Power	Retail Low	Retail High
1985	S/Gas	30,901	34,642
1984	S/Gas	29,184	32,718
1983	S/Gas	26,609	29,831
1982	S/Gas	24,892	27,906
1981	S/Gas	23,176	25,982
1980	S/Gas	21,459	24,057
1979	S/Gas	19,742	22,132
1978	S/Gas	18,884	21,170
1977	S/Gas	17,167	19,246
1976	S/Gas	16,309	18,283
1975	S/Gas	15,450	17,321

Tollycraft 30 Sedan

Year	Power	Retail Low	Retail High
1984	T/Gas	47,209	52,925

Year	Power	Retail Low	Retail High
1983	T/Gas	43,776	49,076
1982	T/Gas	40,343	45,227
1981	T/Gas	36,909	41,378
1980	T/Gas	34,334	38,491
1979	T/Gas	31,759	35,604
1978	T/Gas	29,184	32,718
1977	T/Gas	27,467	30,793

Tollycraft 30 Sport Cruiser

Year	Power	Retail Low	Retail High
1992	T/Gas	80,537	90,288
1991	T/Gas	73,825	82,764
1990	T/Gas	67,953	76,180
1989	T/Gas	62,081	69,597
1988	T/Gas	57,886	64,894
1987	T/Gas	53,691	60,192
1986	T/Gas	51,174	57,370
1985	T/Gas	47,819	53,608

Tollycraft 34 Sedan

Year	Power	Retail Low	Retail High
1980	T/Gas	42,918	48,114
1979	T/Gas	39,484	44,265
1978	T/Gas	36,051	40,416
1977	T/Gas	33,476	37,529
1976	T/Gas	31,759	35,604
1975	T/Gas	30,042	33,680

Tollycraft 34 Conv. Sedan

Year	Power	Retail Low	Retail High
1986	T/Gas	80,685	90,454
1985	T/Gas	74,677	83,718
1984	T/Gas	68,668	76,982
1983	T/Gas	63,518	71,209
1982	T/Gas	58,368	65,435
1981	T/Gas	54,935	61,586

Tollycraft 34 Sport Sedan

Year	Power	Retail Low	Retail High
1993	T/Gas	137,478	154,123
1992	T/Gas	127,167	142,564
1991	T/Gas	116,856	131,005
1990	T/Gas	107,405	120,409
1989	T/Gas	99,671	111,739
1988	T/Gas	94,619	106,076
1987	T/Gas	90,083	100,990

Tollycraft 37 Convertible

Year	Power	Retail Low	Retail High
1985	T/Gas	91,454	102,526
1985	T/Diesel	113,886	127,674
1984	T/Gas	84,551	94,789
1984	T/Diesel	105,258	118,002
1983	T/Gas	79,375	88,985

Year	Power	Retail Low	Retail High
1983	T/Diesel	97,493	109,297
1982	T/Gas	75,061	84,149
1982	T/Diesel	89,728	100,592
1981	T/Gas	70,747	79,313
1981	T/Diesel	82,826	92,854
1980	T/Gas	66,433	74,477
1980	T/Diesel	78,512	88,018
1979	T/Gas	61,257	68,673
1979	T/Diesel	73,335	82,215
1978	T/Gas	56,080	62,870
1978	T/Diesel	66,433	74,477
1977	T/Gas	49,178	55,132
1977	T/Diesel	59,531	66,739
1976	T/Gas	45,727	51,263
1976	T/Diesel	56,080	62,870
1975	T/Gas	42,276	47,394
1975	T/Diesel	52,629	59,001

Trojan 26 Express

Year	Power	Retail Low	Retail High
1983	S/Gas	16,955	19,444
1982	S/Gas	16,107	18,471
1981	S/Gas	15,259	17,499
1980	S/Gas	14,412	16,527
1979	S/Gas	13,564	15,555
1978	S/Gas	12,716	14,583
1977	S/Gas	11,868	13,611
1976	S/Gas	11,021	12,638
1975	S/Gas	10,173	11,666

Trojan 28 Sedan

Year	Power	Retail Low	Retail High
1979	T/Gas	19,498	22,360
1978	T/Gas	17,803	20,416
1977	T/Gas	16,107	18,471
1976	T/Gas	15,259	17,499

Trojan 8.6 Meter Mid-Cabin

Year	Power	Retail Low	Retail High
1990	T/Gas	49,580	55,583
1989	T/Gas	46,160	51,749
1988	T/Gas	43,596	48,874
1987	T/Gas	41,031	45,999

Trojan 30 Sport Cruiser

Year	Power	Retail Low	Retail High
1979	T/Gas	20,056	23,000
1978	T/Gas	17,549	20,125
1977	T/Gas	15,877	18,208
1976	T/Gas	14,206	16,291
1975	T/Gas	13,370	15,333

Trojan 30 FB Express

Year	Power	Retail Low	Retail High
1979	T/Gas	21,727	24,916
1978	T/Gas	19,220	22,041
1977	T/Gas	16,713	19,166
1976	T/Gas	15,042	17,250
1975	T/Gas	14,206	16,291

Trojan 32 FB Sedan

Year	Power	Retail Low	Retail High
1992	T/Gas	82,063	91,999
1991	T/Gas	75,224	84,332
1990	T/Gas	69,241	77,624
1989	T/Gas	64,112	71,874
1988	T/Gas	59,838	67,082
1987	T/Gas	56,418	63,249
1986	T/Gas	52,999	59,416
1985	T/Gas	49,580	55,583
1984	T/Gas	47,015	52,708
1983	T/Gas	44,451	49,833
1982	T/Gas	42,752	47,928
1981	T/Gas	41,007	45,972
1980	T/Gas	39,262	44,015
1979	T/Gas	37,517	42,059
1978	T/Gas	34,899	39,125
1977	T/Gas	32,282	36,190
1976	T/Gas	28,792	32,278
1975	T/Gas	25,302	28,365

Trojan 10 Meter Express

Year	Power	Retail Low	Retail High
1989	T/Gas	74,581	83,611
1988	T/Gas	69,717	78,159
1987	T/Gas	65,664	73,614
1986	T/Gas	61,611	69,070
1985	T/Gas	57,557	64,526
1984	T/Gas	54,670	61,289
1983	T/Gas	51,356	57,574
1982	T/Gas	48,043	53,860
1981	T/Gas	45,558	51,074

Trojan 10 Meter Sedan

Year	Power	Retail Low	Retail High
1989	T/Gas	85,120	95,426
1988	T/Gas	80,256	89,973
1987	T/Gas	73,771	82,703
1986	T/Gas	68,096	76,341
1985	T/Gas	62,421	69,979
1984	T/Gas	57,557	64,526
1983	T/Gas	55,125	61,800
1982	T/Gas	51,883	58,164

Trojan 10 Meter Mid-Cabin

Year	Power	Retail Low	Retail High
1992	T/Gas	98,340	110,246
1991	T/Gas	91,784	102,897
1990	T/Gas	86,047	96,466
1989	T/Gas	81,130	90,953
1988	T/Gas	76,213	85,441
1987	T/Gas	70,477	79,010
1986	T/Gas	65,560	73,498

Trojan 10.8 Meter Convertible

Year	Power	Retail Low	Retail High
1992	T/Gas	114,858	128,764
1991	T/Gas	109,313	122,548
1990	T/Gas	102,976	115,444
1989	T/Gas	96,639	108,340
1988	T/Gas	91,094	102,123
1987	T/Gas	84,757	95,019
1986	T/Gas	77,628	87,027

Trojan 10.8 Meter Express

Year	Power	Retail Low	Retail High
1992	T/Gas	122,441	137,266
1991	T/Gas	113,891	127,680

Trojan 350 Express

Year	Power	Retail Low	Retail High
1995	T/IB/7.4L	136,253	152,750

Trojan 36 Convertible

Year	Power	Retail Low	Retail High
1989	T/Gas	92,789	104,023
1988	T/Gas	86,718	97,218
1987	T/Gas	81,515	91,385
1986	T/Gas	77,179	86,524
1985	T/Gas	72,844	81,663
1984	T/Gas	69,375	77,774
1983	T/Gas	66,773	74,858
1982	T/Gas	63,304	70,969
1981	T/Gas	59,836	67,080
1980	T/Gas	54,633	61,247
1979	T/Gas	48,875	55,414
1978	T/Gas	43,731	49,581
1977	T/Gas	39,443	44,720
1976	T/Gas	37,246	42,229
1975	T/Gas	34,927	39,600

Trojan 11 Meter Exp. (Early)

Year	Power	Retail Low	Retail High
1989	T/Gas	101,083	113,321
1989	T/Diesel	139,511	156,402
1988	T/Gas	95,235	106,766
1988	T/Diesel	130,321	146,100
1987	T/Gas	89,387	100,210
1987	T/Diesel	121,132	135,798
1986	T/Gas	85,210	95,527
1986	T/Diesel	116,955	131,116
1985	T/Gas	81,033	90,844
1985	T/Diesel	111,943	125,496
1984	T/Gas	76,856	86,162
1984	T/Diesel	106,930	119,877
1983	T/Gas	73,515	82,416
1983	T/Diesel	99,412	111,448

Trojan 11 Meter Express

Year	Power	Retail Low	Retail High
1992	T/Gas	136,192	152,682
1992	T/Diesel	190,837	213,943
1991	T/Gas	124,422	139,487
1991	T/Diesel	174,864	196,036
1990	T/Gas	115,175	129,120
1990	T/Diesel	161,413	180,956

Trojan 11 Meter Sedan

Year	Power	Retail Low	Retail High
1988	T/Gas	102,026	114,379
1988	T/Diesel	135,477	151,880
1987	T/Gas	93,663	105,003
1987	T/Diesel	126,278	141,567
1986	T/Gas	86,973	97,503
1986	T/Diesel	120,424	135,004
1985	T/Gas	78,610	88,128
1985	T/Diesel	109,552	122,816

Trojan 370/390 Express

Year	Power	Retail Low	Retail High
1995	T/Gas	161,785	181,373
1994	T/Gas	151,134	169,433
1993	T/Gas	140,172	157,144

Trojan 12 Meter Express

Year	Power	Retail Low	Retail High
1992	T/375D	208,797	234,078
1992	T/550D	237,912	266,718
1991	T/375D	196,282	220,047
1991	T/550D	223,384	250,430
1990	T/375D	184,784	207,158
1990	T/450D	197,925	221,889
1989	T/375D	174,108	195,188
1989	T/450D	185,606	208,078

Trojan 13 Meter Express

Year	Power	Retail Low	Retail High
1990	T/450D	229,594	257,392
1990	T/735D	275,346	308,684
1989	T/450D	215,452	241,538
1989	T/735D	259,541	290,965
1988	T/450D	202,974	227,550
1988	T/735D	242,072	271,381
1987	T/450D	190,496	213,561
1987	T/735D	224,603	251,797
1986	T/450D	178,850	200,505
1986	T/550D	200,479	224,752
1985	T/450D	170,532	191,179
1985	T/550D	183,009	205,168
1984	T/450D	163,045	182,786
1984	T/550D	174,691	195,842

Uniflite 26 Sedan

Year	Power	Retail Low	Retail High
1983	S/Gas	26,883	30,138
1982	S/Gas	24,281	27,221
1981	S/Gas	22,041	25,277
1980	S/Gas	20,346	23,332
1979	S/Gas	17,803	20,416
1978	S/Gas	16,107	18,471

Uniflite 28 Mega

Year	Power	Retail Low	Retail High
1984	T/Gas	32,617	36,567
1983	T/Gas	30,901	34,642
1982	T/Gas	29,184	32,718
1981	T/Gas	26,851	30,793
1980	T/Gas	25,173	28,868
1979	T/Gas	22,656	25,982
1978	T/Gas	20,978	24,057
1977	T/Gas	19,299	22,132

Uniflite 32 Sport Sedan

Year	Power	Retail Low	Retail High
1984	T/Gas	51,819	58,093
1983	T/Gas	46,637	52,284
1982	T/Gas	43,183	48,411
1981	T/Gas	40,592	45,506
1980	T/Gas	38,001	42,602
1979	T/Gas	35,013	39,697
1978	T/Gas	32,451	36,792
1977	T/Gas	30,743	34,856
1976	T/Gas	29,035	32,919
1975	T/Gas	27,327	30,983

Viking Sport Cruiser V38 SC

Year	Power	Retail Low	Retail High
1995	T/Diesel	******	******

Viking Sport Cruisers V39 EX

Year	Power	Retail Low	Retail High
1995	T/Diesel	******	******

Viking Sport Cruiser V42 SC

Year	Power	Retail Low	Retail High
1995	T/Diesel	******	******

Viking Sport Cruiser V45 SC

Year	Power	Retail Low	Retail High
1995	T/Diesel	******	******

Viking Sport Cruisers V52 EX

Year	Power	Retail Low	Retail High
1995	T/Diesel	******	******

Viking 35 Convertible

Year	Power	Retail Low	Retail High
1992	T/Gas	140,782	157,827
1992	T/Diesel	169,110	189,585
1991	T/Gas	121,896	136,655
1991	T/Diesel	156,233	175,150
1990	T/Gas	111,595	125,107
1990	T/Diesel	144,215	161,676
1989	T/Gas	102,582	115,002
1989	T/Diesel	131,768	147,722
1988	T/Gas	97,002	108,747
1988	T/Diesel	123,184	138,099
1987	T/Gas	92,710	103,935
1987	T/Diesel	118,463	132,806
1986	T/Gas	91,851	102,973
1986	T/Diesel	112,454	126,069
1985	T/Gas	88,418	99,123
1985	T/Diesel	108,162	121,257
1984	T/Gas	78,975	88,537
1984	T/Diesel	94,427	105,860
1983	T/Gas	75,541	84,688
1983	T/Diesel	85,843	96,236
1982	T/Gas	69,532	77,951
1982	T/Diesel	79,834	89,499
1981	T/Gas	63,953	71,696
1981	T/Diesel	76,400	85,650
1980	T/Gas	60,519	67,846
1980	T/Diesel	72,108	80,838
1979	T/Gas	57,294	64,959
1979	T/Diesel	67,055	76,026
1978	T/Gas	54,323	61,591
1978	T/Diesel	62,811	71,215
1977	T/Gas	52,626	59,666
1977	T/Diesel	59,416	67,365
1976	T/Gas	49,655	56,298
1976	T/Diesel	56,021	63,516
1975	T/Gas	47,957	54,373
1975	T/Diesel	53,474	60,629

Viking 43 Express

Year	Power	Retail Low	Retail High
1995	550 DD	383,259	429,663
1995	600 MAN	408,670	458,150
1994	T/Diesel	369,123	413,815

Wellcraft 2600 Express

Year	Power	Retail Low	Retail High
1992	S/IO/Gas	31,611	35,438
1991	S/IO/Gas	29,115	32,640

Wellcraft 2700 Martinique

Year	Power	Retail Low	Retail High
1995	S/IO/Gas	47,424	53,166
1994	S/IO/Gas	42,425	47,562

Wellcraft 2800 Monte Carlo

Year	Power	Retail Low	Retail High
1989	T/IO/Gas	32,443	36,371
1988	T/IO/Gas	29,947	33,573
1987	T/IO/Gas	27,451	30,775
1986	T/IO/Gas	25,788	28,910

Wellcraft 287 Prima

Year	Power	Retail Low	Retail High
1993	S/IO/Gas	37,434	41,966
1992	S/IO/Gas	34,938	39,168
1991	S/IO/Gas	32,443	36,371
1990	S/IO/Gas	29,947	33,573

Wellcraft 2900 Express

Year	Power	Retail Low	Retail High
1987	T/Gas	29,947	33,573
1986	T/Gas	28,283	31,708
1985	T/Gas	25,788	28,910
1984	T/Gas	24,124	27,045
1983	T/Gas	22,460	25,180
1982	T/Gas	21,628	24,247
1981	T/Gas	20,797	23,314
1980	T/Gas	19,965	22,382

Wellcraft 3000 Monaco

Year	Power	Retail Low	Retail High
1992	T/IO/Gas	48,746	54,648
1991	T/IO/Gas	44,684	50,094
1990	T/IO/Gas	41,434	46,451
1989	T/IO/Gas	38,184	42,808

Wellcraft 3100 Express

Year	Power	Retail Low	Retail High
1985	T/350G	41,152	46,134
1984	T/350G	36,213	40,598
1983	T/350G	32,921	36,907
1982	T/350G	30,452	34,139
1981	T/350G	27,983	31,371
1980	T/350G	26,337	29,526
1979	T/350G	24,691	27,680

Wellcraft 310 FB Sedan

Year	Power	Retail Low	Retail High
1983	T/Gas	36,602	41,034
1982	T/Gas	34,106	38,236
1981	T/Gas	31,611	35,438

Wellcraft 3200 Sedan Bridge

Year	Power	Retail Low	Retail High
1986	T/Gas	46,812	52,480
1985	T/Gas	41,884	46,956

Wellcraft 3200 St. Tropez

Year	Power	Retail Low	Retail High
1993	T/235G	59,894	67,146
1993	T/300G	69,876	78,337
1992	T/235G	53,239	59,685
1992	T/300G	62,390	69,944
1991	T/235G	48,248	54,090
1991	T/300G	57,398	64,348
1989	T/235G	40,761	45,696
1989	T/300G	49,912	55,955
1988	T/235G	38,266	42,899
1988	T/300G	46,584	52,224
1987	T/235G	34,938	39,168
1987	T/300G	43,257	48,494
1986	T/235G	33,274	37,303
1986	T/300G	39,929	44,764
1985	T/235G	30,779	34,505
1985	T/300G	37,434	41,966

Wellcraft 3200 Martinique

Year	Power	Retail Low	Retail High
1995	T/IO/Gas	83,538	93,652
1994	T/IO/Gas	77,363	86,730

Wellcraft 33 St. Tropez

Year	Power	Retail Low	Retail High
1992	T/260G	58,435	65,510
1991	T/260G	55,143	61,820
1990	T/260G	49,382	55,361

Wellcraft 3400 Gran Sport

Year	Power	Retail Low	Retail High
1992	T/Gas	82,771	92,793
1991	T/Gas	74,735	83,784
1990	T/Gas	68,306	76,576
1989	T/Gas	60,270	67,568
1988	T/Gas	55,449	62,162

Year	Power	Retail Low	Retail High
1987	T/Gas	52,234	58,558
1986	T/Gas	49,020	54,955
1985	T/Gas	46,609	52,252
1984	T/Gas	44,198	49,550

Wellcraft 34 Triumph

Year	Power	Retail Low	Retail High
1993	T/Gas	92,819	104,057
1992	T/Gas	84,677	94,929
1991	T/Gas	78,163	87,627
1990	T/Gas	73,278	82,150

Wellcraft 3500 Corsair/3600 St. Tropez

Year	Power	Retail Low	Retail High
1993	T/Gas	87,650	98,262
1992	T/Gas	79,665	89,311

Wellcraft 3600 Martinique

Year	Power	Retail Low	Retail High
1995	T/Gas	111,956	125,511
1994	T/Gas	100,655	112,842
1993	T/Gas	91,505	102,584
1992	T/Gas	84,850	95,123

Wellcraft 37 Corsica

Year	Power	Retail Low	Retail High
1991	T/Gas	106,994	119,948
1990	T/Gas	97,118	108,876
1989	T/Gas	88,887	99,649

Wellcraft 43 Portifino

Year	Power	Retail Low	Retail High
1995	T/Gas	181,647	203,640
1995	T/Diesel	231,007	258,977
1994	T/Gas	157,364	176,417
1994	T/Diesel	204,416	229,166
1993	T/Gas	151,687	170,052
1993	T/Diesel	180,766	202,653
1992	T/Gas	140,683	157,717
1992	T/Diesel	168,191	188,555
1991	T/Gas	129,680	145,382
1991	T/Diesel	157,188	176,220
1990	T/Gas	119,463	133,927
1990	T/Diesel	146,185	163,885
1989	T/Gas	107,674	120,711
1989	T/Diesel	133,610	149,787
1988	T/Gas	99,815	111,900
1988	T/Diesel	123,393	138,333
1987	T/Gas	93,527	104,851
1987	T/Diesel	117,105	131,284

Wilbur 34 Cruiser

Year	Power	Retail Low	Retail High
1995	S/Diesel	221,484	248,300
1988	S/Diesel	123,508	138,461
1982	S/Diesel	79,398	89,011

Wilbur 38 Cruiser

Year	Power	Retail Low	Retail High
1995	T/Diesel	386,568	433,372
1987	T/Diesel	176,439	197,802
1983	T/Diesel	129,683	145,384

Windy 31 Scirocco

Year	Power	Retail Low	Retail High
1995	T/Diesel	******	******

Windy 33 Mistral

Year	Power	Retail Low	Retail High
1995	T/Diesel	******	******
1994	T/Diesel	******	******

Windy 36 Grand Mistral

Year	Power	Retail Low	Retail High
1995	T/Diesel	******	******

Windy 38 Grand Sport

Year	Power	Retail Low	Retail High
1995	T/Diesel	******	******

Notes

Notes

Notes

Notes

Notes

Notes

Notes

Notes

Notes